Valuation and Dealmaking of Technology-Based Intellectual Property: Principles, Methods, and Tools

RICHARD RAZGAITIS

WILEY
John Wiley & Sons, Inc.

For the late Bill Riley, long time licensing mentor at Battelle.

Published by John Wiley & Sons, Inc., Hoboken, New Jersey.
Published simultaneously in Canada.

This book is a completely revised and expanded edition of Richard Razgaitis's previous book, titled *Valuation and Pricing of Technology-Based Intellectual Property* (978-0-471-25049-4).

For general information on our other products and services or for technical support, please contact our Customer Care Department within the United States at (800) 762-2974, outside the United States at (317) 572-3993 or fax (317) 572-4002.

Wiley also publishes its books in a variety of electronic formats. Some content that appears in print may not be available in electronic books. For more information about Wiley products, visit our web site at www.wiley.com.

ISBN 978-0-470-19333-4

Printed in the United States of America.

10 9 8 7 6 5 4 3 2 1

Contents

Preface

This book is the fourth that I have written for John Wiley and Sons. All of them in some way have been about creating value from technology by identifying opportunities, valuing and pricing those opportunities, and Dealmaking.

The 1999 book, *Early Stage Technologies: Valuation and Pricing*, was my initial effort that developed the Six Methods of Valuation:

(1) Industry Standards
(2) Rating/Ranking
(3) Rules of Thumb
(4) Discounted Cash Flow
(5) Advanced Methods
(6) Auctions

In 2003, I updated and expanded the 1999 book as *Valuation and Pricing of Technology-Based Intellectual Property*. In the same year, I wrote a separate book on Dealmaking: *Dealmaking Using Real Options and Monte Carlo Analysis*.

In the present book, I have expanded most of the material in the three earlier books and cohered it all (I hope) in three core technology commercialization business processes, designated as ***Approaches***. They are: **opportunity Discovery**, **Valuation**, and **Dealmaking**, hence the acronym Technology (or Licensing) **D-V-D**. In particular I have expanded the use of Monte Carlo as an Advanced Valuation Method. The text provides a link to my web site—www.razgaitis.com—that includes spreadsheets used in this book, as well as a means to obtain a free trial of the Monte Carlo software (Crystal Ball developed by Decisioneering, now a part of Oracle Corporation) to enable the reader to run his or her own simulations, and to provide a place for the inevitable errata.

My focus throughout has been on "opportunity Dealmaking," as opposed to litigation contexts. Accordingly, the subject matter of Dealmaking is typically something other than bare patents in a process of sellers and buyers discovering value and enhancing deal structures to their mutual benefit. Technology Dealmaking is that special conjunction of the oldest form of human interaction, trading, with the most modern, technology. The nautical theme of the cover art is intended to be suggestive of this ancient quest for economic benefit through trade in the face of significant risk. The Approaches, Methods, and Tools (A-M-T) here presented are with the intent of being a kind of lighthouse, overarching business principles, not with the aspiration of risk removal, but to support risk-based opportunity discovery, valuation, pricing, and Dealmaking.

Throughout the book, I have made numerous changes and clarifications in the hope of making the points clearer and more useful and fitting together the complete business process of opportunity discovery, valuation, and Dealmaking. Arthur Schopenhauer (1788-1860) in an 1844 edition of his classic book, *The World as Will and Representation* (or *Idea*) originally published in 1818, wrote: "Now, as regards this second edition, in the first place I am glad that after twenty-five years I find nothing to retract; my fundamental convictions have been confirmed, at any rate as far as I myself am concerned."* In his final edition of that book, he changed not a word from text he had written 40 years earlier. From this perspective, his 1844 edition, and his final 1858 edition included his 1818 text unchanged.

In contrast with that genius, I have tried to change anything and everything in my previous writing that I could to make it better and more complete, as well as more interesting, even fun to read. I have made extensive use of everyday terms of art—some might even call it business slang—to be as expressive as possible at the cost, perhaps, of some textual dignity. But Carl Sandburg, that Chicago big shoulders/Tool Maker city poet, said it well: "slang is a language that rolls up its sleeves, spits on its hands, and goes to work." Putting technology to work is what I've tried to do here, using down-to-earth language to do it. I am still not done with that work, but it is the best I can do at the moment. It does not, however, represent my final views on the subject of technology valuation and pricing. I have intended it to be an educational contribution to my profession, not as a proof text on some narrowly defined dispute, but as a systematic discussion of tools, methods, and principles, that can be developed and applied to that most challenging task of developing a model framework for establishing its worth, and reaching agreement with a Dealmaking partner.

Disclaimer

It may not be necessary, but it is probably prudent, to point out what should be obvious: This is not intended as a proof text in support of litigation. The context of the valuation methods considered here and my associated observations and suggestions is in support of opportunity licensing, not enforcement. Further, each licensing and valuation opportunity is specific to the given fact situation; so it is unwise and even misleading to take a passage of static words and assume that it can be applied without consideration of the specific circumstances by the exercise of reasoned judgment.

*Schopenhauer, Arthur, *The World as Will and Representation*, translated from the German by E.F.J. Payne, Dover Publications, Vol. 1, 1969, p. xxi. Although his book on epistemological philosophy is generally far afield from our purpose here, Schopenhauer's core idea that we apprehend not the subject of our consciousness but only a representation of such subject is useful and applicable to our understanding of any valuation model we may use and develop. We will return to this idea in closing observations in Chapter 12.

Acknowledgments

One of the themes of this book is the multidisciplinary context for Technology D-V-D, and the need for active learning. So the list of people I would like to acknowledge is long, but by no means exhaustive. Although I have been involved in putting technology to work since 1965 when I joined the Apollo Program as a "rocket scientist," my work in technology licensing did not begin until the early 1980s when I worked for Battelle Memorial Institute. When I joined its Battelle Development Corporation I was mentored by a special group of long time employees,

Much of my life has been spent in learning. Some would say, I still have a long way to go (which is true, but details on that are more appropriate to a confessional). Here I want to offer heartfelt thanks to you many "teachers" that in some meaningful way contributed to the thinking expressed here.

For 14 years and 2 months, I had the privilege of working for Battelle in Columbus, Ohio. During the early years of this period I had the opportunity of working for Battelle Development Corporation (BDC), a wholly owned subsidiary that had been responsible for commercializing Battelle and outside inventor technology since 1935. During those years at BDC, I happened to be present during the retirement transition of an unusually talented group of individuals who took the time and patience to share with me over a period of years their insights from an incredible breadth of experience. Although the content of this book is mine, I would be remiss not to acknowledge the influences that this unique opportunity afforded me. Bill Riley, to whom this book is dedicated, hired me into BDC. Bill was an endless source of experience-filled marketing and dealmaking stories; many of those stories deserve a string instrument composition to elevate them to more-than-Irish ballads (really more like Homeric Epics). Bill's 29 years with Battelle, long term participation in the Licensing Executives Society (including a term as LES President), and wise memory were, for me, like attending an academy of licensing learning. His recent passing is a loss I feel every time I hear of a funny moment in licensing that I wish I could share with him.

Ken Shaweker was also a 30-year veteran of licensing experience, mostly at Battelle. He was BDC's IP Counsel. As our lead attorney, he was a model of reasoned judgment combined with sagacity in developing solutions to meet worthy business objectives and taught me lot about agreements and people.

Steve Dickerson, another 30-year man and head of BDC for many years, was tireless in his enthusiasm and pursuit of opportunities. In negotiations he was both gracious and quick thinking, a very potent combination.

Dr. Charles Schwartz was, unbelievably, our 50-year man. His breadth and currency of technical insight was astounding; and as to kindness and patience, I have known only one other that deserves mention in the same breath.

Art Westerman ("just" a 40-year man) in addition to his business development skills was a great writer and teacher of business writing (sorry that I didn't learn better than I did).

There were many others at Battelle who were not part of the retirement transition but who were part of my licensing and valuation "faculty": Barry Bissell, Bob Zieg (who as Ken's replacement shared the fruits of 26 years of patent/licensing experience), Bill Huffman, Roland Adoutte, L. Don Williams, Gene Eschbach, and many others.

I owe a very special debt to four very talented administrative assistants whose teachings often had to be by the rescue method: Carol Cremeans, Shirley Russell, Shari Dean, and Mary Ann Dillon.

I am likewise indebted to my experiences and opportunities at Bellcore, now Telcordia Technologics. One of my teammates there, the late Bruce Sidran, was the object of dedication in my 2003 *Dealmaking* book. I miss his friendship and great sense of humor.

For 11 years now I have been associated with a consulting group headquartered in Chicago, initially under the name IPC Group, then Intecap LLC, which then became part of Charles River Associates. The name keeps changing on the door, but most of the people are still there. I would like to acknowledge the special client working relationships I have had with colleagues Dan McGavock and Bob Goldman, and in times past with Brian Oliver and Mike Lasinski. In particular I want to acknowledge two Charles River Associates colleagues, Lew Koppel and Bob Goldman, who made numerous helpful suggestions based on their review of this manuscript. There is a long list of others with whom I have worked however I cannot name them all.

My association with the Licensing Executive Society (LES) has been a constant source of learning from many people who have also become friends. If I start mentioning names, I would never know where to stop. LES is simply an outstanding group of individuals who have universally been both gracious and wise, an uncommon combination.

The origins of these books can probably be traced to a conversation I had with Lou Berneman who, on behalf of the Association of University Technology Managers (AUTM), asked me to teach the valuation section of AUTM's introduction to licensing course. That invitation, and honor, became an annual event for me for some dozen years and lead to my writing the valuation chapter in AUTM's License Practice Manual, which has now been revised. I owe thanks to Lou, AUTM, and in particular the two thousand plus students who have participated in that experience; these many interactions have helped me solidify my own thoughts and defog some aspects.

In my 11 years consulting I have done perhaps 200 or more projects, and given numerous day and multi-day valuation "workshops" for clients. One of the benefits of all these experiences is the learning that takes place in every encounter, every question. Thanks to all of you for the opportunities to serve you by these assignments. Although I have been careful not to disclose anything proprietary from these engagements, the inevitable learning that comes from them has been a lifelong benefit.

Perhaps I owe my greatest learning debt to those many individuals with whom I negotiated, or attempted to negotiate, licensing agreements, including those necessary negotiations with my own teammates. Your reasoned and articulate explanations, of how you viewed the subject opportunities have swirled through my memories many times and continue to do so even now, many years later. It is an axiom of negotiation that Dealmaking is a mutual learning experience. I don't know how mutual it has been, but for me it has been the learning laboratory and my thanks goes out to all of you.

This is not the kind of personal book that causes me to focus on the contributions of my family. But, it has been their encouragement and patience and source of earthly purpose that has kept me going: So to you, Carol (my loyal wife of now two plus years and counting) and children of whom I am so proud . . . Rich, Renda, Christy, Jodi, and Leslee, I say "thanks." These six have all at one time or another asked "What *exactly* is it that you do?" This book is a long answer.

Lastly, my thanks go to Susan McDermott and Emilie Herman at John Wiley & Sons, and Martha Cooley who welcomed me into the Wiley relationship with that first book. Thanks for encouraging my writing, especially when things were going slowly.

CHAPTER 1

Introduction to Opportunity Discovery, Valuation, and Dealmaking

In this opening chapter we will review briefly the key points of ***Technology D-V-D***, namely the ***Approaches of*** opportunity Discovery, Valuation, and Dealmaking, and the valuation Methods and Tools to be developed in this book.

Introduction: *Technology D-V-D*

This book is about three business processes used for transforming technology into money, usually by way of a license agreement. These processes, here referred to as ***Approaches***, are technology: (1) opportunity Discovery, (2) Valuation, and (3) Dealmaking; the overall process is then designated ***Technology or Licensing D-V-D***, where each letter corresponds to the respective ***Approach***.

About half of this book is on the ***Approach*** of Valuation. There are mountains of books on the general subject of valuation in various business contexts; this one focuses on unique issues associated with *technology*.

Technology

One can think of three discrete species of transacted rights: businesses, products, and technologies.

- *Business transactions*. These are usually the outright sale of all assets relating to an operating business including all forms of tangible and intangible property. Such transactions typically include some form of manufacturing or contract-for-manufacturing capability; established sales, marketing, and distribution channels; and, importantly, customers with a revenue history; and all the other elements necessary to operate as a standalone entity for the buyer to take over or integrate into its own operations.
- *Product licensing*. This enables the buyer to duplicate the making of some device, system, or service that has already been completed and proven by the seller. In this situation, the buyer will need to provide the necessary surrounding business assets to realize a profit from the license.

- *Technology agreements*. Such agreements designate transactions for pre or early commercial designs and data, normally without the evidence of large scale manufacturability or possibly even a single legitimate customer. In some cases, the final or best formulation has not yet been established. Another way of thinking of technology is as a work product of research and development (R&D). Put yet another way, R&D is a business operation that has as its successful result technology. Such an R&D work product can range all the way from a raw concept, at one extreme, to the results of many years and many millions of dollars' worth of investigation with comprehensive data books, samples, test results, financial projections, and business plans, as well as outside verification by certification agents and potential customer feedback from trials.

However, the term "technology" is challenging to define exactly. It is meant to encompass the broad meaning intended by its Greek root, *techne*,[1] which designates the craft, skill, and "know-how" associated with making some product or performing some service. This meaning of technology would apply to not yet commercially demonstrated superconductivity inventions based on sophisticated semi conductor physics to software code that has a demonstrated potential of controlling some important business process.

The key ingredient missing from technology licensing that is present in both business and product licensing is a commercial track record. Without such ingredient, the customary approaches to product and business valuations do not work well because the underlying data usually relied upon do not exist. To make this more concrete, consider an automotive example. In early 1999, Ford Motor Company made an offer to buy and ultimately bought Volvo's automotive business (and in late 2008 Ford announced it is planning to sell its Volvo operations). In developing the valuation of this transaction Ford in 1999, as the buyer, and in 2009 Ford as the seller has access to many years of financial and operational data as well as forecasted performance based on such data, and any subsequent buyer of this asset will be able to study the Ford data during its period of ownership. This is the nature of sale of *business* transactions.

Alternatively, Ford could have licensed from Volvo the right to make and sell Volvo cars in the United States in Ford plants based on Volvo proprietary information and patents. Again, in such a situation, Ford would have been able to study an extensive historical basis of the costs and revenues of making a Volvo car, and use such information to develop projections of profitability. This would have been a *product* transaction, because Ford would have had to use its business assets to make and sell the cars.

An example of a *technology* transaction would be Ford's acquisition of the rights to a Volvo invention that Ford could then develop and use in their manufacture of Ford cars, or for some other business purpose. With such technology transaction species, there is often no product or business history because what is being licensed is newly developed and has not yet reached the stage of a product, or the nature of its commercial use would be substantially different in the hands of Ford as the licensee. Although the tools and methods discussed in this book can be of use in business and product transactions, the main objective here is in support of technology licensing.

Technology and Intellectual Property Rights

Technology rights are usually expressed in three forms of intellectual property (IP): patents, trade secrets (also known as know-how, or proprietary technical information), and copyrights. Such IP can be considered as the form by which the technology rights are documented, protected, and conveyed.

It will be assumed that IP protection exists when considering the valuation of technology. There is always some uncertainty about the breadth and strength of such protection, and this uncertainty factors into the value determination. If there are issued patents, there can be some uncertainty surrounding interpretation of claim language or even the validity of the patent itself. If the patents are still pending, then there will be uncertainty about what will be allowed by patent offices in various countries of the world. There can also be uncertainties about trade secrets. It may not be well understood how "secret" the trade secret really is; it could be that many other labs and companies have independently arrived at the same information or soon will do so. Also there is always some risk of inadvertent disclosure of the trade secret by the seller or buyer or by some third party that would damage the value of the underlying technology asset.

The extent and strength of IP protection are dimensions of a valuation. An extreme example of such effect is the absence of value if the inventing organization publicized all the details of its invention in such a way as to preclude obtaining a patent or any other form of IP protection. So the absence of protection can and normally does preclude value (although even with minimal IP protection there can be situations where the seller's commercial assistance can accelerate time to market and create value for the buyer). However, the converse is not true: It is possible to have very strong patent and trade secret protection and still not have much or any value because, for example, of the absence of a market for the product made by the underlying technology (though there can be option value to ownership of a right with no immediately obvious commercial use).

Thus, as a general guideline, some extent and form of IP protection is a necessary but not a sufficient condition for value to exist.

Considerations about which forms of IP should be used in which contexts, and analysis of the strengths and weaknesses of each, are outside the scope of this book. In the valuation examples considered it will be assumed that the technology is protected in some way or combination of ways. When risk issues are considered, or when comparisons are made to reference agreements, then strength and extent of IP protection will be identified as a factor to be considered when performing a valuation.

Technology licensing is becoming an increasingly important transaction category but does not have the abundance of tools and experience available to business and product transactions. This book is intended to contribute to the field of technology valuation.

Technology Opportunity Discovery

In some situations the opportunity for technology licensing is obvious: There is a specific package of IP rights and underlying technology assets that the owner seeks to monetize in some way other than its own commercial development into products and markets. However in many situations, the IP owner has many technologies, perhaps thousands, as a result of significant R&D investments over the years not fully utilized in its own products, or "left-over" technology assets from a major acquisition, or a closing down of a major operating division and the opportunity exists to sell it in parts. In the latter situation there can be more opportunities than can be practically analyzed in detail, and some prioritization must first take place.

In all cases there is the discovery issue of identifying potential commercial applications that may not have been envisioned by inventors or prior business developers. Technology can be created focused on purpose A and instead, or in addition, be valuable for purpose B, or A, B, and C. The challenge and need for a technology owner, is to develop an initial recognition, which is Discovery, of licensing opportunities that are valuable. This business process is the ***Approach*** of opportunity Discovery.

We will cover opportunity Discovery in Chapter 3.

Valuation

The heart of the matter with technology transactions is value. This is sometimes expressed as the "So, what?" question, which is the natural response to any long winded and involved description of the latest and greatest invention. The answer usually begins with a discussion of who in the world will have a happier life because of it, and then how much would that happier life be worth to them if someone were in the business of providing this vehicle of happiness.

For the reasons discussed above, determining technology value is a challenging task. We will consider six Methods, and numerous Tools that derive from such Methods in six separate chapters, Chapters 4 through 9, covering the ***Approach*** of Valuation.

Dealmaking

The vehicle of technology transactions is a contract between a seller and buyer, normally a license. Such license conveys technology rights from the licensor, or seller, to the licensee, or buyer. For simplicity, hereafter the licensor will be referred to as the seller, and the licensee as the buyer.

The transaction between buyer and seller is a trade. Sometimes the trade is as simple as money from the buyer in exchange for assignment of a patent by the seller. In most cases, the trade is much more complex. But it is always a trade. Building on this fundamental idea I have introduced the acronym **TR R A DE™** to structure this discussion. Within the scope of the book, all transactions are founded on the **TR R A DE™** framework:

- TR is used to designate Technology Rights conveyed in the licensing transaction.
- R is the risk involved in any transaction.
- A represents the art behind the opportunity Discovery, Valuation, and Dealmaking ***Approaches***
- DE is the deal economics.

The process of valuation and pricing determines the transaction deal economics, (the DE in our acronym). So, in shorthand form, this book is about TR for DE. The business process of making such happen as trade is here called Dealmaking, our third ***Approach***. Dealmaking will be covered in two Chapters, 10 and 11. As we shall see this ***Approach*** also involves opportunity Discovery, because the technology opportunity discovered in Chapter 3 has to match with the business opportunity to be discovered with/for a prospective buyer.

Depending on the complexity of the transaction, there can be numerous issues and agreements that are included in the Dealmaking and additional to a technology license. For the transfer of physical assets, such as lab equipment or technology prototypes, there may be a separate purchase agreement. For circumstances where key employees are to leave the seller and join the buyer, normally there will be employment agreements. If the seller agrees to provide subsequent technical assistance to the buyer, there will be a separate services or consulting agreement. If the buyer is going to provide a licensed product to the seller for the seller's use in some other product, there will be a supply agreement. Sometimes, the parties choose to create a separate nondisclosure agreement so that it stands independently of the license. In the case of equity transactions, there are numerous other agreements that are needed related to stock purchase, incorporation, and shareholder issues. The legal details of all such licenses and related agreements are outside the scope of this book. Here we will focus on valuation and pricing of "the deal" as a whole unit, understanding there may be one or many legal agreements used to encompass all the deal issues.

Graphic Outline of the Book

A graphic summary of the organization of this book along with the key acronyms we will refer to is shown here:

A-M-T

Licensing D-V-D

	A: Approaches	M: Methods	T: Tools
D	Discovery	The Box NPV v. Risk	Rating/Ranking DCF
V	**Valuation** TR R^k A DE	1. Industry Standards 2. Rating/Ranking 3. Rules of Thumb 4. Discounted Cash Flow (NPV) 5. Monte Carlo; Real Options 6. Auctions	> Rating/Ranking > Rules of Thumb > Discounted Cash > Risk Assessment
D	Dealmaking	Pricing, Structures, Term Sheets Dealmaking-Process Plan B	Rating/Ranking DCF/NPV Monte Carlo Real Options

Taxonomy of Technology Licensing

There are various ways of categorizing the circumstances under which licensing valuation, pricing, negotiation, and dealmaking occur. Although a discussion of the "how to's" of licensing in each of these categories is beyond the scope of this book, it is useful to have a common reference of licensing situations.

Technology licensing can be understood to take place under six situations, as discussed below:

1. *Enforcement Licensing*. The seller (licensor) believes it has the right and opportunity to enforce patent claims, and/or perhaps misappropriated trade secrets, against a buyer (licensee/believed-infringer) whose licensing need is a freedom to practice. In many cases the buyer is already using the technology in commerce and may already be aware of the seller's patent(s). This is sometimes called stick (or "the taxman cometh") licensing. Valuation can occur in pre-litigation contexts, or expert opinion in litigation, or settlement discussions.
2. *Opportunity Licensing*. The seller has a technology IP and possibly other assets that it believes will be of value to a buyer who is seeking new or expanded new revenue opportunities. Such licensing would normally include know-how of some kind. This is sometimes called carrot (or "have I got a deal for you") licensing. Valuation normally occurs in anticipation and in the midst of a negotiation.
3. *Opportunistic* (as distinct from Opportunity) *Licensing*. The buyer seeks out a technology owner for the purpose of securing rights to a technology and perhaps other licensable assets. Prior to such contact, the seller may not have realized that it possessed licensable value, or it may not have been previously willing to license its technology. Valuation typically occurs first by the buyer in anticipation of making the seller an offer, and also by the seller as well as by both parties in the negotiation.
4. *Divestiture Licensing*. The seller is exiting a business area that includes technology and, typically, other assets such as physical plant, property, equipment, people, and trademarks. Traditional M&A (merger and acquisition) activities would encompass this form of licensing, though M&A transactions are normally associated with operating businesses. So in our context, divestiture licensing would more likely be related to technology assets and rights that were unused or underused by the seller and for some reason has become part of the M&A transaction. Divestiture licensing can resemble opportunity or enforcement licensing depending on the circumstances. Valuation typically includes nontechnology elements, such as the value of equipment, buildings, and so forth. Often the value is expressed as a lump sum payable in cash or cash and securities, though there can also be earn out and other future payments.
5. *Partnering Licensing*. The seller is seeking a business partner who will provide certain resources (such as complementary technology, key people, market access, and money) to a joint effort in further R&D, product development, manufacturing, and/or sales. The technology license is normally just an element of a panoply of supply, joint invention, facility access, marketing, and other agreements. Valuation occurs in anticipation of and during the back and forth of partner negotiations and can be expressed in royalty payment or splitting terms, or in revenue apportionment in accordance with some form of a capital contribution calculation, which would include a value for the technology contributed to the partnership.

6. *Startup Licensing*. The seller is licensing to a new business (commonly referred to as a NEWCO as a shorthand for "new company") being formed expressly for the purpose of commercializing the technology by making and selling products and services. Buyers, who may be traditional venture capitalists, private investors, or strategic investors, normally seek many things from the seller, not least of which are the employment of the key people. The closing documents associated with licensing are mountainous and include incorporation papers, corporate bylaws, employment agreements, stock purchase agreements, and the technology license itself. Valuation occurs in the preparation of term sheets in anticipation and in the midst of negotiation of the formation of the NEWCO and for subsequent rounds of investment. Equity is normally the principal valuation consideration.

In the first three categories, the agreement structure and valuation issues tend to be substantially simpler than in the last three categories. To keep our considerations manageable, we will not attempt to include a discussion of all six categories of technology licensing as we go through each of the six valuation methods. In Chapter 10 we will cover the special situation of taking equity as a principal form of compensation, which normally occurs with Startup Licensing, but can occur in other circumstances.

For convenience, most of the illustrations used in this book will use Opportunity Licensing as an assumed context, although the impetus could have originated from one of the other above contexts. It must be noted that enforcement licensing is not the subject of this book. Enforcement licensing is about specific infringement contention of certain patent claims (or, possibly, misappropriation of trade secrets), for a product in commercial use. Such context presumes a bare patent license, no other assets, in a nonexclusive license limited to the field and territory (corresponding to the court's jurisdiction). The contexts we are interested in involve a seller offering a mosaic of assets and rights, which we will later refer to as The Box, in exchange for a structure of cash and noncash payments which may be obligations extending over time and conditional upon subsequent commercial outcomes. Opportunity Discovery, Valuation, and Dealmaking as discussed in this book is far richer and more complex than a litigation context.

High Significance, High Ambiguity Contexts

Another way of envisioning the scope of this book is shown in Exhibit 1.1.

As illustrated, Dealmaking opportunities can be segmented by potential value (high and low) and ambiguity of key business terms (again high and low):

- *Low potential value and low ambiguity*. A significant analytical investment in technology Licensing D-V-D is not usually warranted; the low ambiguity condition corresponds to the substantial availability of business information, such as revenues, margins, market, new production growth potential, and so on. In such circumstances the direct use of comparables and rules of thumb can be all that is needed. Opportunities in this quadrant can be (and need to be) valued and transacted relatively quickly at low Dealmaking cost in order for them to be worth doing.

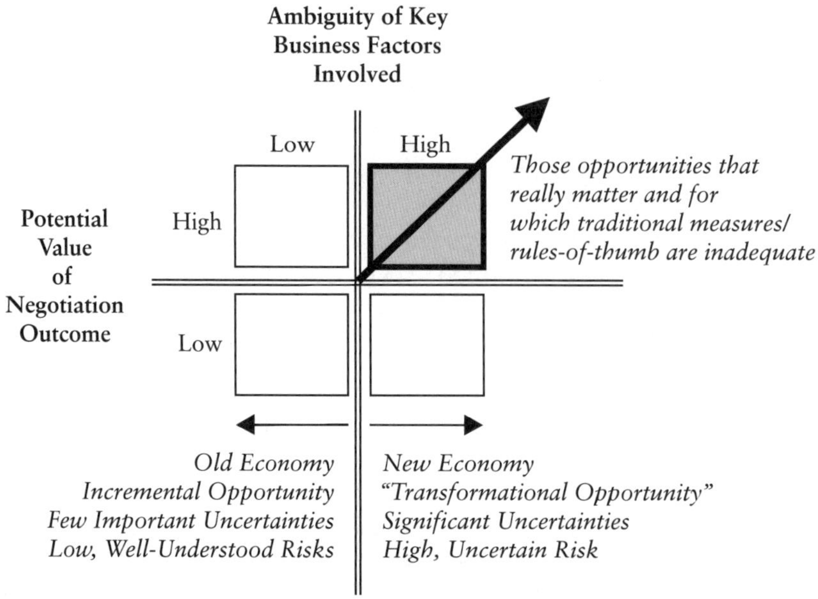

EXHIBIT 1.1 High Value, High Ambiguity Opportunities

- *High potential value and low ambiguity.* A greater investment in Licensing D-V-D is warranted to confirm the abundant business information and rationalize it for valuation, negotiation preparation, and agreement purposes, the Methods and Tools of this book can supplement and assist more traditional valuation tools and methodologies.
- *Low potential value and high ambiguity.* The power (and complexity) Technology Licensing D-V-D can be of value but a high level of effort in its application may not be warranted (if, indeed, the opportunity has low potential value).
- *High potential value and high ambiguity.* This is the "sweet spot" for Technology Licensing D-V-D: there is both a lot at stake and traditional data and methods are likely to be inadequate. This quadrant is sometimes characterized by colloquialisms that express the high potential opportunity with the corresponding, inherent uncertainties in the underlying technology, market, or business operation. For example, "transformational," "game-changing," revolutionary, disruptive, new paradigm or paradigm shift, step change, upset (or "tipping point"), "killer app" (deriving from "killer application," often used in software, or quantum leap[2]). When such terms are used they are a strong indication that the opportunity is high potential value and, though it may not be overtly recognized, high ambiguity (low certainty) often because the transformational model is not achieved by some incremental, obvious new product adoption and growth pattern.

The Perils of Short Cuts

Over the past decade, with the emergence of the Internet and World Wide Web (WWW), the rapidly increasing power at a rapidly decreasing cost of personal computing, the ubiquity of mobile communication (phones, pagers, PDAs, and laptops) provides "the Internet and worldwide connectivity in your pocket." In addition, the corporate information technology (IT) revolution in content availability, data mining, and networking (Ethernet, LANs, VPNs, WiFi, WiMAX, etc.) has together fostered a maelstrom of new business ideas (e.g. Web 2.0) and a premium on decision speed ("Internet time"). For a while it appeared that every new business idea promised to revolutionize how we lived and worked. These ideas were clearly touted as high opportunity and even the ardent believers generally admitted that they had attendant high uncertainties. At work was another force, time ultra urgency. These opportunities were so compelling, it was thought, and so competitively pursued that there was little time to analyze, quantify, or even, it seemed, to think. It was said that no one could do "Ready, Aim, Fire!" It had to be "Ready, Fire! Aim" or, as it was in many cases, just "Fire! Fire! Fire!" and hope you hit something worth the effort. Even our vocabulary reflected the new urgency by the then common usage of "Internet time." Its initial use was in circa 1994. During that year, the *Wall Street Journal* used the term in its writings just four times; in 2000, it was used 43 times.[3] The term conveyed an idea that expressed a behavior that reflected a core belief: The rates of change were so dramatic that time for reasoning was scarce or even nonexistent and the opportunities for success so abundant that the absence of reason was insignificant. Put another way, doing something, anything, had higher value creation opportunity than could be captured by any reasoning process requiring more than the proverbial 15 minutes.

In such absence of reasoned analysis, how were opportunities valued and chosen? Well, the obvious global answer as one surveys the smoldering ruins beginning in 2002 is "not very well." But, specifically, pursuers of such high value/high ambiguity opportunities used two primary methods: (1) simplistic rules of thumb and (2) unstructured auctions. Among the examples of simplistic rules of thumb was the use of $2 million per software "developer" employed in valuing a potential software acquisition target. So, using the first method, if you were considering buying a software company with nominal revenues, but nowhere close to net earnings, with 500 "developers," you would be prepared to pay $1 billion.

The second method was the use of informal auctions. Potential sellers of opportunities had multiple pursuers. This situation enabled them in many cases to play one bidder off against the other in an informal auction process that they, the seller, controlled. This auction was informal because in most cases the buyers did not know who the other interested parties were, or even if there were truly other interested parties or actual bids. Additionally, there were no standardized rules of engagement such as those which exist, for example, in stock or commodity exchanges or even bankruptcy court auctions. The motives of greed for gain and fear of lost opportunity led many buyers to bid and pay for opportunities far in excess of what they now appear to be worth. The examples of such overpayment are legion. Are auctions really markets, and are markets not reliable? The answer to both questions, in the case of informal auctions when there is a frenzy of buyers with money chasing the 'next big thing' is "no." Could not a potential buyer have, instead, resorted to advanced valuation tools and methods such as those that are considered in this book? At the time of the technology bubble in the late 1990s, a common view was "no" because, it was widely thought, that by the time they completed even a cursory analysis the opportunity would have been sold to a buyer unfettered by such concerns who simply looked it over and topped the previous and all competitive bids. A similar

BEFORE A FALL . . .

Merrill Lynch initiated coverage of InfoSpace in December 1999 with a rating of "accumulate-buy" and a price objective of $160. The company's share price fell much faster than its rating.

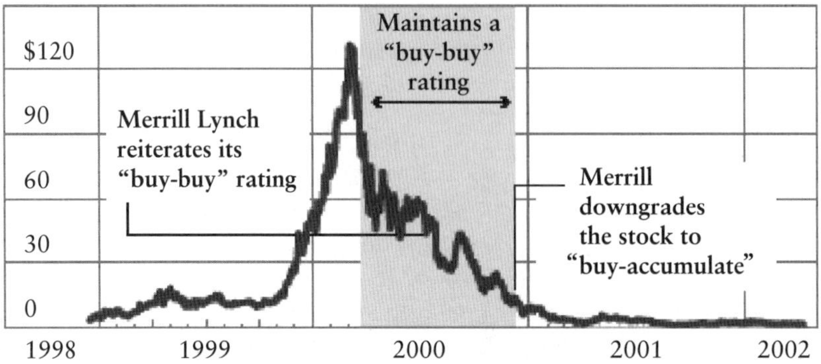

EXHIBIT 1.2 Buy Recommendations by Merrill Lynch for InfoSpace

Source: *Wall Street Journal*: Europe (staff produced copy only by Ravzin, Philip). Copyright 2000 by Dow Jones & Co. Inc. Reproduced with permission of Dow Jones & Co. Inc. in the format Trade Book via Copyright Clearance Center.

propensity to favor speed over reason may have contributed to collapse in value of complex "financial products" created, packaged, and traded in recent years up until late 2008.

Selecting one illustrative proxy for this point is difficult because there are so many to choose from. Exhibit 1.2 presents an easy to understand technology bubble example, namely, the public recommendations by a well known brokerage firm (Merrill Lynch) with respect to a high-flying Internet (dot.com) startup (InfoSpace). We will return to InfoSpace when we consider the valuation of various technology equities.

Consider the following as a benchmark for a poor return-on-investment standard. One can purchase a 12 pack of say, Coke® for about $3.00 in no deposit states or for $3.60 in the five states requiring deposits of five cents per aluminum can. After consuming the Coke, one's "return" would be 95 percent loss of invested capital in a no deposit state (each can is 1/29 of a pound and a pound of recyclable aluminum cans is worth about 40 cents) or 83 percent loss of capital if you live in NY, CT, MA, VT, ME, IA, or OR; for those in Michigan (ten cent deposit) the loss of capital would be only 71 percent, and for Californians (2.5 cents) 91 percent. So, we might say that, on average, the "just-drink-your-investment" experiences a loss of invested capital of 90 percent. For many Fire! Fire! Fire! dealmakers, they would have done better in terms of enjoyment and return on invested capital to have purchased Coke, the soft drink itself (not the company) than many of the 1995–2000 merger and acquisition (or equity) investments, the most recent mania, many of which have exhibited declines in value exceeding the just-drink-your-investment benchmark. This same aluminum can returns have likewise occurred in 2008 and 2009 for certain financial companies. Although financial markets are very different from the technology and Internet examples, there is an underlying similarity, an undervaluation of the price of risk.

We now know that there are allegations that brokerage houses compromised their judgment on stock value by their desire to win investment banking business, which may have been joined with less than well considered merger, acquisition and other Dealmaking advice. Similar motivation and lack of prudence appears also to have contributed to the collapse of multiple forms of investment vehicles created, marketed, and sold by financial companies. Whether, or to the extent, there has been fraudulent or recklessness in making public recommendations of such opportunities, they would not have been effective if the public markets in large part did not find such counsel credible. The point is that investors and dealmakers, with all the reasoning opportunity in the world, believed such prognostications, to their (in many cases) financial detriment.

Dealmaking preparation either by quick and dirty rules of thumb or informal auctions can lead to very damaging results. However, business is about exigency; a scholarly, methodical, patient inquiry into all matters relevant to a potential negotiation is simply not an always practicable option. What is needed are reasonable, powerful, quick-to-apply and -interpret Tools and Methods that can assess opportunities and prepare for negotiation. So urgency in preparation is important, but not to the exclusion of a rational, defendable analysis. Developing a rapidly deployable methodology using valuation tools is what Licensing D-V-D and this book are about.

The Challenge of Close Calls

In most business situations one frequently deals with "close calls," meaning the go/no-go decision with respect to a particular offer is difficult. If we consider for a moment the internal decision of whether to go forward with some particular investment project, it can be argued that the level of analysis should take into account that all that is needed is the answer to the question of should we go forward or not. A common and powerful tool for making such determination is the discounted cash flow analysis leading to a net present value (NPV). In the case of internal project investment decisions, we can perform a simplistic NPV analysis to sort out those obvious opportunities that have strongly positive NPV values and accordingly should be undertaken, and those that have strongly negative values and should be killed.

In Dealmaking contexts, as opposed to internal investment analysis, near zero NPV projections can occur more commonly. Consider for a moment a seller and buyer each using the same data on which they make projections and the same overall business assumptions. Their calculation of NPV will be identical but for small differences perhaps in some secondary assumptions. In this situation, the seller will try to capture in its sales price the entire positive NPV under the argument that so long as the opportunity has any positive value, a buyer should say "yes" to the deal and terms proposed. Thus, sellers are by their self interest offering terms that create near zero NPVs for the buyer, to the extent the market (the population of all potential buyers) permits. If there are multiple prospective buyers who then engage in a formal or informal bidding context, they will each be driven to increase their bids up to the limit of a zero or near zero NPV.

So it is common in Dealmaking contexts that the decision to proceed or not, from both the seller's and buyer's perspectives, ends up being a close call. In contrast then to many internal investment decision making situations, the natural contest and context of negotiations warrants the use of the Methods and Tools we discuss in this book.

Licensing D-V-D and Innovation

The focus of this book has been circumscribed by the term Technology (or) Licensing D-V-D. This subject is interconnected with three other important disciplines. One of them is the law of Intellectual Property (IP). It is such law that enable enforceable ownership rights. Two other important subjects are technology creation and entrepreneurship, which together can be termed "innovation."

A graphic of how the subject of this book interconnects with these other three areas is shown in a Venn Diagram in Exhibit 1.3. It includes the horizontal box

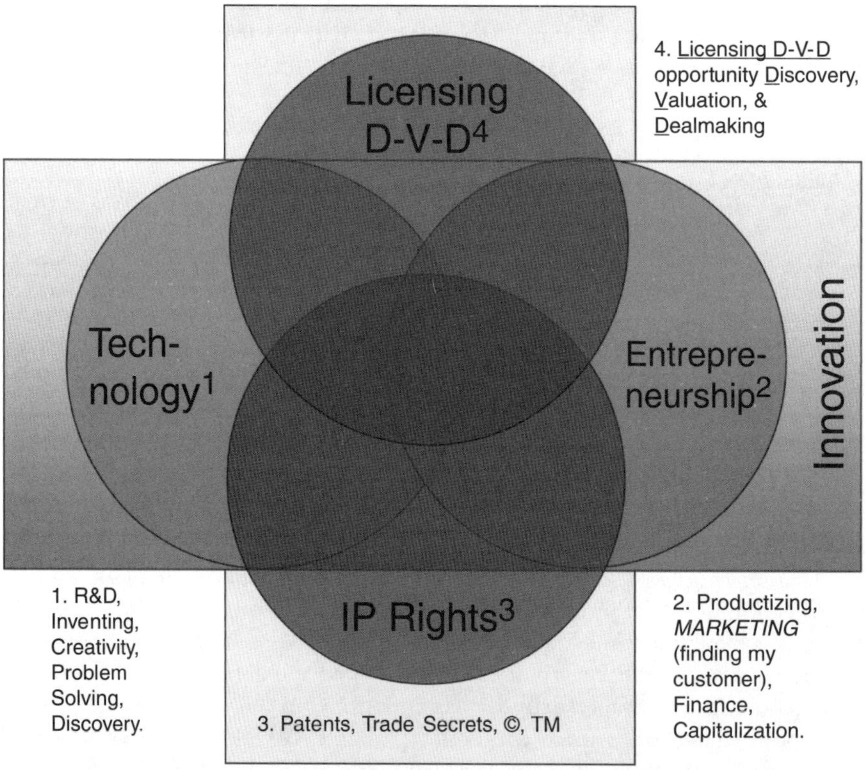

EXHIBIT 1.3 InterConnections of Licensing D-V-D

labeled Innovation, comprising Technology + Entrepreneurship. This is the conventional axis of a technology company's process of creating value for its customers and owners by the transformation of R&D results into products and services. Underlying Innovation is the establishment of IP rights that protect such investment and value.

Licensing D-V-D circle is shown in the Venn Diagram as overlapping all three circles. In some situations, there has been limited entrepreneurship, and Licensing D-V-D builds on Technology and IP Rights. This could occur because a university, institute, or private inventor developed the technology. It could also occur in situations when a company has technology opportunities for which it has not made entrepreneurial investments. In other situations, the technology could have been matured significantly along the Innovation box. In either situation, Licensing D-V-D provides an important commercialization pathway that does not require the technology's creator/owner to undertake commercial development into its own products and services. So, in a real sense, Licensing D-V-D is an always possible alternative to self commercialization. Sometimes such alternative is just an equivalent alternative, other times, a less desirable but necessary alternative, and still other times it is the best of all possible future worlds.

In the sub-sections below we will briefly consider certain proxies for size and scale of the four circles of Exhibit 1.3. We will focus on the most recent published data, 2006 and 2007, for the United States. Our purpose here is not to provide an exact analysis but to give some content and scale to these terms. The values reported below, as in U.S. dollars, are rounded and approximate. The reader is referred to the citations for the exact source data.

"Technology" as Measured by R&D Data

Industrial R&D spending is not exactly the same thing as "technology" as shown in Exhibit 1.3. But, annual R&D spending is a reasonable proxy for at least the *cost*, though not the *value*, of annual new technology creation.

R&D PERFORMED BY INDUSTRY R&D spending is a budgeted category, which is tracked and reported by companies on their income statement as part of a component of its overhead expenses along with sales, marketing, distribution, and administration. The U.S. National Science Foundation (NSF) has most recently reported on R&D Industry spending for the year 2006 in a report issued in August 2008:[4]

- Total spending was $250 billion, 95 percent of which can be grouped into three broad categories:
  - Two-thirds was spent in "DICE" industries, where DICE is my own designation for Digital Information Computing Electronics, which includes software and instrumentation, computer systems design, but not medical instrumentation.
  - 20 percent was spent in "Health" industries, which I have aggregated to include pharmaceuticals and medicines, as well as medical equipment and supplies, in addition to healthcare services.
  - 10 percent was spent on Aerospace, and Machinery combined.

- Total industrial revenues were $6.6 trillion, so R&D spending represented an industry average of 4 percent. 40 percent of total R&D spending occurred in three groups:
  - DICE revenues were nearly $1.8 trillion, so its R&D percentage was nearly 10 percent.
  - Health revenues were under $400 billion, with an R&D percentage likewise just under 10 percent.
  - The revenues of segments Aerospace and Machinery combined were over $500 billion combined, with an R&D percentage of 5 percent.
- There were more than 1 million R&D scientists and engineers in all industry segments; 80 percent were employed in three groups:
  - 60 percent were employed in DICE industries
  - 10 percent in Health industries
  - 10 percent in combined Aerospace and Machinery

There has been an important transformation of the source of such R&D funding. Up through 1978, just some 30 years ago, the U.S. government funded more than 50 percent of total U.S. R&D; the peak percentage was 67 percent in 1964 during the peak spending years on Apollo (and which helped pay my salary as a then "rocket scientist"). In 2006, the year the listed data were obtained, industry paid 72 percent of the R&D bill. That 67 percent government to 72 percent industry is a remarkable shift in less than 50 years.

R&D PERFORMED BY UNIVERSITIES, INSTITUTES, AND RESEARCH HOSPITALS Another very important category of R&D is that which is done at U.S. universities and institutes, including research hospitals. These data have been collected and published annually by the Association of University Technology Managers (AUTM). The most recent data is for Fiscal Year (FY) 2006. For 2006 the total reported R&D ("research") funding was $45 billion. More than two-thirds of such funding was by the U.S. federal government. Nearly 20,000 invention disclosures were reported by 190 survey respondents, which resulted in more than 10,000 new patent applications filed; also during 2006 more than 3,000 U.S. patents were issued (emanating almost entirely on filings in prior years). During the most recent three years, the reporting organizations filed patents on 60 percent of the disclosures received compared to less than 30 percent for years prior to 1995.

TECHNOLOGY DICE AND THE LITTLE ELECTRON Someone has estimated that 70 percent of the U.S. economy depends directly upon the manipulation of the electron. As first that may seem hard to believe, until one tries to list the industry segments that do *not* materially depend upon such manipulation. And it is remarkable to recognize that the discovery of the electron was just over 100 years ago (1897).[5]

TECHNOLOGY AND "CREATIVITY" Technology creation is connected to the encompassing subject of "creativity," the ability to create, or state of being one who creates, from the Latin word *creatus*, meaning to make or produce. Creativity of course exists in many domains outside of technology. When it is used with respect to technology it expresses the idea of bringing something new into being, and often with the flavor of the unexpected, or unpredictable. In this sense, creativity is also a key element of entrepreneurship, though the context is then more about "productization" of a technology, customer/market creation, and new business formation, though the lines blur. Here I have taken the two, technology creation and entrepreneurship, as together being "innovation."

There is a vast literature on fostering technology creativity and entrepreneurship. The reason for such interest, beside just the natural delight in observing it, is the widespread recognition of the importance of technology creation in economic development, meeting human and national needs (real and invented), and competitiveness (corporate and national).

TECHNOLOGY AND "SO WHAT?" Because this book is about discovering, in the sense of recognizing, significant commercial opportunities based on technology, valuing them, and Dealmaking with them, there is an intrinsic issue known as the "So what?" question. Such question arises in many frameworks, and contexts:

- *En emoi?* Ancient Greek for "What is it to me?"
- *Tai, kai?* Lithuanian for "So?"
- *Where's mine?* The classic city politician's expression

Creativity in technology, as opposed to say creativity in the field of art, is about what can the created thing actually do, and why such doing matters. The "So what?" question answer for "technology" differs from the answer for "science." For science the answer[6] is twofold:

1. *Explanation:* "theories that render intelligible and unsurprising phenomena that would otherwise seem incomprehensibly mysterious"
2. *Prediction:* "theories that can accurately and precisely predict the phenomena in their domains, in a non *ad hoc* fashion"

For "technology" the comparable definition is elusive. Using a parallel two factor definition, this is my attempt:

1. It is the craft, and art, of applying "science"
2. It moves toward some useful, economically justified benefit

The "craft/art" component is made actionable by ***Approaches*** (processes), ***Methods,*** and ***Tools,*** or ***A-M-T*** the organizing framework for this book—presented for the purpose of identifying, assessing, and Dealmaking the "useful, economically justified benefit" component.

It is common that with any pronouncement of something new there is an accompanying declaration answering the "So what?" we all ask. We will spend the rest of this book on ***Approaches, Methods,*** and ***Tools*** to prioritize, quantify, and communicate the answer. Here, let us think about a phenomenon of technology classification in terms of perceived significance.

Broadly speaking, claims about "So what?" for technology can be distinguished into two groups as shown under the headings shown in the accompanying table: "A Really Big Deal," and "Not So Big a Deal."

A Really Big Deal	Not So Big a Deal
Major	Minor
Breakthrough	Improvement
Foundational	Enhancement
Transformative	Incremental
Revolutionary	Routine
Next Generation (e.g., G3)	Current Generation (e.g., G2)
Web "N + 1" (e.g., 2.0)	Web N (e.g., 1.0)
Next Wave	Same wave
Quantum Leap[7]	Next Step
Great Leap (forward)	Next Step (up)
Paradigm Shift[8]	Same declinations, conjugations
Game Changer	Same old game, but some new pieces
Tomorrow	Coming later this afternoon
Sea Change	Same old sea
The Pirate Ship that Sailed into the Yacht Club Harbor	*Little Toot*, "the little tugboat that could..." by just trying harder

A great many technology pronouncements use some terms from the left, "Big Deal" column, especially words like "breakthrough." A recent study of company press releases has documented a dramatic increase (one might say, a breakthrough) in the frequency of the use of "breakthrough" to describe some new technology or product. Factiva Consulting Services found more than 8,000 press releases with the word "breakthrough" in just the headline (which, I suppose, if it is a breakthrough it should be in the headline).[9] A potential new software product idea, which idea I am giving away here for no extra charge, would be a word processor (1) that does not bomb with regularity, and (2) automatically sprinkles adjectives from the "Big Deal" column into a just-the-facts description of a new technology; it seems to me this could be a breakthrough product.

There are many challenges in making such "big deal" vs. "not big deal" distinctions:

- There is continuous spectrum from the really really big deal inventions, to the really really small improvements.
- "Technology" can be further subdivided into functional components:
  - Applied research
  - Development, demonstration
  - Manufacturing
  - Marketing
  - Service
  - Product/service continuous enhancement
- Almost everything belongs to some chain of history, meaning very few new technologies are genuinely without prior precedent.

But, perfection is for the next life. Making distinctions as best we can is both useful and necessary, especially when we are trying to distinguish and identify those things, including technology, that are of value: "No greater good can happen to a man than to discuss human excellence every day."[10] We will address the subject of distinctions in Chapter 2 when we consider risk and uncertainty.

BREAKTHROUGH PATENTS To demonstrate the distinction between the above two categories of inventions, let us here consider two breakthrough patents:

1. **2,708,656 (May 17, 1955) "Neutronic Reactor," Enrico Fermi and Leo Szillard**. This patent was awarded to the invention of the chain reaction method of nuclear fission that is the basis by which the more than 100 nuclear power plants in the U.S. (and many hundreds more around the world) operate. Femri and Szillard were giants in the field. The technology embodied in this patent was a clear breakthrough, though economically it is unlikely to have been valuable for the inventors because of the very long period of diffusion of such technology from R&D to commercial use.
2. **2,297,691 (October 6, 1942) "Electrophotography," Chester Carlson.**[11] This was the first of more than 100 patents invented by Chester Carlson, and his commercialization partner, Battelle Memorial Institute, that founded xerography. (The name xerography was "invented" over dinner across the street from Battelle in Columbus, Ohio during a discussion with an Ohio State University classics professor who suggested it because "xeros" is the classic Greek word for "dry" and "graphy" for writing). It was subsequently licensed to the Haloid Corporation which changed its name to Xerox® and founded an entire photocopying industry, and later with its Palo Alto CA laboratory (the famous PARC labs) created significant technologies that led to the personal computing industry. Although the basic xerography patent had expired before first significant commercial sales began (the Xerox 914 copier introduced in 1959), the many important follow-on patents created an important licensable package of IP rights, which led to substantial revenues for Xerox®, Battelle, and Mr. Carlson.[12]

Both of these patents are recognized among the more than 100 inventors (with their patents) inducted into the National Inventors Hall of Fame.[13]

NOT BREAKTHROUGH PATENTS This category is a long one. Let me suggest two as examples:

1. **6,239,919 (December 11, 2001), assigned to IBM Corp**., the annual leader in U.S. patents granted every year for more than a decade. This particular invention is for a reservations system of restrooms in commercial airplanes. Much like at a butcher counter, where you get a numbered ticket, whereupon you wait for your number to be called, this invention provides you a place in a virtual line to use the aircraft's facilities.
2. **6,368,227 (April 9, 2002), "Method of Swinging on a Swing," Steven Olson**. This invention is: "A method of swing on a swing is disclosed, in which a user positioned on a standard swing suspended by two chains from a substantially horizontal tree branch induces side to side motion by pulling alternately on one chain and then the other."[14]

"Entrepreneurship" as Measured by Intangible Value and Venture Capital Investments

There is no simple corresponding measure for "entrepreneurship." One very approximate measure is total intangible value reported on the balance sheets of companies. (A balance sheet is the measure of all a company's assets and liabilities as of a point in time, the year end of its fiscal year. Asset classes include familiar "things" like cash, accounts receivable, which should become cash, physical plant, property, and equipment. While "intangible assets" are a measure of its company value, a broad asset class that is not such a "thing.").

The accounting for intangible value and the interpretation of its practical meaning, is by no means a straightforward subject. One widely cited paper, written for the Federal Reserve Bank of Philadelphia by L.I. Nakamura,[15] estimates U.S. companies invest at least $1 trillion annually in intangible assets. Such a figure is approximately equal to the annual investment in tangible (nonresidential assets).

A more concrete comparison between the R&D component of intangible asset creation and investment in tangible assets can be seen from a *BusinessWeek* study of the 10 largest U.S. companies over the period 2000 through 2005. These companies reported an increase in their combined annual R&D spending of $11 billion or 42 percent over this period, while their capital spending increased by only $1 billion or 2 percent.[16]

Venture Capital (VC) spending is one measure of entrepreneurship investment. VC is high risk investments in companies that cannot readily access debt financing and are not yet public with availability of equity financing. Venture Capitalists (VCs) are making high risk investments in creating entirely new companies or expanding nascent ones. (We will return to this category of investment in Chapter 10). In the period 1995 through mid-2002, nearly 15,000 companies received VC investments. Although the "boom" VC years of 1999–2000 have abated, U.S. VCs still invest about $25 billion a year in 3,000 deals, which corresponds to approximately 10 percent of the total industrial R&D investment discussed above. Such monies are typically not for research, and some would argue there is not much spent on R&D either; this investment is primarily directed to the "Ds" of development and demonstration, especially market demonstration. But for technology or technology application, such investments can be considered as measures of entrepreneurship.

Companies of course make entrepreneurial-like investments in "business development" (biz dev, as it is known), an activity beyond just technology creation. Beyond this, some companies also have a separate initiative generally known as "corporate venturing," for creating entirely new business outside the mainstream of their current operations. Both kinds of company investments are not typically reported even for public companies. However, most technology companies have very senior titled positions such as Chief Technology Officer, or Vice President (VP) of Strategic Development, or some similar permutation. Such people are considered to have important creation responsibilities of businesses and markets that are not presently an important source of revenues and earnings.

The literature of corporate innovation, "creating businesses within the firm"[17] is overwhelmingly large. The subject is the corollary of all the stock picking books published for private investor consumption. Whole consulting industries, creativity workshops, team building, and such exist to help companies be more innovative.

Various companies have from time to time been noted for formal programs of "corporate venturing," also termed "intrapreneurship," including Xerox/PARC, Thermo Electron, and Tektronics.

INNOVATION EXAMPLES One interesting list was developed by *Forbes Magazine*. It published its list of the 85 "most consequential innovations since 1917," one per year.[18] Some examples on this list are:

- 1917, Sneakers (U.S. Rubber introduced "Keds")
- 1924, Frozen Food (Clarence Birdseye)
- 1930, Jet Engine (Sir Frank Whittle)
- 1962, Telstar I (first communications satellite)
- 1972, Ethernet (Xerox PARC)
- 1976, The Personal Computer (Steven Jobs, Stephen Wozniak)
- 1991, World Wide Web (Tim Berners-Lee)

The technology foundation within each of these examples is only an element of their high value "So what?" answer.

DIFFUSION OF INNOVATION There is significant literature on the "diffusion of innovation," meaning the rate and character of technology/innovation adoption. There is a common model known as the S-Curve that we will discuss in Chapter 8.

The classic model was published by Everett Rogers[19] based on a Normal (Gaussian) distribution (which we will cover in detail in Chapter 8) of adopters (buyers) in five distinct groups, who adopt the technology in sequential waves:

- Innovators (2.5 of the of the total)
- Early adopters (13.5 percent)
- Early majority (34 percent)
- Late majority (34 percent)
- Laggards (16 percent)

The cumulative adoption corresponding to a Gaussian rate is an S-shaped curve, with asymptotes at the beginning (slow growth in adoption) and at the end (slow growth at the end), with a rapid growth rate in between.

Any Normal Distribution of adoption rate, however such a *rate* is characterized or sliced, will exhibit an S-shaped cumulative *adoption* curve.

One measurement of adoption has been the time from invention until 25 percent penetration of U.S. households. For the telephone (invented in 1876) it was 35 years for such 25 percent penetration. The television (1927) took 26 years. More recent technologies, especially based on Moore's Law[20] exhibit much faster rates: The PC was 16 years, the mobile phone 13 years, and the Internet 7 years.

An example of one extensive data source[21] on innovation diffusion is given in Exhibit 1.4. The S-shape is the general pattern, but like much of real world data, it is a little messy.[22]

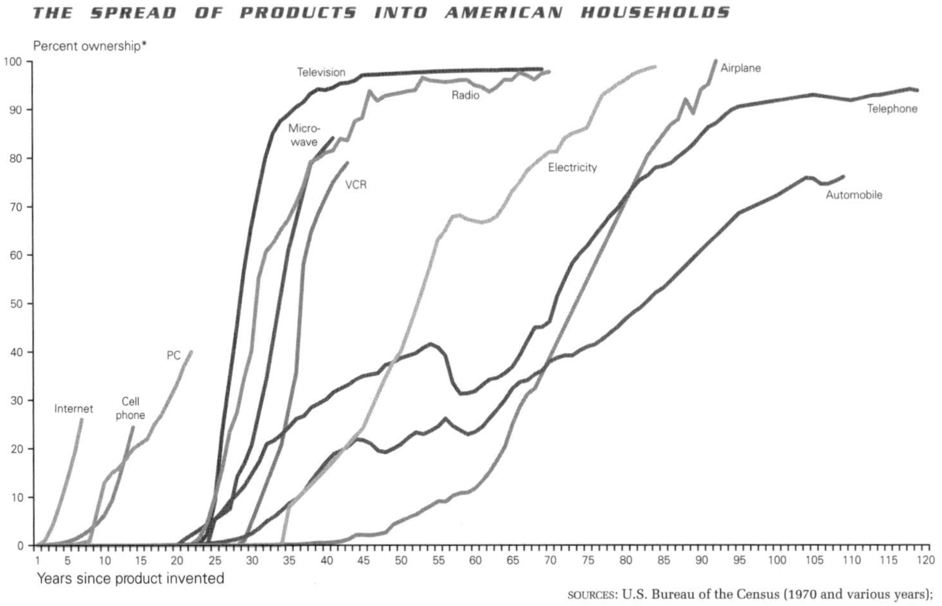

**Percent ownership*refers to the fraction of households that enjoy each product, except for the airplane, automobile and cell phone. *Airplane* refers to the percentage of air miles traveled per capita relative to miles traveled in 1996; *automobile* refers to the number of motor vehicles relative to persons age 16 and older; *cell phone* refers to the number of cellular phones per registered passenger automobile.

SOURCES: U.S. Bureau of the Census (1970 and various years); Cellular Telecommunications Industry Association (1996); The World Almanac and Book of Facts (1997).

EXHIBIT 1.4 Diffusion of Innovation Historical Data

THE "NEW ECONOMY" The subject matter of many business negotiations is changing as fundamentally as the economic structure of the businesses themselves, from being about the value of tangible things such as machines and buildings, to the right to use intangibles such as information and technology. This shift in underlying business value is often characterized by the term New Economy. Although a full discussion of what constitutes such a New Economy deals with broad issues of economic theory and is beyond the scope of this book, it is useful for us to consider some concrete examples. Just over 100 years ago (in 1901) the first U.S. company to emerge with a market value of $1 billion ($1.4 billion in authorized capitalization) was U.S. Steel. ($1 billion in 1901 is approximately equivalent to $40 billion in 2008.) It achieved such valuation primarily through property, plant, and equipment (PPE), three traditional measures of industrial, tangible value. U.S. Steel, which became the company known as USX in 1986, was an icon of the new industrial age and the Old Economy. The company in 1901 owned 213 manufacturing plants, 41 mines, 1,000 miles of railroad and employed more than 160,000 people. U.S. Steel's book value, as measured by accountants and reported on the company's balance sheet was substantially determined by its PPE and closely reflected such market value.

One hundred years later, in 2001, the most valuable company in the United States was Microsoft, an icon of the information age and the New Economy, when it reached a market capitalization[23] (or market cap) of $400 billion. We now know that in 2001 there was a "bubble" over valuation of technology companies, including Microsoft. In 2008, its value had fallen to $200 billion (and less). Its book value of PPE in 2008 is $13 billion, so the ratio of market cap to PPE book is still a dramatic 15 to 1. How can this be? Microsoft's value lies in the very significant intangible value associated with Microsoft's copyrighted software, which is just a string of 1s and 0s, bits, in an archived Microsoft facility; know-how and patents, along with its trademark and tradename value.[24]

Yet another measure of the transformation of the U.S. economy is evident in transportation. In the first decade of the 20th century, ca. 60 percent of companies traded on the New York Stock Exchange were railroads, entities that stored and shipped things with mass. During the first decade of the twenty-first century our market economy is led by companies like Microsoft, IBM, Cisco, AT&T that store and ship massless data bits.

Think of the effect on a negotiation to buy or sell some component of the respective assets of a U.S. Steel in 1901 versus Microsoft in 2001. In the case of U.S. Steel we would be characterizing something tangible using available standards of reference for transactions of other like tangibles to guide both our valuation and negotiation preparation.

Estimates have been made of the value of IP to the U.S. economy. One recent estimate by Shapiro and Hassett[25] is the following: IP in the U.S. is worth more than $5 trillion, which exceeds the nominal gross domestic product of any other nation. One has only to Google "$5 trillion Shapiro" to see how widely cited is this claim. For example, the Global IP Center of the U.S. Chamber of Commerce[26] and even Congressional testimony[27] in addition to amicus curiae briefs filed before the U.S. Supreme Court,[28] and more recently in 2009 in the context of re-introduction of patent reform legislation,[29] where appended to the citation of $5 trillion was a statement that such IP value represented "nearly 70 percent of corporate assets."

"IP" as Measured by Patent Data

IP is more than just patents, but number of patents applied for and insured are usefully quantified figures that are reasonable proxies for the growth in investment in IP.

There are approximately 1.6 million U.S. patents currently unexpired out of more than 6 million that have been issued since 1790, including one to Abraham Lincoln. All these patents, as Judge Randall Rader of the Court of Appeals of the Federal Circuit (CAFC) has pointed out, are gifted to society upon their expiry, more than 4 million so far, and in another decade the total will be approximately 6 million.

In just calendar 2007, the U.S. Patent and Trademark Office received more than 450,000 "utility" (for our purposes "technology") patent applications (nearly 10,000 a week!), and issued (granted) nearly 160,000 (more than 3,000 every Tuesday). Of course the patents applied for in 2007, in most cases, were not the ones that issued in 2007, because of pendency issues. Such figures include both U.S. and foreign inventor filings and issuances for U.S. patents.

In 1964, the referenced year of peak government investment (see the section R&D Performed by Industry earlier in this chapter) as a percentage for industrial R&D, the respective number of applications was under 90,000 and issuances 45,000. So, over this period the number of annual patent applications has increased by a factor of five, and issuances by a factor of nearly four.

The categories of technology patents have also changed. In the early 1980s "software" patents were a tiny percentage of the total; currently they represent approximately 15 percent of all patents issued.

Trade secrets, another form of IP rights, encompass a wide array of know-how valuable to the application of a technology that is not publicly known. There is no comparable registry or tracking means as there is with patents. Yet for many technology opportunities, trade secret IP is an important component of value.

RELATIONSHIP BETWEEN R&D SPENDING AND PATENTS A correlation between R&D investment magnitude and resulting number of patents is problematic at least because trade secret protection of technology does not get counted. Yet, there has been interest in this relationship. One comparison was reported by *Fortune Magazine* of seven large pharmaceutical companies in the period 1996 to 2001.[30] They found that these companies spent a widely varying amount of R&D per patent obtained: from $6 million per patent (Merck, and Pharmacia) to $26.5 and $74.5 million (for Wyeth and Schering-Plough, respectively), with Eli Lilly, Bristol-Myers Squibb, and Pfizer in between these bounds.

As another benchmark, IBM receives about 3,000 U.S. patents a year, and spends about $6 billion annually on R&D. So a simple ratio yields $2 million per patent.

"Dealmaking" (of Licensing D-V-D) as Measured by Licenses and Royalties

There is no known measure of technology Dealmaking across the entire U.S. economy. The U.S. Internal Revenue Service (IRS) has reported on its analysis of corporate tax returns for "royalties" reported. For 2002 the total reported royalty income for active corporations was $115 billion, but this includes copyright royalties for media and natural resources such as oil field royalties. The IRS reported $73 billion for the "manufacturing" sector, and $5 billion for "scientific and technical services." The $13 billion reported for the "information sector" includes copyright media royalties.

The best known source of Dealmaking data is the cited AUTM annual survey. For FY 2006, AUTM reported the Dealmaking data shown in Exhibit 1.5.

The top 25 respondents had a total licensing income in FY 2006 of $1 billion, led by the University of California system with nearly $200 million and New York University with more than $150 million. 26 universities had licensing revenues

EXHIBIT 1.5 Dealmaking Data for AUTM Survey Respondents for FY 2006

FY 2006	Number of Respondents	Total Executed	Startups	% of Total	Small Companies	% of Total	Large Companies	% of Total
U.S. Universities	161	4,192	698	16.7	2,127	50.7	1,327	31.7
U.S. Hospitals & Research Institutions	28	755	66	8.7	289	38.3	321	42.5
Technology Investment Firms	1	16	0	0	0	0	0	0
All Respondents	190	4,963	764	15.4	2,416	48.7	1,648	33.2

between $10 million and $60 million. The top 25 universities had a combined annual license income of $1 billion.

The ratio of R&D spending to current year number of patents ranged from just under $3 million to nearly $50 million for the top 25 universities in terms of license income.

Going Forward

In this chapter we have positioned the scope of this book in the broad context in which it belongs. In Chapter 3 when we discuss the package of assets that a technology owner-seller will offer to prospective licensees-buyers we will use the metaphor of The Box. We will assume that such Box will be encompassing the three lower circles of Exhibit 1.3, namely: (1) the technology plus (2) any available entrepreneurial results, (3) protected in some way by various IP forms. As we will see in Chapters 10 and 11 on Dealmaking, the licensee-buyer will provide consideration in trade likewise using a mosaic of values (which will be referred to as The Wheelbarrow). Such valuation and Dealmaking will be in the context of *opportunity* licensing, the focus of this book.

We introduced the core idea of making distinctions by creating discrete groups. This is a foundational idea for all that follows. In Chapter 2 we will have an expanded discussion on grouping, which, will recur when developing Rating/Ranking, risk classification, and other contexts.

In this chapter we noted the challenges of making forecasts of the benefits of the use/application of a technology. Yet making such forecasts is the basis of determining value, and so cannot be avoided. In Chapter 2 we will consider the effects of risk and uncertainty, factors particularly important to technology valuation.

Finally, we have given some sense of scale of technology. Massive annual investments are made in its creation, and its application to commercial use. All that ongoing investment and risk taking is for the purpose of making the world a better place and rewarding the investors, inventors, and entrepreneurs. Let us try to figure out how important technology opportunities can be discovered, valued, traded.

Additional information is available at my web site: www.razgaitis.com. In any writing, especially a long one, there are inevitable, maddening, errata; I will try to maintain a current list (contributions are welcome: errata@razgaitis.com). Also on the website are certain Excel® templates that are used in later chapters and a bibliography of other resources including interesting, relevant websites. Finally, there is a link to Oracle.com for a free trial of its Crystal Ball® Monte Carlo software that is used extensively in the Advanced Valuation Method (Chapter 8).

Notes

1. Aristotle defined *techne* as a capacity to do or make something with a correct understanding of the principle involved. So this book may be thought, I hope, as a *techne* about the business process of opportunity Discovery, Valuation, and Dealmaking of *techne* opportunities. (*Techne* itself comes from the Indo-European root *tekth* meaning to weave or join, which is the source of the Latin word *texere* meaning to weave or build from which we get the word *textile*.)

2. A quantum "leap" is likely the worst oxymoron in existence. A quantum is the *smallest* possible energy difference in the universe. What a "leap" in such context is meaningless, but the term "quantum" has some sex appeal so the phrase has entered our vocabulary.
3. "How Internet Time's Fifteen Minutes of Fame Ran Out," *Wall Street Journal*, October 28, 2002, p. B1.
4. Source: www.nsf.gov/statistics/infbrief/nsf08313/
5. Attributed to J.J. Thompson. There's an interesting anecdote regarding Thompson's announcement of its discovery: his audience thought he was joking, because it was widely accepted as dogma that nothing smaller than an atom could exist.
6. Prof. Edward Hall, "Philosophy of Science," Massachusetts Institute of Technology, Course QM 24.111, 2 February 2005.
7. See footnote 2.
8. We have a widely cited book by Thomas Kuhn, *The Structure of Scientific Revolution* (University of Chicago Press, 1962), to thank for the introduction of "paradigm" into our common vocabulary. A *paradigm* is the rules of conjugation of verbs and declination of nouns. So a paradigm shift would be that instead of saying "I am, you are, and he is," we might instead start saying "I am, you am, he am," or "I are, you is, and he am." It seems that "you is" is already catching on as we speak.
9. "Some 'Breakthroughs' Deserve the Title—But Not All," *Wall Street Journal,* September 7, 2006. It can be argued that for an announcement to be warranted there is a perfectly appropriate bias toward the "big deal" category; minor inventions may just come into being without much drama.
10. Plato's attribution to Socrates during his post-trial discussions with friends shortly before his death by forced suicide.
11. http://en.wikipedia.org/wiki/Chester_Carlson, www.lib.rochester.edu/index.cfm?PAGE=467, www.ieeeghn.org/wiki/index.php/Inventor_of_Xerography:_Chester_F._Carlson.
12. In my earlier career I was Vice President of Commercial Development for Battelle, and those xerography license agreements were part of our office's files. In a delicious irony, those agreements were all *carbon copies* whose originals had been made in a mechanical typewriter.
13. http://invent.org/, http://en.wikipedia.org/wiki/National_Inventors_Hall_of_Fame,
14. Description from the patent abstract. The inventor made public that he was seeking licensees, whereupon I wrote and requested his term sheet for a nonexclusive license for the field of use of large Lithuanians; so far, five years later, no reply.
15. "What is the Gross Investment in Intangibles? (At Least) One Trillion Dollars a Year!" L.I. Nakamura, Federal Reserve Bank of Philadelphia, Working Paper No. 01-15, October 2001.
16. "Why the Economy is a Lot Stronger Than You Think," *BusinessWeek,* February 13, 2006.
17. See, for instance, Zenas Block and Ian C. MacMillan, *Corporate Venturing—Creating New Businesses within the Firm,* Harvard Business School Press, 1993.
18. "Years and Ideas," *Forbes Magazine*, December 23, 2002, p. 123ff.
19. Everett Rogers, *Diffusion of Innovations*, Free Press, 4th ed. 1995
20. This widely cited "law" is based on a prediction by Gordon Moore of Intel who, in 1965, predicted a dramatic rate of growth in integrated circuit capacity while, at the same time, declining unit price.
21. Federal Reserve Bank of Dallas, 1996: www.nationmaster.com/encyclopedia/Diffusion_of_innovations
22. One is reminded of the cartoon of a university campus physics lecture to dairy farmers in Wisconsin. On the blackboard is a very large, hand drawn circle (more or less). The caption of the wide-eyed professor's opening remarks is: "First, we will assume a spherical cow."
23. Determined by the number of equity shares times the price per share.

24. In both the U.S. Steel and the Microsoft examples, I have used market capitalization as the measure of company value. A more complete picture of total enterprise value would use the sum of equity and debt. In the case of Microsoft, debt is negligible compared to its equity value.
25. Robert J. Shapiro and Kevin A. Hassett, "The Economic Value of Intellectual Property," USA for Innovation, October 2005, p. 3. Dr. Shapiro was Undersecretary of Commerce for economic affairs under President Clinton, and has been a senior advisor to Al Gore and John Kerry during their presidential campaigns.
26. www.theglobalipcenter.com/NR/rdonlyres/ebynkgugywgbp7i6tclq3qotsjqu3xsguy4dj6jxxuyw2iys2uarb7yjtegc52qka4ax4kxv63cyvt246w45knudcoh/gipc_ipbook.pdf
27. Testimony of Kevin Sharer, CEO and Chairman of the Board of Amgen Inc., before the Subcommittee on Courts, the Internet, and Intellectual Property, Committee of the Judiciary, U.S. House of Representatives, April 26, 2007.
28. Filed by the United Inventors Association, on Petition for a Writ of Certiorari, in the matter of KSR International Co., v. Teleflex, Inc. et al., October 16, 2006.
29. Press Club Speech, by Senator Orrin G. Hatch, given March 18, 2009, published http://legaltimes.typepad.com/files/03182009-press-club-speech.pdf.
30. "The 2003 Fortune 500," *Fortune Magazine*, March 30, 2003, based on an analysis by Merrill Lynch.

CHAPTER 2

Risk and Reward

This chapter deals with issues that underlie the rest of this book. The overall purpose of this book is to transform a technology opportunity into a consummated license/sale that creates at least two happy parties. Hence the acronym TR R A DE™ introduced in Chapter 1: Technology Rights exchanged for Deal Economics, all based on a skill or Art, including that of Risk assessment.

The calculation we must make is of what opportunities to choose, and how much to invest, in the face of what uncertainties and risks to gain what reward. Both the seller and the buyer must make these judgments, each from their perspectives and needs. And, ultimately, this process has to reach an agreement for any reward to be realized.

This technology opportunity realization process has to occur within an environment of both high risk and high uncertainty. The high risk environment causes both buyers and sellers to be cautious and skeptical. The high uncertainty environment drains confidence and optimism. These twin villains, risk and uncertainty, are viral enemies of opportunity creation. But there are good twins:

- As necessity is the mother of invention, so is the reward the magnet for investment, and the presence of risk and uncertainty act as barriers to risk-averse, "easy pickings" treasure hunters preserving opportunities for those who can both recognize them and properly price their risk.
- There exist Approaches-Methods-Tools (**A-M-T**) that, though they cannot extinguish risk and uncertainty, can frame an opportunity to enable reasonable judgments to be made.

Uncertainty

Let us think first about what we mean by "certainty." To be certain is to know something concretely, without any aspect of doubt. There is something deeply attractive of *being* certain.

Our living reality is that such *being* is simply denied to us except in the most limited of circumstances. Here are the kinds of things we know with certainty: Four is larger than two, two plus two equals four, and three is between two and four. We also know certain universal relationships with certainty: A circle's circumference is equal to its diameter times a universal constant, π (pi), every place in the universe, at every instant since Creation, without exception. But, consider that universal constant, π, itself. Is it known, is it knowable? The answer, for more 2500 years, is "not yet." It has been calculated to more than 50 billion (!) decimal digits, but its exact value is not known, nor is it knowable. Yet, 3.14 will get you what you need to know in almost every life circumstance.

If we think of certainty in graphical terms, we can put a Euclidian point (the zero size marker) above a time x-axis at a height representing some value measure we know with certainty at this exact moment. *Uncertainty*, in graphical terms is the error bars we have to extend above and below any value point we may attempt to locate. Every bridge you or I have ever crossed has loads (forces) on all its supporting elements that were never exactly known, or knowable, by its designer. If we required certainty from its designer there would be, could be, no bridges.

Ambiguity

In Chapter 1 we made the distinction that Technology Licensing D-V-D is typically a high ambiguity environment. Let us think about what that means in the context of the graphical metaphor of the certainty point and uncertainty bars. If we could know with certainty what the bounds of uncertainty were, the upper and lower edges of such graphical bars, then we have another kind of certainty, absolute knowledge that the value being portrayed lies between fixed upper and lower limits. In certain domains we do know such bounds: Three and π are each bounded by two and four. In the bridge example, we can know that the load on each support strut is bounded by zero and the total weight of the bridge and every possible vehicle and human that could be on it at any given moment (plus their dynamic loads caused by entering the bridge). But the bounded certainty of the numbers example is just a definition, and the bridge example helps very little in sizing a strut because no bridge could be built using such upper bound as the design rule.

So instead of exact error bars above and below our best estimate of the certainty point, we need to think of probability zones. By definition our best estimate value is going to represent our best thinking about the true value of whatever we are calculating. For values diverging above and below such point we will have some basis for believing that such values are increasingly less probable. Even the weather man/woman, with all the instruments and satellite imagery, will most often forecast future rain in terms of probabilities.

The Effect of Time

The given illustrations were about knowing and not knowing now, at one moment in time, by placing our Euclidian certainty point above a particular point above the x time-axis. There are certain business world problems that are about knowing something now, based upon both grasping the past and present into some status document, such as the standard accounting statements. Even the task of knowing something now is not easy. The business news of this first decade of the 21st Century is replete with examples where even such present business knowledge was not only materially wrong, it wasn't even close to being reasonably right.

But Technology Licensing D-V-D is primarily about the future. So, returning to our graphical metaphor, we not only are faced with ambiguity above and below any present value estimate, expressed in probabilities, predicting the future necessarily expands our zone of relative probabilities. However uncertain we are about now, it is hard to conceive of circumstances where we will be anything but more uncertain in some future time.

So by the ambiguity distinction, we mean that (1) we do not have even the knowledge of uncertainty bars above and below any estimated true value, because we do not know, we cannot know, how large those bars are, (2) we necessarily express our beliefs with probabilities, and (3) those probabilities are becoming increasingly diffuse about some future state. What then?

The Golden Mean

One temptation in such predicaments is to abandon any investment in reasoning or judgment, and just guess a value if/as necessary. The polar opposite temptation is to shake one's fist at ambiguity, launch a full scale analytical assault with the objective of creating certainty, against all odds (and, I might add, against all hope). If the latter course is doomed, why not just take the former?

The answer, an ancient one, is that lying between these poles is the wise course of action, because: (1) there are Approaches, Methods, and Tools—**A-M-T**—that can greatly improve on pure guesswork, and (2) uncertainty, though it cannot be eliminated, it can be profitably reduced. There is an underlying deep idea here commonly known as the Aristotelian (or Golden) Mean.

The idea of the mean is that the wisest course of action is usually bounded by unwise extremes. In one sense this can be seen as just a way of compromising or somehow making everyone, or every consideration, equally unhappy. But compromise is not what makes such mean good, let alone golden. The sense is that there is something genuinely true at each extreme, but that the given situation has multiple relevant "truths" that could and should be assessed. So the mean is a representation of the borrowing of some "truth" from each pole region to establish something that is more "true" than either pole considered alone, a kind of "higher middle."

The Mean for High Uncertainty Decision Making

Our present application of the "mean" question is the high uncertainty environment typical of technology opportunities, including the ***Approaches*** of Valuation and Dealmaking. The concept is shown in Exhibit 2.1.

If, then, every art or science perfects its work in this way, looking into the mean and bringing its work up to this standard (so that people are accustomed saying of a good work, that nothing could be taken from it or added to it, implying that excellence is destroyed by excess or deficiency, but secured by observing, the mean; and good artists, as we say, do in fact keep their eyes fixed on this in all that they do), and if virtue (*areté*), like nature, is more exact and better than any art, it follows *that virtue also must aim at the mean* . . . . For instance, it is possible to feel fear, confidence, desire, anger, pity, and generally to be affected pleasantly and painfully, either too much or too little, in either case wrongly; but to be thus affected at the right times, and on the right occasions, and towards the right persons, and with the right object, and in the right fashion, is the mean course and the best course, and these are characteristics of virtue . . . Virtue, then, is a kind of moderation inasmuch as it aims at the mean or moderate amount.[1]

Nothing meaningful can be known, and no judgment is possible.
Can be eliminated (by analysis), and must be to make judgments.

EXHIBIT 2.1 The Polar Perspectives of High Uncertainty Technology Environment

Both poles have reasoned arguments in their support. That is an essential feature of the process of finding the wiser "mean." The "mean" would not make any sense if one pole or the other were completely unfounded. There is no value in finding a "mean" edged by one or two stupidities. The question we face in Exhibit 2.1, and much of our work here, is this: Is there a greater wisdom than that expressed by either pole? Put another way, is there a more persuasive position than that at either pole obtainable by recognizing and incorporating some 'truth' from both poles?

Consider the rightmost pole, uncertainty can be eliminated and must be to make judgments. Is the "can" assertion true about technology, business, about anything? Is the "must" imperative actionable—in the sense that we accept the implied duty because it is doable–in technology, business, or life? The answer to both questions is a general "no," though mathematicians and geometers make this their life calling within the assumptions of their frameworks, and we would like to think the brain surgeon about to operate on one of our kids knows pretty much what he or she is doing and why, and that bridge designer did make some reasonable estimates of structure loads and added a margin of safety so that there is a very low probability that it will come tumbling down during anyone's trip during its projected lifetime.

So, if we were to accept the rightmost pole as being "right," life would pretty much come to a halt because for most situations we would never fulfill our obligation for certainty. But, as a self evident truth, we all understand that this cannot be "right," and we certainly don't behave that way in everyday life.

What about the leftmost pole? Let's consider the context of state-run lotteries, where a prize is awarded on six numbers (Pick Six). Would there be a point in conducting any analysis—other than on the stupidity of playing such lotteries—in choosing six numbers? The answer is a certain "no," but it is a certain answer about a perfectly uncertain world because such world has been designed to be uncertain and defy uncertainty reduction. Such lotteries are perfect random number generators. So any six numbers, are equally "good", even 666666, even repeatedly played every day for the rest of your life. When faced with a world of designed randomness, we are doomed to not knowing, and no **A-M-T** is going to rescue us from that condition.

But is the business or technology world, or life itself, similarly pure randomness? If we really believed this, we would make decisions using the traditional "tool" of random situations, pulling numbers (choices) out of a hat. The pure skeptic has the upper hand in arguments about knowledge, because every belief, statement, or number can be challenged by the absence of certainty. The answer to the skeptic's challenge is the mean is almost always better that the state of absolute ignorance, and so we do what we can to get there.

Einstein's Razor

This then leads to an important follow-on question: How and to what extent are we to perform the analysis suggested by the "mean" in Exhibit 2.1? (So we face these polar choices again and again). One polar response is, consider everything and exhaustively; the other pole would of course be consider just one thing and cursorily. This tension is related to an important idea in science and philosophy. The scientific giant of the 20th Century, Albert Einstein, expressed it this way: "It can scarcely be denied that the supreme goal of all theory is to make the irreducible basic elements as simple and as few as possible without having to surrender the adequate representation of a single datum of experience."[2] This is commonly cited as "Everything should be made as simple as possible, but not simpler," though it is unclear if he ever said exactly this simplified version. This observation is commonly referred to as Einstein's Razor, because it relates to a famous statement by Occam known as Occam's Razor: "*Pluralitas non est ponenda sine neccesitate*"[3] (Entities/ideas should not be multiplied unnecessarily).

The idea behind Einstein's Razor is this: The world is vastly too complicated for humans to account for everything. Simplifications are not just acts of indolence (though sluggards are everywhere). Simplifications are essential for us to grasp complex matters. Our bodies behave this way with respect to all its senses. If we were to be continually conscious of every sensory input, such all-encompassing sentience would overwhelm us, in the same way our thoughts would were we unable to harness them to focus on one thing at a time.

Phronesis (Judgment)

So, how do we decide on what to include and the depth of inclusion on what we are attempting to analyze? The answer is judgment. There is an ancient Greek idea that is exactly on this point: *φρόνησισ*(fro-KNEE or NAY-sis, which is Anglicized to *Phronesis* or sometimes *Fronesis*). It is the conjunction of two words, *fro* (from) + *nous* (head, or seat of reasoning). It is commonly translated practical wisdom (wisdom is about choosing), prudence, or judgment. Such wisdom is a key element of the "A" for Art in our TR R A DE ™ acronym.

In our brief initial consideration, we have at least three contexts where such judgment is needed: (1) What is worth being studied in the first place, (2) What are the appropriate **A-M-T** with models and assumptions for conducting the study, and (3) What can we, should we, best do when we complete such analysis? There is no escaping the need for judgment. It is that critical quality that is not independent of **A-M-T**, but uses what is needed as it is needed to make value judgments about what is worth doing. It is that human capacity we value most in people, particularly those in leadership situations whose decisions affect our well being, and long to establish in our children, even when (during the ages of 14 to 21) this appears to be an intractable possibility.

In the above discussion we have made the distinction between ambiguity and uncertainty. In everyday language ambiguity is freighted with a negative connotation that conflicts with the mentioned core idea, namely that there is something that can be known, including probability estimates, and that based on such, reasonable judgments can often be made. For this reason we will hereafter treat ambiguity as synonymous with uncertainty.

Technology Uncertainty

Although every business process involves uncertainty, for technology opportunity Discovery, Valuation, and Dealmaking, uncertainty is generally greater and more complex. Let us consider some aspects of uncertainty and how they differ for technology compared to normal business practice.

General Issues of Uncertainty

The business environment of operating companies has financial uncertainties of all kinds. The year 2000 technology bubble and the 2008 tumult of companies in the housing business, as well as structured finance products created and sold by financial institutions, has shown how dramatic those uncertainties can be. But with companies, such uncertainties tend to be less dramatic and less extensive than with any given technology. Companies tend to know, or should, how its technologies work, how to operate their manufacturing plant, what IP assets they own and what may be owned by others, who their competitors are and generally what they're up to, and what their customers want and need, and when. There are people who are held accountable for product development, manufacturing, marketing, sales, and IP/legal for each major product category who can be called upon to give a status report of key issues both current and anticipated.

With a technology many if not all of these areas are undergoing development. Further many of these areas are interconnected. For instance, what the market may need or want depends on what the technology can specifically do, and what the costs will be (manufacturability). But manufacturability and such costs depend on how big the market will be. And what the technology can be made to do is a moving target depending on the market pricing, competitive response, and manufacturability. One can picture a large table with all the key technology development leaders trying to nail down who knows anything for sure, and each area deferring its reply until all the others have responded. Technology development requires an iterative simultaneity that is a more uncertain environment than normal product life cycle improvement of incumbent businesses.

Forecast Uncertainty

Creating forecasts is a basic business requirement for both management and investors. Companies with a wealth of historical data on which to base forecasts, provide only limited forecasts to investors, in part because (for public companies) the market lets them get away with it, and, in part because they do not want to take the risk of being wrong and being sued. So a "forecast" for a public company is expressed as something like the next quarter's or year's "guidance," which is usually given as a number range like or "low single digits" of growth and affirmed by phrases such as "we're comfortable with...". Internally, companies of course have made more specific and longer range forecasts, but even in such situations these forecasts typically do not extend for many years, and rely heavily on growth from their existing baseline of financial data.

But technology forecasting lacks the historical data available in customary business contexts, because there isn't any. Because technologies by definition are precommercial, there can be an extended investment period of R&D and market development before even initial revenues occur. Key IP rights may yet be secured. Key technology performance and/or manufacturability questions may not yet be answered. The market may be undefined, with key customer valued features/functions yet to be demonstrated. For technology opportunities to be presently valuable there often needs to be a long tail of future revenues and net cash inflows to compensate for the investment and risk. This then may require forecasts extending for many years into future, starting with no or limited historic data and certain important present uncertainties.

Quantification

Quantification is a term used here to describe the granularity of typical forecasts of financial performance. Established companies have the benefit of aggregation of many technologies into many products and markets as well as territories. So when these companies make forecasts they are not typically doing so at the granular level of any single technology asset. They benefit by the law of large numbers as well as incumbency.

For technology opportunities it is common to consider one-by-each potential market applications for various territorial regions. Such consideration need not be exhaustive, but the value of an opportunity can be critically affected by the difference in perceived value if there is only a single market application in a limited territory verses multiple products in wide geographic market.

Risk

We will consider risk in more detail later in this chapter. But here let us consider how risk and uncertainty are related.

Uncertainty and risk are not the same thing. The word risk is generally used to characterize the possible consequences of adversity that cannot be foreknown.

With companies, there is obvious risk. Any comparison of the top 10 or top 50 companies in terms of market value or revenues decade by decade will show that even companies at the top of their respective industries do not always long endure. But companies once established do have a natural capacity to adapt and stay alive. Leadership can be held accountable for their respective responsibilities. And when a company experiences adversity, the downside of risk, it often has adaptation alternatives such as moving into different markets or selling itself to acquirers. When companies are well managed, the uncertainties under which it operates are low as are their downside risks.

Technology is just naturally riskier. The challenge is not just that we know less about the opportunity; it is that the consequences of that which is known and unknown have more significant negative financial probabilities. Some of such risk is parallel to the risk of holding the equity (stock) of an individual company rather than a mutual fund of multiple companies. But, the technology risk environment is

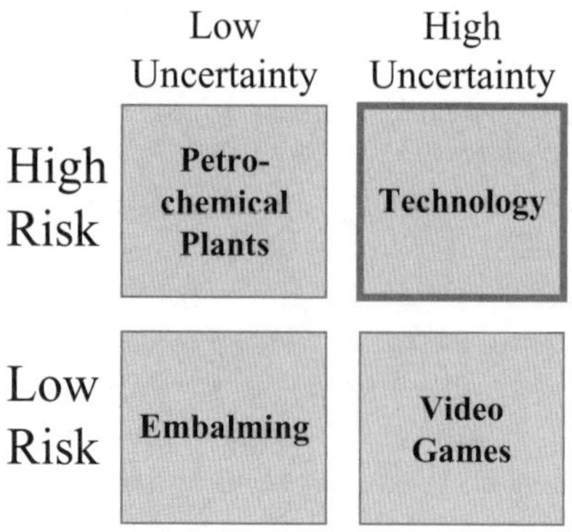

EXHIBIT 2.2 Four Risk-Uncertainty Contexts

more than just individuation. A brand new startup company with an inexperienced management team seeking to commercialize a product for which there is no prior market is simply a riskier situation than a single established, and diversified company, say a GE or IBM (although as we have seen in 2008 and 2009, even IBM, which has lost more than 25 percent of its value in year ending Q1 2009 and GE which lost more than two-thirds of its value in the same 12 month period have shown that being established, big, and diversified is not a guarantor of business certainty or risk-avoidance).

The ideas of risk and uncertainty can be combined in a two-by-two matrix to establish four contexts as shown in Exhibit 2.2.

The distinctions shown in Exhibit 2.2 can be debated, as to what is "low" and what is "high," but the general idea is worth illustrating. Petrochemical plants require hundred million dollar investments. Such expenditures are not made if the uncertainty of technical or market success is high, so they are shown in the low uncertainty column. Their day-to-day risk level can be considered low because they operate in a low uncertainty world. However, the consequences of something going wrong can be very high. We could also put brain surgery in this box.

Mature industries with low capital intensity and limited environmental or human health and safety issues also tend to fall in the low/low box. Video games and some software products can also be in this category. These products can be developed relatively cheaply and quickly (though of course not all manifestations of such product are in this category). The risk here is principally market risk, namely the product just fails to attract customers, although IP risk can be a factor.

Our technology situation tends to be the top right box, both high risk and high uncertainty. This leads to an important common behavior: iterative learning.

Iterative Learning

The technology box of Exhibit 2.2 suggests two interrelated strategies, iteration and learning.

The idea behind iteration is to not decide on the entire course of events but to start by some limited analysis, to develop an initial understanding, and then reconsidering the opportunity. There are a variety of terms and ideas for this. One is developing a *provisional* valuation. Such provisional valuation based on limited initial data, and analysis, would be done for the purpose of a limited commitment, going to the next step, with a measure investment whose risk is constrained.

Another term of art is stage gate product development. The idea here is that at some point in time, there is enough apparent merit in the technology to support taking a limited risk to get to a specific next decision point, called a gate. A very early stage technology could be assessed by a half dozen such gates, which are to be entered and exited one at a time. The idea is to spend a little, to limit downside risk, and learn a little, so the risk at the next gate is reduced.

The second strategy is learning, specifically active learning. With mature technologies one tends to know all that one is going to know, and needs to know, in terms of the basic science and engineering. The learning needed may be in markets and channels of distribution. With premature technologies there is much that is not known that is important, perhaps critically important, to know even about the science and engineering aspects.

Combining a provisional understanding, with some process for spending a little to shrink some important aspect of uncertainty is one way of dealing with the combination of high risk and high uncertainty. This embodies the idea of a quest, a subject we will return to at the close of this book.

In the chapters that follow on Technology, Licensing D-V-D we will understand that every task is faced with uncertainty and risk. We are however making appropriate investments in time and energy to shine some light on the opportunity so that we can reach better judgments at whatever next stage we face.

More on Risk

A dictionary definition of "risk" when used as a noun conveys an idea of possible loss or injury. When used in a technology valuation context, "risk" means that the seller and buyer understand that things could turn out adversely in the context of the projected "most likely" situation assumed when performing a valuation. Risk can be thought of as the likelihood and impact of an outcome less favorable than the "most likely" one.

In this sense risk is tied to the optimism (or pessimism) used to create the valuation. By itself, risk does not have meaning. Like the old vaudeville joke—"How are you doing?" (Answer: "Compared to what?")—risk needs a point of comparison. For example, if a buyer were knowingly to make very optimistic projections of how soon the technology could be brought to market, and of the top line growth in sales and the bottom line profit margins, then there would be a very high likelihood that such a project will not meet such projections. Put another way, this would be a high risk deal for the buyer.

However, if the buyer were instead to make very pessimistic assumptions on time to market entry, sales, and margins, then the risk becomes lower, though it is never zero, because there is always the risk that the entire project could fail prior to the first sale.

Does this variability of risk mean that no rational basis exists for creating valuations and assessing risk? The answer must be "no," or this would be a very short book. There is another dimension to risk not considered in the other examples, namely, the "upside" potential. Generally sellers and buyers are equally interested in upsides as well as downsides. In the optimistic projections the downside (i.e., risk) is large and likely, and the upside small and unlikely In the pessimistic projection, the situation is reversed. Generally both the seller and buyer are interested in grasping and characterizing such upside potential in their projections and valuations; examples of this will be presented in the Monte Carlo Method in Chapter 8.

Consider a simple example. Suppose the seller offers a buyer the right to flip a coin and to be paid by some third party based on the number of successive "heads" that turn up. Specifically, the deal for the buyer is this: If the first flip is "heads," the buyer gets $1 million; if the second flip is also "heads," the buyer gets $10 million (total); and if the third flip is also "heads," the buyer receives a total of $100 million; however, at the first "tails" the game is over. There are the following four payoff possibilities for the buyer who acquires this seller's "technology" (where H stands for heads, and T for tails):

H-H-H = $100 million
H-H-T = $10 million
H-T = $1 million
T = $0

How would a rational buyer characterize the risk and value of such an opportunity? The megaoptimist[4] would say this is a $100 million opportunity with high risk while the megapessimist would say there is a 50:50 chance it is worth nothing. The value of each mode is simply the average of the two subsequent outcomes as each possibility is equally probable.

So, statistically the value of this opportunity is $14 million.

This means that statistically, if a buyer could acquire many such technologies, say 20 or more, it would very likely experience an average benefit of $14 million over the 20 or more "licenses" even though no one license yielded or even could have yielded exactly $14 million because the only possibilities are $0, $1, $10, and $100 million. From this long term/many deal perspective, the buyer should be willing to pay a seller of such rights almost up to $14 million to secure the right to "play" (assuming it does not have to make any other investments or deploy other buyer assets).

Say the parties agree that the buyer will pay $11 million for this opportunity. The most frequent outcome would be that the buyer would lose money on the deal, because half the time the buyer would get zero (tails first), and the other half of the time the outcome would be evenly divided between $1 million and either $10 million or $100 million. Yet, if the buyer can play enough times, then the $100 million prize will occur with sufficient regularity that even paying the seller $11 million would be profitable to the buyer. For the 20-deal example, the buyer would average a profit of $3 million per "license" and, could thereby expect a total profit of $60 million.

Practically speaking, technology licenses require many years before great successes can be realized (failures can come early). Buyers and sellers recognize that in their business lifetimes they will generally not have a statistically significant number of deals that they can be so confident in such statistical methods, though for large corporations doing many deals such analysis is reasonable and appropriate.[5] Accordingly, it appears that buyers generally discount very high but rare upsides in their valuation analysis. Sellers, of course, normally take pains to point out to prospective buyers the existence of the upside potential.

Venture capitalists in particular receive offers that sound like the coin toss payoff example. Here is an actual letter:

> *What we are asking for is Forty Million Dollars ($40,000,000), which will provide the capital needed. . . . As planned, at the end of the two-year period we will have ramped up to 100 percent with an expected pre-tax profit of $211,832,258.*[6]

Risk Categories

Although one appreciates the precision of the projected returns as in the above quoted letter, any reasonable buyer recognizes that what is being pitched here is a very high risk opportunity, or worse. It is useful to consider the kinds of risks that a buying opportunity may entail.

Business planning for future events involves risk. The decision to maintain status quo in a business situation, say by refusing to license, involves risk. Risk is business shorthand for saying that the future may turn out more adversely than our most careful planning and forecasting leads us to believe today. In technology licensing, risk has many potential sources:

- *Technology itself*. Depending on its stage of development, there could be risks associated with R&D activities, product development, and design for manufacture. Unexpected environmental difficulties, rising costs of raw material, or special manufacturing requirements could hamper technological success.
- *The market*. Forecasting market need, acceptance, timing, willingness to pay, and the attendant competitive response can be very challenging, depending on the nature of the technology and the time horizon. Such forecasts naturally tend to under account for emerging, unknown technologies that might compete, or might assist, the commercial value of the subject opportunity.
- *IP issues*. The IP protection of the seller's patentable technology might be incomplete at the time of the transaction, leading to risks associated with ultimately allowed claims. IP of third parties may be required, or useful, to the practice of the subject technology, which may add licensing-patent-avoidance costs to commercial estimates. Trade secret protection could be lost by human error or misappropriation.
- *Government and society*. Government policy, or societal values, can make it difficult or impossible to realize commercial value (take the nuclear power industry as a 30 year historic example.

In fact, any reasonably comprehensive enumeration of risks can be so disheartening as to be disabling, as an ancient (ca. 1000 B.C.) text says:

> *Whoever watches the wind will not plant;*
> *whoever looks at the clouds will not reap.*[7]

Risk is unavoidable, but not all risks are equal. It is possible to characterize the risk of a specific opportunity by specific analysis of the business issues and

EXHIBIT 2.3

Source: DILBERT reprinted by permission of United Feature Syndicate, Inc.

uncertainties. Such a characterization can be used with various valuation approaches, as will be discussed in the next section, to account for the risk. A particularly useful way to deal with risk is through the framework of the buyer's payment structure, which will be referred to as The Wheelbarrow, by using, for example, value heavily weighted by royalties, equity, or conditional fixed payments, where it makes business sense to do so.

What other kinds of risks exist? Fully enumerated, there are at least 36, as Dilbert contends in Exhibit 2.3. However, for our purposes the risks can be grouped into five categories.

R&D RISKS Although there is no bright line of demarcation at the end of R&D and the beginning of design for manufacturing, usually what is meant by "R&D" is the demonstration of a practical means of doing something. In this context, "practical" means that the quality control, the speed, and the cost of making the product appear to be sufficient and the product can be made and sold at a profit.

The nature of R&D is to attempt to anticipate the principal unknowns that require resolution prior to design for manufacturing. The problem is that one can never anticipate the things one does not think of and one can never be sure that everything that should have been considered was considered. There are many famous catastrophes,[8] and lesser ones, that show the danger of R&D hubris.

In some technology licenses the seller purports to provide TR that is complete with respect to its R&D. In other cases, the seller notes known unfinished R&D. In all cases, the buyer in its due diligence needs to consider not only the investment in time and money to complete all the R&D, seller's perceptions excepted, but also to characterize the risk associated with successful completion.

The real risk of failure at the R&D stage is not normally that the technology cannot be made to work but that it is too difficult and costly to be made to work. With rare exceptions, to be commercial it is necessary that the technology is extensively used and, so manufacturing costs are important.

MANUFACTURABILITY RISKS Manufacturability risks refer to all the perils that one faces in creating a production environment that will repeatedly and cost effectively produce the product designed by the R&D process. These risks are associated with converting a technology that has been demonstrated in a limited number of examples at lab scale into something that can be replicated many times at a commercial scale. Also involved in such conversion is the idea that less skilled people will be deployed in the manufacturing process in order to keep costs low.

There are many ways technology can fail at this stage. In chemical processes, R&D is frequently done in a batch mode whereas in many commercial high volume operations, it needs to be done in a continuous mode to be profitable. This can be a difficult transition.

In commercial operations one needs to be concerned with waste product disposal issues. In the R&D process, certain internal recycling operations may have been assumed that in a commercial context turn out to be difficult to accomplish.

In the case of semiconductors, the ratio of good parts to total parts made, or the yield, is the critical factor in the process economics. Although there may be extensive data at the R&D scale on yield, it is possible that when a large scale production facility operates, the yields will not be as high as needed, or that significant additional development will be required to achieve necessary yields.

MARKETING RISKS Even with a product that performs as designed and can be sold at low cost because of efficient manufacture, it is not certain that a sufficient number of customers will purchase the product to warrant its existence.

It is surprisingly difficult to predict what customers will do with respect to a specific offer-for-sale opportunity. This is compounded in technology licensing because at the time of the license the exact nature of the product features and cost may be unknown. Also, the "market" changes its opinion with time. If you asked people in 1990, if they wanted an "Internet," what would they have said? If you asked people in 1985, if they wanted a "fax machine," what would they have said? A "microwave" in 1970? A "PC" in 1980? An "iPod®" or "hybrid" car in 2000?

It is important to recall examples of technology market disappointments as the PC Junior (IBM), Corfam shoes (DuPont), supersonic airplanes (Boeing), Betamax VCRs (Sony), Video On Demand (Time Warner), buying furniture and pet food online, urban WiFi (Earthlink), global fiber networks (Global Crossing), satellite telephones (Irridium), and many others to realize that even very good companies with smart people spending large sums on market research have been humbled, regularly.

COMPETITIVE RISKS When considering the risks associated with a TR buyer making products and selling to its customers, it is easy to lose sight of the fact that this is more than a two-party process. When a technology and its derived products are being evaluated at the licensing stage, assumptions are made about what competitive products will exist when the subject one is introduced and how competitors will respond. All companies are searching to meet customer needs. While a technology buyer thinks it can disadvantage such competitors in the competition for customers, there are known competitors and unknown who are thinking and planning the same thing. This unending stream of suitors for customers is a wonderful situation for the marketplace, but it creates a risky environment for companies making new product plans.

If a technology is going to yield products that will displace currently sold products, one can be sure that the competitors making such products will not stand by and say, "Sure, you go ahead and take my customers because I'll just do something else" (such as go out of business). Competitors have shareholders who expect profits and management who is accountable for same, in addition to salespeople with quotas, along with product managers who are hired and fired based on their ability to create and maintain a competitive edge. All these people and companies are not going to give up without a fight.

Even if a technology is intended to create new products and services for new markets, the competitive response is still there. All companies are looking for opportunities for new revenues and higher margins. If a new product is introduced in a new market, it will spawn a competitive response provided the business looks attractive. When a football coach is watching his first string team beat up his third string team on a Wednesday, he should not assume that Saturday's game is in the bag, as his opponent's first string is also beating up its third string that same day.

LEGAL RISKS One simple example of a legal risk is Prohibition. Early in the twentieth century the government outlawed the making and selling of alcoholic beverages. More recently, the government has put such hurdles in the use of nuclear power as to effectively extinguish for decades that industry in terms of new plants. Designers of new encryption techniques face serious scrutiny for use and export. The cost and therefore, utility, of many chemical products is significantly affected by environmental regulations. In recent years there have been cost penalties and outright prohibitions associated with the use of certain chemicals in packaging (polystyrene cups for example). In the near future carbon-based combustion may face serious competitive disasdvantages.

Another form of legal risk is contained with the very nature of patents. In the United States, approximately 3,000 patents are issued every Tuesday that, for approximately 17 years (20 years from the date of filing), bar the making, using, and selling of a defined and claimed process or product.[9] Because U.S. patent applications are secret until they are issued,[10] and there are literally several hundred thousand such pending applications, it is conceivable that one of those pending applications could mature into a valid, enforceable patent that would prevent one's practice of a licensed technology.[11]

With software technology such patent blocking risks have increased significantly. Although software patentability has been established for some years now, it has not been a significant business issue. It appears that with the increasing proliferation of software tools and processes coupled with the enormous market value of software companies (Microsoft is presently more valuable than General Motors), in the future the blocking effect of software patents will increase the risk of deploying new technologies.

I will include here in the category of legal risk two additional examples, namely regulatory and standards risk. Certain products require government approval to market and even with such approval conformity to the scope of approval. Pharmaceuticals and medical devices are two important technology areas that require government approvals. In the areas of electronics, optics, and telecommunications broadly there exist various standards bodies such as IEEE and ITU (Institute of Electrical and Electronics Engineers and International Telecommunication Union, respectively). Depending on the specific circumstances gaining such approvals may make a material difference in commercial value.

An All Risks List?

Have we covered all risk categories? Consider the Google Initial Public Offering (IPO) document, a legally required filing called an S-1. Google is widely known as being a fabulously successful startup company. We will discuss later in this book some particulars.

In its S-1 filing, Google, as typical of technology startups, enumerated a list of risks that it sought to bring to the attention of potential investors. Space here does not permit including all of the risks they identified; the reader can find the S-1 online. But below are some of the major categories Google used within which was provided a detail description (not shown here). Beginning on page 4 of its S-1,[12] and extending to page 25 (!), are the following risk factors (which I reworded):

1. Competition from Microsoft and Yahoo
2. Competition from other Internet companies
3. Competition from traditional media companies
4. Growth declining and downward pressure on margins
5. Fluctuation in operating results
6. Inadequate continuing innovation
7. Highly dependent upon advertising revenues
8. Dependent on "network members"
9. Growth management
10. Internal controls
11. Migration of financial functions to a 3rd party
12. Brand dependence
13. Proprietary web doc formats limiting search
14. Technologies that block ads
15. Google corporate culture
16. Loss of protection of Google IP
17. 3rd party IP rights
18. International expansion
19. International market access
20. Malicious 3rd party applications
21. Click through fraud
22. Index spammers
23. Privacy concerns limiting Google freedom
24. U.S. and foreign laws limiting Google freedom
25. Loss of services of Eric, Larry, Sergey, senior management team
26. Loss of employees (because they get rich on options)
27. Retention and motivation of employees
28. Eric, Larry, and Sergey operating the business collectively (and therefore may not manage it effectively)
29. Short operating history
30. Scaling and adopting the software architecture
31. Bandwidth limitations

(and this just brings us to p. 15, with another dozen pages of risk factors)

Overall Characterization of Risk

There is no formula that can be used to derive the risk of a technology licensing project. There has been significant study in two related aspects: success rates for new product development and for pharmaceuticals in particular. A study published in *Research Technology Management* summarizes 16 prior studies on the commercial success rates of new product launches; these studies claimed success rates from a low of 40 percent to a high of 67 percent.[13] Further, this study examines data looking at seven stages in the new product development process, starting with "raw ideas" and ending with "economically profitable." The study concludes that the ratio from Stage 1 (raw idea) to Stage 7 (economically profitable) is 3000 to 1: that is, it takes 3,000 starting raw ideas to make one profitable success. Most of the mortality, according to the study, occurs in the R&D process (although that is conditional upon certain definitional issues). Depending on one's interpretation of "completion of R&D", the data suggests that from four to 100 projects are required for one commercial success. These data suggest that both of the following statements are true: (1) 60 percent of new product projects succeed (from Stage 6 to Launch/Stage 7) and (2) 99 percent of ideas submitted fail (from Stage 2 to Stage 7).[14]

An interesting question and relevant issue to technology licensing is this: Do technology licenses have a higher success rate? The argument can be made that the answer is "yes" for two reasons: (1) There exists a willing buyer who, at arms length and without compulsion, elects to pursue the subject opportunity, and (2) By separating the inventing/R&D performing organization from the manufacturing/selling organization, it is possible that a better result will occur, despite "hand off" (tech transfer) issues, because each could be the best at what they do.

Another area in which considerable study has occurred is the development of pharmaceuticals. One widely cited figure is that it takes 10,000 active molecules identified to create (on average) one pharmaceutical sold in the marketplace; this would suggest that the mortality, if that's the right word, in the pharmaceutical development business is approximately three times the 3000:1 findings for typical industrial products. A study attributed to Shearson Lehman Hutton suggested the following ratios at various stages: 20:1 at IND (the filing of Investigation of New Drug), 10:1 at Phase I Clinicals, 4:1 at Phase II, 1.8:1 at Phase III, and 1.2:1 at New Drug Application (NDA).[15] Another study concludes 1 out of 5 INDs received NDAs.[16]

As will be discussed in detail in Chapter 7, the overall commercial risk is normally characterized by one numeric factor designated by the symbol "k." Such "k" is known by a variety of terms: risk factor, hurdle rate, Risk-Adjusted Hurdle Rate (RAHR), and return-on-investment required (or expected); we will generally use RAHR. It is the one value by which all the previously mentioned risks are expressed, and it is used to assess the present value of a prospective future benefit.

Chapter 8 will deal with the Monte Carlo Method, a powerful and more recently developed tool for characterizing risk. With this approach we will see risk expressed as a probability distribution of financial outcomes somewhat like the heads and tails example used earlier.

Just as with the key theme in Arthur Miller's play "The Price" regarding the "price of used furniture,"[23] risk is a perspective. Inventors tend to see risk as primarily embodied in the creation of the original concept, as from their perspective, the risk post invention is, in comparison, small. R&D managers, having a broader perspective, see the successful R&D project as having wrung out most of the risk. Design-for-manufacturing people see the primary risk in creating the cost efficient, reliable "factory" that actually makes things. Marketing people see the identification of customer segments and the cost benefit equation and competitive response as being the real risk. Salespeople see the risk as being what it takes to get a customer to lift his or her pen and sign a purchase order. Lawyers see risk everywhere; it's their calling. And, shareholders don't want to hear about risk; they just want to see double digit percentage growth in share price (or else).

Risk Distinctions and Classification

In Chapter 1 we made a simple distinction between "Big Deal" and "Not Big Deal" technologies. Here we want to consider further making such distinctions. In Chapter 5 on Rating/Ranking we will develop the idea and apply it to valuation.

There is a classic Greek word that grabs what we are seeking to do here: *tagma*, from which we get our word *tag*; in ancient Greek one use was of military ranks and orders. Tagging is an important form of identification, and one that can only be applied to some predetermined identity. Let us consider the following group identification architectures.

EUCLIDIAN GROUPINGS One simple architecture for creating groups is simply to make distinctions without attributing any particular quantitative value to each such grouping. I have termed this Euclidian Groups.

One-Dimensional Groups This is the simplest form of distinction. We simply divide into groups some starting population based upon some distinguishing element. So, were we to divide up a patent portfolio, we could create one set of one-dimensional groups by year of issuance, say: 2000, 2001, 2003, etcetera patent vintage groups. We could also have divided them by the patent class numbers established by the Patent and Trademark Office (PTO). One-dimensional groups can be thought of as arrayed on one horizontal line, with as many distinct groupings as useful in making distinctions. Exhibit 2.1 can be thought of as one example where the "mean" is a location grouping specifically created from the two end-point conditions.

Two Dimensional Groups (Matrix) This is the common management consulting matrix, made famous by Boston Consulting Group, Gartner Group, and many others. Exhibit 2.2 shows independent factors at two levels each to create four distinct combinations. This would be a two-by-two matrix. This can easily be expanded into a three-by-three matrix by considering three levels of each of two variables. This is sometimes referred to as the GE box because of some historical popularization. So a two-by-two matrix uses "high" (H) and "low" (L), and a three-by-three matrix uses "High," "Medium," "Low" (H, M, L). Clearly this can be extended to any number of distinctions. One of the principal attractions is that all such matrices can be readily displayed in two dimensions on paper, such as is done in this book.

Three (and Higher) Dimensional Groups This architecture allows for consideration of three interacting factors. Although it can be displayed graphically on paper, it becomes confusing. So, such groups are normally characterized by notation, such as [x, y, z], where each of x, y, and z can take on the values, say, one, two, or three. This is results in 27 combinations. This can be extended to any number of factors each at any number of levels, though the human capacity to absorb, or use, such distinctions becomes elusive.

VALUE GROUPS It is often useful to consider the implications of value on distinctions made. One way this arises is to think of any particular group as being the value of a technology through sequential stages of development. Another way is to consider its value as a result of the combination of various risk factors coming into play. So, suppose there were ten steps each required to be successful for the commercial success of a particular technology, and it is determined somehow that each individual step, defined in a particular group, had a probability of success of 60 percent. What would then be the overall probability of success?

Here the distinct groups are interrelated to the point of dependence, meaning that a failure in any one of the ten groups (steps) causes an overall failure. If each step has a 60 percent probability of success, the overall success rate is determined by raising 0.6 to the power of ten, which is 0.6 percent, or a 1 out of 165 chance (1/0.06).

In our assessment of risk factors in Chapter 7 we will consider to a limited degree such interaction effects causing a compounding of risk value.

Risk's Connection to Uncertainty

Risk is sometimes considered as an expression of uncertainty. That is, if we somehow had a time machine that could transport the parties to a time 20 years hence with access to all the business effects, favorable and not, of having entered the license and having not entered the license (a kind of Wonderful Life James Stewart movie experience) then the risk would be erased by our privileged future knowledge. Unfortunately for business and valuation purposes (but certainly a blessing in other ways), the future is unknowable to us.

Our purpose here is to consider uncertainty apart from its obvious connection to risk. When performing most accounting business functions, we expect reasonable exactitude and certitude. If one wonders what the cash balance in liquid accounts is at any moment, one does not accept the answer from the treasurer that such a figure cannot be known, or can only vaguely be known. Likewise with raw material inventories: It is either in our control, and therefore on our books, or it is not. If we have it in our control, somebody had better be ready to give a complete and accurate accounting.[17]

Selling is perhaps a little more ambiguous, but each business defines (in accordance with generally accepted accounting standards) a criterion for what constitutes a sale, and thus the sales revenue and backlog at any time is similarly knowable. This belief system forms the basis for having an accounting firm audit a company's books and issue a report that represents fairly the financial position of the company and the results of its operations in the past year on a basis consistent with that of the preceding year (recent headlines not withstanding).

This perspective changes when *pro forma* (projected) business models are created. The need for internal consistency and mathematical accuracy remains (the columns must sum properly, and the assumptions and related calculations must be self consistent), but the need for certitude is further relaxed. However, there is a general understanding that *pro forma* values will be achieved or exceeded or there will be some form of accountability. This causes the responsible parties to be quite conservative, although their managers are known to boost such projections, as has been the source of much of the humor in Dilbert cartoons. In licensing contexts, it is common that the nature of such projections lacks the business history of typical *pro forma* projections. Further, if only a conservative, can't-miss approach is taken, then it is likely that many worthy licenses will be foregone. Although there are valuation tools that specifically deal with this issue, there is an underlying perspective that licensing technology is a risk bearing process, and one can rarely afford the luxury of having a high degree of certitude regarding high value opportunities.

Value and Price

As will be discussed later at length, value is what is determined by the buyer and seller, by some internal method of analysis. Price is what is proposed to the other side of the deal as the basis of negotiation and ultimate agreement.

Pricing intertwines with negotiation, much as it would in selling and buying cars or homes. One can price high and expect to wait a long time for just the ideal buyer for whom such price is acceptable, or price low to attract competitive interest to achieve a rapid sale. One can price a little above the expected final value to leave room for counteroffers and the give and take of negotiation, or one can price firm and inform prospective buyers that no offers less than the stated price will be considered (at least at this time).

Psychology of Negotiations and Buying

The personalities and processes of the seller and buyer significantly affect the perceived value and associated risk of a deal, also the speed (or lack of it) of reaching an agreement. Generally in license negotiations, sellers play the official role of optimists, providing reasoning that leads to higher estimates of future successes, while buyers are the pessimists dedicated to thinking of things that can go wrong. Clearly the respective motivations drive such perspectives: The seller wants to receive a high price, whereas the buyer not only wants to achieve the highest profit possible, but also wants to avoid a situation where the company has paid more than can ever be realized by its commercial efforts.

If both parties conform to their natural inclinations, deals would be rare events. They would occur only in those cases where a pessimist perceives the opportunity more valuable than an optimist! This is similar to the joke about the optimist being one who believes we live in the best of all possible worlds and the pessimist fearing that this just might be true. So, in order for deals to occur, sellers will need to gain a comprehension of the downside that any buyer faces in converting a technology to a business, and buyers will need to grasp that really good things can happen and maybe the overall risks are not as great as they may seem.

From this perspective, negotiation is a teaching process whereby buyers persuade sellers to think less of their technology and sellers persuade buyers to think more of the opportunity.

EXHIBIT 2.4 Subjective Factors Affecting Buyers

"Consumer Products Book"	Mean in Setting A	Mean in Setting B	(B-A/A)
Dress 1	$27.77	$41.50	49%
Dress 2	$21.09	$33.91	61%
Tent	$69.95	$77.73	11%
Men's Sweater	$13.91	$20.64	48%
Lamp	$28.36	$20.64	48%
Electric Typewriter	$131.45	$165.36	26%
Chess Set	$35.29	$43.15	22%

Source: Feinberg, R.A., APA Proceedings, Division of Consumer Psychology, 1982, p.28.

Buyer Perception and How It Can Affect Value

There are many factors that can affect this mutual teaching and persuasion process. For starters, seller professionalism and credibility is important. There is no practical way that a buyer can completely replicate every assertion of a seller without redoing the entire R&D program. If the buyer perceives the seller to be the "Joe Isuzu" of technology licensing, it will either lose interest in the negotiation or so lowball its offers that a deal becomes unlikely.[18]

Exhibit 2.4 shows the results from a study run with two groups, a test group, and a control group.[19]

The results for the control group are shown in the first column under "Setting A." A statistically significant number of individuals were asked, one at a time, to review a notebook describing the seven items shown at the left. Based on such descriptions each individual was asked to say how much they would pay for the item with the understanding that no transaction was to take place. The entire process was repeated for "Setting B", with the results showing that in every case the mean value of willingness to pay was higher than Setting A ranging from a low of 11 percent higher to more than 60 percent higher.

What was different in Setting B? The experimenters placed a "Mastercharge" logo (the experiment was conducted prior to the name change to Mastercard®) on a desk near the notebook. Even though it was clear that no actual purchase was to take place, the interpretation was that the mere presence of a credit card as a means of payment unconsciously influenced the evaluation of the willingness to pay. It is this belief that makes retail stores go to great lengths to display every credit imaginable on their entrance doors and at their counters; they know, or believe, that people will pay more if they can pay with plastic.

How does all this relate to technology licensing? Consider the following two examples. In the first case the seller is an unknown university located well off the beaten path, requiring a planes/trains/and automobiles experience to get there. The principal investigator on the project believes that duct tape and alligator clips are the primary tools of good R&D labs. Moving aside some coffee stained old newspapers, the buyer examines some of the data recorded in pencil on looseleaf paper. For lunch, the prospective buyer is treated to fast food. As the buyer leaves, the principal investigator commends the prospective buyer for having been the first person to have ever bothered to look at the project.

Suppose the exact same technology was instead found in the following setting: Harvard University. Thc buyer has difficulty arranging a visit because, apparently, many other prospects have been previously scheduled. When greeted at the lab, the principal investigator looks as the lab does, impeccable. The latest in data acquisition tools are everywhere. There is a hum of efficiency and excitement among the technicians and grad students. The data is available in electronic form as well as copious and artistic notes in a shelf of lab notebooks. Lunch is at the Harvard Faculty Club and Henry Kissinger stops by to congratulate the principal investigator on receipt of her second Nobel Prize and asks how the new breakthrough invention (being discussed) is going.

Would a prospective buyer come away from the second experience thinking more highly of the opportunity than from the first? Would it make a difference in perception if at the buyer's organization it becomes known that a license is being considered from a prestigious university and a "name" professor?

In 2008 there is a report of research in a very different context, but illustrative of the human side of encounters. The results of a study presented at the annual meeting of the Radiological Society of North America concluded that a radiologist reading an X-ray does a better job of detecting "hard to detect" early stage cancers if the radiologist has the patient's photograph in the file, that is, a physical representation of the human being involved, not just the X-ray image. Specifically, in the experiment, when the radiologist was asked to read the same X-ray three months later and was not provided the photograph (and, presumably retained no memory of his/her earlier reading of the patient), about 80 percent of the original findings (with the patient's picture) were not noted in this second reading. When follow up interviews were held, the researchers discerned radiologist empathy when the photograph was present leading, apparently, to greater care in terms of studying the X-ray.[20]

Litigation attorneys have long known to present to juries as much of a victim's presence and wounds (in the case of a patent plaintiff—his or her sorrowful appearance) as a judge will allow.

The lesson here is that sellers should do all they can to present themselves and the opportunity in the best light possible. This is not to say that one should become Joe Isuzu, because not only would it be ethically inappropriate, it would also be counterproductive. Rather, the seller should make every effort to present as thorough and well considered a presentation as possible. Optimism can be expressed by using scenario projections such as "conservative," "most likely," and "optimistic." The same lesson also applies to the buyer. Typical licenses provide conditional payments to sellers in the form of royalties or equity based upon the ultimate outcome once the technology is in the hands of the buyer. Sellers want to have their technology in the best, most professional (and enthusiastic) hands. So, buyers need to temper their skepticism lest they appear so negative that the seller wonders why they are even interested. However, the same caution against becoming a Joe Isuzu buyer applies.[21]

Technology buyers must have some innate willingness to take risks, or they are in the wrong business. There is a parallel here to the "frontier thesis" of Frederick Jackson Turner. He published in 1893 a famous line of reasoning[22] that an American characteristic was formed by its frontier lines, from the Allegheny Mountains, to the Mississippi River, to and across the Rocky Mountains, crossed in the search for opportunity. He wrote of the frontier life thus created: "coarseness and strength combined with acuteness and inquisitiveness; that practical, inventive turn of mind, quick to find expedients; that masterful grasp of material things, lacking in the artistic but powerful effect great ends; that restless, nervous energy, that dominant individualism, working for good and for evil." It is the seller's hope, that but for the reverence to "for evil," that it finds buyers who look at risk through the opportunity of "frontier" thinking.

Two Final Points on Buying and Selling

A highly recommended book is one of the less famous Arthur Miller plays, (appropriately titled) *The Price*. Like other great works, this play has multiple levels of interpretation. The presented level is the price of some used furniture.[23]

The seller, one of two brothers in the play, has invited a used furniture dealer, an 89-year-old Russian, to bid on the family furniture of his father's estate. There is wonderful interplay between the brother and the savvy buyer. The brother keeps wanting to hear "the price." The buyer keeps providing him insights about the furniture, business, and life in general because, in broken English, "The price of used furniture is nothing but a viewpoint and if you wouldn't understand the viewpoint is impossible to understand the price (sic)."[24]

This apt comment about a viewpoint determining the price summarizes much of what will be later developed in this book. Arthur Miller's play hinges on the realization that value is a function of perspective and, is therefore individual. Two different prospective buyers each following legitimate valuation approaches can come to two significantly different valuations because of widely differing perspectives on what is "most likely" as an outcome and the attendant "risk."

For the seller, the challenge is to find that prospective buyer who, because of some combination of experience, general optimism about the future, relevant assets, and especially with significant needs for new products, will grasp some of the seller's upside enthusiasm. "Hungry" buyers tend to see more opportunity.

He who is full loathes honey,
but to the hungry even what is bitter tastes sweet.

Book of Proverbs, Chapter 27, Verse 7, New American Standard Bible (NASB)

And, finally, pricing is the leverage point of all negotiations. No buyer will ever say to a seller, "This is a great deal, are you sure we would be paying you enough?" That is about as likely as a hockey player apologizing for causing a collision. So, regardless of the price, the seller will hear (even right up to the moment of contract signing) that the price and risk are too high.

"It's no good, it's no good!" says the buyer;
then off he goes and boasts about his purchase.

Proverbs 20:14, NASB

Notes

1. Aristotle, *Nicomachean Ethics*, II.6-7.
2. "On the Method of Theoretical Physics," The Herbert Spencer Lecture, delivered at Oxford (10 June 1933); also published in *Philosophy of Science*, Vol. 1, No. 2 (April 1934), pp. 163–169. [thanks to Dr. Techie @ www.wordorigins.org and JSTOR].
3. 14th Century Franciscan friar William of Ockham.
4. Defined as that person who believes he could douse hell with one bucket—while the pessimist fears that the optimist could be right.
5. A more practical measure is the number of deals in the career horizon of the buyer. Given the increased pressure on near term returns, individuals may be far less prepared to consider statistical returns.
6. Michael S. Malone, *Upside*, September 1992.
7. From the Old Testament book of Ecclesiastes, Chapter 11. The entire paragraph that deals with risk management, and other matters, is as follows: 1 Cast your bread upon the waters, for after many days you will find it again. 2 Give portions to seven, yes to eight, for you do not know what disaster may come upon the land. 3 If clouds are full of water, they pour rain upon the earth. Whether a tree falls to the south or to the north, in the place where it falls, there will it lie. 4 Whoever watches the wind will not plant; whoever looks at the clouds will not reap. 5 As you do not know the path of the wind, or how the body is formed in a mother's womb, so you cannot understand the work of God, the Maker of all things. 6 Sow your seed in the morning, and at evening let not your hands be idle, for you do not know which will succeed, whether this or that, or whether both will do equally well. (New International Version).
8. Two examples come to mind. The first one is home movies of the gyrations and collapse of the Tacoma Narrows bridge that failed less than a week after being opened; there was an era where this was required viewing for every engineering freshman. The second example is of the numerous early aviators with their now-bizarre looking "aircraft" failing with sometimes comic and sometimes tragic outcomes.
9. The life of a U.S. patent is 20 years from filing. Assuming it takes three years to get from filing to issuance, the useful life on issuance would be 17 years.
10. There are exceptions associated with securing foreign patent rights when the application can publish prior to issuance.
11. Although it is possible that the holder of such blocking patent would be amenable to providing a license, there is no assurance that this is the case and the economics of such a second license could significantly harm the overall economics of the original transaction.
12. S-1/A, Amendment No. 7 to Form S-1, Google, Inc., filed with the U.S. SEC on August 13, 2004.
13. Greg A. Stevens and James Burley, "3,000 Raw Ideas = 1 Commercial Success!" *Research Technology Management*, published by IRI, May–June 1997, p. 16-27.
14. Ibid.
15. "Commercializing Biomedical Technology," in *Licensing Economics Review*, June 1991, p. 9, cited an Immulogic Pharmaceutical Corporation presentation at an international conference on Commercializing Biomedical Technologies, held at Harvard School of Public Health, April 1991.
16. Analysis of INDs filed during 1976–1978, published in *Scientific American* (April 2000): 74ff.
17. Of course even in such circumstances, there are practical limits to knowledge because of the cost of knowing compared to the value of such knowing. In the raw materials example, one could include the number of pencils in all the company storerooms and desk drawers as a business asset. In principle, such assets could all be counted and known to whatever degree of certainty one was willing to pay to obtain. In practice, a

principle of reasonableness is applied that pursues such analysis and measurement only insofar as it is really important to the management of the business or the shareholders. There are other examples, such as the ownership of the right to extract oil, where the magnitude of such reserves are not only subject to the market value of oil and extraction technology, but are also in a real sense unknowable.

18. In the late 1980s, the Isuzu automobile company ran a series of television advertisements that made fun of the car salesperson's character by having one Joe Isuzu say the most outrageously puff statements ever heard coupled with small onscreen footnotes providing the corrections.
19. Feinberg, R.A., APA Proceedings, Division of Consumer Psychology, 1982, p. 28.
20. Dr. Yehonatan N. Turner, radiology resident at Shaare Zedek Medical Center in Jerusalem, presented at the annual meeting of the Radiological Society of North America, in Chicago, December 3, 2008.
21. Dear Isuzu Lawyers: I actually like Isuzu cars; I have owned four of them. So, the use of "Joe Isuzu" is not intended as an adverse reflection of the product of the Isuzu Company or its employees, dealers, or shareholders.
22. Frederick Jackson Turner, "The Significance of the Frontier in American History," 1893, published in a reprint by BiblioBazaar, 2008; in essay form it is available on various Web sites e.g., www.fordham.edu/halsall/mod/1893turner.html.
23. Arthur Miller, *The Price* (Penguin Books, 1968), Act I, p. 38.
24. The hidden levels have to do with the price of life paid by two brothers, their wives, and the brothers' parents. The play focuses on the price of the furniture, but the other "prices" keep reappearing. It is a wonderful story.

APPROACH I

Opportunity Discovery

CHAPTER 3

Identifying and Prioritizing Technology Opportunities

Our focus in this chapter is the first "D" of Licensing D-V-D, namely opportunity Discovery.

Our discussion will primarily be from the seller's perspective, but the same basic idea applies to the buyer. With the buyer there is usually a particular "gap" it is trying to fill, either in terms of a product/market or technology that may support existing products and markets. In some cases, a buyer could be "cruising" opportunistically, as is sometimes done with company liaisons to specific university programs.

The ultimate goal of Licensing D-V-D is a deal done with a buyer who is going to deploy successfully the licensed technology. For that to happen there needs to be a transaction structured that both the seller and the buyer find acceptable. The seller needs to identify what it has to offer that it believes will be valuable to at least one buyer, and how best to optimize such offer both for purposes of deal doability (i.e., likely to lead to Dealmaking) and the value that can be realized from such deal. The metaphor we will use for the assemblage of assets that the seller can package and offer is The Box as the container for everything that is being offered to the buyer.

There is another place for opportunity Discovery, and that is on the buy side of a deal. We will focus on the Dealmaking buy side in Chapter 10 where we will discuss pricing, structure, and term sheets. These issues comprise what we will term The Wheelbarrow, as in the carriage by which money is brought by the buyer to the seller.

Seller "Opportunity Space"

A seller's starting position for opportunity Discovery can be thought of as an "opportunity space." Exhibit 3.1 illustrates this idea.

Shown are 15 rows of specific opportunities. For convenience we can think of each row as defined by a specific patent, shown by the ID numbers in the second column. An opportunity could consist of some other form of IP rights such as copyrighted software or know-how/trade secrets, or in combination with a specific issued patent. It is an important corporate practice to identify each opportunity by a numbered designation, a Technology ID (TID).

		Field-Territory					
	Patent ID	1	2	3	4	5	6
1	101						
2	102						
3	103						
4	201						
5	301						
6	302						
7	303						
8	304						
9	401						
10	501						
11	601						
12	701						
13	801						
14	901						
15	902						

EXHIBIT 3.1 Seller Opportunity Space

One obvious approach to the opportunity space of Exhibit 3.1 is to pursue them all, valuing each one (Chapters 4 through 9) and then Dealmaking (Chapters 10 and 11). Even if sufficient resources were available to do this, such a strategy is not normally a wise one, simply because these opportunities will differ in value and deal doability. Further, it is common that companies simply have more opportunities, more rows, than it has available resources to pursue, so the choice will necessarily be to leave fallow some possibilities so the most important opportunities will be brought to fruition.

Grouping

One of the most basic, and powerful, techniques is forming groups or segments, with "tags" (*tagma*) of some kind as we discussed in Chapter 2. In marketing, segmentation has been a powerful business tool for shaping product development. It involves grouping customers and potential customers into like groups based upon key buying distinctives. By doing so, products can be designed, market messages created, channels of distribution established, and pricing set that works best for each such segment-product combination.

In Exhibit 3.1, the boxes shown under the Patent ID column represent groups of related technologies, such as might have been created from a particular R&D project. This is an important task, and for a seller should include the technology asset types that are available and likely to be valuable to a buyer. This can create complex opportunity space maps because, for example, a foundational technology could be valuable, even essential, to more than one row or related groups of rows, and such foundational technology will need to be retained by the seller to support its other business operations not being offered to any buyer.

The columns across the top of Exhibit 3.1 designate combinations of field of use and territory of use. So the columns labeled 1, 2, and 3 could represent a certain field of use/product application in each of three major license territories (say, North

America, Europe, and the Far East). Likewise 4, 5, and 6 could represent a second field of use for the same three territories.

The territorial's distinctions can be important because of the presence or absence of patent coverage, the seller's desire or lack thereof of serving such markets, the commercial utility of the products that would serve those customers, or some regulatory or structural issue associated with reaching a particular territory. Clearly the number of columns can be increased to handle any appropriate degree of granularity. Everything should be made as simple as possible at this stage. If a one world, all world territorial analysis is a reasonable approximation, then doing so is a better course than breaking territories into segments. Likewise technology can often be used in many products and contexts. If these can be compressed into one or two applications and still make at least initial approximations of relative importance then it would be good to do so. The overall goal of Exhibit 3.1 is to have just enough specificity that a high-level assessment of value can identify which opportunities are the more important and, usually, which ones meet some minimum threshold of potential value.

TAPS: Technology Applied—Problem Solved

The next step of analysis in Exhibit 3.1 is to perform what is sometimes termed a "TAPS" analysis, where TA designates technology applied, and PS problem solved.

As discussed, the rows of Exhibit 3.1 should be grouped to represent a technology family. By definition a technology, as opposed to science or some raw idea, is something that can *do something*, perhaps many things, but at least *some* thing. The key step here is to capture in just one or two clear meaning-packed sentences exactly what this *something* is that the grouped technology rows(s) can *do*.

One check point question when a provisional TA definition has been developed is to ask, "How is this different from every other technology known to man?" It's a good idea to capture each and every suggested answer to such question, until the proposals come to a stop or become repetitive. Next to each proposed answer, again for each row, create another column headed by the infamous "So what?" question. The important task now is to drill down on each proposed answer to the "what's different" question by determining why such difference matters, in as concrete terms as possible.

This is not easy to do, and normally cannot be done well in a single sitting, nor without participation by an opportunity team that, ideally, includes inventors, business managers, technology generalists familiar with competing technologies, patent attorneys, and people familiar with relevant markets.

WHAT RIGHTS DO WE HAVE? After some iteration and careful "wordsmithing" there should be a present "best" answer for what's new and why it matters. An important next question is "What rights do we have to offer?" There are two sides to this question. First let us consider what the buyer would think of what we the seller have to offer.

Putting ourselves in the buyer's shoes, even if such buyer is convinced that the opportunity (TA) is terrific, but we had no protection for our technology, what would the buyer conclude? Answer: Let me figure out what it costs me to recreate the technology independently, and use that figure as a cap on my willingness to pay.

Having strong IP protection, which may include multiple patents and trade secrets, makes it more difficult for a potential buyer to envision an independent recreation and increase its risk in attempting to do so.

If IP ownership rights are weak, then a separate task is needed to see what can be done to strengthen them.

The second IP rights issue is more complex and is about a buyer's freedom to practice with respect to third party IP rights now under the control of the seller. A complete "freedom to practice" legal study is normally not appropriate because of the expense of doing so and the uncertainty of exactly the product configuration valued by a buyer; further a buyer will want to rely on its own judgment in such matter (and sellers typically do not provide representations of such freedom to practice for technology licenses even when it has done such analysis). However, an initial assessment of the related patent art will at least begin to scope out which patents could be an issue and identify the owner of such patents. And there can be circumstances where the seller has moved the technology well into the entrepreneurship circle discussed in Chapter 1 including at least initial clearance studies. If such studies are believed relevant to how a buyer would use the technology they can be added to the Box offered to the buyer, but normally on an "as-is" basis, not a representation.

Also in this task, it is a very good idea to make sure that all the inventors have assigned their ownership of the patents to the company, that there have been no grants of such rights to third parties (or if there have, the scope of such rights are known and identified in the opportunity analysis), and likewise with respect to trade secret rights. Such matters can be complicated by publication and presentation activity that has occurred or may be planned to occur.

Trade secret rights may be important to a particular opportunity but may not be codified in the way patent rights are simply because the seller has not been systematic in collecting such information. At the very least, a trade secret "table of contents" should be identified in order to see what it is that could be offered to a buyer. And, for valuable opportunities, the trade secrets themselves need to be documented.

PROBLEM SOLVED From the discussed steps there should then be at least a provisional belief for each of the technology groups, the key technology distinctives of each group, how such technology distinctives distinguish what the seller has to offer compared to all known alternative technologies, the "So what?" significance to a customer of those differences, and clarity as to what rights the seller has that it can offer a buyer.

The next step with the TAPS chart is to express the given findings in terms of "Problem Solved" (PS). A PS description is a plain English paragraph that, in theory, can be expressed in the proverbial "elevator pitch" (i.e, in 30 seconds or so, without presentation handouts). It expresses the answer to some unmet need, which need is either already widely known (say, ultra high capacity electrical battery storage) or could be readily recognized (say, "bomb proof" word processing software, something that would have speeded the writing of this text).

This mapping of TA to PS is also expressed as the conversion of features to benefits, which is another useful way of thinking about this step. Arthur Leavitt has famously said that no one buys 1/4″ drills; they buy 1/4″ holes. Changing the internal feature language of the technology (the ¼″ drills) into the external benefit language of a buyer's customer (the ¼″ holes) is a step toward answering the "So what?" question. As discussed, such an answer needs to then append why these ¼″ holes provide a buyer benefit greater than any other way by which such holes could be made.

The buyer benefit question is often expressed by four tests: better, faster, cheaper, and/or more reliable. For the ¼″ hole example, the "better" could be straighter, smoother, rounder; the "faster" could be reference to how quickly they could be made, or how quickly the holes could be made use of by the buyer's customer; the "cheaper" could be caused by less expensive drills and fixtures, or the material in which such holes are cut or some less expensive aspect of the buyer's customer's end use; and "more reliable" refers to the universal value of having repeatable processes (holes the same size within the specified tolerance for long production runs) and equipment that has high availability and useful life. There is a version of these value tests for software: "good, fast, cheap . . . pick any two." But such software "law" is really about trading off one benefit for another using the same way of doing things. A new method for software development could provide all three benefits, and be a more reliable means of writing code.

RATING/RANKING We will come to a valuation Method and Tool known as Rating/Ranking in Chapter 5. So we will not repeat the details of the Tool here. The Tool is applied by scoring each of the above criteria, or the final "Problem Solved" result. The method of scoring can be as simple as a letter grade, A, B, or C, where an "A" is used to designate for opportunities that have been so "discovered" and will be pursued down the Licensing D-V-D process. A "C" would be used for those that will definitely not be so pursued. So the middle score of "B" would designate either (1) an opportunity that needs additional initial screening to either move it up to an "A" or down to a "C," or (2) an opportunity that will be on hold and later be reconsidered after the "A" opportunities have run their course, or when/if additional resources are made available.

Now, how to make such judgments? The bottom line in business is the bottom line. How much would this opportunity be worth to the ideal buyer as expressed by its willingness to pay for the Box that contains the subject technology? To answer this question fully, requires applying the valuation Methods of Chapters 4 through 9. But we are seeking now to decide which opportunities should be selected for such valuation. So we have a kind of circularity. But circularities are common in life and business. One standard way out of a circularity is to make a provisional assumption for the purpose of determining any approximate range or minimum value.

So we could in this example simply count the total potential sales revenue that a buyer could enjoy over some estimate of the technical or IP life of the technology as manifest in the best/highest "Problem Solved" expression. First cut estimates can sometimes be made using revenue data that can be found in an Internet search for market information. One useful source is the revenue figures of small public companies that sell products similar to the one defined by the "Problem Solved." Commercial market studies are also a source of such information, though they can be expensive. One approach is to call the firm doing such studies and see if you can get a high level estimate over the phone with the understanding that if you go forward with this opportunity you are likely to buy the study.

Although having a total revenue number is not the same thing as net earnings, as will be explicitly clear when we cover the Discounted Cash Flow Method, it is a proxy for value. If one "Technology Applied" group leads to an estimated $1 billion in lifetime revenues and another group is estimated at $50 million, it's a pretty safe bet that the first opportunity is a lot more valuable than the second, even if there are later dramatic changes in these initial guess-timates.

Another approach to rating/ranking that is more subjective but can be equally effective is simply to score the respective "elevator pitches." A specific panel of people can be tasked with hearing each one, and quickly responding with their individual reactions and perhaps participating in a short debate. Some judge then takes the essence of the individual responses and provisionally tags the opportunity with one of the above A, B, C letters. After all the opportunities have been reviewed, then the panel can reconsider them as they are now grouped into the three priorities. There is, for good or ill, a similarity of this process to *American Idol*[1] judging of singing talent. Descriptions of problems that are thought to be solved by technology that may not yet be fully developed is not as simple and obvious a matter to judge as some lunk singing a few bars of "You Are the Wind Beneath My Wings." But with the preparatory work, and the ability to iterate with the panel if there are some close calls, the process can be effective as a screening tool to prioritize resources.

WHAT ELSE IS NEEDED FOR DISCOVERY One question that should be considered for all the "A" and "B" opportunities is what else could be done to shape the opportunity Box to increase its value. Are there some data that could be taken that would make a dramatic change in the value or range of problems that are addressed by the technology? Could these data already exist within the company, or published by others? Is there additional patent protection that could be obtained? Would the addition of specialized facilities or custom test fixtures make possible early market testing by either the seller or buyer? Would the availability of key team members with "head IP" make a difference, where such availability could be permanent employment or a dedicated period of tech transfer?

The key point here is that is that it is in the seller's general interest to offer what a buyer will value highly compared to the seller's own internal use and value. This is likewise true for the buyer. Discovery is not just about uncovering what could have value and be sold, but what could have the most value and be sold.

FACTORING IN DEAL DOABILITY WITH VALUE Returning to our two-by-two matrix, we can envision four combinations of potential deal value with deal doability (ease of finding a potential buyer and likelihood of consummating an acceptable agreement). Exhibit 3.2 illustrates these four possibilities.

As discussed in Chapter 2, the two-by-two matrix is a well established management tool. In the form made famous by Boston Consulting Group (BCG) the two axes are: market share and growth rate. The power of the segmentation into the four boxes, as painful as the choosing may be, is creating a framework for wise choosing. In the BCG model, high-high (HH) represents those products that are "stars" and should be the focus of investment for opportunity realization. In Exhibit 3.2, the "stars" are the "high priority pursuit" opportunities. The BCG low-low (LL)

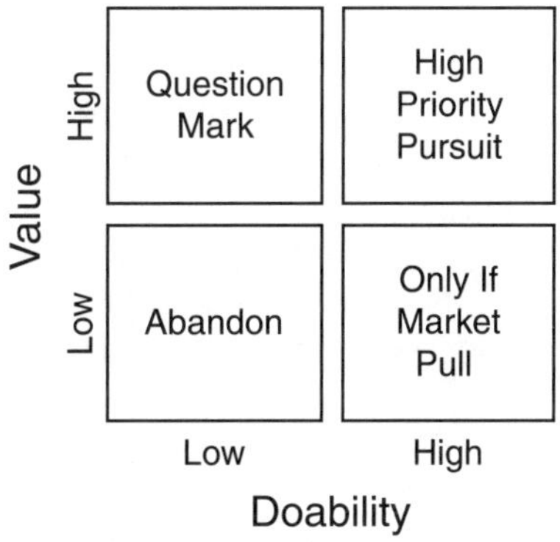

EXHIBIT 3.2 Four Possible Combinations of Value and Doability

were the "dogs" (a regrettable term for all dog lovers), meaning that they should be killed (the idea was euthanasia; from Classic Greek: *eu* [good] + *thanatos* [death], an even more regrettable association with dogs).

The two high market share-low growth (HL) and low share-high growth (LH) boxes, the "shoulders," contain the opportunities that warrants careful judgment. The HL of BCG were deemed the "cash cows" that should be "milked" for return with minimal/no investment. In Exhibit 3.2 this corresponds to the "Only if market pull" box. Finally, the BCG LH, "question mark" is similarly designated in Exhibit 3.2.

Issues that Affect Deal Doability Why is deal doability a factor in value assessment? The answer is the reason this book combines the two "D's" of Discovery and Dealmaking with the "V" of valuation (D-V-D): valuation, by itself, is an internal model (framework) that is not itself directly realizable; it is like a business plan without a business.

What factors tend to cause a Low ranking in deal doability? Here are five:

- High complexity
- People issues
- Inability to demonstrate
- Problematic IP rights
- High initial buyer investment

An example of high complexity would be the seller's need to include in any Dealmaking the sale of land and physical plant, the taking over a team of R&D people, an opportunity that will need multiple areas of breakthrough demonstrations.[2] Even for a high value opportunity (the two top boxes of Exhibit 3.2), such issues will make it hard to find a potential buyer, difficult to work through all the negotiation issues, and in the end a challenge for any buyer to work through all its own internal deliberations and necessary approvals to get to a deal "yes."

Even though our focus here is technology, people issues are important for Dealmaking. Buyers rarely buy a piece of paper. Even a well written patent that is part of the Box is made alive by explanations and background given by inventors or key players in its development. For trade secrets (and related know-how, show-how) the people side is often crucial because of the challenge in documenting everything that is known and important in static text. A common people issue is the loss of some or even all of the team that created the opportunity, which may be why it is on the list of opportunities that can be licensed. A variant of this is that the people are still with the company but are assigned elsewhere and their attention is now on their next new thing; getting their enthusiasm and time on Dealmaking of their "old" opportunity, particularly one which has been designated for, in some way, exiting the company, is sometimes a challenge, and sometimes essentially impossible. There are also those wonderful cases where the principal inventor and his or her team are knowledgeable about the market and competitors, as well as the underlying technology, have great communication skills, interact well with potential buyers, work well as part of a Dealmaking team (more on this in Chapter 11), and, so, make Dealmaking a delight and almost always a success. Then there are those other cases, for which these opportunities deservedly are scored a "Low" in deal doability.

As discussed in Chapter 1, "technology" covers a broad spectrum from an initial discovery through significant entrepreneurial advancement. If an opportunity is only at the "vu-graph" level, that is ideas expressed in presentation charts about what is believed to be demonstratable, it will be difficult for any prospective buyer to overcome the natural fear and doubt about bringing this technology to the market.[3] This point isn't just that doability increases with R&D maturity; that is of course true. The idea is that for every opportunity there are a few key demonstrations, which if they have been done and the results are persuasive and robust, buyers can see how all the remaining pieces/aspects can be put together to make the whole technology-founded business work. If those key demonstrations have not been done, or they have been done but the results are ambiguous, then that tends to lower deal doability.

IP rights are often a key issue in deal doability. When buyers buy businesses, their due diligence is focused on their ability to step into the shoes of the seller, taking over its operations and serving its present customers. IP issues can be important, but they tend to be less so because, after all, there is already an operating business. With technology, a buyer needs to see (in most cases) something that will be commercially important years into the future to pay back for the investment and risk. If competitors can "copycat" the opportunity, or even worse shut it down by imposing their patent rights, the opportunity value will be problematic. Also, with technology, as with a business, the buyer's calculations include the cost and risk of independent development. If the IP rights are questionable, for instance pending essential patent claims that are deemed unlikely to issue in anything like the scope needed for commercial utility, buyers will more likely respond with "Get back to me when those claims issue."

The fifth example anti-doability issue is that of high initial buyer investment. As we have discussed in Chapter 2, and will throughout this book, risk drains value. The higher the initial investment required by the buyer, and the longer such initial investment period, all other factors equal, increases the perception of risk by the buyer. (We will consider in Chapter 10 and Chapter 11 some Wheelbarrow structures that can mitigate to some extent such risks and perceptions). One buyer mantra for business acquisitions is "accretive earnings," meaning that the buyer with the acquisition will have increased earnings in the reference reporting period (the next fiscal year, or sometimes even the next quarter) compared to what it would have reported without the acquisition. Technology acquisitions are almost never accretive in this sense. But to the extent that significant and long-term buyer investments are expected to be necessary, especially with minimal revenue potential from "early adopter" or "lead user" customers, there is a reduction in deal doability even when the effect of such investments is accounted for in terms of deal value (a subject we will address in Chapters 7 and 8).

The deal doability *x*-axis of Exhibit 3.2 can be connected to the value of the *y*-axis by a calculation parallel to probability trees that we will introduce in Chapter 8. If, for instance, the "H" box on the value scale corresponds to $10 million opportunities, as determined by a very high level estimate, and the "L" box on the deal doability scale is thought to designate those opportunities for which there is only a one out of ten chance of getting a deal done at anything close to the perceived value, then multiplying these two factors tells us that the realizable value is only about $1 million.

Decision-Making with the "Corner Boxes" (HL and LH) of Exhibit 3.2 Returning to Exhibit 3.2, the opportunity Discovery issue is now what to do with the occupants of the two "corner" boxes, H value but L doability, and L value and H doability.

One obvious answer is "nothing": Focus on the HH opportunities. Licensing D-V-D is not easy. Even the best opportunities, HH, do not always succeed either in Dealmaking or if a deal is done in subsequent commercialization realization. So why not put all the resources behind the opportunities that look the best of the best, as shown in Exhibit 3.3.

The "Plan A" opportunities of Exhibit 3.3 are those in the HH box of Exhibit 3.2. The "Stop" arrow of Exhibit 3.3 are those in the LL box.

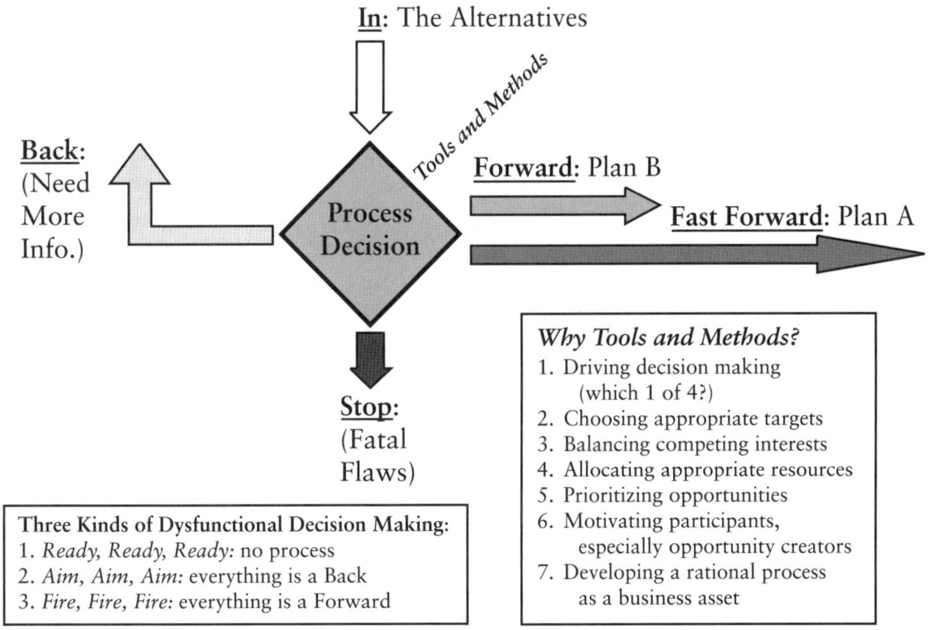

EXHIBIT 3.3 Prioritizing for the "A" Opportunities

The corner boxes, HL and LH of Exhibit 3.2, have to be individually chosen to be either the "Plan B" go forward arrow of Exhibit 3.3, meaning they are worth pursuing, or the "Back" arrow meaning here that they will be pursued only if something new is learned that warrants changing direction. We will return to Exhibit 3.3 in Chapter 11.

The LH box of Exhibit 3.2, low value but high doability, can occur when a prospective buyer "shows up" and initiates Dealmaking. This can occur because of the buyers' interactions with a key inventor, or tracking patents being issued, or simply due to an opportunity scout. The temptation for the seller is to automatically put such opportunity on the "Plan B" arrow of Exhibit 3.3. But there are two questions that should be asked: Does the mere initiation of Dealmaking discussions by an apparently interested buyer really correspond to H doability? It may not for any number of reasons. The Term Sheet Tool introduced in Chapters 10 and 11 can be helpful here to facilitate an early discovery of the likelihood of an acceptable agreement.

The second caution with the buyer-initiated Dealmaking discussion is the question of value. This box is by its provisional classification a L-value opportunity. If there is, without seller initiative, a willing buyer, perhaps this opportunity has been misclassified. This is parallel to the situation where a homeowner adds to a garage sale some old paintings found in grandfather's barn for a dollar each, not knowing that granddaddy had a boyhood friend who became a world famous-painter. We will discuss the example of the "fat gene" in Chapter 9 on Auctions that relates in certain aspects to this point.

Factoring In Risk with Opportunity Discovery In the just concluded discussion we focused, for simplicity, on total potential revenues associated with commercial use of a technology, as a proxy for cumulative net income for a potential buyer.

There are two additional steps that could be taken to improve this estimation and the resulting rating/ranking. The first is to convert potential buyer revenues into new cash flow, and specifically a quantity known as Net Present Value (NPV). NPV analysis will be covered in detail in the Discounted Cash Flow Method of Chapter 7. For now we simply note that highly simplified forms of such Method can be applied to opportunity Discovery to improve the estimate of value to a prospective buyer by a provisional calculation of NPV. Such calculation can shift the rating/ranking we might have obtained by focusing on revenues alone because, as we shall see in Chapter 7, NPV is strongly affected by the magnitude and timing of all the early investments (net cash outflows) as well as the revenues and their timing. An opportunity with very large potential revenues but with such revenues in the distant future, could be less valuable to a buyer than an alternative technology with more modest revenues, but ones that occur early and with a much lower investment.

The second factor that can improve this opportunity analysis is an assessment of risk. Again, as we will see in Chapter 7, risk can be expressly accounted for in the NPV calculation. For opportunity Discovery however, a simplified form of risk assessment can be useful. We can add another column to Exhibit 3.1 for overall risk assessment. Unlike what we will do in Chapter 7, this column would be to establish a preliminary category of risk for each row of opportunity, say using a 1 to 5 scale, where a "1" is very low risk and a "5" is very high. As discussed above such assessment would be made by capturing in a few initial sentences the most important risks as best as they are known. Then a separate assessment is made of the "So what?" of such risk description to assign a 1 to 5 number. The result will be A, B, and C opportunities each paired with a risk number, so the letter gives an estimate of the upside and the risk number the downside. Clearly the A1s are the best, and the C5s the worst.

The two-by-two matrix can be used to refine further opportunity Discovery. For instance, all the individual opportunities in the HH box of Exhibit 3.2, can be mapped against project risk by creating a separate categorization within the HH box of, say, two risk subcategories, L and H. This would then further subclassify certain projects into HHH where the 3rd "H" designates high probability of success (i.e., low risk). This further subcategorization can be particularly useful with the "corner" boxes of Exhibit 3.2, HL and LH; a separate assessment of the opportunity risk can act as a kind of tie-breaker.

The Technology Box

The most basic question in all opportunity identification is "What am I selling?" (There is a relevant joke here: A traveling salesman proudly reports back that he made 10 sales calls that day; and he would have made 15, but someone asked him what he was selling).

The answer to this question is what will be referred to throughout this book as the Technology Box, or the Box; it is where the TR (Technology Rights) resides in the **TR R A DE**™ acronym. In that Box goes everything that the seller is offering, it is what is valued in Chapters 4 through 9, and offered in trade to buyers as discussed in Chapters 10 and 11. A key step in opportunity Discovery is defining the Box.

Both the seller and ultimately the buyer have beliefs as to what should be in such Box. When an early understanding of the Box is not codified, it is not uncommon to find that even well into a negotiation one or both parties are surprised to learn that something they had assumed was part of the deal is not in fact being offered. This discovery leads to setbacks in the negotiation process and, in some cases, a complete breakdown in the relationship. In all cases such a misunderstanding will lead to an error in valuation because valuing a technology needs to be done in the context of all the assets, which includes a specification of the rights being transferred.

Box Associated with Agreement Category

Consider three kinds of licenses: (1) outright sale, (2) non-assert, and (3) limited license.

OUTRIGHT SALE AGREEMENTS In the case of an outright sale, what is being offered is the ownership of the patents and related IP rights, such as trade secrets (know-how). This would appear to be simple: "Here it is, you buy it." However, the buyer and seller can have different perspectives on what "here" and "it" means. The buyer may expect and reasonably need some hands-on learning, often termed "tech transfer" assistance in order to be able to make use of the technology. This could involve months of access to the seller's experts. In special cases, the buyer may even require that certain key employees of the seller become employees of the buyer, because the need for such expertise is perceived to be ongoing and critical to the commercial success of the project. The buyer may also expect to receive ownership of equipment and fixtures that were used in the R&D process. The buyer may also want representations and warranties concerning the seller's rights to the patents and other forms of intellectual property, guarantees that the patents are valid, assurances that the use of the technology as described by the seller does not infringe a third party's patents, and so on. The buyer may also want a representation that it will not require the use of any other patent owned or controlled by the seller even if such patent is not directly related to the technology.[4] Likewise, even with this simple agreement, the seller may expect more from the buyer than just money. For example, the seller may want the retained right to practice the patents or at least to be free from the threat of being sued by the buyer for infringement of the transferred patents and improvement claims (a so-called "non-assert" provision). If the valuation includes royalty or other forms of future conditional payments, the seller may insist on minimums, guarantees, and reversion rights, depending upon future outcomes.

NON-ASSERT AGREEMENTS In a "non-assert" license, the buyer is essentially acquiring freedom from a future lawsuit by the seller. It represents the opposite extreme from the initial example of outright ownership. On the surface, this also appears to be a simple agreement—basically, the buyer is paying for something not to happen. (In reality, the buyer does "get" something: assurance that it has the freedom to practice within the scope of the seller's patents included in the agreement.) Yet despite the apparent simplicity of this type of license, there are numerous elements of the deal requiring clarification as being included or excluded. For example, what about future patents that the seller may invent or obtain? Are such unspecified and even presently unknowable patents included within the scope of the non-assert? Will the non-assert right apply to all countries in which corresponding patents have been obtained? Does the seller have to represent that it will require any competitor of the buyer to pay the seller at least as much to acquire such a non-assert (the so-called "most favored nations" clause)? In turn, the seller may want some form of reciprocal non-assert for the same, related, or completely unrelated technology.

LICENSE AGREEMENTS With a limited license or simply a "license," the grant to the buyer is more extensive than the non-assert but less than an outright sale and considers many dimensions of business practice. Will the buyer be able to make anything it wants under the license or only certain products or categories of products? Will it be able to make, use, and sell, or just one or two of these rights? In which countries will such rights be enabled? How long will the license last? Will the buyer have the right to license third parties (the so-called "sublicensing" right)? Will the buyer be able to sell its right to a third party (assignability)? What will the seller be obligated to provide? Commercial data? Customer lists? Equipment and facilities? Tech transfer support? Improvement inventions? Defense of the patents? Who pays to maintain the patents in all their various jurisdictions? What happens if the patents are later found to be invalid? Can either party terminate the license without cause and cost? If not, under what conditions could termination be effected? Will agreements to supply raw materials or buy or provide finished products be part of the trade? Obviously all these questions require interaction amongst the technical, business, and legal people on each side and should be factored into making a valuation.

The answer to each one of these and many other questions affects the value of the transaction, some more so than others. Accordingly, the specification of the "TR," the Technology Rights which is used here to encompass all such terms, is essential to performing a valuation.

It should also be said that this is not a legal textbook. Therefore the reader is encouraged to refer to many such texts on legal issues to obtain a fuller and authoritative treatment of such agreements. For convenience, future reference to a technology deal will referred to as a "license" as an all-inclusive term covering all three of these agreement categories.

Sell-Side Sources of Value in the Box

The critical starting point of any valuation is defining exactly what is being offered for licensing, the Box. Here we wish to consider what a seller may offer and a buyer may seek in a license agreement as to its potential effect on deal value. In the next section we will reverse the view and consider what a seller may expect and a buyer may offer in consideration for such agreement.

It is useful to develop a shorthand for this discussion: We will use a metaphorical Box and its contents to designate the subject matter of a license being valued. What might such a Box contain? Clearly, we begin with the right to practice the technology being licensed. But even this simple idea contains two very important terms that must be defined: technology and rights.

1. *Technology*. What exactly is the technology being licensed? How does it relate to the issued patents that might be in the Box? For instance, does technology mean that the buyer can use the claims of the licensed patents, however it is able to do so, and only that? Or, is the scope of the technology only incompletely encompassed by the issued patents, wherein some commercially important applications envisioned are not covered by the scope of existing patenting claims? What about pending patent applications whose ultimate claims are not known at the time of the negotiation? What about improvement inventions that might arise at the seller's R&D labs or that the seller may acquire rights to in the future? What does improvement really mean in relation to the technology?
2. *Rights*. This is another term capable of a rich range of meanings. What is the uniqueness of licensed right? Is it exclusive? If so, what are the terms? Does it apply to all potential applications (fields of use)? All territories? For all time? Does exclusivity preclude the seller's right to practice? Is the right to sublicense included in such an exclusive right? What about the right to assign?

It is common that sellers are willing to consider alternative Boxes with respect to the technology and right issues. There are two things that are important about changing Boxes: How does it affect value? How does it affect deal doability?

1. *Valuation*. Any change in the contents of the Box should, in general, cause a change in the value of a license to the Box's contents. Accordingly, without locking on a definition of the content of the Box, it is not possible for valuation to take place by either the seller or buyer. One is tempted to conceive of creating

an à la carte menu by which each element in the Box is individually priced, such that any buyer can self price the deal by the selections it makes, something like this: nonexclusive royalty is 2%; with exclusivity there is a 3% adder (5% total); the sublicensing right is 1%; two years of improvements cost an additional 2% but five years of improvements are on special today for only 3%; and so forth (or the equivalent in present value, lump sum payments).

2. *Doability*. In licensing situations, the number of possible elements is so large, and their value can so interact with the presence (or absence) of other elements, that to create such a valuation model would require an overwhelming level of analysis. Although such an approach works for restaurants and custom-built homes, the idea of a single Box with à la carte pricing incorporating all the possible deal variations is simply impractical for technology licensing. Fortunately there are practical solutions. The obvious solution is for the seller to prescribe only one Box and value it accordingly—as Henry Ford said, you could have any color of a Model-T automobile, as long as it was black. Such a one-size-fits-all approach is likely to be rejected by potential buyers as including more than they want to pay for or less than they need. In many cases, a potential buyer will have very particular interests and values, and will seek a licensing Box unique to its business situation.

Defining the Box carefully is important both for valuation reasons but also to keep negotiations on track. Some buyers will keep asking for more TR until they hear a firm "no" simply as a negotiating strategy: How do we know we got all we can until they are ready to throw us out? (This is sometimes known as the "Brooklyn Negotiating Strategy.") Regardless of the circumstances, it serves both parties well to reach this understanding early, and record such understanding in writing even if in the form of a summary TR table. Such record keeping can be particularly useful when other parties within the buyer's organization join the negotiations at a later stage and presume or feign to presume certain things are included in the deal that have been excluded. Also, at the stage of documenting the TR table it is essential that the parties representing the seller gain organizational unanimity of the scope of what is being offered to avoid creating "take away" situations late in negotiations; such situations are always harmful to the negotiation process and can lead to the breakdown of a pending agreement.

Just as there are deal-breaking requests made by buyers there can be seller TR offers or structures that can be deal-breaking to a buyer. To avoid facing a broken deal after substantial effort, it is in the interest of both parties to work out the deal content issues early in the due diligence process. Another crucial reason for such TR definition is its necessity in assessing Risk (R) and determining the appropriate Deal Economics (DE).

Are there alternatives to the "Henry Ford" and á la carte pricing ways of defining the TR? The answer in many situations is a limited "yes." In general, there are too many elements that can be negotiated that simply cannot be quantitified on a one-by-one basis in an all-inclusive pricing book. But there can be a few alternative TR Boxes deserving analysis. One such situation arises when the technology can be used to make two different products (say, A and B) and in three different territories (say,1, 2, and 3); in such cases it is possible that a limited pricing table can be created along the following lines:

- The TR for "A" and "B" are priced separately for use in all territories (one, two, and three) making a two element pricing structure
- The TR for all products (A and B and any other) are priced separately for each of three territories (1, 2, or 3) making a three element pricing structure.

The former situation makes sense when the buyer is a large international company that is likely to want to pursue worldwide exploitation of one, but not both, products. The latter situation makes more sense when the buyer is a smaller company whose marketing interests are focused in one territory but wants to put the underlying technology to as many uses as possible.

In this example, it is possible (in theory) to conceive of creating a matrix of rights: two products in two rows and three territories in three columns and pricing each of the six resulting cells. It has been reported that term sheets have been offered that have nine products matrixed against nine territories creating 81 cells all for one underlying technology. Such an approach may be workable for special situations such as licensing soft drink franchises in various countries, and it is conceivable for special technology licensing situations such as nonexclusive rights to a medical diagnostic tool protected by worldwide patents. In general, however, segmenting license prices into more than two or three components is rare. And rarer still (in fact, unheard of) would be a TR term sheet that shows the added cost of each of a dozen elements possible in an agreement. Yet it is a good practice for the seller to consider what a particular buyer, or category of buyers, might reasonably want, and prize, as a TR Box.

How is a multiBox opportunity handled? As a starting point for marketing and negotiations, the seller creates a baseline Box of what it conceives is an appropriate configuration of its interests and its target buyers, but with an analysis of one or two alternatives to establish a range of values and an estimate of value sensitivity. Regardless of these choices and complications, the Box must be defined before the valuation process can begin if its result is to have a rational basis.

So far, we have considered technology and rights as two elements of the Box. What else is there? Well, the list is long indeed. The following list provides brief descriptions of additional possible elements that could be appropriate to and included in such a licensing Box.

- *Patents and other intellectual property.* This could include pending patent applications, formalized trade secrets, copyrighted content and software, also even trademarks.
- *Proprietary technical information (PTI).* Although this can be grouped under IP trade secrets, it is useful to consider the wealth of technical (and business) information that is typically created by a seller as being broader than the more restrictive, legal term of trade secrets. Included in such PTI could be laboratory notebooks, unpublished white papers, project plans, management presentations, a selected compendium of published articles whose results are pertinent and valuable to the licensed technology, assessments of competing technologies, market assessments including customer surveys or focus panel results, and the like.
- *People.* There could be individuals employed by the seller who would be interested in joining the buyer and so continuing to stay involved with the

technology. The seller can agree to permit the buyer to recruit selected individuals and even provide inducements to key employees to go with the technology. As part of such transfer, the seller can provide the buyer, and the people transferring employment, the right to use all their "head IP" as it relates to the subject technology. Such seller commitments are subject, always, to the willingness of such people to become transferring employees of the buyer's company, but incentives can be committed to by either the seller or buyer or both.

- *Hardware.* The technology can be expressed in a wide range of physical forms from special raw materials, to models, R&D prototypes, development breadboards, test samples, and so forth, all the way to saleable inventory.
- *Facilities.* This can range from the offerings of a complete operable production plant embodying the licensed technology or a factory that manufactures the licensed technology as a product, down to specialized facilities/infrastructure that can be removed, shipped, and reinstalled at the buyer. Alternatively, a lease arrangement could be used whereby the buyer would use the seller's facilities on a short term or long term basis, or even a "tolling" arrangement whereby the technology seller agrees to sustain a prescribed manufacturing capability on behalf of the buyer.
- *Software.* The seller could have software programs that model the performance of the technology and are useful in R&D and/or production design and/or production control.
- *Customers.* Commercial accounts could be transferrable to a buyer. In other cases, there could be trials with potential customers, or expressions of intent to buy that could be available.
- *Suppliers.* The seller could have identified and even qualified certain vendors who can supply needed materials or services, with the attendant specifications. The seller itself could agree to be a supplier of a needed component (an element that could be a source of high deal value to the seller).
- *External contracts.* There could be sources of funding, including R&D funding by third parties, such as a government agency, which the buyer might acquire as part of the agreement. Likewise, commercial services that are currently provided by the seller could be transferred to the buyer.
- *External licenses.* The seller may have operating permits, government approvals, or other licenses to the subject technology collecting revenues that can be transferred. Alternatively, licensed rights to third party patents could be included here, or under "other IP," and could be an important source of deal value if the seller has the right to sublicense or assign.
- *Patent prosecution and maintenance.* If the patents are assigned (sold), then their prosecution and maintenance normally becomes the responsibility of the buyer. If the patents are only licensed, then the buyer or the seller could undertake the financial obligation, or it could be shared.
- *Infringement enforcement.* A common concern is: What happens after the deal is done if a third party infringes or appears to infringe on licensed claims? A seller/licensor could agree to enforce the licensed patents to ensure the buyer's exclusivity. If nonexclusive, the seller may accept the responsibility to take action against unlicensed third parties who compete with the buyer. In either case there may be some threshold of infringement before the seller would be obligated to take action.

- *Infringement defense.* A different infringement concern by the buyer has to do with the risk associated with its freedom to practice what it licensed from the seller. Though not common with technology licensing, the seller could indemnify the buyer against claims by the third party against the buyer for a specific product.
- *R&D/consulting services.* The seller could provide R&D services (commonly termed tech-transfer assistance) for a transition period, or an indefinite period. A prescribed level of such services could be included in the license, and/or the commitment to provide such services under specified terms.
- *Regulatory support services.* There could be circumstances whereby the use of the technology will require some form of regulatory approval and the seller could be of assistance to the buyer in seeking or transferring such approval.
- *General representations and warranties.* It is, of course, common for the seller to warrant that it has the right to sell or license what it is offering to the buyer, but the seller could offer additional representations and warranties.

Although few agreements have all these elements, it is useful to both the seller and buyer to consider what can, should, and should not be included to maximize the relative value of the opportunity to both parties, particularly for technologies with significant commercial potential. It is especially useful for the seller to create a summary of what is in the Box—or Boxes, in the case of multiple scenarios. This practice allows all the affected individuals within the seller's organization to possess a common understanding of the dimensions of a potential deal. In any case, such a specification is necessary to create a baseline on which a valuation can take place. Further, it is also useful in communicating with potential buyers so that an early understanding can be reached, or the Box appropriately adjusted, to accommodate the deal being envisioned.

These possible elements are not equally important, nor are they unrelated to each other. The IP is, for example, closely tied to both the technology and rights; it would not be uncommon that a license deal would have only these core elements in the Box.

Buy-Side Expressions of Value: The Wheelbarrow

In the previous section, the focus was on the value provided by the seller to the buyer, using the metaphor of the Box, as the contents for the technology, the rights to use, and the related value affecting aspects of a license. Here, we wish to consider how the buyer may provide value to the seller. As before, a metaphor will be useful. Here we use the Wheelbarrow as the metaphor for the carriage of all the value in its various forms that the buyer will provide the seller as the DE, Deal Economics, for its half of the TR R A DE™. The Wheelbarrow will be covered in detail in Chapters 10 and 11 on Dealmaking. Here we will briefly address the Wheelbarrow to aid our discussions of valuation in Chapters 4 through 9.

One frequent measure of the value of a license is the royalty rate, as in "this deal is for a 5 percent license." Atually, a royalty rate by itself is an incomplete description of value. The seller is rightfully concerned about the size of the check that it expects to receive, not the royalty rate used in calculating the amount owed under the license, regardless of the rate, and regardless of whether it is usage-based, time-based, or event-based. To effectively capture the concern of the seller (and buyer), the slang term Wheelbarrow has been utilized in reference to the buyer hauling cash to the seller in a wheelbarrow. Accordingly, while a royalty rate is a common negotiation point, both parties are ultimately concerned with the size of the Wheelbarrow. Here, the Wheelbarrow is used to reflect all of the various forms of value provided by the seller to the buyer. The seller provides a Box of technology, rights, and other deal elements, whereas the buyer provides, in the form of one or many Wheelbarrows, value payments to the seller.

There are two common forms of value contained in such Wheelbarrows: a single payment, such as "the buyer paid $10 million for the license," and a royalty rate. These two payment forms represent polar opposite Wheelbarrow structures, (1) a one-time, paid-up, "lump-sum" license wherein the buyer pays once and can use the technology with no additional payment obligation to the seller, or (2) a pure royalty license where the buyer pays if and as it uses the technology.

1. *Lump-sum license.* A single-payment license, commonly termed a lump-sum or paid-up license, is the simplest valuation structure.[5] It represents a check, or more commonly a wire transfer, usually made simultaneously with executing the license. It represents the only payment that the buyer will make.
2. *Royalty license.* A pure royalty-based license, also known as a running royalty license, is the inverse of the single-payment license: The single-payment license is a fixed sum paid upfront for unlimited (or in accordance with the terms of the license), subsequently free use, whereas the pure royalty license has only payments due on use (make, use, or sell) and only on such use. However, a critical factor in determining value is the royalty base against which such royalty rate is applied. A common negotiation involves a determination of the appropriate base.

In addition to these two common elements, there are many other possible elements that can be used in any combination in the Wheelbarrow to provide value to the seller; here are eight:

1. *Upfront payment(s).* A common value element is the use of one or multiple upfront or license fee cash payments. Upfront payments are unconditional and precede the anticipated commercial use by the buyer. One such payment is made on closing or within a specified number of days of closing (e.g., 30 days). Additional upfront payments could be made at specified dates, such as on the first and second anniversary of the license. In this case, the term upfront is used to specify payments that are committed at deal execution but may be deferred to specific dates after closing.
2. *Annual payments.* Another form of fixed cash payments is the use of annual payments payable on each anniversary of the license for as long as the license is in effect. Sometimes this form of payment is referred to as license maintenance fees or minimum royalties (or simply minimums).
3. *Milestone payments.* Such payments are specified amounts that become due upon the crossing of some milestone event. In the area of pharmaceuticals, such milestones could be the entry into each phase of clinical testing, or any regulatory approval. Other kinds of milestones could be key R&D achievements, and/or the commitment to building a commercial plant of specified minimum

size, and/or the first commercial sale. Such sums are sometimes referred to as "progress payments."

4. *Option payments.* One form of option payment is an initial payment made by the buyer to allow it to conduct additional R&D, or market assessment or other feasibility activities, to enable it to make an informed licensing decision. Such a payment has the effect of compensating a seller for withholding the licensing opportunity from the market during the option period.
5. *Royalty adjustments.* Many creative adjustments have been used with a baseline royalty rate. A wedding cake royalty is one that decreases in rate with increasing sales, such as 5 percent on the first $5 million, 3 percent on the next $10 million, and 1 percent for all additional sales. Such sales could be annual—that is, with each anniversary the royalty again begins at 5 percent in this example—or cumulative (i.e., total sales since the onset of the license).
6. *IP rights.* A grant-back is one type of IP right in which the buyer can provide rights to its own improvements to the subject technology to the seller, either for the seller's own internal use or to enable the seller to offer additional technology to its other technology licensees.
7. *Commitment to purchase goods/services.* The buyer could agree to purchase goods made by the seller at terms that are commercially favorable to the seller in a so-called supply agreement. Another example would be the buyer's commitment to purchase professional services, such as R&D in the area of the licensed technology or some other area. Such an arrangement is common when the seller is a university and the buyer is a large company.
8. *Equity.* The provision of a share of ownership in the buyer can create a source of considerable value, or even the total value in lieu of any cash payments, royalty, or any other form of value in consideration for a license.

Although these eight elements do not exhaust the possibilities, they do reflect commonly used means of creating a Wheelbarrow of value to the seller. We will return to this important subject in Chapters 10 and 11. In general, for less important and less valuable technologies, the parties tend to gravitate to simpler Wheelbarrows (and Boxes). However, as current trends continue into the twenty-first century, technology owners will increasingly recognize their fiduciary responsibility to maximize their return on assets. Also, as time to market urgency increases, sellers will be more inclined to license out even their crown jewels for appropriately large Wheelbarrows. Likewise, we can expect all buyers to consider quite literally the world of technology in-licensing of boxes based on externally created technologies for the prospect that they can become strategic new businesses and, thereby, warrant highly crafted license-in arrangements which tends to make both the Boxes and Wheelbarrows bigger in terms of elements, and it is hoped, value as well. The twenty-first century is expected to become a new economy of licensing by the increasing use of highly tailored Boxes and value optimizing Wheelbarrows for opportunities of high importance to both seller and buyer.

Overview of Valuation Methods

In this chapter we will anticipate the six methods to be studied in Chapters 4 through 9. We will also consider how the use of royalties and equity greatly aid in dealing with high uncertainty valuations. Finally, we will consider the appropriateness of using seller's cost as a valuation method or basis. This is an important issue because it so commonly, and generally inappropriately, arises in technology licensing discussions.

The Need for Judgment

Beginning in Chapter 4, we will consider the first of six valuation Methods. The purpose of this chapter is to provide an overview of these methods and the context of their intended use. Also, we will address the issue of seller's incurred cost as a measure of value.

As discussed in Chapter 2, these valuation Methods require developing models and assumptions for which certainty is an unattainable idealization. But this does not mean that any kind of model or assumptions are equally useful. Drawing on another parallel, in the early days of computers a term was coined to explain bad outputs—GIGO, or garbage in... garbage out. The computer cannot improve bad or false data or improperly crafted algorithms (at least not yet). Similarly, the methods discussed in Chapters 4 through 9 rely on information and application that is as close to mirroring reality as is possible; otherwise, it can be GIGO here too.

Let us illustrate the judgment issue by considering the application of a royalty-based Wheelbarrow. Such royalty is a **rate**, typically expressed as a percentage, which is multiplied against a **base**, typically expressed in dollars (or other currency), which yields a currency payment from the buyer to the seller for the use of the technology typically for some period, such as a calendar quarter. The royalty rate is only meaningful in the context of a specified royalty base. The normal starting point for the determination of the base is the revenue received by the licensee for sales of product or services incorporating the licensed subject matter.

BUYERS AND THE SHRINKING ROYALTY BASE In a negotiation on a royalty rate and base agreement, the buyer will argue for both lower royalty rates and smaller bases. It is common that the royalty base of buyer revenues is reduced by certain specified deductions such as shipping, insurance, returns, and allowances. Clearly buyers like to have this list of allowed deductions long, and sellers want it short.

Beyond these deductions, buyers may argue for further reductions in the base because, the argument often goes, the licensed subject matter contributes to or affects only a part of the overall product that is being sold by the licensee. In such a case, the licensee might reason that the device incorporating the licensed subject matter has four key functions, say each equally significant to its customers and equal in cost to make and so equal in profit margin to the licensee, and the licensed subject matter only enables one of such four functions, then the royalty base should be, according to this line of reasoning, reduced by 75 percent. So, if a royalty was determined to be 5 percent, and the device sold by the license would net $100 after deduction of, say, shipping and returns/allowances, then the licensee would by the above reasoning be proposing to pay 5 percent of just $25, or $1.25 per device sold. The idea of reducing the royalty amount by factoring the base is discussed further in Chapter 11.

Consider the interesting example of licensing in music industry, there are several illustrations of how buyers (music companies) use royalty base creative adjustments.

Say the royalty agreed to for an artist/composer was 10 percent and the expected wholesale price of the CD was $10; it would look like the royalty would be $1 per CD sold. But, not so fast, Ms. Mariah Carey wanna-be. There is a long established practice of allowing deductions of 10 percent of units shipped for breakage. This originated with vinyl records (LPs), which only those born in the first half of the preceding century are likely to remember; this format did break relatively easily. Rather than account for each individual broken record, the practice was widely established that allowed the 10 percent deduction, though from the perspective of the artist/composer this seems high. So, now it appears that the artist 10 percent is applied against $9 yielding 90 cents. Not so. When the CD format was introduced in the mid 1980s, record companies argued that the cost of converting to this new format was significant and, accordingly, a reduction for the high cost of packaging compared to then standard techniques was appropriate. Somehow it became common to deduct 25 percent for such special costs associated with CD packaging. So, now, according to the music company's perspective, the 10 percent would be applied against a further reduced base of $6.75 yielding just 67.5 cents. But, you know, making the artwork and printing of the CD "liner" (the folded insert) is very expensive and we, the record company think it is only fair to deduct this as well. This base-shrinking exercise is a kind of "Where's Waldo?" game.[6] The artist/composer/licensor keeps trying to find his or her base, and the licensee is saying "no it's not there," "no it's not here either," and so forth.

In the case of technology licensing, there are situations where the buyer may propose deducting the cost of goods sold (COGS) to reach the base, or even, in addition, the deduction of certain overhead costs. For reasons discussed in Chapter 10, this is not a recommended approach, nor is it common practice, although from a buyer's perspective the attraction is obvious.

SELLERS AND THE EXPANDING ROYALTY BASE Sellers can (and sometimes do) make the argument that the base, in certain circumstances, be greater than just the revenues associated with licensed subject matter. We will consider the example of ink jet printers and ink jet ink in Chapter 10.

When the seller is doing opportunity Discovery, this question of what is the royalty base can be crucial to an initial assessment of value based upon a royalty rate. Let us suppose that in the opportunity Discovery discussion, it is estimated that a particular opportunity could be very widely used in all automobiles. Without considering what the royalty base would be in the context of a technology buyer, any estimate of a royalty-based value is likely to be flawed. For example, assume there will be 20 million cars and trucks sold each year in the U.S. and they each sell for $20,000, so the round number annual revenue potential for any invention that is used in cars is $400 billion, a very nice figure from the point of view of the seller. Now the temptation could be for the seller to think, "what if I **just** got a 1 percent royalty rate?" (The answer is $4 billion a year). There are two problems with such thought and calculation. The $400 billion is the annual market for automobiles (very approximate numbers), it is not the "license addressable market" (LAM). The LAM has to be what the buyer of the technology opportunity will be realizing, not the entire industry that uses many different components and technologies. If, for example, the technology was a fabulous new connector for the main battery, the licensee would not be the car manufacturers, but one of their suppliers. And such a supplier would likely not even be the battery maker, but a component supplier to the battery maker. So the royalty base would not be total annual revenues of cars, or even batteries, but of the connector component that goes with the battery. Say those components sell for $1, then the potential LAM would be not $400 billion but $20 million, still a substantial figure. However, in a mature industry where battery connectors have been used successfully for about 100 years, it is unlikely, for any number of reasons, that any new technology will supplant all the incumbent connectors. So the license realized market may only be 10 percent of the LAM, or $2 million. Now the question of the royalty rate is important, because there is a big difference to the seller between its initial happiness with the idea of a 1 percent rate, which now would correspond to a royalty of $20,000 a year, or perhaps a warranted 10 percent or $200,000 a year.

Let us consider another example of an expanded base; that of some kind of integrated circuit chip. From a seller's perspective, it would be appealing to collect a royalty on the manufacturer of, say, a chip that incorporates the licensed technology, and also on the device that incorporates the chip, and also on the system that operates by the interconnection of the components, and (while we're at it) on each unit of use of the system. This generally is not possible because of a legal doctrine known as exhaustion of rights, a subject that is beyond the scope of this text. The practical situation, however, in most cases, is that the seller can license at just one point on the value chain, though it may be possible for the seller to choose the point on the chain. So how to choose (when choice is both necessary and practically possible)?

Licensees, for obvious reasons, generally resist paying royalties and seek to push that burden on some other party in the value chain. So, in the above example, if the seller calls on the system integrator and attempts to enter negotiations on a royalty based on the selling price of the system, it is likely to hear that such discussions should take place with the makers of the components who sell to the system integrator. If the seller takes that counsel, it is likely to hear the further suggestion by the component manufacturer that actually the proper party is the chipmaker who supplies the component manufacturer, and so on—this is yet another version of the "Where's Waldo?" game. In many cases, sellers find themselves directed to the smallest, cheapest possible "thing-maker." With increasingly complex technology being embedded deeper and deeper into chips and firmware as well as software, this is not an uncommon situation. From the seller's perspective, negotiating a royalty payment with a chipmaker selling chips at, say $500 each, automatically shrinks the base compared to a device based on such chips that may sell for tens of thousands of dollars, and a system of devices that sells for tens of millions.

It would be possible that the royalty payment to the licensor could be calculated in such a way to yield the same dollar value to the seller. For instance, there could be a 50 percent royalty on the $500 chip, yielding $250 a chip; if four such chips are used in each device, this would have the effective royalty of $1,000 a device, though it would be paid by the chipmaker. Alternatively, at least in principle, the licensor could have negotiated a royalty rate with the device manufacturer of 10 percent on a revenue of $10,000 per device and receive the same $1,000 royalty amount. Thus, if ten such components were required by an integrator to create a system for a network operator, then the licensor would receive $10,000 for each system sold. Thus, in the alternative, the licensor could have licensed the system operator at a royalty rate of 1 percent on, say, a $1 million network system and receive that same $10,000. All such payments are one-time royalties, namely: The royalty is paid one time triggered by the selling event of the respective product on which the base is established. All subsequent use of the equipment by the licensee's customer is then not subject to a royalty.

As one might imagine, sellers might find attractive the prospect of being paid on the use of the above network incorporating the technology rather than on the one-time sale of the chips, the components, or the system. This approach would have the appealing-to-the-seller feature of providing a royalty stream on the ongoing use of the network. This is similar to the example of the ink jet manufacturer making most of its profit on the recurring sales of ink rather than the one-time sale of the printer, and like the appeal of giving away razors to secure the recurring revenues and profits of the razor blades.

Industry practice, and the nature and significance of the technology and the scope of its IP protection, will affect which of the above licensing options will be practicable. In the above chip hypothetical, the seller's presumption was that it **could** conduct Dealmaking at alternative points in the value chain. But, a mere claim of usability does not convince prospective buyers that they need to take such license, because of the availability of alternatives. Further, as we will discuss in Chapter 6, the larger the system produced by the buyer, the more technologies that are incorporated into it and a royalty stacking situation results. No system integration buyer, for instance, can afford to license, say 10 technologies, each at, say a 5 percent royalty on its total revenues, simply because each of such 10 technology owners found it beneficial to license at the end of the value chain.

Exclusivity and Size of Licensed Market

Another important factor affecting royalty rate, and potentially the royalty amount, is the issue of exclusivity and how this may affect the size of the licensed market.

Every licensor wishes for the situation of a high royalty rate and a 100 percent penetration of the potential licensed market, and wants to avoid the converse situation of a low royalty rate combined with a low market penetration. However, the choices facing licensors in most cases are between two intermediate alternatives: (1) do I license exclusively at a high royalty rate to one licensee who in turn will have a modest market penetration, or (2) do I license nonexclusively at a low royalty rate to multiple licensees who in aggregate may reach essentially 100 percent of the license addressable market?

As a general rule, the royalty rate for exclusive licenses is higher than nonexclusive licenses. The customary rationale is that such exclusivity creates higher margin sales for the licensee that enables it to apportion an increased portion of the profits to the licensor. We will consider this effect later in this chapter and in Chapter 6 on the Rules of Thumb Method. Correspondingly, each nonexclusive licensee faces a competitive environment with respect to the same technology because of the market presence of other licensees that has the effect of depressing prices and margins as well as the capacity to pay royalties and still make a fair return on investment.

Let us briefly consider two examples of significant licensing revenues achieved by nonexclusive licensing. Stanford University, on behalf of itself and the University of California at San Francisco, licensed its Cohen-Boyer gene splicing patent to nearly

500 companies and received over the lifetime of this patent more than $250 million in royalties for U.S. practice only.[7]

The other example is quite controversial but nonetheless illustrative of the principle that nonexclusive licensing can lead to a lot of money. The late Jerome Lemelson, and his estate, received in the 1990s more than $1 billion in royalties from nonexclusive licensing from some 800 companies for a method of reading bar codes in managing manufacturing inventory covered by a patent which was issued 38 years after its original submission in 1954. In both these examples, the royalty rates were very low,[8] and correspondingly the payments are low from any one licensee. However in aggregate there are many licensees and products and the total magnitude of royalties is very significant. What is also notable about these two examples is that in the one instance, Cohen-Boyer, all the licenses and royalties occurred as a result of opportunity licensing, whereas in the Lemelson situation all or substantially all of the licenses and royalties are as a result of enforcement licensing (patent litigation or the threat of litigation).

The Effect of Significant Lump Sum Payments

Earlier we discussed how the buyer may seek creative ways of diminishing the royalty base so as to reduce the royalty payment. In a somewhat analogous way, the seller may seek significant fixed payments to minimize their downside risk in case commercialization proves unsuccessful, or of limited success, while retaining upside rights through their royalty interest.

Returning to the music industry let us consider an interesting, recent example. Mariah Carey has been a very popular artist. In the 1990s, she had nine record albums that sold on average 8 million copies each, a very large number, including one that sold 23 million copies. At least since 1991, she is the highest selling female artist according to SoundScan, Inc.[9] In 2001, she entered into a contract with EMI Records to create five new albums. She is reported to have received an $80 million guarantee[10] (which works out to $16 million per album, or more than $1 million per song) of which $21 million was paid upfront at contract signing in April 2001. In September 2001, the first album, *Glitter*, was released; through January 2002 the album had sold just 500,000 copies and had less than glittering reviews. In January 2002, it was reported that EMI would make an additional payment of $28 million to terminate the contract, meaning they paid $49 million for one album (for which production and promotion costs were also significant) that sold 500,000 copies.[11] If we assume that the royalty base on the copies sold was $10, then Ms. Carey received in fixed payments an effective royalty rate of 980 percent ($49 million in payments on $5 million in royalty base), which cannot be what EMI had in mind when they signed the contract. Had her five albums sold her previous average of 8 million copies each, the royalty base would have been $400 million (again assuming a base of $10 per album), which would have meant that her upfront payment of $21 million was just 5.25 percent, and her total $80 million guarantee was 20 percent, of such projected revenues. So, with these assumptions, EMI was guaranteeing Ms. Carey the equivalent of a 20 percent royalty on the sales of five albums at her previous average album sales numbers. However, the guarantee provision, and the termination outcome, resulted in a much higher effective royalty rate, illustrating the risk that a buyer takes when it commits to guaranteed payments.

The Six Valuation Methods

The first method considered, in Chapter 4, is the use of Industry Standards. This is based on the idea of working to find as many relevant agreements as possible that bear some resemblance to the technology and deal in question. For reasons that will be discussed, it is rare that a "right on" comparable agreement is found that can be directly used to infer a value. Rather, an interpretive process works on families of agreements to characterize the nature of the terms agreed to in other agreements so as to give guidance to the subject valuation.

In Chapter 5 we consider the Rating/Ranking Method. This method provides a more formal way of characterizing how one technology and/or one agreement differs from another. It requires a reference agreement or standard in order to base a valuation. For this reason it is normally used in conjunction with the Industry Standards Method.

The use of Rules of Thumb is considered in Chapter 6 as the third method. Such rules, guidelines really, are generalizations derived from observing how parties reached previous agreements. The most common expression is the so called 25 Percent Rule. It establishes a principle for apportioning a percentage of the revenues received by the buyer based on the anticipated profitability.

Chapter 7 presents the Discounted Cash Flow Method. This method introduces the Risk Adjusted Hurdle Rate (RAHR, often designated by "k") as a means for characterizing the overall commercial risk. Using such a risk factor, the magnitude and timing of future cash flow benefits can be analyzed and apportioned between the seller and buyer.

Advanced methods are considered in Chapter 8, principally the Monte Carlo Method. This method is similar to the Discounted Cash Flow Method except that it relies on the probability analysis of estimated ranges to produce a statistical prediction of the expected value. In addition, we will consider in this chapter some other nontraditional perspectives on valuation that deal with high uncertainty and/or long term payoff situations.

Finally, the Auction Method is presented in Chapter 9. In a sense, Chapter 9 brings us full circle back to a market-based approach that is the basis of Chapter 4. However in the case of auctions, the seller creates a market for the specific opportunity being offered for license.

What about Cost as a Valuation method?

You may note from the previous outline that the seller's cost is not considered as a valuation method. Some might consider this as missing the most obvious method. However, with few exceptions (as we shall presently discuss), seller's costs are irrelevant. As the following illustration shows, the seller's cost could be a benchmark as to the buyer's costs to design around the offered license.

SELLER'S COST PERCEPTIONS AND HOW THEY CAN AFFECT THE DEALMAKING PROCESS One common issue affecting a seller's perception of value and price of an opportunity is its costs incurred. There is a logic to this perception because, after all, the cost is what the seller paid for the technology, so why shouldn't the buyer be willing to pay at least the same amount? However, the logic is false in the following sense. What the seller bought was an option to a business opportunity that would result from an R&D success. If the R&D project is a success, then the seller would be foolish to consider its costs as the value. If the R&D project fails or underperforms, then the seller needs to be reminded that it bought an option, and options can go up and go down; in this case, it went down, perhaps even to zero.

Although it is an extreme example, consider buying a ticket in a lottery. If one pays $1 for the ticket, one has bought an option on, say $1 million, if all the little numbers on the ticket line up with all the little balls in the scrambling machine. If they do, the option price of $1 is irrelevant to the ticket's value because it is (in such case) exercisable for $1 million. If the balls do not replicate the ticket holder's string of little numbers, then the option price of $1 is also irrelevant to the ticket's value because it is an option on nothing. So regardless of what happens, the purchaser of a lottery ticket can be certain that his or her ticket will never again be worth $1, because costs are irrelevant. Consider a real-life technology example (one of many). Kendall Square was once a high flying computer company. In August 1993, the company was valued at $360 million and shares were selling for $25 apiece. In October 1994, Kendall Square was selling for less than 5 cents (cents!) a share. In between those dates, one poor soul had invested $65 million in real money.[12] In the more recent Internet and telecom sections, other stock (equity) meltdown examples have demonstrated this point.

In the case of technology that turns out to be a disappointment, sellers sometimes still believe that its cost should invoke a combination of perceived significance and pity on a buyer. Here's another example. In 1990, the investors of Optical Data, Inc. threw in the towel on their $10 million investment made over a nine-year period. A business journal article summarized the decision as follows: "Though it was touted as breakthrough technology, the company was never able to create a market for its products."[13] The resulting patents were being offered at $1 million. Although the linkage between the stated value ($1 million) and the historic costs ($10 million) is not overtly stated, the implication is made that there is a bargain in the offing as the IP can be had for "only" 10 cents on the dollar.[14]

AN EXAMPLE NEGOTIATION DRIVEN BY THE SELLER'S PERCEPTION OF ITS COSTS DETERMINING VALUE For projects that a seller believes will be successful, it tends to view value in a return-on-investment way. Although this is closer to being value based thinking, this idea is flawed as well, as Exhibit 3.4 will illustrate. This example shows how sellers and buyers can misapprehend each other. In one case they miss a deal and in another they reach a deal but through a false rationale.

Shown in the left column is the seller's R&D cost with an added "justifiable" margin that the seller believes it should be entitled to based on its costs. Such a perspective is really based on a manufacturing model of R&D: that selling prices can be determined by some form of "cost plus" pricing, even though such an approach is increasingly rare even for commercial operations.

In the three columns to the right of the dotted line in Exhibit 3.4, the buyer's perceptions of value are shown. For Case A we see three components to such perceived value: (1) the cost if the buyer had to repeat the R&D, plus (2) the incremental cost to avoid the intellectual property barriers surrounding the seller's technology (i.e., patent claims), plus (3) the value of having the head start of picking up the seller's project without attempting to independently recreate the results. In

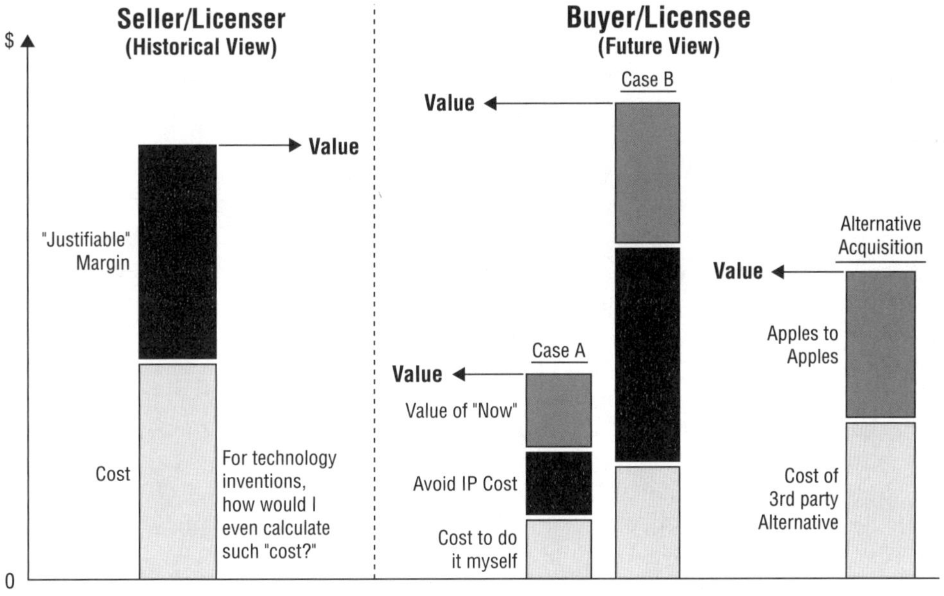

EXHIBIT 3.4 Seller and Buyer Perspectives on Cost and Value

Case A, the buyer's perceived total value is shown as being just below the seller's costs. And here is an illustration of a cost based valuation which is valid. Therefore, the seller's initial reaction will be negative to a buyer's offer of such an amount because it would have the effect of acquiring the technology for less than the seller's own costs. Sellers naturally resist the idea that successful projects can be worth less than they cost. Unless the seller can be persuaded that the buyer's value is in fact an accurate representation of value, then no deal will be done.

In Case B, the same components of value have resulted in a buyer's valuation to be greater than the seller's perception. In this case a deal should be readily possible but only because it so happens that the seller's perception of "justifiable margin" matches the buyer's perceptions of the three components of value that it considered. So the deal is, in a real sense, an accident.

Shown to the far right in Exhibit 3.4 is yet another dimension of buyer valuation.

Every investment that a buyer considers making should be compared to other uses of the investment resources. The decision to acquire the seller's technology should be made only if that decision happens to be the very best use of the incrementally available investment resources. The rightmost column shows that there is an alternative that can be acquired for much less than the seller is offering for the subject opportunity. Because no two opportunities are ever exactly alike, the buyer has to add or subtract an "apples to apples" comparison between the third party alternative and the seller's proposal. In this example, the buyer has concluded that the seller's technology does have an incremental value above the third party's alternative, but not enough to reach the seller's perceived value. If the seller perceives that the third party alternative is something that will affect only this one prospective buyer, then even a demonstration of the basis of such lower valuation will be unpersuasive to the seller. However, if the seller can be convinced that all potential buyers will have third party alternatives like or approximately like this one, then a seller might be convinced that its perception of "justifiable margin" is wrong. This suggestion sets the stage for the first valuation method, the use of industry standards, in Chapter 4.

PROBLEMS WITH COST AS VALUE REASONING There are numerous problems with these lines of cost-as-value reasoning.

- Sellers rarely, if ever, know their true costs. In many technology development projects, the cost accounting of the work leading to the licensable technology is only part of a continuum of investment.
- When the costs are determined for a seller's technology, the value of the starting or infused IP is almost never assessed.
- The seller's development costs often do not correspond to the costs that the buyer might incur in attempting to recreate the technology, because of the differences in capabilities, insights, and approaches.
- The IP rights of the seller generally may make it difficult, and possibly impractical, for the buyer (in terms of investments required, other resources, time delay, and overall project risk) to recreate the seller's technology in a way that the buyer is free to use commercially. So, the replication of the seller's cost is likely to be illusory.
- On the other hand, the seller could have made excessive investments in the development of the technology because of poor choices of approach or other reasons and might thus have a cost basis for the technology in excess of what a reasonable seller should pay, even given the above considerations.
- The risk associated with the commercialization technology is, normally, reduced by the seller's development. Such risk would need to be undertaken by the buyer in an independent development. Even some developments that appear easy turn out to be far more difficult than imagined.
- In some cases there could be an important value of what is sometimes called negative know-how: knowledge of processes or approaches that do not work well or at all. It is possible that the seller's technology incorporates an approach that is the only practical way the technology can be made to work, although independent technical experts who have not participated in the development or the technology might believe, wrongly, that another or many other approaches can be made to work commercially.
- There is the seller's value of now. In most instances, a reasonable buyer is willing to pay a premium to accelerate its time to market.
- Finally, the cost of creating IP is often simply unrelated to its value. As one far afield example, Chuck Close is a famous contemporary artist who paints huge portraitures. Early in his career (1967–1970) he used very highly diluted paints applied by an airbrush technique; he is reported to have painted eight of these amazing paintings with one 60-cent tube of Mars black paint. Technology is not the same as paintings, but the principle is that it is possible to create a valuable technology and not have incurred a commensurate cost.

Yet, if a buyer really believes that its costs to recreate and be free to practice the subject technology are in fact $1 million, including the factors just addressed, which includes the cost to avoid the IP rights of the seller, then this benchmark is likely to be a relevant benchmark.

What do sellers sell? Value. "Price is never the cause of value."[15] Price, or valuation, is the quantification of value. Buyers buy value, not the seller's costs. If the buyer **is** buying the seller's costs, then the implication is very strong that the transaction is not about IP-based technology.

There can be negotiation utility in knowing the seller's costs, although such knowledge and use can be confusing. Let us imagine a technology created by the seller at a cost of $1 million that has, by some combination of valuation methods, a present value of $10 million, the inverse of the mentioned Optical Data Company example. The parties agree that they will divide up the $10 million payment into an upfront component and a royalty component. There might be good reason why the seller would like as a down payment an amount equal to the costs incurred, namely $1 million if it is warranted by the value. This creates a comfortable logic that the seller gets back its costs upfront and will achieve its return on investment from future royalties. In this case, it is likely that the buyer will find this acceptable. However, the logic and comfort of such math only works because the value determined independently of cost turned out to be 10 times the cost. If it is equal to the cost, or worse, then the concept does not work.

Finally a suitable use of cost is for the seller to measure the value generation performance of its R&D function. If over time the seller finds that the cumulative payment received (value) is less than a suitable return on investment (i.e., costs) then the seller should conclude that R&D is not a good business to be in, at least as it has been constituted.

Conclusion

The need to make assumptions and create models and scenarios to obtain a valuation can be troubling. What if the assumptions are wrong? What if the models are incomplete? What if the scenarios were too optimistic or too pessimistic?

The problem is that all these issues are present every day. When buying the stock of a publicly traded company, one is forecasting the future in terms of the company's revenues and profits, the attitude of its customers and competitors, as well as, the skill and staying power of its management, and even the enthusiasm for other investors in bidding up or selling down the stock.

Valuation of business and product licensing transactions is similarly linked to assumptions, models, and scenarios. One huge assumption made in such circumstances is that the past is a predictor of the future. Unfortunately, there are many circumstances in which that has not proven true, and important deals involving the sales of businesses or licensing of products have created adverse outcomes for one party or the other. The purchase of the Snapple business by Quaker Oats and NCR by AT&T, both of which were later sold off, cost shareholders more than $1 billion. In each case the future was not accurately predicted by extrapolating the past, even for a comparatively simple situation of tea in a bottle. Similar though less spectacular examples exist for product licensing. Alas, as the late 2008 meltdown in the housing and automobile markets, and the financial industry and broad equity indices all too dramatically show, we know less about the future than we often think we do.

Also, many key factors in a valuation are not really knowable. Management goes bad. Competition gets good. Customers change their minds. New technology emerges. Government interferes with commerce. Market values which were thought to be rationally based turn out to be so-called bubbles. Such things happen all too regularly. In the case of technology licensing, these uncertainties and risks are compounded with others. The solution is not despair but good judgment. Develop the best model possible, use appropriate methods, exercise judgment (*phronesis*). The result is much better than guesswork, and in many cases provides a surprisingly good answer for both the seller and the buyer.

Notes

1. *American Idol* is a television phenomenon. In early screenings, many thousands of aspiring singers are screened down to an "A" list of potential winners. The ultimate winner, that year's "American Idol," is then chosen by the market for which viewer votes serve as the proxy.
2. It is a general rule of thumb that projects requiring only one breakthrough, with all the related technologies being "off the shelf" or nearly so, have a higher probability of ultimate commercial success than projects requiring breakthroughs in two independent areas, and so forth. One personal example of a many-area breakthrough project was the Apollo space program to land the first men on the moon. The rocket engines (liquid hydrogen and liquid oxygen) were the first of their kind and essential for success; no rocket had ever been built of that size and complexity (7.5 million pounds of lift off thrust, taller than the Washington Monument, three stages), the Lunar Lander itself, space suits, guidance and control, communications and data recovery, etc. There was a reason it cost $20+ billion in 1960s dollars. Buyers can grasp the idea of "we need one miracle right here"; they glaze over when the project needs three independent "miracles" to be successful.
3. In the late 1990s, such vu-graph Dealmaking was done with regularity especially with venture capital startups, because of the frenzy of the time. The more than sobering outcome of many, most, of those deals further proves the rule that "there's many a slip between cup and lip" (a phrase from *Don Quixote*, to which we will return in Chapter 12).
4. Of course what the buyer may desire and what the seller can reasonably provide can be two different issues. In many licensing agreements the seller does not provide IP rights representations/protections for the buyer relating to freedom to practice.
5. Some might argue that a pure royalty rate structure, discussed below, is simpler in that it is a pay-as-you-practice the technology framework, and so it is easier to value and agree to. However, as will be discussed, royalty based structures are long-term agreements and can experience complications because of changing market circumstances.]
6. "Where's Waldo?" is a children's game with the point of trying to find a character, Waldo, hidden in various scenes. It's not as easy as it sounds.
7. Thanks to Kathy Ku of Stanford for this information. Licensing took place for U.S. use only because prior publication precluded the securing of foreign patent rights. Stanley Cohen and Steven Boyer were inducted into the National Inventors Hall of Fame (Akron, Ohio) in 2001 in recognition for their invention.
8. In the case of the Lemelsen licenses it appears that the royalty rates were implied based upon a lump sum payment.
9. According to a *Wall Street Journal* article, "Latest Twist in Mariah Carey Saga; New Multialbum Deal," May 9, 2002, p. B1, the total deal value was $100 million.
10. Ibid.

11. Ibid.
12. Bulkely, William M. "Missing the Boat: Yachtsman Bill Koch Lost His Golden Touch with Kendall Square," *Wall Street Journal*, October 27, 1994, p. 110.
13. "Everything Must Go," *The Business Journal*, Portland, Oregon, January 27, 1992.
14. The irony, of course, is that the patents could be worth much more than the $10 million investment if, for example, the claims covered significant commercial practice by third parties even in products unrelated to the original venture. However, if the patents only protect a product and process that has no commercial value the patents by themselves will have no value, regardless of the cost incurred.
15. Mack Hanan and Peter Karp, *Competing on Value*, AM Acom, 1991.

APPROACH II

Valuation

CHAPTER 4

Method 1: Use of Industry Standards for Valuation

In this chapter we begin our study of the business ***Approach*** of Valuation by development of the first of the six valuation Methods, the use of Industry Standards. As we have introduced in the preceding chapters this book is organized by ***Approaches***—opportunity Discovery, Valuation, and Dealmaking—and six ***Methods*** of Valuation, and multiple ***Tools*** that can be applied in various contexts. The simple graphic included here lays out this architecture.

Here we will first consider what is meant by industry standards and how they can be helpful in valuation efforts. We will also examine their important limitations. Then we will review different possible sources of industry standards data. Finally we will characterize the limitations of this method and introduce the complementary method presented in Chapter 5, the Rating/Ranking Method.

A-M-T

Licensing D-V-D	A: Approaches	M: Methods	T: Tools
D	Discovery	NPV v. Risk	Rating/Ranking DCF
V	**Valuation** TR R^k A DE	**1. Industry Standards** 2. Rating/Ranking 3. Rules of Thumb 4. Discounted Cash Flow (NPV) 5. Monte Carlo; Real Options 6. Auctions	> Rating/Ranking > Rules of Thumb > Discounted Cash > Risk Assessment
D	Dealmaking	Deal Structures Dealmaking-Process Plan B	Rating/Ranking DCF/NPV Monte Carlo Real Options

The Concept and Limitations of "Industry Standards"

The term industry standards is used here to designate the existence of a database of previous deals in a sufficient number and specificity that buyers and sellers can, by reference to such data, agree upon a fair transaction price. The concept conveys the idea of norms or standards that can serve as a guide, somewhat like a complex price book. In some circumstances the concept references an accepted, exact value somewhat analogous to an IEEE or ANSI standard, two widely recognized technology standards bodies (www.standards.ieee.org and www.ansi.org). In most usages, however, the term industry standards is used to designate a value range that can be taken as normative of certain kinds of transactions but for which exceptions can and do occur.

Such norms do exist in many contexts: used cars, corporate bonds, office floor space, peaches, and collector baseball cards. Before considering the utility and limitations of such norms for licensing valuation purposes, it is helpful to understand the circumstances where industry standard norms are usefully applied.

In general, industry standards work well when the item being sold or rented can be characterized by two simple factors—the category and the quality. It also works well when a sufficient number of publicly available, similar transactions that comprise a market history can be determined.

As an example, in the case of used cars, category could mean 1993 Ford Taurus with the quality represented by: four-door, leather interior, all power, 240,000 miles, runs well. In the space of one sentence, it is possible for the prospective buyer to have a reasonably accurate understanding of what is for sale. In this case, probably something that looks pretty bad, but with the possibility of some high maintenance miles left in its life. With a brief telephone call or email exchange, a prospective buyer can rapidly and accurately decide whether this is indeed a purchase of potential interest subject to subsequent due diligence (test drive, mechanic's inspection, etc.) to confirm what is already believed to be true.

The second key aspect of the utility of industry standards is that there also exist a sufficient number of similar transactions and that such information is generally available to buyers and sellers. Continuing with the Ford Taurus example, it is unlikely that any car fitting this exact description has been sold. However, there have been so many Ford Taurus's sold that the database is sufficiently large enough to enable characterization of the effect on value of 240,000 miles even though no one car sold in the database exactly matches this specification. Further, a small industry has emerged which tracks such information and publishes it in various colored "books" and on the Internet. So, both seller and prospective buyer can have a reasonable understanding of what the specific car is worth based upon the agreements reached by many thousands of previous sellers and buyers.

Another example is office space. For the metropolitan New York area there is one firm (Newmark, www.newmarkre.com) that publishes quarterly what amounts to a pricing book for all kinds of office space designated by Manhattan neighborhood. How about "Grand Central"? The weighted average asking rental rate is $33.56 per square foot per year in the fourth quarter 1991, up from $29.82 a year earlier—you can look it up. Are you more a "Sixth/Rock" (New York lingo for Rockefeller Center area) company? Then it's $41.01, up from $39.13. Do you want to rent on "Park Avenue"? You're talking $45.68.[1]

Another example of a valuation blue book is actually bright red with an intriguing title: *What's It Worth?*[2] It is a compilation of more than a thousand summaries of recent decisions and settlements from personal injuries and wrongful death. The alphabetized injury categories range from abdominal to wrist, and cover, in a stream of sad summaries, just about every body part in between a and w (no x, y, z). A herniated disk at LS-51 was worth $1.8 million, but one at C6-7 was $700,000.[3] In the case of the LS-51 disk, an expert panel, a jury, deemed the injury deserving of an award of $2.15 million which led to the settlement paid by a hotel of $1.8 million. In the case of the C6-7 disk, a utility agreed to pay the $700,000 prior to a judgment. This is an unfortunate context, but a valuable resource in assisting injured and responsible parties in determining appropriate financial remuneration. The book contains the judgment of judges, juries, and plaintiffs-defendants on the economic value of something very difficult to quantify. The large number of such cases, and the availability of published information in such matters, makes it possible to use Industry Standards to make comparisons and thereby estimates of the value of a specific injury or life.

An example closer to the subject of this book is the selling and buying of corporate bonds, a debt instrument. For simplicity, consider one class of bonds known as zero coupon bonds or zeros. A zero is simply the obligation of the issuing company to pay the owner of such a bond the face value at the face due date, say $100,000 on January 1, 2010. If the current owner of the bond wants cash now, the owner becomes a seller looking for a buyer. Like the Taurus example, the category here is, simple: a $100,000 zero due January 1, 2010. And, just like the used car example, there exist groups whose business it is to publish market information on what previous sellers and buyers agreed upon for like purchases, depending upon the quality of the bond. An added feature in this example is that there are also groups who provide objective quality measures, called rating agencies, in accordance with established criteria, such as "AAA" or "B" by which the buyer can assess the risk of default. Again, the key elements are present: published market information, large number of deals, and standards by which quality can be assessed.

This is all very nice for bonds and square feet and used cars. The level of specificity enables an efficient market to exist where bonds can be traded with little due diligence. Unfortunately, no such simple "book" or "AAA" rating system exists for the selling and buying of technology. Why not? With certain exceptions, technology transactions cannot be managed like used cars and bonds. One problem is simply that technology almost by definition is unique or at most has few preexisting examples. (There are exceptions to this limitation: A new catalyst material used in a conventional chemical process can be unique of itself but it still belongs to a readily describable category). Another problem is that of describing the quality of the technology in simple, economically relevant terms; the dimensions of technology performance tend to be so numerous and detailed that there is no parallel to "runs good" or "AAA." (Again, a new catalyst material can serve as a counter example). Finally, the number of published similar or "like" transactions is almost always very limited and without such a database of information no "book" can exist.

For business or product licensing, there may be sufficient performance data in which there exists some possible classification and valuation standards such as those expressed in multiples of revenues (such as 1× revenues) and/or multiples of after-tax earnings (such as 15×, also known as the P/E, price/earnings ratio) and/or multiples of the free cash flow (such as 5×). However, even in such cases and with such metrics, the tumultuous and unpredictable world of business still requires substantial specific due diligence and judgment to create a specific valuation. Even on the public stock market, there are huge variations in the P/E multiple based on the market perceptions of future value.

For technology licensing, there are by definition no "standards" for multiples of free cash flow (there may not be cash flow, free or otherwise), of profits (probably none), or of revenues (perhaps not yet, but maybe one happy test customer).

Therefore, one should not expect this chapter to present a notebook of numbers that can be used in every technology valuation. No such all-inclusive notebook exists here or elsewhere. Yet, there is important value in obtaining and understanding market-based data on technology transactions. In almost all technology licensing situations there exist some discoverable previous transactions which can provide useful insight into value, based on what such previous buyers and sellers agreed to. In almost all cases some significant interpretive work will be needed to apply the data to the present circumstance. This will be the focus of the next chapter and Method two, the Rating/Ranking Method.

The Unique-Universal Paradox

There is a paradox that exists with the use of the industry standards method. How can any previous agreement be "like" the opportunity in question? As discussed in Chapters 2 and 3 regarding the Box and the Wheelbarrow, there are so many dimensions to a technology agreement, how can any historic deal be useful in valuing my specific opportunity? Put in yet another way, our dilemma is this: We are seeking not simply to know how other people priced their agreements (however interesting that may be); we want to know, we need to know, how to value and price our opportunity.

Before considering three possible answers to this question, let us directly address the paradox: How can different things be comparable? Let me use the example of foreign films (from a U.S. perspective). In watching many of these films, you find yourself immersed in characters, and plot, that are really different from your own life. The film's evident cultural norms can have features that are very different from our everyday experiences. It is easy to feel that "these people" are "so very different." But, by the end of most such movies, one really concludes that in important ways they are just the same as people I know, and me. At a deep level, they have similar fears and aspirations, disappointments and hopes, depressions and joys. At the end of a well done immersion experience you can easily identify with the characters and their respective dilemmas even though their everyday worlds at an outward level are nothing like your own.[4] Great plays by great playwrights, say *Death of a Salesman* or *The Price* by Arthur Miller, or *Hamlet* (or anything by Shakespeare), survive time and venue differences to connect with us in our circumstances. As C.S. Lewis expressed so succinctly this connectability across time and context: "We read to know that we are not alone." Unless we are reading our own biography, which for most of us is not likely to be literally possible, what we read is never directly about us; but there can be something in the midst of all the differences between a book's characters and the people around us that connects deeply with us. This is the unique-universal paradox, where we encounter unique, distinct experiences so different in their particulars but underneath and inside there is something universal that makes it personal and immediate.[5]

In a licensing context, looking at historical agreements can be something like this. In them, we are looking at final terms agreed to by dealmakers, one selling and one buying, who were expressing a common business language in seeking their self interest, all things considered. Here, the unique-universal paradox means that though no two deals are ever exactly alike,[6] behind the differences are certain business universals such as projected sales and profit, required resources investments, and overall perceived risks and uncertainties that guide the parties in reaching the terms of their agreement. It is this unique-universal feature that we will discuss in this first method of valuation.

Segmentation of the "Industry Standards Method"

The Industry Standards Method, can be thought to comprise three different submethods: (1) the market or comparables approach, (2) paradigm licensing, and (3) rating/ranking. (See Exhibit 4.1.) We shall now consider broadly how each of these three could be applied in technology licensing.

MARKET (OR COMPARABLES) LICENSING One of the traditional approaches to the valuation for anything is commonly known as the market (or, sometimes, the *comparables*) method. The simple underlying idea is that there exists a historical transaction that was valued by other parties that can be used as a direct prediction of the value of the present opportunity. Referring to the above discussion of real property, we can generally determine by public records filed with the appropriate property tax agency the price that was paid for a property together with the legal description of what was sold. If we can find a property that was sold recently that is comparable in size, quality, features, accessories, and so forth, it is likely to be a good indication of the value of our property's value. In residential real property, such comparables are

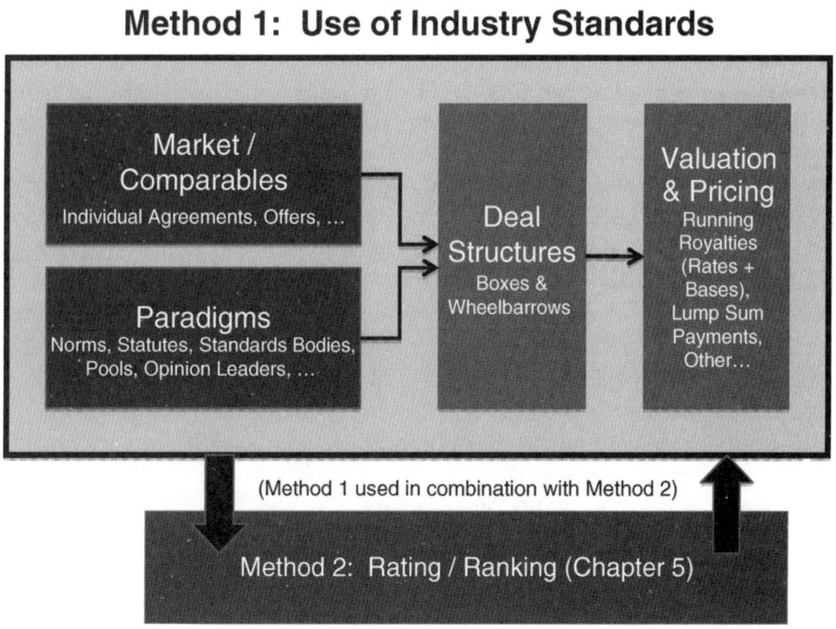

EXHIBIT 4.1 Method 1: Use of "Industry Standards" to Determine Royalties
Source: © 2003 Razgaitis, richard@razgaitis.com.

generally widely available because many homes can be considered as belonging to similar, widely relevant categories such as: four bedrooms, two and one-half baths, two-car attached garage, on a quarter-acre lot, in good condition. In commercial real estate, the situation can be more challenging. In 2002, the Empire State Building in New York City was sold; by definition, there is an inherent uniqueness to this property—it has been designated one of the Seven Wonders of the Modern World, and is a City icon—and by the terms of the sale as there is a pre-existing lease that will extend until the year 2076. Yet there is a cost per square foot and a projected rate of return on the purchase price that can be used to establish a reasonable estimate of value, which was $57.5 million. Taking another New York example, the Mets baseball team, which has a strong component of intellectual property value associated with its trademark and tradename, was valued in 2006.[7] The Mets are at the same time unique, and seemingly beyond a market-based valuation model, yet there are 29 other major league baseball teams, and many other professional sports teams, with which comparisons can be made, as well as return on investment calculations based upon forecasted revenues and profits.

Applying such examples to technology licensing, the market valuation approach is the use of the terms of one or more comparable license agreements to estimate the value of the subject technology licensing opportunity. In some instances one is able to find one or more agreements that appear to be very closely related to the subject opportunity and deal structure. However, even in this fortuitous case one needs to ask whether the price (and terms) of the found agreement(s) reflects present market value. It is possible that the seller in that historic case sold too cheaply, for whatever reason; or, in the alternative, that the buyer paid dearly, perhaps because of something akin to dot-com fever.

In many cases, applying the market valuation approach leads to numerous, say a dozen or more, agreements in the same broad technology category but no one of which, for different reasons, is exactly or near exactly comparable. In this circumstance, one may yet be able to estimate a royalty range from this family of agreements.

PARADIGM LICENSING Paradigm has become a widely used buzz word as a result of one of the most influential books of the twentieth century: Thomas Kuhn's *The Structure of Scientific Revolutions* (University of Chicago Press, 1962). In that scholarly book, which sold more than one million copies (every author's dream), Kuhn applied a term used by linguists to describe how irregular verbs are declined ("I am," "You are," "He is," etc.) to how scientists adopt and cling to models of world (e.g., Ptolemaic geocentric vs. Copernican heliocentric structure, or quantum vs. classical mechanics). Such scientific models, according to Kuhn, become paradigms, meaning they are widely adopted as explaining the way the world works and are not subject to scrutiny any more than we wonder why we say "I am" but "you are" when in both cases we are conveying the idea of being.

Extending the proliferation of paradigm usage into yet another domain, we can consider a segment of the Industry Standards valuation method as being the use of widely accepted standard rates and terms. Paradigm rates exist in many domains. When one eats in a restaurant, there is the understanding that the table server and other wait staff will be compensated for such service by an amount proportional to the cost of the meal, somewhat like a royalty. Historically, such rate was 10 percent, but in the past 20 years or so it has been 15 percent and now one frequently hears 15 to 20 percent as an appropriate range for a tip. Another example of paradigm rates is the maintenance cost of enterprise software. If a company licenses a software product for, say, a payment of $1 million, there is in addition an annual payment (which typically begins after the first year) for maintenance that is based on a percentage of the license fee. Historically such annual maintenance fee was 15 percent of the license fee ($150,000 a year, in our present example); more recently, like table service, it appears to be increasing into the 15 to 20 percent (or greater) range.

Closer to our subject is the area of trademark licensing. There is a general understanding that many such transactions will be valued within widely accepted ranges. One example of this is shown in Exhibit 4.2, taken from a book on trademark licensing rates by Battersby and Grimes.[8] Exhibit 4.2, taken from the first page of their book, shows three products for which trademark licensing of different types could occur: adhesive bandages, afghans (the blankets, not the nation), and aftershave lotion. For each product type there are seven columns that correspond to the various types of sources of trademark value: art, celebrity (such as George Foreman), character (such as Waldo), collegiate, corporate, designer (Ralph Lauren), event (Olympics), and sports (Yankees). Then for each product row, Battersby and Grimes show the range of royalty rates, as determined by a combination of surveying and expert panel, that appear to be widely accepted in the industry. However, notice these values have fairly wide ranges such as 3 to 10 percent or even 1 to 10 percent, so it makes an important economic difference where you end up in that range. Further, Battersby and Grimes point out, as one would expect, there may be certain "hot properties" where rates above the range can occur and in other cases "tight margins" (and, presumably, "not so hot" properties) where the opposite occurs. Two very different examples of hot properties are Jennifer Lopez and George Foreman. Signatures Network Inc. has entered into a licensing agreement with Ms. Lopez for the use of her intellectual property (photographs of her) in T-shirts, posters, calendars, back-to-school items, and other to-be-announced products with sales estimated to reach $20 to 40 million in just six months.[9] Although the royalty terms of this license were not disclosed, it would not be surprising if the royalty rate exceeds the range suggested by the Battersby and Grimes tables because of the then current fervor and fame of J-Lo.[10] (Separately, Ms. Lopez, following a classic field of use licensing model, has licensed her IP for a new fragrance, Glow, various restaurants, and probably thousands of other uses.) However, by 2009 it is likely that female celebrity licensing pricing leadership has diffused to other individuals, although Glow is still on the market. George Foreman, a very different kind of celebrity IP than Ms. Lopez, achieved his own licensing notoriety in 1999 by licensing his name and image to the makers of George Foreman Grills for a paid-up amount of $137.5 million and stock, a gargantuan sum which is probably outside common trademark licensing guidelines.

In the 2008 edition of the Battersby and Grimes book (copyrighted by Aspen Publishers), they have changed the royalty ranges even of such everyday products as adhesive bandages, afghans, and aftershave lotions. For instance, for adhesive bandages, in the 2008 edition the ranges listed for "celebrity" contexts is 7 to 11 percent (compared to 3 to 10 percent in Exhibit 4.2 from 2001), "corporate" is 2 to 6 percent, and "event" and "sports" are 2 to 10 percent. In its preface to the 2008 edition it further cautions that ranges observed for January might differ from that in December.

Licensed Product	Class	Art	Celebrity	Character/ Entertainment	Collegiate	Corporate	Designer	Event	Sports
Adhesive Bandages	5		3–10%	5–10%		8–10%		10–15%	8–11%
Afghans	24	5–8%	3–10%	8–12%	6.5–10%	5–9%	3–8%	10–15%	8–11%
After Shave Lotions	3		3–10%			3–7%	3–8%		1–10%

However

- Hot properties
- Tight margins
- Stacking
- "The Base"
- Still wide ranges
- etc.

EXHIBIT 4.2 Industry Standards Can Work Well in "Standard Industries" Such as Trademark and "Content" Licensing

Source: © 2001 Aspen Law & Business, www.aspenpublishers.com.

Such variability in trademark and content licensing is more prevalent because of the consumer trendiness associated with such products, but it does illustrate the principle that market changes can change the value of rights.

And clearly not every licensing situation falls even within a published range. Consider for a moment the possible celebrity endorsement of another boxer, Mike Tyson, relating to the three items shown in Exhibit 4.2. On an adhesive bandage, I would think rights to Mr. Tyson's IP could command a high end royalty given his close association with such items. However, I would think the use of his name endorsing, say, an aftershave lotion would seem to have less economic value to a licensee. So, even with these comparatively simple licensing deal structures for the use of a person's image and likeness on a well established product category, there remains substantial room for uncertainty. If we were to consider an even narrower classification, say the use of the University of Florida or the Ohio State University on sweatshirts or hats, we could expect to find that the uncertainty shrinks dramatically to fairly standard terms that are widely accepted.

Another example of paradigmatic licensing often occurs with content licensing, such as book, music, and other multimedia publishing. Author royalty rates typically range from 5 to 15 percent, although, like the trademarks discussion, exceptions can occur with hot authors and topics (such as with the separate books by former President Bill Clinton and present Secretary of State Hillary Clinton). Music publishing has similar rates though there is the complication of potential separate royalties for the author of the lyric, the composer of the tune, the performing artist, and the producer. For the lyric, the tune, and the artist, typical royalty rates are also in the 5 to 15 percent range. For a deal which includes the producer, a so called "all in deal," the royalty range is likely to be 10 to 20 percent, but again exceptions occur. Recall that a royalty rate is only meaningful in the context of a royalty base (as discussed in the preceding chapter).

A clear example of paradigm licensing is the royalty for licensing music for recordings. This rate is determined by U.S. statute and is currently capped at eight cents per song per album; in the industry this is known as the stat rate. So when you see an infomercial offering 40 tracks of "one-hit wonders," the promoter paid no more than $3.20 in licensing rights for the copyrighted content per CD, and often they pay even less.

As discussed later, an industry leader can, by their licensing terms, create a licensing paradigm. For a time, IBM offered nonexclusive bare patent licenses to essentially any one of its patents for use in personal computers (PCs) for a 1 percent royalty, any two for 2 percent, and so forth up to a maximum of 5 percent as a way of managing a massive portfolio patents and many licensing negotiations. Although IBM appears not to follow this practice at this time, and there is some uncertainty whether it *ever* followed such recipe, the belief that it had has led some to cite a 1 percent royalty for any one patent in a large portfolio of information technology patents as paradigm rate for licensors with comparable portfolios.

Another occasion where standard licensing terms are often proposed is when the implementation of the technology follows some prescribed standard such as promulgated by IEEE. This can arise because there is a consortium licensing on behalf of its members or because a single company wants to establish a standard set of terms and values for what it believes will be many licensees. An example of the latter type is given in Exhibit 4.3, based upon information obtained from the cited web site (www.bell-labs.com/news/1997/april/29/schedule.html) for licenses to Lucent patents relating to the shown "G" standards, which relate to various compression standards.

In all these disparate examples, the paradigm emerges because there are a large number of transactions involved and they relate to a relatively well defined business model. So the promotion and selling of goods by the use of trademarks, or the creation and selling of music or book content, or the licensing of tens of thousands of IBM patents to the many PC manufacturers, all had to find some way of practically dealing with large numbers of transactions with licensees who were using their acquired rights for comparatively uniform business purposes and benefit. This situation of large transaction numbers in common business situations is what makes paradigm licensing tend to emerge as an industry practice.

EXAMPLE AGREEMENTS USED A third type of Industry Standards method is the use of one or more historic agreements from which one can make systematic comparisons to the subject opportunity even though such agreements may not be directly in the same technology or market application areas. Such systematic comparison constitutes the second method of valuation, the Rating/Ranking method, which we will take up in Chapter 5. As we shall see, Rating/Ranking is a systematic method of making comparisons of the subject valuation opportunity to something else. To the extent that such "something else" is very close to our subject opportunity, the Rating/Ranking method reduces to the market approach discussed above, namely, that we merely point to the "something else" and assert that our opportunity should be valued as that comparable was. Normally, in technology licensing, because of the range of subject matter, and the distinctiveness of the individual Box and Wheelbarrow of each agreement, we find ourselves in a situation where we have identified multiple historic agreements that provide useful insights but no one of them is

EXHIBIT 4.3 Fee and Royalty Schedule for Licensing Lucent Patents for G.721, G.723, G.726, G.727, G.728, and G.729*

Effective April 2, 1997 (Revised)

CLIENT (SINGLE PARTY SUPPORT)**	G.723.1 or G.729A	G.729	G.728	Multi-Function—All Four Stds. Bundled	ADPCM G.721, G726, & G727
Option 1 Unit Royalty Per Channel	**Per Channel**	**Per Channel**	**Per Channel**	**Per Channel**	**Per Channel**
<100 Thousand	$0.42	$0.60	$2.00	$2.58	$2.00
100 Thousand – 500 Thousand	$0.35	$0.51	$1.70	$2.18	$1.70
500 Thousand –	$0.27	$0.39	$1.30	$1.67	$1.30
1 Million	$0.21	$0.30	$1.00	$1.29	$1.00
Fees:					
License Initiation Fee	$50,000	$50,000	$50,000	$50,000	$50,000
Minimum Annual Royalty (Equivalent to 10K Channels/Annually)	$4,200	$6,000	$20,000	$25,800	$20,000
Option 2 Unit Royalty Per Channel					
<100 Thousand	$0.51	$0.75	$2.50	$3.20	$2.50
100 Thousand – 500 Thousand	$0.42	$0.65	$2.15	$2.73	$2.15
500 Thousand – 1 Million	$0.33	$0.57	$1.90	$2.35	$1.90
>1 Million	$0.26	$0.38	$1.25	$1.61	$1.25
Fees:					
License Initiation Fee	$10,000	$10,000	$25,000	$25,000	$25,000
Minimum Annual Royalty (Equivalent to 10K Channells/Annually)	$5,100	$7,500	$25,000	$32,025	$25,000

Option 3

Fully Paid-Up License—License restricted to single party support (client-based) software application for promotional distribution, either separately or as a part of a free software bundle up to a maximum of 10 million channels.

Option 3a	One-time payment of $65,000
Option 3b	Initial payment of $35,000.00, followed by a second payment of $25,000.00, 12 months later, a third payment of $20,000 twenty four months after the first payment.

Fees:

License Initiation Fee $10,000.00

EXHIBIT 4.3 *(Continued)*

CLIENT (SINGLE PARTY SUPPORT)**	G.723.1 or G.729A	G.729	G.728	Multi-Function—All Four Stds. Bundled	ADPCM G.721, G726, & G727
SERVER (Multi-party support)	**Per Channel**	**Per Channel**	**Per Channel**	**Per Channel**	**Per Channel**
Unit Royalty Per Channel	$3.00	$4.20	$14.00	$18.15	$14.00
Fees:					
License Initiation Fee	$50,000	$50,000	$50,000	$50,000	$50,000
Minimum Annual Royalty (Equivalent to 5K Channels/Annually)	$15,000	$21,000	$70,000	$90,750	$70,000

*Lucent Technologies will license the related patents on a personal, nonexclusive, and nontransferable license agreement basis. All fees and royalty Rates are subject to change without prior notice, and Lucent reserves the right to withdraw this royalty and fee schedule in total or in part at any time.
**Quantity discounts are cumulative.

sufficiently close in subject matter or deal terms that we can merely point to its value and reliably use it as our own. In such circumstances, we can use our found agreements with the Rating/Ranking method to develop a reasoned estimate of value.

Sources of Industry Standard Data and Information

There are many different sources of technology licensing industry data. There are individuals, organizations, and even countries that have surveyed license transactions and published the results. Some companies have published what amounts to standard pricing terms for certain of their technology licenses. Court cases can be another source as some license agreements are actually made public. Additionally, there are firms that have developed databases which can be accessed under various arrangements. Finally, there is the opportunity for one to develop one's own industry data book over time.

We will now consider sources of such industry standard data and information organized in the following eight categories:

1. Surveys
2. Proposed or established norms
3. Shopped term sheets, price lists
4. News, publications, and the licensing society/practitioner network
5. Journals, proprietary databases, reports, and consultants
6. Published agreements
7. Court cases
8. Lifetime and organizational learning

In each of the subsequent sections we will consider these various sources and show examples of data that are available. It should be emphasized that these samples are not intended to create a data book on previous licensing deals; this would be a massive undertaking well outside the scope of this book, and when complete it would still not replicate what is available for corporate bonds, office space, or used cars. Rather, the point of the cited examples is to show illustrations of how such information can be found and used for the specific valuation sought.

Survey Results as a Source of Industry Standards Data and Information

There exist numerous surveys of technology license agreements. Some of these have been government sponsored, some gathered by associations, some by companies, and some by individuals. Like all surveys, such data have numerous inherent limitations relating to the nature of the respondents (biased? statistically significant?), the raw data (survey data accurately acquired? relevant to a valuation? sufficient detail?), and the summarized presentation (bias in summarization and statistical analysis? useful information?).

As discussed in Chapter 2, there is a rich mosaic to most licensing transactions involving many different kinds of elements of what is provided by the seller and paid by the buyer. However, most licensing surveys have focused on a single financial parameter: the royalty rate. There are many dangers in thinking of royalty rate as being the determinant of value. As will be discussed in Chapter 11, there are many variables in structuring licensing payments. The parties may agree to a substantial upfront (or other period) payment and, in compensation, will arrive at a lower royalty. There can be cross licenses back from the buyer to the seller that offset an initial royalty valuation so the reported number is very low or even zero. There can be other aspects of the transaction, such as a supply agreement, that have significant enough value to the seller as to warrant low or no royalties.

Furthermore, the royalty rate by itself has a dangerously ambiguous meaning. Sellers and buyers care not about the rate but the payment amount. The conversion is simple: royalty amount = rate × base. The key element is the "base" against which the royalty rate is applied. Take, for example, a computer chip that embodies a commercially significant and patented functionality. If a large manufacturer makes both the chip and the board on which the chip sits and the box into which the chip breathes life and the system that operates only because said chip functionality exists, what is the royalty base? The buyer will suggest the chip itself, which may be a few dollars;[11] in which case the buyer might gladly accept even a 20 percent royalty on even a $100 chip.[12] But the seller could argue that the board and the box have no functionality but for the patented technology on the chip. Compared to the fair market value of the chip alone, the box can be much more valuable. Maybe ten times as much, even 100 times as much or more. Even system solutions based on the patented technology could be subject to an argument that such sales be part of a royalty base. So, what would a 2 percent or 20 percent royalty mean without sorting through such critical matters? It is important to keep in mind that even when royalty rate information can be usefully extracted from published sources, there is more work to be done to complete a valuation.

License Survey Data from Japan

For many years the Japanese government gathered and published license royalty information. These data were obtained because for a period of time, the approval of the Japanese government was needed for any license entered into between a Japanese company and a non-Japanese company. An example of such data is shown in Exhibit 4.4.

As with any survey, (at least) three questions should be asked: Does the survey contain source bias? . . . Data coherence? . . . Utility? Clearly this survey has significant bias just by its scope: The data are solely for licenses with Japanese companies. It is also limited in time as these surveys ended many years ago so they do not reflect current market conditions. Another aspect of bias is not distinguishing between business, product, and technology licensing. All other factors being comparable, product licensing generally would be expected to be more valuable than technology licensing because the subsequent investment required is less, the time to profits is less, as well as the risk is reduced. Grouping such agreements with technology licenses is like performing statistical averages on a combined population of men and women; clearly it is possible to do this in some aspects, but leads to misleading results when extended to averaging of height and weight or other matters. Although technology is not as subject to trends as, say, clothing fashions, one should be careful when comparing valuations across significant time spans. It is widely accepted that patents are more highly valued in the 1990s than they were in the 1970s, due in large part to a trend toward higher probability of enforcement. There can be other factors. In the case of licenses to Japanese companies in the 1970s, it is likely that

EXHIBIT 4.4 **Key Financial Terms of All License Agreements Filed with the Japanese Government in 1975**

Terms of Payment	Classification of Technology	Chemical	Metal	Machinery	Electrical	Others
Initial Payment	Required	100	54	223	119	231
	Not required	65	37	187	119	220
	Less than 2%	5	6	16	32	28
	Over 2% and less than 5%	42	24	119	55	126
Running Royalty	Over 5% and less than 8%	12	8	112	24	119
	Over 8%	7	4	24	11	17
	Others	48	28	80	54	69
	None	51	21	59	62	92
Minimum	Required	38	19	116	35	186
Payment	Not required	127	72	294	203	265
Sub-total		165	91	410	238	451
No Fee, Royalty		16	4	11	2	15
Total		181	95	421	240	466

Source: Science & Technology Agency, Japan. Class A Technological Assistance Agreement for the year 1975.

the technology being transferred was, on average, less advanced and thereby less valuable than technology being licensed today.

On the issue of data coherence, it appears that no attempt was made to characterize the subject matter licensed in terms of business importance (or potential), patent protection (strength, extent, life), or the existence of other forms of consideration (supply agreements, cross-licenses, grant-backs). The information that is available does not quantify the magnitude of the initial or minimum payments, only their existence.

Finally on the issue of utility, how might such information be used to perform a valuation? As an example, consider Exhibit 4.4 as a tool to prepare a valuation of a technology for making a new laser. One immediate limitation is that these data do not contain a laser category. The closest one can get would be to examine the data for electrical licenses which could include electric power generation and distribution, radios and TVs, in addition to who knows what else; the category may not even include a single laser license. However, assuming our way past these questions, let us examine the "electrical" column of data. Provided is a histogram of data for royalty rates: namely, 32 out of 240 total agreements provided a royalty of less than 2 percent, 55 between 2 and 5 percent, 24 between 5 and 8 percent, 11 over 8 percent, 54 with "other" royalty rate, and 62 with no royalty. Which was the most common rate? Zero royalty!

If one considers upfront payments, Exhibit 4.4 discloses that there were 119 electrical agreements which had such payments and 119 which did not; when one considers that two agreements (the next to last row) had no fee or royalty, one would conclude that actually 121 had no upfronts.

So, by this analysis, the most common upfront payment was zero, and the most common royalty was zero! This is not a comforting outcome for a prospective seller trying to use such industry data to price, say, a laser technology license.

Further studying the reported data, what does one conclude? In Exhibit 4.4 under "electrical," the next most common royalty rate was 2 to 5 percent, essentially tied with "other." That is not a particularly helpful statistic. Finally, when one considers all the data, one finds that there were agreement examples for each of the royalty segments from zero to more than 8 percent, including "other." Such a broad spectrum with a gross collection of agreements has so smeared out the original, potentially valuable data that using such a table with our laser example is fruitless.

The root of the immediate difficulty is that there does not exist a small enough category of agreements that can be used to compare with the specifics of the laser.

Even if one considers another category, such as machinery, which does show a majority of agreements with upfront payments and a royalty (in this case between 2 and 5 percent), what does one do with such information in terms of preparing for technology valuation? How would one know whether the subject "machinery" technology warranted more, the same as, or less than the most common 2 to 5 percent royalty range? Furthermore, even within such range there is a significant variation: a royalty rate of 5 percent is two and half times as valuable as one at two percent.

For such data to have the utility of a used car, office space rental, or corporate bonds book it would have to have a much more structured and detailed presentation of information. Gathering and publishing such data would not only require a massive effort, it would jeopardize the proprietary status of such agreements.

Voluntary Surveys

Two more recent surveys are examples of voluntary surveys: McGavock, Haas, and Patin[13] and Degnan and Horton.[14] Both involved mailing out survey instruments to several thousand licensing professionals and tabulating and summarizing the findings. Although the number of respondents was modest (118 in the McGavock survey, and 428 in the Degnan survey), both of these papers provide useful insights into various aspects of licensing practices.

Although the goal of the McGavock survey was to assess the factors that affect value in license agreements, a subject dealt with in Chapter 5, the survey did report certain royalty data. Exhibit 4.5 shows a summary of the licensed out royalty rates by industry from the McGavock survey.

By examining the category of general manufacturing, it can be seen that every column of royalty rate category contains a numerical value (based upon 21 respondents). Any attempt to use such data to value a specific opportunity within this category (which itself is a broad term) is limited because there is reason to believe that royalty rates could be as low as zero percent and, at the other extreme, over 25 percent. In order to understand how the market might value a subject technology it would be necessary to go through a population of these surveyed agreements and perform an agreement-by-agreement analysis to extract specific guidance. It should be noted that the reported data for telecommunications, namely 100 percent between 10 and 15 percent royalty, is a consequence of only one respondent. It should be noted that there is a great deal of useful information in this survey, which

EXHIBIT 4.5 Licensed-Out Royalty Rates as Determined by a Voluntary Survey

	Royalty Rate Category						
	0–2%	2–5%	5–10%	10–15%	15–20%	20–25%	OVER 25%
Primary Industry							
Aerospace		40.0%	55.0%	5.0%			
Automotive	35.0%	45.0%	20.0%				
Chemical	18.0%	57.4%	23.9%	0.5%			0.1%
Computer	42.5%	57.5%					
Electronics		50.0%	45.0%	5.0%			
Energy		50.0%	15.0%	10.0%		25.0%	
Food/Consumer	12.5%	62.5%	25.0%				
General Mfg.	**21.3%**	**51.5%**	**20.3%**	**2.6%**	**0.8%**	**0.8%**	**2.6%**
Gov't/University	7.9%	38.9%	36.4%	16.2%	0.4%	0.6%	
Health Care Equip.	10.0%	10.0%	80.0%				
Pharmaceuticals	1.3%	20.7%	67.0%	8.7%	1.3%	0.7%	0.3%
Telecommunications				**100.0%**			
Other	**11.2%**	**41.2%**	**28.7%**	**16.2%**	**0.9%**	**0.9%**	**0.9%**

Source: McGavock, et al., "Factors Affecting Royalty Rates," *les Nouvelles*, June 1992, p. 107. Reprinted with permission from Daniel M. McGavock, CRA International.

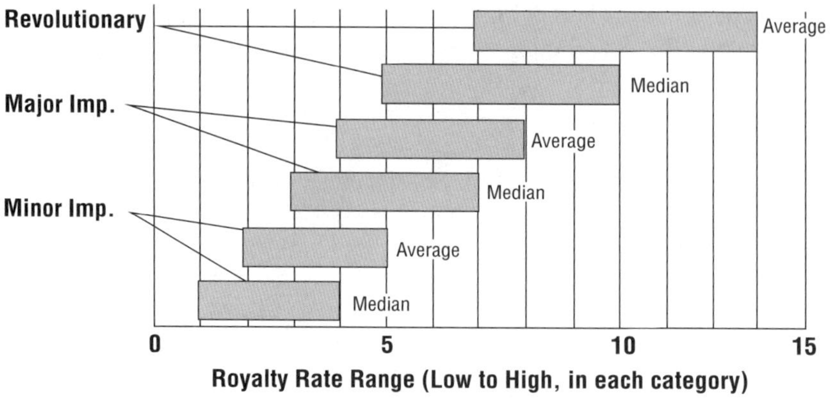

EXHIBIT 4.6 Licensing-Out Royalty Range

will be referenced in Chapter 5; it is just not reasonable to expect surveys by themselves to provide the kind of information that one can use directly in support of a valuation.

The Degnan survey likewise provides useful information that will be referenced in Chapter 5. However, one example cited here is this survey's effort to link royalty rates to an innovativeness scale. The authors designed the following three-level Innovativeness Scale:

1. *Revolutionary*. Satisfies a long-felt need or creates a whole new industry
2. *Major Improvement*. Significantly enhances product superiority in an existing product, process, or service
3. *Minor Improvement*. Creates an incremental improvement in an existing product or service

The authors then used these distinctions to survey and report royalty ranges. Their findings are summarized in Exhibits 4.6 and 4.7 for licensing out and in, respectively.

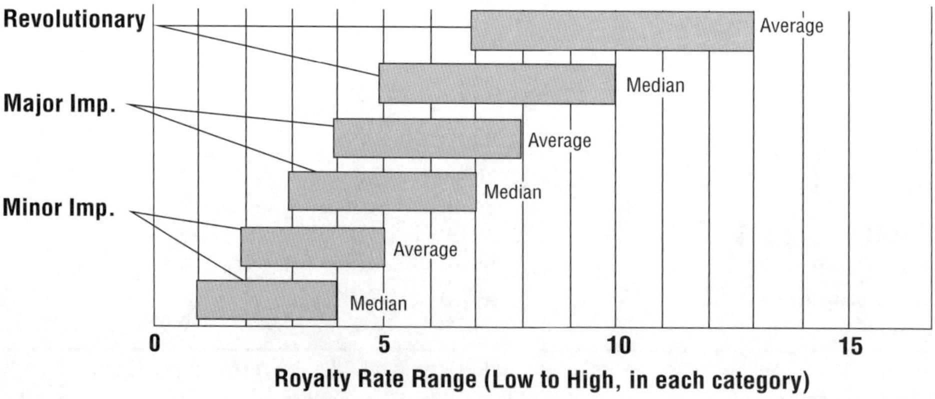

EXHIBIT 4.7 Licensing-In Royalty Range

It appears that the licensing-out rates are higher overall than the "in" rates; this suggests that the licensing-in data more closely correspond to technology, or at least earlier stage technology. An alternative explanation is a simple bias in reporting, where the respondents are of the belief they are paying less for what they license in than what they license out. The high end of the "average" values exceed that of the "median"; this is a result of one or a few very large values acting almost as outliers pulling up the average royalty rate. The key distinction based upon the innovativeness scale shows what would be expected: revolutionary > major > minor. However, the overlap in ranges is notable.

The Degnan survey also contrasted the median royalty rates for pharmaceutical licensing versus nonpharmaceutical licensing. They found that pharmaceutical licensing showed royalty rates approximately double that of nonpharmaceuticals. The reader is referred to the paper for the details. Not captured in these data are royalty rates for licensing contexts where what is licensed is only a portion or component of particular feature/function of an overall product sold by a licensee. As will be discussed in Chapter 10, one way this situation is handled is by adjusting the royalty base against which such royalty is applied such that it is less than the total product revenue. The presumption in these data is that the royalty rates are payment for the complete IP package of rights needed to obtain the respective revenues against which such rates are applied. This latter point is critical to any practical application of data such as Degnan's. When a survey respondent cited, say, a 5 percent royalty rate, such rate would necessarily be with reference directly to the revenues and profits gained by virtue of the license.

Considering again a hypothetical valuation situation for a new laser device, the lack of a specific category of laser licenses or closely related subject matter, the lack of information on all the other important business dimensions, and the wide range of reported royalties all reveal inherent limitation in the use of such survey data, by itself, in determining a valuation. If one uses the licensing "in" table and reasons that the technology is somewhere between "minor" and "major" and focuses only on the median data, these data suggest a royalty range of perhaps 2 to 5 percent. However, recognize that there is no connection between such data and the specific licensing opportunity. Clearly the terms "major" and "minor" are not exact specifications that all respondents would treat in the same way. And of course not all "minor" improvements are equal. There could be patents of vary low value which respondents could have not reported because in their opinion such patents did not rise to the level of "minor."

It should also be noted that these data express an implicit assumption of importance of the invention being licensed even for the "minor" category. There are of course licensing transactions done using a lump sum structure whose value could be very low in royalty equivalent terms.

Summary of Survey Data Limitations for Aiding Valuation

As discussed, such surveys do provide various forms of useful information. However, their capacity to provide guidance in determining a valuation is limited. The primary reasons this is so are as follows:

- These data frequently cite a wide range of possible royalties within each technology category.

- There may be limited characterization available that connects the royalty rate data to the extent and value of the IP: That is, the Box could have been comprised of patents only or patents and important know-how, the number of patents included may not indicate anything significant as to extent of use (related patents are typically included in a package, but there could be only one patent that matters to the buyer), it often is not clear how the technology rights granted relates to the incremental profit that a buyer is projected to enjoy such the making of, high margin product for a large market, and so on.
- The royalty base in some cases may not be clear. Without understanding the base it may be impossible to determine the significance of a royalty rate (royalties based upon the entire selling price of a large assembly, say an automobile, or upon a small component).
- The upfront and other fixed payments may not be defined or correlated to the specific royalty rates.
- Overall there may be lacking a characterization of the many other important terms of a license such as exclusivity, term of the agreement, right to sublicense, improvement rights, etcetera.
- There may be inherent vagueness in product categories: "electrical" would presumably cover an integrated circuit and a curling iron. "Mechanical" could cover everything from a complete automobile engine to a staple remover.
- There are usually an inadequate number of segments of data (because of the scarcity of data). For instance, there are multiple important areas within telecommunications, entertainment/media, pharmaceuticals and medical products, software, and e-commerce. Generally these are omitted entirely or subsumed within categories broad enough to encompass very different types of technology licensing.
- Surveys by their nature contain dated information, which may not be relevant to the present time. Also it is not usually clear how far back in time the data reported by respondents was gathered. And reporting on royalty rates that resulted from agreements entered into over an extended period make it less likely that they can be indicative as a comparable.
- Surveys tend to be influenced heavily by the nature of the survey segment, membership in a particular society, trans-national licensing to a specific country, and so on.
- Many of these agreements likely had other commercially significant provisions that affected the numbers. One of the common elements of licenses between companies is a supply agreement provision; often this takes the form of the licensee agreeing to supply the product to the licensor for use or resale. The pricing of such a supply agreement can be such that it influences the valuation of the license. One extreme would be a licensor's willingness to provide a license for no upfront money or royalty in exchange for favorable pricing under a supply agreement. Without a specification of such terms, it is impossible to interpret the meaning of a table of negotiated royalties. Another example would be the existence of cross licenses.
- There is no characterization of the stage of development of the technology licensed. In some cases the licenses were surely for fully developed products with an already proven market; in other cases, the licenses may have been for unproven inventions still at an early R&D stage.

The observations are not intended to be critical of such surveys. Valuation of technologies is a challenging and important assignment, so every scrap of information is appreciated. However, it is important to understand that such broad surveys have, by themselves, limited usefulness in preparing a valuation.

Proposed or Established Norms

We have previously considered paradigm licensing as one example of established norms. A related source of industry standard data and information is judgment of experts which may be expressed as capturing prevailing values and practices or may be in advocacy of what they believe should be such values and practices. Most licensing practitioners tend to focus on certain technology areas and compile data according to their own experience, by networking with colleagues; and by absorbing published information, develop a formal or informal database of what something might be worth. From time to time various experts are willing to publish their opinions at meetings and in journals. These valuation opinions are generally not statistical but insightful. They exhibit many of the same limitations discussed in the previous section, but they have the advantage that there is a natural segmentation because of the experience and judgment of the expert.

In this section, four examples of such expert judgments are provided. These examples by no means exhaust those available nor are they to be taken as firm and fixed opinions. One of the dangers of publishing anything is that one's opinion may change, but the publication remains throughout the ages. In general be cautious because expert opinions may be dated and may no longer be held by the expert. They are highly contextual (they are judgments based upon the expert's experience however broad or narrow that might have been), and they are subject to interpretation (what an expert meant by a categorization or characterization may not be easily interpreted and applied by others to other contexts). However, obtaining such expert opinion is a useful addition to a database of industry standard information.

Drug and Diagnostic Expert Examples

Because drug and medical diagnostic licensing has been such an important and active area for universities, there have been numerous publications of licensing experiences including valuation. Exhibit 4.8 gives an expert opinion by Tom Kiley who proposed normative royalties in certain pharmaceutical applications (rDNA designates recombinant DNA, and MAb monoclonal antibody).[15]

EXHIBIT 4.8 Another Proposed Table of Industry Standards

Proposed "Standard" Roaylties	Exclusive (%)	Nonexclusive
Developmental rDNA drug	7–10	3–4
Approvable rDNA drug	12–15	5–8
Therapeutic MAb	5–7	3–4
Diagnostic MAb	3–4	1–2
Drug delivery component	2–3	0.5–2

Source: © 1990 by Thomas D. Kiley. *IPH Newsbrief.* Reprinted with permission.

EXHIBIT 4.9 More Tables of Royalty Rates (for the Medical Industry)

Technology/Industry	Earned Royalty	Up-Front Payments	Minimum Payments
Reagents/Process	1–3%	Patent Costs	$2–10K
Reagents/Kits	2–10	Patent Costs	2–10
Diagnostics In Vitro	2–6	$5–20K	2–60
Diagnostics In Vivo	3–8	5–20	2–60
Therapeutics	4–12	20–150	5–20 (Yr 1)
			10–25

Again this is presented not for the purpose of providing authoritative values, but as an example of the availability of published expert opinion. In particular, it should be noted that the 1990 publication date of Mr. Kiley's paper dates the information and, in the rapid pace of this industry, may no longer be reflective of his present thinking.

Another example of expert judgment in this technology area is shown in Exhibit 4.9 based upon a publication by George Korey and E. Kahn.[16] The context for this table was early stage licensing from universities to industry. This example illustrates how such expert opinion can also include other important dimensions of an agreement such as upfront payments and minimum payments.

A useful adjunct to Exhibit 4.9 is the specification of the underlying assumptions; these are specified by Korey and Kahn and provided in Exhibit 4.10.[17]

In Chapter 9, an example will be given of the licensing of an early stage drug compound for an upfront payment of $20 million. One needs to be reminded that expert opinions deal with normative, common situations—events that have occurred

EXHIBIT 4.10 Underlying Assumptions for Table No. 1 [Exhibit 4.9]

1. Upfront payments may be combined and such terms are deal dependent.
2. The high end of upfront payments is usually associated with a "hot" technology in a developing field.
3. Exclusive world wide licenses; anything else diminishes the royalty rates.
4. Licensee holds no equity in licensor. If equity is held or is part of the transaction, then the rates are reduced.
5. There is no claim of infringement by the licensor against the licensee. If a claim exists then the upfront payments can be significantly increased to recapture presumed royalty payments that may have been owed.
6. Terms regarding crediting of any upfront payments toward running royalties are negotiated on a deal-by-deal basis.
7. No significant sponsored research agreements are involved, otherwise the royalties are usually reduced.
8. Overseas licensing rates sometimes command a slightly lower set of rates.
9. Upfront payments are based on 1989–90 dollars.
10. The technology which is licensed may or may not have been issued a patent, but the patent has been applied for and a reasonable opinion exists that the technology is patentable under the laws of the United States and at least one other country.

Source: Reprinted with permission from *Genetic Engineering News*, July-August 1991, p. 4; published by Mary Ann Liebert, Inc., Larchmont, NY.

EXHIBIT 4.11 Example Table of Royalties Developed by Experience by a University Licensing Office

Product	Royalty	Comments
Materials		0.1–1% for commodities; 0.2–2.% for processes
Processes	1–4%	
Medical Equipment/Devices	3–5%	
Software	5–15%	
Semiconductors	1–2%	Chip design
Pharmaceutical	8–10%	Composition of materials
	12–20%	With clinical testing
Diagnostics	4–5%	New entity
	2–4%	New method/old entity
Biotechnology	0.25–1.5%	Process*/nonexclusive
	1–2%	Process*/exclusive

*Expression systems, cell lines, growth media/conditions.
Source: This table was first presented at the Association of University Technology Managers (AUTM) 1989 annual meeting, and is reproduced here with the permission of AUTM and the author. Copyright 1989, Lita Nelsen (MIT).

with sufficient frequency and regularity that it is possible to make generalizations. However, by definition, generalizations do not cover all examples.

Major University Expert Example

As a final example of expert judgment, Lita Nelsen of the Massachusetts Institute of Technology, (MIT) presented her approximate characterization of what buyers were willing to pay sellers such as MIT in a paper presented to the Association of University Technology Managers (AUTM) in 1989 and summarized in Exhibit 4.11. In this case, the royalty rates all correspond to early stage inventions, protectable by patents (because of the need for universities to retain the right to publish).

Repeating aforementioned caveats, these figures are now about 20 years old. Further, they were based upon experience and expert judgment but were in the context of MIT and the level of technology that was being licensed under the licensing perspectives then in place. Put in succinct terms: Your results (and experience) may differ.

What is special about expert opinion is its subjectivity. Experts, like everyone else, filter their data through the lens of their experience and perspectives. However this does not prevent them from seeing patterns and extract generalizations that can be very valuable, particularly for fields such as technology licensing which cannot be easily characterized by statistical means.

Shopped Term Sheets and Price Lists

As will be discussed in Chapter 11, term sheets refer to generally short documents of a page or two that summarize the key financial terms of a proposed licensing transaction. They can originate with either the seller or the buyer, depending on which party is initiating the negotiations. Although a particular term sheet is not normally published, it may become informally available, depending on the approach of the initiator and any associated confidentiality provisions. It is normal business courtesy, apart from any confidentiality provision, not to distribute term sheets one may receive. However, over time an active licensing practitioner can be the recipient of or become exposed to numerous term sheets.

Term sheets, although they are succinct by nature, can be very useful in understanding at least an aspirant's perception of value associated with a particular Box and Wheelbarrow. Because they are brief documents they are often incomplete with respect to all the important deal issues. It may not be knowable whether anyone accepted such terms as were offered. Because they are often the basis of starting a negotiation, it would not be surprising to have even a successful negotiation result with very different terms than contained in such term sheet either because the nature of the Box or Wheelbarrow changed, or there was a change in the perception of value.

Licensing price lists can also be a source of industry standard terms and data. Price lists may be distinguished from term sheets in that there is some presumption that agreements already exist relating to the subject technology and financial terms. Another distinctive element is that price lists are generally publicly available information.

Such price lists, or more accurately pricing tables or pricing categories, become necessary when a seller is in the fortunate position of having to deal with many different buyers and users. Rather than attempt to negotiate individual agreements, the seller in such circumstances prepares a form agreement with financial terms. Although buyers can still seek "exceptions," the seller normally takes the position that it is bound to keep the same terms for all buyers and cannot thereby enter into reduced payment arrangements without having to rebate or renegotiate with all previous licensees. Most Favored Nations (MFN) clauses that the seller has entered into with other licensees could inhibit a seller from offering materially different terms without having to make adjustments in previously entered into licenses.

One use of price lists occurs when a university has developed a technology that it expects to be widely used on a nonexclusive basis. This could occur, for example, as a result of an invention of a fundamental and widely needed diagnostic tool. Another example would be a software technology, such as a speech recognition algorithm. Although such pricing begins to look like right-to-use licenses commonly employed for selling products, in the context of the approaches described here they are for technologies—and lack some combination of packaging, documentation, commercial data, technical and product support, warranties, etcetera. The buyers in such technology licensing understand that what they are obtaining will require further development and adaptation to be usable.

Another context where price lists arise is under the threat of patent enforcement, where a licensor may seek to create a record of royalty rates it was seeking (expecting?) to receive under arms length negotiations. Alternatively, there may be instances where a patent owner is offering more favorable terms than it believes the technology warrants in order to avoid litigation. Term sheets prepared in the context of potential litigation are outside the scope of this book.

In both opportunity and enforcement licensing situations, one should be cautious with the use of pricing data because the seller may have had many other considerations in mind when deciding on a value (such as pricing at a very low level to create momentum to develop the approach as a de facto standard). Nonetheless, the existence of price list values can create an expectation in the mind of buyers that such are industry standards.

One very detailed example is from an actual licensing program for two related patents, one for a digital display and one for LCDs. A price list was widely produced that specified the royalty rates in each of seven categories of products with a different rate for each patent for each category. Example categories included: (1) vehicles, (2) VCRs, CD players, microwave ovens, (3) meters and gauges, and (4) wrist watches, clocks, timers. The royalty rates quoted per patent ranged from a low of 0.125 percent to a high of 7 percent, depending on the product category (this was in the late 1980 time frame). It appears that the distinction in rates was partly a result of the royalty base, and partly the seller's perception of the relative value of the technology rights to the buyer's product.

Another example is the aforementioned IBM practice in the early 1990s of licensing essentially all its portfolio on a nonexclusive basis for 1 percent per patent up to a maximum of 5 percent for all the patents in its portfolio in the field of information handling systems (which did not include manufacturing apparatus).[18] Further such licenses provided an initial payment of $25,000 unless only a single patent was licensed, in which case the payment was $5,000. Although an approach of 1 percent per single patent, regardless of patent or particular application, can appear to neglect opportunities to value specific licenses more highly, IBM at that time had a portfolio of approximately 10,000 unexpired U.S. patents, and this apparently was a cost-effective way of dealing with such numbers and complexity. When a large and important industry player such as IBM creates such pricing, regardless of the rationale or intent, it can broadly influence prospective licenses in other negotiations within the same field, and licensees can, thereby, develop an expectation of paying not more than 1 percent per patent and 5 percent in aggregate for a nonexclusive license. Because of IBMs size and market power when such pricing practices were initiated, there could have been antitrust concerns that influenced pricing.

Another example of price list information arises with licensing under various standards. In formulating standards for methods or products, such as may be developed formally or informally by organizations such as the IEEE, there can arise the situation where patent holders will make rights available to any practitioners of such standard under terms that are widely publicized, in some cases even on the World Wide Web (see Exhibit 4.3).

News Sources of License Agreement Information

Useful license agreement information can sometimes be found in various news publications such as the *Wall Street Journal*, *BusinessWeek* and other business magazines, press releases, business sections of newspapers such as the *New York Times*, proprietary searchable databases such as LEXIS-NEXIS, industry specific journals and publications, and, increasingly, numerous Internet sources of information. As discussed in Chapter 9 regarding the use of patent auctions, there is an increasing amount of data for lump sum payments for patent "lots" (related patents sold as a group).

Some examples of this source of agreement information include:

- Court proceedings disclosed that Duracell had agreed to pay Kodak a royalty of 0.225 cents per battery cell for licensed power-tester/indicator technology.[19]
- LXR Biotechnology, Inc., sold their 19 patents and two dozen pending applications in four technology packages (Cardiosol, Eilrex, Lexirin, & Apoptosis) for $968,829 in a sealed-bid auction.[20]
- Rambus, the owner of certain, SDRAM (synchronous dynamic random access memory, a type of random access memory semiconductor) patents is reported to offer royalties under a "default contract" (presumably as a list price) at 1–2 percent (on a chip basis) and 3–5 percent (for memory controllers). Rambus remains very active in litigation.
- "Gateway paid about $13 million for 47 Amiga patents.... It was a treasure chest."[21]
- Intel settled a patent infringement suit and entered into a cross license with Intergraph by Intel's payment of $300 million.[22]
- Microsoft paid $175 million in 1998 to Citrix for a license to its technology that expired in 2002 for a special kind of "groupware."[23]
- Microsoft paid $100 million to use patents owned by Inprise Corp. (formerly Borland International, Inc.) and, in addition, bought Inprise stock valued at $25 million (about 10 percent of Inprise). Inprise holds some 100 patents relevant to a variety of PC software applications including spreadsheet technology. It was rumored that this substantial payment was affected by a fear that arch rival Sun Microsystems, Inc. might acquire such rights and enforce them against Microsoft.[24]
- Visx, Inc. receives a $250 royalty from doctors every time they use its pulsating lasers (which they sell for $500,000) for vision-correcting laser surgery.[25]
- Artists and record labels (collectively) receive a 3 percent royalty on blank CDs, and two percent on audio CD burners.[26]
- "Tony L. White, chief executive of Applera, told analysts yesterday that the information business [Celera] would be more valuable as part of Applied Biosystems because 'there is evidence that pure data businesses are not viable in this industry.' That is partly because the public Human Genome Project is providing similar data free of charge, he said.... 'Applera has concluded that Celera's information business will probably earn $62.5 million from existing customers over the next four years before interest, taxes, depreciation and amortization. If it does not, Applied Biosystems will make up the difference....' Applied Biosystems will also pay royalties to Celera based on sales of data and of some test kits it sells. The companies said the royalties would amount to about $200 million to $300 million over ten years.[27]
- Microsoft has announced its intention to change its licensing structure to a "subscription" model. As a result of initial discussions with their major clients certain pricing information is emerging. In a *Wall Street Journal* article it is reported that Microsoft's "Office Suite Plan" is seeking annual royalty (subscription) rates in the range of 25 to 29 percent.[28] One large pharmaceutical company said that

under Microsoft's new sales plan its costs would have been "$21 million for software licenses over three years."[29]

- Sony Corp. agreed to pay InterTrust Technologies, Inc. a $28.5 million upfront license fee, in addition to undisclosed royalties, to license all 23 of its U.S. patents (and presumably any foreign counterparts), many relating to digital rights management (DRM).[30] (InterTrust sued Microsoft in 2001 under these DRM patents relating to Microsoft's Windows CP and Microsoft.NET products.)
- A jury awarded a research medical center licensor, the City of Hope National Medical Center, $300 million in what it determined was unpaid royalties by Genentech. Genentech had agreed in 1976 to pay royalties of 2 percent on any product manufactured using a City of Hope patent that enabled inserting human genes into bacteria to produce useful proteins.[31,32]
- In addition to royalty and lump sum information, it is also possible to learn of other forms of payments for rights to IP and IP-based companies. For example, a *Red Herring* article on companies building fully integrated biopharmaceutical systems and sources and magnitudes of investments included the following information (all $ are in millions): Exelixis has received $35 from VCs (venture capital), $125 from public equity, $65 in equity from a strategic partner, and $89 in research funding from a strategic partner for a total of $314; Tularik (from the same sources) received $138, $176, $13, and $160, totaling $488; Human Genome Sciences received $10, $1154, $55, $270, totaling $1489; and Millennium Pharmaceuticals received $9, $1260, $300, $600, totaling $2,169.[33]
- The recorded music industry is introducing new subscription and single payment online listening and recording services in response to the competitive threat of pirated song sources. Although this is a rapidly changing area, FullAudio Corp. had announced their intention to permit CD copying for 99 cents a song, which is effectively a paid-up royalty (presumably for noncommercial use).[34]
- Martek Biosciences, as reported in an article by Christopher Byron in *Red Herring*, appears to be forecasting potential revenues from licensing baby formula additives (DHA and ARA) assuming a royalty rate of 5 percent on the retail selling price of baby formula is attainable from companies such as Mead Johnson (a division of Bristol-Myers Squibb) and Ross Products, a rate that the author of the article says "seems too high ... No well managed company with an established retail brand is likely to surrender 5 percent of its revenues to a third party unless there is some overwhelming reason to do so."[35]
- Industry information can be useful and relevant in illustrating deal structure as well as licensing terms and values. Microsoft with Samsung Electronics Co. is developing a software OS (operating system), code name Stinger, for mobile telephones that will enable them to perform many PC functions and to interface with other devices. Nokia, in partnership with Ericsson, Psion, and Motorola have joined forces to develop a competing next generation mobile phone OS known as Symbian. On top of the Symbian OS, Nokia has developed its own proprietary system it calls Series 60, which it has decided to license to other phone makers for nominal fees including the source code to encourage its becoming a widespread standard. According to a *Wall Street Journal* story, Nokia is charging "just a few dollars a phone on top of the $5 Symbian charges for its operating system."[36] Microsoft has responded that Nokia and Symbian are "underselling" their value, suggesting that Microsoft is seeking higher license fees.

- One can receive daily email briefs from various venture capital funding sources. For just one day, June 25, 2002, one site (www.vcbuzz.com) reported on Vernier Networks (received $24.2 million in Series C round funding bringing their total to date to $34.5 million), Confluent Surgical ($20 million, Series C), Ironport systems ($16.5 million), Paracor Surgical ($16.3 million, second round), Chip Express ($16 million), Qsent ($12 million, Series B), think3, Inc. ($10 million), Princeton eCom ($10 million), Expresiv Technologies, Inc. ($9.8 million), Iridigm Display Corporation ($8 million), Alteer ($4.5 million), Bartech Systems ($3.5 million), Critical Technologies ($1 million), and Vivisimo ($300,000). If you were on distribution for the year 2002 you would have received paragraphs on $12 billion worth of such funding. Like most equity investments, the subject investments are much more than just IP, but these data can be useful in conducting such an analysis as well as being used in performing equity valuations (a subject we will examine in Chapter 10).
- Lastly, another of the many Microsoft litigation examples: They were recently ordered to pay $388 million to a Singapore software company (Uniloc Singapore Private Ltd.) for infringement of anti-piracy registration system patent claims.

Older examples that were cited in the earlier versions of this book are:

- Rodime was reported as having established a royalty rate of 7 percent on disk drives covered by its patent, and IBM took out a license but under unknown terms.[37]
- Microsoft was reported as collecting a royalty of $33 a copy for Windows 3.1, $43 for Windows 95, and between $80 and $90 a copy of Windows NT Workstation.[38]
- Texas Instruments was reported seeking royalties of as high as 10 percent on the price of semiconductor chips ("triple the usual level"), and for licenses applicable to PC royalties in the range of 2 to 3 percent of the PC selling price.[39]

Because such information sources are not generally providing the source material of the subject agreement, but is instead their understanding or what they have been told of what such source material establishes, there is always the question of the reliability of the information. In addition, such stories can omit financially significant factors of the deal Box or Wheelbarrow. Further, because such information arises episodically, it is not readily collected or easily accessible. With increasingly powerful Internet search tools and publishers making available searching of their databases for stories it is getting easier to find news citations of agreements. Also, over time one can collect a significant clip file of such information. Even when the news source is limited in the information provided, it can provide the basis of a search and perhaps the discovery of a source document or more extensive information.

Additionally, such news information can give important insights into market trends, emerging licensing structures, and other potential noteworthy events that could affect valuation. Four examples of such possible noteworthy trends are software licensing, downloadable content licensing, network operating licensing, and so called "reach through" licensing associated with drug discovery tools.

Software value and its licensing has been and continues to be a very significant economic activity, from IBM's mainframe software, to Microsoft's PC software, from multipurpose databases such as Oracle to specifically tailored enterprise applications such as PeopleSoft, from PDAs (personal digital assistants such as Palm's OS) to wireless telephones (or, better, communicators). It has been the source of the great wealth of many "new economy" companies and (despite recent market tumult and declines) 401K portfolios. Discussed above was the example of Nokia's interests in very low cost licensing of its source code for next generation mobile communicators driven in part (apparently) by the desire to prevent Microsoft or some other company from establishing a de facto control point and cost. More recently, Nokia and IBM have announced two ventures to distribute music and other media to mobile communicators and the integration of Nokia's software with IBM's digital media software, basing such software on Java, a Sun Microsystems programming language.[40] Nokia and IBM are also strong supporters of the "Open Mobile Alliance" that was announced in June 2002 which appears to have as one of its objectives, preventing Windows or son-of-Windows from becoming a dominating force. Part of the motivation for the alliance between Nokia and IBM is the development of digital rights management for content, such as music, initially for "light content" (ring tones, logos, and pictures) and later for "rich content" (music, movies, digital newspapers). Matsushita and Nokia have also announced Matsushita's agreement to license Nokia's mobile phone software; terms were not disclosed but were generally noted as being low to encourage widespread adoption.[41] These forces will affect not only software licensing terms and values, but also that of content, light or rich.

Another example relating directly to content is the online delivery of music for listening and/or burning onto one's own CD. The recent legal controversies regarding Napster, MP3.com, and others, reflect the enormous concern caused by the ubiquity of the Internet and the ability to transfer faithfully digital information to literally millions of users around the world, without payment to the copyright owners. It is probably not a coincidence that sales of prerecorded music CDs have declined year after year since 2001[42]) while the sales of blank CDs exceeded (in number) sales of prerecorded music CDs for the first time in 2001. Music publishers are now actively seeking ways of providing reasonably priced access to their copyrighted music to an audience that has become recently accustomed to terms known as free. It now appears that such access will be priced in the range of $1 for the right to listen and burn a single track for one's own, noncommercial collection. Pricing and structure of content appears to be on the cusp of significant changes driven by both technology enablement and market demand.

A third example is network operation licensing. If one has a patent on a way of encoding and transmitting data, the historical and dominant practice has been to license the manufacturer of the "box" that commercially embodies the invention. In this approach, the box maker is paid once for each such box it sells, and a portion of each sale (under a running royalty structure) is likewise paid once to the patent holder. It has occurred to box makers that it might be advantageous instead of simply selling their box and getting a single payment to instead give the box away and get paid on some time or usage basis. For instance during the dawn of xerography, the copiers were so expensive and usage uncertain, that Xerox® established a way of being paid for their copiers on a per copy basis. In a different domain, but by a similar idea, auto leasing is a way I pay the automobile manufacturer a per month and per mile fee in lieu of owning the (what in this example is a quite big) box. In theory, any box maker could seek to do the same thing, subject to the market's interest in paying-as-you go. A technology licensor could under similar circumstance seek to be paid a royalty not by the box maker but the network operator of the box. There are several examples of licensors aspiring and in certain select cases apparently achieving network usage as a royalty basis. Ronald Katz, who is the inventor and owner of multiple patents in the area of telephone interactivity, claims to have obtained license fees and royalties from companies such as American Express, Home Shopping Network, TCI, and MCI.[43] The ability of a prospective licensor to secure usage-based royalties will depend upon the nature of the patent claims or other IP being made available and upon industry practice.

The fourth and final example is of "reach through" licensing. In the new biology that is emerging, proprietary software and hardware tools and databases (content) are being developed that can have important significance in creating new drug discoveries. Suppose, for example, there was a version of a spreadsheet which had proprietary, embedded functions and templates such that when used with published financial information of public companies could reliably predict stocks which were undervalued and, accordingly, if purchased would outperform the market. Setting aside the question of the wisdom of licensing the tool to anyone, such an IP owner could logically expect to have its license fee pegged in some way to the benefit experienced by the licensee in its use. So rather than selling "Excel on steroids" for, say, $1,000, the licensor could conceivably seek some way to receive a share of the profits of the stocks selected by the licensee using the software. This would be a "reach through" royalty. Suppose that instead of a stock selector, there was a hardware/software tool, perhaps together with genomic information, that enabled a licensee to have the equivalent benefit of a stock selector by enabling it to select or design molecules that can cure specific diseases. Although it should be possible to create an upfront and annual fee licensing valuation and structure that could attempt to fairly compensate the inventor/seller, another more direct approach would be to base the royalty on the sales of new drugs discovered or developed by the use of such tools and data. It is likely that prospective licensees will resist such drug-based (reach through) royalties, preferring more conventional payment schema. However, for this fact situation, it is possible that parties could agree to just such an arrangement. One of the uses of the industry standard method is to seek out whether such deal structures have been agreed to and also if the particular circumstances that led the parties to find such an approach is acceptable, in addition to any insights as to specific financial values. Shown in Exhibit 4.12 are 16 examples of license agreements in the bioinformatics area (tools and content for assisting in drug discovery and development); all but examples number 10 and 15 appear to be reach through–structured royalties (note the "yes" in the column headed "royalty payments on products." This table was developed based upon information obtained from public sources.

The examples and associated discussion are not intended to endorse or forecast these as trends. They have been included to expand our understanding of the scope of application of industry standards methodology to structure and not just rates.

EXHIBIT 4.12 License Agreements (Bioinformatics Area)

Licensor	Licensee	Technology	Relevant Date	Upfront Payment	Research Funding	Milestone Payments	Recommendation for Development	Royalty Payments on Products	License Type
1. Martin Karplus & Harvard University	Polygen Corporation	Right to exploit and commercialize a certain computer program and software	12/10/85					Yes	C
2. Columbia University	Molecular Simulations, Inc.	Software programs for calculating and analyzing the electrostatic interactions of protein molecules	07/01/96					Yes, with minimum pmts.	C
3. Genome Therapeutics Corporation	Merck & Co., Inc.	Certain GTC yeast gene patents	7/10/96	Yes				Yes	A
4. Progenitor, Inc.	Amgen, Inc.	Leptin receptor technology	1/16/97	$500K		Up to $22MM		Yes	A
5. SmithKline Beecham p.l.c.	SmithKline Beecham Corporation	Sequencing of expressed genes and development of practical applications	08/14/97					Yes	C
6. Genome Therapeutics Corporation	Schering Corporation	PathoGenome Database containing certain genomic sequence information	09/22/97	Yes	Yes	Yes		Yes	B

EXHIBIT 4.12 *(Continued)*

Licensor	Licensee	Technology	Relevant Date	Upfront Payment	Research Funding	Milestone Payments	Recommendation for Development	Royalty Payments on Products	License Type
7. Gene Logic, Inc.	N.V. Organon	Technology related to high throughput analysis of gene expression and gene regulation	03/31/98	Annual payments	Yes	Yes		Yes	A
8. Synaptic Pharmaceutical Corporation	Kissei Pharmaceutical Co. Ltd.	Novel receptor dentifier	01/25/00	Yes	Yes	Yes		Yes	A
9. CuraGen Corporation	Genetech, Inc.	Discovery of genes that represents potential drugs, drug targets, and clinical markers	04/13/00	Yes	Yes	Yes		Yes	A
10. Cadus Pharmaceutical Corporation	OSI Pharmaceuticals, Inc.	Yeast technology license agreement	05/15/00	$100K, $100K maintenance fee					C
11. MorphoSys AG	Eos Biotechnology, Inc.	Human Combinational Antibody Library technology or antibody generation	06/14/00	Yes		Yes		Yes	B
12. Biosource Technologies, Inc.	The Dow Chemical Corporation	Technology related to the identification and characterization of genetic materials	08/04/00	$10MM	$12MM per year	up to $20MM		Yes, based on sales and added value	A/B

13. Rigel Pharmaceutical, Inc.	Pfizer, Inc.	Technology related to the discovery of novel and selective elements of the IL-4 signaling pathway involved in the modulation of IgE synthesis inhibitor	09/15/00	$2MM	$4.7MM in first 2 years	Payments on discovery schedule.	$500K for human, $250K for animal	2%-4% on human, 1%–3% on animals	A
14. Genomica Corporation	Applied Biosystems	Object model technology license	09/22/00					Yes	C
15. Incyte Pharmaceuticals	diaDexus, LLC.	Computer software for use in the processing and analysis of microarray expression data	11/20/00	$75K annually					C
16. Cambridge Antibody Technology Ltd.	Human Genome Sciences, Inc.	Antibody library and patents	06/05/01	$12MM		Yes		Yes	A

Notes:

(1) License type "A" appears to be a "license option" where the licensee helps develop licensor's technology for future product rights.

(2) License type "B" appears to be a license for an existing body of knowledge and the rights to develop future products resulting from the knowledge.

(3) License type "C" appears to be a license of existing technology to be used for a specific purpose.

Source: M. Michael Carpenter, Workshop at the 1979 LES Annual Meeting.

As with other sources of industry standard data, some precautions should be noted:

- Price lists may not reflect final negotiated values (i.e., the licensor may have been willing to take less than the published list).
- Other business issues may drive price lists. For example, in the IBM case, such practice may have been influenced by IBM's interest in trying to find a cost effective way of licensing such a numerous portfolio.
- Stories citing rates may simply be uninformed or speculative, and may not reflect actual values. (Companies cited in such stories often decline to confirm or deny the values.)
- As previously stressed, the rate depends on the base, and the overall deal economics depend on many factors besides just the royalties themselves.

Nonetheless, gathering such information can provide useful additional insight into market based pricing.

Journals, Proprietary Databases, Reports, and Consultants

There are several publications that regularly contain articles citing technology licensing financial terms, for example: *les Nouvelles* (published by the Licensing Executives Society), and the *Journal of the Association of University Technology Managers* (AUTM).

There is a publication that is dedicated to licensing economics: *Licensing Economics Review*, published by AUS, Inc.

There are various consulting firms that specialize in the valuation of intellectual property that maintain proprietary databases on published or available agreements in addition to tracking and collecting information for such purposes. Recombinant Capital (Mark Edwards), now Deloitte Recap LLC, has presented papers regularly on its study of published agreements. They are mostly in the biotech area and the company has provided increased online access to its long history of deal data. InteCap LLC, now part of CRA International (such as the aforementioned McGavock survey), also publishes regularly and maintains a proprietary database of license agreement valuations. There are numerous other firms offering such consulting and data gathering services.

There are various publications that provide financial information on licensing transactions, mergers and acquisitions of technology companies, financial information on public companies including accounting treatment of IP purchases and sales, and other useful information. *Royalty Rates for Technology* is published periodically by Intellectual Property Research Associates. Intellectual Property Research Associates publishes royalty rates for pharmaceuticals and biotechnology. Business Valuation Resources LLC (BVR) publishes various guides and databases including ones reporting on technology transactions. BVR also includes data such as *Pratt's Stats* (based on the work of Shannon Pratt). CaptialIQ, part of Standard and Poors, provides online screening tools that include transactions financial data. EDGAROnline publishes financial data filed by public companies as well as various aggregations of such data.

Papers are presented regularly at conferences of the Licensing Executives Society (LES) and the Association of University Technology Managers (AUTM) and other tech transfer and IP conferences (such as AIPLA), also at various professional society and industry meetings (such as BIO), as well as general conferences of business valuations (such as AICPA). Increasingly, such presentations are made available in whole or part on society or personal websites, such as my own, www.razgaitis.com. The challenge with these sources, including my own, is finding something new, coherent, and not purely self promotional. But here and there, there is that one insight or nugget that adds to one's toolkit and reference library. And in almost all cases, at meetings of these professional societies you get to meet some very nice people whom you can network with informally about valuation experiences and in some cases concrete information.

Published License Agreements as a Source of Industry Standards

There are a variety of circumstances whereby a license agreement becomes publicly available. In some states, it is mandated that certain license agreements become published under "sunshine" laws. The author was able to obtain a summary of one such agreement covering DuPont's license from the University of Houston for a certain type of superconductor material. This agreement provided that DuPont would pay as much as $5.5 million plus royalties for the patent rights to Professor Chu's invention.[44] Because it may be useful to the reader in other respects, these license terms are summarized in Appendix 4A.

Just as in the circumstance of the legal judgments, published license agreements can be extremely valuable because they provide the complete agreement which conveys a detailed enumeration of all the elements offered by the seller and paid by the buyer.

On the other hand, this superconductivity agreement shows some of the limitations of this approach as well. The inventor was, at the time of the agreement, one of the premier superconductivity researchers and the subject matter of the license was believed to be among the most promising superconductor opportunities. The licensee was highly motivated to branch into what was believed to be an extremely exciting new market. Without comprehending the context of the negotiation, one could easily be misled into thinking that such terms were and are commonplace. Nonetheless, this is a concrete example of the result of a willing buyer and a willing seller reaching an arm's length agreement.

Another circumstance whereby license agreements may become public is when the licensee is a publicly traded company. The Securities and Exchange Commission (SEC) of the U.S. Government maintains a repository of filings of public companies and companies intending to become public. Under SEC rules, such companies are required to disclose transactions that can have a "material" effect on the value of the company as protection for its shareholders. Because of the concern for shareholder suits, some companies interpret "material" quite broadly and so are more likely to publish license agreements. The smaller the company, for any given size license, the more likely the company will be to deem it as "material." There are SEC depositories where such agreements are filed and available to the public (see also, www.sec.gov). Frequently there is redaction present in such agreements, but even in these cases there can be some important business terms inferred. With the explosion of small startup companies in biotech and Internet/e-commerce, there is a surprisingly large population of license agreements available. The aforementioned company Deloitte Recap LLC (Mark Edwards) has acquired and analyzed many such SEC filings with an increasing number of agreements obtained under the Freedom of Information Act (FOIA).

Here we will consider two example agreements that have been published with the SEC. (In Chapter 10 on Equity Considerations, we will consider another agreement demonstrating the particular issues associated with a startup.) These are presented because they show by example one pure royalty license (apparently, no fixed payments), and one non-royalty license (with fixed and conditional payments), and they illustrate the kind of detail one can discover by searching for published agreements.

IBM-Intuitive, Non-Royalty License Agreement

The first agreement we will consider here is a 1997 license between IBM (licensor) and the licensee Intuitive Surgical, Inc. (Intuitive) relating to the use of an endoscope (an optical imaging device used to access a body's interior through a small opening) in the practice of animal and human medicine. A full copy of this agreement is available at www.razgaitis.com. It was obtained from Intuitive Surgical's filing (as Exhibit 10.9) with the SEC of its quarterly financial report (known as a 10-Q) on 3/22/00.[45] This agreement is interesting for several reasons. This is an example agreement made public without redacting the financial terms in an agreement by a very sophisticated licensing organization (IBM), which has reported annual royalties in excess of $1 billion in certain years. The agreement is also an excellent illustration of what might comprise a Box and Wheelbarrow. Following is a summary of some of the agreement's provisions with respect to each:[46]

- Box
  - License is for the rights to practice two groups of defined patents, "LARS" and "ROBODOCS" [Art. 1.8, 9]. The LARS patent portfolio is identified in Exhibit 1 of the license as including nine issued U.S. patents, five pending U.S. patents, and numerous corresponding patents and applications in other countries. The ROBODOCS patents consist of three issued U.S. patents and one Japanese patent.
  - "Patents" are defined to include "all patents which are continuations, continuations-in-part, divisions, reissues, renewals, extensions or additions thereof (or which otherwise claim priority from the foregoing) and their corresponding patents." [1.9 and Exhibit 1]
  - Technical information and other drawings, models, etc. are provided related to LARS patents [as "ASSOCIATED MATERIALS" in Art. 1.1, 2.9]
  - Defined field of use excludes specified medical fields (neurology, etc.) [Art. 1.5]
  - Worldwide and exclusive only within the defined field of use [2.1, 5]
  - Worldwide and nonexclusive for all other non-excluded fields [2.2, 6]
  - For the life of the respective patents [9.1]
  - IBM retains a right to practice [2.3, 7]

- License is subject to rights previously granted to third parties [2.4, 8]
- A limited sublicensing right is included [Art. 5]
- A limited warranty [Art. 7; note the important non-warranty language in this Article]

- Wheelbarrow
  - The payment upon the effective date (closing) of $1 million distinguished as $916,670 and $83,330 for the LARS and ROBODOCS IP, respectively.
  - A subsequent, "trigger" payment of $5 million distinguished as $4,583,330 and $416,670 for the LARS and ROBODOCS IP, respectively, with the trigger event being the earlier of an Intuitive IPO (initial public offering) or a specified date (9/1/98, which date was delayed to 11/2/98 in Amendment No. 1). This payment combined with the closing payments makes the license fee $5.5 million for the LARS patents and $500,000 for the ROBODOCS patents, for $6 million total.
  - Although not directly a Wheelbarrow element, it is interesting to note that closing payments are 20 percent of the respective trigger payments, namely, the deal was 20 percent down with the balance paid on the trigger which was less than one year after the effective date.
  - In addition, there are two payment "kickers," payments which become due upon the achievement of specified milestones. A kicker of $1 million is due after the first year in which sales of all licensed products and services first equals or exceeds $25 million.
  - A second kicker also of $1 million is due after the first year in which sales first exceeds $50 million. Thus, in addition to the $6 million paid at closing and on the trigger, Intuitive could owe as much as an additional $2 million, for a total of $8 million, in the event annual sales of licensed products and services exceeds $50 million, something it is reasonable to assume that Intuitive aspires to occur.
  - Because there is no royalty provision, all Intuitive sales beyond the second kicker event, namely the first year with annual sales of $50 million, are free of any further payment obligation to IBM. Based upon various revenue scenarios that, each party could estimate the effective royalty rate over the life of the subject patents corresponding to this payment structure. Clearly if the total revenues turn out to be small, these payments would correspond to a high effective royalty rate. In the extreme case, Intuitive would have just one year of sales and just reach the $50 million threshold triggering both $1 million payments and then have no further sales. It will then have paid $8 million in "royalties" on a base of $50 million in sales, or an effective rate of 16 percent (ignoring for these purposes the time value of money). On the other hand, if over the lifetime of the patents, Intuitive had cumulative sales of (say) $1 billion, then the effective rate (again ignoring the time value of money) would have been just 0.8 percent.
  - Intuitive essentially bears the cost and responsibility for enforcing the patents (at its election to do so).

The attraction of fixed license payments is that, by their fixedness, both parties understand the financial terms and can more easily plan their businesses. This agreement shows how the parties sought to use the framework of fixed payments to make payments over multiple periods, sometimes for the benefit of the buyer but other times for the convenience of both parties, and to provide conditional fixed payments upon the attainment of future business events which presumably warrant and make affordable such payments. As will be discussed in Chapter 10, one of the key licensing decisions is apportioning the value received between conditional and unconditional forms of payment.

Becton Dickinson and Selfcare, Pure Royalty License Agreement

A second example agreement obtained through SEC filing is between licensor Becton Dickinson and licensee Selfcare, Inc. The full agreement is provided at www.razgaitis.com. Like the IBM-Intuitive agreement this is devoid of redacting and has some interesting provisions illustrating creative use of the Box and Wheelbarrow, as summarized here.

- Box
  - A specified patent, so called Campbell patent [Art 1.2, as given in the agreement identified as Exhibit 10.1].
  - A specified patent, so called Rosenstein patent [Art 1.2 and Appendix A, as given in the agreement identified as Exhibit 10.2].
  - A specified "product" field of use [Art 1.3 of both exhibit agreements and in Art 2.0]
  - A nonexclusive license.
  - No sublicensing or transferability rights.
  - Worldwide license.
  - A release from past infringement by Intuitive (although the existence or magnitude of such past infringement is not stated).
  - There is limited warranty and representation by Becton Dickinson in Art. 9.
  - Becton Dickinson provides a "most favored nations" (MFN) feature in the below described royalty rate [Art. 15]. An MFN provision basically assures a nonexclusive licensee that it will have its royalty reduced to the lower rate that the licensor licenses the same technology to a third party (assuming all other economic factors are materially the same). The language in this article describes a process for enabling Selfcare to receive that protection and benefit.
- Wheelbarrow
  - No payment on closing, or other fixed license fee payments (which suggests that there were known, ongoing sales by Selfcare that would be subject to royalties as given below).
  - Royalty payments in a tiered (sometimes called wedding cake) structure. For sales covered by the Campbell patent from the effective date of the license until a first fixed date (1/1/99), the specified royalty rate is 6 percent.
  - From the first fixed date (1/1/99), the royalty rate for the practice of the Campbell patent increases to 6.25 percent and is due on all incremental sales up to a cumulative amount of $108,667,100, for a total royalty payment of $6.79 million.
  - For sales after the fixed date in excess of the cumulative amount of $108,667,100, the royalty for the practice of the Campbell patent reduces to 5.25 percent for the remaining the life of the agreement. (A traditional

"wedding cake" royalty structure has the royalty rate decreasing with time or sales; this agreement shows first an increase in rate, followed by a decrease).

- The above royalty terms are also applicable to the practice of the Rosenstein patent with the provision, however, there is a full credit allowed when both patents have been used, meaning, that Selfcare only has to pay the (say) 6.25 percent royalty once. However, if they make, use, and sell a product in one country under only Campbell they pay the full royalty and likewise for the Rosenstein patent.
- The royalty base is the "net sales" which is defined in Art. 1.4(a) as being all amounts invoiced (which may be termed "gross sales" or revenues) less (1) cash discounts, (2) transportation and shipping charges, (3) taxes and duties paid, and (4) refunds, rebates and returns. There are also provisions in Art. 1.4 for transactions not at arms length or where the product is not sold but "otherwise disposed of."
- Selfcare indemnifies and holds harmless Becton Dickinson under the terms of Art. 10.

As discussed in Chapter 11, royalty "structures," namely royalty rates that adjust with circumstances, can be used by the parties as economic compromises in their respective positions and to increase the perceived fairness of the terms.

Purchase Price Allocation

Another kind of valuation information available in an SEC filing arises from the need for purchase price allocation. As a result of recent accounting rules, companies making an acquisition must allocate what it paid in three categories: tangibles, intangibles (which could include technology based intellectual property), and goodwill. An example of such allocation calculation is taken from the 2001 annual report of Avaya as shown in Exhibit 4.13 for two Avaya acquisitions in that fiscal year.

Court Cases/Judgments as a Source of Industry Standards

Another source of industry data is patent infringement cases that are the subject of a lawsuit. Many cases settle before final judgment and are thereby usually secret. However, when a judgment is rendered there is the opportunity to study in some detail the specific circumstances that led a court to a subject valuation.

One legal text gives an extensive summary of court imposed "reasonable royalties" ranging from GM v. Dailey for supporting rods for automobile curtains (15 cents per car; 1937 case), to a machine for making paper cups (5 percent of selling price; 1948), to a vitamin (10 percent of gross sales; 1960), to CRT oscilloscopes (10 percent of gross sales, 1977), to vehicle suspension systems (30 percent of net sales; 1986).[47] Another example are court cases. A comprehensive listing of "Remedies"—adjudicated reasonable royalties—is published in a well known resource, *Chisum on Patents*. An example of the decisions reported is given in Exhibit 4.14.[48]

Shown in selected examples given in Exhibit 4.14 are the oldest two cases in the Chisum reported data, going back to 1916. The nine cases selected for this exhibit

EXHIBIT 4.13 Avaya: 2001 Annual Report

ACQUISITIONS

The following table presents information about certain acquisitions by the Company [Avaya] during the fiscal year ended September 30, 2001. These acquisitions were accounted for under the purchase method of accounting, and the acquired technology valuation included existing technology, purchased in-process research and development (IPR&D) and other intangibles. The consolidated financial statements include the results of operations and the estimated fair values of the assets and liabilities assumed from the respective dates of acquisition. All charges related to the write-off of purchased in-process research and development were recorded in the quarter in which the transaction was completed. There were no material acquisitions accounted for under the purchase method in fiscal 2000 and 1999.

		Allocation of Purchase Price[1]				Amortization Period (in years)			
	Acquisition Date	**Purchase Price**	**Goodwill**	**Existing Technology**	**Other Intangibles**	**Purchased IPR&D**	**Goodwill**	**Existing Technology**	**Other Intangibles**
VPNet[2]	February 6, 2001	$117	$48	$30	$16	$31	5	5	5
Quintus[3]	April 11, 2001	$29	$3	$9	$3	$1	5	3	3

(1) Excludes amounts allocated to specific tangible assets and liabilities.

(2) Acquisition of VPNet Technologies, Inc., a privately held distributor of virtual private network solutions and devices. The total purchase price $117 million was paid in cash and stock options.

(3) Acquisition of substantially all of the assets, including $10 million of cash acquired, and the assumption of $20 million of certain liabilities of Quintus Corporation, a provider of comprehensive electronic customer relationship management solutions. The company paid $29 million in cash for these assets.

EXHIBIT 4.14 Case Law Sources of Royalties

Year	Parties	Citation	Patented Invention	Amount (Primary Factors)
1916	Consolidated Rubber Tire Co. v. Diamond Rubber Co.	226 F. 455 (S.D. N.Y. 1915), aff'd, 232 F. 475 (2nd Cir. 1916)	Configuration of rubber tires	5 cents per pound of special rubber stock
1918	McKee Glass Co. v. H.C. Fry Glass Co.	248 F. 125 (3rd Cir. 1918)	Method and apparatus for making glassware	6% of gross receipts
1952	Middleton v. Wiley	195 F. 2nd 844, 93 USPQ 77 (8th Cir. 1952)	Device for cooling draft beer	75 cents per day of use
1972	Sidewinder Marine, Inc. v. Burns	176 USPQ 499 (C.D. Calif. 1972)	Design for boat hull	$125 for 16-foot models, $140 for 18-foot models
1983	Underwater Devices, Inc. v. Morrison-Knudsen Co., Inc.	717 F. 2nd 1380, 219 USPQ 569 (Fed. Cir. 1983)	Method and apparatus for laying underwater pipe for sewer line	$200,000 for project
1986	Bandag, Inc. v. Al Bolser Tire Stores, Inc.	USPQ 211 (W.D. Wash. 1985), aff'd, 809 F.2nd 788 (Fed. Cir. 1986)	Process of treading tires	23.75% of cost of rubber and gum used
1989	Johns-Manville Corp. v. Guardian Industries Corp.	718 F. Supp. 1310, 1316 13 USPQ 2ns 1684, 1688 (E.D. Mich. 1989)	Method and apparatus relating to glass fiberization	Upfront payment of $9,631, 163 plus 10% running royalty
1990	Trilogy Communications, Inc. v. Scope Co.	754 F. Supp. 468, 18 USPQ 2nd 1177, 1213 (W.D. N.C. 1990)	Coaxial cable making apparatus, method and resulting product	0.75%
1996	Joy Technologies Inc. v. Flakt Inc.	954 F. Supp. 796, 42 USPQ 2nd 1042 (D. Del. 1996)	Process for flue gas desulfurization	25% of cost savings from use of patented rather than alternative process

show a range of forms of royalty bases against which a rate or amount is applied, namely: per pound, per day, per product ($125 for a 16 foot boat), per project, and per cost savings. The latter is an example of the 25 percent Rule as will be discussed in Chapter 6. For the royalty percentage examples, shown are cases where it is applied to revenues (the common form) and to costs of a key component. They also show payment structures solely in the form of royalties, solely as an upfront payment, and combinations of upfront plus royalties.

Such data represent the opposite extreme from the survey and expert judgment examples considered earlier: Whereas those surveys and judgments were averages and general, sources from legal cases are specific, narrow, and exact. However, legal disputes more frequently pertain to "bare," nonexclusive patent licensing rather than technology licensing; the Box in such litigation matters is usually only the after-the-fact right to practice nonexclusively one or more patents, often just one or two patents. It is difficult to find a dispute on a directly comparable situation, particularly within a recent time frame. Also one needs to be careful in the interpretation of the finding because there are many factors argued and considered that may or may not be relevant to a pure technology licensing situation.

Some other issues involving the use of court originated royalty data include:

- The patent or know-how involved has been judged as valid and infringed which can make the license more valuable than the case where the validity of patent is unknown and in cases where the patent has not yet been issued.
- The data is very situation specific.
- The data can be old because litigation often starts after manufacturing by an infringer has begun and can take many years. By the time it is available to the public it can be many years after the R&D stage.
- Although we have a legal system that respects the judgment of juries (and judges) valuations in such contexts and by such judgers can be misleading in terms of true market value.
- The biggest limitation is simply that there are very few cases in which the royalty rates (or other financial information) become publicly known because very few cases go to trial and pretrial settlements are commonly confidential.

Despite these limitations, court cases should be considered as a possible source of industry standard insight.

Patent Pools

Patent pools are entities created when multiple parties each own patents that are needed, or are believed to be needed, to make specific products, or practice certain established standards. Example pools are: MPEG-4, MPEG LA, DVD Patent Licensing Program, 1394 Standard (also known as Firewire), Adaptive Multi-Rate Codec, Open Mobile Alliances (formerly the WAP Forum), 3G Licensing, IEEE 802.11 Networking, and many others. Although the issue of forming such pools relates to licensing strategy, for our purposes here they can also be examples of proposed or established royalty rates and/or upfront payments, and licensing structure as their terms are commonly published. However, how the proceeds from such payments to the pool are apportioned to the participating companies based upon their relative contribution may not be published. So such pools can give useful guidance as to a reasonable economic value for a large, and possibly complete, package (pool) of patents it does not guide us as the value of any particular patent whose contribution was important to the pool but was not individually priced.

Lifetime and Organizational Learning

One should not neglect an obvious source of industry standards: one's own experience over time. An active licensing professional will eventually develop a record of first-hand valuation experience based upon deals done as well as deals that could not be consummated. This personal database can be expanded through long-term professional relationships and experience sharing that develops through active participation in societies such as the Licensing Executives Society (www.les.org) and the Association of University Technology Managers (www.autm.org). In addition, there are other societies with significant interest and activities in licensing, such as AIPLA (for IP lawyers), and various pharmaceutical and biotech as well as other technology/industry specific societies and conferences.

In the health profession there is an analogous concept generally termed "evidence based practice."[49] The parallel to our situation includes the idea of building a database of experience, even evidence, using a structured approach to my encounters and learning. This database, however formal or informal, aggregates my experiences and by diary-like notations can capture learning and systematize what can otherwise be a jumble of memories, often unreliable.[50]

Borrowing another idea from a high school teacher notably successful in developing math skills in his students is creating a valuation equivalent of a "math only notebook." The idea is simply this: Start, and no matter what keep, a notebook, in some form, that contains the essence of any valuation event including analyses you have performed, or had performed for you, offers you made or received, or noteworthy deals or deal "nuggets" that you encounter.

A final aspect of lifetime learning is organizational learning. Most of us work as part of an organization with parallel current (lateral) and historic (longitudinal) experiences. In some cases these lateral and longitudinal experiences could be vast, and valuable, and are often not very accessible apart from some systematic effort made to make them so. Shared learnings with peers, and data-mining from files and people, including people who may have retired from active practice, can be a precious source of valuation and pricing insight and experience. With any retrospective analysis there is the caution of being a prisoner of the past way of thinking or doing and current values and terms may simply be different. However, as experimentalists know, all data needs to be scrutinized (scrubbed), digested, and analyzed. The point of historic investigations is not simply to replicate the past, as though that would even be possible, but to learn from it. Likewise, peer-to-peer experience sharing is not about who did better (or worse) but who has learned what from the world and events that surround us.

Average Error[51]

Underlying certain manifestations of the industry standards method is the idea of using averages. For instance, survey results are normally expressed as averages in various categories or segments as we saw previously. Averaging also can occur when one is looking at multiple agreements and one is trying to capture a single, representative value, which may be done by using an arithmetic average (adding them all up and dividing by the total number), or a median value, or even a modal value (the most frequently occurring value).

Do such averages lead us to a more accurate grasp of value? The firm answer is: Maybe.

There are three particularly important aspects of averaging that apply to valuing technology: the law of large numbers, the sensitivity to small distinctions, and the "Tiger Woods phenomenon." To illustrate the first two aspects, consider the following real example. In the early days of commercial aviation, they not only weighed your baggage, they weighed you. Today, despite all the precautions we encounter at airports in a post-9/11 world, no one is weighing anyone.[52] Why not? The answer lies in the combination of the law of large numbers and relative insensitivity to small distinctions. In the early days of commercial aviation the number of passengers was relatively small, in some cases fewer than 20, and the performance of the piston engines pulling relatively inefficient (in terms of aerodynamics and structure) airframes the difference between a full load of, say, a women's club and football linemen was the difference between a smooth takeoff and burning rubble at the end of the runway. With modern jet aircraft carrying hundreds of passengers with enormous performance capabilities the law of large numbers and the relative insensitivity to reasonable variations makes the weight worry largely unnecessary. (Yet, if we outfitted even a modern jet to carry, say, metal ingots, it would be important to know whether our cargo on a particular flight were aluminum versus iron versus uranium.)

In valuing technology we can conceive of examples of both early and modern aviation, namely: There could be cases where we were dealing with just a few relevant agreements with significant variation among them and the amount of money at stake appears large, versus another case where we have many relevant agreements with relatively small variations among them and the total value of the deal is not expected to be large. In the first case, taking an average value as characterizing the group is unlikely to be a reasonable single value to use, whereas in the second case, it might be. Making this concrete, let us assume we have a deal that we perceive to be of total value of about $100,000, and we have found 20 comparable license agreements, all for paid up license fees, scattered between a low of $80,000 and a high of $140,000; taking an average (or median) value as characterizing the industry standard may be a very reasonable act. On the other hand, consider the contrasting situation if we believed that the total deal value over time was going to be in the range of $100 million, and we could only find three relevant, and in this case pure royalty license agreements at 2 percent, 5 percent, and 14 percent (all on some comparable royalty base), taking the average of 7 percent or the median of 5 percent with so much at stake could be seriously misleading. When the numbers are few, and the stakes are high, one is pressed to consider the industry standard method as a collection of individual comparables that is not well characterized by an averaging process.

The third aspect of averaging is what I have called the "Tiger Woods phenomenon." Currently, the professional golfing world is being turned on end by the amazing performance of a still young man by the name of Tiger Woods. His play is simply on a higher plane than his peers. Lance Armstrong demonstrated an unprecedented like dominance in his sport, winning his seventh Tour de France; the now retired Michael Jordan in basketball; Cameron Diaz, Mike Myers, and Eddie Murphy, who were the lead voices in the movie Shrek 2 and received $10 million each for their respective 15 to 18 hours of narration work;[53] and Mike Tyson's household expenses[54] are other examples of performance beyond any normative expectation. It is not likely that any historic averaging would account for these examples. One of the exciting aspects of technology is that a particular invention or discovery could be transforming ("game-changing") in performance or cost reduction. When that happens, historic averages are normally not reliable indicators.

One final, and graphic, example of averaging error is related to us human beings. In many ways one can obtain meaningful averages of the human population, such as the design passenger load on a commercial aircraft just discussed. We can also talk about average life span in some contexts, though that number says nothing about us individually. And in yet other contexts, averaging leads to ridiculous results, such as this: A U.S. resident has (approximately) one ovary and one testicle and lives in Edgar Springs, Missouri, population 190.[55]

Concluding Observations and Cautionary Notes

The power of the method of this chapter is that the valuations are based on market outcomes: real live buyers and sellers reaching agreements by acting in their respective self interest. This can be very valuable when the point of reference is relevant to a subject valuation.

However, with all sources of Industry Standard information, we need to think about the various factors that could affect how the financial information discovered might be applied to the valuation of our present opportunity. Some of the factors we could consider include:

- *The Box.* What do we know about the Box of the reference agreement(s)? How does the Box of the historic agreement relate to the deal under consideration? Are the differences in the relative Boxes significant in terms of their likely effect on deal value?
- *The Wheelbarrow.* What do we know about the Wheelbarrow? Were there elements in the reference agreement(s) not in ours, or vice versa, that are significant? Were there likely to be financially important payment provisions that affect the valuation?
- *Timeliness.* There is an inherent time lag to historic information because it would not be available to us unless it occurred in the past. Does the difference in time of the discovered historical agreement(s) affect its applicability to our present situation? Was the reference agreement(s) done at a time when such deal values were low (or high)?
- *Bias.* If we are using survey or expert sources of data, is there a significant bias in the data set?
- *Actual outcomes.* If we are using expert opinion or published term sheets or price lists, are the valuation opinions or aspirations close to the finally realized deal value?

- *Special circumstances*. Although it is easy for an enthusiastic seller to believe that his or her opportunity is unusually high in value in comparison to some reference agreement(s), is such a belief well founded? Or, conversely, are we as sellers (or buyers) being too quick to peg our opportunity into a historic value range when in fact we have some extraordinary opportunity before us?

As we discussed at the beginning of this chapter, it is rare to find exact or near-exact comparable agreements with the published or accessible information that will be useful in a subject valuation, but sometimes it happens. Even when it doesn't, there is often some useful insight into valuation that comes from the search and study even if there is no close set of comparables. And there are times when we are in a paradigm licensing situation and, thus, even without a specific agreement, we can obtain a useful insight into a valuation range.

Ah, yet, there is this craving somewhere deep inside for norms/standards that can be relied upon. From the time we make selections of what clothes we will wear (is it dress up, or dress down? and if it's down, is it really down?), to how we greet one another (hugs for family and special people, definitely and regrettably no hugs in business encounters, handshakes only upon greeting initially or after some absence and definitely not daily with colleagues), to the structure and etiquette of our meals (soup and salad before entrees, absolutely not after), to every aspect of our respective lives, even the most nonconformist of us. One can even say there is a kind of bizarre haiku of standards and norms surrounding each of us: TCP/IP, XML,CDMA, OC-48, Mac OS, MIDI, MP3, AA batteries, 1 percent milk, kosher, 24 carats, one gallon per flush, 0.08 blood alcohol, April 15, July 4th, 16 ounces, eight to five, 40 hour workweek, 3-1/2 inch floppy, 8-1/2 by 11, #2 pencil, QWERTY, 26 letters, king's English, 88 keys, on key, (do re me fa so la ti do), 33-1/3 rpm, 4/4 time, four-year degree, three-ring binder, three-prong plug, 110 VAC/60 Hz, Sunday, RGB, PG-13, 20/20, 120/80, USDA Prime, shake hands with the right, different fingers in different positions have quite specific communication value, nine innings, 100 yards, par, .357 magnum, 93 octane, 65 mph, 26 miles 385 yards, 8-track, Betamax.[56] Standards and norms are a kind of safe harbor. There are other people who are already there, it's been predetermined as safe, and going there is, if not a best practice it's at least a defendable one (akin to the adage in the pioneering computer decision days, "no one ever got fired for buying IBM." So the desire and search for valuation standards and norms is a natural one. And, in almost all circumstances, it is a reasonable effort to make. But, in valuing technology one should normally not expect to find the easy comfort of a well defined, established standard.

And even when the search for such market-based norms yields close-fitting examples there is an appropriate level of humility. The U.S. housing market has declined by early 2009 approximately $12 trillion (TRILLION!) in aggregate value from what had been believed to be a true market-based value. Consider also the recent examples of the dramatic drop in equity values. Equity values are perfect examples of market-based values, as they are precisely defined and fungible, traded throughout the business day, every business day, throughout the world by many thousands of buyers and sellers who are behaving, it is believed, with economic rationality. Yet the past year has shown that even for highly regarded, stable, diverse industrial companies such as GE, early 2008 equity value has plummeted by 70 percent in a year's time; every 2009 holder of GE equity would gladly trade with anyone using early 2008 values. Even for broad indices, such as the S&P 500, the past year has shown that what was a market value in early 2008 was not what the market perceives it to be today, reflecting a drop of about 40 percent in value, wherein both time periods reflect a belief as to long-term earning potential of the 500 companies comprising the index. Such observations should not dissuade us from the valuation utility of using this first of six valuation Methods we are considering; a little humility often goes well with utility.

The search for the holy grail of an industry standard "pricing book" is not likely to bear fruit (nor does it need to for the search to be valuable). A wide variety of published information is available that will increase the likelihood that examples exist that are reasonably close to your deal. When used cautiously and judiciously, they can usefully contribute to the consideration of value.

In the next chapter we will consider the use of rating/ranking as a semi-quantitative method of making comparisons between a reference (or comparable) agreement and the opportunity being valued. It is a natural extension of the subject addressed in this chapter, particularly for those circumstances when the discovered reference agreements contain enough information that they can be compared to our subject opportunity across multiple aspects that can affect value, as we shall see.

Appendix 4A: Outline of Agreement between DuPont and University of Houston

1. Important Definitions
   a. "*Patent Rights*"—(1) rights in any patents which the United States or any foreign country might grant covering claims to superconductive materials applied for by the University of Houston (UH) as of execution date, and (2) any certain filed applications.
   b. "*Licensed Products*" and "*Licensed Processes*"—products and processes covered by an allowed or issued claim included in any of the Patent Rights. Also includes products, the sale of which would result in contributory infringement.
   c. "*Net Sales*"—the amount invoiced on sales of Licensed Products or Licensed Processes less certain discounts, return credits, taxes, transportations costs, and insurance premiums.
   d. "*Field of Commercial Interest*"—any commercial field in which DuPont can demonstrate financial commitment to research, capital expansion, marketing plans, and so forth.
   e. "*First Commercial Sale*"—can include a sale to U.S. government pursuant to a contract awarded without a competitive bid by a third party.
2. Grant of License

   UH grants DuPont an exclusive, worldwide license to make, use, and sell Licensed Products and Licensed Processes, subject to the following:
   a. UH may make materials for its own research.
   b. DuPont will use its best efforts to introduce Licensed Products and Licensed Processes into the commercial market as soon as possible.

c. Includes the right to sublicense; all sublicenses will include a "best efforts" clause.
d. U.S. government rights.

3. Sublicenses

DuPont may grant sublicenses under the following conditions:

a. At UH's request, DuPont will grant a restricted sublicense to a TCSUH (Texas Center for Superconductivity at the University of Houston) consortium member, who shall pay a reasonable royalty thereof. DuPont will pay UH 75% of sublicense royalties in fields of no commercial interest to DuPont and 50% of royalties in fields of commercial interest to DuPont.
b. At UH's direction, DuPont will grant a sublicense to a third party, regardless of TCSUH membership, in any field of no commercial interest to DuPont. DuPont will pay UH 75% of royalties in such cases.
c. After the earlier of (i) three years after DuPont's first commercial sale (unless DuPont is proceeding diligently toward commercialization) or (ii) eight years after date of patent issuance, UH may direct DuPont to grant a sublicense to a third party in a field of commercial interest to DuPont at a royalty rate no less favorable than DuPont is paying in that field. DuPont will pay UH 50% of royalties so received.

   [NOTE: These features, i.e., 2(d), 3(a), (b), and (c) render the license, in some respects, a "nonexclusive" license.]
d. DuPont may grant sublicenses on its own initiative and will pay UH 75% of all royalties received by DuPont.

4. Payments

In return for the grant of license and rights associated with it, DuPont will pay UH:

a. $1.5 million upon execution of the agreement
b. $1.5 million upon the issuance of a U.S. patent covering the "1–2–3" phase material claimed in the patent applications.
c. At DuPont's option, $1.5 million two years following the date of patent issuance. If DuPont does not execute this option, the agreement terminates with no obligation by UH to refund any previously paid money.
d. DuPont will pay royalties on net sales as determined by agreement between UH and DuPont at the time of commercialization, or in the event UH and DuPont cannot agree, by a third party arbitrator experienced in the field of industrial licenses and royalty arrangements. Added value-in-use by licensed technology is to be a prime factor in determining royalty rates.
e. In the event of cross-licenses, trades, single-payments, or receipt of property, UH and DuPont will agree on the appropriate royalty value, or, failing agreement, submit to arbitration.
f. DuPont will pay the greater of earned royalties or a minimum royalty of $100,000 per year. The minimum is not required until the earlier of (i) the expiration of three years following the first commercial sale (but not before patent issuance), or (ii) five years following patent issuance.
g. Despite U.S. government rights, if DuPont is the supplier to the U.S. government of Licensed Products, based on a contract awarded without DuPont's having to match or overcome a competitive bid, DuPont will pay UH a reasonable royalty.

h. DuPont will require sublicensees to pay royalties on sales even before the grant of patent, provided there is no third party competitor who is not paying a royalty.
i. DuPont is entitled to credits against earned royalties due UH, but only for the third $1.5 million payment and for reimbursement of legal expenses associated with patent filing and prosecution.

5. Patent Filing and Maintenance

UH will prepare, file, and prosecute patent applications. UH will cooperate with, and consider the opinions of, DuPont with respect to such applications. DuPont will pay all expenses relative to such applications, retroactive to the filing of the first application. In the event DuPont decides to cease paying expenses (after the expenditure of $1 million) with respect to particular applications, its rights in such applications will terminate.

6. Records and Reporting

DuPont and its sublicensees will keep accurate records and permit a UH-designated CPA to inspect them upon demand. To the extent permitted by law (e.g., Texas Open Records Act), UH will keep confidential information obtained from such inspections. DuPont will submit semiannual reports of sales and royalties due.

7. Improvements
   a. Any inventions which are "improvements" of the licensed technology will be included in the Patent Rights. For purposes of the agreement, "improvements" are considered additional filings or new applications that would be dominated as matter of patent law by the existing applications.
   b. UH will continue to file patent applications on inventions resulting from Chu-directed work. For three years, DuPont will have a right of first refusal on new patent applications (as opposed to "improvements") covering superconductive materials resulting from Chu-directed work. Other research and researchers at UH are not covered by this right.
   c. DuPont and UH will encourage and promote exchanges of information between Chu and Chu-directed researchers and DuPont's Wilmington Experimental Station. Any contribution of a UH researcher at DuPont will be subject to DuPont's right of first refusal.

8. Infringement

Both parties have the right to pursue legal action against infringers or to otherwise protect the Patent Rights, and either may bring action in the name of the other if the other is an indispensable party. Funding of legal expenses may be derived partially from royalties, and recoveries will reimburse such expenses, and then cover royalties, then be shared equally. Royalties may be partially reduced during the period of an infringement if it has not been successfully abated within six months after it is discovered.

9. Termination
   a. Unless earlier terminated, the agreement will automatically terminate on the expiration of all Patent Rights.
   b. If either party defaults, the other party may terminate by giving notice and the defaulting party does not initiate action to cure the default within 90 days.

c. DuPont may terminate if it decides not to make the payment provided in 4(c).
d. DuPont may terminate without making the payments provided in 4(b) and (c) if the patent is not granted in ten years. UH need not refund the initial payment, and all rights revert to UH. DuPont is relieved of any remaining obligations to pay legal costs.
e. UH may terminate without refunding any payments and all rights revert if DuPont does not make a royalty-bearing sale within eight years after grant of patent and DuPont is not proceeding diligently toward commercialization.
f. After DuPont makes all of its payments required by 4(a), (b), and (c), it may still terminate by giving 30 days notice. All rights revert to UH.

10. General
   a. UH warrants that all interest in the Patent Rights have been assigned to it, and that UH has the authority to license those rights. UH does not warrant that the Patent Rights are valid, that they have any particular scope, or that DuPont may exploit them without infringing other patents.
   b. DuPont indemnifies UH from personal injury and products liability claims.
   c. DuPont may not assign the agreement without UH approval.
   d. UH and DuPont agree to attempt to settle all disputes, claims, etcetera, amicably between themselves. If they fail, they will submit the matter to binding arbitration.

R18/18.11.03.1,2

Notes

1. But, in 2001, the toniest avenues in New York rented for $700 a square foot, according to a *Wall Street Journal* article Nov. 7, 2002, p. C11. This was 25 times the $28 a square foot for the average U.S. shopping mall.
2. Munger, James, P., *What's It Worth? A Guide to Current Personal Injury Awards and Settlements*, 1998 Edition, LEXIS® Law Publishing, 1998.
3. Ibid., p. 95.
4. I invite you to enjoy an especially good such foreign film nominated for an Academy Award in 2002: *Son of the Bride*; it is an Argentine film with many culturally specific events and yet when it is over we can see ourselves and people we know in a similar, yet deeper, way.
5. Thanks for this example belong to Richard Brown, who for some 30 years has taught various incarnations of "Movies 101" in New York City.
6. There exist comparatively rare situations where one could identify a historical agreement that can approach being essentially the same as one's subject opportunity. For instance, a licensor can offer a bare patent license (such as a non-assert) on a nonexclusive on a one-time payment basis to an industry comprised of very similar actual and prospective licensees.
7. For those of you with some extra money and interested in becoming baseball owners, a Doubleday, 50% owner, had been expecting an appraisal in excess of $600 million, noting that the Boston Red Sox had then recently been sold for a reported $720 million and Forbes valued the Yankees at $730 million, though such value includes more than just the brand/IP value; according to FutureBrand, the Yankees are the most valuable sports-franchise brand in the U.S. at $338.8 million (according to

a *Wall Street Journal* summary, July 8, 2002, p. A20.) Forbes publishes valuations of major league baseball teams, estimating in 2006 the Mets were worth $604 million, third highest in major league baseball, substantially the value argued for in 2002: http://www.forbes.com/2006/04/17/06mlb_baseball_valuations_charts.html?

8. Battersby and Grimes, *Licensing Royalty Rates*, 2001 Ed., Aspen Law and Business, 2001.
9. *New York Post*, June 18, 2002, p. 31.
10. It is probably a powerful indication of unique value when the public associates a person or product by an unusual, single name such as J-Lo, Elvis, Madonna, Bono, Cher, Sting, or Prince (or, now more accurately, by an unpronounceable name of the artist formerly known as Prince). On the other hand the unique name Liberace does not seem to have much traction these days, and "Raz" has not done much for me.
11. Buyers characteristically play a game I've called the "Where's Waldo™ of Licensing?"—shrinking the domain of the licensed technology down to the most microscopic scope possible so that almost any royalty rate, even 100 percent, does not constitute a significant payment.
12. For the moment we are ignoring the issue of how one would determine the appropriate "price" of the base, as in this example the manufacturer is "selling" the chip to itself.
13. "Factors Affecting Royalty Rates," Dan McGavock, David Haas, and Michael Patin, *les Nouvelles*, June 1992, p. 107, published by the Licensing Executives Society International (LESI).
14. "A Survey of Licensed Royalties," Stephen Degnan and Corwin Horton, *les Nouvelles*, June 1997, p. 91, published by the Licensing Executives Society International (LESI).
15. Tom Kiley, *IPH Newsbrief*, April 1990, and published in *Licensing Economics Review*, September 1990, p. 4.
16. George D. Corey and Edward Kahn, "Biomedical Royalty Rates: Some Approaches," *Genetic Engineering News*, July-August 1991, p. 4; also published in *Licensing Economics Review*, December 1990, p. 13.
17. Ibid.
18. This information is based upon a one-page summary prepared by IBM in 1993 entitled "IBM Worldwide Patent Licensing Practices." This practice was also cited in a paper by David Guenther and John Wills, "A Survey of PC Technology Royalty Rates," *les Nouvelles*, December 1995, p. 200. It is the author's understanding that this does not constitute IBM's current licensing practices.
19. *Wall Street Journal*, July 27, 1999, p. B5.
20. LXR Biotechnology press release, October 25, 2000.
21. *Wall Street Journal*, August 21, 1999.
22. "Intel settles patent suit with software makers," Reuters, April 15, 2002.
23. *BusinessWeek*, May 22, 2000, p. 136.
24. "Microsoft to Pay Inprise $125 Million to License Products and Form Alliance," Don Clark, *Wall Street Journal*, June 8, 1999, p. B13.
25. *Wall Street Journal*, May 26, 1999, p. 1.
26. *Wall Street Journal*, November 2, 1999, p. B1.
27. *New York Times*, April 23, 2002 "Celera Genomics in Surprise Appointment," story by Andrew Pollack.
28. *Wall Street Journal*, March 12, 2002.
29. "New Microsoft pricing looms," Rebecca Buckman, *Wall Street Journal*, June 24, 2002.
30. "InterTrust Signs Licensing Deal," *Wall Street Journal*, May 23, 2002, p. B8.
31. "Jury Rules Against Genentech in Research-Royalties Lawsuit," David P. Hamilton, *Wall Street Journal*, June 11, 2002.
32. "Genentech Faces $500 Million Charge," David P. Hamilton, *Wall Street Journal*, June 25, 2002, p. D4.

33. "Knowledge is Power, but Pills are Profits," Stephan Herrera, *Red Herring*, May 2002, p.72.
34. "Listen.com Deal to Advance Effort in Music Licenses," Nick Wingfield, *Wall Street Journal*, July 1, 2002, p. B5.
35. Bryon, Christopher, "Smart Babies, Dumb Investors," *Red Herring*, July 2002, p. 94–5.
36. "Facing Big Threat from Microsoft, Nokia Moves to Share Its Software," David Pringle, *Wall Street Journal*, May 22, 2002, p. 1.
37. "IBM to Make Patent Payment in Rodime Case," *Wall Street Journal*, Nov. 2, 1990, p. B2.
38. "Microsoft's Earnings Hot Streak Cools," *Wall Street Journal*, July 18, 1997, p. B6.
39. "A Chip Maker's Profit on Patents," *New York Times*, October 16, 1990, p. C1.
40. "Nokia to Join with IBM in 2 Ventures on Software," by Steve Lohr, *New York Times*, July 10, 2002.
41. "Matsushita to Use Nokia's Cellphone Software," story by David Pringle, *Wall Street Journal*, July 11, 2002, p. B6.
42. Reported by SoundScan in Billboard, July 13, 2002, p. 6.
43. "Ron Katz, Enforcer," by Seth Lubove, *Forbes*, August 25, 1997, p. 78.
44. "DuPont Stakes Claim on Superconductor Rights," *Science*, Vol. 241, p. 1156.
45. Although we will discuss the recently publicized problem of confusing and unreliable financial data, such problems have not extended to license agreements that have been filed. Companies will regularly redact certain information for competitive (or perhaps embarrassment avoidance or other) reasons, but what is submitted is generally taken as a faithful representation of the agreement between the parties. One always wonders if there are other related agreements, sometimes called side letters, which are not filed or otherwise disclosed that exist that have a material effect on the valuation of the deal being disclosed. The problem with side letters is that there is no way to prove their nonexistence (short of having access to the complete files of the respective parties, which is not going to happen).
46. Just to state what should be obvious: I am not a lawyer and, accordingly, I am not giving here, or anywhere, a legal interpretation but, rather, a businessperson's understanding of what is being sold and bought in exchange for what consideration.
47. *Patent Licensing*, Harold Einhorn, Section 3.03, Royalty, 1990, p. 3-11ff; another, classic authority is: *Chisum on Patents* by Donald S. Chisum, Lexis Publishing, August 2005.
48. Donald S. Chisum, *Chisum on Patents,* Vol. 7, Lexis Publishing, August 2005, "Remedies."
49. These summary comments derive from a telephone discussion with Dr. Suzanne Bakken, Professor of Medical Informatics, Columbia University School of Nursing, an authority on evidence-based advanced practice nursing, but do not do justice to the vast literature available in that discipline.
50. There is an epic novel of gargantuan length, such that almost no one on earth has actually finished it, including me, that has as its deep thought that the past is both far more and far less accessible to us than we think. Marcel Proust in *Remembrance of Things Past*, also and perhaps better translated as *In Search of Lost Time*, expends some 3,000 pages to demonstrate the strangeness of memory and our forming present meaning from it. Creating some system for recording valuation and pricing memories as described in the next text paragraph can help circumvent much of that strangeness.
51. Yes, this is a play on words.
52. Yet even today, in small airplanes, such as four- or six-passenger, single-engine piston aircraft, the pilot is, or should be, doing such weight assessment when approaching a full load for the same reasons discussed in the text.
53. "An Animated Conversation," authored by Tom King interviewing Dreamworks' Jeffrey Katzenberg, *Wall Street Journal*, May 17, 2002.
54. As reported by Mr. Tyson's accountant and introduced in the U.S. district court in New York (reported by Sports Illustrated), his expenditures for the three-year period 1995

through 1997 included: automobiles/motorcycles $4,477,498, pet expenses (pigeons and cats) $411,777, lawn care $748,367 (but it was for three houses, so it only "averaged" $249,456 per house), and cash and personal expenses $7,794,103; Sports Illustrated, 2002.

55. According to the 2000 U.S. census data, Edgar Springs has replaced Steelville, Missouri as the human center of gravity for the United States, reported in National Geographic, May 2002; I am not aware of a specific scientific source of the other statistic cited.
56. Adapted from a sidebar "The Poetry of Standards," *Wired*, January 2002, p. 89.

CHAPTER 5

Method 2: The Rating/Ranking Method, and Tool

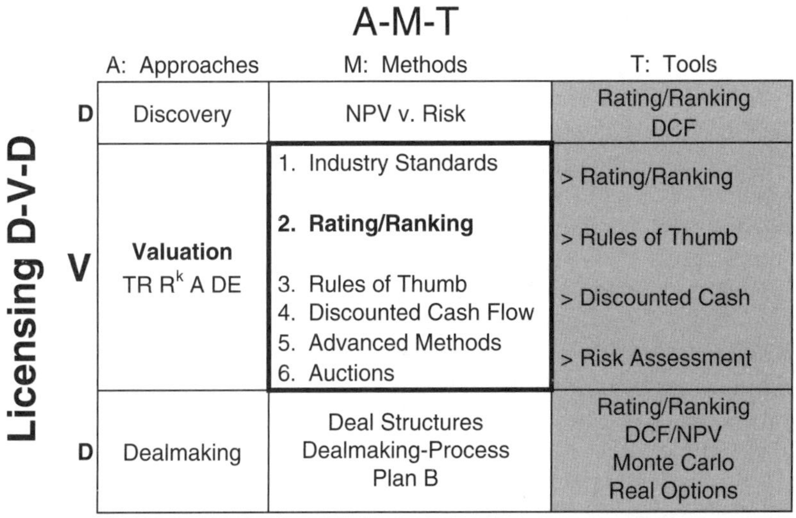

A-M-T
A: Approaches
M: Methods
T: Tools
Licensing D-V-D
D
Discovery
NPV v. Risk
Rating/Ranking
DCF
V
Valuation
TR R^k A DE
1. Industry Standards
2. Rating/Ranking
3. Rules of Thumb
4. Discounted Cash Flow
5. Advanced Methods
6. Auctions
> Rating/Ranking
> Rules of Thumb
> Discounted Cash
> Risk Assessment
D
Dealmaking
Deal Structures
Dealmaking-Process
Plan B
Rating/Ranking
DCF/NPV
Monte Carlo
Real Options

In this chapter we will consider the second of six valuation Methods, that of Rating/Ranking. As a valuation Method, Rating/Ranking requires the pre-identification of a reference or comparable agreement or cluster of such agreements. For this reason this method is closely associated with Industry Standards, Method 1, covered in Chapter 4. One of the observations on the use of Method 1 is the difficulty in identifying exact or near-exact comparable agreements. There are other concerns about solely considering Method 1 approaches to valuation. One such concern, one that is always present with any method, is the risk of distortion, or even disablement, of judgment. As we have discussed, considering agreements which are deemed comparable is a compelling instinct for both technology sellers and buyers, though as we will discuss in Chapter 11, sellers and buyers may "see" very different populations as being comparable. Like any other quick-to-compel idea or "fact," the result can be a misguidance that, upon a broader reflection, could have been avoided. Another area of concern is the difference between the past and now, let alone the past and the future. Another kind of compelling instinct is "pastcasting": extrapolating the past as a kind of sovereign determinant of what will happen now and in the future.[1] One expression of such pastcasting, some times referred to as "groupthink," occurs when peers with similar backgrounds and experience are firmly, unanimously, and, as it too often turns out, wrongly convinced about confident predictions about even the then present conditions, let alone the future. Andy Grove, former CEO of Intel has said: "When everybody knows that something is so, it means that nobody knows nothin'."[2]

Rating/Ranking, as we will see, is a systematic way of using available agreements and consideration of the key determinants of value, to improve the comparability of available experience to the subject valuation project. This can help minimize pastcasting as well as groupthink and balance that compelling instinct to seize and lock onto what might only be the appearance of "the obvious."

Earlier, when we discussed valuation as a business process, we introduced the taxonomy of Approaches, Methods, Tools (AMT). Although Rating/Ranking is here treated as one of six valuation Methods, it also finds utility as a Tool that supports other valuation methods we will consider, as well as guiding Approaches that can be followed in opportunity Discovery and dealmaking. We will introduce the uses of Rating/Ranking as a Tool at the end of this chapter, and apply it in subsequent chapters on Methods 3 (Rules of Thumb), 4 (Discounted Cash Flow), and 5 (Monte Carlo and Real Options Advanced Methods). We introduced previously that Rating/Ranking as a Tool can be useful also in the Approaches (business processes) of opportunity Discovery (D) and Dealmaking, which along with Valuation comprise our Licensing D-V-D acronym. At the end of this chapter we will expand upon the use of Rating/Ranking for Discovery of licensing opportunities. In Chapter 11, we will demonstrate how Rating/Ranking can be used in Dealmaking to identify higher value dealmaking propositions and dealmaking target companies.

Rating/Ranking as a valuation method can appear to lack a foundational quantitative framework which can lead to the criticism of it as leading to arbitrary or unreliable conclusions, or worse, that it all too readily permits someone to "slant" an outcome and cloak it as a methodology. The underlying IP of technology licensing is often sophisticated science and engineering using a high degree of precision and concreteness. We would naturally like to evaluate such assets with comparable exactitude. Method 1 (Industry Standards), through its reliance on existing agreements, has a comforting concreteness, though often weak on exactitude; Method 6, Auctions, also exhibits concreteness and gives some basis for belief in exactitude, as we will discuss in Chapter 9. With Methods 4 (Discounted Cash Flow) and 5 (Advanced Methods) we will consider detailed, complex, and concrete financial models, with scenarios and trade off analyses, even to the application of advanced mathematical tools such as Monte Carlo and Real Options, including Black-Scholes (for which a Nobel Prize has been awarded). However, in this chapter and the next, Methods 3 (Rules of Thumb), we will develop methods that rely more obviously and directly on judgment. Judgment is a necessary element of all valuation methods. Every method relies in some way upon assumptions and specific calculation models. The danger of "slanting" an outcome can be inflicted on any valuation method. In fact, the systematic nature inherent to Rating/Ranking has as one of its benefits that it reveals underlying judgments and can make more evident unintentional, or intentional, mis-valuations.

As in other chapters, we will highlight as examples how Rating/Ranking can be used as a ***Tool*** by shaded text entitled "The Toolkit."

Ubiquity of Rating/Ranking

Let us first recognize that Rating/Ranking is a widely used methodology for reaching value judgments, even, or especially, when dealing with hard-to-quantify distinctions, such as:

- A regularly appearing type of news story is headlined by "Best X" where X designates the place(s) "to Start a New Business," or "Raise a Family," or "Retire," or (and I'm not making this up) "Romantic Cities for Baby Boomers."[3] There is a world database on happiness established by rating/ranking some 100 countries on a ten point happiness scale.[4]
- *U.S. News and World Report* regularly publishes its ratings and rankings of various academic programs of colleges and universities[5] and medical care offered by hospitals by specialty.[6] *Moody's Economy* has created a business vitality index for 379 metropolitan areas considering measures of general economic condition, household income, labor availability, and regional cost structures; their top 10 includes Austin TX (#1), Corvallis OR, Raleigh NC, Orlando FL, and two Dakota cities—Sioux Falls SD and Fargo ND (who knew?).
- In a specialized and emerging form of rating/ranking, medical professionals use a ten-point pain rating/ranking method for characterizing pain, the so called fifth vital sign (after temperature, pulse, blood pressure, and breathing). Such scale, shown in Exhibit 5.1, sometimes known as the Wong-Baker FACES pain rating scale or the "Universal Pain Assessment Tool" (UPAT), uses graphics of six facial expressions. (The use of facial expressions has been found to be a meaningfully accurate way to measure something otherwise not readily quantifiable and can be used with patients over a wide range of ages and levels of sentience). The UPAT, shown below, by "coding" the face ratings to a ten-point scale shows

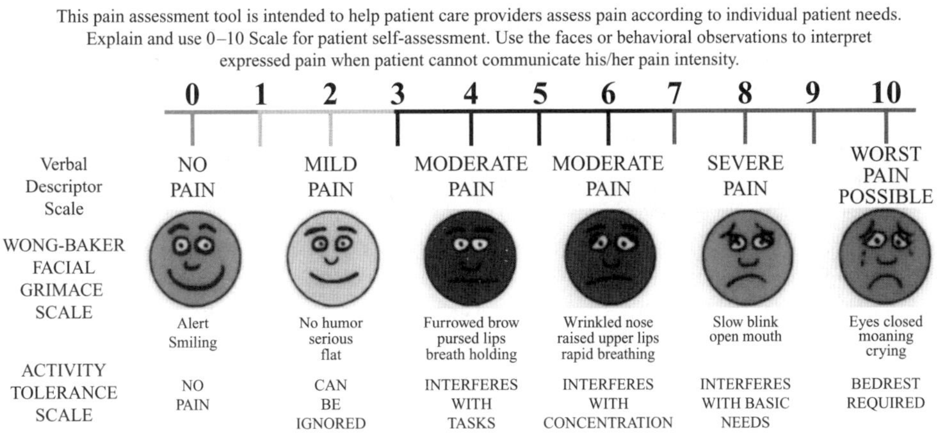

EXHIBIT 5.1 Universal Pain Assessment Tool

Source: UCLA Pain Management Clinical Resource Guide (http://www.anes.ucla.edu/pain/FacesScale.jpg).

how iconic and quantitative expressions of rating/ranking can be used together, which in this case allows for a quantitative value to be coded in a patient record as well as deal with "in between" responses.

- Edmunds (www.edmunds.com) provides a ranked numerical quality ranking for every automobile, new and used, by a ten-point scale, although its use of one decimal place distinctions makes this effectively a 100-point scale. *Consumers Reports* reviews of automobiles uses filled circles to characterize iconically the quality and reliability of various sub-systems. Netflix® and Apple's iTunes software asks its users to rate movies and songs by clicking on the number of stars, one through five stars. The website Amazon.com similarly invites visitors to rank products it sells on a one-to-five star basis, as does versiontracker.com for all the software for which it provides download access.
- Smokey the Bear, the icon of the U.S. Forest Service, has for 50 years reminded us that "only you can prevent forest fires" and weighted such reminder by providing a five-level fire danger scale: no, low, medium, high, and extreme.[7] In the wake of the U.S. terrorist attacks of 9/11 there now exists a Department of Homeland Security (DHS) which characterizes risk by a five color rating/ranking system: green (low risk), blue (guarded), yellow (elevated), orange (high), and red (severe).[8] The U.S. Federal Emergency Management Agency (FEMA) has applied a similar color-based rating/ranging system for ascribing security risks for various facilities.[9] The U.S. Transportation Security Agency (TSA) has proposed a controversial three-level airline passenger rating/ranking system based upon seven (or more criteria) into three categories: passengers deemed "red" are barred from boarding flight ("no fly"), those designated "yellow" receive extra screening, and those rated "green" endure only the customary inconveniences.[10]
- The value of Google, currently ranked in the top 20 most valuable companies in the world (measured by market capitalization), is founded primarily on its rating/ranking of search queries. PageRank™ was developed and patented (U.S. 6,285,999) by Google's founders, Larry Page and Sergey Brin, now each multi-billionaires, while Stanford University graduate students prior to their becoming college drop-outs and licensees of the invention. PageRank is a proprietary algorithm used by Google that performs a very sophisticated kind of Rating/Ranking of untold billions of web pages, ever growing in number, by considering more than 500 million variables and two billion terms.
- At the other extreme, another example of a Rating/Ranking method is Benjamin Franklin's "decision algebra." He is reported to have developed this decision-making tool over his lifetime and used it in many different contexts. When faced with a decision he would create two columns, one for the "yes" outcome and one for the "no" (he lived in simpler times). Then in each column he would list every reason or argument that would support the respective "yes" or "no" outcome. (Presumably he did some compression so that he did not end up with the same reason expressed multiple times in different ways). Then he would select one reason / argument from, say, the "yes" column and cross it off and at the same time cross off as many "no" entries as needed to be of equal "weight" to the "yes" entry being crossed off. He would continue to cross off equal weights of reasons until one column had no more reasons left. Then he would examine the other column to find at least one good, un-crossed-off reason supporting that decision (say, "yes"), unbalanced by any entries supporting the opposing

decision ("no"), and so he would then chose "yes." Franklin Rating/Ranking can be directly applied to the Approaches of opportunity Discovery and Dealmaking.

- Sailing has a long history of risk and reward in the face of conducting trade over the highly variable wind and wave conditions of the open seas; it is no accident that there are terms such as "trade winds" and "ply one's trade" ("ply" derives from the ancient Greek word for ship: πλιο, *ploio*). A rating/ranking scale developed more than 200 years ago that is still widely recognized is the Beaufort Scale. This scale (shown in Exhibit 5.2) classifies and ranks all possible wind speeds into 13 groups (zero through 12) based upon observable phenomenon on land or sea. The scale provides a standardized way of communicating weather observations and sailing risk. And, with experience, sailors have been able to apply such rankings to their decision strategies (to sail or not) and ship management (from arraying the right amount of sail area, to securing all cargo, to readying a "ditch bag").[11] Applying Beaufort Rating/Ranking to the Approach of opportunity Discovery for trade by sailing, both very low values and high values would be unfavorable rankings—the former because our ship is not going to get anywhere quickly, the latter because our ship and its cargo and souls is in danger of never being seen again. Related to extreme sailing conditions including coastal danger is the Saffir-Simpson, five-category Hurricane Scale.[12] Category One has wind speeds in the range of 74 to 95 mph, and the highest Category, Five, has wind speeds exceeding 155 mph. Such categories are sometimes condensed into smaller groups, as is common with rating/ranking; for hurricanes it is common to simply group them into two: "major" (Categories Four and Five), and not major (One through Three).
- Nuclear accidents are characterized by an eight-level scale developed in the 1990s, known as the "International Nuclear Event Scale" (INES), as a means of creating a global comparison of such events and their human health implications: ranging from zero (no safety significance) to seven (major accident). Similar to the Saffir-Simpson Scale there is a sub-classification: INES zero is characterized as only a "deviation" or "anomaly," INES one–three are "incidents," and INES four–seven are characterized as full-fledged "accidents." The 1986 meltdown of the runaway reactor at the Chernobyl Plant in the then USSR was, understandably, a seven.[13]
- Criminal Punishment. Judges in our criminal justice system have the responsibility of deeming just punishments for a diverse range of individuals convicted of a diverse range of crimes. Regrettably, the number and variety of convictions has created the societal need for a classification system, based upon the character of the criminal and the nature of the crime. Crimes can be categorized as misdemeanors or felonies, a distinction that goes back to feudal times; they are further subdivided into, for example in the state of Virginia, four classes of misdemeanors and six classes of felonies, so if one is guilty of a Misdemeanor 4 the punishment cannot exceed $250, escalating to death or life imprisonment and a fine of $100,000 for a Felony 1. Likewise, convicted individuals are themselves classified in addition to their particular crime. In the U.S. Federal System, the sentencing guidelines in 2005 treated six different categories of criminal histories as determined by "criminal history points" which are, in turn, then mapped against 43 different crimes ("offense levels"), so that a person whose individual history puts them in Category II and their particular offense a Level 13, they should

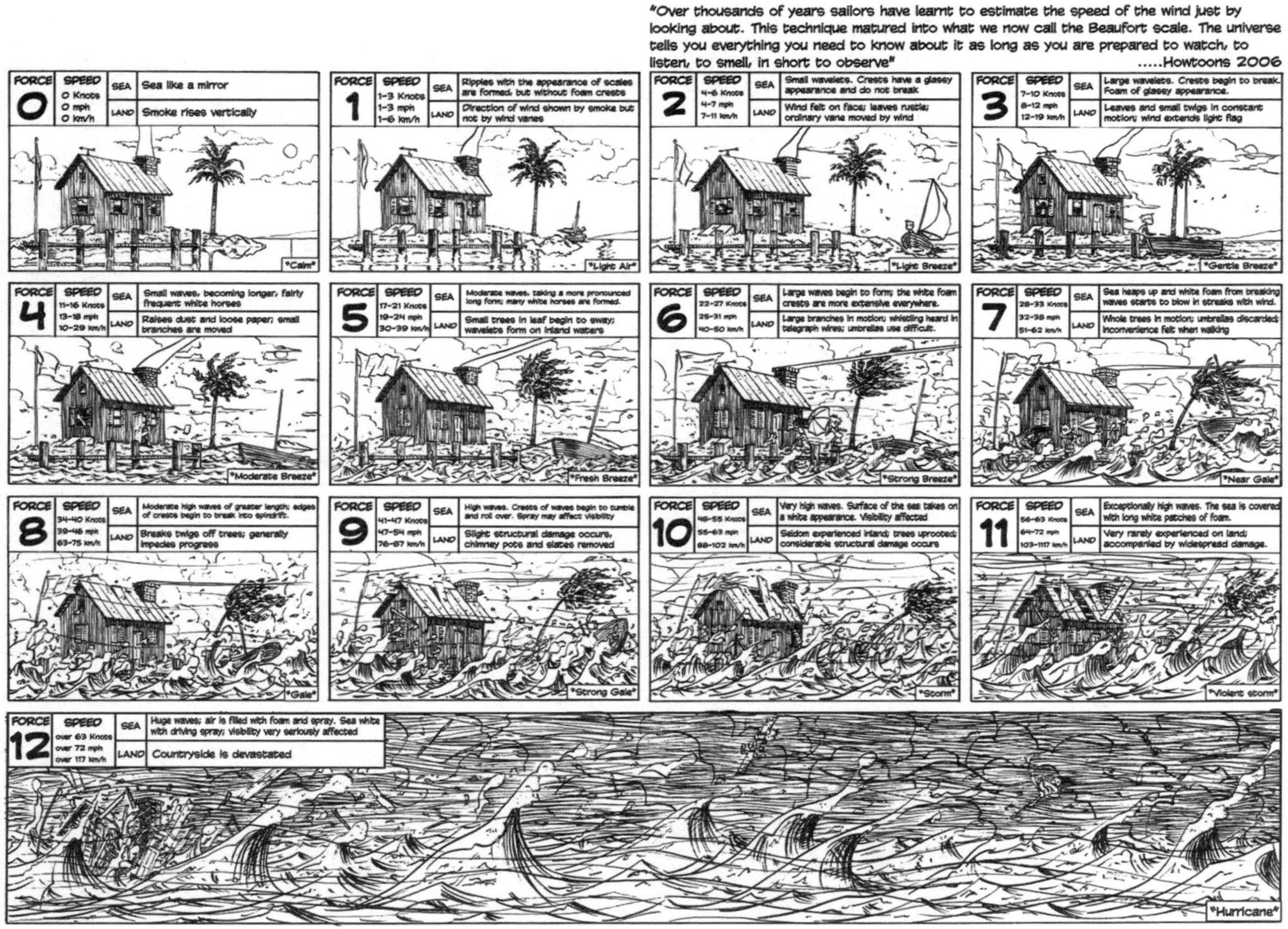

EXHIBIT 5.2 The Beaufort Scale

Source: Howtoons.

receive a prison sentence in the range 15 to 21 months. This same sentence range, 15 to 21 months, is the guideline for an individual with a more extensive criminal history—Category V—convicted of a lesser offense—Level 10. For high category criminals creating higher level offenses, say a VI committing a 29, the punishment guidelines goes up by a factor of approximately ten (incarceration between 151 and 188 months). Such sentencing guidelines are an example of Rating/Ranking by Classified Value, which will soon be discussed, using here two primary factors, criminal history and seriousness of the particular offense. In principal, such rating/ranking is more likely to result in a consistent way of treating all kinds of criminals and all kinds of crimes.

- Ending our examples on a less ominous note, baseball, like most sport endeavors uses rating/ranking for young prospects, for established professionals ("starter," "franchise player," "allstar"), and even for retired players ("hall of famer," "first ballot hall of famer"). The interest in rating/ranking approaches appears to be on the increase because of a popular book, *Moneyball,*[14] and the explosion of interest by adults playing "fantasy baseball" where they draft and "play" their own individually and uniquely configured teams. One rating/ranking tool used by fans playing fantasy teams is PECOTA, which stands for Player Empirical Comparison and Optimization Test Algorithm (yes, that's the real name); it's been claimed to be "deadly accurate," though one hopes this is meant metaphorically. The underlying idea is comparing by a PECOTA rating/ranking any given player's performance to comparable players using a database of statistics of players who played at least one season in the Major Leagues since 1946, yielding more than 20,000 (!) batter seasons.[15]

Behind some of the above examples lies a physical law or principle that can, arguably, make more defendable each classification. But even in such cases, the boundaries are neither exact nor uncontestable. With some classification systems, arguments about a rating/ranking decision is never ending: why isn't [FILL IN THE BLANK[16]] in the baseball hall of fame? But, nonetheless, we find such distinctions both possible and meaningful, not necessarily unarguable, and that's good enough for many purposes.

Overview of How Rating/Ranking Can Be Used in Valuation

There are two general instantiations of Rating/Ranking as a valuation method, which I shall characterize here by (1) Factor Assessment and (2) Classified Value. It is useful initially to consider how this chapter's development of the Rating/Ranking Method can ultimately be applied in these two ways. Although both embodiments of Rating/Ranking are similar in that they require starting with comparable transaction agreements, they use such information and methodology in different ways.

Factor Assessment

Rating/Ranking can be used to value a particular technology licensing opportunity—which we will call "B"—in comparison to some preexisting technology license agreement (a comparable), or group of such agreements—which we will

	Factors				
	F1	F2	F3	F4	F5
B | A =	H	0	L	L	0

EXHIBIT 5.3 Illustration of Factor Assessment Using the Rating/Ranking Method

designate by "A"—by considering each *factor* that materially affects the value of *any* technology license agreement. The result is a valuation by means of a factor-by-factor relative comparison of how licensing opportunity B differs from the known, reference financial value of A. How such factors are determined and their comparative effect on the value of B with respect to A will be developed later in this chapter. A simple conceptual form of the result of such Factor Assessment is shown in Exhibit 5.3.

The comparison of prospective agreement B with respect to the historical agreement A is designated here by the symbol B|A, namely: B in comparison to A. In each above cell some expression of such comparison is expressed below each respective factor number (F1 through F5 in the above example). Each such factor (F1, F2, etc.) represents one distinct influence upon the value of a technology, such as the size of the market addressable by products. The relative significance of each factor for technology B in comparison to A is expressed in the corresponding cell by some measure. Such measure can be something simple such as "H" (or "+") for higher, meaning that B is perceived to be more valuable than A with respect to the corresponding valuation factor such as addressable market size, and likewise use "L" (or "−") for relatively lower, or a blank or "S" (for same) or "0" (for no difference). Later in this chapter we will consider alternative comparison expressions. In such a Factor Assessment approach, we are ***rating*** B with respect to A (in some way) for each valuation factor we consider to be material.

To complete such analysis, we would then need to combine all our individual factor ***ratings*** into an overall rating and use that rating to guide us in valuing B, given A. In the above example, B is perceived to be a net lower in value because it is neutral (i.e., approximately equal) on two of the important factors, higher in value in one factor, and lower for two factors assuming, as we are for this illustration, that all such factors are equal in significance. Later we will consider how such valuation factors might be weighted to reflect greater or lesser financial significance.

Classified Value

The Rating/Ranking Method can also be used in a systematic way to create value *classes* that are more versatile in their application than the considered Factor Analysis. To illustrate this concept of Classified Value, let us use the five common letter grades familiar to us that classify a student's performance in a college class—A, B, C, D, and F (or E); so here "A" and "B" mean something very different than in the discussion about Factor Assessment. As we will discuss later, the number of such distinct classes depends on the desired precision of the result and the available number of Industry Standard agreements with the relevant financial information.

Continuing with this example, we need access to a population of past agreements with widely varying valuations from which we can form, in this example, five groups. The "A" group representing the highest value technologies based on available prior agreements, ranging down to the lowest value "F" group. Again the details should not concern us here, but "A" could represent licenses with running royalties greater than ten percent, and "F" those with royalties between zero percent and 0.5 percent, and "B," "C," and "D," representing ranges such as 7–10 percent, 3–7 percent, and 0.5–3 percent, respectively. Such class distinctions would of course depend on the particular population of comparables available to us. Classified Value requires many more comparable agreements than Factor Analysis, because they are needed to characterize each of however many distinct categories we deem appropriate and because we are seeking to acquire a *generalized* characterization of value for a certain type of technology.

Once such classes are established we can then value some new licensing opportunity, here designated as "NEW," by comparing it to the members of each of these five groups (A through F) and identifying which group opportunity NEW most closely corresponds by considering all the relative valuation factors that make each class distinctive. As in a college class, where there is some weighting on homework, midterm exams, the final exam, and perhaps class participation to rank each student relative to the current and previous populations of students, so here there would be some form of weighting market size, profitability margins, time to market, completeness of the IP package, and so forth.

Exhibit 5.4 is an illustration of how a population of three "F" category agreements, six "D" category agreements, and so forth, can be used to establish a category value (in this example, the described range of royalty rates for each corresponding classification). Any opportunity to be valued ("NEW") would then be placed in the most appropriate category based on how it best fits to the corresponding population of agreements.

With the above Classified Value embodiment of Rating/Ranking we are establishing ***ranks*** of comparables and then, by locating our NEW licensing opportunity within the most appropriate class we are establishing a value (or value range) based on its relative **ranking**. Implicit in this process is that the agreements in each classification share certain characteristics that caused them to exhibit the financial outcome (the shown running royalty range); if there is no rational cause and effect between any agreement and the outcome, there will not be a basis for making a comparison with the to-be-classified opportunity.

As we will see in this chapter, and can anticipate from this discussion, Factor Analysis comparing a potential transaction ("B") with an existing one ("A") is simpler to implement, and thus more readily done, than Classified Value where a potential

	Category				
	F	D	C	B	A
Royalty Range	< 0.5%	0.5% - 3%	3% - 6%	6%-10%	> 10%
Agreements	*F1*	*D1*	*C1*	*B1*	*A1*
	F2	*D2*	*C2*	*B2*	*A2*
	F3	*D3*	*C3*	*B3*	
		D4	*C4*	*B4*	
		D5	*C5*	*B5*	
		D6	*C6*		

EXHIBIT 5.4 Illustration of Classified Value Using Rating/Ranking

transaction ("NEW") is assigned an appropriate group among pre-created classes of value (or value range) based on numerous existing transactions.

Groups and Grouping as a Fundamental Knowledge Forming Process

It is helpful to begin our development of the Rating/Ranking Method by first thinking about a fundamental idea—namely, that of forming groups or matching "like with like." This is such a common idea that there are many everyday words used for such assemblages of "like" things: groups, categories, classes, clusters, families, populations, genres, tranches, and more colloquially, buckets, with their associated verb forms such as grouping, clustering, classifying, and even bucketizing and tranching. *Tranches*, from the French word for slice (*tranche*), is commonly used for distinguishing groups of securities by their relative risk level, a purpose that fits well in our valuation context.

The immediate issue in forming groups (tranches) is dealing with individual uniqueness. Even a simple snowflake is said to be unlike any other ever formed. With people, we are cautioned early and often of the perils of stereotyping (another term for grouping). Even mass manufactured items are not truly identical despite best efforts to make them so; in fact, business processes such as Six Sigma have been created to minimize such variability while recognizing that total elimination of any item-to-item variation is not exactly possible. How, then, is it meaningful to form, identify, and then characterize any group of distinguishable individual members?

The first part of the answer has to do with the motivation for forming groups. The world is too vast, too complicated, too detailed for us to exist in it without some means of simplifying it. Creating groups out of discrete entities is a necessity to grasping reality. Almost every noun would be meaningless if we did not recognize that unique examples are usefully subsumed within classifications.[17] The answer to the second part, how can this be done, relates to the ability to make judgments either objectively or subjectively. Let us consider some group-making examples.

1. *Biology*. In the study of biology, we immediately recognize the existence of species, a way of describing groups, such that all cows are different but they can for many purposes be treated as the group "cow," which is different from the group we know as "horse," despite certain physical similarities. For various purposes, however, both cow and horse groups are subdivided into other groups, using some key distinguishing feature; for certain purposes it is worth distinguishing a Clydesdale from a Thoroughbred, and much money is invested in distinguishing among Thoroughbreds between "winners" and "hayburners." Biologists have systemized such distinctions for all living entities by the Linnaen Classification system (named in honor of Carl Linne, b. 1707), which distinguishes groups by species, of which about 1.5 million have been identified so far.

   Underlying such classification enabling systematic studies, we know that every material thing is discrete. Every object you and I have ever seen or known is made up of just three things: two quarks (named "up" and "down"; scientists do have a sense of humor), and the electron. Discreteness is not just a human predilection. Those three fundamental things in turn make up the 100 or so elements, which are assembled into a myriad of different molecules. In human biology, just four of these molecules (designated by the letters G, C, T, A, the first letter of nearly unpronounceable chemical acids) define literally who we are by means of a helical sequence (DNA) of three billion (for humans) such G-C or T-A molecule pairs that, among other things, create the 100 trillion individual, distinct cells that comprise our body. Everything in the universe, including us, and possibly time itself, is made of discrete, individual units. In a universe of discreteness, at the level of such discreteness, there are not any "tweeners."

2. *Music.* We understand that tones are perceptions of vibration frequencies in the range of our auditory capacity, and can be any arbitrary frequency in such range. However, we have settled on specifically identified notes—which we identify, in Western music, by letters A, B, C, ...G, and their flats and sharps—so all the music we know is made up of just seven (or 12 counting sharps and flats) notes in any given "key." ("A," for example, is defined by the discrete value of 440 Hz). Music can only exist if the continuum of sound frequencies has been made discrete into particular frequencies, which are then used as building blocks of tunes.

   But further, we recognize that musical pieces (sequences of notes) can themselves be classified by "genre" such as folk, country, rock, classical, and so on... In the social networking system known as MySpace®, it currently provides 127 such identified musical genres by which one can describe one's likes and dislikes. Gracenote®, used by Apple's iTunes and others, creates even more finely categorized ranks by identifying 1800 genres including "nerd core hip hop" (perhaps an acquired taste). So, even though each piece of music is by definition unique, and there appears to be literally millions of different musical pieces in Western music alone, we find it useful to have a means of making distinct groups that allow us to classify (***rank***) any new musical piece. Further, we can then ***rate*** each musical number within each ***rank*** by applying some objective (or, in the case of music, more likely subjective) standard.
3. *Patents.* A patent is by definition a discrete, unique entity. Being unique it is individually identifiable, currently by a seven-digit number. The U.S. Patent and Trademark Office (USPTO) has issued more than seven million such patents since 1790, a number which grows by about 3,000 a week. Yet, despite each patent's inherent uniqueness, the USPTO creates (some) order out of this vast number, by a classification system whereby each patent is assigned to one or more groups (classes and subclasses) of "like" patents by technology (or "art"). In 2006, there were approximately 470 technology classes ("primary" or "original") further subdivided into 159,000 subclasses.
4. *Dead Celebrities.* There is value associated with a famous individual, or institution, being linked with a product or service. Although by definition, each individual is unique, for valuation purposes it is possible to create discrete categories. This example is simpler with deceased celebrities as there is a fixed 'body' of work. Various organizations provide rating/ranking services on such individuals. Perhaps the most well known is the Q Score, developed in 1963 by Marketing Evaluations, Inc. Every two years the commercial attractiveness of some 150 deceased celebrities is assessed by surveys conducted with a panel of U.S. consumer households, using a four level scoring system: very good, good, fair, and poor. The results are then expressed as a Q score, which can then be sliced and diced by socioeconomic ranges associated with the respondents. So, although Edward G. Robinson (forever known by his movie line "you dirty rat"),

Jacques Cousteau (undersea exploration), and Chris Farley (let's call it lowbrow humor) all received the same Q score (23). Mr. Farley scored quite high (26) in another metric, "negative Q score," and there is no doubt very different scores for different categories of respondents.

5. *Businesses*. A company (corporation) is a legal creation of a discrete entity that has been created for some business purpose.[18] It is said that every company exists to find and serve a customer. For most companies, this means serving some population or category of individuals or other companies, not an assemblage of individual customers. This leads to customer groups, commonly known as market segments, such as "early adopters," or "soccer moms" (or "NASCAR® dads"), "boomers," "Gen X," and "DINCs" (double income, i.e. two working adults, and no children). The core idea is that a company needs to find a category of individuals toward which it can address its find-a-customer energies because, in most circumstances, it is simply impractical to consider a company's customers as unique individuals. Of course the identity of each customer purchase may be known, and may need to be known; but, in most circumstances, a company cannot operate effectively by creating, selling, and supporting products unique to each of their thousands of customers.[19]

   This process of identifying a company's target market segment(s) is considered to be one of the important developments in forming a strategy, because it enables a company to organize itself around a coherent mission, namely creating and making products that satisfy the needs of its target segment(s) better (in some important ways) than its competitors. How can a segment (group) be meaningful when every individual in it is unique, as we all are? This becomes possible when and if some key identifying feature, or features, are approximately common within a group, but which is distinguishable from another or all other groups, and such feature (or features) can be connected to something actionable by the company seeking to serve a segment. Distinguishing features can be geographical (residents of large metropolitan areas), demographic (middle age career females, or very high net worth retirees), psychographic (individuals who seek environmentally friendly products), or some other category. Creating such market segments does not mean that, say, *every* "middle age, affluent career female" is alike but that as a group there can be a sufficient similarity in certain products each such group of women want that it is useful to think of the group as a single entity for purposes of product development and marketing.

6. *Debt Securities*. A bond is a debt instrument that embodies the promise of a specific debtor to pay a specific lender an amount(s) of money in the future in exchange for some lesser amount given to the debtor now. Such debt obligates the debtor to repay regardless of what happened to the debtor or the money lent. For loans to companies the lender is "senior" to a holder of an equity (stock) interest and has priority over equity holders in any recovery even in the case of bankruptcy. Most debtors are likely sincere in their promise to repay. However—and when it comes to human, or corporate, behavior there is always a "however"—not all promises carry the same probability of fulfillment, either in terms of capacity or intentionality. The U.S. government is borrowing money all the time under the promise of repayment (and as of early 2009, it will owe more than $11 trillion). Because such loans (securities known as T-bills, notes, and bonds) are backed by "the full faith and credit" of the U.S. government, and

its underlying economy, and there has been no record of default in more than 200 years, such government securities are perceived as low in risk as is likely to be found in human existence; this perception is commonly characterized by referencing the interest rate associated with a U.S. government security as the "risk free rate of return."[20]

Would it make sense for a lender to offer loans to all prospective borrowers at the same interest rates as U.S. government securities? Although we will consider this question in some detail in Chapter 7 for the Discount Cash Flow Method (Method 4), it should be obvious that making distinctions about the types of loans and borrowers is necessary for prudent lenders. Yet the number of bonds are so numerous, and the market for them so widespread and active, the marketplace has created opportunities for companies to create order out of chaos by assigning all rated bonds into various risk categories. An important class of such rating/ranking companies is Nationally Recognized Statistical Rating Organizations (NRSROs) recognized by the U.S. Securities and Exchange Commission. Three major NRSROs are Moody's Investor Service (Moody's), Standard and Poor's (S&P), and Fitch Ratings. Exhibit 5.5 shows a comparison of the classification systems used by these three companies. Considering the three "long term" columns (generally used for debts longer than one year), all three NRSROs distinguish ten tranches for aggregate classification known as "investment grade" debt and ten tranches (except Moody's which uses nine) for the riskiest aggregation known as "speculative" (colloquially referred to as "junk") debt.

Exhibit 5.5 is an example of the Classified Value instantiation of Rating/Ranking. The purpose of such ratings is to guide potential investors in pricing such bonds by scaling the required rate of return with the risk of default, and by gaining insight by the use of market comparables for like rated bonds. Any new debt being issued can then be individually classified as belonging to one of the above tranches and, so, of comparable risk and value. Exhibit 5.6 is an example of how each tranche correlates to first year default percentages based on data embedded in a *Wall Street Journal* article about a particular type of debt instrument known as a Collateralized Debt Obligation (CDO).

We will consider these ratings in more detail in Chapter 7 in our discussion of risk and return. In 2007, many of such CDO classifications were found to be unreliable. And, so, we will return to this example and others in Chapter 12 in our consideration of uncertainty and judgment matters.

7. *Equities.* Stock shares represent partial ownership interest in the issuing company. Unlike bonds, there is not even a promise of financial return on such ownership, and as such they are generally considered to be riskier investments associated with greater potential rewards. There are numerous equity analysts of publicly traded stocks whose work is to classify all equity investment opportunities in the industry they cover into various categories for investment guidance purposes. A simple, three level tranching is, buy / sell / hold, or, equivalently expressed by other terms, outperform / perform / underperform. Such analysts review massive amounts of financial data for each ranked company to compare, for instance, current after-tax earnings to current stock price (P/E ratio), growth in revenues, earnings, and costs, market positioning, capital intensity, and so forth. At the end of all such considerations, the judgment that is sought is this: Is buying (or selling) this particular equity at its present price a wise use of

Moody's		S&P		Fitch		
Long term	Short term	Long term	Short term	Long term	Short term	
Aaa	P–1	AAA	A–1+	AAA	A1+	Prime
Aa1		AA+		AA+		High Grade
Aa2		AA		AA		
Aa3		AA–		AA–		
A1		A+	A–1	A+	A1	Upper Medium Grade
A2		A		A		
A3	P–2	A–	A–2	A–	A2	
Baa1		BBB+		BBB+		Lower Medium Grade
Baa2	P–3	BBB	A–3	BBB	A3	
Baa3		BBB–		BBB–		
Ba1	Not Prime	BBB	B	BB+	B	Noninvestment Grade Speculative
Ba2		BB		BB		
Ba3		BB–		BB–		
B1		B+		B+		Highly Speculative
B2		B		B		
B3		B–		B–		
Caa		CCC+	C	CCC	C	Substantial risks
Ca		CCC				Extremely speculative
C		CCC–				In default, with little prospect for recovery
/		D	/	DDD	/	In default
/				DD		
/				D		

EXHIBIT 5.5 Comparison of the Debt Ratings Used by Three Large NRSROs

capital? This question is commonly answered by grouping all "buy" (or "strong buy") ranked equities into a Classified Value tranche, and distinguishing such tranche from other equity tranches (e.g., "hold" or "sell" or any other actionable distinction). As we will discuss later, there are numerous examples were such judgment later proved unreliable. But this only leads us to reassess our categories and the bases used for rating/ranking, but not to abandon either hope or this methodology.

Charles Schwab, the financial services company, has developed a proprietary rating/ranking tool that groups some 3,000 publicly traded stocks into five

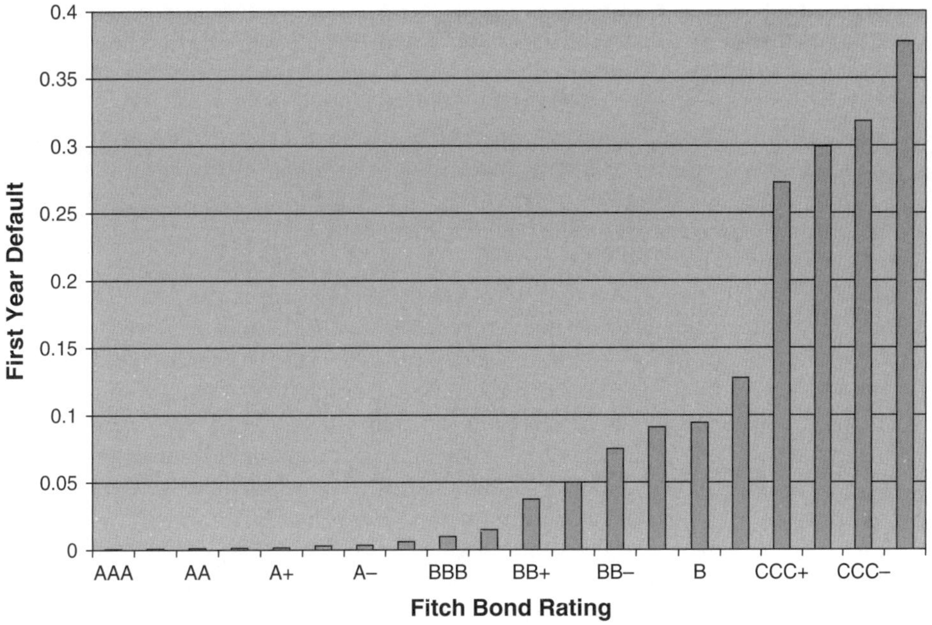

EXHIBIT 5.6 Projected First Year Default Percentage for Fitch CDO Ratings

Source: Based on data contained in "Wall Street Wizardry Amplified Credit Crisis," *Wall Street Journal*, December 27, 2007, p. 1.

categories: 20 percent top ranked stocks as "A" stocks, 20 percent high ranked stocks as "B," 20 percent as "C," 20 percent as "D," and 20 percent as "E." According to the company, it uses a computer program to automatically assess these stocks based upon 24 different factors. As with the above bond ratings, such approach is an example of Classified Value Rating/Ranking.

A different approach used by equity analysts providing stock picking advice also uses five tranches: strong buy (also assigned a value 1.0), moderate buy, hold, moderate sell, and strong sell (value 5.0). Such expression of rating/ranking is not constrained by any fixed percentage in each of the five categories. A common use of these rankings is in assessing the perceived investment attractiveness of a specific stock compared to some norm; websites providing investor resources, such as www.moneycentral.com/investor, can then be searched for a specific equity, such as Apple, Inc. (AAPL): as of this writing, AAPL has a rating/ranking of 21 analysts, with a mean recommendation of 1.74 (1.0 is "strong buy," and 2.0 is "moderate buy"). Each analyst performs some version of Factor Analysis Rating/Ranking comparing the given equity to a baseline equity portfolio for which the recommendation would be "hold," suggesting that such portfolio would be expected to appreciate at overall market average rates.

Morningstar, Inc. is a company whose business is rating/ranking of stock and mutual fund investment opportunities. It uses a five star rating system for stocks based on the perceived attractiveness of the investment at the current stock price. Morningstar also rates the business risk of corresponding company. The comparative risks are distinguished as below average, average, above average, and speculative. The premise of value of a Morningstar rating/ranking derives from its ability to provide excess returns above some broad index such as the S&P 500. Morningstar reports such results for several investment strategies based on purchasing "five star" rated equities and selling them when they reach "three star" or "one star" ratings based (presumably) on an increase in the stock's price making subsequent investment unattractive. For 2006, Morningstar's reported trailing year, time-weighted returns for either of these two strategies for each trailing year (one through five) exceeded the corresponding S&P 500 value.[21]

Although the details of such debt and equity rating/ranking methodologies are proprietary, the tranching is published (in some cases only to subscribers) so, the results can be tracked and evaluated. In the above example given by Morningstar on equities it ranked, the predictive value compared to, say, an S&P 500 basket of equities, appears to be modest. In 2007, the rating/ranking of mortgage backed debt aggregated and sliced in CDOs has been seen to have woefully under-predicted initial default rates (one important expression of risk). This has led the NRSROs in many cases to dramatically revise downward their rating/rankings of such instruments. This certainly provides evidence, if one needed it, that not all rating/ranking expressions are predictive or useful. Yet, here is a prediction: the models used to create such rating/rankings will be revised and improved, and will again be relied upon, perhaps with more humility by both the tranchers and the users, especially with financial instruments (such as CDOs) for which experience has been limited.

What about commercially available valuation rating/ranking of technology IP? For reasons discussed in Chapter 3 (regarding "the Box" and "the Wheelbarrow") each dealmaking asset can be complex in both its offering and desired form of payment, very unlike both bonds and equities which are widely rated/ranked as discussed above. There have been certain organizations who claim to be able to value in some way the selling price of an individual patent by some universal scoring methodology. However the absence of a market transparency such as exists with stocks and bonds makes it impossible to know whether any of such proposed systems reflects what even bare patents are valued by sellers and buyers. (This matter will be addressed again in Chapter 9). This circumstance then leads us to the need to create a rating/ranking methodology that we can develop and apply on technology IP which we wish to offer for sale or which we are seeking to buy.

The Toolkit

Creating segments or groups is a tool applicable to many purposes. It can be used to distinguish types of technology commercialization risks, products that can be formed from an underlying technology, markets to which products can be sold, and so forth.

As we will discuss in later chapters, identifying and analyzing segments can lead to a deeper understanding of risks and opportunities, but this potential virtue is always balanced by the additional complexity introduced.

Using Rating/Ranking to Value Technology: Factor Assessment

Given this weight of diverse examples of the Rating/Ranking, how might we use it as a methodology for valuing any particular technology? Let us first consider the simpler instantiation, namely "factor assessment."

The five elements that comprise the Rating/Ranking Method are as follows:

1. Scoring criteria
2. Scoring system
3. Scoring scale
4. Weighting factors
5. Decision table

Scoring Criteria

Examples of criteria that are used in licensing valuations are market size, patent protection, and stage of development. A further discussion of useful criteria is given later in this chapter in the section entitled, "Developing Criteria for Using Rating/Ranking for Valuation of Technology."

Scoring System

Many different kinds of scoring systems are used, and the choice is a matter of taste and experience. Perhaps the most common system is the one to five point system, similar to the one to five stars scoring examples, with five as the best, one as the worst, and three representing equivalence to the reference condition or some kind norm or average. Its appeal may be related to people's familiarity with college GPAs. It is also very simple as there are only two levels "better" and two levels "worse" than the reference condition (the score of three).

Such scale is sometimes referred to as a Likert Scale, named after Rensis Likert.[22] One limitation with the above one to five point system is dealing with in-between values. In surveys—a common manifestation of Likert Scales—it is often useful to compel responses to one of the five numbers. However, in valuing technology, finer distinctions can be drawn, which of course can be expressed by decimal values (3.5 and so forth). Another alternative is to use a one to seven point Likert scale. Here a four represents equivalence to the reference condition, five is "better," six is "much better," and seven is "outstanding" (and vice versa for three, two, one), thus permitting three levels of "better" and "worse."

Others, more digitally inclined, seem to prefer the zero to ten point scale. For obsessive compulsives, a zero to 100 point scale is a possibility.

Right hemisphere people seem to lean toward nonnumerical methods. The simplest such approach used is H/M/L for high/medium/low (i.e., better, same, or poorer) which forces the decision to one level better and worse. A variant of this approach is to use symbols such "+" for "better," "++" for "much better," "=" for comparable, and similar negative signs for "worse" and "much worse"; this has the same effect in terms of levels as the one to five scale but avoids attaching numerical significance to the outcome. An average of votes or factors in the one to five scale system could result in being midway between a 4 and 5 and, so expressed as a

4.5; in the "+" expression approach this would have to be expressed awkwardly as "midway between a + and ++." On the zero to ten scale, a like outcome could be "eight."

For the Crayola® regressives there is even the possibility of colors: green for "better," blue for "much better," yellow for "worse," and red for "much worse" (no color, or white, for equivalence to the standard). Alternatively, for each factor both the comparable and the subject opportunity can each be judged with an appropriate color using some general notion of all typical valuation opportunities. With such alternative approach, the comparable license could have an abundance of green factors. Regardless of the approach the use of colors is effective when presenting findings to either young children or management (there's a Dilbert®-like cartoon yet to be written here). Although generally less useful for valuation purposes, color-based rating/ranking can be very useful for opportunity Discovery and Dealmaking because red can be used to designate a "fatal flaw" and blue a truly outstanding opportunity (such as a one out of 20, top five percent rating), and yellow can flag a key unresolved issue which by further investigation might be converted into a positive green or a fatal red. Opportunities, or Dealmaking targets, represented by mainly yellow and green rated factors are likely not worth pursuing.

A multidimensional representation of rating/ranking can be illuminating. A simple form common in management consulting is the two-by-two matrix, creating four quadrants. The two columns could then represent "high" and "low" (say) intrinsic value assuming no risk, and the two rows then representing "high" and "low" risk, with the comparables centered at the middle. Then each factor, say F1 through F6, is in the appropriate quadrant or even micro-positioning within each quadrant. An alternative is a three-by-three matrix (which is the format of the game "tic tac toe") with the comparables occupying the middle square. Then a labeled tick mark for each factor is assigned to one of the nine cells. Whether using two-by-two or three-by-three matrices we are, by this representation visually portraying how the subject opportunity ranks and rates comparable to the comparable or comparables positioned at the center with respect to the important value factors. A variation of this visual tool would be to locate multiple comparables, or groups of comparables, in the various squares. So if one had available, say five potential comparables from a Method 1 analysis, one could locate them in respective cells of, say, a three-by-three matrix. If the valuation data and risk profiles of the five comparables were very similar then they could all belong to a common cell, in which case it would be best to use the middle cell as above. However if there was notable variability in the valuations and overall risk profile these five might be located in three or more different cells. Then each relevant valuation faction of the subject opportunity would then be located in the appropriate cell in comparison the locations of the five comparables. The visual result then guides a judgment as to how best to weight and compare the available comparable valuation data.

These multidimensional mappings are a kind of Likert Scale showing better-than or worse-than but using graphical displays. Additional dimensions can be added by using denotations with circles or other shapes of whose relative size represents other rating/ranking factors or certain general aspects of the analysis such as confidence level. Another way of expressing Factor Analysis would follow the format shown in Exhibit 5.7, which is an abbreviated chart from a *New York Times* portrayal of the

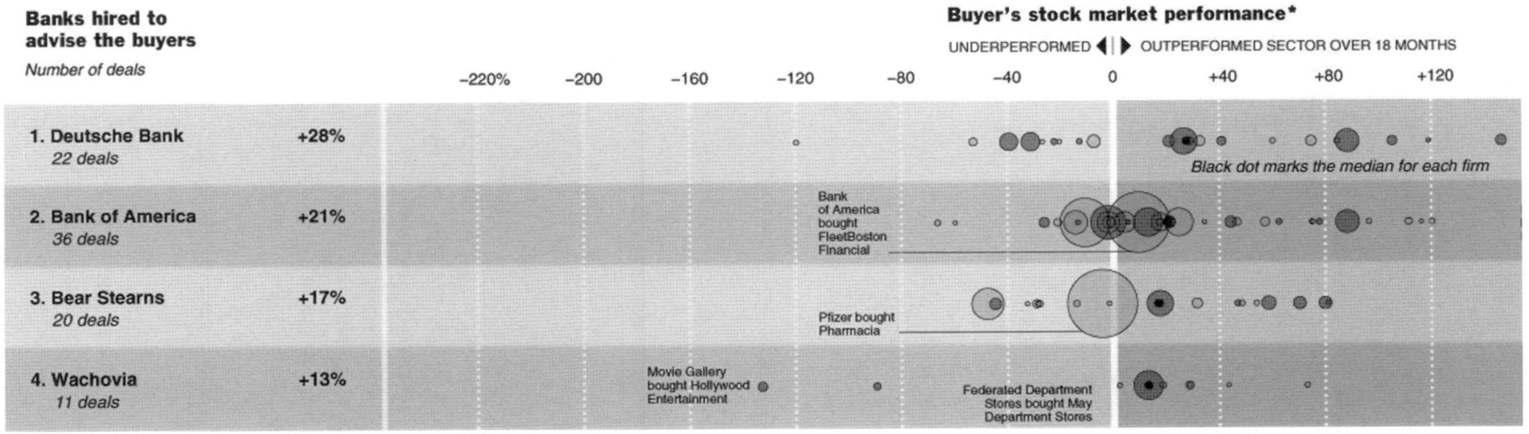

EXHIBIT 5.7 A Multi-Dimensional Likert-Like Assessment of Merger & Acquisition Returns

Source: "Looking Back, How Good Was That Deal?," *New York Times*, August 9, 2007.

relationship between an M&A (Mergers & Acquisition) buyer's stock performance and the investment bank who acted as their adviser.

Applying such format to Factor Analysis of Rating/Ranking each row would represent a distinct valuation factor, with the zero center-value at the top of the chart being the ranking of the comparable with respect to each such factor, and a single circle representing the ranking whereby the diameter of the circle could represent the weighting (importance) of such factor and one could use color for the circle to represent confidence level of the ranking (blue being metaphysical certitude, metaphorically speaking, down to red as best guess).

Although there is some arbitrariness about the choice of a scoring system, it is actually important and serious to select one and to standardize it. The power of Rating/Ranking increases with experience and a database of previous determinations. It would defeat some of the value of the method to make ad hoc selections of scales.

The advantages of a Likert Scale are:

- Clearly scores opportunities above and below a reference point (such as a comparable), which is the essence of the rating/ranking method.
- Can create any number of levels above and below the reference point (a five-point scale has two above and below, a seven-point has three above and below, etc.), allowing any level of precision desired or warranted.
- Numerical normalized result can be used to create priorities when evaluating a portfolio of opportunities.
- The individual scores on each of the factors can be used in preparing for a negotiation.
- It just looks like a serious process, perhaps because of the echo of college grading.

Some issues with the use of Likert Scale are:

- Quantification can be misleading ("exactly what do I do with a 4.0?").
- It does not overtly reflect the catastrophic effect a fatal flaw can have on value. Suppose on an IP protection score, an opportunity receives a 1 because it has none, but it scores high on all other factors. Just determining a weighted average score will obscure the fact that the opportunity is likely to have no (or little) value.[23]
- It can too easily let mediocrity slide by on each of the factors so that the results are commonly "better than average" (like Garrison Keillor's Lake Wobegon, where all the kids are above average), something like "gentleman's C's."

Ten (or 100) point scales have certain advantages for valuation approaches of rating/ranking:

- In many contexts, from political punditry to quantifying a dining experience, it seems somehow more natural to ask reviewers or a panel to express their bottom line opinion on a zero to ten scale.[24]

- The best available comparable license, or the average of the available comparables, need not be ranked as a 5. If it is believed that such comparable is a relatively lowly valued opportunity compared to the range of opportunities commonly valued by the rating/ranking team, one can "assign" such comparable a ranking of (say) 3.
- Midpoint scoring is less ambiguous than with Likert scores. On a five-point Likert Scale, a 4.5 score can perhaps represent a halfway point between a "better than average-4" and a "much better than average-5," but what then does a 4.2 or a 4.8 mean? Using a ten-point scale, there is an implicit proportionality with all scores making rational distinctions for 11 cardinal numbers as well as any intermediate decimal value.

The advantages of the four-color (Crayola) scheme is that it overcomes some of the previously listed disadvantages:

- Fatal flaws are red and obvious.
- Avoids quantification battles and misuse of quantification results by Likert or ten-point systems (but does not avoid the need for making distinctions).
- Highlights by the factors scored as yellow those questions that could be usefully analyzed further to understand why they're not green or what key information is missing that could be found by further investigation.
- The use of blue to designate which factors, if any, strongly favor the subject opportunity or its reverse because the comparable license is itself blue with respect to this factor.
- It is a great management communication tool.

The multidimensional expressions have similar visualization advantages to the color approach:

- On a single page one can readily apprehend a summary of a lengthy analysis.
- Enables many creative means of expression by using tick marks of various shapes, sizes, and colors.
- Finds particular utility as a "sanity check" (when the Rating/Ranking analysis has been completed, factor by factor, and one examines the summary of one's conclusions does it appear to cohere, or does it cause one to reexamine certain of the factor analyses).

The disadvantages of the color and multidimensional schemes include:

- The better-than and worse-than categories can be too broad to be meaningful.
- There is an inherent fuzziness about the ranking compared to Likert ten-point systems.
- It is not easy to express a bottom line answer as some calculation of average with one of the quantitative schemes.
- Although all rating/ranking schemes have as one of their challenges being the conversion of the outcome of the analysis into valuation dollars, this challenge is perhaps greater with these graphical systems.

Scoring Scales

Two types of scoring scales can be used: subjective and objective. Subjective scales merely ask an expert or expert panel to consider the described circumstance through the "eyes" of each of the criteria and assign a score based upon the selected scoring system (i.e., one to five). Objective scales can be created when enough experience has been gained with predicting values using Rating/Ranking and comparing such predictions with actual outcomes. After numerous experiences, it is possible to estimate (or in some cases derive) numerical scales; when derived scales can be created they are commonly known as influence coefficients. It is possible to use a mixture of subjective and objective scales for any given rating/ranking valuation.

When subjective scales are used, an expert panel of some sort has to be established. Setting up such a panel requires some thought and planning. If the number of people on the panel is small, say two or three, the panels tend to operate by consensus rather than by vote. This seems to work best when all the parties are in the same room and participate in an active discussion and debate before proposing scores and reaching consensus. If a larger number of people are involved, then voting and averaging seems to work better. In such cases it may be difficult to assemble everyone in the same room and commit the time to hear all opinions and debate. However, when voting remotely, it is possible, even likely, that such voters will not have considered important aspects of certain matters, calling into question how much weight to attach to their vote.[25] Sometimes political necessity requires the larger panel. Decision making in large groups has been the subject of much research, though none known in the context of technology valuation. The recommended approach would be a panel of three to five persons, at least half of which (two to three) are regular participants in such technology valuation processes, and the balance are other needed experts and stakeholders. The optimal result is a weighted opinion of the regulars over the experts and stakeholders.

Weighting Factors

The weighting factor is used as a means of assigning a higher importance to some criteria and a lower importance to others. For example, one could choose ten criteria to be scored and deem that one particular criterion (say, market size) is twice as important as any of the other nine; in this case, the score for the market size criterion would be doubled, effectively (but intentionally) counting it twice. What should be carefully avoided is unintentionally counting the same idea or criteria multiple times. This might happen if one criterion was "market size," another was "projected sales," another was "likelihood of use for other applications," and another was "likelihood of sales in other countries"; this is tantamount to scoring "market size" four times. With the use two-by-two or other matrices With multidimensional schemes should as two-by-two matrices such weighting can be expressed by the size of the tick mark such as circles of varying diameter to express relative importance as factors. With a little careful thought, which is exactly what the Rating/Ranking Method is designed to aid, an impressive amount of useful information can be displayed on a single chart. Exhibit 5.7 given above is one such example. A famous, and highly admirable, charting example is one done in 1869 by Edward Joseph Minard of Napoleon's retreat from his disastrous invasion of Russia 1812–3, reproduced in

Edward R. Tufte's excellent book *The Visual Display of Quantitative Information*, 2nd Ed. (Graphics Press, 2001); the Minard chart can be seen on Mr. Tufte's web site: http://www.edwardtufte.com/tufte/posters. Although the "valuation" portrayed in Minard's chart is of a very different kind than our interest here, one can grasp the complex story and see the essence of the cost (more than 500,000 men on the side of the attacking French grand army) and the key drivers of the campaign's failure (long supply routes and bitter cold).

Decision Table

The end result of a rating/ranking process using one of the quantification schemes is a column of raw scores entered by the expert(s) next to each criterion, which is then multiplied by the respective weighting to obtain a weighted score, and then all the weighted scores are added to determine the rated/ranked score. For convenience, often the rated/ranked score is normalized so that, for example, on the one to five score system, an "average" score would yield a 3.00. This simply makes interpretation easier.

The issue then becomes this: How does one actually put a result to use and aid a valuation? It is helpful to consider what is being accomplished by the Rating/Ranking Method. In essence, we can visualize the process as creating an "industry standard" in the following sense. The method requires a comparable or reference agreement or cluster of agreements in order for the scoring to take place because each score is always in the context of a point of reference. A comparable deal could be one specific technology which was licensed under known terms, or a general understanding of a population of related (in the sense of belonging to a category) technologies licensed. In effect, this method assumes that the technology being valued "belongs" to the category of the comparable deal. The scoring and calculations are means of creating quality or value differences from the comparable deal. The result is similar to saying the technology being valued is "like" a 1995 Ford Taurus, but its overall quality differs from the norm of that category by the rating/ranking score.

With multidimensional schemes there are several ways to quantify the result. The most obvious is applying a ten-point scale as a judgment to finally-determined locus. So, for instance, in a three-by-three matrix, if every factor for the subject opportunity is determined to be in the top/right-most cell (the most-favorable cell of the nine), then such a result can be assigned the value of 10, representing the highest possible score, where the comparable is a 5, and the bottom/left-most cell is then a zero. With a normal outcome where various factors end up all over the place, some judgment as to average would be required. If both the comparable and the subject opportunity have been ranked (in comparison to large, unspecific population of valuation projects), then both the comparable and subject opportunity can be similarly scored. The specific score assigned in either case is not itself noteworthy because such score will need to be translated to a valuation, as will be discussed.

At one level, rating/ranking as a valuation method can appear to be so ad hoc and so subject to intentional and unintentional biases that it is a pointless exercise. However, as we reviewed in the beginning of this chapter, Rating/Ranking is how decisions are often made in many highly complex situations. There is usually no differential equation or computer program that can answer our questions about value or choice and, so, we must rely on some method of applying judgment with available facts or other points of comparison.

Here are eight reasons why the Rating/Ranking Method is used and valued:

1. It causes one to prepare for negotiation by thinking through the relevant factors that make up licensing value.
2. It facilitates discussions with other valuation experts as it focuses on the key components of value and what is known (and not known) and good (and not good) about the subject technology.
3. It can be useful in explaining to nonexpert stakeholders how the valuation was reached.
4. With experience, the method increases in value. As one sees more and more outcomes and develops more experience with rating and ranking, the structure of the method enables one to make more insightful comparisons. The method becomes a tool for creating a storehouse of one's own licensing experience.
5. It is easy to use and can, with a good benchmark(s) and appropriate criteria, yield useful results.
6. For all its subjectivity, it is a tool in the toolkit of the licensing professional and no tool should be ignored (and, in this regard, it complements the more quantitative methods considered in Chapters 7 and 8).
7. It can lead to strategies for increasing the value of the technology by identifying important missing components of a potential deal, or reducing the risk (uncertainty) by further research or inquiry to improve a low score on a particular criterion.
8. During or after negotiations, an already completed Rating/Ranking valuation can be useful in assessing the need for a re-valuation, or a "Plan B."

Developing Criteria for Using Rating/Ranking for Valuation of Technologies

One of the critical steps in employing the Rating/Ranking Method is selecting appropriate criteria. Like other aspects of this method, the identification of such criteria is a matter of judgment. For the method to be effective, one generally seeks to use five or more criteria.

A set of criteria widely cited in legal contexts is the 15 "Georgia Pacific Factors."[26] These were developed by a court for the purposes of determining a reasonable royalty.[27] These factors are presented in Exhibit 5.8. Bob Goldscheider has written an extensive review article on the use of such factors in litigation contexts.[28]

Factors 1 and 2 are expressions of the first method we considered, the Industry Standard Method. Factor 8 is applicable to Rating/Ranking and will be also considered in the Discounted Cash Flow Method and the Monte Carlo Method (Chapters 7 and 8, respectively). Factor 11 is primarily relevant in the context of a litigation matter. Aspects of Factors 12 and 13 will be considered in Chapter 6 under the Rules of Thumb Method, although these are also legitimate matters for use in the Rating/Ranking Method. Factor 14 is itself a summary statement of the use of this Rating/Ranking Method. Factor 15 is the outcome of the valuation process and so can for our purposes can be considered as the objective, not a criterion. From

EXHIBIT 5.8 Georgia-Pacific Corp. v. U.S. Plywood Corp. Factors Applicable to the Determination of Reasonable Royalties

1. The royalties received by the patentee for the licensing of the patent in suit, proving or tending to prove an established royalty.
2. The rates paid by the licensee for the use of other patents comparable to the patent in suit.
3. The nature and scope of the license, as exclusive or non-exclusive; or as restricted or nonrestricted in terms of territory or with respect to whom the manufactured product may be sold.
4. The licensor's established policy and marketing program to maintain his patent monopoly by not licensing others to use the invention or by granting licenses under special conditions designed to preserve that monopoly.
5. The commercial relationship between the licensor and licensee, such as, whether they are competitors in the same territory in the same line of business; or whether they are inventor and promoter.
6. The effect of selling the patented specialty in promoting sales of other products of the licensee; the existing value of the invention to the licensor as a generator of sales of his non-patented items; and the extent of such derivative or convoyed sales.
7. The duration of the patent and the term of the license.
8. The established profitability of the product made under the patent; its commercial success; and its current popularity.
9. The utility and advantages of the patent property over the old modes or devices, if any, that had been used for working out similar results.
10. The nature of the patented invention; the character of the commercial embodiment of it as owned and produced by the licensor; and the benefits to those who have used the invention.
11. The extent to which the infringer has made use of the invention; and any evidence probative of the value of that use.
12. The portion of the profit or of the selling price that may be customary in the particular business or in comparable businesses to allow for the use of the invention or analogous inventions.
13. The portion of the realizable profit that should be credited to the invention as distinguished from non-patented elements, the manufacturing process, business risks, or significant features or improvements added by the infringer.
14. The opinion testimony of qualified experts.
15. The royalty that a licensor (such as the patentee) and a licensee (such as the infringer) would have agreed upon if both had been reasonably and voluntarily trying to reach an agreement; that is, the amount which a prudent licensee—who desired, as a business proposition, to obtain a license to manufacture and sell a particular article embodying the patented invention—would have been willing to pay as a royalty and yet be able to make a reasonable profit and which amount would have been acceptable by a prudent patentee who was willing to grant a license.

Source: 318 F. Supp. 1116 (S.D. N.Y. 1970).

this perspective, that would leave 10 of the 15 Georgia-Pacific Factors that could be directly applied in a rating/ranking approach: numbers 3, 4, 5, 6, 7, 8, 9, 10, 12, and 13.

In the Degnan and Horton survey cited in Chapter 4,[29] one of the surveyed questions was directed toward the use of such Georgia-Pacific Factors in performing

EXHIBIT 5.9 Frequency of Use of Georgia Pacific Factors by Licensing Professions According to a Survey

Importance of Factor	Licensing-In	Licensing-Out
1. Nature of the Protection	4.3	4.2
2. Utility Over Old Methods	4.2	4.2
3. Scope of Exclusivity	4.1	4.1
4. Licensee's Anticipated Profits	3.0	3.4
5. Commercial Success	3.7	3.7
6. Territory Restrictions	3.7	3.5
7. Comparable License Rates	3.6	3.7
8. Duration of Protection	3.3	3.1
9. Licensors' Anticipated Profits	2.6	3.1
10. Commercial Relationship	2.6	3.6
11. Tag Along Sales	2.1	2.1

Source: Stephen A. Degnan and Corwin Horton, "A Survey of Licensed Royalties," *les Nouvelles*, June 1997, pp. 91–96. Reprinted with permission from *les Nouvelles*.

valuations. The respondents were asked to rank each factor on a one to five scale with 5 designating very important and 1 not important; this in itself was a rating/ranking exercise. The results are shown in Exhibit 5.9. The two columns deal with the two licensing situations: selling and buying. The factors are ranked from highest to lowest, so the factor numbers do not correspond to the numbering of Exhibit 5.8.

The McGavock survey discussed in Chapter 4[30] also asked its participants similar questions. The findings on this matter are presented in Exhibit 5.10.

One massive list of 100 factors was developed by Tom Arnold.[31] Although Mr. Arnold did not present his list in the context of employing a formal rating/ranking approach, he did enumerate a comprehensive list of points to consider. Mr. Arnold's paper is provided in Appendix 5A and summarized in Exhibit 5.11. In this author's experience, 100 criteria are simply too many.

The separate assessment of 100 factors would be a long process with the results difficult to grasp and adequately characterize a reasonable predictive value. However, the list and article are commended as a reference in the consideration of which criteria are to be selected. (And, consideration of 100 factors would not set a record).[32]

For many licensing situations, the most important criteria include:

- *Estimated attainable market size and overall product profit margins.* Together, these two factors will strongly influence the earnings (commonly designated EBIT, Earnings Before Interest and Taxes as will be discussed in Chapter 7), which has a very strong influence on the value of a license.
- *Strength of the IP protection* (patents, trade secrets, copyrights, and trademarks). For exclusive licenses, this criterion plays an important role in creating defendable, unique products (and, thereby margins higher than commodity levels). For nonexclusive licenses, buyers consider this criterion because it affects what they would have to do if a license agreement is not entered into.

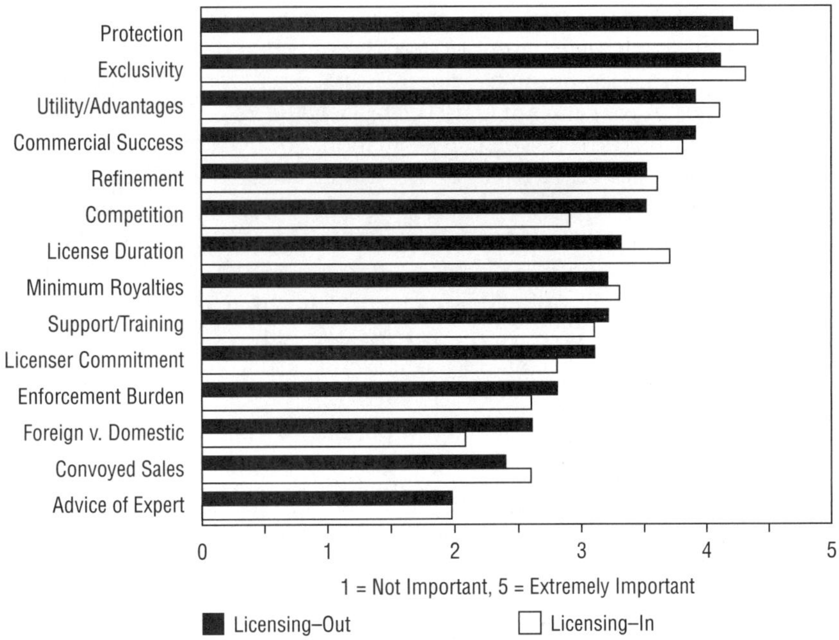

EXHIBIT 5.10 Importance of Various Factors on Royalty Rates

Source: McGavock, et al., "Factors Affecting Royalty Rates," *les Nouvelles*, June 1992, p. 109. Reprinted with permission from Daniel M. McGavock, Managing Director, InteCap, Inc.

EXHIBIT 5.11 A Checklist of 100 Factors in Setting the Value of a License: A Summary of the 100 Factors

Category	Example Factors	
I. Intrinsic Quality	Stage of development	Significance of the invention
	Marketability	Type of license
II. Protection	Scope of protections	Enforceability issues
	Contractual commitments	
III. Market	Market size	Distinctiveness of market
IV. Competition	Scope of protected market niche	Third party alternatives
V. Licensee Values	Grant-backs	Manufacturing, market, capital
VI. Finances profit	Manufacturer's margin	Costs of warranty negotiation
	Degree of design-around possible	Expected follow-on sales
VII. Risk	Exposure to liability suits	Technical obsolescence
	Exposure to patent validity suits	
VIII. Legal	Force majeure clauses	Favored nation clauses
	Duration of license	
IX. Requisition	Government restrictions on royalty and other terms	Currency movement restrictions

Source: Howrey, Simon, Arnold, & White LLP, Houston, Texas; paper presented at workshop at LES U.S.A./Canada Annual Meeting, Los Angeles, California, October 1986; published in les Nouvelles, March 1987, p. 34. Reprinted with permission from *les Nouvelles*.

- *Breadth of the IP protection*. This criterion addresses the economic impact of working just outside the patent or other IP protection. It is important to know, for example, that even in the case of a strong patent, one can operate outside the boundaries of the claims at (say) only a small decrease in some performance metric, or a small cost penalty; such a situation would clearly lower the value of a license in comparison to a circumstance where such a penalty were massive, or if practical operation was impossible. Also the completeness of patent coverage can be considered as part of this factor. Although one can never know what unpublished patents are pending nor, of course, new ones that may be filed, one can consider the risk of needing patent rights from a third party to practice the subject technology IP. Such risk can be assessed by considering the number and scope of prior art patents in the relevant technology areas. Likewise the value of know-how/trade secrets can be assessed. Although like unpublished patents it can sometimes be difficult to predict how difficult it would be to do independent re-creation of such know how IP.
- *Stage of development*. This criterion addresses three interrelated issues: How long will it be until the licensed invention will be producing profits? How much additional investment will need to be made prior to commercial introduction? What is the overall development risk?
- *Market environment*. Any invention being developed for commerce enters some kind of business environment. Is it in a generally growing market (or not)? Are there strong and aggressive competitors? Are there existing channels of delivery or will entirely new infrastructures have to be developed (for instance, to create value for a hydrogen burning auto engine technology, one would also need hydrogen "gas" stations, hydrogen mechanics, etc.).

Referring again to the McGavock survey in Exhibit 5.10, although there is some variation in perspective between seller and buyer, overall both sides appear to place the highest importance on "protection," "exclusivity," and "utility/advantages," and lowest importance on "advice of expert," "convoyed sales," and "foreign versus domestic."

Looking deeper at the importance of "protection," the Licensing Foundation (www.licensingfoundation.org), a 501c3 nonprofit creation of the Licensing Executives Society of the United States and Canada (LES), has conducted annual surveys questioning its membership on various important aspects of licensing. In the data taken for 2006, the following question was asked: "How important are the following types of IP in creating a competitive advantage for your organization?" The IP categories considered were: patents, know-how, trade secrets, copyrights, and trademarks. The respondents (LES members) are not primarily involved in non technology IP such as copyrights critical to music and other publishing industries, nor trademarks such as prevalent in the clothing industry. The respondents were asked to rate each form of IP on a modified five-level Likert Scale: Extremely Important, Moderately Important, Mildly Important, Not Important, or Not Applicable. The most important IP form identified was patents, which were rated as "extremely important" by 83 percent of the respondents; less than 6 percent of the respondents rated patents in the combined three lowest ranks (not applicable, not important, or mildly important). The next highest ranked form of IP was "know-how": 46 percent ranked it as "extremely important," 34 percent as "moderately important," and

12 percent as "mildly important." Next in ranking priority was "trade secrets" which was identified by 31 percent, 25 percent, and 18 percent, extremely important to mildly important, respectively.

These Licensing Foundation data also compared such responses by industry segment, and by size (large versus small, distinguished at 500 employees). Regarding the importance of patents, as might be expected the healthcare industry and the "small" companies exhibited a somewhat higher percentage as "extremely important": 89 percent and 88 percent, respectively. With respect to the relative importance of know how and trade secret IP the industrial segment put a higher priority on these forms: 58 percent and 74 percent as "extremely important."

When considering the relative importance of the strength and breadth of IP one needs to account for the relative importance of all the forms of IP as they are perceived to relate to the specific licensing situation. With pharmaceuticals where composition of matter patents are commonly sought, strong patents carry great weight. Likewise (generally speaking) patents which effectively cover some digital signal processing standard such as those established by the IEEE are more important than a patent covering just another way of operating an electronic circuit. On the other hand, a technology relating to a complex industrial manufacturing process is likely to exhibit greater value dependence on the know-how and trade secrets in the licensing package. However, there is no simplistic weighting recipe that can cover all IP asset situations. In each case the weighting as well as rating of the IP included must be assessed.

The selection of specific criteria, the scoring system, and weighting should be tuned for the particular industry in which the valuation is being made. Thus, there are multiple levels of expert judgment required with the Rating/Ranking Method:

- Selection of benchmark agreement or category of agreements
- Selection of criteria to be used
- Scoring system (what warrants a score of 4?)
- Weighting factors for each criterion which are used to multiply the raw scores
- Interpretation of the result (discussed later in this chapter).

This may appear daunting. Yet, with experience and expert help inside and outside the organization, this method can be very useful.

The Toolkit

Such Rating/Ranking scoring, weighting, and deciding method can be used in other Licensing D-V-D contexts. In Chapter 3, we discussed the difficulty of opportunity identification with technology when so many unknowns exist as its feasibility and market need. Yet some *Process* for deciding which opportunities are worth pursuing, even for analysis, is needed in most contexts simply because there are more potential ideas and opportunities than there is time and resources to pursue. Rating/Ranking, even on a highly preliminary basis, can be a ***Tool***

(*continued*)

(*Continued*)

to create two broad groups: those opportunities which are believed, on the basis of such analysis, to be worth pursuing at least initially, and those which are not.

In Chapter 7 we will see the important role that the quantification of risk plays in determining the value of a technology. Rating/Ranking will be illustrated there as a way of identifying risk categories, each of which are ascribed a different risk measure.

In Chapter 11 on the *Process* of Dealmaking one of the important tasks is prioritizing which potential buyer or even categories of potential buyers are best suited for extracting the value for the technology under consideration. Rating/Ranking is a useful Tool for distinguishing among many potential buyers.

Illustrations of Applying the Rating/Ranking Method

Consider an instance where one is attempting to value a new laser device for optical communications. The first step is to find a comparable, or an individual license agreement or group of agreements to which such a device generally "belongs." One would conduct reviews of one's own company files, search for published information (as discussed in Chapter 4), look for SEC filings (also Chapter 4), network with colleagues, and/or hire consultants who have developed license agreement databases or who are expert at conducting searches for finding comparable agreements. By some means, one must find at least one comparable in order to begin.

For the sake of this example, let us consider that this search has found an excellent comparable: a different technology for making a comparable laser device was found to have been licensed for $1 million upfront, and 5 percent royalty on the sale price of the entire laser device, with no rights to improvements, no grant-back rights, and no other significant financial factors. Further, let us assume that the criteria selected are as shown in Exhibit 5.12. As shown, it was determined that there were three different levels of weighting: one, two, or three. For this marketplace, the experience and expert opinion was that factors, two, four, and five which were notably more important than one and three, and significantly more so than six. Also

EXHIBIT 5.12 Example Use of Rating/Ranking Method

	Weighting (1-3)	Score (1-5)	Weighted Score
1. Market Size	2	3	6
2. Product Margins	3	5	15
3. IP Strength	2	4	8
4. IP Breadth	3	3	9
5. Stage of Development	3	2	6
6. Market Environment	1	3	3
TOTALS	-	-	*47 [1.12]*

as shown, the scoring system used was the one to five scale. Multiplying the score times the weighting determines the rightmost column, the weighted score.

By adding all the weighted scores, the result is 47. However, the result needs to be scaled in comparison to the benchmark with all the weightings. Had all the scores been 3, the total weighted score would have been 42. In other words, based on this scale and score, the subject opportunity was perceived to be only a little better than the comparable (12 percent to be exact, though this is not an exact process, corresponding to an average score of 3.36). Allowing for the uncertainty of the process, this finding would suggest that the subject opportunity should be worth only a modest amount more than the reference agreement or category.

Scores of rating/ranking factors can be usefully displayed in charts. Below we will consider two types: radar, and the infamous two-by-two matrix.

Let us first consider a nine-factor radar analysis. A more refined rating/ranking analysis than that which was shown could include the following factors associated with the projected commercial introduction of products from a technology:

(1) Annual revenues
(2) The margins (profitability) associated with such revenues[33]
(3) The market environment as it is expected to affect growth rates and overall sustainability of the business
(4) The stage of development of the technology insofar as affects the time to revenues
(5) The IP "moat" as characterized by the expected IP barriers to competitors (affecting revenues, margins, or growth)
(6) IP "risk" as characterized by the potential cost of needing third party patent licenses or designing around the patent claims of others
(7) The R&D risk assessing the potential for technical failure prior to commercial introduction
(8) Manufacturing risk relating to the ability to produce in commercial significant quantities at commercially necessary costs and specifications
(9) A market risk associated with the uncertainty of the revenue and margin projections

Exhibit 5.13 is an illustrative example using a ten-point scale; for the four "risk" factors, a high score means low risk.

Factors one through five, from the "12 o'clock" to the "5 o'clock" positions relate to intrinsic dollar value, where this example shows high scores. From "7 o'clock" over to "11 o'clock" the risk factors are shown, which factors affect the likely realization of the intrinsic value; in this illustration, the R&D and manufacturing risk are shown as being very high.

Another format for rating/ranking uses a matrix. Here one axis (in the example shown, the *y*-axis) is used to portray intrinsic value (the magnitude of the dollars expected to be derived from the technology assuming everything works). The other axis can be used to show any other key variable, most commonly some measure of risk. Now each rating/ranking factor has two coordinate numbers associated with it (x, y), one measuring intrinsic value (y) and one measuring risk (x). In Exhibit 5.14, five factors each characterized by a value pair are shown again on a ten-point scale: revenues (3, 8: scored 8 on value, but 3 on risk, meaning the revenue potential is

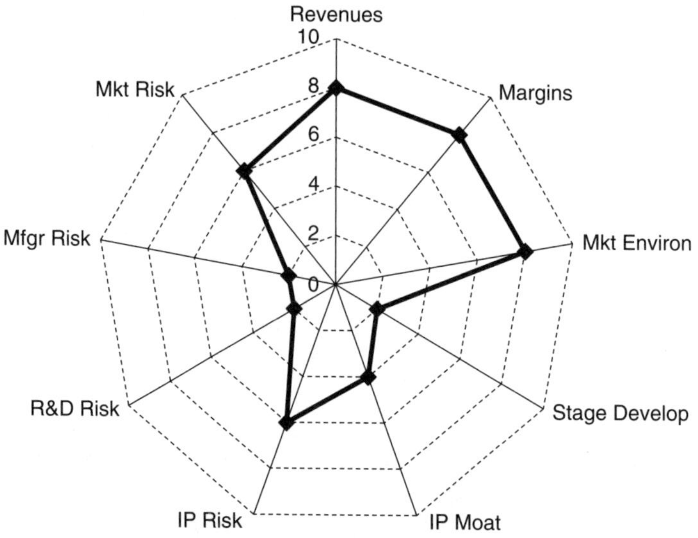

EXHIBIT 5.13 Radar Display of a Nine-Factor Rating/Ranking

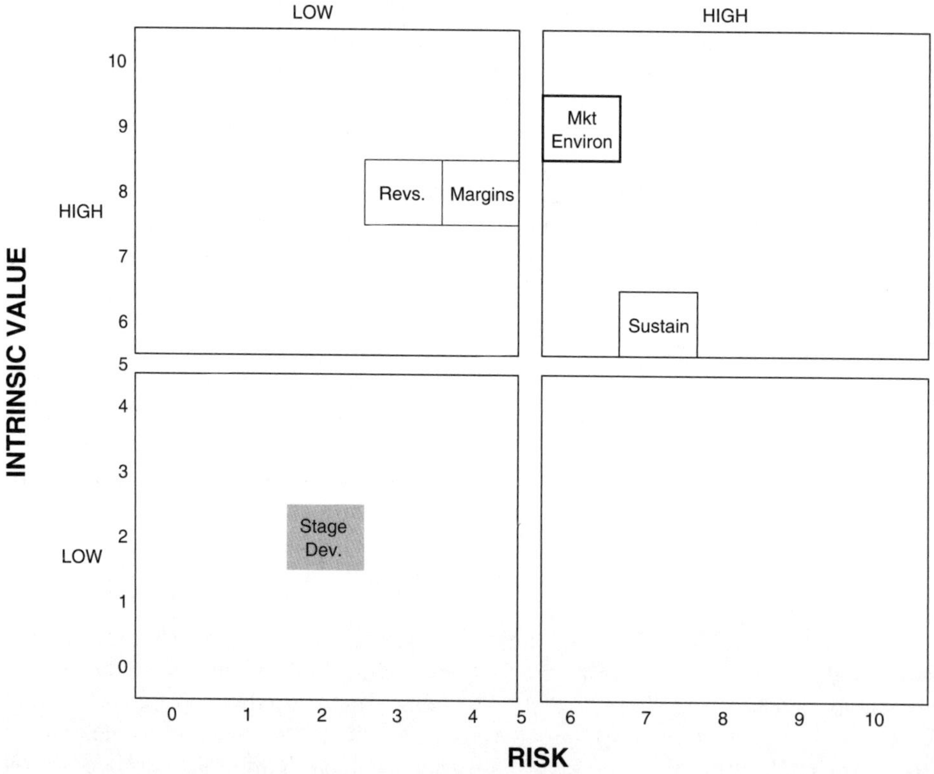

EXHIBIT 5.14 Matrix Display of Five-Factor Rating/Ranking

large, but the risk of realization is high), margins (4, 8: believed to be as attractive as the revenue estimate, but slightly less risky to achieve), market environment (6, 9: which includes a measure of the risk of third party patents), sustainability of revenues and margins (7, 6: which measures the effect of the IP "moat"), and stage of development (2, 2: which measures both the time to revenues and the R&D and manufacturing risk).

As just shown, each of the five factors reflects the related combined opportunity-risk. By the ten-point scoring (11 levels counting zero), each of the four main quadrants has 25 cells (five-by-five matrices within each quadrant). The top right quadrant is commonly referred to as the "star" quadrant, following a format popularized by BCG in their management consulting practice[34] but widely used in many contexts;[35] factors sited here signify high risk-adjust value, which in this illustration relates to the market conditions, not specifically the technology being valued. The bottom left quadrant is known as the "dogs" quadrant (clearly named by a cat lover); factors located here mean that they are both adverse in terms of value and risk, a bad combination. The top left and bottom right are the question marks; in the case the risk is very low but so is the relative value, where in the other case it is the reverse, which is the common quadrant for attractive technology opportunities (high potential value, but high risk).

Issues in Interpreting Value from a Rating/Ranking Result

In Exhibit 5.12, the result of the rating/ranking method was essentially parity with the benchmark. What if the result had turned out to be much higher? Suppose the total score had been 4.0. What should one do with such a value?

One approach is to do a simple linear normalizing ratio: 4.0/3.0 = 1.333. Multiply each of the economic terms of the comparable agreement by the ratio 1.333 to yield a valuation. So, in this example, such an approach would yield a valuation of $1,333,333 as a market based upfront payment, and 6.67 percent as the corresponding running royalty.

The reality of using such a ratio as a direct multiplier depends upon the reasonableness of the assumption of a linear scale. Does a score of 4.0 compared to the comparable reference of 3.0 really mean that the subject technology is four-thirds as valuable? What would a score of 1.0 mean? (Remember a score of 1 was effectively a zero; it was the lowest possible outcome). It could be argued that 1.0 scoring technology would be worth nothing, not 33 percent of the comparable. On the other hand, a 5.0 by this math could only be worth 67 percent more than the comparable license value, whereas by our scoring system a 5 would suggest something much more valuable than the comparable.

It is often helpful when translating a rating/ranking score to a value to go through each of the criteria that was scored and look at how it affects value. For example, if the total gross profitability of a deal (defined as market size multiplied by average margins summed over the commercial life of the products made from the technology) is estimated to be one-half of the comparable, and if the other criteria are scored as good or even somewhat better than the comparable, then a deal is likely to be doable with an upfront payment of approximately half as much, namely $500,000 and likewise for the royalty. This translation between score and value will be considered in detail in Chapter 7, once discounted cash flow analysis has been introduced. As we shall see, the use of the Discounted Cash Flow Method is a very powerful technique for assessing the impact of market size, margins, timing, and risk upon license value. This is another example where two valuation methods can work well in combination.

However, if one were to try to resolve this question without resorting to other methods, how would one convert a 4 into value compared to a 3? Like many of these matters, there is no simple answer. If there had been a benchmark license of a comparable technology that had been a 4 itself, then it would have been used and the subject technology would have shown a parity score suggesting that the value of the 4 benchmark license was an appropriate place to start. However, by definition, the best we could find in this example is the benchmark that led us to score this opportunity as a four. What is needed is some combination of license agreements in other areas, or equivalent experience and expertise with another panel that can begin to characterize the sensitivity to the value of such scores. With study and experience, one can begin to grasp, at least qualitatively, how the market reacts to opportunities that are "better" or "much better" in various criteria. A valuation expert panel could be convened to examine a series of published agreements using an established rating/ranking method for the purpose of sorting them out by score from low to high. Then by comparing their rating/ranking scores to their actual valuations (recall that one chooses the benchmarks because one has the data needed), it is possible to develop a correlation, however approximate, between rating/ranking score and value, at least with respect to the selected family. In the absence of other information, such correlation would be a useful place to begin to assess the value of a 4 in the subject case. The deal structure (the Wheelbarrow) is also an aspect of comparability, and can have a significant influence on value. If, for example, one is presently valuing an opportunity that is envisioned to be offered as an exclusive license extending to all fields and territories including multiple patents and know-how, and all the comparables are for nonexclusive licenses for a bare, single patent, the Rating/Ranking Method can assist in making some relative judgements about market size and margins, for example, as was done above. However, the comparables in such case are likely to be of little aid in guiding the valuation because the deal structures are so different. Ideally one looks for comparables that are comparable not just in technology and market but also deal elements. When this is attainable, it is expected that rating/ranking of an opportunity will evidence results that are fairly close to the comparable. Of course this is not always true but one expects it to be true more often than with comparables which have very different deal structures.

In general the closer the comparables are to the subject opportunity the easier it is to estimate valuation by rating/ranking. When the finding by rating/ranking is dramatically different from the comparables, either much more favorable or much less, then there is a higher degree of uncertainty of interpreting the result in financial terms. Consider the following example. Suppose the best assemblage of comparables we can find are pure royalty license with modest variations centered around a one percent royalty relative to an obvious product base. But when applying rating/ranking to our subject opportunity, every factor we consider causes us to believe that we dealing with a Likert 5 (or a "blue" or a "top/right" cell). Although this outcome leads to a helpful insight that the subject opportunity should be worth much more than a 1 percent royalty, the problem stems from the age-old question, "How much (more)?" Five times (i.e., 5 percent)? Ten times? It can be difficult to say, though as we will see after considering the DCF Method (Method 5) there are some direct ways of quantifying the value of the relatively larger market or profitability.

A caution is needed on the use of numerical scoring approaches for the special case of a fatal flaw. If one critical rating/ranking factor has a fatal flaw, say patent protection has been irretrievably lost and there are no other forms of protection, then one can obtain a misleading result by assigning a value of 1 to such factor. For this situation, some modification to the approach is needed. One way this can be treated is with a color scoring system where a "red," for example, eliminates any value to the opportunity being analyzed. Another approach is to multiply the scores, rather than add them so that the effect of a 1 or a zero can be dramatic. Yet another approach is to discard the analysis when confronted with a genuinely fatal flaw.

Another caution is pastcasting, an issue we discussed at the beginning of this chapter. Rating/ranking helps avoid one common manifestation of pastcasting, namely too readily assuming that the subject opportunity is just like a certain one from the past and, so, it should be worth what that one got. Systematically considering each of the underlying factors can identify some important difference, either favorable or unfavorable, that can be all too easily missed on an initial view. But there is another kind of pastcasting risk that is not so easily addressed: What if (1) the deal that was done in the past was, in retrospect, done foolishly, resulting in too high or too low a valuation, or (2) the world has changed dramatically even with respect to wisely transacted past deals. With respect to the first risk, bad historic deal valuation, it is common to assume this way under the argument of the "efficient market hypothesis," especially with professional buyers and sellers. We know from the tumult of the financial markets in 2008 and into 2009 and the technology markets of 2000 that even highly traded equities with abundant public information and extensive professional analysis that "bubbles" occur and in such events the past are not a good basis for forecasting. In like manner, though possibly the consequence of different causes, technology dealmaking can produce a data set of past Dealmaking that is not indicative of what would have occurred under current conditions. The second kind of risk, a changed world, can be argued to be another manifestation of poor human judgment. But, the landscape of technology by its nature changes rapidly, and often in ways that astonish even the most astute and carefully prepared deal valuation team. There was a time when superconductivity appeared to be the next "transformative opportunity." Gene therapy was another. Telecom and datacom, and first generation Internet businesses experienced a market "transformation" from, say 1999 to 2002 that very few predicted. Prices paid in the late 1990s for such now considered "dot bomb" opportunities look sadly comical even as early as 2001. The reverse is also true. In a widely cited story, IBM, in developing the technology which became the PC, did not believe the size of that market would ever be notable and, so, they were very willing to have the operating systems (OS) developed by an outside company (think Microsoft) as well as the chipsets (Intel). In a short time, the PC market exploded into units of hundreds of millions per year and the "Win-Tel" (Windows/Microsoft-Intel) monopoly became fabulously profitably and IBM a minor player in the PC market that they ultimately exited entirely by selling what remained of their business to Lenovo.

The more graphical representations of rating/ranking shown in Exhibits 5.13 and 5.14 are very effective at portraying the key value and risk factors but, as with the above discussion, there is no simple mathematical or algebraic method of converting these scores into a royalty rate or upfront payment. However, as one develops a history of performing such valuations and thereby a database of such scoring compared to value received, then it becomes increasingly possible to do pattern matching where a given opportunity can be seen as being very comparable (in radar or two-by-two quadrant coordinates). Developing such a database for the purposes of making direct comparisons leads us to a discussion of Classified Value Rating/Ranking.

Using Rating/Ranking to Value Technology: Classified Value

In the discussion of Rating/Ranking in the form of Factor Assessment, we developed a valuation estimate of our particular technology valuation by developing the factors, weightings, and scoring specific to such technology and the particular comparable(s) available. This approach is in my experience the most common utilization of rating/ranking. But it has three of the following disadvantages:

1. It requires setting up the analysis (comparables, factors, weighting, etc.) for each valuation project. Though clearly there is a great deal of methodology reuse possible for subsequent projects, each valuation has an inherent specificity to it.
2. There is likely to be some inconsistency from valuation project to project by the specific choices made in factors and weighting and so forth, as well as the important scoring tasks. Some variation of course can arise from the specifics of the opportunity. However other variations can arise because different people have been involved or simply a lack of consistency in defining terms or considering factors. This is similar to grading a large stack of student exams: By the time one has finished the last paper graded it can easily be that one's standards of scoring has evolved from the first ones scored, necessitating a second pass through the stack to be sure that everyone has been graded on a consistent basis.
3. If performing rating/ranking on only a one-by-each Factor Assessment process, one can easily lose any learning that occurs by connecting whatever became the valuation outcome as a result of dealmaking outcomes with the rating/ranking process score.

In the Classified Value instantiation of Rating/Ranking, the above issues can, in principle, be improved upon at the cost of a larger upfront investment in developing a formal methodology. Classified Value has the promise of establishing a taxonomy of valuation tranches such as that shown in Exhibit 5.5 for debt instruments, or "A" through "E" or one to five star ratings for equities as used by Schwab and Morningstar, respectively. If such a meaningful taxonomy can be established, then each particular valuation project need only determine which tranche is the corresponding best "fit" and, thereby, the value determined.

Classified Value Rating/Ranking is most attractive as an approach when (1) one is doing many valuations and (2) there is a well established means of creating value tranches. Consider the example of trademark licensing of various Major League Baseball team marks. There is a limited population of different teams (30) and licensees in addition to associated licensed products (hats, sweatshirts, etc.). It would make sense for any licensing program to develop a rational system based on Classified Value such that any potential licensee and product for any particular team can readily be ascribed a unique value, one presumably where the World Series Champion (Tampa Bay Rays for 2008) or large market notable teams (New York Yankees for any year) is worth substantially more than poorly performing teams (Tampa Bay Rays in 2007, but definitely not 2008) or small market teams (Milwaukee any year).

For technology licensing, developing Classified Value taxonomies is more problematic because it is more challenging to create universal standards by which any particular technology valuation project under any particular terms can be dropped into some clear and distinct pre-identified value tranche. However, at least informal versions of such Classified Value systems are common such as when a company with IP assets assigns certain patents to an "A List" (or designates patents as their "proud patents"), and others to a "B List," with the rest unclassified or by implication on some less valuable "C List." Although such broad tranching may not be associated with specific valuations, it would be expected that the range of value expected from any license would be at distinctly higher levels for such "A List" patents, whereas the response to a "C List" licensing opportunity may be a much more cursory effort as well as a lower value.

As we considered in the preceding chapter, some technology licensing situations involve relatively or even exactly standard terms to many potential licensees. This could arise when nonexclusive licenses are being offered for licensees seeking rights to a patent(s) needed to practice as standard and the licensor has agreed with the standards body to offer licenses under so called RAND terms (Reasonable And Non-Discriminatory, or FRAND, for "Fair" + RAND). In some circumstances, a term sheet is published in which the Classified Value taxonomy is overtly expressed for any potential licensee.

Another kind of Classified Value approach was reportedly followed by IBM when licensing its myriad of patents. As discussed in Method 1, at one time, IBM was reported to have made available almost any and every one of its 30,000 patents under the following terms: 1 percent royalty for a license to any one patent, 2 percent for two patents, and so forth, to a cap of 5 percent for all the patents (with certain IBM patents excluded), all for nonexclusive "bare" patent licenses. This expression of Classified Value was premised on the simple idea that two patents, any two patents, were twice as valuable as one, and so forth, up to a maximum of 5 percent. This approach is difficult to justify in terms of business benefit to the buyer—if I need two patents to make some given product, will this double my earnings and so support double the royalty?—but was done, as (and if) it was, to simplify and standardize a large licensing program.

The challenge in developing an all-encompassing Classified Value system for technology licensing is that such licensing valuation is normally much more complicated that rating/ranking bonds or even equities. The primary factors that affect bond and equity rating/ranking can be obtained from accounting statements and analysis of the established industry and markets in which the company whose debt or equity is being classified. With a company there is normally a well established history of past performance, a multiplicity of products/services and customers, that provides some base of economic performance and a kind of "mutual fund" of sources of revenues and profits. With a technology license, there is normally limited established financials because it is nascent or incomplete in some way, and it tends to be more of a single point success or failure.[36]

Another kind of Classified Value approach can arise when there are a substantial number of potential comparable agreements. Implicit in all the discussion in this chapter has been that there is either a single, "poster child" comparable, or a set of agreements which are narrowly distributed around some mean or median value. If this is not the case, it is difficult to understand which comparable one is being used as the point of comparison. However, there are circumstances where there exists a large population of published agreements for the same market applications (such as a specific disease) and/or technology for which there is significant scatter in the values reported. One way such data can be used is to create a Classified Value system from these divergent comparables. A simple way would be to assign the comparables to one the four colors discussed above, or on a one to five star ranking based on their expressed deal value. Then a comparison can be made to the populations within each (say) one to five star ranking to reach a judgment as to which is the most rational ranking for the subject opportunity.

Uses of Rating/Ranking with Approaches and as a General Tool

As we have discussed, Valuation can be considered as the second ***Approach*** of a three-stage Licensing D-V-D business process: opportunity Discovery (D), Valuation (V), and Dealmaking (D). The Rating/Ranking Method can be usefully applied to aid decision making at both the opportunity Discovery and Dealmaking stages.

So, one business ***Approach*** for which Rating/Ranking can be applied is to systematize how opportunity Discovery is conducted. Because technology valuation is normally performed in the context of multiple opportunities, either simultaneously or sequentially available or both, it is useful to consider how rating/ranking can be used in portfolio analysis. How might Rating/Ranking help us with both valuation and deciding what to do with a portfolio of opportunities? Put another way, how can this method be used for both valuation of a specific opportunity and for sorting and categorizing many opportunities presently available to us or as will become available to us over time?

We are already well familiar with one such application of rating/ranking for portfolio categorization, and that is academic performance. As a general rule, one would imagine, or like to believe, that A and B high school graduates are candidates to become college students, and C (and lower ranked) students are candidates for something else, with notable exceptions which tend to establish the rule. Similarly, A and B college graduates tend to be good candidates for graduate school, and C students not. Prospective employers make similar ranking categorization when they seek top 10 percent students, or any other range specification based upon academic performance. We even tend to label top students by "he (or she) is a top student" ("top" being a ranking outcome) or "an A student" or "just a C+ student."[37] We even resort to poker chip measures by talking about a "blue chip [i.e., highest value] student."

In commercializing IP a common difficult choice is which of many disclosures do I take action on and file patents, or take steps to preserve as trade secrets, and subsequently to commercialize by manufacture or licensing. Another common context is choosing a particular commercialization approach for already selected projects (IP/technologies). This choice might be forming a startup versus licensing, or licensing nonexclusively to the industry versus exclusively to a strategic partner, or licensing for all fields of use or licensing separately for each field. In such circumstances, Rating/Ranking can be systematically used to ascribe perceived value to each alternative under consideration. As with the qualifications given for its use with valuation, Rating/Ranking does not lead to certifiable "right answers." Subject to the assumptions and the judgment of the raters/rankers, it leads to generally better choices. In the context here of choosing a "best" path, the ultimate realization is also dependent upon the implementation skill and industry. Returning to a baseball metaphor, Ted Williams, who is generally attributed to be one of the greatest hitters of all time and one of the greatest students of hitting, claimed the deepest secret of hitting he got early in his career from a conversation with another outstanding hitter, Rogers Hornsby (1897–1963), and it is simply this: "Get a good pitch to hit."[38] Choosing by Rating/Ranking is just this simple: grasping what a "good pitch to hit" looks like, and doing everything one can to get opportunities to hit one. Neither Hornsby nor Williams ever batted 1000 (100 percent), but their averages would have been a lot lower, even with their prestigious talent, had they been swinging at everything that came their way or swinging without purposeful choosing.

Whatever rating/ranking choosing structure is used, the key is to focus one's limited energies on the highest (and few) opportunities, be they ten's, A's, five-stars, or "blues" (the color associated with outstanding opportunities). The next lower group can be pursued opportunistically, and beyond that is that painful, divided line which separates the group of technologies for which no further licensing resources will be assigned.

Closing this thought with two baseball anecdotes. Ted Williams, cited previously, and now deceased (though frozen awaiting some future life restoration technology), plotted his prospective batting average for each possible pitch in his strike zone. The home plate is approximately seven baseballs wide and Ted Williams's vertical zone was 11 baseballs high, making 77 possible pitch locations that could count for strikes. Mr. Williams computed his prospective batting average for each of those 77 locations from a fabulous high of .400 (40 percent of his official at bats leading to hits) in the middle of the plate down to a poor .230 for the farthest "low and away" strike.[39] Even as great a hitter as Williams was, perhaps the very best, he would have had a short and uninspiring career if he swung at many of those low and away strikes; and he never hit 100 percent even on his best located pitch.

A final baseball example of the difficult process of deciding on which players have a chance to make it at the highest level of the profession: "Major league teams scout about 500 amateur players a year, sign 40 (ca. ten percent), and hope four to six make 'the bigs' (ca. ten percent of ten percent = one percent; 'bigs' is baseball slang for The Major League). It's the hardest job to do in all of baseball except playing the game."[40] So it is in managing technology opportunities.

There is no simple short list of criteria (factors) that can be used to screen and prioritize opportunity Discovery. Common screening factors include:

- *Inventor(s).* Is there a track record of success? Is the inventor available to assist in developing the technology and dealmaking, and usefully so? Will the reputation of the inventor help or hurt dealmaking opportunities?
- *Technology.* Does it really work (at whatever level of development it has reached)? How do we know? Would an unbiased third party appraisal affirm a "yes"? Does it solve a long standing need (problem resisting a solution)? Does it appear "foundational"—meaning that it can create a diverse industry of potential applications? What level of convincing demonstration will be needed, and what investment of resources of time, people, facilities, and money will it take to reach a commercial convincing demonstration for a licensee or investor or a ready for manufacturing design team?
- *Protectability.* Is the technology protectable by patents? If so, what is the scope of anticipated allowed claims (composition of matter vs. article vs. process)? Is there relevant prior art that could affect the freedom to practice? Is there know-how/trade secret protection that is likely to be valuable and sustainable?
- *Market Potential.* How big is the potential market, how soon (really), and how fast will it grow? How is the problem solved today? What other alternatives exist for solving the problem (either now or anticipated)? What will be the competitive response? What is the evidence that there is substantial customer demand and the subject technology and its IP satisfies such demand in a valued and sustainable as well as unique way? Are there structural issues in the market channel?

As with valuation, each of such factors can be used with a numerical or non-numerical rating/ranking scheme, with the results summarized by a single or pair of numbers, or a graphical representation (such as the two-by-two matrix, or a radar diagram). With experience and a database, such rating/ranking can be evolved into a Classified Value system, where an opportunity can be fit into a tranch based on the similarities of the factor scoring.

Similarly with Dealmaking, Rating/Ranking can be used to identify the highest potential product applications, or markets, and end user categories. When considering potential licensees (or investors), a long list of candidate companies who broadly fit into such markets can be screened and prioritized by performing rating/ranking of each such candidate using the following categories:

- *Strategic Fit.* Does the technology align with the future of the company either from its own self characterization or by understanding the market drivers affecting the company? Is there synergy with other technologies/core competencies that the company is known to have? Does it align with a growth/investment area of the company?
- *External Focus.* Does the company have a track record of Dealmaking for technology at a comparable stage of development? Does the company have as a strategy acquiring companies and technologies to fuel growth or reach new markets?

- *Capacity.* Is the likely cost of a license (or investment) plus the needed further investment within the financial capacity of the company? Is the opportunity too small to be of interest to a company that size? Is the company overwhelmed with startup/new product launch opportunities? Does the company have recent startup successes evidencing such know how and willingness?
- *Access.* How will one "knock on the door" to propose that this is that company's lucky day? What contacts exist that can get the technology a fair and rapid hearing?
- *Reputation.* Is this a company with a strategy that you will be honored to be affiliated with?
- *Long-Term Relationship.* Would a deal for this technology be a once-in-a-lifetime event, or could it lead to other possible licensing, or other relationships?

When assessing outcomes from a portfolio of technology investments (opportunity Discovery), or a short list of potential licensees (Dealmaking), one can expect a notable number of failures. But the word failure conveys a mental image that it should have been otherwise, namely that failure is nonrealization of what should have been. But when investing in a portfolio of opportunities, particularly technology, it is so highly probable that such nonrealizations will occur that it is not appropriate to consider such outcomes as something less than what they should have been. From any portfolio of investments in R&D, or investments in technology marketing and licensing, it is expected that some individual opportunities will be more valuable than had been anticipated, some about as valuable as anticipated, some less, and some will become nonperforming assets (NPA), not failures; for some reason it helps to be able to say: "Well, that blue-green laser invention appears to have gone NPA." Even airlines use "hull loss" as a euphemism for "crashed."

Developing and applying a rating/ranking opportunity selection tool can be strategically valuable and itself proprietary. Exhibit 5.15 shows a simple three-level Likert Scale used on a "Technology Evaluation Worksheet" developed at a regional meeting of the Association of University Technology Managers (AUTM).[41]

Another, more graphical approach is to use a "dashboard" model similar to the structure of Exhibit 5.7. Here each row would represent a decision making factor for new opportunities. This would include valuation factors such as we have considered earlier in this chapter—market size, market profitability, time to market, et cetera—and other factors relevant to any technology adoption: synergy with existing technologies and markets, suitable internal champion, fit with long term strategic initiatives, and so forth. Then by marking each opportunity on the appropriate horizontal locus one can achieve a useful graphical display.

Another Approach for which Rating/Ranking is useful is in prioritizing Dealmaking opportunities. Considering first the circumstance of a technology seller interested in finding an exclusive licensee. Clearly not every potential licensee is equally likely to find such opportunity of serious interest, nor are even all the ones potentially interested likely to put a high value on the opportunity. Because technology licensing normally requires a substantial due diligence effort by the buyer, and the seller of the buyer, it is impractical (in many circumstances) to launch such a licensing campaign with expectations of serious negotiations with dozens of potential licensees.

EXHIBIT 5.15 Technology Evaluation Worksheet

Invention Title: ____________________

Inventors: ____________________

Docket # __________ **Date:** __________ **Associate:** __________

Commercial Potential	(+)	(0)	(–)*
• Ability to define product (i.e. what is for sale?)	__	__	__
• Perceived need	__	__	__
• Identity of end user	__	__	__
• Market size	__	__	__
• Maturity of market	__	__	__
• Competitive advantage/product differentiation	__	__	__
• Prospective licensee(s) identified	__	__	__
• Liability considerations	__	__	__
• Predisposition of industry to licensing	__	__	__
Inventor Profile			
• Cooperative/will serve as champion	__	__	__
• Industry contacts	__	__	__
• Realistic expectations	__	__	__
• Success with previous disclosures	__	__	__
• Credibility/recognition in field	__	__	__
• Research funding and direction	__	__	__
• Conflicting obligations	__	__	__
Scientific/Technical Merits			
• Invention is adequately defined in disclosure	__	__	__
• Supporting data are available	__	__	__
• Utility shown (i.e., solves a problem)	__	__	__
• Core technology versus improvement	__	__	__
• Features of invention versus limitations	__	__	__
Proprietary Position/Patentability Issues			
• Patentability of invention (new, useful, non-obvious)	__	__	__
• Breadth and strength of claims	__	__	__
• Freedom to practice (i.e., other dominant patents?)	__	__	__
• Possibility of reverse engineering	__	__	__
• Ability to detect infringement	__	__	__
• Ability to withstand litigation	__	__	__
• Known prior art exists	__	__	__

EXHIBIT 5.15 *(Continued)*

Stage of Development	(+)	(0)	(-)*
• Only a concept	__	__	__
• Reduced to practice/prototype available	__	__	__
• Manufacturing feasibility (facilities, equipment, etc.)	__	__	__
• Clinical data available	__	__	__
• Inventor cooperation required	__	__	__
Avenues of Commercialization			
• License to established company	__	__	__
• License to start-up company	__	__	__
• Access to venture capital	__	__	__
• Package with other technologies	__	__	__
• License to inventor	__	__	__
Financial Analysis			
• Cost of patenting	__	__	__
• Financial support from licensees	__	__	__
• Possibility of sponsored research	__	__	__
• Anticipated license/royalty income	__	__	__
Total:	__	__	__

Comments:____

____

____

____

____

____

____

Recommendation: _____ Needs further research

_____ Return to Sponsor/Inventor(s)

_____ Patent application

_____ Market without patent

*Ranking Codes: (+) favorable (0) neutral (–) unfavorable

Source: Reprinted with permission from Stanford University. 1995.

Perspectives on Rating/Ranking as an Approach with Licensing

There are two common reactions to the use of rating/ranking as a valuation method. The relativism inherent to the approach leads some to conclude that the use of the method merely reflects underlying biases rather than some rational, defendable approach to value. Although to be sure, rating/ranking can be used as a construct for making "the answer" come out as one wants, such a criticism can be leveled against essentially every valuation method in that they all to some degree rely on an assumed model of an envisioned future and assumed values. So in this respect, even the use of discounted cash flow models expressed in spreadsheets, as we shall see with Method 4, is not immune from bias.

In fact, the presence of bias is actually a benefit of rating/ranking because it should become apparent and in some way characterized by virtue of the articulation of the key valuation characteristics, as we shall see later in this chapter. Rating/ranking is based upon the determination and assessment of the key assumptions that are expected to affect valuation. In this respect it is similar to the stage gate product development process, which is presently taken as the best-in-class approach to new product development. In the stage gate process, a critical element of managing new product development is articulating the assumptions about what will be achieved in the future as specifically as possible with respect to the key aspects that will affect performance and value.

Another criticism that is waged against rating/ranking is its relativism. By definition, rating/ranking requires a comparison. So, rating/ranking cannot be done on a blank page. But this requirement of a reference point, or points, is by no means a flaw of the method; the method is intended to make as rational as possible a comparison between a subject opportunity and one or more reference points. As we shall see in this chapter, such comparison extends the value of Method 1, the use of industry standards. Later, we shall see where it can be used to increase the value of other methods.

Returning to the issue of bias, rating/ranking is frequently used with expert panels where multiple perspectives can uncover defendable and weak biases, as will be discussed later.

So, my response to those who might contend that this method is so inexact and ungrounded as to be valueless, is that in general it can be done systematically and skillfully to provide valuable insight on relative value.

At the other extreme, there could be some who expect more of rating/ranking than they should. Holders of this view could become paralyzed by analysis and argument seeking a level of precision or confidence that is unreasonable (recall the Aristotelian admonition not to seek more from a method of searching for truth than it is capable of giving). Although as we shall see, rating/ranking can lead to a numerical value, the source of the value is an accretion of judgments. So, we should not be lured in calculating as many significant digits as possible in the hope that this will lead to greater valuation utility.

Between these two extremes is our ancient Greek idea of FRO-knee-sis (*phronesis* = judgment). It requires *phronesis* to perform rating/ranking, and to determine when enough (analysis) is enough, and to apply the result in order to determine value.

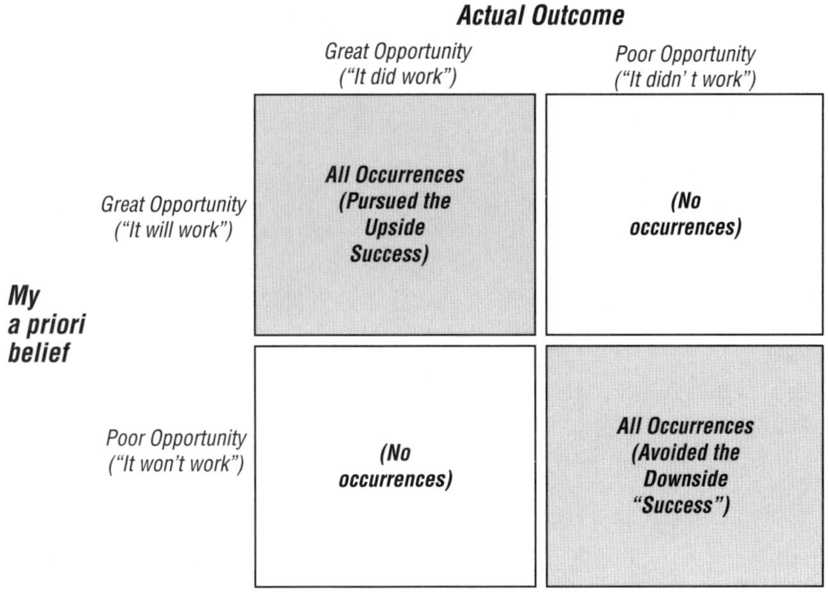

EXHIBIT 5.16 Certainty World

Source: © 2003 Razgaitis, richard@razgaitis.com.

Looking at this from another perspective, consider a world that I will call "Certainty World" (CW). CW is that environment where I can anticipate outcomes with certainty. Consider arithmetic and geometry. When we proceed with the addition of a column of numbers, we proceed with the mental framework that we are in CW: the addition will lead to a result which we a priori believe will be the value representing the sum of the numbers added; if it turns out not to be so, we immediately recognize the situation as a correctable mistake, and it is our aspiration and expectation that such mistakes would be, apart from inadvertent human error, unexpected. Similarly, if we are trying to determine the hypotenuse, C, of a right triangle of sides A and B, we expect it to be determined by the relationship $C^2 = A^2 + B^2$, namely the Pythagorean Formula. CW can be diagrammatically illustrated as shown in Exhibit 5.16.

The top row of this figure reflects the condition when we a priori believe that a specific opportunity will turn out to be favorable. In CW, what actually transpires, like the calculation of the hypotenuse, is what we expected, commercially favorable outcomes. In other CW cases, we will find those opportunities where we hold the a priori conviction that an unfavorable commercial outcome will occur and, in CW, so it is; so we have the favorable result of avoiding just those opportunities as shown in the bottom right hand cell. The other two cells, top right and bottom left, never occur in the crystalline certainty of CW. Rating/ranking is not like CW. Most of life is not like CW.

At the other extreme is "Uncertainty World" (UW). This is shown in Exhibit 5.17.

In UW, no matter what gymnastics we go through in an a priori analysis, the results turn out about half the time as we expected and about half the time the

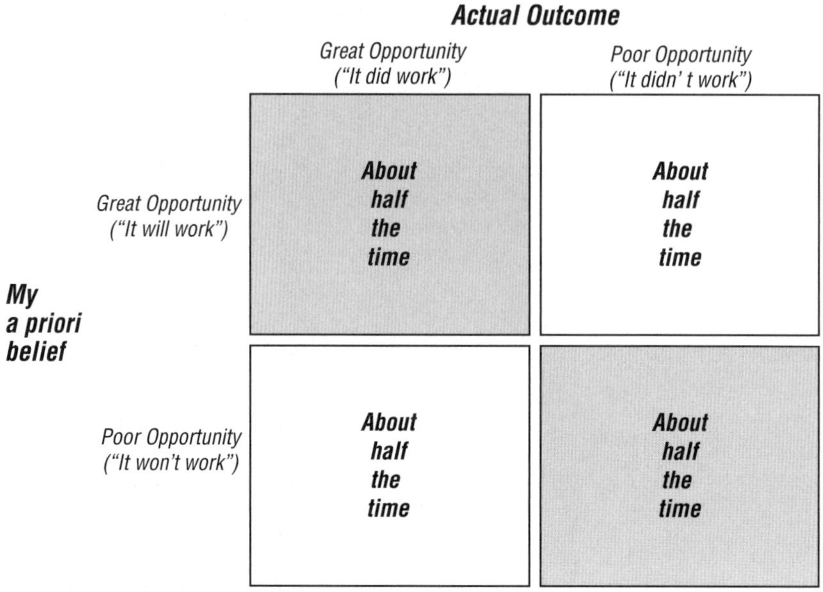

EXHIBIT 5.17 Uncertainty World

Source: © 2003 Razgaitis, richard@razgaitis.com.

opposite of what we expected. Coin flipping is a perfect illustration of UW. If I am trying to conjure up an a priori perspective on how your coin flip will turn out, and you are using a trusted coin, no matter what differential equations I use, experts or mystics I consult, I will discover about half the time I will be right and the other half wrong. A more interesting illustration of UW is the stock market. Because the stock market represents, at least in theory, a perfect expert system, each stock is priced perfectly at its true present value, though almost no one seems to believe this. Here is a test I shall call the SUW—for Stock Uncertainty World—Challenge pick ten publicly traded stocks for which you hold an a priori belief, on whatever basis, represent a good opportunity relative to their price, meaning that you believe they will outperform on average, then pick ten more for which you hold the opposite a priori belief, namely that they will be poor performers, and ten more that are randomly selected. Track these three tens of stocks for say ten years and my prediction is that their financial performance will be indistinguishable as a portfolio because of stock picking on a price-weighted basis in UW.

The underlying belief in the value of rating/ranking is that it can be applied to technology valuation because such an activity is neither CW nor UW but, rather, "Probability World," PW, as shown in Exhibit 5.18.

Rating/ranking, like many human activities, is about making reasoned, systematic a priori judgments with the belief that such choosing is justified over time, most of the time, or at least an economically significant percentage of the time. The key attribute of PW, which drives people who love CW crazy, is that there are times when despite the most careful of analysis some of our a priori positive outcome choices turn out to be duds and vice versa; CW lovers tend to say that rating/ranking "failed" in such circumstances. Actually rating/rankings does not fail when exceptions occur

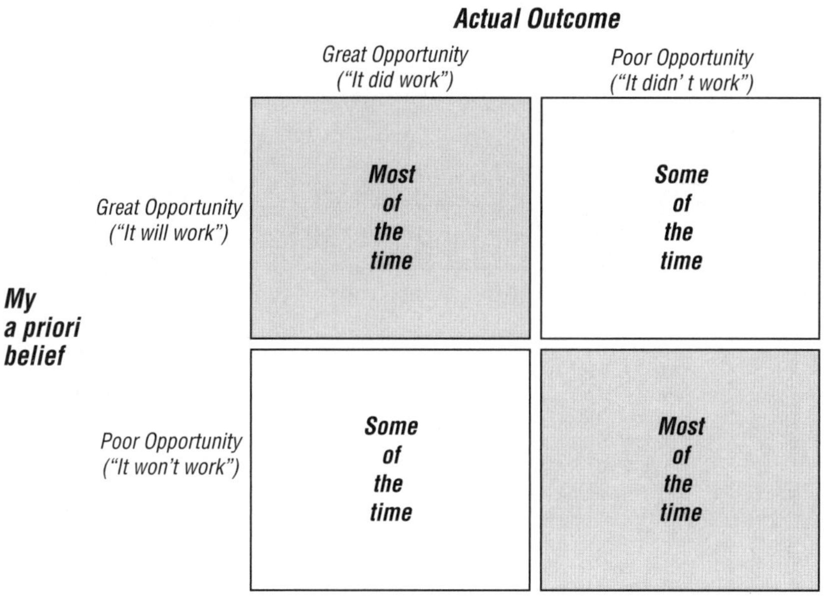

EXHIBIT 5.18 Probability World

Source: © 2003 Razgaitis, richard@razgaitis.com.

because it, and we, live in PW; it fails when our rating/ranking process is either so flawed that there turns out to be no economically valuable correlation between a priori analysis and actual outcomes or the process has been applied to a UW context, such as coin flipping or stock picking. Technology, markets, and IP protection normally reflect PW conditions.

Knowledge, Uncertainty, and Humility

Does the application of the rating/ranking method *reliably* provide *reasonable* PW assessment? Let us return to three, serious, very public rating/ranking failures: technology equities ca 2000, mortgage bond ratings ca 2007, and hedge fund and related insurance risk ca 2008.

As discussed earlier in this chapter, bond (debt) instruments undergo rating/ranking for repayment risk by companies who are recognized to have such capabilities (NRSROs) using their respective proprietary methodologies. In 2007 and 2008, there is a widely perceived failure of rating/ranking of secured mortgages and credit card receivables, especially those that have been grouped into CDOs (Collateralized Debt Obligations) and resold, in some cases many times over. An example of what has happened as of the end of 2007 is shown in Exhibit 5.19.

NRSROs have responded to the emerging data on newly "nonperforming" home mortgage loans by revising their rating/rankings. Standard & Poor's Ratings Services has in the last few months of 2007 lowered its ratings on approximately 1,000 tranches embedded within more than 300 CDOs.[42] Altogether, Standard & Poor's, Moody's, and Fitch Ratings have issued approximately 20,000 debt downgrades of

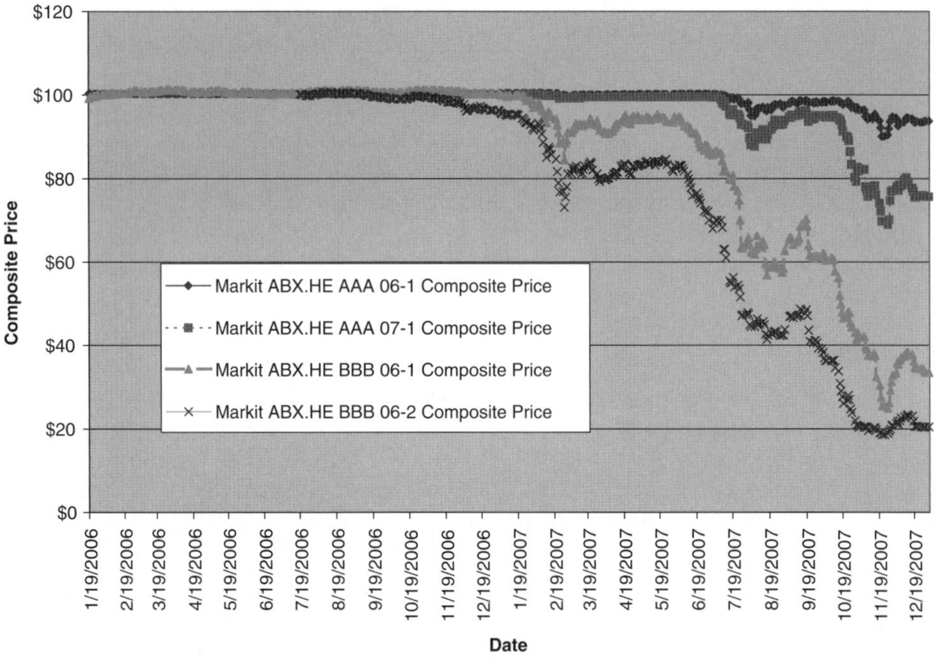

EXHIBIT 5.19 Effect of Unexpected Market Tumult on the Value of Rating/Ranking of U.S. Mortgage Bonds

Source: "U.S. Mortgage Crisis Rivals S&L Meltdown," *Wall Street Journal*, December 10, 2007 (page one).

securitized assets just in 2007, nearly ten times the number of downgrades issued in 2006.[43] Some of these lowered ratings have been dramatic, going from AAA (the highest rating, comparable to the sovereign debt of the U.S. Government) to "junk" (below "investment grade") overnight, which is a downward adjustment of more than ten tranches (see Exhibit 5.5). This has created great market unrest in part because of massive economic losses and in part because it calls into question the reliability of the new ratings as well as those which have not been re-rated, and even the reliability of any rating/ranking system. Terms like "market meltdown" and "bubble" collapse are being used to characterize the aftereffect of these changes.

The years between my first valuation book (*Early Stage Technologies: Valuation and Pricing*, Wiley, 1999), and the previous edition (*Valuation and Pricing of Technology-Based IP*, Wiley, 2003) almost exactly bracketed the previous infamous equity "bubble" primarily associated with technology companies. Although equities are inherently more risky than bonds, and there does not exist a comparable 20-level rating/ranking classification such as Exhibit 5.5 nor is there a recognized rating/ranking industry as with NRSROs, there is a direct parallel in that numerous companies were publicizing "strong buy" (their highest equity rating) and equivalent characterizations of many equities which turned out to have little or no value. The U.S. technology equity bubble experienced a drop in total value of nearly $7 trillion,[44] which represented about 75 percent of then U.S. Gross Domestic Product (GDP)—a huge drop in value, to say the least. The U.S. housing market appears to be plummeting in early 2009 to a market value approaching $13 trillion below its recent peak in the summer of 2007, which is close to 100 percent of the current GDP.[45]

So, in very recent history we have two demonstrated sudden, massive failures of rating/ranking in what is generally perceived as being well understood business assets, stocks and bonds. What, then, should be learned from this? Is it that rating/ranking as a valuation method is fatally and unpredictably flawed? How does such outcomes comport with any belief that rating/ranking provides PW (Probability World) determinations?

One simple answer could be the reminder that these were PW not CW (Probability World, not Certainty World) best estimates, and there is always some probability that all such estimates will be "off." But, "off" by (an aggregate) of hundreds of billions of dollars, or even trillions of dollars? Twice? Within a seven-year period?

The primary lessons here are familiar life lessons: garbage in /garbage out (GIGO); never assume the obvious is true;[46] dishonesty is so grasping it would deceive God Himself, were it possible;[47] maturity is the capacity to endure uncertainty.[48] Let us consider these in turn.

- *Every valuation method, and human endeavor, is based on certain critical assumptions.* If such assumptions have been badly created, a single valuation method may not make the result evident—at least not without the presence of judgment, a critical element in all valuation work. As we will discuss in Chapter 7 concerning the Discounted Cash Flow Method, which is considered to be "the gold standard," bad assumptions lead to bad results despite being presented in high precision (using many significant digits) in each of hundreds of spreadsheet cells for dozens of scenarios. Even highly exact mathematical calculation does not, by itself, assure that the results are meaningful. Rating/Ranking is likewise subject to deeply flawed predictions if important underlying assumptions are wrong or key factors are not included.
- *The standard of reasonableness for key assumptions can be subject to wide error.* Assumptions can be deemed reasonable because they conform with experience (pastcasting). The projected default rates for home mortgages were thought to be low as they have been in the past. However, in recent years the percentage of household home ownership had increased significantly as home loans were enabled by more aggressive lending standards and even, in some cases, the absence of documentation of such simple issues as income of the borrower. In the period 2001–2003, the average percentage of subprime loans was approximately 7 percent. During the next three-year period, 2004–2006, subprime loans represented about 20 percent of all residential loans.[49] Did the bond rating/ranking models properly account for this effect upon default rates?
- *Another standard of reasonableness is "everybody else says so," a standard that every parent of a teenager has heard more than once.* In the case of the technology equities bubble of 2000–2002 there was an obvious red flag in the P/E ratio (the stock price divided by trailing annual after-tax earnings, all on a per-share basis).[50] Historically, the aggregate P/E ratio of U.S. equities is typically below about 20.[51] At its peak in 1999, the P/E ratio of the stocks listed on NASDAQ, a closer measure of technology stocks, had a P/E ratio of over 200, more than ten times a historic P/E benchmark. Yet, instead of these high P/E values breeding

caution and "sell" rating/rankings, there was a widespread belief that the old rules of thumb for P/E ratio no longer applied to technology companies relying primarily on intangible assets (including IP) to produce revenues and earnings. Once one deems the valuation of highly value comparable companies as being reasonable estimates of true value, then it is all too easy to use an overvalued asset as an overestimating valuation guide.

- *And, sadly, outright human dishonesty is a common cause of rating/ranking failure, as with any other predictive activity.* As with the "snake oil salesman" of the Old West, there are some who promise glorious outcomes not only without a factual basis but knowing that such are utter falsehoods. The technology stock bubble led to new laws enhancing criminal liabilities for finance fraud (Sarbanes-OxleyAct) and a Presidential "Corporate Fraud Task Force" that became a growth industry for criminal prosecutions. The latter task force was formed in 2002 and by mid-2007 had obtained 1,236 corporate fraud convictions, including 214 CEOs and presidents, 129 VPs, and perhaps most appallingly 53 CFOs and 23 corporate lawyers.[52]
- *A more benign issue has to be with respect to subjectivity.* Research into human decision making has opened up a whole field of behavioral economics. This has been famously recognized by the awarding of the Nobel Prize for economics in 2002 to Daniel Kahneman, a psychologist who claims never to have taken a class in economics. Prof. Kahneman and his co-investigator for much of his work, Dr. Amos Tversky, showed that in many circumstances people do not make judgments in accordance with rational, *homoeconomics* models. In a certain sense, these general findings support the value of Rating/Ranking as a valuation method, and the subject of our next chapter—valuation by Rules of Thumb. However, it is readily possible, perhaps inevitable, that subjective factors will influence valuations determined by Rating/Ranking, because of the choices made for the factors considered, the relative weighting applied to various factors, and of course the scoring of each factor. This is where an expert panel helps, and the friendly questioner who challenges assumptions; as was quoted at the beginning of this chapter, the former CEO of Intel observed that if everyone claims to know the same thing is true, it is likely that no one knows anything.
- *Humans seek certainty; but in all practical circumstances it is elusive:*[53] through chances various, through all vicissitude, we make our way.[54] Forecasting the future is necessary to operate any business, and conduct any technology valuation. Although the future is never knowable, there are some factors affecting valuation, and some valuations themselves, which we can reasonably believe are more subject to uncertainty than others. There is a reason why lower ranked (higher risk) bonds, such as "junk," carry with them higher nominal rates of return. Innate uncertainty should lead us to humility, and humility to reexamining assumptions, seeking the wise counsel of others, considering alternative valuation methods, and providing a margin for error and a premium for risk taking. A common January publication, evidencing the need for humility, is various favorite "top ten" lists of worst predictions for the preceding year.[55] There is never a shortage of excellent candidates.

And, yet, there is a long history of rating/ranking leading to trusted and highly useful results. Returning to the rating/ranking example of corporate bonds by S&P,

the below table shows the default rate on the payment of such bonds over a recent 15-year period as a function of the original S&P bond rating, where those rated BBB or better are "investment grade":[56]

Original Rating	Default Rate (%)
AAA	0.52
AA	1.31
A	2.32
BBB	6.64
BB	19.52
B	35.76
CCC	54.38

Conclusion

The Rating/Ranking Method is the most overtly subjective of the six methods we will consider. However, as we shall see, all methods contain a certain amount of subjectivity because they deal with the unknowable future. Because the application of a rating/ranking method must be fact and content specific, it is not possible to identify a universal set of criteria that can be applied in all circumstances.

Rating/Ranking works best when it is systematized and applied by a panel of "regulars" who develop a history of making such judgments. It is greatly aided by feedback from actual values received (favorable and not). Over time, an organization can develop a very powerful set of enabling tools for expert panels to apply.

It should be recognized that this process is very similar to that followed by focus panels and other formats that companies use to test market acceptance and enthusiasm for new drugs. It is also used with proxy juries in preparation for trial before the actual jury. It is used with prospective voters on issues as well as subjective factors associated with political candidates. It is even used on odors. It turns out that for many purposes, the human nose is the most appropriate instrument to assess favorable and unfavorable odors. Companies concerned about such matters work very hard to develop an expert "smell panel" that is used again and again to perform similar rating/ranking exercises. So, rather than thinking of the Rating/Ranking Method as a "smelly business," it should instead be considered as a structured way to "scent opportunity."

To gain a more elevated appreciation of the Rating/Ranking method, we can rightly claim it as an expression of an important philosophical concept which is succinctly expressed in Latin as *mutatis mutandis* (derived from the word mutate and means, literally: "things having been changed that need to be changed," namely, we have adjusted, or mutated, as needed to make things applicable); so if someone reacts to this method as being ad hoc, you can reply, "au contraire, *mutatis mutandis*."

The method has to commend it three important values: It directly links to market value while characterizing the differences, it is useful preparation for marketing and negotiation by causing one to sharpen thoughts about strengths and weaknesses, and it is a useful way of defending both a valuation and a process to internal stakeholders.

In the next chapter we will consider another powerful technique: the use of rules of thumb. In many respects this method will be based on a subjective judgment because the "rules" are guidelines and need to be applied case by case. In this respect, the Rating/Ranking Method will apply in the next chapter as well.

Appendix 5A: Factors in Pricing License

A checklist of 100 important considerations in setting value of technology license

By Tom Arnold and Tim Headley

Source: Arnold, White & Durkee, Houston, Texas: paper presented at workshop at LES U.S.A./Canada Annual Meeting, Los Angeles, CA, October 1986. Reprinted with permission from *les Nouvelles*.

There is cost, risk of (i.e. hope for) profit and risk of loss involved:

- In licensing early or concept-only technology vs. matured and proven technology development
- In scale-up from prototype or pilot plant to production model or commercial plant
- In commercial manufacture and marketing
- In patent or know-how litigation and commitments to enforce rights
- In license nonexclusives and in license exclusions
- In licensee competition with the licensor
- In third party competition and new leap-frogging developments
- In guarantees of costs, quality, or production rates of the licensed operation
- In favored nations clauses
- In the cost and quality of the technology transfer itself
- In everything in the license

The total price for a technology may be structured in the forms of commitments and guarantees plus total or partial payment in equity, debt, front money, postponed sums certain, minimum royalties, running royalties, and so on. But in the ultimate sense the total price is primarily a balance in the hope/risk of profit and loss by the two license parties.

Each of the following listed considerations affecting the setting of the price on a technology, should be reviewed by both sides in the context of hope/risk, in arriving at that balance.

If reviewed before and during a negotiation, these considerations will help a party put his own value on the technology and will forewarn him of the thinking on the other side—thinking for which he should be forearmed when entering the negotiation.

Because many of the considerations are a mixture of intrinsic quality, strength of protection, market niche, financial and other factors, grouping them under headings can be misleading and beget redundancy. We feel, however, the headings and groupings help the reader a bit in spite of such inherent shortcomings.

Intrinsic Quality

1. The stage of the technology's technical and market development. Barely conceived? Reduced to practice? Commercially proven?
2. The intrinsic quality of the technology as a marketable quality, reliable technology.
3. The perceived utility by the buyer or user of the technology or its product.
4. The value to the licensee or its country of educating the licensee employees in the technology. Often developing nations will subsidize a technology-transfer or a licensee-research clause in a license in order to get their citizens technically trained and gainfully employed in a technology.
5. Perceived value of continuing access to technical help and ongoing research and development by the licensor and/or other licensees, including reputation of the seller for innovation and technical development.
6. The possibility of profiting from the good reputation of the licensor.
7. The need for the licensor's technology in the licensee's operations.
8. Pioneering invention or mere slight improvement?
9. Ongoing technical services by the licensor.
10. Whether the technology arose as a byproduct of other R&D. (This does not truly change the intrinsic value of the licensable technology, but it seems to have a psychological influence which, when properly advocated, does sometimes affect what a licensor will take.)
11. The type of license (patent, know-how, trademark, copyright, mix, etc.).

Protections and Threats of Protection

1. The scope and reliability of the protections of the technology, be it patent, trade secret, trademark, copyright or chip protection, and so forth.
2. Whether there is a favored nations clause.
3. Precedent, the value in money and other considerations being paid by, or offered as acceptable from, other licensees, particularly if they are likely to be partly competitive.
4. Reputation of the seller for defending its invention and for technology protection.
5. Contractual commitment of either party to protect the technology, or risk of nonprotection.
6. Can the offered patents or secrets be designed around (and at what cost in time, money, legal risks or technical risks)?
7. Enforceability of capacity, volume, location, geographic restriction or field-of-use clauses or other restrictions against competition.
8. Is this license a compromise of a suit for patent infringement or misappropriation of trade secrets, etc.?

Market Considerations

1. Size of the total relevant market and licensee's likely share.
2. Distinctiveness of the market niche of the licensed subject matter; differentiation of licensed product (e.g. if ten companies are making a soft, stretchable quality of polyethylene as commonly used for garment bags, would a licensee pay more for a license for a nonstretchable film strong enough for use as shopping and grocery bags?)

3. Demand for the product of the technology in the licensee's potential market at various potentially available prices and product quality as well as styles (e.g. the same invention may have a bigger market in a Cadillac than in a Volkswagen or vice versa).
4. Geographical location of licensee's manufacture or sales base.
5. The importance of a second source of supply in the market. Many is the market where two quality competitors will sell nearly three times as much as one alone.
6. Changing market trends in competition.
7. Dynamism of the market.
8. Trade cycles.
9. General state of the economy.
10. The possible extent to which the demand for the licensed product may be depressed by unemployment, union attitudes, et cetera in the primary marketing area of the licensee.

Competitive Considerations

1. The nature and extent of the third party competition with the licensee.
2. The nature and extent of licensee competition with the licensor and/or reaching markets not served by the licensor.
   a. Will the licensee serve markets the licensor cannot effectively serve or will the licensee serve competitively the licensor's own markets, et cetera?
   b. Whether and to what extent gray market goods of the licensee will compete with the licensor's products.
3. The scope of the market niche which is protected, and the cross-elasticity of the market within and without the protected niche (i.e., the degree of exclusivity of the license of the inherent market niche).

Value Brought to the Table by the Licensee

1. Capital, marketing talent, and other values brought to the table by the licensee.
2. Grant-backs of research and development by the licensee.
3. The possibility of acquiring an equity interest in the licensee.
4. Manufacturing and marketing capability of the technology recipient: Whether the licensee has greater talent and capacity effectively to make or to market the invention in the subject market, or to use the technology, than the licensor.
5. The degree of economic and industrial development, the labor and capital availability and cost, and so forth, in the licensee's country.

Financial Considerations

1. Manufacturer's margin. For example, a unique agricultural chemical, medical device or pharmaceutical may often be priced in response to value to the customer, independently of cost of manufacture and sale or competitive prices. Perhaps the farmer can be given a three dollars return in increased crop yield for one dollar of cost to buy the product, and the manufacturer can still sell such a chemical, if protected, at eight or eighteen times its manufacturing plus sales costs. A much higher royalty (33 percent of retail price in one of my cases) is justified in such a case than when the manufacturer's margin is forced to be one or two percent.

2. Cost of the license negotiation and the technology transfer itself, and profit on that cost. Licenses for small markets often cost more to negotiate than the license is worth.
3. Potential for profits at royalties at X percent, Y percent, and Z percent, each to the licensor and the licensee.
4. Availability and cost of capital and labor.
5. Tariffs.
6. Taxes and related considerations—capital gains vs. ordinary income. But "capital gains" as such seems destined to disappear under U.S. Tax Reform Act of 1986.
7. The amount of the licensor's expected cost savings, risk savings, and other burden savings, which follow from licensing a given market in lieu of developing it himself.
8. A comparison of the projected license net income against the potential for profit by the licensor's service of the same market.
9. Can the offered patents be designed around? Or the secrets be independently duplicated?
10. The burdens on the licensee inherent in its developing the same or competitive technology by its own effort are:
    - Cost of licensee R&D
    - Time for licensee R&D
    - Quality of licensee R&D result
    - Unresolved infringement, environmental and other legal risks involved in likely licensee R&D result
    - Technological risks in likely licensee R&D result
11. What did the technology cost the licensor to develop? This should be disregarded except insofar as it helps evaluate the cost of the licensee's competitive development of the same technology.
12. Cost and risks of enforcing patents or trade secret rights.
13. Cost of warranty service.
14. Cost savings in avoiding litigation to enforce a patent.
15. Costs of obtaining and maintaining local or foreign patent and trademark protection. (Really, not relevant.)
16. Cost of training the licensee's employees; risk that the planned training may prove inadequate.
17. The seller's cost of continually upgrading the project.
18. The nature and type of obligations to be assumed by the licensee under the contract; e.g. books to be audited by the competing licensor, licensor quality control burdens, royalties to be made on sales before goods paid for, force majeure clause.
19. Policing costs: accounting audits, quality control tests/inspections.
20. The probability of the license being profitable for the licensee.
21. The amount of expected profit or saving incurred by the licensee, including any likely monopoly profit.
22. Different costs in the different countries involved:
    - Of capital (either equity or debt capital)
    - Of labor
    - Of raw materials

23. Traditional royalty rates in the industry—a factor relevant more to negotiating tactics and psychology than to what is fair or economically reasonable for the subject technology. Be imaginative in developing reasons for departing from tradition. Precedent-priced technology is often wrongly-priced technology.
24. The profit plan; the traditional profit margins in the industry. But again, be imaginative in finding reasons for departure from tradition.
25. Estimated cost of adapting the technology to planned applications like 220 volt power in lieu of 110, etc.
26. The structure and time spread of payments of equity, sums certain, royalty minimums, running royalties, payments to be of large sum certain in spite of market failure by licensee, etc.
27. Accounting simplicity.
28. The potential for and availability of barter and local manufacture arrangements to cover currency control problems and the like.
29. Follow-on related sales, the profits thereon.
30. The buyer's right to duplicate the seller's technology in subsequent projects.
31. Inflation, in some countries running at 400 percent annually.
32. Varying international exchange rates.
33. The prices (equity, sums certain, royalties) being asked by sellers of competitive or similar technology. Recent industry licensing rates and practices for similar products and processes.
34. Anticipated sales volume of licensed products.
35. Contract administration costs, comfort, and convenience.
36. Division of projected profits, as for example 25 percent to 50 percent, which is common for the licensor, and perhaps 50 percent to 75 percent, which is common for the licensee who usually has much more at risk.

Particular Risk Considerations

1. Exposure to product liability suits.
2. The licensor's risks and costs of litigation against the licensee, in lieu of license, for example, risk of loss of royalties from existing licensees if the patent is held invalid.
3. The risk of cost and other burdens upon either party who assumes to police patents and sue infringers.
4. Risk of having to perform uncompensated technical study or training services to verify performance guarantees and specifications.
5. The risk of loss or prior license royalties if the patent is litigated and held invalid. The potential for this risk biases toward an early litigation—which in turn puts at risk all the royalties that might have been collected, usually at lower rates, had the patent never been risked in court.
6. Licensee's credit position.
7. Licensee's willingness to be audited—perchance by a competitor.
8. The risk of a diminished quality of future R&D if the licensor does not manufacture.
9. The reliability of clauses protective against product liability lawsuits, particularly in connection with trademark licenses.
10. Exposure to charges of infringement of rights of others.

11. The risks of the licensee's developing the same or competitive technology by its own effort.
12. The risks of the licensee's developing the same or competitive technology by its own effort.
13. Uncertainties in cost, time, legal quality and technological quality of licensee R&D result, if independent development is selected in lieu of license.
14. Risk to the licensor and value to the licensee of the licensor's guarantee of performance in the following:
    - Time of plant erection
    - Quality of product
    - Production capacity
    - Cost of product
    - Enforcement of patent and know how protections and exclusivities
    - Indemnity against infringing third party patents
    - Et cetera
15. Apart from the guarantee (which is often an incomplete remedy for failure of performance), the licensee's perception of the true reliability of the following:
    - Time of performance
    - Quality of product
    - Production capacity
    - Cost of product
    - Enforcement of protections and exclusivities
    - Indemnity against infringements of third party rights
    - Et cetera
16. The potential licensee's:
    - Cost of defending an infringement suit
    - Risk of damages
    - Risk that the license price if any will go sharply up after a litigation
    - Risk of injunction with no license available at all
17. The term of licensee lock-in (as by a plant design frozen in steel and concrete).
18. The risks of technological obsolescence.
19. Can the offered patents or secrets be designed around (and as aforesaid, at what cost in time, money, legal risks or technical risks)?
20. Risk of erroneous estimates of licensee employee training.

Legal Considerations

1. Force majeure clauses.
2. Legal enforceability of restraints on competition.
3. Whether the patent value has been or will be enhanced by a judicial reexamination and decree. Patentees frequently should decline to license or price a license very high before the first litigation, hoping to precipitate an early litigation with respect to an infringer suffering poor litigation equities, thereby to enhance the subsequent license value of the patent(s).
4. Duration of the license, of payments of sums certain, of the royalty payments, of the obligation of confidence—all of which commonly should be different terms.
5. Favored nations clauses.
6. The risk of, or opportunity for, suit by the licensee to invalidate patents at times and forums of his choice—he may not stay hitched.

Government Regulatory Considerations

1. Licensee's government's restrictions and law on royalty rates, royalty terms, and so on.
2. Legal restrictions on currency movement.

Notes

1. One common type of anti-pastcasting is a kind of humor characterized by "it seemed like a good idea at the time," where observed outcomes were obviously bad that not only is there little danger in emulation there is a present incredulity about "what were they thinking?" Unfortunately for our valuation purposes bad thinking in the past is often not only not obvious it may not be knowable to us.
2. Said in an interview with *Fortune* magazine in 2005, cited by Janet Rae-Dupree, "Innovative Minds Don't Think Alike," *New York Times*, December 30, 2007.
3. www.bestplaces.net.
4. Veenhoven, R., "Average Happiness in 95 Nations 1995–2005," World Database of Happiness, RankReport 2006-1d worlddatabaseofhappiness.eur.nl
5. http://colleges.usnews.rankingsandreviews.com/usnews/edu/college/rankings/rankindex_brief.php
6. http://health.usnews.com/sections/health/best-hospitals
7. Officially this is known as the National Fire Danger Rating System (NFDRS). There is an actual underlying calculation based upon two primary factors—the speed at which a fire started will spread, and the fuel available on the surface. A calculation of 81 or greater receives the "extreme" rating, 61 to 80 the "high" rating, and so forth. www.dem.ri.gov/programs/bnatres/forest/pdf/firewthr.pdf
8. www.dhs.gov/xinfoshare/programs/Copy_of_press_release_0046.shtm
9. www.fema.gov/txt/plan/prevent/rms/426/fema426.txt
10. www.tsa.gov/assets/pdf/Secure_Flight_PRA_Notice_9.21.04.pdf
11. Underlying the above 13 groups are laws of fluid mechanics, including: The force exerted by wind goes with the square of the speed, but the power (capacity for driving objects for good or for ill) goes with the cube of the speed. So a Beaufort 7, median speed 35 mph, compared to a Beaufort 3, with a median speed of 10 mph, creates more than 12 times the loads on one's boat, and nearly 43 times the energy for harm.
12. Herbert Saffir was a structural engineer whose work in South Florida made him very familiar with hurricanes. He developed the scale for hurricanes as a predictive tool for damage primarily to low cost structures worldwide for the United Nations. The scale was extended in the 1970s by Robert H. Simpson, a former director of the National Hurricane Center. The scale has been a vital communication tool that has been used to change and unify building codes and has saved lives. Perhaps as a reward, Mr. Saffir lived into his 90s, 1917–2007, and Mr. Simpson is still living at 95. Source: *New York Times*, Obituaries, Nov. 24, 2007.
13. www.npp.hu/biztonsag/INESskala-e.htm
14. Michael M. Lewis, *Moneyball: The Art of Winning an Unfair Game*, W.W. Norton & Co., 2003. *Moneyball* is primarily about the use of rating/ranking of baseball players for the purpose of winning as cheaply as possible. The general manager of the major league Oakland Athletics, Billy Beane, is a primary character in the book.
15. And in the artful and descriptive world of baseball player assessment there are many examples of rating/ranking characterizations. One of the most famous is the "Mendoza Line": named after Mario Mendoza, a poor hitting major league shortstop whose batting average over his career was only 215 and in one sad season was 198. No batter wants

at any time to be near the Mendoza Line. Another, even worse ranking is attributed to Billy Beane, general manager of the Oakland Athletics who, when considering prospects who had a "troubled" history, would say "put a Milo on him," named after a trouble-some former front office employee, and would designate someone that they would not seek.

16. Like former Chicago Cubs third baseman Ron Santo, or the late Thurman Munson of the Yankees.
17. Consider nouns such as car, house, and student. Although there are a finite number of unique cars, at least when new, there is a significant variation between, say, any Ford and any Ferrari. Yet for many purposes, we can usefully group all such examples within one category, as at a highway rest stop, by signage directing all "cars" to a particular exit. 'Houses" by virtue of their one-by-each manufacture tend to be even less alike than "cars," yet such noun exists because despite the wide variability in individual structures there are circumstances when they can be usefully considered as all members of the same group, as on a form used for a mailing by which a "house" is distinguished from an "apartment." An example of a group for which every member is unique is "student." But, again, there are contexts where all members can be usefully described by such group term ("faculty" vs. "student" or "alumni" vs. "student"). There is a deeper, and ancient, discussion behind any such example, namely the Platonic "forms." Plato introduced, or at least made known in Western literature, the idea that every unique example expresses an unseen, perfect form. So when one sees some particular horse, say one named Widowmaker, Plato called us to apprehend the "horseness" form from which any horse, including Widowmaker, was expressed. So, in a sense, Rating/Ranking is about seeking the Platonic form from which a given real-world embodiment is expressed.
18. For our purposes the terms business, company, and corporation are synonyms for entities established to conduct some commercial enterprise, as are other comparable entities which may be formed as legal partnerships or operate as sole proprietors.
19. Two kinds of exceptions to this can be noted. One exception is where a company has few, large customers, such as the commercial aircraft division of the Boeing Company; it is quite possible, and probably necessary to consider each airline as a distinct customer. Another exception is associated with "the long tail" phenomenon associated with Internet retail relationships such as Amazon or Netflix; the Internet and relational databases have made it increasingly feasible to profitably serve small niche interests.
20. The U.S. government's stellar "AAA" credit rating, which it has held since it was first assessed in 1917, may change. Moodys Corp. on January 10, 2008, issued a warning that the debt issued by the U.S. government may be downgraded because of increased repayment risk associated with factors such as healthcare and pension costs. If it falls to AA+ (S&P Grading), it will equal the bond quality for the state of Nebraska's public debt, but still be rated more favorably than, say, Malaysia (A-) or Bulgaria (BBB+), based on published S&P sovereign debt ratings August 15, 2007.
21. For example: the buy at five stars and sell at one star for trailing one-year return was 17.4%, sell at three stars was 23.3%, compared to the S&P 500 one-year return of 15.8% (all based on 2006 data). Source: http://news.morningstar.com/articlenet/article.aspx?id=183630&_qsbpa=y
22. Often spelled "Likkert," as I did in earlier editions; however, the proper spelling appears to be with a single "k."
23. This can be overcome, to a degree, by multiplying each of the factor scores instead of adding them. This has the effect of splaying out the differences and rightfully punishing an opportunity that scores only a "one" on one or more factors. However, the numerical result is not easy to normalize and visualize in terms of meaning.
24. One manifestation made famous by the McLaughlin group where the question to the panel is often by posed by John McLaughlin regarding some political question as: "On

a zero to ten scale where zero is 'no chance' and where ten is 'metaphysical certitude' where to do you rank the possibility of X doing Y?"

25. Such discounting of remote participants is increasingly justifiable in this multitasking age where the temptation to check (and respond to) email, surf and who knows what else, results in such individuals not fully apprehending the analysis and discussion taking place.
26. Georgia-Pacific Corporation v. U.S. Plywood Corporation, 318 F. Supp 1116 (S.D. N.Y. 1970).
27. The expression "reasonable royalty" in the context of litigation is a term of art that refers to a payment determined in litigation to be adequate compensation for infringement of a patent. The expression, as it used in opportunity licensing, which is the scope of this book, means a royalty which is reasonable.
28. Robert Goldscheider, "Litigation Background for Licensing," *les Nouvelles*, March 1994, pp. 20–33.
29. Stephen Degnan and Corwin Horton, "A Survey of Licensed Royalties," *les Nouvelles*, June 1977. p. 91.
30. Dan McGavok, David Haas, and Michael Patin, "Factors Affecting Royalty Rates," *les Nouvelles*, June 1992, p. 107.
31. Tom Arnold, "Factors in Pricing License," *les Nouvelles*, March 1987, pp. 19–22. Adapted from a paper presented at a workshop at LES U.S.A./Canada Annual Meeting, Los Angeles, CA, October 1986.
32. C. M. Meston and D. Buss, "Why Humans Have Sex," *Archives of Sexual Behavior*, Vol 36, 2007: 277–507, claim research results that lists 237 reasons that motivates people to have sex (who knew?). The research based on survey responses from Texas college students used a five-level rating /ranking methodology in their work.
33. In subsequent chapters we will consider two such measures, EBIT for Earnings Before Interest and Taxes, and EAT for Earning After Tax.
34. BCG developed the matrix to map market share versus growth rate. Those products a company had that were in the high-high quadrant were the stars, those in the low-low were the dogs. The ones in the high market share but low growth rate were the cash cows (to be milked for cash, not for further investment). Finally, the ones in the low market share but high growth rate were the question marks.
35. For example, the two-by-two matrix has been used to distinguish customer love for a company and its products: Linda Tischler, "How Do I Love Thee? Let Me Plot the Graph," *Fast Company*, July 2004, p. 94. The quadrant for "high" love and respect was occupied by Starbucks and Nelson Mandela. The "low" for love and respect had salt, corn flakes, and Hyundai. The two "corner" quadrants, high love but low respect had the VW Beetle and the low love but high respect had Chevrolet.
36. Of course a given technology can have multiple ways it can be used to make different kinds of products and even services, and in different territories. However, the volatility associated with future outcomes tends to be larger simply by virtue that there are certain common, core features of such technology on which all such potential applications are dependent. There are technology licenses, such as nonexclusive licenses to patents that cover some standard for which there are already many licensees and products, for which uncertainties as to value are low.
37. This discussion brings to mind the advice given by one retiring small college president to her replacement, a first time president: "Be nice to your 'A' students because one day one of them will return and head your physics department; but also be nice to your 'C+' students, because one day one of them will donate ten million dollars to this college so you can have a physics department."
38. Ted Williams, "The Science of Hitting," quoted in *Sports Illustrated*, June 21, 2002, Scorecard.

39. Taken from a chart originally published in a series of articles written by Ted Williams and John Underwood published in *Sports Illustrated* in 1968 and the basis of Williams' book, *My Turn at Bat*, 1969.
40. Allard Baird, General Manager of the Kansas City Royals Major League Baseball team, quoted in the *New Jersey Star Ledger*, March 25, 2001.
41. At the Western Regional Meeting of AUTM in August 1994 the focus was on methods for technology assessment. The chart given in Exhibit 5.15 was developed from this meeting. Kathy Ku, Director, Office of Technology Licensing, Stanford University, was the source for this document originally published in Technology Access Report, December 1994. Reprinted with permission from Stanford University, 1995.
42. "S&P Slashes Its Ratings on $6.8 Billion in CDOs," *Wall Street Journal*, Dec. 18, 2007.
43. According to research from Deutsche Bank.
44. The Wilshire 5000 is the most comprehensive of the well known equity indices, including nearly every U.S. publicly traded company. It reached its peak value, nearly 15,000, on March 24, 2000 at a total market capitalization of $17.25 trillion. By July 18, 2002 it had dropped to just above 8,000, reflecting a loss in market capitalization of $7 trillion to a value of $10.03 trillion, and the extinguishing of more than 1,000 companies. Enron, as one notable example, went from $51.5 billion on Wilshire high date down to zero.
45. "The Great Adjustment Is Well Under Way," *BusinessWeek*, April 13, 2009, p. 6.
46. Attributed to William Safire, author and long-time columnist for the *New York Times*.
47. Attributed to George Bancroft, 1800–1891.
48. Attributed to John Huston Finley, 1904–1995.
49. Source: "Inside Mortgage Finance," reported by the *Wall Street Journal*, January 17, 2008.
50. The P/E ratio has long been considered the most basic factor for assessing equity values. Its importance has often been ascribed to Benjamin Graham, 1894–1976, mentor of Warren Buffet at Columbia University. Graham is famous in part because of his classic investment book: *The Intelligent Investor*, Harper Business, described by Mr. Buffet as "by far the best work on investing ever written."
51. http://www.multpl.com/
52. U.S. Department of Justice Fact Sheet, "President's Corporate Fraud Task Force Marks Five Years of Ensuring Corporate Integrity," July 17, 2007.
53. For those seeking to delve into this at a very deep level there are some excellent treatments of Goedel's Completeness Theorem. Kurt Goedel, a contemporary and friend of Albert Einstein (there would have been a pair to have a stimulating lunch with), proved at a very fundamental level our inability "to know."
54. *The Aeneid* by Virgil, 70–19 BC. Quotation cited in the front matter of Benjamin Graham's *The Intelligent Investor*, Collins Business, 2003.
55. A notable record holder has been William Safire, senior editorial writer for the *New York Times*. He has been forecasting that Cuba's Fidel Castro will "leave the political scene" in the subsequent year, for 33 years running. He has re-upped his prediction for 2008.
56. Data is Standard & Poor's Corp., reported in *BusinessWeek,* April 8, 2002, p. 40.

CHAPTER 6

Method 3: Rules of Thumb to Determine Valuation

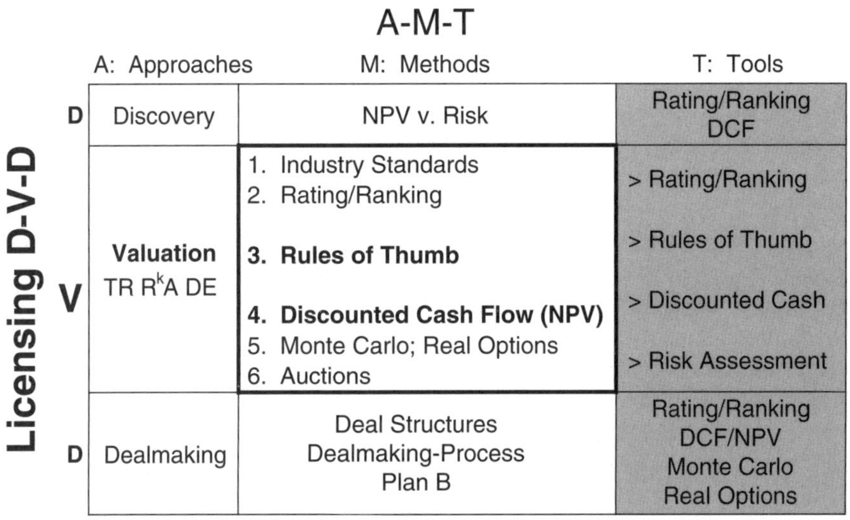
A-M-T
A: Approaches
M: Methods
T: Tools
Licensing D-V-D
D
Discovery
NPV v. Risk
Rating/Ranking DCF
V
Valuation TR R^k A DE
1. Industry Standards
2. Rating/Ranking
3. Rules of Thumb
4. Discounted Cash Flow (NPV)
5. Monte Carlo; Real Options
6. Auctions
> Rating/Ranking
> Rules of Thumb
> Discounted Cash
> Risk Assessment
D
Dealmaking
Deal Structures
Dealmaking-Process
Plan B
Rating/Ranking
DCF/NPV
Monte Carlo
Real Options

This chapter will consider another method for using market data to value a technology. The focus will be on identifying and using suitable market-based "rules of thumb" as a tool in value assessment. Also in this chapter we will consider how rules of thumb are used throughout our ***A-M-T*** framework shown: as a ***Tool*** in the ***Approaches*** of opportunity Discovery and Dealmaking and in support of other valuation ***Methods***. As with Method 2, Rating/Ranking, considered in the previous chapter, Rules of Thumb has broader utility than strictly as a valuation Method.

The term "rule of thumb" has come to mean a useful guideline for decision making based on numerous experiences. A simple example used with first-year college students is: two hours of study outside of class for each hour spent in class. There are similar such rules in every walk of life that serve as useful simplifications of complex phenomena and behaviors. They tend to be reasonable approximations, not unbendable laws, so "rules" is probably a poor though well established term; "guidelines" may be a better word as it more accurately reflects the idea behind the method.

Rules of thumb are closely related to a more formal idea known as a heuristic. A dictionary definition of a heuristic method is: "involving or serving as an aid to learning, discovery, or problem-solving by experimental and especially trial-and-error methods."[1] The idea of a heuristic method (or simply, heuristic) as used here is the desire to develop a simple valuation principle that can be conveniently and quickly applied to many different types of specific situations and one that can be flexibly applied to publicly available data. The origin of such an idea is the belief that valuation negotiations between numerous willing buyers and sellers have some rational, underpinning principle that can be discovered and applied. By their nature, heuristics are guides, or starting points.

Financial rules of thumb become everyday obvious once one begins thinking about them, much like buying a particular automobile and then seeing the same model everywhere. One's personal investment percentage in equities, versus fixed income securities such as bonds, should be determined by subtracting one's age from 100 (or 110).[2] One should not borrow more than 2.5 (two to three) times one's annual income for a house, wisdom that would have served borrowers and lenders well during the 2006–2008 period. Commissions paid to selling agents range from 5 to 10 percent (realtors earn historically 6–7 percent, more recently, at less than that percentage, investment bankers at 3–7 percent, though scaling downward with increasing deal size). Stocks of publicly traded companies sell for price/earnings ratios of (on average) 15 (historically) which guideline was widely considered archaic during the boom in technology equities in the period 2000 to 2002 and now, again, appears to be reasonable (with still notable exceptions, especially for rapidly growing businesses or ones with uncharacteristically low current earnings). In retail businesses, a 10 to 15 percent unexpected decline in sales will eliminate 100 percent of the store's planned profits. Acquiring ownership of a company typically costs a "control" premium of 30 percent.[3] Consulting firms sell for 1 to 1.5 times annual sales, though IBM acquired PricewaterhouseCoopers, shortly before it was to be spun off as a company called Monday, for 0.7 of annual sales.[4] Corporate software annual maintenance agreements cost 15 to 20 percent of the upfront license fee. An employee's benefits package costs 20 to 30 percent of the employee's salary. Area managers of music concerts typically get 30 to 40 percent of T-shirt dollars. Movie studios are reported to allocate up to about 40 percent of gross receipts for the combined costs of the producers, directors, and stars. When major league baseball teams can keep the aggregate cost of their players' salaries to less than 50 percent of total revenues, an actual current-year profit is reasonably possible. When N couples have dinner, they'll split the check 1/N, regardless of who ate or drank more (exception: If one of the couples are particularly slender and fastidious bookkeepers; then the bill will be itemized by person, including the weighted sales tax and tip, and which bookkeepers will not be invited to the next time).

The Toolkit

Workers in the practice of their art just naturally develop rules of thumb. We are all innately summarizers and generalizers of our experience.

With experience, licensing professionals, R&D managers, and M&A Dealmakers develop a formal or informal litany of rules of thumb. As noted in our discussion of Method 1, Industry Standards, one category of comparables is one's own personal experience. For instance, someone who has engaged in years of industry specific licensing can recite often by rote from memory what certain kinds of opportunities are likely to worth. However, as discussed with Method 1, the world undergoes change, sometimes dramatically. History records the failure of many a military campaign, and leader, who fought the last, or wrong, war to his mortal end.

The most famous heuristic, or rule of thumb, for licensing valuation is known as "the 25 Percent Rule," although as we will see each word in this descriptor is not exactly true: it's not "the," nor is it always "25 percent," and it is not a "rule" but a "rule of thumb" (guideline as to a starting point). In this chapter the 25 Percent Rule, will be defined, the rationale behind the rule will be analyzed, and specific examples will be considered. Situations that require values other than 25 percent also will be discussed. We will also discuss at length certain improper usage of the 25 Percent Rule.

Foundations of Rules of Thumb

The existence and wide use of a term such as the 25 Percent Rule is itself an indication of an important fundamental idea. The undergirding idea of a valuation rule of thumb is that the total value created from a deal (license) should be equitably apportioned between the seller and buyer; the DE of TR R A DE™ can also be thought of as Deal Equity, where equity refers to creating attractive value for both parties in Dealmaking.

An agreement reached by a willing seller and buyer is a value-creating event. For the moment, without considering who keeps what portion of the value created, it is important to recognize that a deal necessarily creates the expectation of a gain. Were this not so, neither the buyer nor the seller would be willing to enter the agreement. (We are not considering the case of involuntary licensing, such as in the settlement of a lawsuit, where a gain unjustly realized is being reapportioned between the parties).

How Is "Deal Equity" Determined by Rules of Thumb?

The question arises, is there a general observation, (or rule of thumb) that can be made about how sellers and buyers seem to reach agreement on splitting such gain? Put another way, on average what do buyers and sellers both agree is deal equity? Clearly cases where either the buyer or seller claims "it's all mine" can be dismissed. We are considering values for which the seller will receive more than zero percent and less than 100 percent of the total gain resulting from a deal. Well, how about 50 percent, where the seller and buyer split the gain 50:50? Except for some unusual circumstances, this rarely happens. In order to understand why, it is useful to analyze four elements behind the idea of rule of thumb.

Total Value. As a result of the transaction, the buyer will be able to create a product(s) or provide a service(s) that will produce a stream of revenues and a profit. (The presumption throughout this book is that the "buyer" of the license becomes the "seller" of the products made from the technology and, so, receives all the proceeds from all the sales, a portion of which must then be redistributed to the licensor/seller.) Generally such profits will occur over a period of many years.

Apportionment. The second element is apportionment, or in colloquial terms, the split. This is the heart of the rule of thumb as applied to valuation. For the 25 Percent Rule, the apportionment is 25 percent of the total gain to the seller, and 75 percent to the buyer. This particular value seems to be arbitrary so it leads to the logical question: On what basis is 25 percent fair? For the moment, we will only assert that enough buyers and sellers believe that this particular value is fair that it has risen in stature to a commonly used guide; a deeper discussion of this issue will take place later.

Investment. The third element is investment. The seller has made the investment in order to bring the technology to its current state. From this state, the buyer alone, or in some circumstances with participation from the seller, must make subsequent investments to create a product and business. When two parties to creating a business begin at the same point, it is common to apportion the rewards in the same manner as the total investment: Whoever does most of the work gets most of the reward—it is a principle as old as antiquity. Because in a licensing transaction the two parties by definition did not begin at the same point, there was a period when only the seller was investing and there will be a period when only the buyer is investing. In addition to the timing of the investments being different, the magnitude of the investments is almost certainly going to be different, as will be the risk undertaken in making such investments. Therefore, it should not be a surprise that a 50:50 split rarely occurs.

Risk. The aforementioned sentiment brings us to the fourth and final element: risk. Not all investments deserve the same return. Although this principle will be examined in quantitative detail in Chapter 7, the relevant point here is that higher risk investments, typically borne by the seller, deserve a greater return in proportion to the magnitude of such investment than the lower risk investments that will be borne by the buyer, all other factors being the same. There is a prevailing failure rate of all new technology projects that begins at conception. Although failure can and does occur at all phases, including after market introduction, it is generally the case that the fallout rate of new ideas is highest during the research and development stage, which normally precedes a licensing event.

Practical Application of the 25 Percent Rule

In order for any valuation rule of thumb to be of use, there has to be a way that both the buyer and seller can estimate the first two elements: gain (value created) and apportionment. In general, there are two ways gain arises, cost savings and new profits. The cost savings type is realized because the licensed technology enables the buyer to make a product or provide a service more cheaply than without the technology. In the new profits case, the buyer will be able to charge more for a product already being made (because it has some new performance benefit as a result of enabling the licensed technology) or it will create an entirely new product or even product category. (A variant of the new profits case is sustaining existing profits which—but for the subject license—would erode and disappear because of market changes, competitive alternatives, or some other reason). We will first consider the cost savings application.

Cost Savings Example of the 25 Percent Rule

Although the cost savings situation occurs less frequently than the new profits case, it is easier to understand and apply, so it will be presented first. And as will be discussed later, the cost savings situation is somewhat less prone to misuse of such rules of thumb.

Consider a seller offering to license technology that will enable the buyer to operate a factory (or some other business process) at lower cost. For simplicity, let us assume that both the seller and buyer agree that if the technology can be successfully deployed in a factory floor environment, it would save the buyer-manufacturer $100 per unit made, where such $100 savings is net of any necessary implementation cost, so it represents a true decrease in a buyer's variable cost.

Setting aside temporarily the issue of upfront payments or other forms of nonroyalty compensation, what would be an equitable apportionment of this $100 savings? If the seller argues for receiving 100 percent of the $100 benefit per unit made, the buyer will rightly point out there is zero (or negative) incentive to incorporate the technology. Likewise if the buyer argues for keeping the entire savings, there is no incentive for the seller to transfer a rightful possession. What about a 50:50 split of the savings? From the point of view of the buyer, this is unlikely to appear reasonable as there are numerous business responsibilities that the buyer alone typically bears and are required for there to be *any* benefit:

- Making the technology fully design-ready for manufacturing
- Purchasing, installing, and conducting shake-down of manufacturing tooling
- Sample making and test marketing
- Creating and maintaining finished goods inventory
- Creating specialized products for specific customer requirements
- Marketing the product (advertisements, collateral materials, trade shows)
- Selling the product (salespeople, 800-numbers, processing orders)
- Shipping and distributing the product (warehousing, tracking, reordering)
- Handling returns and allowances
- Collecting payment (that's why it is called accounts receivable)
- Performing the accounting, paying the royalties

Also, there is some value of business incumbency that such buyer brings to the table. In the assumed situation, the buyer is already making and selling product, so it has customers as well as suppliers and has established at least some competitive position with respect to competitors. Regardless of whether the buyer has developed a significant patent portfolio or is protected by a fortress of trade secrets, the buyer will reasonably expect that its presence in the marketplace has some non-negligible value, beyond the costs and risks noted above associated with technology adoption.[5]

If two parties decided to go into business and split the profits 50:50, it would be expected that they would likewise split 50:50 all the investment, risk exposure, and day to day work to make the business successful. In the above licensing example, it is perfectly legitimate to consider the seller and buyer as going into a business to produce $100/manufactured unit of gain. Thinking of the transaction in this way, are the seller and buyer making equal contributions to creating this new $100/unit? In most circumstances, the situation is that the buyer is recognized to contribute more than the seller to the $100 realization. (Later in this chapter, circumstances will be considered where the seller deserves 50 percent or even more, but these are not common situations.)

The 25 Percent Rule states that an equitable split of the $100 savings is $25 to the seller and $75 to buyer as a starting point. Thus, in this simple example, and in the absence of adjustments specific to the circumstance the royalty rate would be $25 per item manufactured, with some provision in the license to account for the effects of monetary inflation and perhaps changes in the savings benefit over time.

Before going further in the use of the 25 Percent Rule, it is useful to think through the rationale for the specific apportionment of 25:75. The following are six different ways of looking at why this apportionment could be perceived as fair to both the seller and buyer.

"That's The Way It Is" Perspective

One simple way to look at the 25 Percent Rule is to simply say this particular apportionment is what numerous sellers and buyers have agreed to, or appear to have agreed to, in many different transactions and there is nothing more to be learned by thinking about it. This perspective is exactly the how technical analysts, sometimes called "elves," look at stocks and the overall stock market: The market has spoken, deal with it.

The Going Concern Perspective

As enumerated above, there is a long list of business processes that the buyer must possess and apply in order to realize the benefit from the technology. Many if not all of the processes are business assets that the buyer has developed prior to the transaction and which will be leveraged to create value out of the technology. The 25 Percent Rule then asserts that 75 percent of the work that has to be done to go from a raw idea to the customer's cash in hand will be done by the buyer using extensive business assets it has previously and independently developed, which are also necessary to commercialize the subject technology.

The Golden Rule Perspective

In a famous and lighthearted restatement of the Golden Rule, "He who has the gold makes the rules," there is the recognition that in many transactions a willing buyer can exert considerable leverage in a transaction. This is generally because there are more goods, services, and technologies seeking buyers than there are buyers seeking goods, services, and technologies. The money in the hand of the buyer is readily transformable into many different kinds of assets and opportunities. From this perspective, the deal will have to look attractive or buyers will look elsewhere to make their investments. This perspective suggests that buyers will look for opportunities where they can realize most of the gain in their own pockets, and they will continue to scan for sellers until they can find a suitable opportunity in which this will be true. Put simply, if a buyer is considering the subject technology (Plan A) and an alternative (Plan B), and the seller of Plan A insists on a 50:50 split of the future gain, and the seller of Plan B will settle for a 25:75 split, the buyer will have no difficulty in deciding which deal to pursue (all other factors being the same).

Related to this "golden rule" concept is consideration of the seller's alternative to entering a license agreement. If the seller is happily and profitably exploiting the technology commercially, it can view "the gold" offered by a prospective licensee-buyer quite differently than if it has, for all practical purposes, no ability or intention but to offer the technology as-is for licensing.

The 3-Times Impetus Perspective

Buyers tend to include payback multiple in their decision making. Buyers (in business) think in terms of every one of their payments resulting in a multiplied return. The more complex the circumstances, the more unclear the timing and likelihood of the return, the higher the multiple has to be in order to be worth making the deal. It has been observed in other contexts that buyers frequently need to be convinced that they will benefit at least about three times the cost of getting the benefit (although the author is not aware of any formal study of this phenomenon). However, it has been observed in diverse settings that to induce buyers to proceed with projects, they need to be convinced (if only by an introspective mental calculation) of a 3-times return on the immediate costs, assuming all goes according to plan. Applied in this context, the commitment to pay a royalty equivalent to 25 percent of the cost savings is another way of saying that the buyer is getting back three times what it is committing to pay on each unit being manufactured.

The One-Quarter of the Way Perspective

Yet another way of looking at the 25 Percent Rule is that it is the recognition that "technology" is only about one-quarter of the way to a product.[6] How might this be? One could assert that creating the technology of a new product or service is one big step. Making it manufacturable is a second big step. From this perspective, then, manufacturing and selling the product are the third and fourth big steps. Therefore, it can be argued, creating the technology is one of four big steps to commercialization and, thereby, receives one quarter or 25 percent of the gain.

Continuing with this perspective, an argument for a 33 Percent Rule, would be based founded on technology that has already advanced to include aspects of the manufacturing component, so the "technology" is actually one-third of the way.[7] There is of course an arbitrariness to this perspective, as a technology owner can assert that its creation was not a one-step job, but involved basic science, engineering analysis, lab testing and iteration, and final design. (To which the buyer can respond: If the rest is so easy, why don't you do it yourself?) The specific situation, as we will discuss, can adjust a valuation heuristic to account for relative value additions.

The R&D Tax Perspective

One can think of technology as the product of a research and development (R&D) organization. When a company's own R&D department creates technology, normally there is no license payment or royalty made by the manufacturing group or the respective business unit that puts the technology into commerce. However, on average there has been a payment made by all the business units for such R&D technologies. This is commonly done by "taxing" a company's sales in accordance with industry norms and the company's strategy (being the lead innovator justifies more spending; being a follower requires less R&D spending). Put another way, in any given year, earnings before interest and taxes (EBIT, a fundamental measure of a company's profitability) could be increased by the amount spent that year on R&D.[8] The most recent annual survey by Battelle Memorial Institute, a survey it has conducted for 35 years, estimates 2006 R&D spending by U.S. industry to be $207.5 billion.[9] According to the U.S. Department of Commerce, the total industry profits for U.S. "nonfinancial" companies was $814.3 billion. Remarkably, the ratio of R&D spending by nonfinancial companies is almost exactly 25 percent of total industry profits. The direct comparison to this discussion would be to form the ratio of $207.5 divided by the sum of the R&D spending and total profits ($207.5 + $814.3 = $1022, all in billions), which is 20 percent.[10]

Perspectives on the 25 Percent Rule

Regardless of the validity or weight of the previous arguments as to why 25 percent has emerged as a commonly cited rule, the fact is that the phrase 25 Percent Rule (and the idea behind it) is widely recognized in the licensing community. It appears in almost every article about valuation. It has been cited, in different forms, in court cases. For example: "As a general rule of thumb, a royalty of 25 percent of net profits is used in license negotiations."[11]

Bill Lee has written a very succinct summary of the history of the 25 Percent Rule.[12] It has a long history, with many claimed fathers. His paper summarizes values ranging from 25 to 33-1/3 percent and it is cited in an "authoritative treatise on licensing,"[13] in an article by Larry Evans,[14] and by a Japanese author, Yoshio Matsunaga,[15] and in an article by Edward P. White, who cites the value range as 25–35 percent.[16]

In a paper by Goldscheider, Jarosz, and Mulhern, the authors provide a history of the 25 Percent Rule going as far back as 1938 where the Sixth Circuit Court of Appeals heard expert testimony that asserted the inventor was entitled to a proportion ranging from 10 to 30 percent of net profits.[17]

It is likely that examples of 25 percent profit-sharing arrangements with the asset owner can be found dating back to the Middle Ages in feudal times where the serfs had to dedicate two days a week (29 percent, which is midway between 25 and 33 percent) of farming service to the feudal lord.[18]

However, it is important to note that there are other points of view. Buyers can argue, especially when dealing with very early-stage, speculative technology that 25 percent is simply too high to make business sense. Such reasoning is this: (1) the seller has not moved the technology even to the end of the R&D stage, and/or (2) the costs (and risk) of getting through "manufacturability" are huge (especially in comparison to the R&D), and/or (3) the costs (and risk) of marketing and sales are large, and/or (4) this is a low margin, competitive business that does not provide the profitability to support a 25 Percent Rule.[19] The net result of such an argument could be a proposal from the buyer that amounts to a split smaller than 25 percent.

On the other hand, sellers can, in some circumstances, argue: (1) this technology is ready to manufacture (or nearly so), and/or (2) there will be almost no incremental costs or risks in marketing and sales, and/or (3) this is or will be a very high margin (high profitability) business in an exploding market. The net result of this point of view could be a proposal that reflects a 33 percent split or even higher.

And regardless of the relative weights of the seller's and buyer's argument, the application of any heuristic rule such as 25 percent requires the agreement as to 25 percent *of what*. In simple situations the "of what" is that which, but for the technology license, would be unavailable cost savings or new profits to the buyer. However, in other situations the technology is part of an overall manufacturing process under development to minimize total variable costs or of an integrated product for which revenues are received for a bundle of features/functions.

The key point here is that 25 percent, and to a lesser extent 33 percent, has emerged as a commonly cited number that appears to be helpful in many negotiations. However, it is not a rigid "rule," despite the use of the word next to "25 percent." The specific circumstances of each valuation should be analyzed to determine whether it deserves more, the same as, or less than that given by the 25 Percent Rule. One useful tool for conducting such an analysis is the Rating/Ranking Method (discussed in Chapter 5). An effective way of using rating/ranking for this purpose is to use as a comparable agreement one which is known (or believed) to have resulted in a valuation and agreement that reflects the use of the 25 Percent Rule. Then by conducting a rating/ranking scoring process, one can develop a perspective as to whether the present valuation is wisely guided by 25 percent or by some other number. And, as will be discussed later in this chapter there are some limitations of its application that should be recognized.

Use of the 25 Percent Rule for Apportioning New Profits

In our initial discussion of the 25 Percent Rule, the example used was a cost savings of $100 per unit. In most licensing situations, what is being licensed is more appropriately considered as creating new revenues rather than reduced costs. How would one apply the rule to such a situation? The 25 Percent Rule for this case can be stated as follows: The royalty in percent of net sales price should be one quarter of net sales after deduction of (1) cost of goods sold (including depreciation of relevant plant and equipment), (2) appropriately allocated general and administrative cost, (3) appropriately allocated marketing and sales cost, and (4) any other appropriate costs (but not including interest, taxes or dividends). Let us now consider each of these elements.

Net Sales Price

Why, after all the discussion of dividing profit or gain, does one base the royalty on sales? Rather, it would seem convenient for the buyer and seller to agree that the buyer will simply pay the seller a royalty of 25 percent (or some other percentage) of its pretax profit, as such a figure includes the deduction of the appropriate costs. This actually is a bad idea. Companies pay taxes on their pretax profit.[20] So there are (well) paid people at such companies to make every effort to reduce the taxable exposure. Further, companies of any reasonable size create operating groups onto which costs are allocated with wide discretion and such allocations determine profitability for such groups and individual products. Basing a royalty on a number that is calculated "low" (i.e., below the top line, namely that of sales) on the income statement is just not a good idea. For this reason, almost without exception sellers insist that the royalty be based on the easiest-to-measure number: sales revenues. The term "net sales" will be discussed in Chapter 11, but "net" in this context does not refer to net of operating costs but of certain direct costs associated with delivering the sale, such as shipping and insurance. So the split of the value is determined by an appropriate analysis of the profits, but it is *administered* by a payment of a separately determined percentage (typically a royalty rate) of the revenues.

Appropriately Allocated Cost of Goods Sold

Cost of goods sold (commonly designated COGS) refers to the direct costs of producing the product or service. It typically includes the cost of raw materials, the direct labor of converting the materials to the product, the depreciation cost of the necessary manufacturing equipment, and so forth. A portion of all such costs are unambiguously connected to the making of the product from the technology. Some of the costs are calculations derived from many circumstances, such as two products, one based on the licensed technology and one not, being made on the same machine in the same building. How should the depreciation costs of machine and building be allocated between the licensed product and all other uses? Like all cost allocation issues, there is some degree of interpretation and opinion involved.

The number that results from subtracting COGS from net sales is called the "gross margin." It is a very important barometer of profitability and, as such, is widely reported and studied. However, the reported values for gross margin are not always to be relied upon. It is believed that some public companies engage in reporting lower gross margins by finding ways to increase the calculated cost of goods sold so as to dissuade competitors from entering a business because of the attractiveness of high reported gross margins; another example of a rule of thumb is that if your gross margin is more than 50 percent you will be attacked by competitors.

Also, upon seeing "juicy" gross margins a company's customers are likely to become more aggressive in their purchase negotiations. Finally shareholders, who always want to see costs minimized, are especially vigilant for overhead (SG&A—sales, general, and administrative) costs, so some companies interpret certain gray area costs as being COGS. There are also motivations to overstate gross margins as we have recently learned in the postmortem of various company collapses. Companies reporting high gross margins tend to be more attractive to investors, even for the same value of EBIT, because of a belief that the present SG&A costs can be reduced as a percentage as the company grows and after incurring certain one-time expenses such as a new launch of a major new product. These uncertainties in real gross and other margins are serious complications to valuation because the gross margin is a very useful measure of the profitability of a technology or business. Sellers are at a valuation and pricing disadvantage if they are unable to make accurate estimates of the potential gross margin of a product. Conversely, buyers who are likely to have a much better estimate of their potential gross margins are motivated to understate them.

Two points should be made here: (1) basing royalties on gross margins, rather than net sales, is fraught with accounting (and other) perils and should rarely, if ever, be done, and (2) there is some inherent uncertainty (putting it charitably) when surveying gross margins data on public companies.

Other Allocated Costs

As one goes lower on the income statement, there is increasing room for, shall we say, discretion in allocating costs. Below the gross margin line are the general overhead (sometimes known as SG&A) and other expenses of running a business. Considering an appropriate allocation of sales cost for, say, a drug being licensed, the result can be very different if the drug will be sold through an existing sales force, or whether an entirely new sales force has to be created, or through some combination of the two. Other issues relating to general allocations will be considered in the next section, which covers specific examples.

Restatements of earnings, which amounts to corrections in previously reported, audited financial statements has been a "growth industry." For the nine-year period 1997 to 2005 there were 3,642 such restatements, but 1,200 restatements were for just 2005 alone.[21] In Chapter 7 on the DCF Method we will address further some of the perils of reliance on accounting statements, particularly as one descends further down a company's income statement from its recognized revenues down to gross margin, net margin, and after-tax profits.

Examples of Applying the 25 Percent Rule to New Profits Licensing

Considering first a generic example, let us take the following "data" from the marketplace and apply the 25 Percent Rule. Considering the case where the buyer has revenues of $100, and "profits" of 7.54 percent, what would be an appropriate royalty from the application of the 25 Percent Rule? We will assume for this example that the appropriate costs have been included in the income statement leading to the reported profit figure.

The calculation of such "profit" number begins with the revenues, deducts all the direct costs (COGS, as defined above), indirect costs (SG&A), and other costs (such as interest expense and restructuring or other extraordinary costs), and finally provision for taxes (both federal and state/local). The final number, often referred to as EAT for earnings after tax, represents the net gain from operations after all bills have been paid. It is the figure to be distributed to the shareholders (the owners) or to be retained by management for reinvestment in the company, or any combination of the two.

One way to apply the 25 Percent Rule is to start with such after-tax profit and work backward. The 25 Percent Rule should be based upon a pretax profit which is known by a variety of terms: EBIT (Earnings Before Interest and Taxes),[22] operating profit, even "gross profit"; here we shall use EBIT. The immediate question is why the 25 Percent Rule should be applied to pretax profits. The answer is that the royalty is an expense of operations and like any other expense of operations it is a deductible business expense that reduces taxable profits. Further, the seller receiving such royalties will have to pay tax on such moneys (depending, of course, on the kind of entity the seller is and its particular tax situation in any year in which it receives such royalties). Additionally the value of the technology's contribution should not be influenced by the way the buyer has financed its operations. In addition, the value "25" in the 25 Percent Rule has evolved because parties used such EBIT value as the basis for the calculations.

To convert from after-tax to pretax dollars, one divides by the factor: "1 – T," where T is the effective tax rate of the reporting organization as a decimal value. Although the value of T depends upon specific circumstances, including the effective tax rate of the respective state/local government, for illustration purposes the factor 0.40 will be used. Thus, dividing 7.54 by 0.6 (which comes from 1 – 0.4) results in 12.57 percent pretax earnings.

Using the 25 Percent Rule on these data, taking 25 percent or one quarter of the value of 12.57 percent, would result in a royalty of 3.14 percent of sales.[23] Such payment would become a revenue line to the seller and an expense line to the buyer, reducing the buyer's pretax profit to 9.43 percent (by simply subtracting 3.14 percent royalty from the 12.57 percent EBIT) which results (by multiplying 9.43 percent by 0.4, the assumed effective tax rate) in an after-tax profit of 5.66 percent. Thus in this example, the seller would receive 3.14 percent of sales, and the buyer's after-tax income would be reduced from 7.54 percent of sales to 5.66 percent of sales for those sales subject to the royalty.

So, on an after-tax basis, the 3.14 percent royalty "cost" the licensee 1.88 points of profit because such 3.14 percent was a deductible business expense.

Performing such a calculation on a company's total profits on which to apply the 25 Percent Rule does not normally produce an appropriate result. This is because in this example the gain has included businesses with widely varying profitability, as well as those that do not use technology to any appreciable degree and those that have a high reliance on technology. Also, the calculation did not take into account the specific marginal costs (COGS and SG&A) of adding the licensed technology into the product mix of the licensee. The calculation also did not take into account those portions of costs of goods sold and the related SG&A that were marginal to adding the licensed technology into the product in that it assumed all such costs were incremental/marginal. A much more useful result is obtained when the reference profit numbers are closer to the technology being valued, as will be shown.

Applying the 25 Percent Rule to Specific Companies

In any specific valuation, one should attempt to perform the calculation on an income statement that most closely approximates the expected profitability of commercializing the subject technology. There are two general ways of doing this: bottom's up or benchmark. Bottom's up means that all the terms of the income statement are estimated from first principles. So the COGS would be calculated by considering the actual costs of raw materials required, the labor costs required, the capital equipment and the associated life of such equipment, the number of salespeople and related nonpersonnel costs, and so on. For new technologies it can be quite difficult to make accurate estimates of such costs. Also, in many circumstances the seller is somewhat unfamiliar with the licensed application, which is why the seller is licensing rather than going into manufacturing.

The other approach is to find benchmark data from published sources. This is very similar to what was done in Chapter 4 to find a published agreement approximating the subject valuation and then using the Rating/Ranking Method of Chapter 5 to estimate valuation differentials based on the particular situation.

Thus, the first task is very similar to what was done in performing the Rating/Ranking Method, namely, finding a benchmark or comparable. Rather than using an all-industry composite as was done in the preceding section, it would be much better to be focused on the industry and companies that typify those that will be commercializing the subject technology.

Let us consider a technology whose value in the marketplace is believed to be comparable to that of digital signal processors (DSPs) today. DSPs are a special-purpose semiconductor. Given that assumption, what guidance might the 25 Percent Rule provide? To answer that question we would need to identify public companies for which DSPs are an important business. There are many online screening tools available to do this. One powerful example is CapitalIQ (www.capitaliq.com), which will be used to illustrate initial steps in the process.

Screening tools are all based on a similar idea of applying criteria to whittle down the universe of possible companies to an appropriately focused list. In CapitalIQ the area of semiconductors is grouped within its industry classification of "information technology," which has more than 100,000 companies. By adding to the screening criteria the requirement that the company in its short business description, included both "DSP" and "devices," shrinks the number to 43. It is often useful to also apply income statement criteria such as a minimum annual revenue to screen out companies so small that their financials may be distorted by its heavy investment in growth. Likewise negative EBIT values although possibly significant indicators of a marketplace environment are not useful for a 25 Percent Rule application because the result would be a less than zero implied royalty rate. Using $25 million as the minimum annual revenue and a positive EBIT further reduces our population to just the eight companies shown in Exhibit 6.1.

The total revenues and EBIT of these eight companies is shown at the bottom line of Exhibit 6.1, and the EBIT in dollars and as a percentage of revenues. For purposes of illustration we will assume that these eight companies, based upon the

EXHIBIT 6.1 Semiconductors and Other Components

Company Name	Total Revenue ($mm) [LTM*]	EBIT ($mm) [LTM*]	EBIT %	25% Rule Implied Royalty Rate %
Taiwan Semiconductor Manufacturing Co. Ltd. (TSEC:2330)	11,265.8	4,014.9	35.6%	8.9%
Xilinx Inc. (NasdaqGS:XLNX)	1,922.3	486.0	25.3%	6.3%
Okmetic Oyj (HLSE:OKM1V)	95.6	11.0	11.5%	2.9%
Marvell Technology Group Ltd. (NasdaqGS:MRVL)	3,282.4	204.1	6.2%	1.6%
Cirrus Logic Inc. (NasdaqGS:CRUS)	191.0	7.34	3.8%	1.0%
Synplicity Inc.	74.9	1.98	2.6%	0.7%
Zenitron Corp. (TSEC:3028)	686.0	18.1	2.6%	0.7%
CEVA Inc. (NasdaqGM:CEVA)	38.6	0.211	0.5%	0.1%
TOTAL	17,556.6	4,743.6	27.0%	6.8%

*LTM = Last Twelve Months, which corresponds approximately to 2008.

last twelve months of data (which is approximately 2008 in all cases), is a reasonable reflection of the value potential of the subject technology.

Now the question is which EBIT percentage one would use, given that they range widely, as they typically do, here from less than 1 percent to more than 35 percent, with an average value of 27 percent. Clearly a prospective buyer would likely find 25 percent, or any percent, of the 1 percent EBIT an acceptable starting position, but can one just choose a favorite "poster child" and its value?

Two common benchmarks as a starting point are the mean value, and some proxy for an upper level performer. Using the mean value of 27 percent, and applying the 25 percent rule results in an implied royalty rate of 6.8 percent as shown in the right-most column. As is typical in such compilations, the mean value of the group does not yield the same implied royalty rate as the median company. In Exhibit 6.1 the median is bracketed by Marvel and Cirrus with EBIT percentages of 6.2 and 3.8 percent, suggesting a royalty rate in the 1.0 to 1.6 percent range.

There is often a basis for reasoning that the proxy for value for the new technology is greater than the median of incumbent technology. The argument goes likes this. Once a product is introduced, a company is inclined to keep selling it so long as to provide a positive contribution to margin, namely that its EBIT is greater than zero because its startup costs are sunk and it presently contributes to both overhead costs and overall margin. So if one looks at the entire portfolio of products comprising the revenue and EBIT dollars of a particular company, there is a spectrum of performers from "stars" to "dogs." So its average EBIT under-reflects its aspirations for new products, as the portfolio is "weighed" down by its historic dogs but needs to be continuously upgraded with new stars. So, by this reasoning, an opportunity presented to a company that would be at or below its current EBIT performance is unlikely to be of high commercial interest.

Another factor in such argument is that the margins on incumbent products (after a startup period) tend to erode over time as the technology matures and competitive alternatives emerge. Another factor is that for a new technology opportunity being added to the product mix, there is some efficiency in the use of overhead costs such that the *marginal* EBIT will be better than the average EBIT even if it were an average performer.

On the basis of such reasoning, and in the absence of contrary indications, sellers argue for EBIT percentages corresponding to upper half values such as the top quartile or quintile values. In Exhibit 6.1, the upper quartile is comprised of the top two companies, Taiwan Semiconductor and Xilinix, at EBIT percentages of 35.6 and 25.3 percent, respectively, and implied royalties (using the 25 Percent Rule) of ca. 6 to 9 percent as shown.

Further Refining Benchmark Categories

In the previous section's example, the benchmark category was obtained by selecting the most appropriate grouping in one indexed source of data (*BusinessWeek*). A better benchmark could be obtained by creating one's own grouping based upon an analysis of the subject technology. This could be done by identifying about ten specific companies that appear to be closely related in technology, industry, and business model to the deal being valued. Start by identifying (1) companies to which the technology is being marketed, (2) competitors of such companies, (3) companies of like SIC or NAICS code (a standardized classification system used to index companies), (4) companies found from Internet or library searches that make products like or similar to those produceable by the technology, and (5) companies from lists such as those compiled by *BusinessWeek* and others such as Ibbotson, Bloomberg, Thompson Reuters, Capital IQ, Business Valuation Resources, and free online sources such as the "finance" sections of Google and Yahoo. Google, for instance, provides financial data on more than 190 companies within its "semiconductor" category.

All such data should consider multiple time periods (if available). Certainly whole years should be used, because there are seasonal effects. Multiple years should be considered to average out unusual fluctuations.

The data should then be analyzed to see if some companies should be dropped from the calculation because, for example, they had losses or their business performance was suppressed because of other factors. There may also be cases where the top performers might be excluded: the "Tiger Woods" effect. Other reasons could include extraordinary performance due to a huge new marketing initiative, or the realization of profits from the sale of a division, and so forth.

All of this can consume a significant amount of time and requires critical thinking. For this reason it is common to employ consulting experts to develop some or all of this type of information or to provide an expert pair of eyes to review an internally prepared analysis. The economic significance of the valuation in question has to be used to determine how much effort should be expended. If a particular opportunity cannot conceivably be worth more than, say, \$100,000 in total, then it is not prudent to spend \$25,000 worth of time or consulting to develop a ten member benchmark category. On the other hand, if the opportunity could be worth \$10 million, it is worth making a serious effort to develop a thorough economic framework in preparation for negotiation.

EXHIBIT 6.2 Example Applications of the 25 Percent Rule

Raychem Annual Report, 1991	$K	%
Sales	1,249,512	100
COGS*	643,357	52
Gross Margin	606,155	48
SD&A	447,607	36
R&D	140,196	11
EBIT**	18,352	1
Interest	8,090	
Restructuring	3,697	
Other	9,674	
EBT†	(3,109)	(0.25)
	Now What?	0.25%?
		(0.06%)?

Morgan Matroc Annual Report, 1991 European Company	£M	%
"Turnover"	454.0	100
Other Inc.	2.2	
	456.2	
"Operating Costs"	405.0	89
EBIT	51.2	11
"Investments"	(1.4)	
"Finance Charges"	8.7	
EBT	43.9	10
	Now what?	2.5%?

*Cost of Goods Sold (all "direct" costs of making the product).
**Earnings Before Interest and Taxes.
†Earnings Before Tax.

Source: Raychem & Morgan Matroc Company Annual Reports. Reprinted with permission.

Using a Specific Company's Profitability for the 25 Percent Rule

Another approach to finding a benchmark for the 25 Percent Rule calculation is to identify one single company instead of looking at a category. In this section, two examples will be considered: Raychem and Morgan Matroc.

In Exhibit 6.2, the income statement for Raychem for the year 1991 is presented. In previous examples, the starting point was the after-tax profit numbers. A more accurate method is to look at the income statement and examine how the profitability number was reached. Recall that the definition of the 25 Percent Rule introduces the ideas of "appropriate" deductions from the sales number. In the Raychem example we see the following deductions from sales: COGS (Cost of Goods Sold) of $643 million or 52 percent of sales, SD&A (Sales, Distribution, and Administrative) of $448 million or 36 percent of sales, R&D of $140 million or 11 percent of sales, leaving an EBIT of just $18 million or 1.5 percent of sales.

Below the EBIT line, there are two other deductions: interest expense (paying lenders of capital employed by Raychem) and "restructuring costs" (presumably nonrecurring costs associated with some significant change in business operations). Together, these two additional charges result in a net loss for the year of $3 million, shown as EBT (Earnings Before Tax).

Now, assuming that Raychem 1991 is the appropriate benchmark, how would one apply the 25 Percent Rule? Clearly, applying the 25 Percent Rule to the EBT line would result in no royalty at all, which makes no sense. However, one cannot just arbitrarily pick a favorite line on the income statement and take 25 percent of that number as the appropriate royalty calculation.

What about the appropriateness of the interest and restructuring cost deductions? Restructuring costs, like other extraordinary costs, are by their nature not reflective of normal business operations. Although they may be a legitimate deduction for tax computation purposes, it is not reasonable to deduct these costs from the profitability calculation for computing royalties. Adding such costs back increases the EBT line to $10 million or 0.8 percent of sales.

What about interest costs? Generally it is not appropriate to deduct such costs before applying the 25 Percent Rule. The idea is that a company obtains capital from lenders and equity holders in accordance with its financing strategy. However, the corporate financing strategy should not be used to affect the profitability calculation for use with the 25 Percent Rule.

Exhibit 6.2 also shows the 1991 financial data for Morgan Matroc, a UK company. This is an example of a sparse income statement. "Turnover" corresponds to sales. "Operating costs" encompasses COGS, SG&A, and R&D. The lack of detail shows how difficult it can be to use financial reports to analyze the real operating economics.

By studying an income statement, judgments can be reached about the appropriateness of the charges against profitability in the context of the subject valuation. For example, the COGS shown is 52 percent. If estimates can be made of the COGS that will occur for the subject technology, then this figure could be adjusted upward or downward to more accurately reflect the prospective situation. Although adjustments could also be made for SD&A (more commonly termed "SG&A"), and R&D, it is more difficult to rationalize. One could argue that R&D costs are really being incurred to develop other products for the company—products which will not be subject to the royalty and so will not benefit the seller. From this perspective, R&D costs should not be deducted. On the other hand, R&D covers a bundle of activities associated with keeping products up to date with enhancements, new models, and so forth, and such costs will benefit the seller because they will tend to keep the technology up to date and commercially useful. So, generally speaking, it does make sense to allocate some R&D costs prior to using the 25 Percent Rule. Further analysis could reveal appropriate adjustments in such costs if the company is incurring extraordinarily lower- or higher-than-average costs in those business segments that make products closely related to the technology being licensed.

Likewise, adjustments in SG&A could be made because, for example, the company incurs very large sales costs on average, but will not incur them for the subject technology (or vice versa). Again, a detailed analysis should be performed to determine norms for such costs and to compare them to the specific income statement being analyzed.

If we conclude that the COGS, SG&A, and R&D are appropriate allocations, and the restructuring is not, then the bottom line EBIT is 1.5 percent of sales, so the 25 Percent Rule suggests a royalty of 0.37 percent. However, such a low value of EBIT would not be credible to an opportunity licensing situation: why would a buyer aspire to enter such a low performing business?

Considering a pharmaceutical example, in Exhibit 6.3 is the income statement of Eli Lilly for the year 2000.

EXHIBIT 6.3 Eli Lilly Income Statement

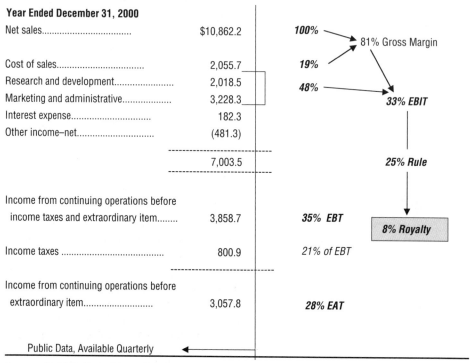

Year Ended December 31, 2000		
Net sales	$10,862.2	**100%**
Cost of sales	2,055.7	**19%**
Research and development	2,018.5	**48%**
Marketing and administrative	3,228.3	
Interest expense	182.3	
Other income–net	(481.3)	
	7,003.5	
Income from continuing operations before income taxes and extraordinary item	3,858.7	**35% EBT**
Income taxes	800.9	*21% of EBT*
Income from continuing operations before extraordinary item	3,057.8	**28% EAT**

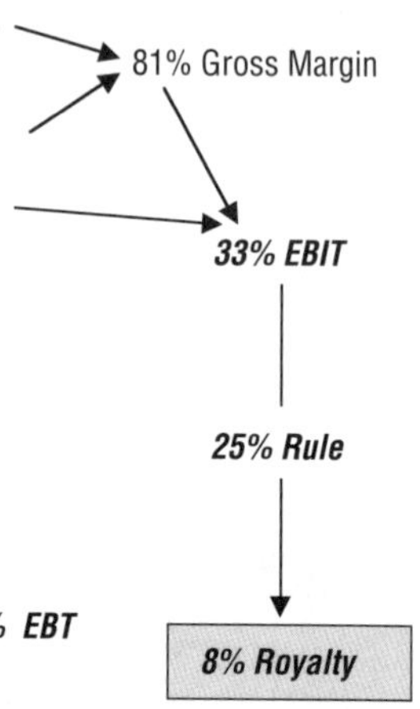

Public Data, Available Quarterly

Source: © 2003 Razgaitis, richard@razgaitis.com.

As is characteristic of pharmaceutical companies, the value of COGS (shown by Lilly as "cost of sales") is very low as a percentage because the direct cost of the chemicals and packaging in making a drug is (like perfume, beer, and Crayolas®) quite low (in the latter three examples, the cost of the packaging is frequently greater than the cost of the contents). What is very costly are the selling and marketing costs, because of the high cost of "detailing" drugs to doctors and hospital formularies and advertising, and because of the high cost of developing new drugs (as shown in the R&D expense of more than $2 billion or 18.6 percent of sales). If all such costs were included in calculating an EBIT for licensing purposes, and the 25 Percent Rule applied, the resulting royalty would be, as shown, approximately 8 percent. However, for such a licensing situation a number of substantial adjustments would need to be applied. As discussed elsewhere, the R&D cost in large part can be reasoned not to belong as a deduction for 25 Percent Rule calculation because it is an expense Lilly is incurring to develop other, non-royalty-bearing products; arguably, some of such costs would or could be relevant to enhancing and sustaining the licensed product and as such should be included. The marketing and sales costs are another matter requiring careful attention. It would be normal for a licensor to approach candidate licensees who are already established at selling into the markets relevant to the technology opportunity. So, for instance, if the seller has a new wonder drug for heart disease, it would make sense to target pharmaceutical companies who already have an established sales and marketing force targeted to cardiologists. This being the case, the seller can then reason that the only cost that should be deducted from the gross margin should be the incremental cost of marketing and selling the drug, not the apportioned total cost of the existing marketing and selling infrastructure. Eli Lilly would argue, with some justification, that someone has to account for the basic infrastructure; for example, one cannot expect to hop on an airplane by paying only the small incremental cost of the fuel consumed to carry your additional weight to the destination under the argument that the airplane and pilot would have been there anyway and so the costs should not be allocated to your ticket.

There are additional factors that should be considered in applying the 25 Percent (or other valued) Rule. One large factor is the stage of development, or degree of completion, of the technology at the time of the license. Licensing in the pharmaceutical industry is a perfect example of this issue. There is a long and very expensive process required by companies and the FDA (Food and Drug Administration) of the U.S. Government to obtain government approval to sell a drug to the public. In a 1994 interview with Merck's CFO (Chief Financial Officer) published in the *Harvard Business Review*, Judy Lewent characterized in general terms that "roughly one in 10,000 explored chemicals become a prescription drug" and "we need to make huge investments now and may not see a profit for ten to 15 years."[24] If the license valuation is occurring prior to even the first phase, then Lilly would rightly argue that the cost, time-to-market, and risk (FDA satisfaction as well as market risk) do not warrant 25 percent.

Another factor that can arise is commonly termed royalty "stacking." Staying with the Lilly example, suppose the seller is licensing a proprietary time-release drug delivery system for a pharmaceutical that Lilly has already licensed from a third party. When Lilly sells the drug in the marketplace, it is going to receive one revenue payment for the drug in the bottle, which includes the chemical composition and the delivery means. Accordingly, even if Lilly agreed to pay a 25 Percent Rule royalty, it could not do so to each of the two licensors. An even more compelling situation can be envisioned by considering a telecommunication switch or a computer that has perhaps dozens or hundreds of patents governing its operation. If such a manufacturer had to pay 25 Percent Rule royalties to four licensors, it would be left with no profits. Accordingly, the application of such rule has to generally consider 25 percent, or whatever is the appropriate apportionment, in the context of all the enabling technology. This does not mean that all relevant licensors share equally (*pari passau*), because their economic contributions are very unlikely to be equal. Nor does it mean that any one needed licensor can justifiably command the full 25 percent in a standoff situation.

There are multiple sources of EBIT information available. Every public company must report such information quarterly (so called 10-Q's) and annually (10-K's) to the Securities and Exchange Commission (SEC) of the U.S. government. However, as recent events have shown, these numbers that are already difficult to interpret because, for example, of the different ways companies treat extraordinary costs, have been in certain cases simply invented fraudulent values designed to mislead investors. In currently unfolding events, Worldcom apparently eliminated billions of dollars in current years expenses by treating them as capital costs for the apparent purpose of portraying a higher gross margin and net income to investors; if one were licensing to them, such a maneuver would actually work to their detriment because

EXHIBIT 6.4 Operating Margin Data (Ibbotson Associates)

Operating Margins

Average Sales	Small Cap $320M	Mid Cap $780M	Large Cap $2.9B
Latest (1995)			
90th Percentile	34.38%	38.36%	40.48%
75th Percentile	21.91%	29.17%	31.29%
→ *Median*	*13.15%*	*17.69%*	*20.51%*
25th Percentile	8.12%	11.18%	13.64%
10th Percentile	3.87%	7.14%	9.18%
Industry Composite	11.22%	14.69%	18.80%
Five Year Average (ending 1995)			
90th Percentile	31.35%	35.40%	39.23%
75th Percentile	20.07%	25.89%	27.64%
→ *Median*	*2.33%*	*16.50%*	*18.50%*
25th Percentile	7.65%	10.59%	12.91%
10th Percentile	4.29%	6.61%	8.32%
Industry Composite	11.00%	13.69%	17.35%

Source: Ibbotson Cost of Capital Yearbook, Ibbotson Associates, 1995.

it would argue for a higher royalty. It is expected that over the next year or two there could be substantial restatement and correction of recently filed income statements and over time improved uniformity of how revenue and costs are interpreted and applied. In the meanwhile, it makes an accurate determination of licensing EBIT more challenging.

One source of EBIT information is Ibbotson Associates (now part of Morningstar, www.morningstar.com). An example of their data is shown in Exhibit 6.4.

Shown here are example single-year and five-year quartile EBIT values ("operating margins") and for three categories of company sizes based on market capitalization. As discussed here and elsewhere, normally the licensed subject matter is intended to improve the operating performance of the licensee. In such case, the appropriate EBIT is not the median of the respective industry, or even that of the licensee, but some higher value reflecting a realistic expectation of the economic advantage anticipated. Shown in this chart is the 75th percentile as a proxy for such higher-than-average performance expectation. So, using 75th percentile and the five-year average for the small cap company, the corresponding EBIT is 20 percent and the 25 Percent Rule would then suggest a 5 percent royalty rate. However, Ibbotson bases their operating margins on revenues less costs but not less the cost of depreciation and amortization, which tends to inflate the resulting value. If the licensee has to build an expensive facility to practice the technology, the depreciation cost is a legitimate deduction from their projected revenue.

Other sources of EBIT value include Bloomberg, which publishes a wealth of current and historic information on company financials, Capital IQ (www.capitaliq.com), the Almanac of Business and Industrial Financial Ratios,[25] and Schonfeld & Associates,[26] both of these latter organization publish corporate financial ratios by industry as determined from more than four million tax returns (schedules C and S) filed with the U.S. Internal Revenue Service (IRS).

The "Pure Play" Analysis

All of the above examples were based upon public data for companies making multiple products. Although some useful information can be obtained by analyzing clusters of related companies, it would be better to find financial data on companies that make essentially only products similar to those being planned under the subject valuation. This is the notion of a "pure play."

The approach is similar to the previous discussion except that the search for benchmarks (comparables) is confined to just the products in question. In many cases this search yields very small companies.

Although such examples exhibit the usefulness of pertinent costs, there are other issues that require interpretation of the data. First, such companies can be rapidly growing which causes significant growth costs of funding inventory, advanced sales in addition to marketing, and so forth. This can bias the profitability to lower values. Also, because they are small, such companies can be subcritical and are thereby incurring a higher percentage of SG&A and R&D than a larger, more established company might incur. Finally, many smaller companies are privately held and their financial data can be harder or impossible to find.

Nevertheless, even with these cautions, it is a good idea to find some examples of pure plays to supplement the analysis.

The Use of a Bottom Up Income Statement Estimate

All of the approaches to finding EBIT values and applying the 25 Percent Rule rely on data available from existing companies. Another, more complex, approach is to prepare an income statement for a hypothetical business unit (or company) created solely to make products from the subject technology. This process is sometimes referred to the making of a *pro forma*, that is, a forward-looking, estimate of business performance.

Preparing such a pro forma would require a mature understanding of how manufacturing, marketing and sales, R&D, and overall administration of such a new business would operate. If the technology is at an early stage, there may need to be substantial assumptions about how the product would be manufactured. Often this leads to a scenario approach to financial modeling: namely, two or three different models are developed (such as optimistic, pessimistic, and most likely) based upon different manufacturing approaches and efficiencies. Similar assumptions would likely need to be made about pricing and other elements of an income statement.

Outside experts knowledgeable in the industry are frequently necessary to be able to determine usable numbers. Depending upon the potential significance of the licensing deal, such expenditure may or may not be warranted. When such an investment is made, it can provide a very useful cross-reference to the EBIT data obtained from industry analysis.

Technology buyers typically have an important valuation advantage as they are more likely to have good estimates on the costs of making the technology into a business, although they may likewise have to use a scenario approach because of substantial uncertainties.

One potential benefit of both buyers and sellers performing this type of analysis is that it can lead to creative ways of structuring a license so that the royalty rate could be adjusted based upon future events. For example, this can happen through the use of a royalty or lump-sum "kicker." A baseline royalty (fixed payment sums) is calculated assuming a more conservative outcome for manufacturing cost (for example). Then, if it happens that the more optimistic manufacturing costs come true, because the yield is higher or the process is faster or the raw materials are cheaper, then there is an additive royalty (or payments) known as a kicker. Thus, an agreement could be structured with a 3 percent royalty on all sales providing that the product is made in accordance with Scenario A (the more conservative scenario); however, if Scenario B results, then the buyer agrees to pay a kicker royalty of an additional 2 percent (making it a 5 percent royalty) to reflect the added profitability resulting from the more favorable outcome.

Such approaches can be creative ways of dealing with highly uncertain situations by sharing risk. However, to avoid subsequent disputes it is critical that the provisions are carefully specified so that it is clear when the kicker becomes effective.

A Universal Rule of Thumb Chart

A graphical portrayal of the 25 Percent, and any other, Rule along with the related valuation adjustments is shown in Exhibit 6.5.

Shown along the inside left scale are percentage values for the rule of thumb starting at 5 percent, in 5 percentage point increments to a maximum of 50 percent. The highlighted value for 25 percent merely illustrates the starting point concept of the 25 Percent Rule.

Shown along the top axis are the projected EBIT values of the commercial use of the subject technology starting at 10 percent, then 15, 20, 30, 40, and 50. Using the "rule" and "EBIT" values fixes a royalty rate because, by definition, the royalty rate is simply equal to the "rule" multiplied by the "EBIT." So, for example, looking at Exhibit 6.5 for the row corresponding to the 25 Percent Rule and below the column headed by the project EBIT of 20 percent we would expect that 25 percent payment to the seller of a 20 percent EBIT realized by the buyer corresponds to a royalty of 5 percent, which is just what is seen within the highlighted box. That is, a royalty of 5 percent paid by the buyer-licensee to the seller-licensor acts just as an additional cost of manufacture for the licensee of 5 percentage points, reducing its EBIT from what it would have realized, namely 20 percent, to what it now realizes, namely 15 percent; thus it has "shared" with the licensor, 25 percent of its EBIT, which is precisely what the 25 Percent Rule assumes.

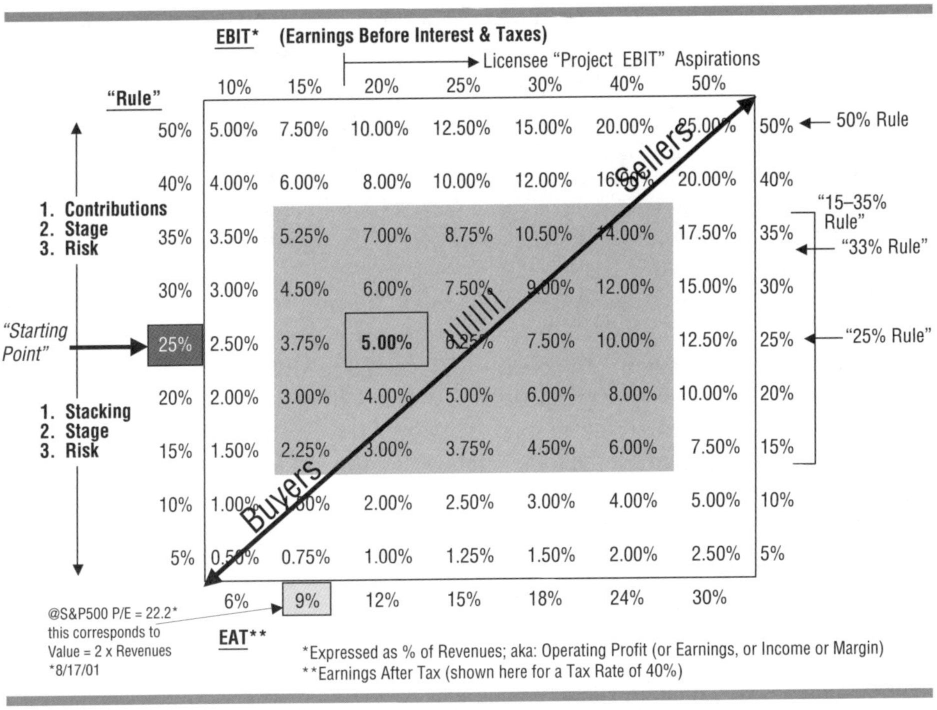

EXHIBIT 6.5 Universal Rule of Thumb Chart
Source: © 2003 Razgaitis, richard@razgaitis.com.

All the other values within the outer frame are similarly just the product of the rule percentage on the left axis and the EBIT percentage across the top. So, for example, a 4 percent royalty would be appropriate if (1) the appropriate rule was a high 40 percent on a low projected EBIT of 10 percent, and (2) the appropriate rule was a low 10 percent on a high projected EBIT of 40 percent, and (3) for the case of a 20 percent rule with a 20 percent EBIT. Clearly there are an infinite number of combinations of rule and EBIT that would yield a 4 percent (or any other) royalty.

Shown along the right axis are various rules that have been cited as discussed previously in this chapter, namely: the 33 percent rule, the 15 to 35 percent range, and the 50 percent rule. Along the very left of the chart is shown how sellers and buyers would reason such rule value up or down in consideration of relative additional contributions by the seller or the buyer (the latter is sometimes referred to as the stacking issue), the stage of development, unusual risks, and any other relevant factors.

Shown along the bottom of the chart are the corresponding licensee earnings after tax (EAT) corresponding to the commercialization of the project. For illustration purposes, a nominal tax rate of 40 percent[27] has been used in making the calculation so that:

$$EAT = (1.0 - 0.4) * EBIT = 0.6 * EBIT$$

Noted by the EAT value of 9 percent, for a price/earnings ratio of 22, which was what the S&P 500 showed in 2001, the market value would correspond to twice the annual revenues. This is determined simply as follows:

Market Value/Annual Revenues = (P/E Ratio) * EAT = 22 * 0.09 = 2 (approximately)

Put in words, if investors are willing to pay a so-called P/E multiple of 22 for a company whose EAT was 9 percent (which would correspond to an EBIT of 12 percent for a tax rate of 40 percent), then they are valuing the company at the equivalent of twice its annual revenues.

Finally, on Exhibit 6.5 is shown a diagonal line between the upper right corner and the lower left corner. Sellers clearly hope that their licensing opportunities are toward the upper right corner, justifiably large rules of thumb, because of the specific circumstances, for opportunities that will be very high in EBIT, again because of the specific circumstances. Although buyers are generally also seeking high EBIT opportunities, their perspective of the value may well be more toward the lower left corner as they see less of a relative contribution by the seller than the seller perceives and may be more pessimistic about its EBIT potential in the face of all the costs of doing business, the power of their customers to push down prices, and the general competitive environment. Some of the pushing back and forth along this diagonal can be just the respective posturing of buyers and sellers in their negotiation assertions. However, there is, by this Rule-of-Thumb Method a basis for making a reasoned defense of the advocated, reasonable royalty rate.

Other Percent Rule Values

The 25 Percent Rule, though widely cited, may not be appropriate in many licensing situations. One can easily conceive of circumstances where the technology being sold is very far from commercialization, in terms of investment and time required, for an outcome that is not predicted to be commercially significant; it is unlikely that a buyer, under such conditions, would be willing to pay as much as the 25 Percent Rule computation. The Rating/Ranking Method could be used to scale the 25 Percent Rule downward.

On the other hand, there are also circumstances whereby the seller deserves and should receive more than the 25 Percent Rule. Software licensing can easily involve significant contributions by the seller in creating something more akin to a product. Further, a seller could agree to complete the software that expresses the technology (invention) inclusive of documentation and training manuals and activities, as well as provide ongoing telephone hot line support for the buyer, and perhaps, even commit to providing upgrades. When a software licensor delivers substantially turn-key software it is commonly termed a "reseller agreement." Such seller-buyer relationships can approximate wholesale/retail sales: the wholesaler provides the finished product and the retailer owns and manages the storefront and the direct one-to-many retail selling environment. Under these circumstances, the appropriate split of the gain may be a 50 percent rule, or even more than 50 percent.

The Rating/Ranking Method used on one or more benchmark agreements, or clusters of agreements, can guide both the seller and buyer in determining a fair split of the gain. The closer the benchmark agreement is to the subject valuation, the more accurately the Rating/Ranking Method can be used. In Chapter 7, an additional tool will be presented.

Some Misuses / Misapplications of the 25 Percent Rule

The appeal of ease-of-use of the 25 Percent Rule can lead to its use in ways that are not correct. One of the most obvious misapplications is, as discussed already, a licensor assuming that it is entitled to 25 percent of a licensee's EBIT regardless of the number of patents and potentially other licenses that may be essential to using the given technology commercially. The concept behind the 25 Percent Rule is that such 25 percent (or whatever the proper percentage) is for *all* the IP/technology needed, including IP that the licensee may need to provide. To do otherwise, would readily result in a licensee being obligated to pay 50, 75, 100, or more percent of its EBIT to two, three, four, or more licensors.

A flawed variant of the above error is to assume that the then current licensor is entitled to 25 percent of whatever is left of EBIT after previous licenses by other parties, including IP from the licensee's own R&D programs. Such a model would mean that the royalty rate for each individual license would depend upon the order in which the licensors showed up to negotiate.

Another error that can arise has to do with the royalty base against which the 25 percent (however adjusted) is applied. In the cost savings illustration we considered it was implicit that the entire $100 cost savings was due solely to the subject licensed technology. This made the 25:75 dollar split straightforward. With the more common situation of technology for new products, determining the royalty base can be a complicated issue. Consider the situation where the technology being valued and licensed relates to a component of an overall system (or "Box"), where the only anticipated revenues will be for such overall system. Depending on the significance of the component to the commercially valuable features of the system, applying the royalty determined by the 25 Percent Rule to the EBIT of the system can result in a significant over payment to the licensor. For the example we considered with Method 1, Industrial Standards, if an automobile manufacturer seeks a license for a battery connector it would be foolish to consider an application of the 25 Percent Rule to the EBIT of the finished automobile.

A fourth, more subtle error arises by neglecting the effect of a significant delay from the time of the license to initial realization of commercial value. Recall that our 25 Percent Rule example began with splitting a $100 cost savings. Implicit in this approach is that the licensee will be able to experience its 75 percent benefit immediately or very soon after the license. Although not all cost implementations are rapid, the 25 Percent Rule does not explicitly account for the effect of time implementation. If the technology, on either a cost savings or new revenue opportunity, requires a substantial time, and even financial, investment by the licensee, then the effect of a royalty based on the 25 Percent Rule is a much more significant relative proportion of the profits being paid to the licensor than implied by the "25 percent" apportionment. In the next chapter when we have introduced the Discounted Cash Flow Method we will illustrate this effect.

Other Valuation Rules of Thumb Used (or Have Been Proposed)

As in any other profession, there are used or proposed various heuristics (rules of thumb) for various situations. In this section we will consider several such examples. The examples which follow can also be thought of valuation Tools (as part of our ***A-M-T*** metaphor), in that they can provide guidance in deal structure and Dealmaking tradeoffs. First, I must offer an apology and a caveat. I seek to credit the source of any specific insight or suggestion to recognize the contributions of others; for the examples given here, I simply do not recall where or how I first became aware of them and know of no written citation. The caveat is this: These rules of thumb do not have the widespread agreement that the above-described 25 Percent Rule (and its variants) has. In fact, as I argue below, in some cases these "rules" may not be economically supportable. So, my inclusion here is not necessary to endorse them but to codify what has been sometimes asserted.

Upfront Fees as a Royalty Down Payment

As will be discussed in Chapter 7, a down payment of 5 to 10 percent of the total value is a widely used criterion in non–risk-averse situations, such as home or car purchases with a reasonable credit history and ability to pay. Such a value provides some assurance to a lender that the borrower has some capacity to pay in proportion to the amount borrowed (5 to 10 percent), also that such down payment will be large enough in proportion to what is borrowed to dissuade a borrower from abandoning the purchase and walking away. In addition, it indicates that in the event that the borrower does abandon the subject item the lender has some cushion that it can use to regain at least full value of what was lent. In application to licensing when the Wheelbarrow is primarily a running royalty return, it is common that the licensor will require and the licensee accept a license fee that acts as a down payment on such future stream of royalty payments in the range of 5 to 10 percent of their net present value (NPV), a concept that is developed in the next chapter. Although our context is clearly distinct from a lender-borrower situation, the underlying motivations have some similarity. The licensor reasonably wants to see some initial investment capacity by the licensee that is evidence of and in proportion to the ultimate projected royalty payment. Also, the licensor normally wants the licensee committed to the commercial success of what is licensed and, so, seeks some "skin in the game" in the form of license fee as evidence of the licensee's commitment.[28] Finally, in the event of the licensee's termination, the licensor logically wants the opportunity to recover the originally projected NPV by having received such upfront fee and possibly other fees, particularly when the licensee has terminated for reasons unrelated to the commercial merit of the opportunity.[29]

Another upfront fee rule of thumb is one year's mature royalties. In this manifestation, a forecast is made of future revenues subject to royalties and the royalty amounts year by year. Typically, there is an initial period of no revenues, followed by a ramp-up period reaching maturity where the subsequent projected growth corresponds to overall market growth at steady market share. The royalty amount of one of the early years of steady, market growth at its equilibrium market share is then used as the upfront license fee. As will be shown in the next chapter, depending upon the timing and risk of such maturity, the one year's mature royalties could easily fall within the same range as the 5 to 10 percent rule of the preceding paragraph.

Exclusive versus Nonexclusive Royalties

As discussed earlier, when the Box is an exclusive deal, the Wheelbarrow royalties are normally higher than if the Box had been a nonexclusive deal. One rule of thumb that has been used is that market appropriate exclusive royalties are double the nonexclusive royalties, all other things being equal (which they rarely are).

Referring back to the Degnan and Horton survey in Chapter 4, we saw data based on a survey that compared exclusive versus nonexclusive royalty rates. It is difficult to make a generalization based on these results because of the range of overlap, but it is reasonable to see how two to one, exclusive to nonexclusive, could be consistent with these data.

Considering the application of the 25 Percent Rule, such 2:1 rule of thumb suggests that the margins associated with an exclusive right are double those associated with a nonexclusive right. Referring again to Exhibit 6.5 showing the general application of the 25 Percent and other rules to various EBIT levels, one can envision pairing EBIT columns that differ by a factor of two to yield royalty calculations corresponding to exclusive and nonexclusive terms.

This interpretation of margin doubling by exclusivity is a simplification, and possibly an erroneous one, of various possible business situations. Consider the following situation. Licensee A sells its products only to Customer one, with whom it has a special relationship. Prospective Licensee B sells its products broadly into the same market as A, to Customer two through ten, but none to Customer one. Under these facts, it is possible that Licensee A's margins could be unaffected by the presence or absence of Licensee B and, accordingly, would have the same capacity to pay a royalty under a nonexclusive license.[30]

Conversely, one can conceive of a situation where Licensee A is a high-end product provider (a kind of Lamborghini), and Licensee B is an aggressive competitor whose corporate strategy and culture is to be the lowest cost, low-margin market share usurper (think Wal-Mart). In this circumstance, the nonexclusive license to A and B could result in a drastic reduction in (or complete elimination of) A's margin and ability to sell any product and thereby pay royalties.

So, this 2:1, exclusive: nonexclusive, "rule" is a gross simplification that presumes, according to a 25 Percent Rule model that there is a halving of margins by the presence, or potential presence of a directly competing licensed product.

Minimum Royalties

As will be discussed in more detail later in this book, minimum royalties are fixed dollar sums payable quarterly or yearly for the term of the license. They may begin in the initial year of the license or they could be deferred to some later time. As the term is generally used, such royalties are scaled in some way on the parties' expectations of the running royalties, sometimes termed earned royalties to distinguish them from minimum royalties. The magnitude of such minimums is less than the expected earned royalties in the corresponding year.

The rule sometimes proposed for settling on a minimum royalty structure is that they should be 25 to 50 percent of the anticipated earned royalties for the corresponding year with the observation that licensees strongly prefer the 25 percent and licensors the 50 percent, but that establishes the range of negotiation. The idea behind the rule is that the licensor deserves some protection against a less than stalwart market introduction by the licensee and the licensee needs some cushion of less than full royalties as a fixed obligation because things may not go as smoothly as projected for reasons outside its control.

In some cases such a rule, and minimums in general, are inadequate to protect the reasonable licensor's interest. One example would be in pharmaceutical licensing. By any reasoned projection, the minimum royalties scaled on projected earned royalties could be quite distant because of the regulatory hurdles. A licensor entrusting a blockbuster opportunity to a licensee would reasonably want some form of significant milestone, progress, and/or annual payments (subjects to be discussed further in Chapter 11) to not only assure licensee due diligence but also to obtain an earlier return on its having-been-made-earlier investment. Such payments could be so significant, that the minimum royalty provisions could be negotiated at much lower rates than suggested by this rule.

Another factor affecting the reasonableness of this rule is the reasonableness of the projected royalties on which the 25 to 50 percent minimums rule is applied. As will be discussed in the next chapter, revenue and royalty forecasts are frequently done under multiple assumption sets, called scenarios. The parties may, in the alternative, agree to minimum royalty amounts corresponding to the projected earned royalties for a most conservative, or minimum outcome, case under the reasoning that if the licensee is not making at least this royalty payment it will not want to even retain the license, which is a reasonable way of dealing with a future uncertainty. Harmonizing these two approaches, such 25 to 50 percent minimums rule is equivalent to saying that the most likely forecast of royalties is two to four times greater than the most conservative scenario.

Payment for Uncovering Underpayment of Royalties

License agreements are normally self-policed. Licensees compute on an agreed upon frequency, quarterly, semi-annually, or annually, what they think they owe the licensor and submit a payment with a brief report. Most license agreements provide for audit rights of licensors of licensee's records to confirm that such payments were in accordance with the terms of the license. The cost, at least initially, of such audit is borne by the licensor. It is not uncommon, for various reasons, some pure and some not, for such audits to lead to the discovery of an underpayment by the licensor.

A commonly negotiated practice for underpayments greater than 5 to 10 percent is that in the event of the discovery of such underpayment the licensee must pay for the cost of the audit in addition to making up such underpayment. The concept behind the provision is that the licensee should have the business skills and processes in place to accurately pay under the terms of the agreement since it negotiated with the licensee the agreement itself and it has access to all the business records associated with its own operations. Besides, as they say, this is not rocket science, and one assumes that accountants know how to account. So, when anything other than a trivial underpayment occurs, then it is only reasonable that the licensee whose fault it was then be required to pay the audit cost as a kind of tuition in learning how to manage its accounts payable function properly and reimburse the licensor for its investment and trouble. For this reason, licensors strongly favor the 5 percent figure.

Late Payment Penalties

Agreements should have very clear dates when royalty and other payments are due to the licensor. Most agreements establish a late fee penalty in the event of late payment, perhaps as part of broader provisions defining licensor termination rights.

Typically, such late fee penalties are expressed by reference to a prime rate established by some publication or source, plus points. A late payment penalty in the amount of 2 to 4 points above the defined prime rate may be used (so, for a prime rate of 4 percent, such rate applied to the magnitude of late payments would then be 6 to 8 percent).

The logic behind the provision is clearly to encourage timely payments in accordance with the agreement. From a licensor's perspective, such provision is to avoid becoming a technology provider and commercial bank to the licensee.[31] A licensee, particularly a financially troubled one, may resort to viewing all its accounts payables as potential sources of short term financing, an action which could be quite adverse to the licensor's business interests even with the 2 to 4 points premium. (In such instances, the licensor may invoke its termination rights under some provision of a material breach, a subject outside the scope of this book.)

Summary Points on the Use of the 25 Percent Rule

In the previously cited paper by Goldscheider, Jarosz, and Mulhern,[32] the authors seek to find experimental evidence of the 25 Percent Rule. They were able to obtain average royalty rates in each of 15 industries using the database of RoyaltySource.com, and used such data to compare to the average operating profits of the corresponding 15 industries using data from Bloomberg. By ratioing the average royalty rate (say 5 percent) with the average operating profit (say 20 percent), both expressed as percentages, one can calculate, within the framework of such approach, the inferred Rule (so, using my example, 5 percent/20 percent = 25 Percent Rule). Then the authors averaged each of the 15 industry-inferred rules, and found the result close to the value of 25 percent, which is a comforting finding. However, I am compelled to have the reader recall the discussion on risks of averaging at the end of Chapter 4, and the discussion of the Box and Wheelbarrow in Chapter 2, to realize that such approach is interesting but does not itself give empirical proof. Such empirical evidence would require a large sample of directly correlated (paired) royalty rates with expected (or actual) operating profit at the time of the concluded deal. Developing such an empirical understanding would be very useful to valuation practice, but, regrettably, there does not presently appear to be a practicable means for developing such empirical evidence.

Nonetheless, the existence and use of the 25 Percent Rule gives credence that at least many people hold to the view that it is a starting point for valuation in many licensing situations.

Some cautions in the use of the 25 Percent Rule:

- *The appropriate number is not always 25 percent.* The figure "25" (and 33-1/3) has emerged as a common generalization and is many times a useful initial calculation. However, one should always consider whether more or less than 25 percent of the gain is the appropriate reward for the seller.
- *The base against which the 25 percent is applied is subject to judgment.* The idea of the base against which 25 percent is applied is that the gain (profit) should be divided 25:75 between seller and buyer. However, determining the gain requires analysis. In the cost savings approach, it is important to determine the costs of operations without the benefit of the subject technology, and the costs with the technology or as compared to the next best alternative.
- *A pro forma income statement needs to be created.* In the case of new sales, the result of the 25 Percent Rule should be expressed in terms of a royalty against sales so as to create an auditable system. Likewise, in the case of cost savings, some conversion is necessary so that the royalty can be paid on something that is counted in an accounting sense and adjusts for inflation. However, the 25 Percent Rule itself does not provide any guidance on distributing value paid to the seller between upfront payments and running royalties.
- *The 25 Percent Rule does not provide guidance on upfront payments.* The 25 Percent Rule suggests how future savings or profits should be divided between seller and buyer. In normal circumstances there is an upfront license fee paid by the buyer. In order to determine what an appropriate upfront figure should be, some additional methodology is needed. In Chapter 7 some tools for doing this will be reviewed.

Some positive aspects of the 25 Percent Rule that make it popular and worth using are as follows:

- *It gives a feeling of fairness.* Because it is based on apportioning anticipated gain, it creates a basis for considering the respective contributions of the seller and buyer.
- *It is based directly on resulting benefits.* The 25 Percent Rule is focused on the EBIT line in the income statement, which is an appropriate measure of the direct benefit of the subject license (subject to potential adjustment in allocated costs).
- *It can be the basis of an early agreement.* Parties beginning a negotiation can sometimes agree to agree that their negotiations will be governed by the 25 Percent (or some other) Rule. This can be helpful in determining mutual expectations at any early stage and in reaching closure.

Toolkit

In the previous chapter we noted that rating/ranking can also be a ***Tool*** that usefully assists the rule of thumb Method. As shown in Exhibit 6.5 and discussed in the accompanying description, there are several factors that should be assessed in adjusting the numerical percentage of the 25 Percent Rule such as: technical and other risks, the present or likely need for third party IP (including IP of the licensee), time and investment required by the licensee to realize cash inflows. Assessing the effect of all such factors to determine a rule of thumb percentage can be aided by combining a rating/ranking analysis described in Chapter 5 with the Rule of Thumb Method. Likewise rules of thumb can be applied to the Rating/Ranking Method by weighting various valuation factors. For instance, it is commonly believed that "the market" plays a more important role in commercial success than "the technology"—broadly considered. And for startup companies, "management" is frequently given equal or more weight than "the market." The reasoning behind this is that wise management will "find" the market, and the market will "find" the technology. In certain contexts, such as pharmaceuticals, IP rights issues are critical both from a freedom to practice standpoint (withstanding third party patent infringement claims) and also to defend against competitors (infringers). Such judgments can be used to weigh appropriately each factor considered in a valuation.

In the next chapter on the Discounted Cash Flow Method we will see how judgment, often in the form of rules of thumb, is useful to preparing pro forma income and cash flow statements. And in the Chapter 8 on Advanced Methods we will propose how a Monte Carlo Method valuation might use a version of a 20th to 30th percentile range to determine a net present value of an opportunity.

Although our focus here has been on the use of rules of thumb for valuation, as already noted there are many different uses of various rules of thumb as a Tool in support of deal structuring (Chapter 10) and Dealmaking negotiations (Chapter 11), and earlier (Chapter 3) in opportunity Discovery.

Conclusion

Rules of thumb and specifically the 25 Percent Rule are widely used in valuation situations. At the close of 2008, there has been a very public application of such "rule." Pirates off the coast of Somalia captured a world scale, Saudi-owned oil tanker and held it for ransom. At the time of its capture, the market value of the crude oil so captured was approximately $100 million. The pirates, who perhaps as regular readers of the technology valuation publications, concluded that a reasonable value for the return of the tanker to the Saudi Arabian government was—can you guess?—$25 million. This became a matter of substantial negotiations leading to a Dealmaking event at the reported price of $3 million. However, by the time of such Dealmaking event the market price of crude oil had, remarkably, halved, so the 25 Percent Rule figure would have been approximately $12 million, so the final negotiated figure was approximately 25 percent of the 25 Percent Rule value. And, upon departure of the pirates, variously numbered to be two dozen, capsized one of their ships in their haste to escape, and did so with the loss of six pirates, or approximately 25 percent of the pirates.

Like the previous two methods, Industry Standards and Rating/Ranking, the 25 Percent Rule, or any heuristic-based method, requires judgment in its use and is situation specific. The next chapter continues the analysis of the income statement but with more sophistication. Estimates of the actual cash flow of a business will be made. Then, by using certain simple accounting equations, such future cash flows will be discounted to reflect their timing and risk.

Notes

1. *Merriam Webster's Collegiate Dictionary*, Tenth Edition, 1994.
2. According to Charles P. Kindleberger, a retired MIT economist and author of a classic economics text: *Manias, Panics, and Crashes: A History of Financial Crises*, 1978, as quoted in the *Wall Street Journal*, July 25, 2002, p.1.
3. "Let's Talk Turkeys" [in an article about the numerous difficulties of mergers and acquisitions], *BusinessWeek*, December 11, 2000, p. 44.
4. "IBM Boosts Consulting Service with $3.5 Billion PWC Deal," article by William M. Bulkeley and Kemba Dunham, *Wall Street Journal*, July 31, 2002.
5. Of course such characterization is situation specific. The value of incumbency could be negligible if the buyer was failing in its business because its costs were too high. A buyer could also have a poor reputation for product quality or delivery. At the same time, the seller could have strong brand value associated with the technology (although this is less likely with a cost savings approach).
6. Duke Leahy has made this point in talks he has given.
7. This discussion should not be confused with relative magnitude of investment made at these various stages. The timing and risk of investments need to be weighted along with magnitude.
8. As with all generalizations this of course is not exact. Some of "R&D spending" supports even current-year products and their associated revenues. But, generally speaking, R&D spending is primarily directed to creating new product and service revenues (or preventing the erosion of such existing revenues) in years beyond the year of investment.
9. Jules Duga, "Globalization Alters Traditional R&D Rules," *R&D Magazine*, September 2006, p. G1. Total U.S. R&D spending was estimated to be $328.9 billion, with industry being the source of 63.1% of spending. www.battelle.org, www.rdmag.com.
10. This example leads to the same definitional ambiguities encountered in Chapter 1 as to what is "R&D." Because this discussion is intended to be only illustrative, one should not attempt to be precise on the appropriate fraction of R&D that corresponds to "technology" as used here.
11. W.L. Gore and Associates v. International Medical Prosthetics, 16 USPQ 2nd, p. 1257.
12. William Lee Jr., "Determining Reasonable Royalty," *les Nouvelles*, September 1992, p. 24.
13. "The Basics of Licensing," The Licensing Executives Society, 1982.
14. Larry Evans, "Turning Patents and Technology into Money," *Licensing Law and Business Report*, Clark Boardman Company, 1979.
15. Yoshio Matsunaga, "Determining Reasonable Royalty Rates," *les Nouvelles*, December 1983.
16. Edward P. White, *Licensing—A Strategy for Profits*, Licensing Executive Society, 1990.

17. Goldscheider, Robert; Jarosz, John; and Mulhern, Carla; "Use of the 25 Percent Rule in Valuing IP," *les Nouvelles*, December 2002, p. 123n13. The 1938 citation in their paper is: Horvath v. McCord Radiator and Mfg. Co. et al., 100 F.2nd 326, 355 (6th Cir. 1938).
18. An even older, and weightier, example can possibly be traced to the Old Testament of the Bible. In Egypt (ca. 1800 B.C.), Joseph on behalf of Pharaoh used the storehouses filled during the seven years of plenty to acquire the live stock and land of the people, which was then "licensed" based on 20 percent of seed (profit) obtained from its farming (Genesis 47:23). In the Mosaic Law (ca. 1400 B.C.), God instructed the people that the crop land, which all belonged to God, was to lie fallow (a Sabbath year) after every six harvest years and after seven Sabbaths there was to be a two-year Sabbath rest. So in 100 years, there would be 14 regular Sabbath years and two additional Sabbath years, making the profit sharing, so to speak, as 16 percent. However, in addition, there was an annual tithe of 10 percent, so the 84 harvest years yielded nine-tenths of the total harvest, or 75.6 percent to the farmer and, so to speak, 24.4 percent to God. (There were additional tithes that have been the subject of some 2,000 years of scholarly debate that we will not consider further here).
19. Although this last claim is really a circular argument, because the 25 Percent Rule is applied to profitability values.
20. An exception occurs when there are losses from previous years being carried forward, a frequent situation with startup or early stage companies. Although even in these cases companies prefer not to consume the tax credit any faster than necessary. There can be circumstances where such companies are positioning themselves for other investors and actually want to increase their taxable profitability because it can dramatically increase the value of the company for sale. However, as a seller, it is advisable not to base the royalty on a number which can be computed in different ways for different purposes.
21. Source: Glass Lewis & Co.
22. And not, as some have recently suggested, Earnings before Irregularities and Tampering.
23. This calculation assumes that the licensee is an all-equity company with no debt so there are no interest payments (or other excluded costs or adjustments) to account for in working an after tax to EBIT calculation. And, yes, 7.54 percent was selected to make the royalty come out to 3.14 percent.
24. "Scientific Management at Merck: An Interview with CFO Judy Lewent," by Nancy A. Nichols, *Harvard Business Review*, January–February 1994, p. 89.
25. Troy, Leo, *Almanac of Business and Industrial Financial Ratios*, 31st Annual Edition, CCH Inc., 2000.
26. Schonfeld & Associates, Inc. *IRS Corporate Financial Ratios*, 15th Edition, Schonfeld & Assoc., January 2001.
27. The income tax rate for companies varies in a complex way during the history of a project because of how early losses can be carried forward, and various other tax treatment issues, which are beyond the scope of this book.
28. Depending upon the stage of development of the technology, and the scope and cost of further development required, such upfront license fee could be dwarfed by the investment that will be required just to get the technology into the marketplace. In such circumstances, the licensor may also seek evidence in addition to, or in some cases in lieu of, such upfront licensing fee.
29. When the licensee is a large company, a technology license could be one of many commercial opportunities that they then elect to pursue. Even with genuine commercial development intentions, companies change their priorities and what was once core to their strategy can now become peripheral, or their capital investment budget can be reduced by adverse business outcomes and cause them to drop certain projects that they had previously intended to commercialize. And, there are other cases, where such

licensees simply plan on having a certain degree of project mortality, sometimes referred to as R&D Darwinianism (survival of the fittest) and so it can be that abandoning a license is a planned possible outcome right from the start. In still other cases, licensees have no serious intention of commercializing the technology themselves and are seeking only to make it unavailable to competitors and the marketplace for the lowest possible cost.

30. It could be argued that the presence of Licensee B will, at some point, become known to Customer one and lead Customer one to seek competitive bids from Licensees A and B for its purchase of license subject matter and thus drive down margins. Such a situation is possible but may never occur for any number of reasons (Licensee B does not wish to serve Customer one, Licensee B does not have the manufacturing capacity to supply one in addition to its other sales, etc.).
31. It can be argued that the licensor is, to some extent, already providing working capital to the licensee by virtue of the delay in royalty payment, from the licensee's receipt of revenue, based on quarterly, semi-annual, or annual royalty payment schedule.
32. Robert Goldscheider, John Jarosz, and Carla Mulhern, "Use of the 25 Percent Rule in Valuing IP," *les Nouvelles* (January 2003), p. 123ff. This paper is an empirically based attempt of discerning broad scale evidence of the 25 percent Rule.

CHAPTER 7

Method 4: Discounted Cash Flow Method to Determine Valuation

A-M-T

Licensing D-V-D

	A: Approaches	M: Methods	T: Tools
D	Discovery	NPV v. Risk	Rating/Ranking DCF
V	**Valuation** TR R^k A DE	1. Industry Standards 2. Rating/Ranking 3. Rules of Thumb **4. Discounted Cash Flow (NPV)** 5. Monte Carlo; Real Options 6. Auctions	> Rating/Ranking > Rules of Thumb > Discounted Cash > Risk Assessment
D	Dealmaking	Deal Structures Dealmaking-Process Plan B	Rating/Ranking DCF/NPV Monte Carlo Real Options

In this chapter, we will consider our fourth valuation ***Method***, the Discounted Cash Flow (DCF) Method, sometimes referred to as the Net Present Value (NPV) Method or the Income Method. As we shall see, the term DCF (or NPV) Method refers to the same basic idea, namely: determining in today's dollars the perceived value of future net cash inflows enabled by the licensed technology by quantifying the (1) magnitude, (2) timing, and (3) risk of all such future cash inflows and outflows. Such present value quantification of the net economic benefit associated with the licensed technology is then expressible as IP payment(s) in various forms as running royalty payments, upfront lump sum payment(s), or any combination of upfront payments, annual payments, running royalties, or other forms of consideration as discussed concerning the transfer of the Wheelbarrow in Chapter 3.

As shown in this chapter's first exhibit, the DCF/NPV ***Method*** is the fourth of six methods that comprise the ***Approach*** of Valuation. Technology ***Valuation***, the ***V*** of Licensing D-V-D shown in the middle row of the above Exhibit, is that ***Approach*** that quantifies what a technology opportunity is worth in economic terms. The term

Approach is used to categorize a core business process—in Chapters 4 through 9, a determination of value by following one or more ***Methods***.

The DCF Method we will consider here will also lead to specific ***Tools*** that can be used to support other methods of valuation, and the ***Approaches*** of opportunity ***Discovery*** and ***Dealmaking***, the two ***D***s that bookend the acronym *Licensing D-V-D*. The sections of this chapter that relate specifically to identification of ***Tools*** will be shown in shaded text.

In Chapter 5 on the Rating/Ranking Method, we saw how Rating/Ranking can be used as a ***Tool;*** similarly, in Chapter 6 we noted that Rules-of-Thumb can be used as a ***Tool.*** Both of these previously introduced ***Tools*** will be used here in support of the DCF Method. And, in turn, we will see how the underlying principles of the DCF Method lead to two additional ***Tools***: Discounted Cash calculations and Risk Assessment.

Overview of the DCF Method

The DCF Method is much more mathematically based than our previous methods. However, it is founded on a very simple idea: In the business world, something is worth what it can generate in cash over its life. Suppose you were offered, say, a ten year license that is forecast to yield annual cash returns (new cash inflows net of all expenses) of $1,000. What would such a license be worth, or putting it in negotiating terms, what should be the most one should *be willing to pay* for the right to such a license? To use a phrase from the poet John Keats, albeit from a different context, the DCF Method answer to this question is founded on the idea that "everything is worth what it will fetch."[1] The "fetch" here, is the $1,000 per year for ten years, which, by this method, is discounted (hence DCF) to the present time as the Net Present Value (NPV).

The Three Key Inputs Needed to Calculate DCF Values

This $1,000 per year example clearly specifies two of the three key inputs needed for the application of the DCF Method, namely the magnitude ($1,000) and timing (at the end of each year for ten years) of such net cash inflows. Although these two inputs determine the total net cash inflow *expected*, here simply a total of $10,000, this would not represent the present day, lump sum value of the technology. There are two reasons for this. First, the cash flows occurring at the end of each of the next ten years will be denominated (per this example) in $1,000 of the U.S. currency (or any other currency of payment) as it is worth on such respective date. Thus, such payments will not add up to $10,000 worth of *present* value because of the effect of inflation, an effect we will quantify in this chapter. But beyond the issue of inflation is absence of absolute assurance that each annual cash flow will occur in the amount projected ($1,000), or for *each* of the ten years, or even for *any* of the ten years. In addition to accounting for inflation, which itself deflates the present value of such $10,000 of projected future cash inflows, any buyer will further discount[2] such sums by some measure of *risk*—which together with magnitude and timing comprise the three key inputs of the DCF Method.

We will consider what is meant by risk in detail later in this chapter, but here let us illustrate the idea by considering the experience of downhill skiing. If you are led to the top of a ski slope for your first skiing experience, looking down to the serenity of the ski lodge with its log fire and plentiful cappuccino, you see just before you the awaiting thrill of gravitational acceleration down a slick white surface littered with freshly fallen predecessor skiers, edged by immobile trees, and an absence of any obvious brakes on those two narrow slabs under your boots. Hearing a stranger's encouragement that "you'll be fine" is like hearing that there is no risk of those ten $1,000 cash flows not occurring. However, you take note of the angle and undulation of the slope dropping away from you, and the speed and adventures of those who have gone down before you some of whom are now in the parlance of the sport, in a "face plant" with their possessions scattered about in a "yard sale." If you wisely did your homework, you would also know to look for markers that designate the slope by the simple blue circle which means suitable for beginners (aka: "bunny hills"), as opposed to those marked by double black diamonds with trail names like "Elevator" or "Sayonara." This important thinking ahead about what unpleasantries could happen to your body in skiing, or your future cash inflows in licensing or R&D or M&A transactions, is known as *risk assessment*. And Sayonara is what sometimes happens with technology investments; and the return-on-investment Elevator is sometimes going up, and, well, you get the idea.

In the present example, the projected $1,000 in net cash at the end of each of ten years was a given assumption. As we will see, such yearly net cash flows normally must be calculated from the creation of a *business (financial) model* together with *business (financial) assumptions*. Such assumptions may be single-valued "best estimates," or multi-valued (also known as "what ifs"), or they can be derived from a defined perspective of future events known as a *scenario*, such as "optimistic," "conservative," "baseline," or some other defined characterization.

The acronym we have been using throughout the ***Approach*** of valuation is **TR $\mathbf{R^k}$ A DE™**. Earlier we identified the **TR** as representing Technology Rights and the **DE** as Deal Equity (or Deal Economics). In this chapter we will consider in detail the $\mathbf{R^k}$ in the middle of the acronym. The **R** stands for Risk, and the **k** relates to a quantified assessment of risk. The symbol k, commonly termed the discount rate, arises from traditional finance because the specific value of k acts to *discount* the present value of projected cash inflows. As we will discuss, for technology licensing, risk is generally a more significant and complex consideration than tradition finance settings and so we will introduce **RAHR**, for Risk Adjusted Hurdle Rate, although such term can be used interchangeably with k in the DCF equations to be developed.

So, the DCF Method requires the creation of a financial model with quantified assumptions, which together yields the projected (1) timing and (2) magnitude of net cash flows, both outgoing and (hopefully) incoming. The Method then requires (3) the quantified risk assessment in the form of a value for RAHR (or k).

Net Present Value and the DCF Method

The Net Present Value (NPV) is the single value quantified benefit of an ownership right in an economic opportunity, be it a share of equity or a technology license right. It is the *present* single number that expresses the total expected value of all future net cash inflows. A company's equity expressed by the present selling price of a share of stock is exactly the market's determination of the NPV associated with each share. That is, owning a share of stock entitles one to all the benefits of future earnings on a per share basis that the company may expend in direct dividend (cash) payments to equity owners and/or the expected benefit of the company's reinvestment of retained earnings either in future dividends or an increase in the price of each share of stock (equity). And, so, the price per share of stock, known commonly as the P/E Ratio (the share price divided by the earnings per share) is really just a particular expression for the NPV of the company on a per share basis of all the future Discounted Cash Flows (DCFs). The total owner's equity, commonly termed "the market cap," is determined by multiplying the price per share by the total number of shares outstanding. This market cap value plus the value of all outstanding debt then determines the "enterprise value."

Because the use of the DCF Method is long established and widely published in equity analyses we will first consider such applications. Although equity and technology rights valuations have many parallels, there are certain differences with equity considerations. For equity applications of the DCF Method:

- The economic value is typically determined on a per share of stock basis although for mergers and acquisition, the value of the entire company, all the equity (the market cap) and outstanding debt, is the ultimate measure of total value.
- The company is assumed to exist indefinitely into the future.
- The value realized is some combination of dividends paid out and/or stock price increases as a result of the company's retained earnings that have been fruitfully reinvested.

Despite these differences, the DCF Method is widely and properly used for the valuation of both technology licenses and equity investments.

The underlying principle for any equity valuation, or any valuation of a future benefit (as in a technology license), is "weighing" it in present terms. This is what is accomplished by the DCF calculation for each future cash inflow, and outflow, and then all such DCFs are summed up to determine the NPV. With an equity, what is known (one hopes) is the current net earnings after all expenses and taxes, usually expressed for the trailing 12 months (LTM, for Last Twelve Months). The future earnings are of course not presently known, or knowable in the sense that present earnings are known. But businesses, and investors, must make projections as best they are able to do so. Based on such projections, the NPV and thereby the fair current share price can be determined. In this book, I will treat projections and forecasts as synonyms, though a distinction could be made by reserving the word "projections" for a forecast based upon an analysis of current trends.

Historically, such a P/E Ratio has been about 15.3,[3] meaning that buyers are willing to pay 15 times the current year's after tax earnings. So in the example beginning this chapter, if the current year's earnings per share were $1,000, then such P/E Ratio would indicate that a buyer would be willing to pay $15,000 to own such share. Now why is this larger than the technology licensing situation where we above concluded that a buyer would pay *less* than $10,000? One reason, as already discussed, is that the equity is presumed to represent a share of ownership in perpetuity, not some finite period such as ten years. But a more significant factor is that the normal expectation for an equity is that the earnings will grow over time, so the current year's earnings ($1,000) are a floor not a level expectation. Additionally, as we will discuss, generally speaking there is the belief that the risk associated with an equity investment is less than a technology license.

At any given time some stocks evidence a P/E Ratio substantially greater than 15, and during the period of the late 1990s many stocks, even the average stock listed on the NASDAQ, were valued at substantially more than this historic figure. The high P/E valuation occurred because (1) buyers believed that the growth in earnings would be substantially greater than the rates expected for equities with traditional P/E Ratios of 15, and/or (2) there would be someone willing to pay more in the future for whatever reason, including irrationality. This split in the rationality of P/E Ratio derives from a combination of extraordinary optimism about the future (forecasting extraordinary earnings growth), and by the faith that subsequent buyers will, for whatever reason, pay even more for a share of stock. The NPV calculation represents the rational model of the equity value even though some underlying assumptions may be very optimistic, whereas the "future buyer" basis of valuation (in "bubble" situations, some would say, the "future fool") represents a belief in understanding the psychology of would be buyers together with the assumption that such future buyers will not be using an NPV basis for determining their willingness to pay. There is a well known quote attributed to Benjamin Graham, a historical giant in the field of stock valuation, which goes: "In the short run, the stock market is a voting machine, but in the long run it is a weighing machine." This useful distinction highlights the difference in the sought for rationality of a NPV calculation versus what may happen in some psycho-drama Dealmaking environment.

NPV Historic Examples Used for Technology Equity Valuations

In Chapter 4 in our consideration of the use of comparables in valuing a license (Method 1), we noted that one of the limitations is that prior transactions may be comparable in terms of technology and IP rights, but can be noncomparable in terms of valuation. This was because of some aspect of irrationality associated with a given prior transaction; the parties "voting" back then may not be representative of any party willing to "vote" now or in the future. When we later address Method 6 in Chapter 9, we will consider how "voters" today can both value and purchase the license through an auction method.

In this present chapter on the DCF Method, we will apply the DCF "weighing machine" which values opportunities by the magnitude, timing, and risk of earnings that they are expected to be able to produce. But, as we will see, risk assessment plays a crucial role in such "weighing" and that such assessment is itself a kind of "voting" process.

As we noted in Chapter 4, there are many published license agreements, some of which can be useful in estimating the value of IP rights. Because in this present chapter we will be developing DCF models, the question naturally arises do published DCF analyses exist that can be helpful guidelines and information sources for use in this method? It turns out that such DCF analyses, which may well have been used to enter into such published licenses, are almost never published; the few examples that exist are sanitized illustrations used in presentations or privately shared during Dealmaking.

However, equity analysts do sometimes support their valuations of technology companies by publishing certain key DCF assumptions. Although there are certain important differences between the valuation of an equity and a technology license, it will be useful for our purposes to consider the below equity valuation examples.

THREE FUEL CELL EQUITY NPV FORECASTS In the final year of the twentieth century, which closed on December 31, 2000 (not 1999), a notable peak occurred in the value of "technology stocks." One proxy for such stocks is the NASDAQ exchange because it is comprised of many technology companies, including midsize and even smaller ones. The highest value of the NASDAQ composite index occurred on March 10, 2000 when it closed at 5049. Two and a half years later, in October 2002, the index stood at 1114, approximately what it had been in August 1996, less than four years prior to its peak in March 2000. The loss in market value of all the NASDAQ listed companies was 80 percent from the 2000 peak to the 2002 minimum, representing a total equity loss of more than $4 trillion, an astounding loss of value.

Because, in principle, such stock valuations were and are made based on a DCF analysis (assuming that investors are buying the right to receive a distribution of future earnings or the right to sell such right to others who are themselves buying this right), it is reasonable to ask whether the year 2000 technology market tumult, and in particular the evaporation of $4 trillion in equity value in two years of the NASDAQ listed firms, reflects a fundamental flaw in the DCF Method.

Fuel Cell Energy, Inc.: A Fuel Cell Equity DCF Example To illustrate how DCF methods are used, and some pitfalls, let us consider such a DCF analysis performed by one analyst during the twilight of technology equities innocence at the end of the year 2000, just as the NASDAQ was plummeting. Published on December 18, 2000 in *Red Herring*, one primary source of technology company information at that time, was an analysis of fuel cell company stocks.[4] I have selected this example, instead of the multitude of "dot bomb" or telecom stories which were and are plagued by other kinds of issues, including, in some cases, outright fraud, so as to have an illustration that just focuses on certain keys of a DCF analysis. Here in this article is the analysis of a Lehman Brothers analyst concerning a then small company, Fuel Cell Energy (FCE), a company then (reportedly) "the leading developer of . . . stationary [fuel] cells . . . which is poised to be the first to commercialize them [stationary fuel cells] in 2001."[5] At the time of the article, FCE's stock had increased 791 percent to $73.50 in the *year* ending October 2000, which is quite a spectacular gain for one year in comparison, say, to returns on, say, U.S Government Treasury Bills at 5 percent, particularly since the company was not expected to be profitable until 2006.

However, the Lehman analyst expressed the following view of the future: When FCE does become profitable (per the projection) in 2006 when its revenues (not earnings) were forecast to be $1 billion, its market value then would be five times such revenues (not earnings), making the 2006 market value of the company $5 billion. The Lehman analyst then discounted such future value using a discount rate (RAHR) of 17.5 percent to determine the October 2001 value (one year hence the publication of the analysis) of FCE and then divided by the outstanding shares, concluded such "one year target price" of FCE is $124, or a projected increase of 69 percent (= 124/73.5) over the then present share price. So, one could have chosen to buy a T-Bill and receive a guaranteed increase of 5 percent, or buy shares in FCE at higher risk (reflected by the discount rate of 17.5, together with the other assumptions) for the prospect of a one year 69 percent return.

What has happened to FCE? As of 2008, it is still in business with annual revenues of more than $70 million, though well below the $1 billion in the above forecast, and it is still unprofitable, with its stock is selling for less than $10 a share, which corresponds to less than $40 a share in comparison to the $73.50 share price in October 2000 as the stock has split 2:1 twice since the above analysis. Its stock has lost approximately 50 percent of its value since the 2000 analysis. *Red Herring* magazine itself has not fared as well, having entered bankruptcy in 2003, subsequently selling its name and brand assets. And, in 2008, Lehman itself went bankrupt, though for reasons unrelated to technology equities (but for other even more seriously erroneous economic forecasting).

Ballard Power Systems: A Second Fuel Cell Equity DCF Example Another example from the same article was the Merrill Lynch view of another fuel cell company, Ballard Power Systems. Although Ballard was then continuing to report losses, Merrill Lynch projected Ballard's earnings to be $24.22 a share in the year 2013 (13 *years* hence). Then using a 25 multiple on those earnings (namely a P/E multiple of 25) to project Ballard's market value in 2013, and using a 15 percent discount (RAHR) rate to bring such value back to the present, Merrill Lynch projected a Ballard stock price in October 2001 (one year hence) of $150 a share, an increase of 44 percent above its 2000 share price ($104 at the time of the analysis).[6]

So, if the 17.5 percent discount (RAHR) rate associated with the projected 69 percent return of FCE was too risky, one could presumably opt for the 15 percent rate associated with the projected 44 percent rate of return and instead have bought Ballard.[7]

What happened to Ballard? It too is still in business in 2008 with revenues of approximately $70 million, but unprofitable, and a stock price of less than $5 a share, that is, about 5 percent of the value it had at the time of the 2000 analysis. And in 2008, Merrill Lynch ceased to exist as an independent company having sold itself under conditions of exigency to Bank of America.

Impco Technologies: A Third Fuel Cell Equity DCF Example A third example from this same article is an analysis by First Albany regarding Impco Technologies, another company then heavily involved in the fuel cell market. First Albany projected Impco's 2006 earnings of $2.86 a share and a P/E multiple on such 2006 earnings of 45. First Albany then discounted such projected future value using a discount (RAHR) rate of 20 percent to project a one year Impco target price increase of 100 percent.

Impco no longer exists as a standalone company. In 2006 it was reorganized into and became part of Fuel Systems Solutions, Inc. And in 2007, First Albany ceased to exist, having sold its name and part of its operations, and reformed the balance of its operations as part of Broadpoint Securities Group Inc a company with negative enterprise value as of early 2009.

THREE DOT COM EQUITY VALUE FORECASTS The above fuel cell examples are interesting for several reasons. The company valuations were more akin to technology valuations because of the early stage of fuel cell technology and market development. They also show the choices that are made by expressing various values of RAHR (15, 17.5, and 20 percent) based on a belief about the risk of the underlying assumptions being realized. Finally, they also show that use of DCF analysis requires one to make predictions about the future, often a humbling experience. If the assumptions are not realized, because of some technology or market or other failure or difficulty, then the projected value will not be realized.

Also, the demise of all three investment analysis firms whose employees made the above projections (Lehman, Merrill Lynch, and First Albany), and that of the publication in which they were made (*Red Herring*), all for reasons unrelated to the projections, is symptomatic of the uncertainty and risk associated with business in general, and in the case of the above projections, technology in particular.

However it would be wrong to lay blame on such forecasts upon the DCF Method, even if they had been reasonable valuations. Forecast errors can arise in any valuation, including the use of the DCF Method, by simple "if/then" calculations, which though mathematically correct (that is if the "if" then the "then"), if there lacks any reasonable basis for a critical "if," the entire assembly of assumptions as a whole will lead to meaningless forecasts. Beginning with MicroStrategy we will consider three such examples.

MicroStrategy, Inc.: Five Giant Assumptions Consider the following example from a *BusinessWeek* story also from the year 2000.[8] In this article are the calculations of the then CEO of MicroStrategy, Inc., Michael J. Saylor, justifying a $30 billion valuation for his company. Here is what he is reported to have said:

(1) In 2010, U.S. consumer spending will be $11 trillion annually.
(2) Wireless e-commerce will be the means by which 33 percent of such $11 trillion spending occurs.
(3) MicroStrategy Inc., via its website strategy.com, will be the means by which 25 percent of such 33 percent of such $11 trillion annual spending (in 2010) will occur.
(4) MicroStrategy will be paid a 1.1 percent sales commission on all such sales. (Now, a brief intermission for some math: The above four assumptions yield 2010 MicroStrategy revenues of $10 billion).
(5) The market will value MicroStrategy in 2010 at a multiple of three times annual sales (3 times $10 billion = $30 billion, QED).

Therefore, MicroStrategy should be worth $30 billion, though it is not clear why the market should put such value on MicroStrategy in 2000, 10 years before all these outcomes were assumed to be realized. Selecting a risk-adjusted discount rate appropriate to this set of five assumptions would be a challenge.

What has happened to MicroStrategy? In 2008, the company still exists, providing business intelligence software products, with more than $300 million in annual revenues. However, along the way, they have had a bumpy road: Their stock fell from its all time high of $333 a share in 2000, the time of the above projections, to a low of $4.20 in 2002. They have recovered from such low to an enterprise value in 2008 that exceeds $600 million, or 2% of the $30 billion calculation made in 2000.

InfoSpace: How to Forecast $1 Trillion in Market Cap Value In 2000, published in *The Industry Standard*, itself now bankrupt,[9] the CEO of InfoSpace, Naveen Jain, was interviewed regarding the reasonableness of projections that InfoSpace was on its way to a $1 trillion market cap. InfoSpace's business model was to garner a "tax" on all e-commerce transactions that it enabled; according to Jain: "We have 2,500 paying partners. Every time you go to NBCi looking for a plumber we get paid.[10] Every time you go to Go Network (since shut down) looking for a phone number, we get paid. We are probably the only partner to both Disney and Playboy at the same time." InfoSpace's share price peaked at $1305 in 2000 and collapsed to less than $3 in 2002.

In 2008, its enterprise value is somewhat over $100 million, short of $1 trillion by a factor of 100 million.

Sun Microsystems: "What were you thinking?" Sun Microsystems is one of Silicon Valley's iconic companies. Founded in 1982 by Stanford University students who later themselves become icons for innovation and success (Andy Bechtolsheim, Vinod Khsola, Scott McNealy, and soon joined by Bill Joy from Cal Berkeley). It developed UNIX based operating systems (SOLARIS) and hardware platforms (SPARC) and later a ubiquitous language (JAVA) as well as many other innovations. During the late 1990s and into 2000, Sun's equity was highly valued by "the market" (Methods 1 and 6), by comparison to alternative companies (Method 2), and by research analysts using various DCF models (Method 4).

In a 2002 *BusinessWeek* interview with Scott McNealy, the CEO of Sun Microsystems looking back at the market's valuation of Sun in this same year, 2000, of the mentioned fuel cell projections,[11] he was asked: "Sun's stock hit a high of $64. Did you think what tech stocks were doing two years ago was too good to be true?" Mr. McNealy, in an amazingly candid answer, replied: ". . . . two years ago [2000] we [Sun] were selling at 10 times *revenues* when we were at $64. At 10 times revenues, to give you a 10 year payback, I have to pay you 100 percent of revenues for 10 straight years in dividends. That assumes I can get that by my shareholders. That assumes I have zero cost of goods sold, which is very hard for a computer company. That assumes zero expenses, which is really hard with 39,000 employees. That assumes I pay no taxes, which is very hard. And that assumes you pay no taxes on your dividends, which is kind of illegal. And that assumes with zero R&D for the next 10 years, I can maintain the current revenue run rate. Now, having done that, would any of you like to buy my stock at $64? Do you realize how ridiculous those basic assumptions are? You don't need any footnotes. What were you thinking?"

In 2008, Sun was still in business, with a market capitalization of more than $6 billion, though its stock price has been in a multi-year decline to just a few dollars a share on an equivalent basis,[12] about where it was in 1995. In early 2009, Sun was purchased by Oracle Corp. for a little over $7 billion. So what went wrong? As we discussed in Chapter 4, comparables valuation depends on rational comparables. The essence of a "bubble" is that entire markets are wrongly overpriced. The DCF Method can suffer the same fate of predictive error for similar reasons: using unfounded, or ill-founded, assumptions and scenarios to make projections.

TELECOM EQUITY FORECASTS IN THE PERIOD OF Y2K[13] AND "BUBBLE" ECONOMICS As a final category of equity valuation forecasts, let us consider what has become known as the telecom industry deriving from the break up of the old AT&T in 1984 into a long distance providing parent (AT&T) and the so called seven "Baby Bells," including Bellcore, and by the late 1990s numerous new entrants providing communication networking service. In parallel with the internet/dot com speculation that grew during the late 1990s and collapsed beginning in March of 2000, there were incredible increases in the equity value of such telecom companies. Fueling this rise in telecom values were the forecasts of equity research analysts supported by, for a time, dramatically increasing revenue and earnings reported by publicly traded companies.

Such equity research analysts had developed comprehensive, sophisticated DCF models of all the major companies and many increasingly numerous new entrants in the telecom industry supporting (in most cases) the current, (then) high stock values and projecting (in many cases) dramatic earnings growth in (1) "double digits" (trade lingo for greater than 10 percent but less than 20 percent, Compound Annual Growth Rate (or CAGR) and (2) CAGRs greater than 20 percent.

During this period, the unit costs of telecom were declining rapidly. What had been $20 a minute for overseas calls in the 1920s had dropped (in the United States) to below $1 a minute by the 1990s, but by the late 1990s the decline had accelerated to just pennies and dimes a minute, with parallel declines and even elimination of "roaming" charges on mobile telephony. How then can any reasonable DCF model forecast dramatically increasing earnings when the unit revenue rates are declining? The (then) proclaimed answer was the projection of almost unimaginable growth rates in usage, primarily by "data" meaning packet based communications of voice and every other form of content over the internet to computers, fax machines, landline and wireless telephones, pagers, PDAs, and smartphones. The statistic that was widely quoted during this period was demand (bandwidth) growth rates which were doubling every 100 days, approximately every quarter, which corresponded to nearly an annual growth rate of 7 to 8 times the previous year.

The second high level explanation was the cost savings by industry consolidation, so called "roll ups." If company A buys company B, and the costs associated with all of B's revenues can be, say, halved because of integration into A (so called "synergy"), then the earnings of B in the hands of A can be dramatically increased even without revenue growth. If, for example, B had revenues of $100 and all-in costs of $80 yielding net earnings of $20, and those costs could be halved to $40, the corresponding earnings available to A would triple from $20 to $60 (i.e.: $100 less $40 of all-in costs of B as operated by its new owner A equals $60). This wonderful, in-principle-gain would only be realized by A after an initial investment in Dealmaking to acquire B, expending integration costs of B into A, and other so called one-time costs associated with the dramatic cost cutting at B. Over time, as many different A companies started competing to acquire various B companies, the premiums paid to consummate these deals also became significant, eroding the earnings gained by the acquisition.

Embedding such growth rate and cost reduction assumptions into a DCF model of even a very large revenue based company, such as one of the former Baby Bells (SBC, NYNEX, Bell Atlantic, etc.) or long distance providers (old AT&T, MCI, Sprint), led inevitably to very attractive forecasts of future earnings and, thereby, dramatically increased value of their underlying equity.

What turned out to be dramatic was not the earnings growth but the cataclysmic failure of essentially all such analyst DCF models. But what failed was not the DCF Method, but the models that had been expressed using such Method. In these models one of the primary causes of the failure to forecast value could be traced to the assumed "data" growth rate doubling every 100 days. If such rate was ever true, it was for a very limited period for certain companies. However in a short period of time there was a glut of bandwidth (capacity) because everyone was behaving in the mode "if you build it, they will come."[14] This all led to enormous overcapacity and, accordingly, dramatic price erosion, and, ultimately, massive fraud as certain company leaders used "creative accounting" to meet or even exceed the forecasted earnings growth, which led to a kind of validation of the wildly aggressive DCF projections, which led to even more fraud to keep the "results" in line with expectations. The "poster child" for this was Worldcom which, when the dust all settled in bankruptcy, had to restate $11 billion in previously audited and published revenues as having been entirely an illusion. Its CEO at the time is now serving a 25 year prison sentence, while countless thousands of employees lost their jobs and investors dealt with the evaporation of billions of dollars of equity value.

Do These Examples Show Some Innate Flaw in the DCF Method?

The DCF Method, and the associated RAHR tool, is only as good as the thinking that goes with it and the assumptions that model the underlying projections.

Given the above examples, and one can find innumerable others, is there a fatal flaw within the DCF Method? The Method is sometimes maligned by characterizations of it being guesswork or merely a tool for coming up with whatever number one is seeking. Even such highly respected business world authorities as Jack Welch, CEO of GE from 1981 to 2001 has (I believe too casually) said, in response to the question "What decision model can be used to launch a technology at the right moment?"

> ...*you will never know exactly how the market will respond, nor will you ever be 100 percent certain about the viability of your technology*. And forget discounted-rate-of-return analyses. *[Emphasis mine] With a new technology, those numbers fall somewhere between guessing and wishful thinking?*[15]

(But, Mr Welch has also said: "I was afraid of the Internet...because I couldn't type."[16])

One should be cautious in, shall we say, discounting Mr. Welch. GE is the only remaining original member of the Dow Jones Industrial Index, a last-company-standing testament to its longevity, ranked highly in all surveys of innovation, respect, brand value, and just about every other business metric while being one of the largest, most diverse companies in the world with a market capitalization of nearly $300 billion, ranking it second in size behind only Exxon-Mobil Corp., while spending about $150 billion a year to run its business (all 2008 figures). Such annual costs include $4 billion for R&D and nearly $20 billion a year on capital expenditures, all of which are GE investments on behalf of its shareholders to create an even more valuable company in the future. The critical job of anyone with the fiduciary duty of managing the capital of others is to allocate it efficiently. And, although it is generally true that one can "never know exactly" anything about the business future it is inconceivable that such expenditures are planned and authorized without massive use of DCF Models. (And, in 2009, wherein GE's stock has dropped some 70 percent in value over the past two years, and it has lost its coveted and rare triple-A debt rating, whether any boast about the lack of utility in financial forecasting is of comfort to its shareholders).

However, at the end of this chapter we will return to DCF misuse issues, which issues do exist, as they do with any valuation method or indeed the basic business disciplines of both accounting and finance; behind every tool there hides at least one fool, and one malevolent. As we discussed in the previous chapters on Method 1, Industry Standards, and Method, 2, Rating/Ranking, these accusations of unreliability or—even worse—tools of deceit can be, and are, raised against these methods as well. But misuse—whether or not intentional—is not a valid charge against a business method. A surgeon who is negligent in his/her implementation of an accepted medical procedure does not invalidate the procedure, no more than a three-year-old with a chisel and block of wood demonstrates some impossibility of a sculptor making art by such tool and medium.

The DCF Method is not "wrong" because predictions from its use did not come true. The Method is tied to assumptions about tomorrow, and such tomorrows are never knowable things. The key to the DCF Method is developing reasonable assumptions including risk assessment. Because in the DCF Method such risk assessment is expressed by a single number, the risk adjusted hurdle rate (RAHR) where the resulting NPV determination is highly dependent on the value selected. As we have discussed, risk is also embodied in the assumptions that comprise a scenario, specifically, some coherent view of the future.

In the three fuel cell examples given, there is a reason why projected one-year rates of return are so high (44, 69, and 100 percent): The attendant risk was high. You wanted risk free in 2001? You should have invested in 10-year U.S. Treasury notes and earned a 5 percent return; it's as close to risk free as is humanly available, or so it seems. You wanted the potential of greater return? Any analysis using RAHR values in the range of 10 to 15 points (percentage points) above a risk free rate is an automatic "heads up" that one is venturing into an investment that could fall far short of its projected returns and even become a total loss.

In the other four examples we considered, discernment of risk lies primarily within the assumptions themselves. The MicroStrategy, InfoSpace, and Sun examples did not present DCF (NPV) results derived from large RAHR values. Had they done so, the over-predicted NPV values would have been less dramatic. Rather they exhibited an unfounded "if only" error, that will be addressed later in this chapter. The telecom industry example did use RAHR values driving a DCF calculation but as we will show in this chapter, if the assumptions are too high by huge factors, even high RAHR values will not rescue the model. And in certain instances equity values were based on false "data" provided deceitfully for the purpose of creating inflated values.

The DCF as a method enables us to express quantitative wisdom about the present value of the future, accounting for risk. This does not mean that any mathematically correct calculation is equally valid or at all wise.

So, does the existence of bad financial predictions prove that any valuation methodology, or specifically the DCF Method, is flawed beyond utility? Clearly my answer is "no," or this would be a very short chapter and book. But the examples that we have spent some length in considering should lead us to be humble and cautious. Humility is generally a good thing in analytical endeavors because it causes one to question assumptions, to consider alternatives, perform tests of reasonableness, to not take the first result that exits a calculation as the final and only or even a reliable answer. We all make mistakes. Even being rescued from spreadsheet simple math errors because software like Excel does that work for us, it is easy to mess up a formula so the model is not doing what you thought it was. One can all too easily overlook something and never notice its absence; as it is said, it is hard to make a list of things you haven't thought of. Developing reasonable assumptions and having them fit together to make up a coherent scenario is always a challenge.

So is a well developed DCF model "true," in the sense of being exactly right? From the standard of truth underpinning mathematics and geometry the answer is "no." We don't permit arguments against the Pythagorean Theorem of the kind "well that's just your opinion." Within the framework of Euclidian geometry we can prove with certainty that for right triangles c^2 equals a^2 plus b^2. Likewise 5 plus 4 equals 9 in base 10 every time, everywhere. But in business, we do not live in a framework that enables forecasts with certainty. And even in geometry there exist other frameworks where c^2 is greater than a^2 plus b^2 and mathematical bases where our familiar base 10 math does not apply; for a right triangle on the surface of a sphere $c^2 > a^2 + b^2$, and in base eight $5 + 4 = 11$. If we held business operations to some philosophical truth standard, we could accomplish little more than filling out our expense reports, in base 10. Decisions have to be made, commitments undertaken, risks accepted. So it can be said: "A (financial) model is always wrong [in the sense that it will not reflect exactly how things will turn out], but not useless."[17]

Humility and wisdom combined with the DCF Method is an extremely important valuation methodology and a Tool useful in many other contexts.

Basic Financial Concepts

In this section we will derive and apply the foundational DCF equation. As we will see, one simple equation enables us to determine a present value of any forecasted cash flow at any future date based upon the perceived risk. By summing up all such discounted cash flows we can then determine the Net Present Value (NPV) which, by this method, is the value of the technology.

The key concept required to use the Discounted Cash Flow Method is the equation for converting future cash payments into their present equivalent, taking into account the time such payments would be made and the risk associated with their being paid. A very simple derivation provides useful result.

Derivation of the DCF Equation

If one lends, or invests in, an entity A dollars—let's use $1,000 as the example—and expects a k rate of return (such 5 percent), then after one year, one expects to receive the following:

Money received a year from now = A + k × A, where A is the amount given at the beginning of such year, and k the annualized rate of expected return. Using the $1,000 and 5 percent values:

$$\text{Money one year from now} = \$1{,}000 + 0.05 \times \$1{,}000 = \$1{,}000 + \$50 = \$1{,}050.$$

Calculating the money due two years from now is obtained by repeating the above calculation using the end-of-year-one value, $1,050, for a second year of interest, as follows:

$$\begin{aligned}\text{Money two years from now} &= \text{Money one year from now} \\ &\quad + \text{the additional benefit of another year} \\ &= \$1{,}050 + 0.05 \times \$1{,}050 = \$1{,}050 + \$52.50 \\ &= \$1{,}102.50.\end{aligned}$$

Expressing this process in symbol terms, we have:

$$\begin{aligned}\text{Money two years from now} &= (A + k \times A) + (A + k \times A) \times k \\ &= A \times (1 + k) + A \times (1 + k) \times k \\ &= A \times (1 + k) \times (1 + k) = A \times (1 + k)^2,\end{aligned}$$

where A in the example was $1,000 and k is 5 percent (or 0.05 when used in equation form). So, using this formula,

$$\text{Money two years from now} = \$1{,}000 \times (1 + 0.05)^2 = \$1{,}000 \times 1.1025 = \$1{,}102.50,$$

which is the same value obtained by doing the calculation one year at a time.

Now, extending the formula to three years adds another factor of (1 + k) or, in this example (1 + 0.05), so the formula is:

$$\begin{aligned}\text{Money three years from now} &= A \times (1 + k)^3 = \$1{,}000 \times (1.05)^3 \\ &= \$1{,}000 \times 1.157625 = \$1{,}157.63.\end{aligned}$$

The generalized formula then can be expressed as follows:

$$B_n = A_n \times (1 + k)^n$$

where A_n is the money invested at the beginning of the analysis period, B_n is the money received after n years, and k is the expected annual rate of return (or return on investment, in any case always expressed as a decimal). In finance textbooks, A_n is usually designated by PV for present value (i.e., money now), and B_n as FV for future value (i.e., money returned after n years).[18]

However, our purpose here is to do the reverse: calculate the present value (A_n) of a known future amount (B_n). The above equation can be re-expressed as follows:

$$A_n = B_n/(1 + k)^n,$$

which is obtained by solving for A_n.

When used in this fashion, B_n is the money at the end of year n and A_n is the present value of that money for the chosen value of k. Normally the term used for A is DCF for Discounted Cash Flow, B is simply the value of the money in year n, which may be designated by GCF for Gross Cash Flows (i.e., undiscounted value in year n), and k is the factor that discounts any GCF into its present DCF value. For this reason k is normally termed the discount rate.

When we consider B monies that will result from the commercialization of technology, we normally do so from the perception of something more than discounting. We seek to take into account the risk that something dramatically unexpected and adverse could occur. Accordingly, here, we will primarily use the term "risk-adjusted hurdle rate," or RAHR, in place of k. When we do so, the RAHR merely replaces k in the above equation.

The normal valuation situation is that the buyer agrees to pay to the seller a prescribed amount of money at a defined date, perhaps as a denominated value (as here with \$1,000) or perhaps as a percentage of some other specified quantity, as with a royalty percentage, of that year's revenues. So, rather than calculating the future value of the present \$1,000, one is calculating the present value of a future payment of \$1,000, as follows using the assumption such payment is made at a 5 percent discount rate:

$$DCF = GCF/(1+k)^n = \$1{,}000/(1+0.05)^5 = \$1{,}000/1.27628 = \$783.53.$$

Expressed in this way, the idea is simply that in today's dollars, the value of receiving \$1,000 five years from now is \$783.53 if the k value is 5 percent. The reason the \$783.53 is called the Discounted Cash Flow is that one has reduced or discounted the value of the future \$1,000 payment by virtue of the fact it will not be received for five years and the belief that there was a 5 percent loss of value in money each year either through inflation alone, or (more commonly) through a combination of inflation and opportunity cost, given alternatives for investing the money.

With this single simple equation, $DCF = B_n/(1 + k)^n$, and a computer software spreadsheet program such as Microsoft's Excel, one can create some very complex financial models as will be shown in the next sections. However, before doing so, an in depth understanding of k, or as more commonly used here the Risk-Adjusted Hurdle Rate (RAHR), is needed.

For the simple situation of a single payment, as shown in the above example, the Net Present Value (NPV) is exactly equal to the DCF value of \$783.33. Commonly in licensing situations there are multiple payments expected. In such cases the NPV will then be the sum of all the individual DCF values where each single payment is calculated using the above simple equation.

When looking at the value of a licensing opportunity from the perspective of the buyer, the early years of the license typically involve net cash outflows because of investments the buyer must make in the technology, before the cash flows turn positive in later years. So, for the buyer, typical DCF values in a financial model are both negative and positive. When the NPV is calculated by summing the DCFs the result can then be either positive or negative. For very large RAHR values the more distant positive GCFs are more highly discounted, compared to the near term negative GCFs; conversely, for low values of RAHR the distant GCFs are relatively less discounted. For many financial models there is a crossover value of RAHR, for which the NPV is exactly zero. This particular RAHR value is known as the hurdle rate because the perceived risk has to be something less than such RAHR for the NPV to be positive, and, the project should only be considered if the NPV is positive. So in this sense, this particular RAHR value is the "hurdle" that the opportunity must be able to jump over.

The key to this process is determining an appropriate RAHR value.

The Toolbox

One of the powerful features of the DCF Method is that it can be used as a ***Tool*** with any other valuation ***Method*** or ***Approach*** to move money forward or back in time. For instance, if, using the Industry Standard Method of Chapter 4, the parties agree on a royalty of 5 percent but for some reason want to defer or move up some or all of certain royalties, the above DCF equations can be used to convert such moneys into equivalent value but at different times.

In some agreements, the seller definitely prefers to receive substantial early, fixed payments in lieu of some of its downstream royalties. These DCF equations can be used to restructure equitable financial agreements into equivalent forms with different payment times and amounts.

Various Perspectives/Contexts for Risk and RAHR Values

There are three main considerations in determining an appropriate RAHR value: (1) inflation, (2) alternative available rates of return, and (3) risk of return. Inflation is the deflation in the value of a fixed denominated currency. $1,000 today is worth more than $1,000 a year from now even if one was absolutely certain to obtain it.

However, inflation is not the only consideration. Every buyer with investment monies is seeking, in some way, to maximize its return by consideration of a range of possible investments. Although the universe of strategic investments for any buyer is not infinite, typically there are multiple alternatives, each having a different set of projected cash outflows and inflows forecasted year by year, and a unique risk profile. This range of opportunities, together with an assessment of its cost of capital—the investment monies that it would be committing to commercialize any technology—will govern its decision making about any specific opportunity.

Even for opportunities that look extremely attractive because of large, projected positive GCFs, a buyer will want to consider if it has properly considered the associated risk.

INFLATION AND K Essentially with no exceptions, money in all countries of the world for the last 100 years has experienced inflation and is expected to continue to do so indefinitely. Inflation simply means that it will take more dollars to buy in the future what less dollars could buy today. The rate of inflation has significant implications for long term investments with modest expectations for rates of return. There are multiple measures (standards) by which inflation is calculated. The measure commonly reported as it is designed to track consumer spending is known as the CPI[19] for Consumer Price Index; there are actually multiple versions of the CPI distinguishing, for example, between urban and rural consumers; since January 2007 these data are now collected and reported to six significant figures. Economists often use a different measure known as the GDP (Gross Domestic Product) deflator. Although there are people for whom the difference between various measures of inflation is their life's work, for our purposes these are distinctions without a difference.[20] A market measure of inflation is available with an inflation protected U.S. government bond known as a TIPS (Treasure Inflation Protected Security).

For the five years 2003 through 2007, in the United States, the average CPI was 3 percent (3.05 percent). The time period of our interest is the future where no "data" exists, even to one significant figure. Fortunately, on this point, the range of uncertainty appears to relatively insignificant for our purposes and we will consider 3 percent as a reasonable future projection. Thus, accounting for inflation our DCF equation is expressed as follows: $A = B/(1.03)^n$, where B is the value of money to be received at the end of n years, and A, which is the present value or DCF, is then calculated to be the exact equivalent value of such money in today's dollars. So, considering the example of $1,000 to be received five years hence we have:

$$\text{DCF} = \$1{,}000/1.03^5 = \$1{,}000/1.15927 = \$862.61.$$

To put this in words, providing inflation continues at 3 percent then someone promising to pay $1,000 five years from now is really promising $862.61 in terms of value in today's dollars. (Note: We can perform the calculation the other way around and say that $1,000 today is equivalent to $1159.27 five years from now using exactly the same factor of 1.15927 obtained from calculating 1.03^5). Another term used to describe the $862.61 is Present Value or Net Present Value (or NPV) which means that today, the perceived value of $1,000 five years from now is exactly $862.61. When considering a *single* future payment, DCF and NPV are exactly the same concept and equation. When dealing with multiple future payments, then the *sum* of *all* the DCF values is exactly the NPV of the opportunity; examples later in this chapter will make this clear.

A key idea with DCF and NPV is the following. If a company is considering conveying a right, such as a license, in return for a promised future payment, and the appropriate RAHR (i.e., k value) is used, then it is assumed that the promise to pay B in year n or the present payment of the DCF are exactly equivalent. In the previous example, if it is perceived that the 3 percent value of k is appropriate, then there should be no preference between $1,000 five years hence or $862.61 now. The test of this perception is a buyer offering the seller the choice of these two situations and being indifferent to the selection made.

The DCF concept is a foundational idea in licensing transactions because it is innate that some comparison needs to be made between dollars now and dollars in the future or over time. The buyer will experience the commercial benefit of the license over a period of years and must characterize that benefit in terms of a willingness to pay a lump sum on closing and/or royalties or annual payments over time in order for the project to be worth doing. When a license is being granted for a single lump sum (so called "paid ups," a useful shorthand for "paid up licenses"), then the entire future benefit to the buyer is being consolidated into one single, "present day" number. However, even when there is no upfront license payment, the buyer typically performs a spreadsheet calculation of the prospective income including anticipated royalty payments. This will enable the buyer to determine whether the overall returns, net of royalties, will be sufficiently attractive to make the additional, needed development investments, given the perceived risk.

The inflationary value of k, here taken to be 3 percent, reflects no real gain (or loss) in value given the *assumption* that the inflation rate will remain constant over the period. Thus, \$862.61 is actually identical to \$1,000 five years hence, under the circumstances of constant 3 percent inflation.

In business contexts, however, there are numerous investment opportunities that provide greater-than-inflation returns and such returns are used to calculate the value of money for various times and risks.

There is a very very old, but still pretty good, joke that goes like this:

Al (spoken to his friend Ben): "How are you doing?"

Ben (after a long, thoughtful pause, replies): "Compared to what?"

The "compared to what?" reply is exactly our question here. Any prospective buyer (licensee) has to have, and will have, in mind some range of alternative possible investments. In this sense, a buyer's risk assessment is following a process much like Method 1, the use of Industry Standards (comparables), namely: What other investments have been made, or could now be made, that would provide me attractive returns for various levels of risk?

RISK FREE The worldwide risk free benchmark tends to be rates of return available to holders of debt back by the full faith of the U.S. government. T-Bills (for Treasury Bills, one category of U.S. debt) mature in less than twelve months and are one common "risk free" standard.[21] Different U.S. debt maturities, which are all generally considered risk free, have slightly different rates of return. A standard one year equivalent rate known as the CMT (Constant Maturity Treasury) Index is regularly published by the government.

Historically, the "coupon" rate of return[22] on a T-Bill converted to a one year maturity has been in the mid single digits, commonly ranging between 3 and 7 percent.[23] Taking the average CMT Index over the 13 year period 1995 through 2007, but excluding the unusually low rates for the years 2002 through 2004, (rates which were low as a result of government policy to aid in the recovery of the economic downturn post-2000) the result is 5 percent (5.03 percent).

Although the future is never certain, based upon recent history, a discount rate of approximately 5 percent is generally considered the risk free rate of return that every owner of cash perceives. Using such rate, if one had \$1,000 that could be committed for five years, a risk free investment could be reasonably expected to yield the following result:

$$B = \$1,000 \times (1.05)^5 = \$1276.28.$$

That is, an owner of \$1,000 today would expect to receive no less than \$1276.28 in five years.[24]

Of course nothing in life is risk free or guaranteed, and the future is never known; however, a T-Bill (or other form of government debt) is backed by the full faith of the U.S. Government so barring default of the United States, the T-Bill will be paid at the face value return rate (5 percent in this example). Of all investments available, T-Bills are considered to be the most secure (one would be tempted to say a "gold standard"; however, the United States no longer bases the value of its currency on the value of gold).

Another investment opportunity that may be considered equally secure to a T-Bill is the repayment of existing debt; assuming one is able to do so without penalties for early repayment and ignoring any tax benefit associated with debt payment, then the investment value of such payment is exactly the interest rate of the debt being paid off. In business contexts, this is not generally an appropriate point of reference because businesses choose to borrow money because they have investment opportunities that are expected to provide greater returns than the debt payment rate.

Staying with the government risk free example of 5 percent, a payment of $1,000 promised five years in the future by a buyer would be considered by the seller to have the present value as follows:

$$\text{DCF} = \$1{,}000/(1.05)^5 = \$783.53.$$

Remember that for our earlier calculation the present value (DCF) of $1,000 five years hence was deemed to be $862.61, for a k of 3 percent, and here, with a k of 5 percent it is deemed to be $783.53, or $79.08 less. Why would $1,000 five years from now be worth $79.08 less than the previous inflation-based calculation? The answer is because there exists an alternative means of investing money that is (in principle and principal) risk free at a k of 5 percent, so that it is possible to produce $1,000 in face value five years hence by the present investment of $783.53, not $862.61. In other words, the larger the investment opportunity that's available, expressed in terms of k, the smaller the amount of money required today to produce specified value in the future (such as the $1,000 in these examples).

For example, an offer by a buyer to pay $1,000 five years hence instead of $862.61 now would be unacceptable to a seller because however reliable the seller's promise it is almost certain to involve more risk than the risk free rate of 5 percent underlying such calculation.

PROMISED, BUT NOT RISK FREE RATES Let us now consider another kind of "compared to what?" investment opportunity.

Corporations borrow money just like the U.S. government and, like the government, they issue bonds that pay interest to attract capital for investment in its business. However, because the guarantee of payment is the promise of the issuing corporation secured only by a promise to pay (as opposed to some security like a mortgage on a factory building) investors (lenders) correctly perceive a higher risk. This then requires corporations to pay a higher rate of return than a T-Bill in order to persuade investors to take that risk and lend the corporation money. The premium that corporations must pay in order to attract investment depends in large part upon the perceived financial soundness of the corporation as to its capacity to repay the debt.

The magnitude of the difference between what a corporation must pay to attract debt capital and the risk free rate is expressed as a "spread," either in percentage points or, for small spreads, in basis points (one percentage point difference equals 100 basis points, or BP). Although bond holders hold priority with respect to equity holders in the event of a failed business there are other parties, such as employees, who are ahead of bond holders and in any case a corporate failure can easily lead to insufficient funds to meet any obligations. So even the black-and-white-in-writing promise to repay a loan can have no or low value when repayment is due. As

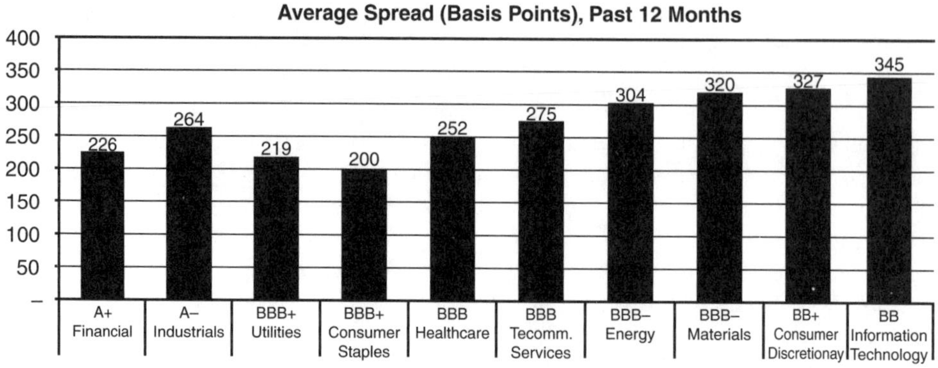

EXHIBIT 7.1 Average Spread for Various Technology Sectors and S&P Bond Ratings
Source: Capital IQ, June 2008, for the preceding 12 months. Basis Points (BP) are defined as one-hundredth of a percentage point; so 100 BP = 1 percent. Spread is in reference to a baseline (standard); S&P average ratings are computed by Capital IQ by averaging the issue level S&P credit ratings within a given Sector

we discussed in Method 2, Rating/Ranking, there exists rating agencies that assign commercial debt into one of some 20 distinct categories based upon perceived risk, for the purpose of guiding investors as to its risk category so that the market can establish a spread appropriate for any given category.

For very low risk corporate bonds, so-called "investment grade," the spread is in the range of 1 to 3 points (i.e., percentage points), or 100 to 300 BP. So, for a risk free U.S. government debt of 5 percent, such investment grade debt would be available in the range of 6 to 8 percent (100 to 300 BP, above the government debt). GE, one of the few major industrial companies to hold the coveted, highest rating of "AAA," can find investors in its bonds at the lower end of this spread. (It should be noted that during the period late in 2008 and early in 2009, unusual market conditions have occurred that may not always be consistent with these general characterizations).

Exhibit 7.1 shows the variation of such high grade debt over a recent period of 12 months for various industry sectors.

Returning to our example of the promise to pay $1,000 five years hence, and using as an example a spread of 300 BP, or a discount rate of 8 percent we find:

$$\text{DCF} = \$1000/(1.08)^5$$
$$= \$680.58, \quad \text{or} \quad \$102.95 \text{ less than the risk free rate of 5 percent.}$$

Large, established companies are like huge ships: They have enormous inertia—established product lines and customer relationships, production facilities and vendors, extensive intellectual property and other competitive barriers, established customers, multiple product lines, strong and deep management teams, and so on—that protects them from short term ups and downs, making them less risky for bond holders (unless they run aground in some metaphorical way).

For smaller companies with few products, limited barriers to competitors, or companies that are new to their primary markets, as well as companies that are troubled in some way, the risk tends to be substantially greater and spreads for bonds higher and more widely ranging from 5 to 25 points, or even more for seriously troubled companies (i.e., discount rates of 10 to 30 percent, or even more, above a risk free base of 5 percent). As we discussed in Chapter 5, debt perceived to be high risk occupies the bottom half of rating agencies rankings and is generally known by the term "junk bonds," rated below Baa3 by Moody's Investors Service or BBB- by S&P. The term "junk" is unfortunate because it conveys the idea that its object has no value or even negative value (because you have to pay some disposal cost); however, such higher risk bonds have value exactly because their issuers promise to pay higher returns, not because of some charitable disposition but because the debt is of higher risk and the market requires a premium to take such risk.

Considering General Motors (GM) and GE we can see two contrasting examples of market pricing of debt. GM is an example of a very large, established company that has devolved into a highly troubled company the market perceives as having significant risk of entering bankruptcy and defaulting on its equity and debt. In September 2008, one of the most actively traded bonds was a GM bond maturing in January 2011 with a coupon (interest rate) of 7.2 percent. It was rated at Caa2 (Moody's) and Ccc+ by S&P, which classifies it well into the high risk category ("junk"). One rule of thumb is that CCC rated bonds have approximately a 25 percent of default, a significant risk level for a bond. This high risk GM bond traded in the marketplace at $64 per $100, corresponding to an annual yield to maturity of more than 29 percent. By late 2008, GM's economic situation had worsened dramatically; one of its bonds, maturing in July 2033, was selling for just 19 cents on the dollar, equivalent to a yield of 44 percent. This deterioration in GM in just three months is not just a representation of high risk; it reveals that investors are now not seeking high returns in the face of uncertainty but are acting in this manner because of significant evidence that economic failure, bankruptcy, will occur. In contrast, another actively traded bond during the same September 2008 period was issued by GE Capital Corp with a maturity of May 2018 and a coupon 5.63 percent. The GE bond traded at $98, corresponding to an annual yield of just below six percent. Although, GM and GE are both extremely large companies with storied histories, they are clearly at opposite ends of the "promised but not risk free" spectrum as demonstrated by the risk premium the market requires to acquire their debt.

CORPORATE COST OF CAPITAL Businesses who are either buyers or sellers of technologies have to consider not only risk adjusted discount rates, but also that they themselves have to turn to others to gain necessary capital and justify investments previously made. Corporations are legal entities that typically acquire investment monies from both bond (debt) and equity investors, although some cash rich technology companies carry zero debt. When one considers the total rate of return a corporation must pay back to its investors, it is necessary to account for the returns expected by holders of both bond (debt) capital and stock (equity) capital. (For a state owned university, or other not-for-profit, cost of capital considerations are less straightforward, but they too must have some equivalent measure in order to properly manage their capital).

Equity investors rightly expect a higher rate of return because they own a less secure right of return than a bond holder. Accordingly, a corporation's weighted average cost of capital, known as its WACC (Weighted Average Cost of Capital), is typically higher than its debt alone. For the corporation to grow and prosper it seeks

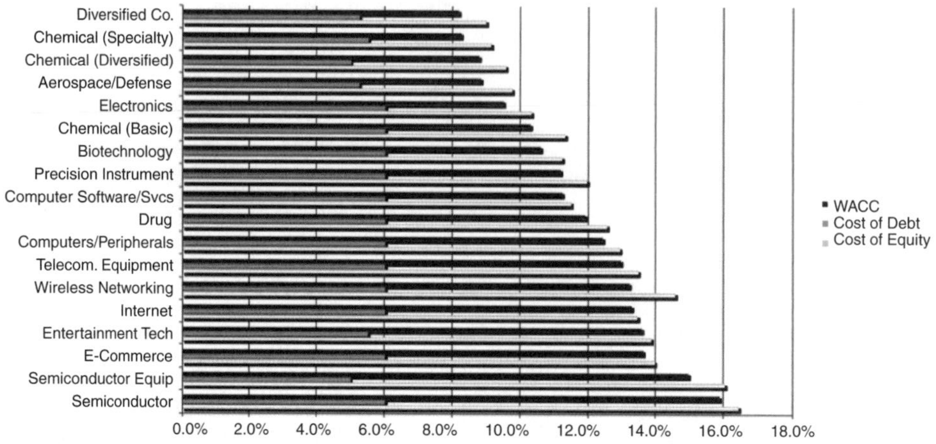

EXHIBIT 7.2 Median Cost of Debt, Equity, and WACC for Various Technology Sectors
Source: as of this writing, the values shown were obtained from: http://pages.stern.nyu.edu/~adamodar/New_Home_Page/datafile/wacc.htm.

to earn rates of return on its investments in growth opportunities, such as mergers and acquisitions (M&A), R&D expenditures (technology creation), or technology acquisition by in-licensing, that exceed its WACC because, if it does not over the long term, it is on a path to going out of business.

The calculation of WACCs requires some model, such as the famous Capital Asset Pricing Model (CAPM), and historical data such as the variability of the corporation's equity, typically expressed by a parameter known as its "beta" (b). The reader is referred to standard finance books or Shannon Pratt's *Cost of Capital*[25] for details on WACC calculations. The development of WACC models and the resulting calculations are not essential to our consideration here.

For illustration, the Stern Business School of New York University regularly publishes WACC data for various industry sections. The results for the median values in January 2008 of selected sectors with significant technology dimensions are shown in Exhibit 7.2.

Shown in Exhibit 7.2 are the calculations for the cost of equity and the resulting WACC values that range 8 to 16 percent for the median companies in the shown sectors. If we were to look at individual companies within each respective sector we would observe even a wider range of variation, especially for higher WACC rates as there are limits as to how low the WACC can be, given the availability of risk free bonds at 5 percent.

For illustration purposes let us use a discount rate corresponding to the approximate middle of the sectors, or 12 percent.

With this value, the present value of $1,000 five years hence is as follows:

$$DCF = \$1{,}000/(1.12)^5 = \$1{,}000/2.0133 = \$567.43.$$

Compared to the DCF value of $783.53 obtained for a risk free government debt of 5 percent, this calculation shows that from the point of view of the corporate cost of capital (we are using 12 percent as the illustration), the present value of $1,000 five years hence is $216.10 less.

Data on the cost of capital for various industry classifications is available from multiple vendors, notably Ibbotson's cost of capital publications (now part of Morningstar).

CORPORATE RETURN ON CAPITAL The goal of any corporation is to provide a return on capital that exceeds its cost of capital (WACC). This is exactly parallel to what a savings and loan does: It has to (on average) earn a return on the loans it makes to home buyers which exceeds the rate it pays to depositors that provide the capital to make such loans.

So a Chief Financial Officer (CFO) of a business seeks to select internal projects for investment—such as possible M&A, R&D, and technology in-licensing investments—that will earn a return on capital that exceeds the company's WACC. The resulting corporate return on capital is the company's economic report card.

Return on Equity (ROE) is considered to be one important metric on the report card. The numerator is simply the after tax earnings of the company. The denominator is the average equity (common stock owners) during the period in which such earnings occurred.

ROE data is readily available on individual public companies. The NYU Stern Business School annually publishes ROE data for various sectors, a selection of which is shown in Exhibit 7.3.

As might be expected, there is a substantial year-to-year variation in such data as a result of the market environment for the respective sectors. Using an ROE value of 15 percent as an approximate middle point value, we can make a comparative

EXHIBIT 7.3 Median 2006 Return on Equity (ROE) Data for Various Technology Sectors

Industry Name	ROE
Computer Software/Svcs	18.02%
Drug	17.37%
Telecom. Equipment	16.83%
Computers/Peripherals	16.63%
Securities Brokerage	16.35%
Semiconductor	14.33%
Aerospace/Defense	12.74%
Precision Instrument	10.83%
Semiconductor Equip	10.51%
Internet	9.37%
E-Commerce	8.71%
Biotechnology	7.34%
Healthcare Information	6.39%
Electronics	6.13%
Telecom. Services	5.43%
Wireless Networking	−0.26%

Source: http://pages.stern.nyu.edu/~adamodar/New_Home_Page/data.html (2006 data).

calculation as to the perceived present value of a $1,000 return five years hence:

$$DCF = \$1,000/(1.15)^5 = \$497.18.$$

Essentially, the value of $1,000 five years from now is, to an extent, in the eye of the beholder, who has available various other means of converting money today to money tomorrow. The higher the available alternative returns (k value), the lower any fixed future amount appears to be worth today. In mathematical terms, the DCF of a fixed, future sum declines with increasing k.

Although this seems to trouble people, the rationale behind it is very straightforward. If George is a business person who considers investments solely in T-Bills (at a k of 5 percent), then George will correlate money now with any future year by the factor $(1 + 0.05)^n$ whether George is on the receiving or granting side of an investment decision. This factor is simply the way of creating monetary equivalence between now and year n from the point of view of George, who does business buying and selling T-Bill investments at five percent returns. If Sally is a business person who considers investments solely in corporate bonds at a k of 15 percent, then Sally correlates money at different time periods with the factor $(1 + 0.15)^n$ simply because to Sally that is how future money "looks" today (and Sally will need the inner constitution to deal with increased risks she is taking to secure such higher return). Because licenses typically involve a business either on the selling or buying side (or both) a k value of 15 percent, plus or minus a few points, is typically the way money is viewed by the parties.

It should be noted that in addition to the various approaches to calculating a WACC value, such as previously discussed, its value also depends upon the magnitude of a company's investments. In general, companies have more internal proposals for investment that can be funded by its investment funds, however it is categorized internally as "capital funding," "R&D," "special projects," and so forth. If the company were to reduce its investment pool of dollars by, for instance, reduced borrowing, its balance sheet would improve in the eyes of lenders, though perhaps not equity investors, and in principle its borrowing costs and WACC would decrease. For each additional investment it undertakes, it needs to raise or consume additional capital causing, in principle, an increase in its WACC. Thus when considering a particular investment from a large portfolio, a company faces a *marginal* WACC (MWACC) value, meaning the WACC that corresponds to the next call on investment dollars. Because such MWACC increases with the magnitude of a company's investments at any given time there is always some limit on the number of projects that are economically justifiable even if the need of such project is genuine and other people and other resources are available.

CORPORATE EXPECTED RETURNS FOR ITS INVESTMENTS The previous two subsections considered discount rates associated with what a corporation has to pay for its capital (WACC), 12 percent in our example calculation, and what a corporation returns, or can return, to its equity investors (ROE), 15 percent in our example calculation.

Both the corporate WACC and ROE numbers can be thought of as representing a kind of mutual fund cost and return because in both cases these figures, even if they are for a particular company, such company has many technologies and products. If a company is trying to assess what discount rate it should use to measure the value of one particular technology investment, be it an R&D project or an in-license, then it is expected that it will require an additional return premium because of the risk associated with any single investment.

Why is this the case? The answer turns out to be essentially the same reason that an individual stock is more risky than a mutual fund. The corporation borrowing money invests it in many different kinds of projects: energy efficiency to reduce utility bills, opening a new sales office overseas to increase sales, building another plant to increase production volumes (and consequently revenues) based upon anticipated higher demand, and R&D projects that will produce entire new products that will be sold at a profit. A large company could easily have thousands of investments of all types being made in any given year. Even though each of these investments might have been made with the expectation that they would succeed in returning an investment of 15 percent or more, it can be expected that some of these investments will turn out to perform more poorly than expected—in some cases returning 10 percent, in others perhaps 5 percent, in others zero percent (i.e., zero net gain), and in still others the entire investment will be lost (i.e., a 100 percent loss). If money is lent to a corporation at the individual *project* level, then the risk of the investment is higher than if the money is lent to the *corporation* to be applied to all its projects, because in investment of diversified projects it is highly unlikely that all of them will turn out poorly. Another way to look at this is as follows: If one wants to make a conservative $1,000 investment in corporate bonds, one could invest $100 in each of ten different companies all in different industries rather than invest all the money in just one company.

However, in a technology licensing situation, a corporation would logically conclude that the overall risk of creating a profitable business is higher than, say, the risk of investing in insulation to reduce its utility costs. Accordingly, corporations typically consider each investment as belonging to a risk category and require higher risk investments to exhibit higher rates of return. For the purposes of illustration, consider the case where a corporation has concluded that investments for an R&D or licensing project of moderate risk the appropriate RAHR is 20 percent. Therefore we have:

$$\text{DCF} = \$1{,}000/(1.20)^5 = \$401.88.$$

In other words, for a RAHR of 20 percent, an upfront investment of $401.88 must show a return of $1,000 in the fifth year. If this were deemed a comparatively high risk project, say an RAHR of 30 percent, the result would be $269.33.

TECHNOLOGY VENTURE CAPITAL (VC) RISK Another category of technology investor is venture capitalists, or as they are commonly known VCs. VCs invest in technology only in the sense that it is the beginning underpinnings of a business it seeks to create via a startup (aka NEWCO). VCs often say they invest in management, because the judgment of the leadership team is the critical element in navigating the high risk environment of creating a NEWCO out of nothing, even when it begins with great looking technology. In contrast, when the buyer is a company such as we considered above, it has an incumbent management, business operations, products and customers, so the technology it is buying is for a predetermined objective. With a NEWCO, its management must make critical determinations, and iterations, in finding its customers and expressing the technology in products (including services). So VC investors have the advantage of being unbound from the constraints of being an incumbent, so they can be nimble and quick, like Jack in the nursery rhyme, but they do so in an even higher risk environment.

VCs who are too optimistic in valuing technology quickly find themselves providing very low returns on investment and unable to attract capital to make subsequent investments. VCs, raise money in "funds" from high net worth investors and from high risk segments of large, traditional investment pools. Typically such funds are raised during a recruiting period. If a VC firm is raising Fund I, then, as the joke goes, their track record is in front of them. Potential investors would examine the performance history of the individuals raising the money and the business model for its subsequent investment and reach a judgment on whether to take the risk. When a VC firm is raising Fund IV, investors tend to look at the financial performances of Fund I and Fund II as well as some preliminary results from Fund III. From such examples, investors make a judgment on what kind of return might be expected from this new fund and how such return compares with all the other VC firms also seeking investors.

Although the volatility of returns in the VC industry is high, investors appear to expect a return of at least 20 percent from the portfolio of investments made by any given fund. When the IPO (initial public offering) market is active, and/or when midsize and large companies are in an acquisition frenzy, the top tier VC firms exhibit returns of 40 percent and greater, net of the expenses. During the Internet/telecom/Y2K mania closing the twentieth century transition, VC returns of more than 100 percent occurred.[26] This of course attracted more VC firms and investors which, coupled with the collapse of the technology "bubble" in the early years of this century, the closing or near closing of the IPO markets, and the more cautious M&A market, have caused substantially lower and more volatile returns.

Data compiled by Thomson Reuter's and published as their Private Equity Performance Index (PEPI) is given below in Exhibit 7.4 averaged over various ending periods from March 31, 2007 through March 31, 2008.

However, considering the "early/seed" VC investments, the annual returns during the most recent five years have been, in aggregate, in the range of 5 to 11 percent.

EXHIBIT 7.4 **Thomson Reuter's PEPI Data: Investment Horizon Performance through 3/31/08**

Fund Type	1 Yr	3 Yr	5 Yr	10 Yr	20 Yr
Early/Seed VC	10.6	4.9	4.8	34.0	21.2
Balanced VC	8.8	13.1	12.7	14.8	14.6
Later Stage VC	30.4	13.1	11.1	8.6	14.4
All Venture	*13.3*	*9.5*	*9.1*	*17.2*	*16.8*
NASDAQ	−5.5	4.3	11.0	2.2	9.4
S&P 500	−6.4	3.8	9.1	1.8	8.5
All Venture (through 12/31/07)	*20.9*	*9.7*	*8.7*	*18.3*	*16.7*
All Venture (through 3/31/07)	*15.8*	*9.8*	*2.7*	*20.9*	*16.4*

Source: Thomson Reuters/National Venture Capital Association (www.nvca.org/pdf/PerformanceQ108FINAL.pdf). The Private Equity Performance Index is based on the latest quarterly statistics from Thomson Reuters' Private Equity Performance Database analyzing the cashflows and returns for over 1860 U.S. venture capital and private equity partnerships with a capitalization of $678 billion. Sources are financial documents and schedules from Limited Partner investors and General Partners. All returns are calculated by Thomson Reuters from the underlying financial cashflows. Returns are net to investor after management fees and carried interest.

However, for the ten year data which period includes the technology boom period of 1998 through early 2000, the returns are dramatically higher (34 percent), and even over a 20 year horizon they have exceeded 20 percent.

Regardless of the current experience in such returns, when VCs look at individual startup or early stage investments, that is, when they are investing in the formation or initial substantial capitalization of companies (NEWCOs) to productize some technology, they will need to see projected returns on their investment well above 20 or 30 percent because (1) there are VC management costs which dilute the returns to their fund investors, and (2) it will happen that not all their investments will pan out as planned, as recent history has amply demonstrated. (There is a rule of thumb in the risk capital industry that says: "All surprises are negative." It's a pessimistic outlook, but people who have been managing such investments over many years attest to its general validity.) Accordingly, when a technology seller is negotiating a license with a VC buyer, the VC may require a RAHR of 50 percent or more in order to attract their investment. Using such values in the example of $1000 in five years results in the following expression:

$$\text{DCF} = \$1{,}000/1.5^5 = \$131.69$$

Compared to the DCF calculations shown in Exhibit 7.4, such NPV value appears to be very low. Put in other terms, such a VC rate requires a potential return as follows:

$$\text{Return on Investment (ROI) in Year 5} = \$1{,}000/\$131.69 = 7.6\text{x}$$

A technology owner (seller) in such a VC negotiation may feel an injustice as an investor (buyer) seeking to receive more than 7x (seven times, also known colloquially as a "7 bagger") their investment in just five years.

However, what a VC is likely to claim is that, based upon (often painful) experience, using a minimum RAHR threshold of 50 percent is needed to produce investment portfolio returns that, after VC costs, are adequate to induce investors to make such risky investments. There is another factor at work in such high risk situations: There is almost zero probability that any investment of $131.69 will yield $1,000 in five years. Unlike the T-Bill example, or even the corporate bond example, what will happen is unknowable to any human. The technology based startup could easily fail completely consuming all the original investment (in this example, $131.69). There is some chance that it could be wildly successful producing a 40 times return (a "40 bagger"); Microsoft, for example, was a 400 bagger from its initial public offering (IPO) date to mid 1998. Risk capital investors expect that a reasonable number of their startup investments will be 10 baggers and more. Given that some investments will be totally lost, some must be 10 or more baggers in order to yield, on average, an attractive return.[27]

SUMMARIZING NINE POINTS OF VIEW OF RISK FACTORS: K AND RAHR The values calculated in the preceding sections are summarized in two exhibits below. Exhibit 7.5 shows the present value (NPV) of the promise to pay $1,000 five years from now, based upon the nine different "compared to what?" benchmarks discussed above.

Exhibit 7.5 presents the basic DCF equation discounting a future revenue, here $1,000, at one future date, here five years hence, yielding the NPV, the value now

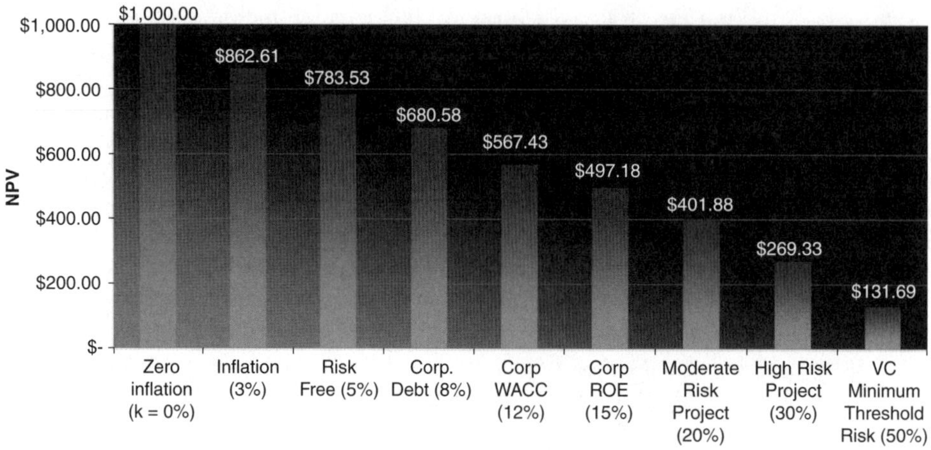

EXHIBIT 7.5 The Effect of Various Discount Rates on the Present Value of $1,000 Five Years Hence

in today's dollars. The only difference in the nine values shown in the vertical bars is the perceived risk associated with presumed payment.

Now a simple interpretation of these results from the perspective of a company CFO considering a technology investment would be: the most a CFO would be willing to pay for the promise of a return of $1,000 five years hence is the value shown at the top of the vertical bar associated with the appropriate risk benchmark.

An alternative interpretation is as follows: For the amount being invested as shown at the top of the bar toward a projected return of $1,000 five years hence, the corresponding hurdle rate, or measure of risk, must be not greater than the percentage shown at the bottom of the column. In other words, if the project that promises a return of $1,000 in five years and requires $497.18 in investment today, the risk or discount rate or hurdle rate, should not exceed 15 percent. If the discount rate exceeds 15 percent, then per the DCF calculation the CFO should not expect to see the needed return on such $497.18 for the risk being undertaken. This perspective is what leads to the use of the term Risk Adjusted Hurdle Rate (RAHR).

The perspective of a CFO investing in a project, be it R&D or a technology in-license, is exactly the same as the seller (licensor) of a technology viewing the promise of its buyer (licensee) making a promise to pay a lump sum. The difference could be in the discount rate used. A CFO might well use a rate such as the example 20 percent, because the return is predicated solely on the particular project being successful.

As we will discuss in Chapters 10 and 11, using the DCF method to discount future payments can be done by both the buyer and seller, and they can be done using different RAHR values. A seller viewing a payment promised by the buyer five years hence for the technology being sold could use a lower discount rate, such as 12 percent, because such payment is unconditional, the buyer is creditworthy, and the seller's WACC is 12 percent. Alternatively, the seller could use some other discount rate based upon its "opportunity cost," namely the return it could reasonably expect on it being paid today and then making a CFO-like investment of its own.

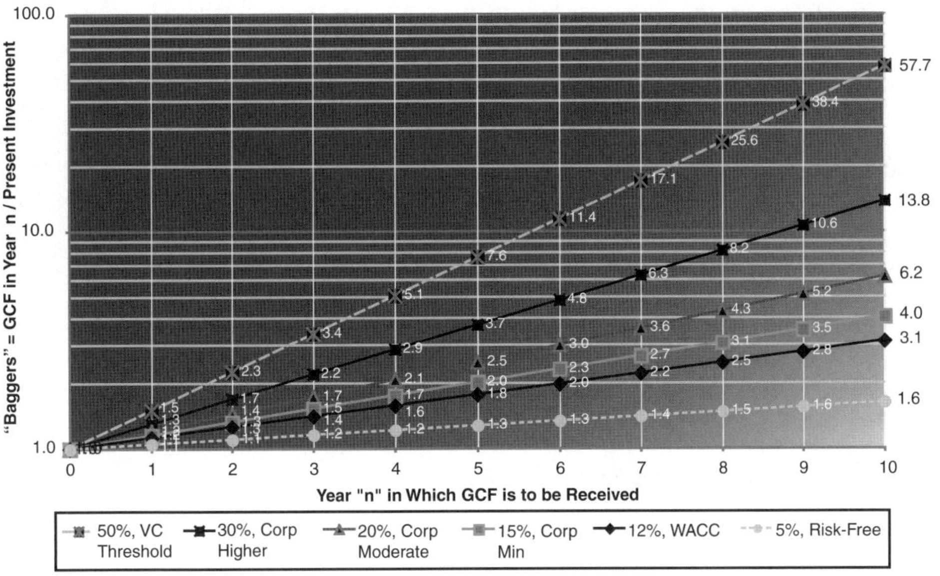

EXHIBIT 7.6 Ratio of Required Future Return to Present Investment (the "Bagger") as a Function of RAHR

The basic DCF equation can, alternatively, tell us what return must be projected in order to justify the risk to be undertaken. To illustrate this graphically, we will show the ratio of future return to the present investment, such future return occurring in any one year, ranging from one year hence to ten years hence. Such ratio is the bagger discussed, where the numerator is the GCF in the subject year divided by the dollar amount invested today, in present dollars. Exhibit 7.6 provides this comparison. This exhibit can be best understood as portraying the required one time, future liquidity event payment needed for any given year and RAHR value in terms of dollars invested as a lump sum today.

For clarity, only six of the nine RAHR values used for Exhibit 7.5 have been plotted. The lowest RAHR value plotted, five percent corresponding to "risk free," is shown by the short dashed line, the highest, 50 percent corresponding to "VC threshold," by the long dashed line, and the four corporate RAHR values (12, 15, 20, and 30 percent) discussed above are shown by solid lines.

Considering the RAHR = 30 percent line in Exhibit 7.6, we can see that the required projected return as a lump sum, must be 3.7x in five years, or 13.8x in ten years. The liquidity payment concept is that the party making the one time initial investment will receive a onetime payment at the end of the respective year. So, for a corporate internal R&D investment or a VC investor, the liquidity payment would be the lump sum that the technology should be worth to some third party buyer as of the respective year, to be just worth investing, given the respective RAHR presumably when the technology has matured into a product with a market and established profitability. Every technology buyer, be it a corporate licensee/assignee, or a VC, can be considered to be an intermediary between the current technology owner and some subsequent customer. For a corporation such subsequent customer could be the companies or individuals to which it sells products year-by-year, or some other company to which the then mature, or more mature, technology will be sold. For VCs, their customer is usually either the public via an IPO (Initial Public Offering) or a "strategic buyer" (a company who acquires the NEWCO).

Clearly for high RAHR values and/or distant liquidity dates (high n values) the bagger values become extremely high. For the RAHR value of 30 percent that will be used in subsequent examples in this chapter, if the only realization is a lump sum payment at the end of ten years, such payment must be 13.8x the present lump sum investment. Another perspective can be highlighted by estimating the n value for a three bagger: from Exhibit 7.5 we can see that it is approximately 2.5 years for RAHR = 50 percent, ca four years for 30 percent, six years for 20 percent, eight years for 15 percent, and ten years for 12 percent; there is clearly a big difference between achieving a 3x return in 2.5 years versus ten years. We will return later in this chapter to the situation of high RAHR values, or distant returns, or both, as such circumstances are special challenges for the use of the DCF Method.

The Toolbox

The DCF equation developed above—$DCF = GCF/(1 + k)^n$—can be used as a ***Tool*** with other valuation ***Methods***, or ***Approaches*** (such as opportunity ***Discovery*** or ***Dealmaking***). For instance, a common opportunity ***Discovery*** decision is deciding "Is it *worth* it?" (where "it" is a value realization quest under consideration). The above DCF relationship can be used as a rough (so-called "quick and dirty") guide. If one needs to commit, say, \$100,000 to advance a technology from its present state toward some licensable outcome (ignoring, as always, all sunk costs) then the value in lump sum form of such outcome should exceed: GCF (Gross Cash Flow, the dollar amount expected and denominated in such future year) $\geq 100{,}000(1 + RAHR)^n$, where RAHR is the Risk Adjusted Hurdle Rate and n is the number of years from now that such realization is expected to occur. If the technology is in near-ready-to license condition, and there is reason to believe it to be licensable (as discussed in Chapters 1–3), then a possible estimate would be RAHR = 20% (0.20) and n = 1 year. Substituting such values yields: GCF $\geq$ \$120,000, where GCF is the then (one year hence) minimum value of the anticipated realization from a licensee justifying making the further investment in the project.

If, on the other hand, the technology is in an early and incomplete stage of feasibility demonstration, whereby \$1 million is the estimated further investment required, then RAHR may be 50% and n = 3 years, yielding: GCF $\geq$ \$3.375 million, which means that a reasonable expectation should be that the opportunity should realize this amount (as a lump sum) three years hence, or the project is not worth doing.

Suppose, both of the above possibilities were reasonable estimates of the associated investment, risk, and reward. In accordance with our assumptions, both of these options have the same NPV, zero, that is they are just at the minimum threshold of being worthy of investment if in the case of the first approach the expected future yield is \$120,000, or in the second approach the future yield is \$3.375 million. The management decision is then which minimum outcome is the more likely to be *exceeded*, namely with an NPV greater than zero, and as large a positive value as possible? If the answer turns out to be the second option, say an NPV of \$1 million (i.e. an expected value realization of \$4.375 million), compared to a (say) best guess NPV for the first option of \$300,000 (realization of \$420,000), then a follow up decision has to be made as to which is worth more given the consideration of investment. With the first option, using these hypothetical values, the NPV is \$300,000 from an incremental risk capital investment of \$100,000 (assuming the technology has zero value but for such incremental investment) whereas in the second option the NPV of \$1 million requires the investment of \$1 million and three years. The option-specific risk factors (RAHR values) put these two alternative returns on the same basis, so the choice becomes risk independent. The use of the DCF tool does not answer the question as to which is the best choice, but it defines, within the framework of the assumptions, what each choice means in present value terms.

The DCF ***Tool*** is very useful in ***Dealmaking***, specifically in considering alternative payment amounts and structures. A common ***Dealmaking*** issue is the timing of payments to be made by the buyer. For example, the technology seller may have offered a technology for series of three "upfront" payments of \$1 million upon signing and on each of the first two anniversaries, followed by running royalties. The buyer may counter with, for example, a signing payment of \$500,000, with four anniversary lump sums of \$750,000 each with the seller's royalty terms. The question for the seller is, how different is the buyer's offer from what was proposed? For purposes of this analysis we will assume that the RAHR is 10 percent. The NPV to the seller of its proposal was: $\$1 + \$1 \times 1.1 + \$1 \times 1.1^2$, or \$3.31 million. The NPV offered by the buyer is: $\$750 + \$750 \times 1.1 + \$750 \times 1.1^2 + \$750 \times 1.1^3$, or \$3.48 million. So, for these assumptions, the buyer has actually offered more than the seller proposed, presumably because the buyer's cost of capital (or its perception of project risk) is sufficiently high that it is highly motivated to defer cash outlays.

A similar use of the DCF ***Tool*** arises when considering a lump sum, paid up license in the alternative to a running royalty paid over time. The approach is the same, namely: discounting each year's anticipated royalty payment by an appropriate RAHR factor to compute an NPV value. The RAHR value could represent the perceived risk of receiving such annual royalties, or the opportunity value to the seller because of investments it could make in other areas with a lump sum payment.

Quantification, Classification of Risk

Returning to the **TR $\mathbf{R^k}$ A DE™** acronym where **TR** designated Technology Rights, and **DE** Deal Economics or Equity, now we are prepared to consider further the symbol $\mathbf{R^k}$ representing "Risk expressed in terms of k" (or RAHR). Critical to translating Technology Rights into Deal Economics is an understanding and judgment of the risk associated with converting the technology rights conveyed into a stream of profits. As we have seen, the DCF Method determines value based on the timing, magnitude, and risk of all future cash flows attributable to the technology being valued. Further, the basic DCF, or NPV, equation expresses the entire project risk by a single factor, the Risk Adjusted Hurdle Rate (RAHR).

As we will do throughout this chapter, we are seeking a single valued RAHR that will appropriately account for the risk of the entire technology commercialization opportunity. At the end of this chapter, and more so in Chapter 8, we will develop a methodology whereby the RAHR is not a static, single value over the life of the project.

In previous discussions we considered how such RAHR values affect NPV for various contexts. In this section, we will address more carefully how a RAHR value can be determined. As we will see there are generally guidelines, but such guidelines require judgment. Two tools that assist making such judgment are (1) reference to comparables, as a type of industry standard for risk, (2) use of rating/ranking to compare and contrast a given project's risk to available comparables or standards, and (3) rules-of-thumb based upon some codification of experience. In this sense we can apply here as ***Tools*** the principles underlying Valuation Methods 1, 2, and 3. But first, let us consider another approach to determining RAHR.

Risk Adder Concept

One possible way to develop a RAHR value would be by following a parallel to what has been done with equities. Earlier we mentioned in passing the Capital Asset Pricing Method (CAPM) whereby the market expected rate of return for an equity is equated to a risk free rate plus a risk premium associated with the volatility of the particular equity compared to the market, measured by a parameter known as its beta.

This approach for equities is also used to add expected returns for other factors such as a size premium or a country risk premium. The basic idea is that one looks at the various kinds of risks associated with a particular equity and then quantifies each such risk and sums up all of them to determine what should be an appropriate overall risk adjusted return for the stock.

The parallel for technology valuation would be to take the rating/ranking factors we considered in Chapter 5, and assign some risk percentage points appropriate to each kind of risk and add them up to get a total.

For example, we could start with a corporation's targeted rate of return of, say, 15 percent. Such value would be the risk associated with all the corporate investments in aggregate. Any particular project could then be assigned a size premium risk, because it might totally fail losing its entire investment, of, say two points. Then because the technology is still at a lab "bench," and hasn't been demonstrated at a pilot plant scale, we might add three points of R&D risk. Then there could be certain manufacturability risks because of some new aspect of production that could add, say, one more point. Then there is the marketplace with its uncertainties as to willing to pay in terms of unit pricing and total demand, again because there is something unknown about the products from the subject technology compared to what is known about the corporation's incumbent products and markets. This could add five points. We could also add competitive risks associated with intellectual property barriers such as a less than complete patent estate or uncertainty as to what claims and scope of claims will be allowed. This could add four points. The result would then, for this example, look like this:

$$RAHR = \text{Corporate Baseline} + \text{Individual Risk "Adders"}$$
$$RAHR = 15 + (2 + 3 + 1 + 5 + 4) = 15 + 15 = 30 \text{ percent}$$

Although in this example such values are without quantified support, the process for developing such estimates can use rating/ranking or rules-of-thumb as ***Tools***. For instance, a company could develop a somewhat standardized way of rating/ranking each risk category by making comparisons between the subject opportunity and the comparables that exist based on its prior investment history.

The meaningfulness of performing such a rating/ranking based RAHR adder analysis depends upon having a database history of prior investments and risk issues, and having expended some effort to systematize the facts and circumstances behind such history.

The adder concept is appealing because of its obvious flexibility of scoring and inclusivity of any risk type consideration. However, there is a hidden assumption that is not parallel to the Rating/Ranking Method of valuation in Chapter 5. For example, we can reasonably say that if the market created by the technology under consideration is larger than our family of comparable agreements the value of the technology could scale in some direct way. This concept works if the technology is the *raison d'etre* of achieving the large market size. Similarly, with profit margins we expect rating/ranking results to scale with increases in such margins.

However, risk does not work in this simple additive way. Whenever we are adding things up, we are assuming that what is being added is the same thing, apples with apples, oranges with oranges, and that each unit being added is independent of the others. Risks are not like apples, or oranges. They are not wholly independent, nor can they simply be added.

A man named Evel Knievel achieved some fame years ago for jumping on his motorcycle over all kinds of objects, like buses parked side by side. Risk for Evel was associated with not being able to land on the down ramp after soaring over the last bus while still in control of his motorcycle such that he could stop without he and his bike being broken into pieces. If we consider his risk as being related to the number of buses, which seems like a quite reasonable approach, can we keep incrementing his risk by one unit for each bus? Evel, it turns out could jump one bus with the ease that normal people can pour coffee. Two buses? No problem. Five buses? He can do that too at essentially no, or very low risk. But there is an n + 1 bus that is, as they say, one bus too far, for which the risk is extremely high; and at n + 2 there is essentially no chance of making it without injury or death.[28] How would any additive process properly calculate this? Further, in addition to the number of buses there are other factors that likely affect risk, such as: wind, engine performance, tires, or run out length after the down ramp, starting ramp height and length, et cetera. Could we develop some independent number for each of these and other risk categories and add it to the number of buses?

The bus jumping example is extreme because of the bimodal outcome: Either Evel makes it without injury or he doesn't. Technology commercialization can have a range of outcomes from wildly successful, to a solid win, to "we're glad we did it," to "it was not that great an idea after all," to "please don't ever remind me that we tried this."

A related way of determining RAHR is instead to use a classification method, similar to that used by rating agencies for equity values and debt, as we discussed in the background of Valuation Method 2.

Risk Benchmarks: Bonds, Equities, and Technology

As we saw in Chapter 5, risks associated with debt instruments (bonds) tend to be well established because of rating/ranking performed usually for each bond issue by agencies that provide such assessments as their business model. In addition, there is an active public market for bonds that are resold prior to the maturity that provides a market based valuation much like equities. Finally, bonds tend to be comparatively low in risk because they are direct promises to pay a maturity amount together with an interest coupon. Yet, as we also saw there have been significant risk assessment errors, so these categories of investments are neither risk free nor risk certain.

Equities tend to have an even greater uncertainty as to the risk, although the variation in risk from low to high can be very wide. Utilities such as electric power generating companies have a long history of stable earnings and, thereby, low risk associated with their stock, even lower in risk than bonds issued by companies in challenging business situations. Equities also have very liquid, completely public markets, and small armies of research analysts making assessments of risks and potential returns. Such markets and expert judgments can be, and regularly are, widely off the mark, as was the case with many NASDAQ listed companies as became evident in the post March 2000 period.

For technology licensing, or M&A of nascent technology companies, there is no public market providing any pricing guidance, or for that matter misguidance, and there are no research analyst reports or rating agency classifications. In some circumstances the market size for the technology is speculative because the products being contemplated are not higher performance versions of incumbent products. There are often also significant unknowns with respect to the ultimate performance of the technology itself, and/or the manufacturability in commercially necessary volumes of products embodying the technology.

In Chapter 9 we will consider technology auctions as a valuation method. As we will see there are certain, limited circumstances whereby a public value has been placed on various technologies offered for sale. However, unlike the situation with equities, or bonds, there is usually no public data as to revenues, let alone profits, associated with the use of the auction technology. So even if we were to find some auction based values for comparable technologies, there is no ready way of knowing the economic significance of ownership as we generally are able to do with public equities or with public markets for many kinds of bonds.

So as a general rule, we can consider most bonds and equities as being of lower risk than a technology, but we are missing the recipe for how much greater the RAHR for any given technology should be compared with what bond or equity risk. It should be noted that there are very high risk bonds and equities, so risky that their market value is nearly zero. Companies entering bankruptcy for example, may still have their stocks and bonds traded on a public market, finding buyers albeit at huge discounts in value. The debt and equity risk of companies in or near such straits would correspond to extremely high risks, far above those that we will consider for technology opportunities.

In the eyes of the technology seller, especially in the eyes of the inventor-seller, the risk associated with obtaining a profit from such rights can appear to be very low. This can be attributed to two primary factors. First, the seller has an intimate understanding of all the difficulties that have been overcome in bringing the technology to its present state (and in many cases it has been a multiyear or even decade-long trail of tears interspersed with transitory joys). Secondly, it is human nature to underestimate the complexities that await the recipient of one's work product. This is particularly true in high technology contexts because the science embodied in the **TR** can be extraordinarily complicated while the seller's expectations of the buyer amounts to "all they have to do is make it and sell it." Although making and selling may not involve differential equations (although sometimes it does), even simple process steps involve risk.

In the eyes of the technology buyer-company the same opportunity can appear to be high risk, especially a company which is considering a technology expected to yield products that are to be sold to customers the company does not presently serve, and/or require expert application of science and engineering that it has not previously applied. Such a company recognizes that even after a successful R&D program, there are important subsequent phases including design for manufacturing and the manufacturing itself, marketing and sales, distribution, service and support, and so forth, all in the face of ever-changing market circumstances and competition from other companies. Every one of these areas can involve some, or even substantial, risk.

As we have seen, increasing risk perception causes buyers to discount future value using larger values of RAHR. To use the DCF Method, we require some means of specifying—estimating is really the better idea—the risk of a particular technology commercialization opportunity. Not all of them will look alike in terms of risk, just as not all bonds or equities look alike. In fact, the risk variation with technology is generally very large compared to these other, more conventional and marketable, investment categories.

In Chapter 5 when we considered the Rating/Ranking Method, we identified key factors by which distinctions could be usefully made and scored in some way. If one wants to make a comprehensive list of all possible drivers of technology value, and the risks associated with each one, the result will be so complex, even harrowing, that there will be no actionable way out.

What is needed is some way of developing a reasoned estimate for a RAHR value that can be general enough to apply to the infinite variety of technology commercialization opportunities.

Risk Classification Concept

An alternative approach to the adder concept is to develop a parallel to the rating/ranking used by firms that classify the risks of bonds or that used by research analysts to classify equities into categories of "buy," accumulate," "hold," and so forth.

For technology commercialization the two factors that tend to be given the most weight in terms of the risk are the market demand and the success of the technology in the sense that it "works," namely what is apparently demonstrated in the laboratory can be scaled up, harnessed for manufacture, and made safely in large quantities at a sufficiently low cost. These of course are not the only factors, but they tend to be uppermost in the minds of investors usually in the form of the three commonly asked questions:

1. Is it [the technology] real?
2. Does anybody [the market] want it?
3. If so, is it worth doing [the NPV value question]?

Of course the scope and strength of the IP protection is another category of factors. In general these relate to the technology owner's ability to forestall, inhibit, or block a competitor from offering a "like" product. In some situations, such as composition of matter claims for pharmaceuticals, such IP rights can make a huge difference in achieving a competitive advantage. But even in these situations—think of a cholesterol inhibitor—there are alternative pharmaceuticals that have similar biological benefits and which are outside the strong IP rights of this example. For electronics or software technologies, for example, there are likely to be ways that a company with the subject IP rights will be able to offer some kind of a competing product in the marketplace.

Another category of key factors includes the know-how and data that have been developed by the seller. Although such know-how and data itself can be an important form of IP rights, its existence can also reduce the technology risk.

In the risk classification structure presented below, it is assumed that the IP rights provide a level of protection to the technology being licensed such that there are reasonable grounds to prevent an "in kind" competitor, namely one using the same technology to make the same product(s) as that being offered for sale. But it is not assumed that there will not be products offered by competitors that do something like what the subject technology is expected to.

Exhibit 7.7 presents, in the author's experience, how various categories of investment/licensing opportunities are viewed by technology investors. These RAHR estimates are very approximate values based upon buyers' general perceptions of the required rate of return, or the associated risk, of commercializing the technology. These values are not hard and fast numbers, but reflect commonly used values. This information can be useful in negotiations between buyers and sellers to share perceptions of risk and the associated RAHR. Such discussions can help parties understand why they look at the same opportunity and see different values and, in some cases, may aid by removing some of the uncertainty and lowering the RAHR, thereby increasing the perceived value to the buyer. This subject will be discussed in more detail in Chapter 11.

The final category in Exhibit 7.7 introduces a third factor of risk, that of forming a startup company (NEWCO) with a new management team, which category is most often associated with "venturing" kinds of risk. A 1987 case study on hurdle rates used by venture capitalists provides another perspective.[29] Looking at the opportunity to invest from startup to IPO, these authors suggest the following RAHR values at "seed stage" (raw idea, pre-business plan) > 80 percent, "startup" 50 to 70 percent, "first stage" (existing company but with limited or no customers) 40 to 60 percent, "second stage" (to fuel growth) 30 to 40 percent, "bridge" financing

EXHIBIT 7.7 Approximate Values of Risk Adjusted Hurdle Rate Used in License Negotiations

Characterization of Risk	Approximate RAHR (k value)
O. "Risk-free," such as building a duplicate plant to make more of a currently made and sold product in response to presently high demand.	Approximates the corporate rate of borrowing, which can be in the range of 8–18%
IA. Very low risk, such as incremental improvements with a well-understood technology into making a product presently made and sold in response to existing demand.	15–20%; discernibly above the corporation's goals for return on investment to its shareholders
IB. Low risk, such as making a product with new features using well-understood understood technology into a presently served and understood customer segment with evidence of demand for such features.	20–30%
II. Moderate risk, such as making a new product using well-understood technology to a customer segment presently served by other products made by the corporation and with evidence of demand for such a new product.	25–35%
III. High risk, such as making a new product using a not well-understood technology and marketing it to an existing segment or a well-understood technology to a new market segment.	30–40%
IV. Very high risk, such as making a new product with new technology to a new segment.	35–45%
V. Extremely high risk (sometimes known as "wildcatting," borrowing an expression from the oil exploration industry), such as creating a startup company to go into the business of making a product not presently sold or even known to exist using unproven technologies.	50–70% or even higher

(to carry to an IPO) 20 to 35 percent. It should be remembered that these rates reflect the added risk of creating a startup company, which approximately corresponds to the situation for the bottom two entries of Exhibit 7.7.

The reader is cautioned that the phrase characterizing each risk category in Exhibit 7.7 is a simplification for purposes of illustration of what must be a case specific analysis. There are many dimensions to risk; the characterization of Exhibit 7.7 is focused on just two: the technology risk and the target market segment. A buyer could ascribe a low RAHR value to a potential opportunity because it perceives that the risk of *not* adopting the subject technology or entering the target market is significant relative to the long term well being of the company. In the other situations, the buyer may possess inside information from known customers on the high value already placed on potential products or have valuable insights as to how the technology can be scaled commercially.

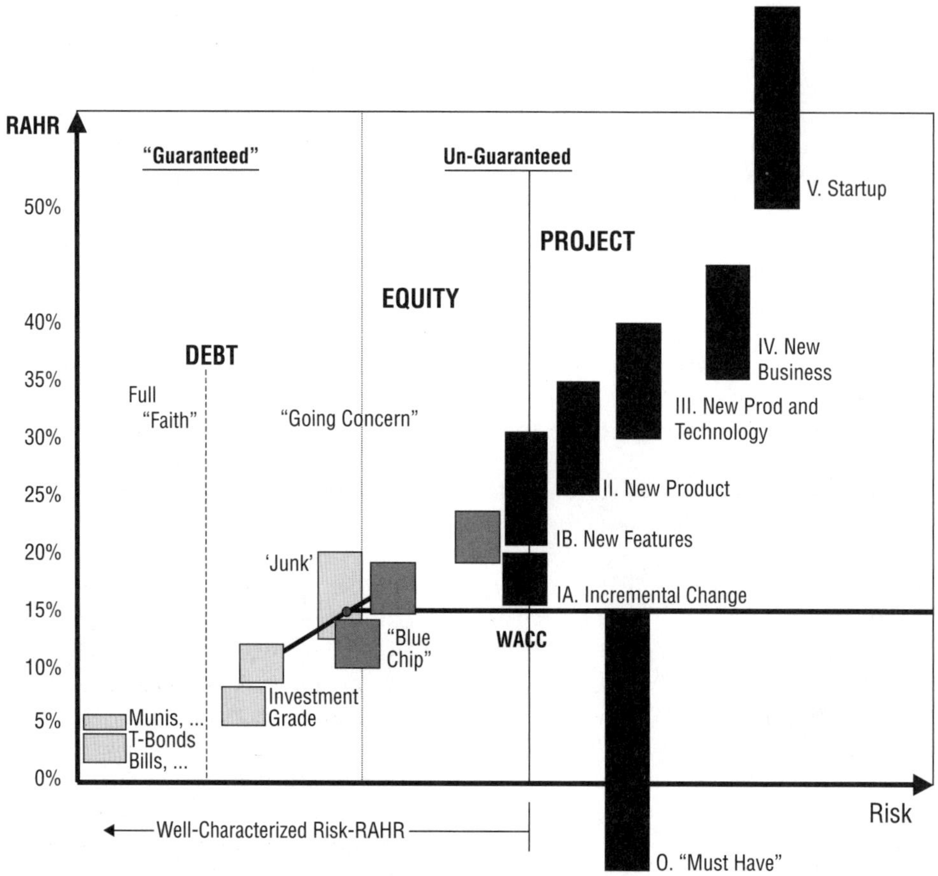

EXHIBIT 7.8 RAHR vs. Risk: Types and Values
Source: © 2003 Razgaitis, richard@razgaitis.com.

A graphical portrayal of such RAHR values together with other benchmark rates is given in Exhibit 7.8.

This exhibit seeks to show how investors expect and receive higher rates of return for high risk investments. The leftmost group represents debt forms of investments (bonds). These are traditionally considered as guaranteed, but such guarantees are only as good as the guarantor as the recent debacle in mortgage-based investments such as the CDOs discussed in Chapter 5 displayed. In the case of the governments, the full faith and power of the respective government or agency stands behind the repayment and the risk is generally considered to be very low. Next up the risk ladder are corporate bonds. As discussed previously, they are rated by various agencies into a dozen or more categories from very low risk to extremely high risk; for risks above some demarcation such bonds are considered junk (meaning not appropriate for investment grade purposes where the risk of loss of capital is supposed to be extremely low).

Overlapping somewhat the debt categories are the equity classes of investments (stocks). Such investments are viewed as riskier than bonds because returns are not guaranteed, and any claim on the assets of the issuing company is inferior to the claim of bond holders. However, the lowest risk stocks are less risky than the highest risk bonds, because bond holders are at risk in a default situation even though they have a preferred place with respect to equity holders in any recovery of assets. Also, bonds can be sold prior to maturity (when they would be redeemed by the debtor[30]) and when they do so they sell at the then market price that takes into account the then perceived risk of default and rates of return available from alternative investments. So, the debt and equity areas of the figure should overlap but have not been shown to make the figure more readable. As an equity is perceived to be more risky, the expected rate of returns by investors goes up, as shown by the fuel cell valuation examples at the beginning of this chapter.

The next category is the project investments we have just been considering and have summarized in Exhibit 7.7. Like the equity type investments, these are not guaranteed. They are generally considered to be more risky than equity investments because, for one reason, they are investments in a single project whereas equity investments in a typical company involve investment in multiple company projects and the company has some momentum of an incumbent business. So one would expect less investment failure with a company investment than a single project, although one can conceive of companies "at death's door" that are in extremely high risk circumstances. In such circumstances, the investment risk in a particular project under consideration is less, even substantially less, than that in a distressed company; again this overlap has not been shown in order to make the chart readable. The Roman numerals on each of the vertical bars correspond to their designation in Exhibit 7.7 and are a kind of rating/ranking categorization of risk, similar to that discussed in the previous chapter used by NRSROs (discussed in Chapter 6) such as Moody's, Fitch, and S&P for rating bonds, or, more fancifully, the designations used at ski resorts to characterize the danger (risk) or various categories of slopes (blue circles for beginners, squares for intermediates, and diamonds and double diamonds for experts).

The horizontal line designated WACC represents an important corporate finance concept which is the Weighted Average Cost of Capital. A company's WACC is the average cost of capital based upon their particular balance between debt and equity coupled with the market's expectation of return given the company risk. In principle, it represents the floor of a company's expected rate of returns for its own investments. So, companies not only seek high rate of return projects, they are highly motivated, on average, to exceed their WACC return on the portfolio of investments.

However, there are some projects that companies undertake which are shown by the O category of "Must Have." For instance, suppose the government passes a law that requires companies that make a chemical, say benzene, to reduce ambient emissions of benzene. On a return on investment basis for the subject project, a financial analysis could yield an NPV that does not meet any of the above criteria, or even a negative number because there will be no or an inadequate return (because, for example, no increase in benzene revenues are expected despite an increase in production costs), but, nonetheless, the company must comply or get out of the business.[31] In such a circumstance, the company may look at a range of compliance solutions, all of which have projected returns below their WACC.

Another, less obvious example is the anticipation of "transformative" market opportunities. As discussed earlier, fuel cells continue to receive commercial interest as nonpolluting transportation engines and even to provide portable electronic power for laptops and the like. A maker of conventional internal combustion engines perhaps coupled with motors powered by battery capacity (so called "hybrids") could face a situation soon where on a return on investment prospect it would just as soon stick with improving its conventional engine but knows (or believes) that if it does not make some investments in fuel cell technology, regardless of the immediate prospective return (but mindful of the total investment and potential ultimate, total return), that it will be out of business like the proverbial buggy whip manufacturer. A related current example is the change in product mix being offered and planned by U.S. automobile companies. The high return on investment product categories has been, until recently, pick-up trucks and SUVs. However as cost of crude oil has reached new record highs, and is approximately 10x what it was in the early 1990s, the price of end product gasoline and diesel fuel has also increased dramatically, driving consumers toward vehicles with higher fuel economies, and leaving unsold inventories of trucks and SUVs on dealer's lots. Accordingly, automobile companies are changing their investment strategies to develop more high fuel economy vehicles. The risk level associated with such new technologies and vehicles is almost surely higher than had been perceived for the recent strategy of investing heavily in trucks and SUVs. However, the world has changed, or at least appears to have done so. The risk of creating high fuel economy vehicles is higher than had been the risk associated with trucks/SUVs but is now less than the risk in making future investments in trucks/SUVs because of the change in buyer preferences. The challenge facing these companies is, can they now reasonably forecast positive returns at discount rates that exceed their WACC.

The Toolbox

Creating distinct risk classifications, and quantifying such classes, is a ***Tool*** useful to other Valuation ***Methods***, and to the ***Approaches*** of opportunity ***Discovery*** and ***Dealmaking***.

Opportunity Discovery, as we discussed in Chapter 3, requires making judgments about both go/no-go actions, and prioritization of those selected to go forward as to the appropriate level of resource investment and time urgency. Because such decisions have to be made early in the life of a technology development program, the level of uncertainty is of course higher than during a typical valuation process such as we are considering here. However, judgments must be made on some basis, or one is reduced to selection by lottery or inventor resume or who can scream the loudest. One can, alternatively, use two forms of risk classification: (1) a table such as Exhibit 7.7 assuming that the technology opportunity will achieve a level of success whereby a more formal valuation is needed either to support more significant internal investments or for Dealmaking, and (2) a calculation like that done in the risk-adder discussion above that assesses the risk of getting to the point where Exhibit 7.7 would apply.

For Dealmaking, having a model for quantified RAHR value enables one to make concrete financial judgments as to the implications of moving payments forward or backward or making them more or less conditional. Such a risk model can also aid a seller in assessing the potential deal value for a royalty based or other conditional payment structure as may be licensed to different potential buyers each with distinct complementary assets.

Risk Calculation Example

We can combine the risk adder and risk classification concepts discussed above with the Rating/Ranking Tool from Chapter 5 to establish a more systematic way of estimating a reasonable RAHR. In Chapter 5 we reviewed the use of Likert Scoring using a 1 to 5 or 1 to 7 scale. With the 1 to 7 scale, a 4 designates a middle value, so there are three integer scores that can be used to designate less than such 4, namely 1 to 3, and 3 greater than 4, namely 5 through 7.

In the top half of Exhibit 7.9 is an example of Likert scoring for relative risk, using the one to seven scale, for each of the four valuation factors shown on the left of the table—Technology, Market, IP Rights, and NEWCO (management/startup). Across the top are shown the seven RAHR categories used in Exhibit 7.7, with the corresponding RAHR range also from Exhibit 7.7. So for the lower risk categories, such as the first three columns, the Likert scores are all less than 4, the middle range of risk. The NEWCO risk is low for the non-NEWCO Categories because it is assumed there are in place experienced, incumbent management teams lodged within companies with infrastructure and well honed business procedures; however, some management risk (a 2) is included for Risk Classifications III and IV because new markets are being addressed.

The bottom box in Exhibit 7.9 shows a possible calculation methodology based upon the Likert scoring, as follows:

EXHIBIT 7.9 RAHR vs. Risk: Types and Values

		Risk Classification						
		Corp Risk Free	IA	IB	II	III	IV	IV
	Likert 1–7	10–18%	15–20%	20–30%	25–35%	30–40%	35–45%	50+ %
	Technology	*1*	*2*	*4*	*5*	*5*	*5*	*5*
	Market	*1*	*2*	*3*	*4*	*4*	*5*	*5*
	IP Rights	*1*	*1*	*2*	*2*	*3*	*4*	*2*
	NEWCO	*1*	*1*	*1*	*1*	*2*	*2*	*6*
Weight	*Corp RAHR*	*15%*	*15%*	*15%*	*15%*	*15%*	*15%*	*15%*
10	Technology	0.3%	1.3%	5.3%	8.3%	8.3%	8.3%	8.3%
10	Market	0.3%	1.3%	3.0%	5.3%	5.3%	8.3%	8.3%
10	IP Rights	0.3%	0.3%	1.3%	1.3%	3.0%	5.3%	1.3%
20	NEWCO	0.7%	0.7%	0.7%	0.7%	2.7%	2.7%	24.0%
	RAHR	16.7%	18.7%	25.3%	30.7%	34.3%	39.7%	57.0%

For the Technology risk calculation for the left column corresponding to "Corporate Risk Free," the value shown, 0.3 percent, is determined by the following:

- Technology Risk Addition = (Likert Score)^2 * Weight/30 * 1/100 = 1^2 * 10/30 * 1/100 = 0.003 = 0.3%
- The "Weight" factor is the relative importance given to each of the four shown risk factors as shown in the leftmost column. For this example, all the risks are weighted equally except the NEWCO risk which is double weighted in comparison.
- The Market, IP Rights, and NEWCO risk additions are similarly calculated.
- The four calculations are added together and to the baseline Corporate RAHR of 15 percent to yield, for this column, a RAHR value of 16.7 percent.
- The remaining columns follow the same methodology and differ only by the Likert scoring which increases as shown because of the increasing risk of the respective classifications.
- The calculation has been arranged so that the lowest scored risk of 1, 1, 1, 1 corresponds to a modest increase above the Corporate baseline, namely 1.7 points above the assumed 15 points, and the highest scored risk of 7, 7, 7, 7 yields about 100 percent. The squaring of the Likert score is a method of accelerating the increase in RAHR for higher risk scores.

The approach shown by example risk model in Exhibit 7.9 can be useful in several contexts. When dealing with a large number of valuations there is an opportunity to develop an expert panel not only for risk assessment of multiple opportunities but also to create a learning database that can be applied to subsequent valuation projects. Another reason for following such a procedure is when small RAHR distinctions can make an important difference in whether to proceed or abandon an opportunity and/or a substantial investment will be put at risk; in such circumstances it is worth trying to understand the risk elements and characterize them as carefully as possible. A third reason is to handle unusual risk combinations. For instance, suppose an opportunity has negligible technical, market, and NEWCO risk, but substantial IP Risk, and such IP Risk is important because if barriers to competitive market entry are weak or nonexistent there are strong, fast following competitors with very low cost structures. For such case, we might have a Likert score of 1, 2, 6, 1, respectively, which would yield an RAHR estimate of 34 percent; this result would be dramatically greater than the minimal IR Risk calculation shown in the left-most column of Exhibit 7.9 (1, 2, 1, 1) corresponding to a RAHR of 16.5 percent.

The weighting for the four risk factors of Exhibit 7.9—10,10,10, and 20, where the NEWCO risk element is weighted the highest—can be adjusted based either on the particular technology being valued or to reflect the nature of the industry. One way to make this adjustment is to ask: if all factors are rated at the same innate level of risk, say a Likert 2 or 3, which factor do I really worry about the most? For startup situations, the prevailing answer tends to be the NEWCO risk category, reflecting the combination of the management team and all the key startup business decisions. In other situations, the Market risk category may be weighted higher because of the difficulty in finding and keeping customers, so called "customer sat" (satisfaction), also because "Quality in a service or product is not what you put into it. It is what the client or customer gets out of it." (The quotation is from world renowned business management authority Peter Drucker about the role of quality, but it is applicable in principle to features/functions that may be expressed by a product or service because of the underlying technology). In other industries, the difference between having success and abject failure is in critical differences made possible by the underlying technology. And, as discussed, in yet other contexts, the patent or trade secret protection is the "but for" condition for commercial success.

An Example Cash Flow Projection from a License

The previous sections of this chapter considered simple situations; the present value of one future payment, or the converse of one future payment derived from a single initial investment. One simple formula was used to make such present-to-future (or vice versa) dollar conversions requiring only two other factors: the time to the future payment (n, usually expressed in years) and the RAHR or k value.

The bad news is that such single payment calculations are not sufficient to treat most real life license valuations. The good news is that with the one trusty equation $\{DCF = GCF/(1 + RAHR)^n\}$ and spreadsheet software such as Microsoft Excel,[32] it is relatively simple to deal with as many future payments and upfront investments as necessary.

The reason why multiple payment calculations are necessary is that the buyer, and possibly the seller, will be experiencing multiple cash flows over time. In a typical licensing transaction, the buyer performs (and the seller should perform) a calculation of the future economic benefit of obtaining the subject license agreement. The buyer does this by creating a prospective income statement, known as a *pro forma* because it is being projected into the future and is, by necessity, somewhere between a wild guess and (closer, hopefully to) a well founded as well as reasonable estimate. The pro forma income statement provides a year-by-year cash stream to the buyer over the projected life of the technology being licensed. In order for the buyer to rationalize the present value of such future cash flows, it is necessary to use a RAHR.

Multiple payments over time can also affect the seller's deal economics. Clearly in a running royalty structure, some form of annual royalty GCF inflows to the seller are expected. In addition there could be lump sum payments, conditional or unconditional or both, at various dates. Such structures could vary from one potential buyer to another, or as a result of negotiations with one particular buyer. So the seller needs some way to make rational comparisons of such various alternatives and computing an NPV (Net Present Value) is the way to do it.

The way this is handled is to compute each year's revenues in that year's dollars, for example, the calculation for (say) the year 2015 estimates the revenues for 2015 expressed in 2015 dollars and all the costs for that year are also in 2015 dollars so the net cash produced by the business also is expressed in 2015 dollars. Then, in a separate calculation, those 2015 net cash dollars are converted back to current dollars using the DCF equation with the appropriate RAHR value and n. Finally, all the DCF values for each year are then added resulting in the total present value of the future benefit of commercializing the technology. As part of such calculation the investment costs in the early years need to be considered; any upfront or progress payments to the seller are also included as part of such costs. When all the projected cost outlays and revenues have been estimated and converted to present value (that is, all the DCF values positive and negative have been added), then the result is the NPV. Incidentally, there are embedded NPV formulas in spreadsheet programs such as Excel that can perform this calculation in one step, although this is not recommended because it is useful to see the year-by-year DCF values and, computationally, the use of computer spreadsheets makes it easy to perform. Also, it is all too easy to make a mistake in the inputs to such built-in NPV formula and it is not obvious from the output that the result is wrong. And, as will be shown later, there are certain enhancements—such as the mid-year convention—which does not exist in such built-in spreadsheet NPV formulas.

Illustration of Buyer's NPV Based Upon Various RAHR Values

Shown in Exhibit 7.10 is a hypothetical example of gross cash flows (GCF) that would be experienced by a buyer as a result of commercializing a licensed technology. This exhibit assumes that the buyer invests a total of $10 million by the end of the sixth year from the date of the license, and then receives a total of $136 million from the end of the seventh year through the end of the twentieth year, netting $126 million (136 less 10). The $10 million invested is assumed to be: $1 million in one lump sum at the end of Year 1, $1 million at the end of Year 2, $2 million at the end of Year 3, and so forth. Similarly, incoming net cash flow begins at the end of Year 7 in the amount of $1 million, then at the end of Year 8 an additional $4 million comes in, and so on.

Each year's cash flow can then be discounted using the RAHR value to determine the *present* value of such future payment. The first row of the upper and lower figures of Exhibit 7.10 considers the simple case of k = 0%, for which the DCF is identical to the GCF. Such an example would correspond to a world of zero inflation where no alternative investment opportunities were available that could produce a greater than zero return, clearly an impractical example.

As is sometimes convenient for long project periods, the forecast is broken into two (or more) periods, Years 1 through 10, and 11 through 20 in Exhibit 7.10. Although we are focused on the NPV of the entire opportunity, it is sometimes useful for reasons we will discuss later in this chapter to calculate also the totals for each of the row-separated periods as shown in the rightmost column of the upper figure and the two rightmost columns of the lower figure. The vertical dotted line between Years 6 and 7 is highlighting the crossover point in the forecast from net cash outflows to net cash inflows.

The second rows of Exhibit 7.10 shows the effects of k = 5%. This assumes a so-called risk free investment, assuming such is available at 5 percent per year. From such a perspective, the present value of the $10 million in net cash flow projected for the Year 17 is worth only $4.4 million. The $10 million in net cash flow projected for the Year 9 is worth more, namely $6.4 million. The cash outflows projected at the end of Years 1 through 6 are treated in exactly the same way, so, the $1 million spent at the end of Year 2 is only $900K in present dollars, and the like amount spent at the end of Year 6 is even less at $700K. The net effect of this perspective is that the buyer will enjoy the net benefit of $63.8 million in present dollars, taking all the projected DCF inflows and subtracting all the DCF outflows. This $63.8 million is known as the NPV, which is simply obtained by adding all the DCFs, and because

Year	RAHR, k	1	2	3	4	5	6	7	8	9	10	Total 1-10
GCF	0%	$ (1)	$ (1)	$ (2)	$ (3)	$ (2)	$ (1)	$ 1	$ 5	$ 10	$ 13	**$ 19**
				Net cash outflow years ("investment")				Cash inflow years…				
DCF	5%	$ (1.0)	$ (0.9)	$ (1.7)	$ (2.5)	$ (1.6)	$ (0.7)	$ 0.7	$ 3.4	$ 6.4	$ 8.0	**$ 10.2**
DCF	15%	$ (0.9)	$ (0.8)	$ (1.3)	$ (1.7)	$ (1.0)	$ (0.4)	$ 0.4	$ 1.6	$ 2.8	$ 3.2	**$ 2.0**
DCF	20%	$ (0.8)	$ (0.7)	$ (1.2)	$ (1.4)	$ (0.8)	$ (0.3)	$ 0.3	$ 1.2	$ 1.9	$ 2.1	**$ 0.2**
DCF	30%	$ (0.8)	$ (0.6)	$ (0.9)	$ (1.1)	$ (0.5)	$ (0.2)	$ 0.2	$ 0.6	$ 0.9	$ 0.9	**$ (1.4)**

Year	RAHR, k	11	12	13	14	15	16	17	18	19	20	Total 11-20	Total 1-20
GCF	0%	$ 14	$ 15	$ 15	$ 15	$ 14	$ 13	$ 10	$ 8	$ 3	$ -	**$ 107**	**$ 126**
		Cash inflow years…											
DCF	5%	$ 8.2	$ 8.4	$ 8.0	$ 7.6	$ 6.7	$ 6.0	$ 4.4	$ 3.3	$ 1.2	$ -	**$ 53.6**	**$ 63.8**
DCF	15%	$ 3.0	$ 2.8	$ 2.4	$ 2.1	$ 1.7	$ 1.4	$ 0.9	$ 0.6	$ 0.2	$ -	**$ 15.3**	**$ 17.3**
DCF	20%	$ 1.9	$ 1.7	$ 1.4	$ 1.2	$ 0.9	$ 0.7	$ 0.5	$ 0.3	$ 0.1	$ -	**$ 8.6**	**$ 8.8**
DCF	30%	$ 0.8	$ 0.6	$ 0.5	$ 0.4	$ 0.3	$ 0.2	$ 0.1	$ 0.1	$ 0.0	$ -	**$ 3.0**	**$ 1.6**

EXHIBIT 7.10 Discounted Cash Flows as a Function of the Year and RAHR Value

it is determined using a k value of 5 percent this value is appropriate only to a risk free investment. One further point of interest, by comparing the total for the first 10 years with the second 10 years we can see the ratio is about one-fifth, namely \$10.2 million to \$53.6 million (10.2/53.6 = 1/5.3). The primary reason for the difference in ten-year totals is due to the GCF value being negative for the first six years.

The remaining DCF calculation rows of Exhibit 7.10 show the effect of higher values of RAHR: 15, 20, and 30 percent. Such values reduce the NPV of the opportunity from \$63.8 million (for k = 5%) to \$17.3 million (RAHR = 15%) to \$8.8 million (RAHR = 20%), and to \$1.6 million (RAHR = 30%). Because the projected positive GCF values (i.e., net cash inflows) occur far into the future, peak GCF does not occur until the end of the Year 12, and the discounting effect of larger values of RAHR is huge. From the buyer's perspective, the cash outflows occur early and are comparatively likely, whereas the inflows occur late and are not at all certain. Assuming the risk of this opportunity corresponds to a value RAHR of 30 percent as an appropriate return for the buyer, given the risk, then the NPV calculation concludes that the seller is entitled to 100 percent of the \$1.6 million. From the seller's perspective such a small figure does not seem fair given that the buyer should have \$126 million in the bank after the project is completed, if all goes according to the model. The buyer's response to the seller is likely to be, "You, instead, receive all your return in the form of royalties paid on the inflow GCFs starting at the end of Year 8 and continuing through the end of Year 19."

Comparing the total DCF values for the first ten years with the second ten years, we see that the ratio changes dramatically with RAHR value. As the RAHR value increases, not only does the NPV decrease but the positive DCF values shift to later, and more highly uncertain, years. For a RAHR value of 5 percent, approximately 84% of the total NPV value (of \$63.8 million) occurs in Years 11 through 20. For RAHR of 15 percent this back-years shift increases to 88 percent (of a reduced NPV of \$17.3 million) and for 20 percent the last 10 years yields 98 percent (of the NPV of \$8.8 million).

Another ratio worth noting is the NPV values for the three RAHR values that could be considered (in this example) by a company evaluating its potential return. Comparing the NPV values for a 15 percent and 30 percent RAHR the ratio of projected returns is more than a factor of ten (\$17.3 million divided by \$1.6 million).

Computing Royalties from a Rate of Return Perspective Using DCF

There are several perspectives possible on the splitting of the NPV resulting from the use of the DCF Method. The most straightforward perspective is that the buyer and seller reach a common understanding of the rewards, the timing of such rewards, and the overall risk of receiving the rewards as would occur if the parties agreed on a DCF table like that shown in Exhibit 7.7 with an appropriate RAHR value. Continuing with this example, if it is assumed that the buyer contends and the seller agrees that the appropriate RAHR value to be used to determine the buyer's justifiable return is 30 percent, then *all* of the \$1.6 million NPV shown in Exhibit 7.10 (resulting from using RAHR = 30 percent) belongs to the *seller*. This is built on the assumption that the buyer concluded that it is entitled to all the benefits of a RAHR value of 30 percent. Exhibit 7.11 is based on the model given in Exhibit 7.10. Starting just below the row of "years," the first row is simply a repeat of the Gross Cash Flows

EXHIBIT 7.11 Value of the Opportunity Shown as Apportioned between Buyer and Seller (Assuming RAHR = 30%)

Year		1	2	3	4	5	6	7	8	9	10	11	12	13	14	15	16	17	18	19	20	Sum
GCF		−1	−1	−2	−3	−2	−1	1	5	10	13	14	15	15	15	14	13	10	8	3	0	126
Royalty	28% (on basis of GCF)						0.28	1.39	2.78		3.62	3.9	4.17	4.17	4.17	3.9	3.62	2.78	2.23	0.83	0	37.84
Net GCF		−1	−1	−2	−3	−2	−1	0.72	3.61	7.22	9.38	10.1	10.83	10.83	10.83	10.1	9.38	7.22	5.77	2.17	0	88.16
DCF Buyer	30%	−0.8	−0.6	−0.9	−1.1	−0.5	−0.2	0.1	0.4	0.7	0.7	0.6	0.5	0.4	0.3	0.2	0.1	0.1	0.1	0	0	0
DCF Seller	30%							0.04	0.17	0.26	0.26	0.22	0.18	0.14	0.11	0.08	0.05	0.03	0.02	0.01	0	1.57

(GCF) paid to the buyer by its customers for sale of products made by the licensed technology. The next row is a calculation of the GCF amounts to be paid by the buyer to the seller as a royalty. The way this royalty payment is calculated involves an iteration between the second, third, and fourth rows of Exhibit 7.11. The third row shows the GCF retained by the buyer after payment of the royalty to the seller. The fourth row shows the DCF of such net buyer's GCF using k = 30% as the hurdle rate, which in this instance can be thought of as the buyer's rate of return.

Because the underlying assumption of this example is that the buyer has proposed that it is entitled to a 30 percent return on investment and the seller has agreed, the fourth row discounts the net GCF of the third row. The iteration takes place by adjusting the royalty rate used in the second row so that the sum of the DCFs of the fourth row, that is, the NPV to the buyer, is identically zero. Such iteration can be done by hand by substituting trial values of the royalty rate until the NPV becomes zero or, much more easily, by using the Goal Seek function of the spreadsheet usually available under the Tools menu in Excel.

What this example shows is that for a royalty of 28 percent on the basis of the GCF received by the buyer, the net cash flow retained by the buyer produces a return on investment of 30 percent. The buyer will net (if the plan comes true) in GCF terms $88.16 million, $10 million in investment, offset by $98.16 million in cash inflows. Using RAHR = 30% for all the gross outflows and inflows results in an NPV of $ zero, which means the seller obtained 30 percent return on investment (ROI). The seller will receive a total of $37.84 million in royalties paid out in Years 7 through 19 as shown. If the seller's perspective of the risk of such payments is also reflected by RAHR = 30%, then the seller perceives the present value of these royalties as shown in the fifth row: namely $1.57 million, just as was determined previously. Put another way, if the buyer counterproposes to the seller that instead of paying royalties yearly and a single, upfront payment is made, the seller should be entirely indifferent as to whether it receives the royalties shown over time or the $1.57 million upfront payment (providing the seller's perception of k is 30 percent).[33] It should be noted that the above royalty rate calculation was, for convenience, performed on the GCF which is typically a much smaller number than revenues as discussed earlier. So a royalty rate based on revenues, as it normally done, would be much less than the shown value of 28 percent.

EXCESS EARNINGS CONCEPT The above example, where the seller lays claims to 100 percent of the NPV (because, the model assumes, the buyer is receiving its full, appropriate return by the value of the RAHR used), is a special case of the DCF Method known as the Excess Earnings (EE) method. EE is really not a method, but a way of using the DCF Method to apportion the NPV, namely: to provide the buyer its return through the RAHR used, and provide the seller the entirety of the positive NPV. The use of EE usually arises when there is a factual basis for ascribing a specific rate of return (RAHR) to the buyer, as might be the situation based on some comparables analysis for returns on investment not based upon IP rights where the returns are expected to be higher.

The royalty rate in this example is based upon the gross cash flows received by the buyer. Such cash flows result from taking the sales revenues and subtracting all the seller's costs in producing and selling the products. Royalties should normally be based upon sales not on cash flows; therefore in any agreement between the parties, there would need to be a separate calculation that would convert the royalty rate from 28 percent based on cash flows to an amount based on sales. Although this will be discussed later in this chapter, for illustration purposes let it be assumed that gross cash flows of this example were 20 percent of the sales: That is, 80 percent of the total sales dollars were consumed in expenses, taxes, and the like. This means that a royalty of 28 percent based upon cash flows that comprise 20 percent of sales revenues is exactly equivalent to a royalty of 5.6 percent based on such sales revenues (which is how royalties are expressed). A quick demonstration makes this clear:

Sales Revenues = 100
Cash Flow = 20 (for the assumption that cash flow is 20% of sales revenues)
28% royalty based on Cash Flow = 5.6%
Alternatively, a 5.6% royalty based on sales also = 5.6.

Excess Earnings Concept Applied to Alternate Rates of Return Another kind of EE model as it has been applied to technology licensing uses a more complex analysis. The basic idea is apportioning the NPV above some corporate WACC baseline, say 15 percent, into two components: (1) that which arises from a company being in the same general business area but with the use of the technology, and (2) that which is achieved by virtue of applying the subject technology. The difference between the latter (2) and the former (1) is deemed the "excess earnings."

The idea behind such apportionment is that the seller's value in providing the technology is measured by such excess earnings, and not the total NPV. This excess earnings approach is used by company analysts to discern what assets a company deploys in its business contributions to what magnitude of its earnings.

Let us illustrate the idea by using a per unit revenue, profit, and royalty structure. One simple example of an excess earnings argument applies to the selling of sweatshirts on a college campus. Suppose one innocently goes into business of making and selling a standard quality sweatshirt with the name and logo of the local college imprinted on it for $12. The college licensing office sends a cease and desist letter because you have infringed their trademark. But you have ordered 1000 sweatshirts, so you call on the office to negotiate a license. The college might then argue along these lines:

Without our license, you could only sell these sweatshirts for $10 each. Because you are selling them for $12, the difference of $2 must be entirely attributable to the college's IP because the only distinction is the imprinting. (And, let us assume that your costs whether lettered or not is $9 a sweatshirt). So, the college argues your excess earnings of $2 is its royalty because you would have earned just $1 without its IP.

The key assumption in this simple example is the sweatshirt is the same product and can be sold either with or without the licensed IP. In technology licensing, this cornerstone "either with or without" assumption is suspect, as perhaps it is even for the simple sweatshirt example, but we can conceive of examples where this might be the basis of a reasonable analysis. Consider a commodity polymer manufacturer selling, say, poly-ordinary, for $1 a pound, making 10 cents a pound profit. A licensor shows up and says that its technology can use the same process and cost to make say, poly-amazing, which can then be sold for $1.20 a pound. According to the simple application of excess earnings concept, the technology licensor claims it is entitled to a royalty of 20 cents a pound because of the 30 cents a pound profit for poly-amazing the licensee has earned—in the sense of "deserved"—just 10 cents.

We can readily think of two variants of this polymer situation. One obvious response of the manufacturer is that it is not in business to convey 100 percent of all profit improvements to someone else and remain contented with its 10 cents a pound "commodity profit." The second variant is a market change is underway whereby the demand for poly-ordinary is declining and its profit will be squeezed in both magnitude and percentage to essentially zero.

For the first variant, the buyer will insist on participating in the excess earnings, perhaps arguing for a 25 percent rule so that it will pay 5 cents as a royalty, retain 15 cents of the excess profit, and of course its 10 cents baseline profit.

For the second variant, the seller will insist that the buyer has no sustainable business "but for" a license to poly-amazing and, thereby, the buyer is entitled to some fair proportion to the entire 30-cent-a-pound profit.

Regardless of the context, using this application of excess earnings requires the construction of at least two financial models, and critical assumptions about "either with or without."

INCORPORATING UPFRONT AND ROYALTY PAYMENTS IN A DCF MODEL Other variations of royalty payments can be similarly calculated. For example, suppose the parties agree that the seller should receive an upfront license fee of $100K. Now the costs to the buyer would increase by $100K at time zero (at the beginning of Year 1) and so the royalty payments would have to be reduced in order to provide the same 30 percent return on investment to the buyer. This case is shown in Exhibit 7.12.

In the first row (below the "Year" row) the column for "Year 0" (representing the date of execution of the agreement) a $100K expense to the buyer is shown in rows 2, 3, and 4, and a $100K revenue to the seller appears in row 5. The royalties paid by the buyer will need to be reduced in order to provide the same 30 percent ROI due to of the initial $100K payment. Performing the Goal Seek function results in a royalty of 26 percent corresponding to the cash flow basis, which is two points less than the 28 percent for the no-upfront payment case in Exhibit 7.10. As shown in row 5, the NPV of the seller is also unchanged in this example because both the seller and buyer are using the same k value of 30 percent to calculate DCFs. Expressing such 26 percent of cash into a royalty rate based on revenues, as was already done, results in royalty as commonly expressed, as a percentage of revenues, of 5.2 percent. In Chapter 10 we will address the issue of an appropriate royalty base against which a royalty rate is multiplied to determine a royalty payment. In the Goal Seek example of Exhibit 7.12 it is convenient to determine a "royalty" based upon GCF because this is how the example has been constructed.

COMPUTING ROYALTIES FROM A 25 PERCENT RULE PERSPECTIVE In Exhibits 7.11 and 7.12, it was assumed that the value of RAHR = 30% provided a fair return to the buyer so that all the excess DCFs, that is, the NPV, was the value attributable to the seller and that this value could then be provided in royalties only, in an upfront payment only, or in an infinite number of lump sum payments and royalties as long as NPV for the *buyer* was $0 with a k of 30 percent.

Another perspective on this approach is that the value of RAHR = 30% (or whatever final value is deemed appropriate) be "neutral" to the buyer, and not

Year	RAHR, k	1	2	3	4	5	6	7	8	9	10	Total 1-10
GCF	0%	$ (1)	$ (1)	$ (2)	$ (3)	$ (2)	$ (1)	$ 1	$ 5	$ 10	$ 13	**$ 19**
				Net cash outflow years ("investment")				Cash inflow years...				
DCF	5%	$ (1.0)	$ (0.9)	$ (1.7)	$ (2.5)	$ (1.6)	$ (0.7)	$ 0.7	$ 3.4	$ 6.4	$ 8.0	**$ 10.2**
DCF	15%	$ (0.9)	$ (0.8)	$ (1.3)	$ (1.7)	$ (1.0)	$ (0.4)	$ 0.4	$ 1.6	$ 2.8	$ 3.2	**$ 2.0**
DCF	20%	$ (0.8)	$ (0.7)	$ (1.2)	$ (1.4)	$ (0.8)	$ (0.3)	$ 0.3	$ 1.2	$ 1.9	$ 2.1	**$ 0.2**
DCF	30%	$ (0.8)	$ (0.6)	$ (0.9)	$ (1.1)	$ (0.5)	$ (0.2)	$ 0.2	$ 0.6	$ 0.9	$ 0.9	**$ (1.4)**

Year	RAHR, k	11	12	13	14	15	16	17	18	19	20	Total 11-20	Total 1-20										
Year	**0**	**1**	**2**	**3**	**4**	**5**	**6**	**7**	**8**	**9**		**10**	**11**	**12**	**13**	**14**	**15**	**16**	**17**	**18**	**19**	**20**	**Sum**
GCF	−0.1	−1	−1	−2	−3	−2	−1	1	5	10		13	14	15	15	15	14	13	10	8	3	0	126
Royalty	26% (on basis of GCF)						0.26	1.3	2.61			3.39	3.65	3.91	3.91	3.91	3.65	3.39	2.61	2.08	0.78	0	35.43
Net GCF	−0.1	−1	−1	−2	−3	−2	−1	0.74	3.7	7.39		9.61	10.35	11.09	11.09	11.09	10.35	9.61	7.39	5.92	2.22	0	90.47
DCF Buyer	−30%	−0.1	−0.8	−0.6	−0.9	−1.1	−0.5	−0.2	0.1	0.5	0.7	0.7	0.6	0.5	0.4	0.3	0.2	0.1	0.1	0.1	0	0	0
DCF Seller	30%	0.1						0.04	0.16	0.25		0.25	0.2	0.17	0.13	0.1	0.07	0.05	0.03	0.02	0.01	0	1.57

EXHIBIT 7.12 The Effect of a $100K Upfront License Fee on Example Given in Exhibit 7.8

reflective of an adequate rate of return. In other words, the buyer could argue that the 30 percent is simply that value of RAHR for which the project is just worth doing, and if the buyer does not obtain the benefit of some or most of the excess NPV, then the buyer will not seek the license or undertake the project.

From this perspective the 30 percent is not an adequate rate of return but is the appropriate way of creating a neutral consideration of all future cash flows in the context of the overall perceived risks. From this situation, the logical follow-up issue is how the NPV above 30 percent, namely the $1.57 million in this example (Exhibits 7.7 through 7.9) should be divided between the parties. Here is where the Rule of Thumb Method can be used as a ***Tool*** with the DCF Method: The $1.57 million could be divided using a 25 percent split or any other split factor.[34] Using the 25 percent split, this would say that the seller's share of the $1.57 million NPV is $393K (25 percent) and the buyer's share is $1.18 million (75 percent). From this perspective, the royalty rates can be recalculated as shown in Exhibit 7.12. Using the Goal Seek function and setting the outcome sought to 1.18 results in a royalty of 5 percent on the basis of cash flows in addition to the $100K upfront payment.

To recap, there are two basic perspectives that can be employed in using the DCF Method to provide a valuation:

1. A RAHR value that includes the effect of risk and justifiable returns (given the contributions of the buyer to achieving commercialization) so that the resulting NPV belongs to the seller either in the form of royalties only, upfront only, or a combination
2. A RAHR value that provides only the appropriate present values of all the future benefits, given the risk of the project, so that the resulting NPV should then be divided between the buyer and seller in a way that reflects their comparative contributions

The first perspective, sometimes referred to as an "allocated return" approach, can be grounded by analyzing what the buyer and comparable companies can expect to receive as a return for the deployment of the particular assets involved in the license. For instance, the buyer could deploy numerous kinds of assets such as cash, plant and equipment, design engineers, proprietary design tools and approaches, trademarks, patents and trade secrets, and so forth. For each asset so deployed, one could perform an analysis of the magnitude of such asset and the appropriate market-based rate of return. The outcome of such analysis would be a weighted-average, market based rate of return. Done in this way, the logic of the process would then say that all of the excess NPV should belong to the seller. Such determination is essentially what is meant by the Excess Earnings "method."

Thus, if one used such grounded methodologies for each of the two perspectives, one would expect the resulting value to be the same. That is, if one performed a reasonable "allocated return" analysis and found RAHR = 30%, so that the NPV of $1.57 million belonged to the seller, and then separately did an analysis of the appropriate "risk adjusted" perspective, one would expect that the RAHR would be less than 30 percent. In this way, when the NPV was divided between the buyer and seller (using, for example, a 25 percent split) the seller would still be entitled to an NPV of $1.57 million. Exhibit 7.14 shows how this could develop. The top set

EXHIBIT 7.13 Using the 25 Percent Rule to Apportion the NPV (RAHR of 30 percent)

Year		0	1	2	3	4	5	6	7	8	9	10	11	12	13	14	15	16	17	18	19	20	Sum
GCF		−0.1	−1	−1	−2	−3	−2	−1	1	5	10	13	14	15	15	15	14	13	10	8	3	0	126
Royalty	5% (on basis of GCF)							0.05	0.26	0.51		0.66	0.72	0.77	0.77	0.77	0.72	0.66	0.51	0.41	0.15	0	6.95
Net GCF		−0.1	−1	−1	−2	−3	−2	−1	0.95	4.74	9.49	12.34	13.28	14.23	14.23	14.23	13.28	12.34	9.49	7.59	2.85	0	111.95
DCF Buyer		30%	−0.1	−0.8	−0.6	−0.9	−1.1	−0.5	−0.2	0.6	0.9	0.9	0.7	0.6	0.5	0.4	0.3	0.2	0.1	0.1	0	0	1.18
DCF Seller		30%	0.1						0.01	0.03	0.05	0.05	0.04	0.03	0.03	0.02	0.01	0.01	0.01	0	0	0	0.39

EXHIBIT 7.14 Same Net Outcome of Two Perspectives of RAHR

Year		0	1	2	3	4	5	6	7	8	9	10	11	12	13	14	15	16	17	18	19	20	Sum
Allocated Return Perspective: 30% Return on Investment to the Buyer																							
GCF		−0.1	−1	−1	−2	−3	−2	−1	1	5	10	13	14	15	15	15	14	13	10	8	3	0	126
Royalty	26% (on basis of GCF)						0.26	1.3	2.61			3.39	3.65	3.91	3.91	3.91	3.65	3.39	2.61	2.08	0.78	0	35.43
Net GCF		−0.1	−1	−1	−2	−3	−2	−1	0.74	3.7	7.39	9.61	10.35	11.09	11.09	11.09	10.35	9.61	7.39	5.92	2.22	0	90.47
DCF Buyer	30%	−0.1	−0.8	−0.6	−0.9	−1.1	−0.5	−0.2	0.1	0.5	0.7	0.7	0.6	0.5	0.4	0.3	0.2	0.1	0.1	0.1	0	0	0
DCF Seller	30%	0.1							0.04	0.16	0.25	0.25	0.2	0.17	0.13	0.1	0.07	0.05	0.03	0.02	0.01	0	1.57
Risk-Adjusted Perspective: 25% Rule Split of NPV between Buyer and Seller																							
GCF		−0.1	−1	−1	−2	−3	−2	−1	1	5	10	13	14	15	15	15	14	13	10	8	3	0	126
Royalty	26.0% (on basis of GCF)						0.26	1.3	2.6			3.38	3.64	3.9	3.9	3.9	3.64	3.38	2.6	2.08	0.78	0	35.36
Net GCF		−0.1	−1	−1	−2	−3	−2	−1	0.74	3.7	7.4	9.62	10.36	11.1	11.1	11.1	10.36	9.62	7.4	5.92	2.22	0	90.54
DCF Buyer	20.40%	−0.1	−0.8	−0.7	−1.1	−1.4	−0.8	−0.3	0.2	0.8	1.4	1.5	1.3	1.2	1	0.8	0.6	0.5	0.3	0.2	0.1	0	4.7
DCF Seller	30.00%	0.1							0.04	0.16	0.25	0.25	0.2	0.17	0.13	0.1	0.07	0.05	0.03	0.02	0.01	0	1.57 1.57 0

of rows shows that for a 30 percent allocated return to the buyer, the seller receives 100 percent of the $1.57 million which results in a royalty of 26 percent (on the basis of the cash flows) plus an initial $100K license fee. In the bottom group of rows, the seller experiences exactly the same return: $1.57 million NPV with a RAHR of 30 percent. However, in this case a RAHR of 20.4 percent provides an NPV which, when split 75:25 (buyer:seller), provides the aforementioned $1.57 million for the seller and $4.70 million for the buyer. Notice that for this latter case the royalty rate remains unchanged, so the payments made by the buyer to the seller do not change. Also unchanged is what the buyer receives and the buyer's perspective of risk (RAHR = 30%). What has changed is that the RAHR value has become 20.4 percent instead of 30 percent as in the top table.

From a negotiation perspective, the seller should be indifferent as to which of these perspectives is employed and can tell the buyer: "Either we discount all the GCF at 30 percent and I (the seller) keep *all* the NPV, *or* we discount the GCFs by 20.4 percent and we *split* the NPV 75:25 buyer:seller."

Although either interpretation and use of DCF can be employed, the normal method is the former: the RAHR value used includes the effect of the buyer's profit so 100 percent of the resulting NPV belongs to the seller. This is the implicit perspective behind the previous table of RAHR values in Exhibit 7.7.

Additional Considerations for Calculating DCF

In all the previous examples, a single value for RAHR was used to discount both the buyer's outflow GCFs and inflow GCFs. When one uses a risk free value of k such as 5 percent, so that dollars tomorrow are made to look like dollars today, then it makes sense to use such k value on all the GCFs. However, what about the case when the parties agree that an appropriate RAHR value is 20 or 30 percent?

Using Different RAHR (or k) Values for Cash Outflows and Inflows

There is a logic to structuring financial models so as to discounts the outflow GCFs at the risk free rate (such as 5 percent), or at a buyer's WACC rate (say 15 percent), while the inflow GCFs are discounted at the appropriate RAHR. The rationale for this distinction is as follows: From the buyer's perspective, the outflow GCFs are much more certain than the inflow GCFs. This is because it is known that the prescribed outflow GCFs will be required to complete development of the technology, purchase manufacturing equipment, gear up for production, prepare marketing materials, train the sales force, conduct an advertising launch campaign, and so forth. However, the inflow GCFs will depend on the willingness of customers to buy the product, which is considered to be less knowable and subject to far less control than making expenditures. For this reason, outflow GCFs logically could be discounted by a k value appropriate to inflation, or the cost of capital, and the inflow GCFs discounted by a RAHR value appropriate to the overall risk of project success. So, in the discussed example, the outflow GCFs could be discounted at k = 15 percent and the inflow GCFs at RAHR = 20% or 30% or whatever the appropriate number.

In some cases, the outflow GCFs are not even discounted by this lesser amount (15 percent). This is a result of considering how the outflow estimates are made.

Consider a simple case where the only investment required is in people and the seller computes such cost as follows: In Year 1, 10 people will be needed at \$100K/person in salary, benefits, and supplies, for a total of \$1 million. If Year 2 requires these same 10 people, then it could be expected that, because of inflation and merit increases each person would cost the seller \$115K. Thus, the estimate of \$1 million spent in Year 2 has *already* accounted for the cost of the 10 people in Year 2 currency. Consequently, to discount or not to discount the outflow GCFs depends upon how such estimates were made.

Despite the logic of this two-valued k approach, it leads to unusable results when applied to long-term projects such as shown in Exhibit 7.7. The resulting problem is shown in Exhibit 7.15. Discounting all the Exhibit 7.7 outflow GCFs at 15 percent causes the NPV of all such outflows to be −\$6.1 million, with the minus designating that it is an outflow. The gross total outflow was actually \$10 million over six years, but discounting all the inflow GCFs at 30 percent causes the NPV of all such inflows to be only \$5.6 million, even though the total GCF was \$136 million. So such downward adjustment in the NPV of the cash outflows actually makes this project have an overall negative NPV for the 30 percent RAHR case.

The reason this effect is so dramatic is a consequence of one of the key assumptions of the DCF Method, namely that the RAHR value, however it is chosen, is used to discount all future cash inflows. When the RAHR value is high, and the commercial life of the project is expected to be long, and needs to be long to provide a return on investment, one is confronted with the very low, even negligible, present values of distant cash inflows.

Of course the mere fact that the use of 15 percent for cash outflows results in a negative NPV for the project as modeled does not mean that such approach is incorrect simply because the outcome tells us the project is not worth doing. Some projects are not worth doing, and when our best thinking comes up with this result it should not be dismissed as an unacceptable calculation.

Fortunately, in many cases the outflow GCFs are made over a sufficiently short period of time, such as two or three years, so that the DCF values obtained are reasonably unaffected by the choice of k as was discussed earlier in the chapter. In such situations, the modest complication of different inflow and outflow k values is not used. The simplification is justified partly because the RAHR value applied to the inflow is sufficient to account for this effect, and since this estimating process is sufficiently tenuous such attempts at precision are not justified. However, it is proper and more accurate to discount cash outflows (investments) at rate appropriate to their value, such as the marginal cost of working capital, and discount cash inflows (returns) at a value appropriate to the project risk.

Use of the Mid-Year Convention

There is one additional refinement to be considered. As developed earlier in this chapter, the equation $DCF = GCF/(1 + RAHR)^n$. Normally, both cash outflows and inflows are made more or less uniformly throughout a year, not just all at once at the end (or beginning) of the year. Accordingly, the outflow GCFs of Year 1 occur monthly during the year, not all at once at the end of the year. Likewise, the inflow GCFs for, say Year 10, occur throughout the year, not all at once at the end of the year.

EXHIBIT 7.15 Effect of Discounting Cash Outflows at a Lower RAHR than Inflows

Year	k	1	2	3	4	5	6	7	8	9	10	11	12	13	14	15	16	17	18	19	20	Net
GCF	0%	−1	−1	−2	−3	−2	−1	1	5	10	13	14	15	15	15	14	13	10	8	3	0	126
Outflow DCF	15%	−0.9	−0.8	−1.3	−1.7	−1.0	−0.4															−6.1
Inflow DCF	30%							0.2	0.6	0.9	0.9	0.8	0.6	0.5	0.4	0.3	0.2	0.1	0.1	0.0	0	5.6
																						−0.5

The way this phenomenon is usually handled is by means of the so-called "mid-year" convention. How this works is as follows: All the outflows (or inflows) of a year are assumed to have occurred throughout the year; for purposes of computing a DCF one can consider them to have occurred halfway through the year. Thus, the time period of the outflow GCFs for the first year occurred actually at mid-year, so that n = 0.5 for Year 1. Likewise for Year 2, all the outflows occurred at n = 1.5, and so on. Thus, the DCF equation becomes:

$$DCF = GCF/(1 + RAHR)^{(2n-1)/2}, \text{ so for } n = 1 \text{ for Year 1, the exponent equals 0.5; for Year 2 } (n = 2), \text{ the exponent equals 1.5, for Year 3 it equals 2.5; and so on.}$$

To be even more precise, which is rarely warranted, one could make monthly estimates of outflow and inflow GCFs and discount by a monthly k. Normally the mid-year convention is as precise as needed, given all the other uncertainties associated with making such estimates.

Use of Terminal Value Multipliers

One approach to financial modeling is to extend the projected period to some less-than-expected life, perhaps 5 to 10 years, and then use a multiplier of the DCF value for the final projected year to account for the forecast value of all the remaining value to the end of life of the opportunity. (Such end of life would be the earlier of the projected expiry of the IP rights, such as patent life or estimated life of trade secrets, or other IP form, or of the technology life itself).

With equity analysis, a common perspective on such terminal value is the assumption of a perpetuity, meaning that the final year GCF will occur annually thereafter without end. It turns out the DCF calculation for a perpetuity has an appealing simplicity, namely:

$$DCF_n = GCF_n/k$$

where GCF_n for year n is assumed to be constant for all future years, k is the appropriate discount rate for the risk associated with such constant future GCF, which risk is presumed to be comparatively low because the calculation made is only appropriate when it is reasonable to assume a stable revenue and earnings environment. The above equation is actually a simplification for a well known formula known as the Gordon Formula for dividends where the growth rate in dividends (here our GCF_n) is assume to be zero.

So if our original example of $1,000 per year for 10 years were instead such a perpetuity and the appropriate k value at that time were 5 percent representing rate of inflation, the 10th year DCF would simply be:

$$DCF_{10} = \$1{,}000/0.05 = 20 * \$1{,}000 = \$20{,}000$$

To convert such DCF terminal value in the 10th year to a present value one would then apply the RAHR equation as done before. If we assume a RAHR value of 15 percent for the project, then the present value of the 10th year terminal value would be:

$$DCF_0 = \$20{,}000/(1 + RAHR)^{10} = \$20{,}000/1.1510 = \$4{,}944.$$

As we have discussed, technology opportunities are finite-lived, not perpetuities. But the parallel idea is that such an estimate can be an approximate way of estimating the value of the remaining technology life beyond the specifically forecast period.

The straightforward approach is simply to create a financial model that extends over all the years of the projected technology life, as bound by the shorter of the underlying IP rights or the useful life of the technology itself either in its operational benefits or market demand. In the examples given, we did exactly this by projecting to the 20th year, showing the forecast revenues declining to GCF = $3 million in the 19th year and $0 in the 20th whereupon the technology or its IP, or both, have been assumed to have no remaining license value to its seller.

If one believes the forecasted financial values for some initial period, say Years 1 through 10, are much more reliable than the believed-to-be-reasonable but less certain values forecast for, say, Years 11 through 20, then one approach is to separately determine an NPV value for each of the two 10-year periods. Although the effect of the RAHR calculation of DCFs "automatically" discounts the GCF values in the second 10-year period more highly than the first, it is sometimes useful to consider the contributions to the total NPV by treating each of the 10-year periods separately.

The use of a terminal value multiplier is taking this segmentation approach one step further by direct consideration of only the first period, in our present example of 10 years, and then adding a lump sum to such value as an estimate of the contribution of the second10 year period.

A buyer performing a similar DCF Method analysis may reason, and argue, that *any* multiplier representing a terminal value for all years after Year 10 is both pure speculation and presumptuous of there being any remaining value in the technology being valued. The seller's argument and reasoning could be supported by the innate nature of the technology, say composition of matter patents on an important pharmaceutical, and the likelihood of a long enduring market, and, of course that the severe RAHR discounting of such distant cash flows has already accounted for any such "speculation."

Segment and Scenario Analysis

For almost every technology valuation there are alternative ways of looking at the opportunity that affect how a financial model based on the DCF Method can be constructed and, thereby, the NPV determination. We might classify these alternative ways of looking at things as shown in the following six points:

1. Adjusting the RAHR based upon further analysis such as the risk classification example of Exhibit 7.9
2. Changing the value of one of the assumptions ("inputs") such as the rate of growth in revenues, as we will consider later in this chapter and in detail in Chapter 8
3. Systematically changing the value of one of the assumptions to examine the effect of such range of values upon any of the calculated "outputs," especially the NPV; this is sometimes called "sensitivity analysis" because it leads to an understanding as to the relative importance of the assumption upon any key output; we will see in Chapter 8 how the Monte Carlo Method is particularly powerful in this regard

4. Changing the basic structure of the financial model in some way, such as by the inclusion of upfront and/or periodic IP lump sum payments and/or running royalties
5. Creating multiple sub models by looking at the opportunities by considering multiple, discrete "segments"
6. Defining possible "scenarios"—coherent models of the alternative future environments—and the set of inputs appropriate to each such scenario, to create multiple output sets

In the next two sections, we will consider how segments and scenarios can be helpful to the DCF Method.

Improving Upon Uncertainty

It is axiomatic that one does not know what the future will bring, except, as the joke goes, death and taxes. But the interesting question is this: Are all forecasts—call them guesses even—equally uncertain? Or, put in a positive sense: Is it possible to reduce uncertainty by more careful analysis? The question is not can uncertainty be shrunk to certainty; it is: Can uncertainty be shrunk by wisdom, by some ***Approach***, ***Method***, ***Tool*** (**AMT**), and if so, how, and at what cost versus what gain?

Putting the root question yet another way, is there any **AMT** better than the use of the proverbial dart board, or randomly drawing names or numbers out of a hat? If not, random drawings are cheaper and easier, and dart boards more fun, than the work of any DCF Method, or any Method for that matter.

Let's consider a context where the dart board answer may be just as good as any **AMT**. For a number of years, the *Wall Street Journal*, publication ran a quarterly contest pitting various expert equity analysts against the "selections" of a literal dart board. At the end of the contest period, one of the analysts would of course have selected equities that performed the best, but only randomly would the best analyst beat the dart board's selections. Let us assume these limited trials, and many others like them, were a valid demonstration of the principle that an expert using whatever **AMT** he or she wanted cannot systematically make better economic forecasts of the future than random selection. Does this make the case that uncertainty in our context of technology valuation cannot be improved upon?

The answer is "no." Here's why. The equity analysts were not making forecasts against any *tabula rasa*, a blank slate. They were compelled to make a forecast to *beat* the forecasts of the market, as evidenced by the then selling price of every equity that they picked for being *more* valuable than the market then said it was, as reflected in its stock price. So this is an example of a very severe test: outsmarting an exceedingly expert system that has established the present value for every publicly traded equity. There is even a near religious argument—generally part of "the efficient market hypothesis"—that claims it is not statistically reasonable to assume that anyone, by reason, can "beat" the market because the present price of any publicly traded equity already reflects everything that can be discerned about the future affecting its value.

Consider a different experiment more parallel to our purposes: 10 equity analysts are locked in a room free to choose among a thousand companies with their own unique financial data or revenues and costs, but without knowledge of any of the present equity values as would be determined by a public market. The test now is this: Could these 10 analysts on average, identify the more valuable companies compared to a dart board selection? This answer is "yes." The reason is, here the dart board has no intelligence upon which it can "act"; it has only the list of a thousand companies. And the analysts are not trying to beat an expert system; they are trying to pick the best investments.

Technology investing, be it R&D, M&A, licensing, or some other manifestation, is like the latter example—no available expert system of pre-established valuation—in contrast to the former example (publicly priced equities). Here's a demonstration of the widespread conviction of this conclusion. If the above conclusion were not true, then every company investment committee could, and should, be eliminated as an unnecessary cost and a "basepath clogger,"[35] so that all investments are authorized by random selection, one after the other until the available investment budget is committed. No company, no CFO, believes such random selection would improve their technology investment scoreboard. Absent some established, reliable pricing standard, such as a public market, some **AMT**, has to exist and be applied to create wisdom and enable choosing well.

However, in the field of business, even the most powerful **AMT** applied by the wisest of individuals does not create certainty with respect to future predictions. Any prediction about tomorrow is subject to some form of uncertainty. For things that obey the laws of classical physics—gravity for example—we can take such uncertainty as zero because we assume such laws will be unchanging day to day and insofar as is knowable there have been zero exceptions since the beginning of time. Economics, sometimes called the dismal science because its predictive and explanatory power is something much less than achieved in classical physics, lacks the exactitude and certainty of, say, calculations for gravitational effects.[36] Such predictive limitations in domains classical economics, or the more nitty gritty of technology business, should not lead to either despair or inaction, but to care in the application of **AMT**, and a measured humility in its results.

In Exhibits 7.11 through 7.15 above, the GCFs for each forecast year were taken as a given. We considered the effect of risk that such GCFs would not occur by the RAHR values discounting GCFs to DCFs and summed to yield the NPV. This approach takes account of uncertainty only by the discounting effect of RAHR on the given GCFs. A more common approach is to consider various possible GCFs. This could be done by changing one or more of the inputs to the GCF calculation, say, by an alternate, higher cost in some particular year or throughout the period, lowering the respective GCFs. Or we could consider a situation where the revenues would be higher and the costs unchanged so the GCFs would be higher than shown in Exhibits 7.11 through 7.15. A more general approach is through the use of segment and scenario analyses.

A scenario is a self-consistent, conceived future outcome.

Segment Analysis

One powerful marketing tool is classification into segments. In the world of consumer products, we are all seen to belong to one or more segments toward which products are marketed, even by those whose product is their candidacy for elected office. We are perhaps baby boomers, or young urban professionals, or soccer moms, or first adopters, or Latinos, or adventure seekers, or dozens of other such segments, or combinations thereof. Consumer products are commonly designed from the ground up with a particular segment in mind, which in turn determines the channel of distribution, advertising and promotion, pricing, service, and every other product attribute.

As we discussed in Chapter 3 on the ***Approach*** of opportunity Discovery, segmentation also applies to the recognition of likely commercial value of a technology. The DCF Method can directly apply such segmentation analysis. For instance, let us consider how we might set up a DCF Method to value a polymer technology acquisition (or license). We could simply consider in aggregate all the potential revenues and the time of such revenues and subtract all the anticipated investment and operating costs to forecast year-by-year GCFs as we have used in the examples of the previous exhibits. But if such revenues were derived from distinct product applications and sales in various territories, we could likely improve our forecast accuracy by a segment analysis. For example, we could say the technology is expected to have distinct commercial applications in (1) medical disposables, (2) machinery housings, and (3) structural brackets. Further, we could believe that such applications could use our sales channel based in North America (A) but with strong representation in Western Europe (B), and the Far East (C). Combining these two triads of possibilities leads to nine combinations, where each of the three territories will exhibit sales from each of three product categories.

In Exhibit 7.10, the GCF forecast for Year 5 was a negative $2 million. Let us assume this Year 5 value was the result of revenue forecast of $10 million offset by $12 million of costs. One obvious way that the $10 million revenue forecast could arise is by simple consideration of the capacity of a manufacturing plant based on the subject technology in the fifth year after the planned development. This consideration alone would not account for market demand needed to convert production capacity into revenue dollars. So, it might be implicitly assumed, based on some general benchmarks such as prior experience, that such capacity could be fully sold at the assumed unit price.

In most circumstances, an improved forecast for demand can be developed by a segment analysis by considering, for instance, the nine combinations discussed previously, e.g.:

1. Revenues for the medical disposable product category, by each of the primary territories (North America, Western Europe, and the Far East)
2. Revenues for the machinery housing products in each of these same territories
3. Revenues for structural bracket applications in each of the territories

Forecasting revenue by these distinct product and geographical segments is likely to lead to a more refined thought process as to pricing, demand, competition, market timing, necessary sales channel structure and investment, marketing and sales costs, et cetera. Available internal or external studies on one of more such market segments may be available and useful in guiding forecast judgments.

What about pursuing segment analysis at a more granular level, say, by individual country in Europe and Asia and by state or region in the United States or even by individual industrial customer, and/or by subcategories or products such that we have 20 or 30 or more individual subforecasts which are then aggregated to yield a Year 5 revenue? There is no universal answer on how far to pursue segmentation. Usually there is a significant gain in shrinking uncertainty by the first level of segmentation, with the law of diminishing returns being activated as one pursues ever more granular distinctions. The answer as to how far to go is similar to the question we will address at the end of this chapter about the DCF Method as a whole: comparing the benefit of achievable reductions in uncertainty with the cost of gaining such reductions. When the benefit is high and the cost is low, or vice versa, the choice is obvious: Do the analysis in the former circumstance and don't in the latter. Then the gain is likely to be high along with the cost of obtaining the gain, and vice versa, the choice is more a matter of experience.

When a segment analysis is extended to fine scale detail it is often called a "bottom-up" analysis, to distinguish it from the "top-down" approach of just considering a few, macro level categories using more global assumptions. Such a bottom-up analysis can be illuminating because it leads to a consideration of the perceived value to each selling opportunity and the alignment with marketing and sales activities that will ultimately be necessary to realize the projected NPV. Even when the investment is made in a bottom-up analysis, it is usually useful to perform an independently developed top-down analysis to serve as a reasonableness check, particularly if one has data of other product introductions into such broad market categories.

Scenario Analysis

Scenario and segment analyses are similar in that they seek to reduce the uncertainty in forecasts by more carefully considering the components or subcomponents that comprise any given forecast. Segment analysis seeks to find those components of a total that can possibly be better understood from some fundamental consideration of the particulars of each component. Scenario analysis looks at forecasts from the viewpoint of different possible future "worlds" that could affect any or all of such segment components.

As an example of a scenario analysis, let us consider the cost side of the Year 5 forecast discussed immediately above, namely: revenues of $10 million and costs of $12 million, resulting in a negative GCF of $2 million. One of the important costs in making any polymer is the raw material cost. Polymers are made (primarily) from petroleum sources, just as gasoline, diesel fuel, tars, and an incredible variety of everyday products. Forecasting the raw material cost could be done by considering various scenarios such as: (1) business as usual, corresponding to a constant growth rate in unit raw material cost based upon knowable recent data, or (2) a higher than historic growth rate in costs in anticipation of increasing demand for petroleum resources from rapidly emerging economies such as the BRIC countries (Brazil, Russia, India, China), or (3) a dramatic increase in raw material costs because of the increasing scarcity in supply as reserves are depleted and/or dramatic changes in environmental treatment and disposal costs associated with converting the raw material into polymers.

Another example of scenario analysis could relate to the cost of capital needed to build world class polymer plants. By Year 3 or 4 when a large capital commitment is needed, there could be various conceivable cost-of-capital scenarios that would have an important impact upon capital costs.

Scenario analysis makes discrete classifications of the wide range of future possible business outcomes. In this example, we could envision a polymer technology that, if successfully developed, will meet new levels of impermeability, high-temperature resistance, and strength, at costs equal to the present, poorer-performing polymers. Further, our analysis of certain market needs focuses on its potential application for medical disposables (benefited by improved impermeability and high-temperature resistance), machinery housings (benefited by high-temperature resistance and strength), and structural brackets (benefited by higher strength properties). With these optimistic assumptions we can create a coherent, high-outcome scenario that projects that the polymer technology will be successful in all three markets and in all three territories (assuming, for instance, that environmental restrictions or other local governmental requirements do not inhibit the application of the technology for any of these products in any of the territorial segments). Once this high-outcome scenario has been defined, together with all the underlying assumptions and supporting data justifying such assumptions, then a projection can be created for each of the nine combinations and the DCF analysis can proceed as before. It may be possible to aggregate all the revenues and costs for all three applications and territories so that a single DCF analysis can be done. If the cost ratios vary from application to application, or territory to territory, or the growth in revenues likewise depends on the specifics associated with a particular combination then one needs to perform a separate DCF calculation for each such distinct situation and then add them together. The most complex situation would be if a separate DCF analysis were required for each of the nine cells.

Next, we can consider a much more conservative perspective of the range of applications of the polymer technology. For instance, we could observe that the key breakthrough we have demonstrated and characterized is the property of chemical impermeability and, although high-temperature operation and higher strength appears to be also realizable, there are some additional challenges to be overcome. Further, it is noted that there are competitive alternatives emerging that could provide comparable temperature and strength performance. These clouds on the horizon cause us to believe that there is a real possibility that the only product application that we will achieve market success with is medical disposables. Finally, based on previous experience we may conclude that the ability to penetrate medical markets in the Far East is unlikely to bear fruit. We call this set of cautious beliefs the low-outcome scenario. Here we might just use the previously developed calculations unchanged, but taking only the values for combinations "medical" in North America and Western Europe.

As you can expect, there is usually a middle level set of assumptions, often called the base scenario. This scenario is generally considered to be the most likely outcome. In some cases it is determined by a corporate protocol for being somewhat conservative so there is a reasonable likelihood that what occurs exceeds such base prediction; people do not like to be disappointed.

Depending on the specific situation, one can create any number of such scenarios. Two is the minimum, and three is common, but four or five would not be unreasonable. The basis for choosing the number is driven by the number of distinct, rational possible future outcomes that can be characterized and analyzed by generally self consistent assumptions, and the justified level of effort given the magnitude of the opportunity.

The question then arises as to the RAHR, or k, to be used with the GCFs of the scenarios to determine the NPV. One way to make this calculation is to use a corporate cost of capital rate. The use of a corporate cost of capital discount rate then requires a probability estimate to be applied to each resulting NPV calculation to account for the respective risk. This is sometimes called the "decision tree" method or "decision analytics" but it is really a simple "probability tree" calculation. We will return to this method in Chapter 8.

Another way to calculate NPV using scenarios is to use the same RAHR value as used for the base case. This assumes that the risk of the project is the same for all the scenarios considered, then only the uncertainty exists as to which (if any) scenario will "come true." As an example, let us consider that the GCF values shown in Exhibit 7.10 represent a "base case." And let us assume that a further analysis of these GCFs results in a "high" scenario whereby all the positive GCFs are higher than such base case by a factor of 1.2, and the "low" scenario where they were only 0.8 times as large as the base case, and all the negative GCF values (the net investments) were identical for all three scenarios. If these three scenarios were all considered to be equally risky, and relatively high in risk such that a RAHR value of 30 percent was appropriate, the result would be: NPV High = \$7.2 million, NPV Low = 0.4 million, and the base would be unchanged from that shown (\$1.6 million). In this example, our risk is assumed unchanged, although our uncertainty has increased corresponding to the three scenarios considered to NPV ranging from a low of \$0.4 million to a high of \$7.2 million. We will return to this idea in Chapter 8 when we apply a more versatile, and powerful, analytical method, namely Monte Carlo.

Cash Flow Projections

Creating an annual cash flow projection is a fundamental requirement for performing the DCF Method discussed in this chapter. There is some bad news and some good news. The bad news is that done properly, creating a cash flow model is a daunting task, as it involves numerous assumptions involving future sales, the cost of raw materials and labor, the cost of the manufacturing plant, distribution costs, sales and marketing costs, efficiency of manufacture (yield ratios), administrative costs, product development and R&D costs, taxes (federal, state, and local), working capital, inventory, and any and every cost associated with producing the revenue.

The good news? The good news is that for purposes of valuing technology for a license negotiation, there are so many inherent uncertainties involved that it is often possible with some skill and experience to create a useful business model without resorting to a highly detailed calculation of individual costs. Further, publicly traded companies provide quarterly and annual reports of key financial data which can be used for insight. We will in this section use as examples financial data from three very different kinds of technology companies—Eli Lilly, a pharmaceutical company; Texas Instruments (TI), a semiconductor manufacturer; and 3M, a diversified industrial and consumer product company.

In the previous examples, the gross cash flows were simply assumed. In order to perform a valuation, it is necessary to make estimates of cash flows. How does one obtain the future cash flows year by year?

Income Statements

One of the foundational financial reports of any company is its income statement. This statement provides insight to management and investors as to the revenue, costs, and earnings of the business, and it is the basis for paying federal corporate income tax, as much as one's own personal income tax is determined by aggregating total revenue and deducting certain allowed business expenses yielding a taxable net income against which the tax rate table is applied.

However, for purposes of a DCF analysis, standard income statements alone are inadequate because they are designed to be a current year snapshot of the performance of a long established going concern. One primary limitation is that a major investment cannot usually be treated as a current year cost. This is because as an accounting principle, such an investment should be allocated over a period of years reflecting the anticipated useful life. Similarly, the tax code establishes how such investments can be "expensed" (treated as a cost) against current year revenues. As a simple example, if a particular new project requires building a new facility and needs production equipment requiring a current year investment of $10 million, as well as the anticipated life of such facility is 10 years, a standard accounting treatment is to depreciate such investment by establishing an annual cost of $1 million.

Although this approach is useful for certain business purposes it is inadequate for a DCF analysis because we need to account explicitly for the $10 million upfront investment in a financial model because such cash outflow occurs in one year. There are two ways to do this: (1) Begin with an income statement and make the adjustments necessary to create a cash flow statement, or (2) simply create a cash flow statement from the start. The former approach can be useful when there is a useful understanding of how the subject project is expected to perform financially after some startup period.

Cash Flow Adjustments

This first approach, basing a cash flow analysis on an income statement, is performed in two steps. Step 1 is to create an income statement projection; step 2 is to use the "net income" obtained at the bottom of the income statement (the origin of the term "the bottom line"), and adjust it to create a year-by-year cash flow statement. In simple form, income statement is established as follows:

- Revenues (sometimes termed Sales or, in Europe, Turnover)
- Less Cost of Goods Sold (known as COGS)
- Equals Gross Margin (GM)
- Less all appropriate overheads (known as SG&A, for Sales, General, and Administrative, and relevant R&D, which together are "Total Overhead" below)
- Equals Earnings before Interest and Taxes (known as EBIT, and below EBITA for Earnings Before Interest Taxes and Adjustments)
- Less interest expense and other adjustments, which for our purposes are typically negligible, and provision for taxes (PFT)
- Equals Earnings after Tax (known as EAT)

A cash flow statement, the second important company financial document, starts with the data and EAT from the above income statement and adjusts the figures to determine GCFs, as follows:

- Start with Earnings after Tax (EAT) off the bottom line of the income statement
- Add back all depreciation and amoritization expenses which were embedded in COGS and/or SG&A or other, because these are not current year cash outlays,
- Subtract the increase in working capital (required to grow the business), all lump sum investments for acquisitions, license fees, spending of any plant, property, and equipment
- Equals Gross Cash Flow (GCF)

The treatment of spending (costs) can be confusing. Broadly speaking a company has two kinds of costs:[37] (1) "expense items," and (2) capital investments. The first kind of costs appear in the income statement, either under COGS, if it is directly related to making the product for which revenues are obtained, or under one of the overhead categories. The second kind of costs occur as a current year expense, because the company has to in fact pay for such costs in current year currency, but the income statement only includes a portion of such costs in that first year, allocating the balance of such costs to multiple subsequent years corresponding to the projected useful life or in accordance with tax regulations.[38] Such capitalized expenses for long-lived assets are then "written down" by some principle of depreciation (for tangible assets, such as plant and equipment) and amortization (for intangible assets, such as patents, know how, and goodwill). Depreciation and amortization are dependent on the specific assets involved and allowed periods of such write down, all of which tend to be industry specific; these accounting treatments and tax matters are beyond the scope of this book.

Cash Flow (GCF) Corporate Examples

To illustrate how GCF data can be estimated, let us consider two public technology company financial statements.

ELI LILLY Returning to the example of Eli Lilly, a large pharmaceutical company, introduced in Chapter 6, Exhibit 7.16 shows how their cash flow statement is calculated from their income statement, using data contained in their public filings.

Eli Lilly is somewhat unusual in that it shows a decrease in working capital (WC) requirements, when normally growing companies exhibit an increase in WC. Also, it should be noted that all such cash flow calculations should be made for licensing purposes with costs and adjustments that are appropriate to the subject opportunity being valued so that other, extraneous financial effects do not influence the analysis.

Eli Lilly, as typical of pharmaceutical companies, has high overhead costs and comparatively low COGS costs. Its overhead is high in part because of the heavily regulated environment it must work within, as essentially all its products required specific federal approval (by the FDA) to be sold, and also by the high selling costs associated with "detailing" the pharmaceuticals to doctors, pharmacies, hospitals, and other points of sale. Also its R&D expenses tend to be very high because of the laboratory-intensive nature of discovery and long development periods before revenues are actually achieved.

Year Ended December 31, 2000	**Op. Income Statement**
Net sales	$10,862.2
Cost of sales	2,055.7
Research and development	2,018.5
Marketing and administrative	3,228.3
Interest expense	182.3
Other income--net	(481.3)
	7,003.5
Income from continuing operations before income taxes and extraordinary item	3,858.7
Income taxes (Note 11)	800.9
Income from continuing operations before extraordinary item	3,057.8

Cash Flow Statement

Increases to Cash Flow

- Dep/Amor **435.8**

Incr or Decr to Cash Flow

- WC **+ 777.7** (normally a negative, for a growing business)
- Other (change in deferred taxes, gains on sales, asset impairment, etc.) **(539.8)**

Net Operating Cash Flow

3,731.5

EXHIBIT 7.16 Eli Lilly Cash Flow Calculation

Source: © 2003 Razgaitis, richard@razgaitis.com.

3M 3M (also known as Minnesota Mining and Manufacturing) is a "diversified chemical company" categorized in SIC code 2813 though it manufactures and sells 60,000 products, making it a remarkably diversified company. In 2002, it had its 100 year anniversary. Exhibit 7.17 shows its financial data for the last three years of its first 100 years (1999, 2000, and 2001).

These financial data (all dollars in thousands) summarized in Exhibit 7.17 are 3 year averages for 3M's annual filings with the U.S. Securities and Exchange Commission (SEC) from a standard financial report known formally as a 10-K, or simply 3M's annual financial report. The upper box of Exhibit 7.17 represents 3M's income statement, after some category simplifications have been made. The first line is the revenues (also known as sales). Subtracting from such sales are a series of cost categories that are shown in italics. The first cost is generally called COGS for cost of goods sold, or sometimes COS for cost of sales. This cost represents the direct cost in labor, materials, and equipment (expensed and capitalized) incurred during the period that produces the revenues that 3M receives. The net of revenues and COGS is commonly known as the gross margin, and is a measure of the innate profitability of the products sold. For 3M, averaged over 3 years over all their revenues, we see that their gross margin, weighted over all their 60,000 products, was just over 47 percent of their total revenue. The other costs are often called overhead because they are necessary costs to manage the business but they are not directly associated with the products and services sold that produced the revenues. Two common components of such overhead cost are sales, general, and administrative (SG&A) as well as research and development (R&D). These costs are sometimes lumped together as overhead. For 3M, together these costs are 30.8 percent of revenues. When such overhead costs are subtracted from the gross margin, the result, shown in Exhibit 7.17 as $2.6 billion (16.3 percent), is termed EBIT for earnings before interest and

EXHIBIT 7.17 3M Flow Calculation

Income Statement 3-year Avg (1999–2001)	$ thousands	Revenue Ratios
Revenues	$16,184	100.0%
COGS	($8,554)	52.9%
Gross Margin	$7,630	47.1%
SG&A	($3,912)	24.2%
R&D	($1,080)	6.7%
Total Overhead	($4,992)	30.8%
EBIT	$2,637	16.3%
Interest	($82)	
EBT	$2,555	15.8%
Provision for Tax	($877)	34.3%
EAT	$1,678	10.4%
Operations Adjustments to Income		
Dep & Amor	$1,005	6.2%
All Other Adjust.	$165	1.0%
Purchases PPE	($1,048)	6.5%
Net Adjustments	$122	0.8%
Cash Flow	$1,800	11.1%

Notes: COGS = Cost of goods sold; SG&A = Sales general and administrative; R&D = Research and development; EBIT = Earnings before interest and tax; EBT = Earnings before tax; Dep & Amor = Depreciation and amortization; PPE = Plant, property, and equipment (new investments). Because of rounding not all numbers add and subtract exactly as shown.

Source: © 2003 Razgaitis, richard@razgaitis.com.

taxes, and sometimes called operating profit, though different companies ascribe the term operating profit to different places in their income statements. For 3M there is a small net interest expense that reduces their income to the shown EBT, earning before tax, value. The provision for tax is based on 3M's tax return that, for a large company operating in many states and countries, is determined from a very complicated calculation. Shown is the provision of 34.3 percent of EBT (not revenues) based on the average of their three most recent years. Finally we have EAT, earnings after tax, which is often called the bottom line. Such earnings are then available to pay dividends to shareholders or to be retained by 3M for future investment or some combination of both. Such earnings are a new resource to the company—the reward from its customers for the capital and human assets deployed in their service.

In the lower box of Exhibit 7.17 we have the operations adjustments to the income statement to determine the actual cash flow that occurs. (There are also adjustments for other business functions such as financing operations that are not relevant to our purposes here). As discussed earlier, when capital investments made have multiyear benefit they are depreciated or amortized over time. When 3M determined their COGS and other costs that are contained within this income statement, such costs included depreciation and amortization expenses ascribed to each year based on investments made in some earlier year. So, in the income statement such depreciation and amortization reduced the calculated revenues received from 3M's customers by an amount that was not a literal cash expense in that year. In order to determine the actual cash flows we must then add back to the EAT number bottom line of the income statement the amount that had been deducted for such noncash costs. For 3M, and for many other companies, the adjustment is dominated by the depreciation and amortization costs as shown in Exhibit 7.17. All the other adjustments, including increases in accounts receivable and changes in inventory levels, are in 3M's case relatively small as shown.

To sustain its revenues and margins, 3M has to make new investments. For a completely static situation, one can conceive of a company's new investments each year exactly offsetting its depreciation and amortization amounts, sustaining the same total value of plant, property, and equipment. In practice, even for a mature company, the new investment differs from such depreciation and amortization either because the company is planning to grow, it is becoming more capital intensive, it is exiting certain businesses (and revenues), or it is becoming less capital intensive. In the 3M example, the investment in new plant, property, and equipment (PPE) of $1.048 billion almost exactly offsets the depreciation and amortization amount of $1.005 billion (within ca. 4 percent). The net effect of all such adjustments determines that the average cash inflow to 3M was $1.8 billion or 11 percent of revenues (averaged over the 3 years 1999–2001).[39] If 3M's revenues and costs all arrived and left in small unmarked bills, a scary thought in these trust-challenged times, we should see in the company shoebox on the 365th day of their fiscal year that $1.8 billion cash inflow (having started the year with the shoebox empty).

The values for the categories shown in Exhibit 7.17 vary widely depending on the industry in which the company operates and the individual company itself. Some industries, such as software and pharmaceuticals, characteristically have very low values of COGS and very high values of SG&A and especially R&D, although there can be significant company-to-company variation within any given industry segment. Other industries, such as commodity chemicals or consumer electronics, tend to have very high values of COGS and lower values of SG&A and especially R&D, again with company-to-company variation. Likewise, companies with high capital investments, such as are associated with a multibillion dollar semiconductor chip manufacturing facility or large polymer factory, have significant depreciation expenses as those large capital investments are written down over their useful lives. Intangible investments under recently adopted accounting rules can also, in certain industries and companies, represent significant annual deductions to income.

Corporate Examples of Income Statement Ratios

GCF forecasts start with the creation of an income statement. One approach to creating an income statement is to perform a bottom-up analysis specific to the subject technology, analyzing how each revenue dollar will be obtained, every component of COGS, preparing a complete business management plan with all the staffing and overhead costs, and so forth. This can be a very complex and lengthy task, and yet have high degrees of uncertainty because the technology development process is still active, the commercial products not yet fully defined or finalized, the customers and their demand and willingness to pay only estimated, the competitive response unclear, and so forth.

An alternative approach, one that is much simpler, is to rely on cost ratios from proxy companies as being indicative of what will be experienced by the subject technology after some startup period. Each public company reports quarterly its income statement values from which ratios can be computed. Many sources now provide useful summaries of these data.

Let us now look at four technology companies to see how this might be done:

- Two companies with gross margins (GM) of about 75 percent or greater, Eli Lilly as a pharmaceutical example, and Microsoft primarily a software example.
- Two companies with GM of about 50 percent, 3M a diverse products company, and Texas Instruments (TI) primarily a semi-conductor company.

In Exhibit 7.18 are data made available by Google Finance for annual results for three sequential 12 month periods.

The left column categories are as we have used to date: COGS are Cost of Goods Sold, GM is the Gross Margin (revenues net of COGS, but before overhead costs are included), SG&A (Sales General & Administrative) and R&D are the two primary overhead costs which added together are the Total OH (Overhead). EBIT (Earnings Before Interest and Taxes, or EBITA Earnings Before Interest Taxes and Adjustments) is obtained by subtracting the Total OH from the GM, PFT (Provision for Tax) is a percentage of EBIT, and EAT is the Earnings After Tax (sometimes "net income"). Income statements tend to also have numerous adjustments or inclusions of other kinds of nonoperating costs as shown in Exhibit 7.18. For technology valuation purposes these are usually ignored.

The percentage ratios shown in Exhibit 7.18 are calculations made from the Google supplied data normalized on the current year revenues except for PFT which is the ratio of the PFT dollars divided by the EBIT dollars and shown in italics to distinguish the ratio from all the other data which use the total annual revenue of the relevant year.

The two companies on the left side of Exhibit 7.18 are examples of very high gross margin technology businesses. This is another way of saying that their COGS is relatively low. The two companies on the right side are approximately typical of high performance technology companies for which manufacturing (COGS) is a comparatively significant expense. There is a corresponding inversion between the COGS and Total Overhead (OH) ratios: Eli Lilly and Microsoft experience high overheads (greater than 50 percent, and substantially greater than their respective COGS), whereas 3M and TI have overheads in the mid to low 20 percent range (much less than their respective COGS). The EBIT line is a commonly considered to be the measure of operational profitability. Except for the high values for Microsoft (ca. 40 percent), the range for the other three companies is relatively narrow (21 to 27 percent, for year ending 2007). (Investors "EAT" off the Earnings After Tax, and here the variation in percentages is affected by the various tax circumstances for each company: for year ending 2007, the EAT for Microsoft is 28 percent, TI 19 percent, Eli Lilly 16 percent, and 3M 14 percent.)

> 75% Gross Margin (GM) Companies

	12 months Ending 12./31/07		12 months Ending 12/31/06		12 months Ending 12/31/05	
Eli Lilly						
Revenue	$ 18,634	100%	$ 15,691	100%	$ 13,858	100%
COGS	$ 4,249	23%	$ 3,547	23%	$ 3,224	23%
GM	$ 14,385	77%	$ 12,145	77%	$ 10,634	77%
SG&A	$ 6,095	33%	$ 4,890	31%	$ 4,284	31%
R&D	$ 3,487	19%	$ 3,129	20%	$ 2,691	19%
Other OH Exp	$ 926	5%	$ 707	5%	$ 717	5%
Total OH	$ 9,582	51%	$ 8,019	51%	$ 6,975	50%
EBIT	$ 3,877	21%	$ 3,418	22%	$ 2,942	21%
PFT	*$ 924*	*24%*	*$ 755*	*22%*	*$ 1,132*	*38%*
EAT	$ 2,953	16%	$ 2,663	17%	$ 1,810	13%
Microsoft						
Revenue	$ 51,122	100%	$ 44,282	100%	$ 39,788	100%
COGS	$ 10,693	21%	$ 7,650	17%	$ 6,031	15%
GM	$ 40,429	79%	$ 36,632	83%	$ 33,757	85%
SG&A	$ 14,273	28%	$ 12,256	28%	$ 10,789	27%
R&D	$ 7,121	14%	$ 6,584	15%	$ 6,097	15%
Unusual Exp	$ 536	1%	$ 1,728	4%	$ 2,462	6%
Total OH	$ 32,623	64%	$ 28,218	64%	$ 25,379	64%
EBITA	$ 18,499	36%	$ 16,064	36%	$ 14,409	36%
Adjustments	$ 1,602	3%	$ 2,198	5%	$ 2,219	6%
EBIT	$ 20,101	39%	$ 18,262	41%	$ 16,628	42%
PFT	*$ 6,036*	*30%*	*$ 5,663*	*31%*	*$ 4,374*	*26%*
EAT	$ 14,065	28%	$ 12,599	28%	$ 12,254	31%

Approximately 50% Gross Margin (GM) Companies

	12 months Ending 12./31/07		12 months Ending 12/31/06		12 months Ending 12/31/05	
3M						
Revenue	$ 6,739	100%	$ 6,463	100%	$ 6,206	100%
COGS	$ 3,510	52%	$ 3,336	52%	$ 3,298	53%
GM	$ 3,229	48%	$ 3,127	48%	$ 2,908	47%
SG&A	$ 1,394	21%	$ 1,275	20%	$ 1,274	21%
R&D	$ 363	5%	$ 351	5%	$ 359	6%
Other OH Exp	$ 23	0%	$ -	0%	$ 5	0%
Total OH	$ 1,780	26%	$ 1,626	25%	$ 1,638	26%
EBIT	$ 1,449	22%	$ 1,501	23%	$ 1,270	20%
PFT	*$ 453*	*31%*	*$ 495*	*33%*	*$ 411*	*32%*
EAT	$ 963	14%	$ 1,006	16%	$ 859	14%
TI						
Revenue	$ 13,835	100%	$ 14,255	100%	$ 12,335	100%
COGS	$ 6,502	47%	$ 6,996	49%	$ 6,319	51%
GM	$ 7,333	53%	$ 7,259	51%	$ 6,016	49%
SG&A	$ 1,681	12%	$ 1,697	12%	$ 1,471	12%
R&D	$ 2,155	16%	$ 2,195	15%	$ 1,986	16%
Total OH	$ 3,836	28%	$ 3,892	27%	$ 3,457	28%
EBITA	$ 3,497	25%	$ 3,367	24%	$ 2,559	21%
Adjustments	$ 195	1%	$ 258	2%	$ 196	2%
EBIT	$ 3,692	27%	$ 3,625	25%	$ 2,755	22%
PFT	*$ 1,051*	*28%*	*$ 987*	*27%*	*$ 582*	*21%*
EAT	$ 2,641	19%	$ 2,638	19%	$ 2,173	18%

EXHIBIT 7.18 Income Statement Data for Eli Lilly, Microsoft, 3M, and Texas Instruments

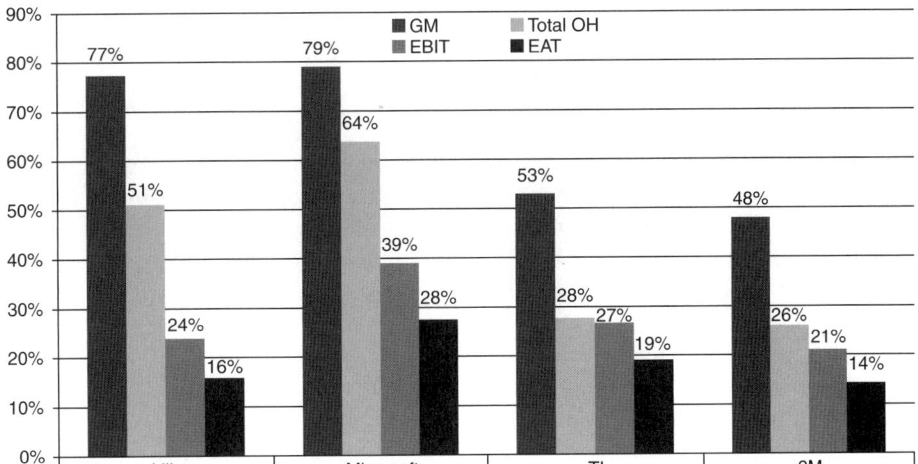

	Lilly	Microsoft	TI	3M
GM	77%	79%	53%	48%
Total OH	51%	64%	28%	26%
EBIT	24%	39%	27%	21%
EAT	16%	28%	19%	14%

EXHIBIT 7.19 Income Statement Ratios for Eli Lilly, 3M, and TI

The dollar data are directly available from Google Finance and other free online sources, from the individual companies, and proprietary data vendors such as Capital IQ, Bloomberg, and Ibbotson Associates (now part of Morningstar). It is often useful to use such data from industry peers in the segment of most relevance to the technology being valued. The proprietary data vendors can be especially useful for this purpose as they express all the reported data in a common classification and format, and they do so for literally thousands of companies representing various industry classifications (such as SIC codes, or more recently NAICS codes).

The key income statement ratios for these three companies shown in Exhibit 7.18 are compared for Year Ending 12/31/07 in Exhibit 7.19.

One of the additional useful features of Google Finance and similar sources is that they provide data for peer companies. So, for instance, for TI Google identifies 10 peer companies including National Semiconductor, STM Microelectronics, Fairchild Semiconductor, and so on. So by focusing an income statement analysis on one peer company, such as one might do by using TI, a ready comparison can be made with any number of related companies by, in turn, analyzing their income ratios.

Developing a GCF Model Based Upon 3M Data and Ratios

The specific opportunity being valued in the context of a negotiation can itself differ substantially from the norms of the selling or buying company. In the 3M example we have been considering, COGS, and appropriately allocated SG&A and R&D overheads for each of 3M's products no doubt varies widely because its products span so many industries and product applications from stationery to automotive, from electrical to medical, for business, government, and consumer customer categories. In theory, a company with a product line having a gross margin greater than zero provides some economic benefit to the company because it makes an overhead contribution; in practice, every product requires some overhead, if only the distraction of thinking about it and reporting on it, such that once a product's gross margin erodes to low values it is likely to be killed. 3M's objective for its R&D and business acquisition groups is obviously to create new products with very high gross margins. So we should not assume that a new opportunity being considered by 3M as a buyer will be characterized by the average gross margin, EBIT, and cash flow values shown in Exhibit 7.17; except for certain unusual circumstances, buyers are seeking to acquire opportunities with substantially higher financial ratios than their current average.

Accordingly, the financial model for any given opportunity needs to be specific to that opportunity. No universally applicable set of financial parameters exists. For purposes of the examples in this chapter, we refer to the 3M ratios because they are reasonably illustrative of a broad range of valuation opportunities. However, even if the buyer (or seller) was 3M itself, the appropriate parameters should be analyzed so that they are specific to the opportunity and as accurate as possible.

Now, we turn our attention to how, using 3M data as a benchmark, we can construct financial models. Following our principle of making our model as simple as possible, but not simpler, we consider two primary issues that affect the value of an opportunity during the transition from Dealmaking until operations at the 3M benchmark are expected. In contrast to purchasing of equities in the stock market, in most Dealmaking contexts such transition period involves additional investment by the buyer and a delay to the realization of the anticipated financial performance anticipated by the 3M benchmark we are using. This need for subsequent investment is the distinction between taking ownership of, or having proportional rights to, the fruits of a going concern, such as would be the case in purchasing all or some of the shares of, say, 3M versus buying from (or selling to) 3M a technology or nascent product line that has the potential of exceeding the 3M financial benchmarks but is presently only in the lab, or beginning manufacturing operations, or having initial "beta" sales.

For the purchase of a going concern, we can make first order estimates of the value of an enterprise by assuming that the cash flows now being generated will continue in perpetuity. It turns out the formula for present value A, of an annual cash stream GCF in perpetuity is simply:

$$NPV = GCF/(RAHR - CAGR)$$

Where RAHR is again the risk adjusted hurdle rate, and CAGR is the compound annual growth rate (where such CAGR must not be too close in value to RAHR for the equation to be valid).[40] For a going concern, especially a 100-year-old going concern with 60,000 products, such RAHR is a relatively low number. For simplicity, using an RAHR of 9 percent and a CAGR of 5.3 percent based on 3M's historic, 10-year growth rate in earnings per share, means that the present value of 3M, in accordance with the simplified assumptions described, would be 27 times the $1.8 billion cash flow calculated in Exhibit 7.17, or $49 billion. In 2003, 3M's market capitalization (total value of outstanding equity shares) is $44 billion, and its outstanding debt is approximately $2 billion, so its enterprise value is $46 billion, which is essentially identical to the simple calculation based on an RAHR of 9 percent.

What makes this calculation simple is the going concern assumption of a large, many product entity such as 3M. This is because its present financial performance can be reasonably understood and reasonably projected to continue in the future. In many negotiations, however, even of a going concern, what is being sold and bought is something that has the prospect of performance substantially greater than evidenced today and requires investment and nurturing by the buyer. It is this combination of (1) prospect, (2) nurturing, and (3) investment that makes calculating contingent value so much more complicated, and interesting, and negotiating agreements so much more challenging.

First, let us consider the investment that is estimated to be required of the buyer, and the time period of that investment, in order to create a business that can be thenceforth sustained from the overhead investments (a total of 30.8 percent of annual revenues based on the 3M data). Such investment is sometimes called the "CapEx" cost, for capital expenditures for depreciable assets (PPE) in addition to other expenses and labor that will be required during a startup period. Thus, during the startup years of our financial model, there normally needs to be included such CapEx and additional overhead investment to complete R&D, prototype manufacturing, test the market, develop sales channels and customers, scale up production, and fully staff the then going concern.

By analyzing multiple companies over multiple time periods, one can make reasonable approximations of such ratios. By further analyzing how companies prepare their cash flow statements, also part of the public record, it is possible to make some ballpark estimates for the key adjustments to the income statement: depreciation (which is not a current year expense) and increases in investment required (for working capital or other purposes).

With even more effort, one could make estimates from first principles of what it will cost to manufacture the licensed technology. To do so would require domain expertise in manufacturing for the subject area, also in marketing, sales, and general administration. Where the opportunity warrants such increased investment in analysis, such expertise can be found within one's own organization or, more likely, by employing outside consultants.

A final source of such information is the buyer. Because they are in the business of commercialization, buyers normally have the resources, experience, and the need to develop such detailed projections. Although it is not reasonable to expect the buyer to provide the seller complete access to their records and projections (particularly if the seller is negotiating with multiple prospective buyers), it can be in both parties' interests to share reasonable projections for the purpose of conducting win-win negotiations.

A "Baseline" GCF Template

It is common practice to develop a cash flow model, needed to forecast year by year GCFs, using the combination of income statement and making adjustments to income using the cash flow statement. As we have seen, income and cash flow statements are widely publicized because they are basic accounting documents that publicly traded companies must provide quarterly. So there are literally thousands of companies making available their financial information, all of which can be retrieved for historic periods as well.[41]

By analyzing such available reports, it is often possible to use certain ratios to aid in creating a GCF model for a technology. In this section we will show an example of how this could be done. An alternate approach is to create a bottom-up financial analysis of the costs and benefits associated with the rights to use the technology being value as would be done in a formal business plan prepared for investors. And, of course, both a ratio and a bottom-up analysis can be done as a reasonableness test on each other. Doing a bottom-up analysis is typically a very significant effort, easily requiring months of effort, which may not be justified by either the magnitude of the investment required or the knowledge of how the technology will be commercially used. If a company is licensing out a technology it had evaluated for its own use in a business, it may have already done such a detailed analysis. Also, a seller who has done numerous licenses in the same general area may be able to readily adapt a prior financial model to the specifics of the subject technology valuation.

It is useful for didactic purposes to standardize on a financial model of cash flows. Our challenge in developing such a model template, as is the challenge for negotiation purposes, is to hit the right level of complexity. The world is an extremely complicated place that is made all the more complicated by any consideration of all the things that could happen in the future. We actually do not want to attempt to consider all possibilities because we would leave ourselves with an insoluble problem, which even were it solvable, would be unintelligible and impotent to help our negotiation process.[42] Such a situation would be akin to our listening to a fool asking a question that seven wise men cannot answer. However, we can oversimplify a model, or a question, so that the answer is easily achieved but lacks bearing because of how we have trivialized the context. This situation would be like gaining an understanding of a simple answer for which no one is asking the underlying question. With the exception of very simple problems that can be solved exactly even considering all factors, we are normally faced with this challenge of choosing an effective level of analysis that incorporates a reasonable, important level of complexity without weighing ourselves down with details that add little meaningful information or encumber our finite ability to grasp reality or projections of reality.

There is no single right place to locate our analysis on this simplicity–complexity space. Further, it is often difficult to make good judgments at the beginning of an analysis of what to include and what can be safely ignored or greatly simplified. This predicament is akin to the paradoxical aphorism of "you can't read a book once" (meaning you have to read it and see the whole picture before you can really "read it" and grasp how it all fits together); to some extent this point also applies to financial analysis—through experience it becomes ever easier to know what to include and what can be ignored. In Chapter 8 we show how the tools associated with the Monte Carlo method can aid us in ignoring those variables whose impact on NPV is inconsequential.

This modeling design problem is not unique to financial analysis. Even "exact" equations do not directly apprehend reality, but only certain idealized representations of reality. (There is a genuine philosophical question as to whether we would know reality if we saw it, because we are always dealing with representations.)[43] The explanatory power of models depends on whether such representation is adequate for control, prediction, and decision making. This axiom is true in physics, combustion, biological systems, psychology, economic policy, and virtually every human endeavor involving complex behaviors. Albert Einstein (1879–1955), known for many pithy quotes had one that is applicable here: "Every problem should be made as simple as possible, but not simpler." This is the guidance we seek to follow in the examples considered throughout this book.

A simple, but illustrative, example of how ratios and judgment can be used in the framework of an income and cash flow statement to create GCF forecasts is shown in Exhibit 7.20.

The exhibit reflects a 10-year projection divided into two segments: the first five startup years, and the last five mature years. The distinction between the startup and mature periods is that during the mature period we assume revenue growth is determined by a constant value of CAGR, all the other parameters are determined as fixed ratios as shown. Also, the CapEx investment is exactly equal to the current year depreciation and amortization, maintaining a constant total asset value. During the startup period, we are creating the transition financial model between the initial time at which it is assumed that no revenues exist and that additional CapEx and overhead investment is necessary to complete R&D and manufacturing, as well as market development to launch the product. Other important aspects of this template are:

- Total startup costs, which can be considered as the investment to launch a self-sustaining business, are assumed to be equal to the annual revenues for the first mature period year (Year 6 revenues = $200 million).
- CapEx, which includes any IP acquisition costs, those costs that are deemed to require depreciation (or amortization for IP costs) over the estimated life of such assets. The total CapEx during the startup period is estimated to be 50 percent of the total startup costs, a total of $100 million, that will be expended as shown during the startup period and depreciated on a straight-line basis over 10 years from the year of investment.
- The tax rate is 34 percent (of EBT). Note there is a calculation of the carry-forward losses during the first 3 years that is credited against taxes due in Year 4.
- The combined COGS and overhead cost ratio is assumed to be 70 percent after the first three years, which is approximately 14 points less than the 3M 3-year average, leading to an EBIT value of 30 percent. This assumption is made because it is assumed that the opportunity under investigation will cause the buyer (3M or some other company) to improve its average current economic performance.
- The CAGR is assumed to be 12 percent and applicable after the 5th year.
- No account has been presently made for any terminal value. Accordingly, the analysis cuts off at the 10th year with no additional value ascribed.
- The increase in working capital requirements is assumed to be 10 percent of the growth of subsequent year's revenues (to fund receivables and inventory and all other purposes).
- The entries for overhead costs in Years 1 to 3 are assumed as shown taking into account the total costs for Years 1 to 5 added to the assumed total of $200 million.
- An NPV calculation is listed for the RAHR of 15 percent, showing that the modeled opportunity has a large positive NPV of more than $35.88 million for this

	Assumed Ratios	Year 1	2	3	4	5	Startup Total	6	7	8	9	10	Mature Total	10-Year TOTAL
		Startup Period						Mature Period						
Revenues		*0.00*	*2.00*	*15.00*	*70.00*	*170.00*	257.00	*200.00*	224.00	250.88	280.99	314.70	1270.57	1527.57
CAGR, Current Yr		-	*650%*	*367%*	*143%*	*18%*		*12.0%*	*12.0%*	*12.0%*	*12.0%*	*0.0%*		
INCOME STATEMENT														
Dep-Amor(1)	*10*	0.20	1.20	4.20	8.20	10.00	23.80	11.1	12.3	13.7	15.2	16.9	69.3	93.11
All Other(2)		*3.00*	*8.00*	*15.40*	40.80	109.00		128.89	144.46	161.91	181.46	203.37	820.09	
Total Costs, $	*70.0%*	3.20	9.20	19.60	49.00	119.00	*200.00*	140.00	156.80	175.62	196.69	220.29	889.40	1089.40
Total Cost, %		-	*460%*	*131%*	*70%*	*70%*		*70%*	*70%*	*70%*	*70%*	*70%*		
EBIT		(3.20)	(7.20)	(4.60)	21.00	51.00	57.00	60.00	67.20	75.26	84.30	94.41	381.17	438.17
PFT (of EBIT)	*34.0%*	0.00	0.00	0.00	2.04	17.34		20.40	22.85	25.59	28.66	32.10		
EAT		(3.20)	(7.20)	(4.60)	18.96	33.66	37.62	39.60	44.35	49.67	55.64	62.31	251.57	289.19
Carry forward loss		(3.20)	(10.40)	(15.00)	3.96									
CASH FLOW AJUSTMENTS														
Dep, Amor(1)	*10*	0.20	1.20	4.20	8.20	10.00	23.80	11.1	12.3	13.7	15.2	16.9	69.3	93.11
Incr WC(3)	*10%*	0.20	1.30	5.50	10.00	3.00		2.40	2.69	3.01	3.37	3.37		
CapEx(4)		*2.00*	*10.00*	*30.00*	*40.00*	*18.00*	*100.00*	*11.1*	*12.3*	*13.7*	*15.2*	*16.9*		169.20
GCF		(5.20)	(17.30)	(35.90)	(22.84)	22.66	(58.58)	37.21	41.70	46.67	52.29	58.96	236.84	178.26
	RAHR													
DCF	*15.00%*	(4.85)	(14.03)	(25.31)	(14.00)	12.08		17.25	16.81	16.36	15.94	15.63		
NPV	35.88													

Notes

1 Depreciation + Amortization assumed (a) 10 years, straight line, (b) 50% of startup investment (balance is non-PPE investment)
2 "All other expenses" for Years 1–3 are assumed to be the values shown; Years 4 and 5 are determined using the assumed total cost ratio of 70%.
3 Increase in Working Capital (WC), to fund receivables, inventory, and other purposes is assumed to be the shown percentage of the increase in Revenues year over year
4 Startup period CapEx assumed to total 50% of startup total costs; during mature period CapEx is assumed in each year to be equal to the depreciation + amortization

All values that are both italicized and underlined, are assumed values.

EXHIBIT 7.20 Baseline GCF Template

discount rate. Using a conventional discounted cash flow (DCF) approach and the Excel Goal Seek function one can determine that the RAHR corresponding to an NPV of zero is 27.55 percent. Thus, for perceived RAHR below this threshold value there will be a positive NPV and the project will be deemed worth doing, and vice versa for values above 27.55 percent. Thus if we used a RAHR value of 30 percent as in the previous examples in this chapter, this project would not be worth doing, unless some of the costs can be eliminated.

- The revenue projection is based on the assumption that zero revenues will be achieved during the first project year, and modest market-testing revenues in Year 2. Revenues in Year 3 are still assumed to be small and correspond to production from prototype (semiworks scale) manufacturing equipment. Based on the assumed revenue growth, significant CapEx investments are made in Years 3 and 4 to support the large projected revenue increases in Years 4 and

For our purposes, we use as the baseline template for our demonstrations in this chapter and Chapter 8 using the Monte Carlos Method, the financial model as shown in Exhibit 7.20. For the reader's convenience, an Excel downloadable version of this exhibit is available at "Dealmaking Resources" at the author's web site, www.razgaitis.com.

Modeling Startup Revenues

GCFs all begin with revenues, also referred to as sales, or the 'top line'. Because of the compounding effect of RAHR on discounting GCFs the onset, growth, and maturation of revenue models often plays a very important role in determining NPV.

The early years are the most significant in this regard because the effect of discounting GCF to DCF is smaller than for the late project years, especially for 10 or 20 year projections.

The effect of a delay in positive GCF values, even one year can make a significant difference. Referring again to the model of Exhibit 7.10, let us quantify the effect of a one year delay of all the GCFs from Years 7 through 19 so these values become the GCFs for Years 8 through 20, and we simply assume a zero GCF for Year 7 (where we originally have $1 million positive GCF). So the GCF for Year 20 that had been $0 in the original model of Exhibit 7.10 becomes $3 million, because the Year 19 GCF has been delayed on year. The total GCF for the 20-year period is unchanged ($126 million), but now the one year with a GCF of $0 is Year 7 instead of Year 20. Just this one year delay inserted between Years 6 and 7 causes the NPV for RAHR = 30 percent to decrease from a positive $1.6 million to a negative $0.2 million, leading to a "no investment" decision assuming this RAHR value is appropriate.

Similar to the effect of a delay in positive GCF values is the rate of growth of positive GCF during early years. This period is commonly referred to as a "ramp-up" or "startup" period. After some period of a few years it is common to experience an annual growth rate in revenues that can be characterized by a fixed annual percentage, commonly termed the Compound Annual Growth Rate (CAGR). After some further period of time the growth rate (CAGR) is likely to diminish, become zero, and then a negative value during product maturity. And ultimately the revenues for the subject technology can be expected to decline to zero either because the IP rights are no longer being used to generate revenues or the entire product category has expired. These various revenues periods can be seen in Exhibit 7.10:

- Years 7–9 experience very high growth rates (CAGR > 100 percent)
- Years 10–12 have CAGR values of 30, 8, and 7 percent, respectively
- Years 13–14 have "flat" GCF, corresponding to a CAGR of 0 percent
- Years 15–19 have negative values of CAGR of −7 percent for Years 15 and 16, and then declining more rapidly is a reverse ramp-up down to GCF = $0 in Year 20

Because NPV is most dependent upon the startup GCF revenue years, and the early CAGR-characterized years, it is worth considering how these might be modeled.

We now need to consider the time to initial revenues, and the growth profile of those revenues during a (it is hoped rapidly growing sales) ramp-up period before we can make reasonable approximations for future revenues using CAGR estimates and other income statement ratios. The growth of revenues from new product introduction has been widely studied. The profile of revenue growth is generally modeled by an S-curve, also known as a sigmoid shape, as shown in Exhibit 7.21.

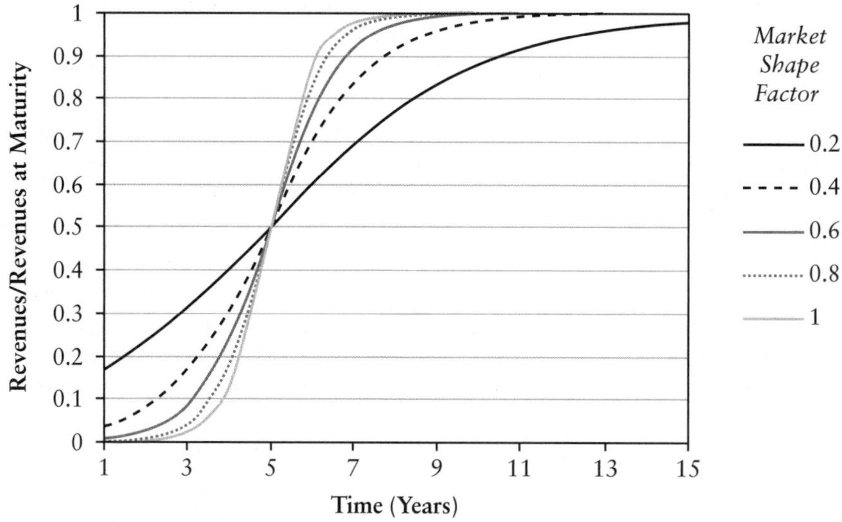

Based on the Fisher-Pry Model, with 50 percent penetration at the 5th year

$$\frac{\text{Revenues for year } t}{\text{Revenues at Maturity}} = 1 + \tanh\,[(s(t - t_{50})]$$

Where t_{50} is the year for 50 percent penetration, and s is the market shape factor

EXHIBIT 7.21 S-Curve Revenue Growth Model: Fisher-Pry

Shown in Exhibit 7.21 is the Fisher-Pry equation from which the shown curves were derived, all for an assumed 50 percent penetration at the fifth year, and for the five different market shape factors, s. As shown, for low values of s, the market response is slow to start but grows rapidly to maturity near to the t50 year (in this case, the fifth year). For high values of s, the market response is early to start, but grows slowly to maturity.

Other S-shaped adoption curves are shown in Exhibit 7.22. Shown here are two closely related relationships known as Pearl-Reed and Gompertz. Instead of prescribing a year of 50 percent penetration, these relationships use a factor, a, termed a location coefficient in addition to s, a market response (shape) factor. Unlike Fisher-Pry, these curves do not cross over each other, meaning that a curve corresponding to a particular market response factor will always reflect sales above the curve corresponding to a smaller value of s.

These (or other) new product introduction models can be used to project the rate of market penetration and revenue growth for a new product opportunity. They are more important to a financial model when the startup phase of an opportunity is anticipated to be long (say 10 years or more). For short startup phase opportunities, however, manual, annual estimates, or even straight-line estimates, can work reasonably well for valuation purposes. Again, we favor simplicity when it does not cost us an important degree of understanding.

The revenue projection shown in Exhibit 7.20 can be compared with the three S-curve production adoption models previously depicted in Exhibits 7.21 and 7.22. The comparison with the assumed revenue projection of Exhibit 7.20 is shown in Exhibit 7.23.

In the table at the top of Exhibit 7.23 are the baseline template revenues for the first 6 years. Below such assumed revenues are the Fisher-Pry, Pearl-Reed, and Gompertz models in table format. Under the tables is a graph depicting the assumed values in the Baseline Template and the three startup revenue models already discussed. As can be seen, all three of these models can be adjusted to follow closely the assumed revenue growth rate during the startup period, although the Gompertz model underpredicts the revenues during the initial 3 years. With research and experience, it may be possible to establish an independently developed model with corresponding coefficients to derive startup revenue projections. Using the Goal Seek function in Excel one can iterate on the twin parameters of any one model to reduce the difference to zero in total revenues through the first six years.

Revenue projections are commonly made from either a top-down or bottom-up basis, and from making use of segment and/or scenario analyses. The top-down approach starts with some perception of the size and growth of the total market either based on experience or market studies or research. From this perception, estimates are made as the capture (or "penetration") that the subject opportunity will evidence as some percentage of such "addressable" market. A bottom-up approach starts with an analysis of how many customers exist of each type, the corresponding sales channel model that will reach such customers (number of salespeople, the sales cycle, and so forth), the units of the product that can be sold as a function of unit pricing. This model then builds up from individual accounts to an overall total revenue projection. Revenue projections are often made from both a top-down and bottom-up perspective and then compared as a test of reasonableness. An initial

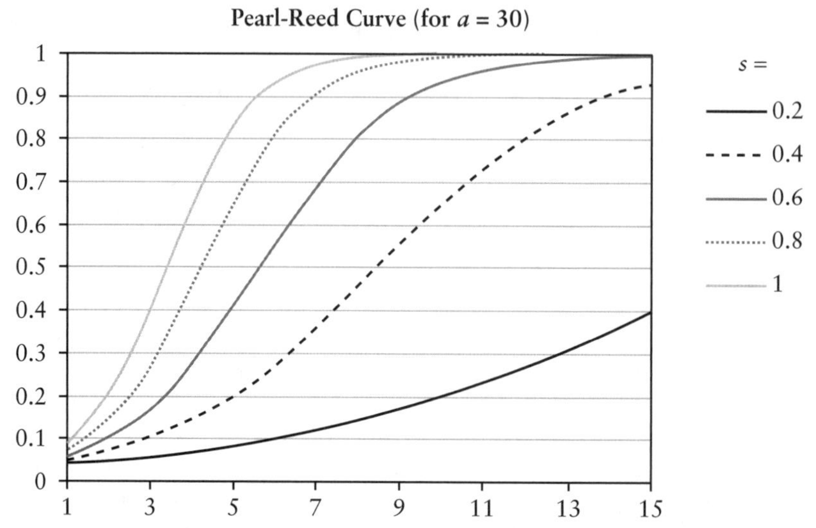

$$\frac{\text{Revenues for year } t}{\text{Revenues at Maturity}} = 1/[1 + \text{a} \exp(-st)]$$

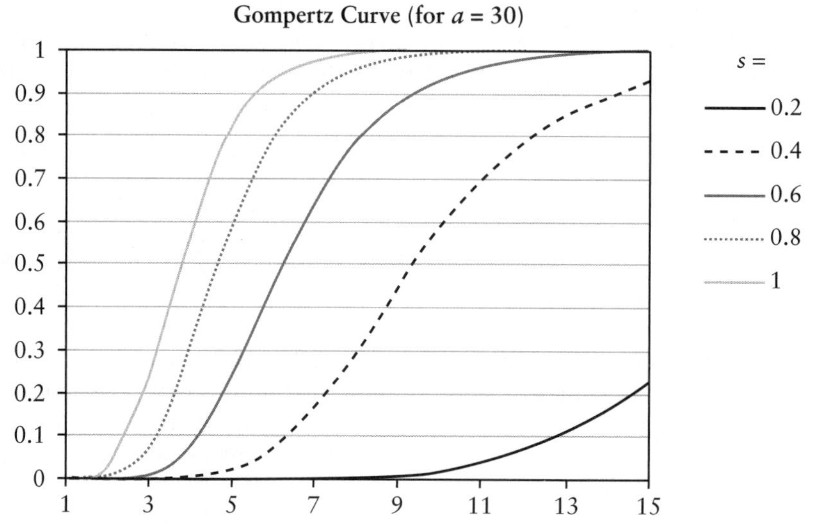

$$\frac{\text{Revenues for year } t}{\text{Revenues at Maturity}} = 1/\{\exp[\text{a} \exp(-st)]\}$$

EXHIBIT 7.22 Other S-Shaped New Product Adoption Curves

bottom-up analysis, for example, may lead to a revenue projection in excess of a reasonable projection of market share based on a top-down analysis of the overall market. Or an initial top-down model may have missed the effect of significant revenue potential available from certain large customer segments. The three S-curve models discussed and shown in Exhibit 7.23, provide another means of testing for

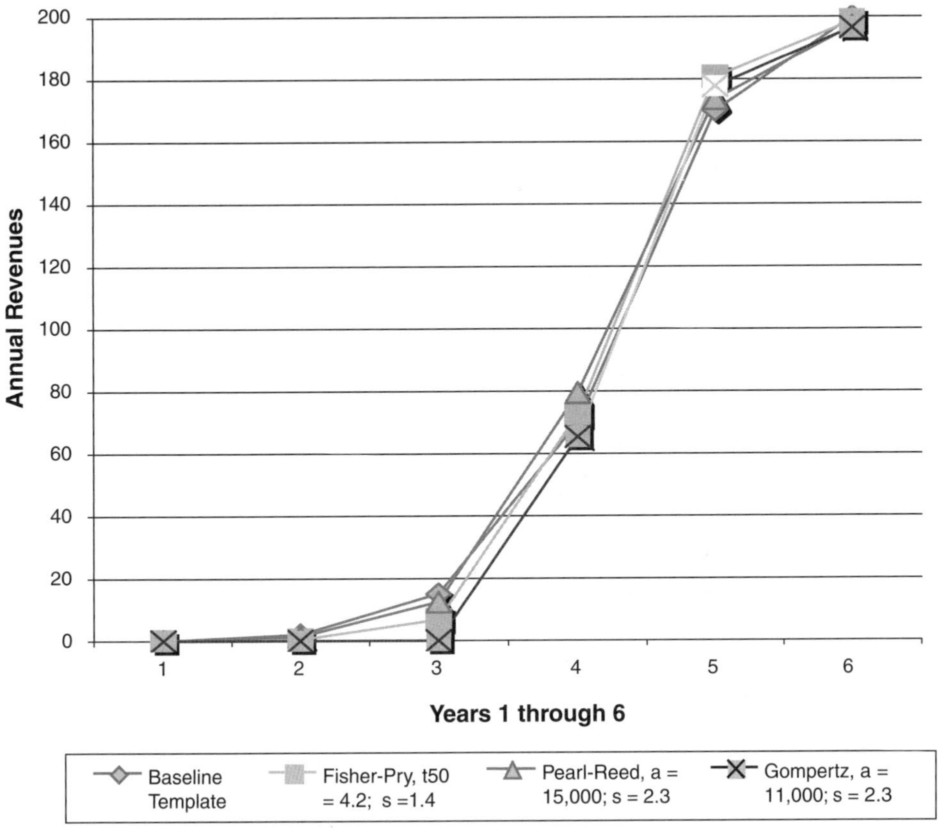

EXHIBIT 7.23 Baseline GCF Template Compared with S-Curve Models

reasonableness. By tracking actual results and correlating such results to solve for the pair of factors required in any of the three S-curve models considered (such as a and s for Pearl-Reed and Gompertz), one can develop a database of examples that can be used to develop new opportunity revenue models or test for reasonableness such models developed by a top-down or bottom-up approach.

The baseline template of Exhibit 7.20 is an example of how the DCF Method can be developed based upon a two-period analysis: a startup period, in which revenues and costs are year by year estimates, and a standardized growth period where income and cash flow statement ratios are used from an appropriate peer company or companies. These two periods are separated into the left and right half of Exhibit 7.20. A third period can be estimated by adding a terminal value calculation as discussed previously, or by directly modeling a continuing maturity and/or decline period such as was done in Exhibit 7.10 for Years 15 through 20. Any number of segments or scenarios can be used to improve the forecast accuracy of the assumptions shown in Exhibit 7.20.

As we have demonstrated in this chapter, once a financial model has been established, the specification of a RAHR value then permits the direct calculation of the NPV. In Chapter 8 we will use this baseline template to illustrate how the Monte Carlo Method, one of the Advanced Methods, can be used to examine the sensitivity of NPV to each different input variable and any dispersion in value of such input.

The Toolbox

Timing of projected cash inflows has an important influence on most technology valuations regardless of the valuation ***Method***. This can be most readily demonstrated using the DCF Method by simple adjustment of the year by year projected revenues, or costs. Because costs, including investments, are expected to track closely with revenue projections—although in early years of a technology development there can be significant costs before there are any revenues and of course for adverse outcomes costs can occur with even zero revenues—it is often useful to give consideration to revenue models. This is particularly the case for technology valuation because the starting revenues are typically zero or modest in comparison to that anticipated.

The diffusion of technology innovation has been widely studied with common reference to a 1962 book by Everitt M. Rogers.[44] In that widely cited writing Rogers identifies a rapidly growing adoption *rate*—characterized by buyer categories "innovators," "early adopters," and "early majority" with ever increasing rates of adoption, followed by a decline in adoption rate by "late majority" and "laggards." Then such adoption rate characterization is graphed on cumulative basis. The results are the s-shaped curves discussed in this chapter.

Using one of the s-shaped startup models can be a useful tool to make growth revenue estimates.[45] In some circumstances the startup period can last decades. Examples would include household penetration (adoption) of microwave ovens, DVD players, personal computers, or, going forward, of plug-in hybrid automobiles. It can be useful to seek out startup revenue data for comparable technologies and/or market applications with which to begin to make model estimates. Performing a DCF Method calculation of the NPV effect of different startup revenue models can then be a useful complement to other valuation ***Methods*** such as Industry Standards (Method 1) or Rules of Thumb (Method 3).

Other Issues to Be Considered with the DCF Method

The DCF Method is very widely practiced in many kinds of business contexts. Its theoretical foundation and practical power is widely recognized. But, as we have discussed in closing the previous chapters on other valuation Methods, there are some "howevers" and cautions to be recognized. In this closing section of this chapter we will consider some of these.

Zero or Negative NPV Projects

Although, in principle, a less than zero NPV technology investment should not be undertaken because it is forecast to be a capital consumer not a return on investment provider, for the given level of risk (RAHR). However—and there's our word—a buyer may apply reasoned judgment to go forward on such a project overriding a negative NPV projection. How so?

Denial is always one answer. (And, as the joke goes: "da-nial" is not just a river in Egypt). Passion is another; love is not mathematical, nor is in-the-moment euphoria. (Which commonly leads to a post-mortem highlighted by "What were we thinking?")

But are there *reasoned* bases for going forward on negative NPV projects?

THE "DEAN'S RULE" As discussed already in the context of college admissions, there can be limited circumstances where a resource manager such as a college dean is simply given a limited ability to make instinctive choices that simply fall outside of policy guidelines used to govern the vast majority of situations. Choosing to pursue a negative NPV project is, in this sense, going against "the book." Depending on the manager's track record, and the magnitude of the investment put at risk—or misdeployed as the DCF Method tells us—there can be limited circumstances where such decisions are given DCF forgiveness.

THE "KING FERDINAND RULE" When Christopher Columbus sought funding from the King of Spain he was at least twice refused. Upon the latter refusal he was reportedly ready to depart to France to try "selling" his plan that (1) ships properly built and outfitted could make it to "the Indies," that is, Southeast Asia, and (2) this would be a very profitable alternative to the long and costly alternative trade routes.[46]

We do not know what caused the King and Queen to initially reject and ultimately agree to fund the project, but fear of a competitor's success was no doubt part of the calculation. But also there was the innate belief in a great potential reward for achieving an alternate trade route outside the control of many parties unfriendly to Spain. So, the Columbus offer was indeed that of a "transformative," "game changing" technology, but of unquantifiable economic value. But the business world is awash with the economic failures of "transformative," "game changing" technologies: the SST (Supersonic Transport), Irridium (low earth orbit communication satellites), www.pets.com (and many other "dot bombs"), AI companies (Artificial Intelligence), and the everyman airplane or even car-plane.

THE "OFFER I CAN'T REFUSE RULE" Another type of zero or negative NPV project that is accepted by buyers is the "have to have" kind. Several examples can illustrate this type. A government entity creates a legal duty with regard to some environmental issue that must be met by some date or the company has to shut down its operations. Even though the NPV of the particular project will be negative according to a traditional model that projects, say, no new revenues but only new costs, the real issue is that the company's future revenues will be even smaller, perhaps zero, if it does not make such investment. So taking into account the loss of revenues as a certain future, the license of the technology will create additional revenues compared to such loss and create a positive NPV even though the final revenues for the company may only equal the revenues it now has.

Another version of this "have to have" investment is market obsolescence. Technology-based companies typically face obsolescence as a way of life. Protecting its markets against competitors, or loss of perceived value by its customers, requires continual investment in R&D, M&A, and/or technology acquisitions. Any given opportunity may be deemed necessary though it's specific NPV calculation yield a non-positive value. Of course, not all projects for all time can fall into this condition or the company is simply restraining the inevitable.

THE "LOOK-SEE RULE" A buyer may rationally make an investment in a negative NPV project because of a perceived need to launch a high risk initial effort toward some long-term goal that is broader than just the one project being considered, and the investment sums involved are affordably modest. When doing so, investments are not really rationalized on a DCF basis on the specific investment project, but on some Rule-Of-Thumb Method (Method 3), such as allocating a certain percentage of its revenues investing in long term speculative areas; or on some Industry Standard Method (Method 1) such as a willingness to spend some lump sum, say $1 million, to begin to frame out what would be a long term and later justified investment. Such investments have sometimes been termed "mad money," meaning a modest investment, and risk, based on an instinct.

Encompassing such a rationale is some larger initiative of which the subject project is just a part. If an NPV were to be constructed on such overall initiative, it would be positive in order to make sense. Because the larger enterprise may be outside the purview of the technology seller, it may have no ready way of assessing how its technology may contribute to such positive NPV.

THE "BIG PICTURE RULE" Any large business has so many interacting divisions, technologies, and investment opportunities, that no single DCF Model can encompass all the operational decisions management must face in wisely allocated always scarce capital. Accordingly, one must break down problems to be solved into discrete subordinate elements.

One of the first questions to be answered in any DCF Model is the exact identification of what is being valued. As was discussed in Chapter 3, defining the Box, exactly what is being offered for sale, is a critical first step. Whatever the outcome from the selling and buying of a subject technology, there is almost certain to be some effect upon multiple other aspects for the seller and buyer, which effects are not directly computed within the financial model of the DCF Method.

One of the important business strategy themes of recent decades, and one that has become so foundational as to be a kind of mantra, is that of focus and coherence: a company should build itself around its core strengths like spokes in a wheel so that each initiative is helped by other company capabilities and businesses and in turn reciprocates such help. The idea is to strip out those outlier businesses, even if profitable, not only because they are a management and investment distraction but also because the business game is won by marshalling massive strength at significant existing and emerging opportunities. This strategic practice complicates the use of a DCF Method because a NPV result from a particular initiative does not encompass all the related benefits that a buyer may gain. Especially when considering how the technology fits and supports all the other buyer's business activities.

Although a buyer should have a superior position by which to make such NPV calculation of its additional benefits to acquiring the technology, the complexity of the analysis can make its quantification difficult. This effect may be accounted for by the use of an appropriate royalty base. Returning to the laser example, if the licensed subject matter is the lasing element only, the buyer will likely gain the benefit of selling entire laser components as a result of having such new element. By using the selling price of the entire component, and appropriately adjusting the royalty, the seller can be fairly compensated.

Accounting for such additional value is normally much more uncertain than the products made directly by the licensed technology. As in the case of the terminal value issue, in many instances this effect is deemed too distant or speculative to be included. However, it is always a reasonable question to ask: What is the total benefit of the licensed technology? If the answer is a significant enhancement of other businesses, then a zero or negative NPV individual project can be not only justified, but highly valuable.

Although this discussion is specific to negative NPV projects, the "big picture rule" is also relevant to highly positive NPV projects which, by virtue of this consideration, are even more positive than a forecast made by a model specific to a particular technology.

THE "THROW DEEP RULE" There is a story told of how the U.S. Government chose to authorize the challenging and costly superconducting supper collider project during President Reagan's term. The story goes that proponents for and opposed to launching the massive investment had prepared detailed presentations supporting their respective positions, including matters of advanced particle physics. Before the presentations had barely begun, President Reagan had heard enough, walked out of the room, with a closing comment of "throw deep," an apparent reference to a high stakes football play. The people left in the room were left with divining what decision had been made and ultimately interpreted the comment as a "yes" for funding.

There are those opportunities that will energize an enterprise into new areas for which a "throw deep" decision is made, even if the NPV is predicted to be negative, even if an NPV calculation has been made.

High RAHR Values and Long Project Durations

Previously in this chapter we have seen how technology opportunities forecast to yield more than $100 million in GCF over its life, was present valued at less than two million dollars because of the compounding effect of a high RAHR value over a long period. Exhibit 7.24 shows an important interaction between the number of years (n) between now and the time a GCF of $1,000 is to be received and RAHR value.

The values are shown on two RAHR lines: 15 and 50 percent, corresponding to a possible corporate project discount value and a VC investment value. For short periods of time, such as three years, the impact of different values of RAHR is comparatively small unless the RAHR value is large, such as the VC figure. What this exhibit shows is simply this: When dealing with short investment periods, the

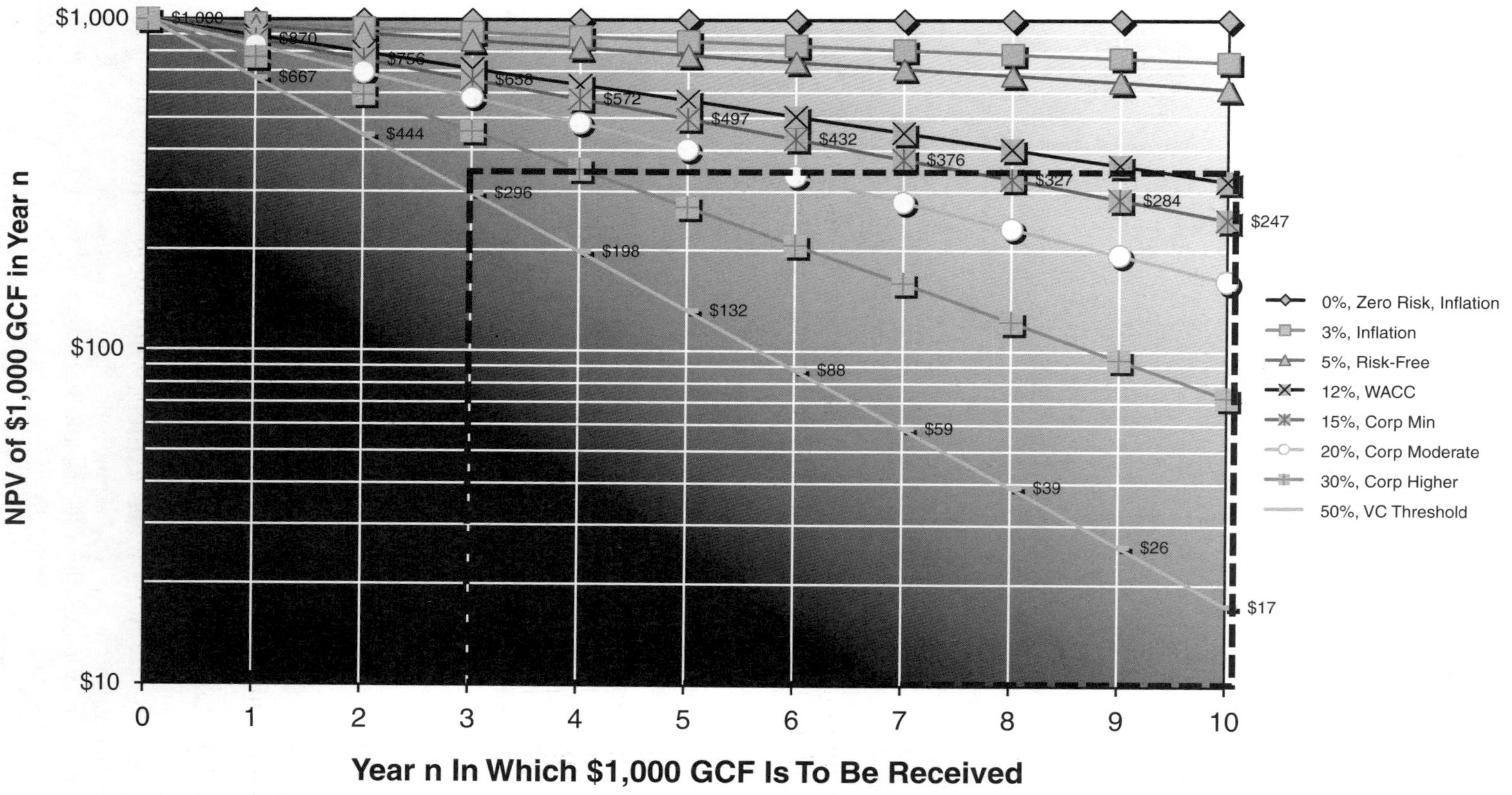

EXHIBIT 7.24 Effect of RAHR Value and Time (n) on the NPV of $1,000 GCF To Be Received in Year n

uncertainty in appropriate RAHR (or k) is not highly significant in determining the value of an opportunity, but when the investment periods are longer, say seven years or more, then the value of RAHR plays a critical role in the perception of value. This observation is what makes the prediction and assessment of returns associated with inherently long term projects, such as a new pharmaceutical, a challenge using a DCF method. In the same way, and for the same reason, for long periods of time the NPV value declines significantly even for comparatively modest RAHR values.

Shown in Exhibit 7.24 is a dashed-outline box. Although its demarcation is a matter of judgment, any combination of RAHR and n within such box creates an NPV value of less than 20 percent of the GCF value for any of the shown years and is likely to make relatively unattractive any opportunity valued by the DCF Method—unless the preponderance of the project GCF inflows occur in the early years such that any of the more distant cash flows are not critical to the overall value of the opportunity. One of the advantages of the Advanced Methods of Chapter 8 is to value opportunities so that the effect shown in Exhibit 7.24 is accounted for by other means.

Risk Dynamics

Normally, RAHR is not a static value over the investment life of a given opportunity. As the subject technology is advanced one normally expects to learn more, get closer to commercialization, and reduce the total risk, although in some cases the more one learns the worse it looks. And, not infrequently, technology commercialization projects have episodes of what are, or appear to be, risk reduction or even elimination accomplishments soon followed by some setback or discovery of a new challenge or risk. This is not a field of work well suited to people with paranoid or schizophrenic inclinations.

Considering the more favorable outcome of a project, as additional investments are made its risks reduce, and the value of the technology should increase, all other factors being equal, because of both stage of development considerations (discussed in Chapter 6) and a reduction in appropriate RAHR. Empirical evidence and examples are not readily available in most cases because companies do not normally publish histories of all their projects, including commercially unsuccessful ones.

Two categories of examples do exist. One is that VCs usually invest in "series" or rounds of funding. The initial round would be known as the A Series, and the initial pricing of the common stock is set at a common share price—such as $1/share–based on the valuation and number of shares authorized. One example where such data is available is the FDA approval process for new drugs.

Another example can be found in the pharmaceuticals industry. There is a highly regulated process by the government (FDA) for gaining approval to offer pharmaceuticals. There exists data as to the number of drugs entering different phases of development. Shown in Exhibit 7.25 are data from a *Scientific American* article that studied the history of what happened to new drugs entering the approval process (by the filing of an IND, Investigation of New Drug) in 1976–78 (which early period is needed in order to be able to follow the history).

Shown are the data for the drugs successfully entering each subsequent gate: Phase 1, 2, and 3 clinical trials, New Drug Application (NDA) applied for and granted (enabling sale). As shown, only 20 percent of the drug candidates that began the

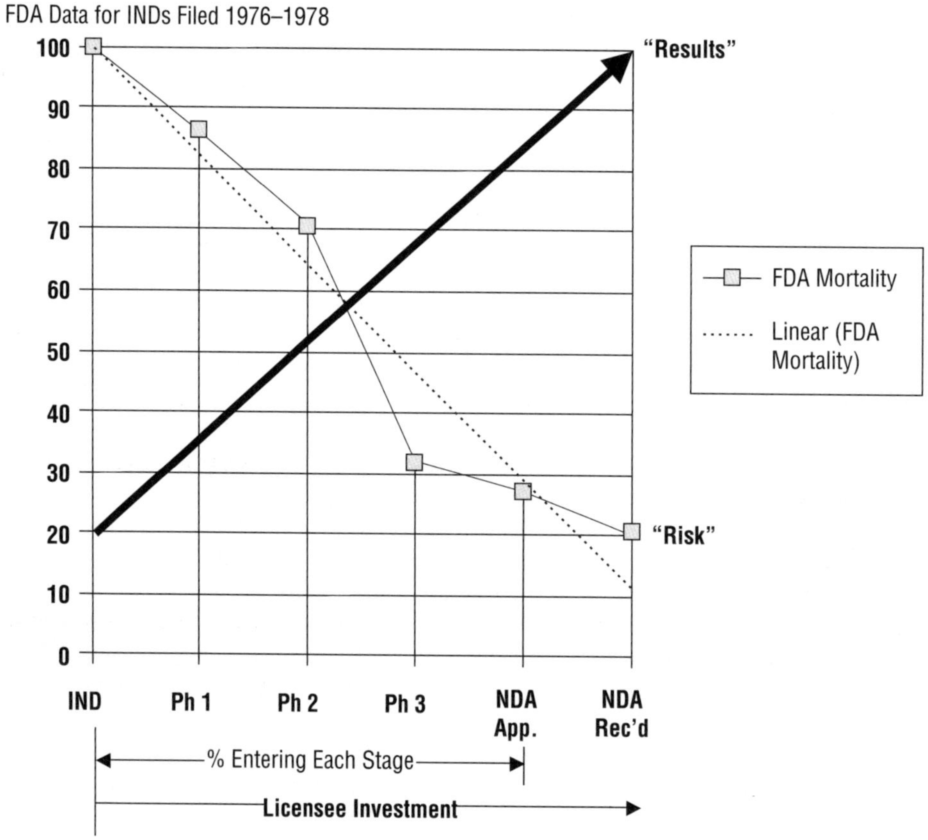

EXHIBIT 7.25 **Product Development as Results-Creating and Risk-Reduction**
Source: Scientific American, April 2000, p. 74.

process emerged with approval to be sold. If the licensor makes the investment and takes the risk of advancing the opportunity closer to FDA approval and hence commercialization then the appropriate RAHR for a license valuation will decrease and, correspondingly, the value of the projected cash flows will increase.[47]

Normally, multi-year investment projects are not funded irreversibly for all future years. Any investor, be it a CFO, a department profit and loss (P&L) manager with investment discretion, or a venture capital investor, initially committing to fund a new project opportunity does so knowing the perceived risk, and thereby the appropriate RAHR, is not static, fixed-for-life. During, say, the first investment year, it is expected that initial results will reduce at least some aspects of the risk, such as the technical (or R&D) risk, and perhaps also the market risk as the time to market introduction has been shortened by (ideally) at least one year. The risk, then, associated with the investment required in the second year should be perceived to be less than that used in the original DCF Method calculation.

Alternatively, things could go poorly during that first year—the R&D results are slower than expected or show less attractive performance or higher costs, or further market research could indicate this is a less attractive opportunity, or for some other reason. This would indicate that the RAHR associated with making follow on investments should be higher than that used in the original DCF Method calculation. Such effect could then mean continuing with the project no longer makes financial sense, and so it is restructured or terminated.

So, should one attempt at the time of developing the original DCF Method calculation to account for such varying RAHR year by year values? The general answer is "no." Although there is no mathematical law against doing year-by-year adjustments in RAHR in a DCF Method model, the underlying concept of RAHR and the DCF Method is that the value used is in some sense a weighted average value for the entire investment period. If we use the corporate target rate of return for all the investment cash outflows, such as 15 percent in the previous example, and the RAHR of 30 percent for all the cash inflows, we have accounted for, on an overall average basis, the expected ups and downs of a new opportunity creation.

In Chapter 8 we will consider how to value opportunities with dramatically changing risk profiles using Real Options, one of the Advanced Methods. By such method, we are effectively "slicing up" the financial model into segments of years. Each with its own incremental investment and risk model associated with the then forecasted future cash flows. For our purposes here in Chapter 7, we are treating risk as determined by the overall assessment of the investment project and assuming that such investment is being committed irreversibly. This ascribes a single RAHR value to the project as a whole.

Bad Data

Although the DCF Method can be applied to financial models based entirely on a bottom-up analysis of revenues and costs, it is common to use publicly reported accounting data to supplement such analysis or as a proxy in place of such analysis. The question then arises, how "good" is such data.

The first issue of "goodness" is the comparability of the publicly reported data to the subject technology valuation. As we discussed with the Industrial Standards Method (Method 1), comparability is not easy to apply to technology. In part this is because any particular technology tends to have certain key distinctives, but also because technology financial data is scarce. Startup technology companies are typically private and do not report their financials. Companies large enough to be public often have multiple products and even distinct businesses that are not individually reported upon in their public documents. Even if/when a comparable or group of comparables is found, one has to consider whether the reported financials are truly representative of the costs and profitability of a related technology. The public company could be overspending on SG&A because of a particular marketing or business development strategy that may be transitory, or even ill advised. There could be significant performance or maintenance issues unique to that company's products. Looking behind the financial data of any particular company, and looking at its peers, can lead to a better understanding as to what is behind the reported numbers. Detailed reports by analysts of the financials of the comparable company or the industry peers can provide further insight.

A second issue of "goodness" relates to the practical usability of public financial data. One affront on usability is caused by "restatements." Companies can make mistakes preparing their financials and so they publish after-the-fact corrections known as restatements; not all of these are innocent (more on this below). For the years 2004 through 2006, there were on average 600 annual restatements for exchange traded public companies.[48] The good news is that the rate of restatements declined in 2007 compared to 2005 and 2006. Another financial data challenge is "one time" effects. Such "one time" effects appear to be happening with some regularity. They could be caused by "restructuring," often a euphemism for the close-down of some failed business, but could also be the result of an "extraordinary" gain or loss such as the winning or losing end of a large law suit. Another challenge is dealing with simple obscuration. Public companies have the burden of reporting material financial data to the public; that's their deal for being public. However, companies do not want to make it any easier for competitors, and in some cases customers and employees, to know any more than necessary about internal operations and profitability. So the really pertinent information for a technology comparable may be subsumed in some aggregated reported figures.

Then there are the footnotes of financial reports to be considered. Companies may take certain accounting actions to increase their cash flow, unrelated to their actual business operations. One technique is to sell their accounts receivable, which accelerates, in the current reporting period, their cash flow. Capitalizing certain expenses has the same effect because it reduces the current period costs, leading to higher GCF for the same revenues.

Finally there exists "bad data" in the moral sense as to those responsible for its production. There, is now, and, sadly, always will be some outright fraudulent financial reporting. A recent fraud scorecard has been published relating to the President's Corporate Fraud Task Force. In July 2008 Department of Justice (DoJ) reported that since July 2002 convictions have been obtained against 214 chief executives, 128 VPs, and 23 corporate counsels.[49] Perhaps even more remarkably, 63 CFOs (chief *financial* officers) have been convicted during this period.[50] A significant number of these individuals have served or are serving prison sentences, some as long as 25 years; prison stripes, for some, have become a new form of business casual. The numbers of convictions, now well north of 1,000 and still counting, has led even the SEC to do a segmentation into five types, and whose instincts are self evident: the "Grifter," the "Borrower," the "Opportunist," the "Crowd-Follower" and the "Minimizer."[51]

Potential Manipulations and Misuse

The DCF Method is not uniquely subject to "Grifters," and others. However, the complexity of a particular financial model can be such that conscious fraud can be a challenge to uncover. There are other, more common temptations and misuse that we will consider here.

WORKING BACKWARDS TO GET "THE NUMBER" In the beginning of this chapter we cited a Jack Welch quote that expressed doubt on the value of DCF models and results. In closing this chapter we might as well consider another, even more famous, business world giant—Warren Buffet, sometimes known as the Oracle of Omaha.

Mr. Buffet's rise from modest circumstances to a builder of incredible long term value owning many different, and different kinds, of companies is storied. In addition to his great business success he remains modest, interesting,[52] and determined to give away more than $50 billion of accumulated wealth without drawing a lot of attention to himself.

He has been asked countless times to share his business "secrets." One common manifestation of the question is along the lines of "what hurdle rate [RAHR] do you use to decide on the best use of capital?" (As CEO of Berkshire Hathaway he oversees more than $30 billion in cash [2008] and is ultimately responsible for the capital allocation of some 20 companies). He has been an absolutely consistent champion of the simple idea that businesses are about providing returns to investors. Yet if one searches for his capital allocation criteria, a specific hurdle rate, or a table of such rates for various situations, none is known to exist. Recently, in a forum at the University of Pennsylvania Wharton School, famous for its business analytic orientation, he was asked about this issue. His reply:

> *The smaller capital expenditures, or even fairly large ones at the subsidiaries, they just do them themselves. They don't need me, because if some guy comes in to me and talks about something in the yarn plant or something in Georgia, what the hell do I know about it? I mean, they can always present it in a way that makes it look good. If I say the internal rate of return we demand is 15.83, it'll be 15.84. I mean, you just can bet on it. I've never seen a project that doesn't meet your hurdle rate, you know, if they really want to do it. We don't go through those charades.*[53]

What? The man who considers his primary task being the best allocation of capital does not rely or trust results from the DCF Method?

Berkshire is galvanized on "returns," namely earnings that exceed the capital investment. All the "chairman's letters" (Mr. Buffet) are available online.[54] By searching them for the word "returns" one finds it occurs throughout the letters. In Berkshire's "owners manual," first written for shareholders in 1996 by Warren Buffet and his colleague Charlie Munger of the company's guiding principles concludes [my commentary in brackets]:

> *Intrinsic value [in effect, the NPV] is an all-important concept that offers the only logical approach to evaluating the relative attractiveness of investments and businesses. Intrinsic value can be defined simply:* It is the discounted value of the cash that can be taken out of a business during its remaining life.
>
> *The calculation of intrinsic value, though, is not so simple [we know]. As our definition suggests, intrinsic value is an estimate [it is indeed] rather than a precise figure, and it is additionally an estimate that must be changed if rates move or forecasts of future cash flows are revised. Two people looking at the same set of facts, moreover — and this would apply even to Charlie and me — will almost inevitably come up with at least slightly different intrinsic value figures. That is one reason we never give you our estimates of intrinsic value [but they do measure value by such DCF Method]. What our annual reports do supply, though, are the facts that we ourselves use to calculate this value.*[55]

Warren Buffet's intrinsic value determination, namely the NPV value determined by the DCF Method, is what in the end yields those returns so fundamental to Berkshire's reason for being.

So why the absence of a specified hurdle rate (RAHR)? The answer is embedded in the Wharton Q&A, namely: If you quote a RAHR value as a necessary investment threshold then every proposed use of capital will have a DCF Model structured to exceed it.

In the early 1990s as the venture capital industry was beginning to expand its influence there emerged a growth industry in business plans seeking such investors. Although we will discuss venture capital investing in Chapter 10, this setting provides a further example of "design for the objective" DCF models. VCs, as they are known, at that time tended to use as cut off for consideration business plans that did not project at least $25 million in annual revenue run rate by the end of their third year. In a very short time, everyone knew the guideline, after which, no matter what, business plans were crafted projecting some number greater than $25 million.

One clear, and deeply wrong, response is to jumble anything and everything to make the result meet "the number." With complex financial models this is all too easy to do because it is extremely difficult for one not party to the analysis to be unable to find deeply and perversely hidden machinations.

A second, somewhat less regrettable approach is simply to boost ("juice") the assumptions in an otherwise fair DCF model to get to "the number." Again this is easier to do with complex models as in some cases a little "tweaking" of many assumptions can make a dramatic change in the predictions.

This approach may be justified by an attitude of "nobody knows what will happen anyway," or "you have to have a little optimism or you won't get out of bed." However, each time and to the extent that assumptions are extended to be more favorable there is a countereffect upon the RAHR value because there is an increased risk that such a projected outcome is unlikely to occur. In the next chapter we will use a more powerful mathematical tool that can quantify such decrease in probability of the outcome occurring.

A third approach is to create a new, coherent scenario of how the world would have to look for "the number" to be achieved. Defining a specific scenario that warrants a DCF model is a matter of judgment. Sometimes scenarios are defined early in the process of analysis and never reconsidered as understanding of the opportunity grows.

Working backwards from "the number" can lead to an inventive way to restructure the business plan. Although this can be simply another version of "juicing," there are circumstances where necessity does drive invention and a justifiably better business concept and financial model is created.

An example of potentially fruitful restructuring of the model is putting more emphasis on speed to market, because time to positive cash flow plays an important role in both increasing the NPV but also earlier revenues ideally combined with deferring some investment needs can also decrease the risk. Sometimes when a business plan is initially put together various team members build in some extra conservatism as "elbow room." Sometimes such conservatism also reflected a lack of urgency in completing development and getting the technology/products in the hands of customers, even just some initial ones for validation and cash flow.

One of the powerful results possible from a DCF Method is a gaining a deeper perspective on opportunity value which aids not only valuation but may also lead to a change in an overall business strategy. The core belief in our economic system is that returns are enhanced for everyone by the flow of capital from less profitable uses to more profitable ones (on a risk adjusted basis). This has to mean that capital is starved for those less attractive return-on-investment (low NPV) opportunities with the compensating gain that those opportunities that can provide greater returns on investment will get more investment. This is why we call this economy "capitalism," not "socialism."

If a project cannot be rescued by a dramatic redesign, then a lot of future pain and disappointment can be avoided by finding a different opportunity. Coachable business analysts are ones who can think it possible that their plan is not the best use of time and capital, and go on to something else.

The Warren Buffet caution about prescribed RAHR values, as the earlier caution by Jack Welch about DCF calculations is simply the realization that the human temptation is to make a "quick fix" and less inclined to the re-thinking of a potential redesigned business model or simply abandonment.

SEGMENT/SCENARIO EXPLOSION Excel spreadsheets once created can be recreated following different assumption sets, segments or scenarios, and varying assumptions over a range of values using Excel's TREND function to create an incomprehensibly fat file of possible future worlds. Remember that the goal of any valuation method is to develop a succinct model of what something is worth, perhaps simply as a single NPV value, or royalty rate so that an opportunity pricing can be codified in a page or two as a term sheet summary of the deal economics.

Too many segments, scenarios, and case studies can lead to "paralysis by analysis" and inhibit the ability to express judgment. We have also seen these inspiring posters with some beautiful picture and a short text extolling the virtues of teamwork or some such behavior. There is a website that offers anti-motivation posters, mostly in humor, called "demotivators." There is a particularly apt one for this DCF Method danger:

> *Madness does not always a howl. Sometimes it's the quiet voice at the end of the day saying, "Is there room in your head for one more?"*[56]

In summary, application of DCF methods is powerful and useful even with the limitations associated with long durations and high RAHR values, and it can be combined with a segment and scenario analysis to address different possible outcomes and overcome the risk-adjusted heavy discounting of future, risky cash flows. However, the calculations quickly get complex and are subject to difficulties of deciding what relative probabilities to ascribe to each set of scenario assumptions. Although the amazing power afforded by spreadsheets such as Excel can easily support essentially any level of analysis to which one is inclined to subject oneself, what happens is the results are obscured by the complexity and very little insight is available to negotiation planning and decision making. Further, self-, or other delusion is all too easy with a proliferation of "what if's."

Making financial complexity easier to both analyze and grasp is exactly what the Monte Carlo method addresses, which is dealt with in Chapter 8.

HUBRIS We began Chapter 7 with some equity valuation examples that ended up being wildly off the mark. The key conclusion of these examples is the DCF Method is not wrong because it was used (or misused) to make such forecasts. The results can be no better than the model plus the assumptions.

In closing this chapter it is a good idea to return to this subject and deal with the temptation for *hubris* that, in our context, is the overweening attitude of certainty about one's NPV result to the extent of being intolerant of any examination as to the underlying DCF Method that gets to that result. "Spreadsheet hubris" is a natural temptation. After one has invested significant hours creating, tweaking, comparing, checking, modifying, a model, and applying segmentation and scenario analysis, one tends to believe the result is both meaningful and "right." But it is a very good practice to keep in mind three things: (1) Any model can only be a *representation* of even a present reality let alone an omniscient lens into the future, (2) there's a reason that assumptions are called "assumptions"; we cannot know the future, and though we're paid to make better than random judgments about it, it is innate that things will turn out not exactly as we had thought no matter how careful and exact the calculation; and (3) we're human so it is very easy for simple typographical or cell calculation mistakes to occur and be missed even upon review.

However elusive certainty is, knowledge is attainable. Knowledge with humility gives space to useful observations (even corrections) of others, even by the other side in a negotiation, as we will discuss in Chapter 11.

Conclusion

The DCF method requires delving into the origins of expected profit from the use of the licensed technology. If this is done primarily by reliance on ratios, such as EBIT as a percentage of revenues projected by year, then the DCF Method has made use of such percentages as a type of ***Tool*** based on certain Rules of Thumb. Likewise the DCF equations can be used as a ***Tool*** which enables moving payments in time, such as reduced royalties, to create a larger upfront license fee. The DCF method can also provide insight into the sensitivity of the value to perceived risk (RAHR).

If the DCF Method is implemented by a detailed analysis of each component of the income and cash low methods, then it can provide significantly more insight, if there is a reasonable basis for making such analysis, than the use of proxy percentages, which is an application of the Rule of Thumb Method as a Tool for DCF analysis.

For the valuation of significant opportunities, the DCF Method is often used in addition to other methods to increase one's insight into value and confidence in the calculated result.

The DCF Method has an inherent combination of uncertainties and certainties. The uncertainties of course underlie any financial model, the assumptions needed as inputs to the model, and of course any forecast of the future. The certainties derive from the exact mathematics of the spreadsheet calculations and NPV result. Focusing on the certainties can lead to hubris. Obsessing with the uncertainties can lead to despair or, even worse, disparagement of the entire Method. But the essential reality of business is the responsibility for creating value for customers, employees, and owners—which are the audiences to which a CEO is responsible (Customers + Employees + Owners = CEO) in the face of uncertainty and risk. CEOs and everyone who supports the mission of any business are responsible for creating "alpha"-returns that exceed what investors can get from making comparatively low risk "mutual fund–like" investments. The DCF Method is a powerful, mathematically founded weapon that when wisely deployed can assist this mission.

Summarized below are the equations developed and used in this chapter.

- A or DCF = $B/(1 + k)^n$, where A or DCF is the present value of a future gross cash flow B, or, $A = B/(1 + k)^{(2n-1)/2}$, using the mid-year convention
- $B/A = (1 + k)^n$, where such B/A ratio is known as payback or baggers
- $B/A = (1 + k)^{(2n-1)/2}$, using the mid-year convention
- NPV = the sum of all the DCFs (noting outflows offset inflows)

Sources of Information to Develop Business Projections

There are a tremendous number of books, papers, and data sets that relate to the DCF Method, ranging from accounting and finance textbooks, to books and other writings on financial ratios, to published income and cashflow statements on thousands of companies. A representative example of such resources is given at my website: www.razgaitis.com.

Notes

1. John Keats, in a letter to Benjamin Bailey, March 13, 1818.
2. For the moment we will exclude from consideration the possibility that these end-of-year net cash inflows could be *greater* than $1,000. As we will see later in this chapter, most cash inflow forecasts have some possibility that the expected value will be exceeded under more favorable than expected circumstances.
3. The S&P 500 stock index has traded at an average price-to-earnings multiple of 14.5 for the 128-year period 1872 through 2000 (source: *Economic Review*, Publication of the Federal Reserve Bank of Kansas City, http://www.kc.frb.org/publicat/ ECON-REV/PDF/4Q00Shen.pdf).
4. "Sector Watch: Fuel Cells Fire Up Alternative Energy Stocks," by Beverly Goodman, *Red Herring*, December 18, 2000, p. 234.
5. Ibid.
6. Ibid.
7. However, because such analyses were done by two different people using two different sets of assumptions, and there is no universal RAHR scale, there is no assurance that the 17.5 percent RAHR used here with FCE really reflects a higher risk assessment than the 15 percent that was used with Ballard.
8. "Wireless Plaything," by Timothy J. Mullaney, *BusinessWeek* E.Biz, July 24, 2000, p. EB21.
9. "InfoSpace Evangelist," by Cory Johnson, *The Industry Standard*, March 20, 2000, p. 79.
10. I wonder how many plumbers have been so hired? And, in any case, NBCi in 2008 is simply a portal into NBC television programming.
11. "A Talk with Scott McNealy," by Editor-in-Chief Stephen B. Shepard, *BusinessWeek*, April 1, 2002, p. 66.

12. Sun (JAVA) had a 2:1 split in December 1999 and again in December 2000, and a 1:4 reverse split in November 2007.
13. Trade reference to "Year 2000." The years leading up to 2000 exhibited a frenzy of software updates because of the fear that legacy software would not properly account for years beyond 1999 (because in the early days coding was commonly done using just two digits for the year, e.g., after 99 would come exactly zero). It appears that the dot com "bubble" that collapsed in 2000, along with much of the telecom stock value, along with the completion of most of the Y2K software updates was "the perfect storm" of technology value collapse.
14. The famous and often-quoted line from the movie *Field of Dreams*. And, like a lot of lines in movies, the outcomes only happen in movies.
15. "When to Talk, When to Balk," *Ideas The Welch Way*, by Jack and Suzy Welch, *Business-Week*, April 30, 2007, p. 102.
16. www.brainyquote.com/quotes/authors/j/jack_welch.html
17. Thomas Wilson, Chief Insurance Risk Officer, ING Group, quoted in the *Wall Street Journal*, August 22, 2007, p. D10.
18. The value of k has to be based on the same time period as n in order for these equations to work. In all the examples provided, n was expressed in years; so, the value of k was given in annualized (yearly) values. One could use monthly periods, but in such an instance the k value would be interest expressed per month; for example, the future value (B) of a present sum (A) could be:

    $B/A = (1 + k)^n$
    For k = 12% on an annualized basis and a period of five years, one obtains
    $B/A = (1 + 0.12)^5 = 1.76$

    Equivalently, one could consider this same example as consisting of 60 monthly periods, such that n = 60. However, in such a case, k must be expressed as the monthly interest rate. Here, the equivalent monthly value of k is 0.9489 percent or 0.009489, so that

    $$B/A = (1 + 0.009489)^{60} = 1.76$$

19. ftp://ftp.bls.gov/pub/special.requests/cpi/cpiai.txt
20. Inflation plus time creates a dramatic effect. Over the past 100 years, in the United States, the cumulative effect of inflation is a factor of approximately 20: $1,000 at the time of 100 years ago would be worth just $50 today. One example of when inflation could be material to a technology license is Listerine® (the mouthwash). It was originally licensed April 20, 1881 for a fixed rate of $20 per 144 "bottles," which amount was negotiated down to $6 per 144 b four years later. It is believed that Pfizer, who makes and sells the product, continues to pay a royalty to the estate of the licensor. A middle class city dweller income in the 1880s was less than $1,000, compared, perhaps to the average of the middle quintile today of approximately $50,000. So, what was $6 in 1885, is about 12 cents today, or less than one-hundredth of a cent per bottle which may about what it costs to print just the name "Listerine" on the label.
21. As of this writing a one year T-Bill is no longer available. Six month T-Bills and two year "Notes" (as they are called) are available. However, the government now publishes an index known as CMT for Constant Maturity Treasury in which the various rates paid on the various treasury bills and bonds is converted to a constant, one year equivalent maturity.
22. A government T-bill pays the "coupon" rate of interest in two semiannual payments. So a $1,000 T-bill, with a five percent coupon, would pay $250 in each of two semiannual payments until maturity. Because such T-bills can be sold at any time prior to maturity,

the actual yield can be greater or lesser than the coupon rate because the selling price is unlikely to be exactly equal to the $1,000 maturity value.

23. The average coupon rate on a 10-year Treasury note was 7.25 percent for the 42 year period 1960–2002. Since 2002, the rate has declined to average less than 5 percent.
24. To be strictly accurate, the risk-free debt of comparison should be a U.S. five year bond, which normally provides a higher rate of return than the one year CMT rate. However, for our purposes the differences between such risk free one year, five year, and even ten year rates are not significant.
25. Shannon P. Pratt, *Cost of Capital, Estimation and Application*, 2nd Edition, John Wiley and Sons, Inc., 2002.
26. And in keeping with such high rates of return are high risks for VC's, their investors, and the management, employees, vendors, and customers of their invested companies. The average VC returns has been 41 percent in 1995, declining year after year to 18 percent in 1998, then surging to 160 percent in 1999, returning to 23 percent in 2000, and becoming negative (−20 percent) in 2001, and continued to be negative in 2002. By 2004, the one-year returns again exceeded 10 percent, and in 2005 it exceed 20 percent, according to data compiled by the National Venture Capital Association (www.ncva.org).
27. One question that naturally arises is how much of such expected gain is "real," in the sense of a true increase in purchasing power, and how much is simply a reflection of the deflation in the value of currency. The answer for high RAHR projects in periods of low inflation is "almost all of it." Specifically, for the example of three percent inflation, we can start with $1,000 now and calculate that such sum would only be worth $862.61 in five years. In other words currency five years hence is worth 86.261 percent of the same nominal value of currency today. So, for the 50 percent RAHR example, that calculated a present investment of $269.33 yielding $1,000 in five years, to make an inflation corrected comparison, such investment actually yields $862.61 in five years because the difference between $862.61 and $1,000 is the deflated value of the same denominated money. In inflation-corrected terms, the return on investment for a 50 percent RAHR is then 3.20 ($862.61/$269.33), not 3.71, and the effective RAHR or return rate is 26.2 percent.
28. http://espn.go.com/abcsports/wwos/e_knievel.html: On May 26, 1975, in front of 90,000 people at Wembley Stadium in London, Knievel successfully cleared 13 double-tiered buses but upon landing went flying over the motorcycle's handlebars. "Once he plummeted to the stadium floor, the momentum from the jump continued to pull, scrape and smear him for another 20 yards with his Harley in tow. But Knievel's problems did not end there. When his body finally came to a stop, the Harley landed directly on top of him. As a result, he broke his hand, re-injured his pelvis and had a compression fracture of a vertebra. Despite his condition, Evel was determined to, and did, walk out of the stadium." After the crash, he announced his retirement. However, just five months later on October 25, 1975, Knievel successfully jumped fourteen Greyhound buses at Kings Island, Ohio.
29. "A Method for Valuing High-Risk, Long-Term Investments: The Venture Capital Method," Harvard Business School Case Study, 9-288-006, published 1987, Rev. 6/89, Harvard Business School, Cambridge, MA.
30. Certain bonds can also be "called" by the debtor prior to maturity.
31. Of course the scope of the analysis could be expanded to include a financial analysis of losing the incumbent business, and on such basis conclude that the investment in the project has a high rate of return.
32. There are many proprietary spreadsheet software products available, including Apple's recently introduced Numbers. And with LINUX there are an increasing number of "shareware" and very low cost spreadsheets. However, Microsoft's Excel is widely considered to be the "gold standard." It is stable, robust, and has many extensions and templates available because of its long life and widespread adoption.

33. The seller's appropriate k value is normally different, and lower than the buyer's. The buyer is using the k value to scale risk and reward of a future investment. The seller is moving money expected to be paid in the future to the present. The discussion of such k values and how they relate to the weighted average corporate cost of capital is outside the scope of this book.
34. It should be noted that this is not the same use of 25 percent as the 25 Percent Rule of Chapter 6. The 25 Percent Rule applies to the split of EBIT.
35. A wonderful baseball term for a slow footed runner who, once they get on base, clogs up all base running possibilities. In business, basepath cloggers are all those infrastructure people and systems that do not add value but inhibit the speed at which things can get done.
36. One current example of the interface of uncertainty between science and economics has to do with the NPV of any future societal consequence of inaction, such as the issue of global warming. If the "cost" of inaction on global warming is (somehow) calculated to be $1 trillion 100 years from now, what is the economically justified present investment to avoid such cost? There are (at least) two competing economic theories (prioritarianism and utilitarianism) that lead to dramatically different discount rates (e.g., 6 percent versus 1.4 percent) leading to dramatically different NPV values ($2.5 billion versus $250 billion), leading to very different conclusions as to how much present expense is justifiable.
37. This discussion is a highly simplified treatment of management and financial accounting. There are entire professional disciplines and thousands of pages of standards and tax regulations that deal with all the particulars of the subject. Following the Einsteinian Principle of things should be made as simple as possible, but not too simple, developing cash flow projections for technology valuation faces its primary uncertainties in making reasonable estimates of revenues, development costs, and operating cost ratios that are not significantly affected by the myriad of possible accounting issues.
38. Tax issues are incredibly complicated. Companies in general pay income tax at both the federal and state level, and other tax districts as well, so called "subnational" taxing authorities. Certain kinds of expenses, including depreciation and amortization expenses are allowed deductions before the tax is applied. However, there exists a blizzard of tax adjustment issues such as carryforwardlosses, or tax abatement concessions, which affect the tax percentage calculation (PFT, for Provision for Taxes). This can create a significant difference between "statutory" rates and "effective" rates. Because each company has its own unique tax issues, and tax credits or concessions it may possess, any benefit it has by virtue of its "effective rate" are typically deemed by the company to be its own advantage. The marginal U.S. federal tax rate in 2007 for corporate income above $18.3 million is 35 percent. The various state tax rates vary in the general range of upper single digits (say 5 to 8 percent), putting the combined rate at over 40 percent. There is no simple answer as to what rate could or should be used for a technology GCF forecast. Typical practice appears to be reducing the statutory rates somewhat because deductions and allowances are normal, to values in the mid-30 percent range.
39. In addition to the shown investment in new PPE, 3M also invested in the purchase of new businesses, which is not shown; also it realized modest gains on the sale of previously acquired PPE and businesses. For simplicity, I have not shown these or other investing and financing activities that also had an effect on cash flow. The entries shown are the ones that correspond most closely to cash flow from operations, which is the focus of our interest.
40. For CAGR values 2 percentage points less than RAHR, the perpetuity equation calculation results in an error of only ca. 2 percent. For example, for a CAGR of 13 percent and an RAHR of 15 percent, the perpetuity calculation over-predicts the true NPV by ca. 1.2 percent. As the difference between CAGR and RAHR values increases, such over-prediction reduces to zero.

41. However, as we shall discuss, companies periodically "restate" their revenues or transform their businesses making it problematic to rely heavily on income and cash flow statements many years in the past.
42. Consider the simple everyday situation of a falling leaf, a much more complex question than Newton's falling apple. What would it be like to develop the system of equations that would accurately model a particular leaf falling from any particular branch under any condition of wind, sleet, snow, or hail? All the kings horses and all the kings men, and every Intel processor made in history harnessed by the world's smartest scientists, cannot solve that simple problem at an exact level. On the other hand a child with a $10 digital watch, a glass of lemonade, and several summer afternoons of observation lying on the warm grass can get an understanding of the answer that is reasonably, and surprisingly, accurate.
43. See Arthur Schopenhauer's classic work entitled: *The World as Will and Representation*, [or *Idea*] Dover Publications, 1969 translation from German by E.F.J. Payne of the work originally published in 1819 and a second edition in 1844.
44. Everitt M. Rogers, *The Diffusion of Innovations*, originally published in1962 and currently in its 5th edition, 2003, published by Free Press.
45. There are, of course, notable exceptions to S-Curve technology diffusion. Of the barrier type are examples where standardization, informal or formal, are simply unlikely to be abandoned. The QWERTY keyboard is a commonly cited example, also included is which side of the road we drive on, where the accelerator and brake pedals are located, and why we spell "enough" instead of "enuf." At the other extreme there are "game changers" whose adoption profile is more vertical than S-shaped, especially those associated with dramatically lower costs as well as unique performance advantages. Mobile phones would be one possible example, although the "product" was transformed by the introduction of bundled services and unlimited usage.
46. He was wrong on both counts. Columbus and everyone knew the world was round, but he had underestimated how big it was. He had no idea that North and South America occupied what he thought was an uninterrupted ocean between Western Europe and Eastern Asia. And what happened between the New World and the Old could hardly be called "trade."
47. They will also increase because presumably the time to market has shortened.
48. www.treas.gov/press/releases/reports/FinancialRestatements_1997_2006.pdf
49. www.usdoj.gov/opa/pr/2007/July/07_odag_507.html
50. www.cfo.com/article.cfm/9608130
51. http://sec.gov/news/speech/2008/spch090908lar.htm
52. Three examples of "interesting." He chose to remain in Omaha, avoiding the lure of various bastions of capitalism, and still lives in a modest house he has owned for fifty years. He participates in charity auctions in which he contributes, among other things, his (empty) wallet, a prize always the subject of hot bidding; and, by the way, he is giving to charity more than $30 billion through the Bill and Melinda Gates Foundation. When the Yankees broke off negotiations for a long term contract renewal with Alex Rodriquez, one of baseball's all time great players, Mr. Rodriquez met with Warren Buffet, a huge baseball fan, to develop a strategy for smoothing over the situation and restarting negotiations.
53. Posted by a blogger based on an interview with Warren Buffet at the University of Pennsylvania's Wharton Business School in May 2008: http://sgxinvestment.blogspot.com/2008_05_01_archive.html.
54. www.berkshirehathaway.com/letters/letters.html
55. www.berkshirehathaway.com/ownman.pdf
56. www.despair.com.

CHAPTER 8

Method 5: Advanced Valuation Methods

Monte Carlo and Real Options

A-M-T

Licensing D-V-D

	A: Approaches	M: Methods	T: Tools
D	Discovery	NPV v. Risk	Rating/Ranking DCF
V	**Valuation** TR R^k A DE	1. Industry Standards 2. Rating/Ranking 3. Rules of Thumb 4. Discounted Cash Flow (NPV) 5. **Monte Carlo; Real Options** 6. Auctions	> Rating/Ranking > Rules of Thumb > Discounted Cash > Risk Assessmemt
D	Dealmaking	Deal Structures Dealmaking-Process Plan B	Rating/Ranking DCF/NPV Monte Carlo Real Options

Chapter 7 presented a mathematical structure for performing valuation using projected, or *pro forma*, income and cash flow statements, together with equations and methodology to assess the present value of future sums based upon timing and risk. Such Discounted Cash Flow Method is the most mathematical valuation approach considered thus far. It is well established as a standard valuation tool used in many contexts from bonds to equities to technology asset sales and licenses.

In recent years, more sophisticated methods of valuation have been developed and are being applied with increasing frequency. In this chapter, two such advanced methods will be considered: Monte Carlo (or Probabilistic) and Real Option Methods.

The Monte Carlo and Real Options ***Methods*** are the fifth of six methods that comprise the ***Approach*** of Valuation. Technology ***Valuation***, the ***V*** of Licensing D-V-D, is that ***Approach*** that quantifies what a technology opportunity is worth in economic terms. The term ***Approach*** is used to categorize a core business process—in Chapters 4 through 9, a determination of value is found by following one or more ***Methods***.

As in previous ***Method*** chapters, our development of the valuation ***Methods*** in this chapter will also lead us to identify specific ***Tools*** in support of other methods, and the ***Approaches*** of opportunity ***Discovery*** and ***Dealmaking***, the two "***D***'s" that bookend the acronym ***Technology/Licensing D-V-D***. The sections of this chapter that relate specifically to identification of ***Tools*** will be shown in shaded text.

Both Monte Carlo and Real Options Methods are based upon the Discounted Cash Flow Method. They are similar methods in that both are based on cash flow models derived from specific assumptions about revenues and costs. However, they differ from the DCF Method of Chapter 7 in important ways. With the Monte Carlo Method, one is not constrained to make single value (or "point") predictions of key variables such as revenues, costs, or even the technical risk of success; instead, estimates are made of ranges of outcomes with associated probabilities. Surprisingly, in many cases this turns out to be easier to do than making discrete value projections, and it can provide a deeper, more cogent insight than a multiplicity of scenarios following the classic DCF Method.

The second **Method** considered in this chapter is Real Options. Calculations using the DCF Method play an important role here as well. When dealing with long-lived projects, particularly when the expenses are significant and early, and the projected returns are far into the future, the use of a single Risk-Adjusted Hurdle Rates (RAHR, or k) tends to make such projects look economically unattractive because of the heavy discounting that takes place by the DCF Equaiton:

$DCF = GCF/(1 + RAHR)^n$, where GCF is Gross Cash Flow in year n, and DCF is the Discounted Cash Flow, which when summed for all projected years yields the NPV (Net Present Value). Alternatively, using the mid-year convention, the exponent is not the year n but the mid-year as determined by: $2 * (n-1)/2$, so, for example, for year 10, using the mid-year convention, the exponent is 9.5 not 10.0.

When n or RAHR is large in the above DCF equation even large, gross cash inflows in distant years results in a small or even negative NPV for the opportunity. Option methods can be useful in such circumstances.

We will begin this chapter by considering as another "advanced" method the Probability Tree Method, or sometimes referred to as the Decision Analytics Method. To introduce the use of probability trees, we will first return to the issue of scenarios and the DCF method.

Modified Discounted Cash Flow Method

Let us consider again the DCF Method example introduced in Chapter 7 as Exhibit 7.8, shown below as Exhibit 8.1

The NPV of the GCFs (Gross Cash Flows) ranged from \$1.6 million to \$126 million, shown in the right most column, for the five different RAHR (or k) values: 30, 20, 15, 5, and 0 percent, for three periods: Years 1 through 10, 11 through 20, and 1 through 20. As was discussed in Chapter 7, one of the challenges in using the DCF Method is that a single RAHR value is used for all future cash flows which, when (1) the project life is long, and (2) the risk assessment at the time of valuation leads to a comparatively high RAHR value, the distant DCF values for even substantial projected cash inflows contribute very little to the NPV. Exhibit 8.1 demonstrates this for the row corresponding to RAHR = 30 percent: no single year DCF value exceeds \$1 million, even though the projected GCFs are \$10 million or greater for each of the nine year periods beginning with Year 9.

Year	RAHR, k	1	2	3	4	5	6	7	8	9	10	Total 1-10
GCF	0%	$ (1)	$ (1)	$ (2)	$ (3)	$ (2)	$ (1)	$ 1	$ 5	$ 10	$ 13	$ 19
		Net cash outflow years ("investment")						Cash inflow years...				
DCF	5%	$ (1.0)	$ (0.9)	$ (1.7)	$ (2.5)	$ (1.6)	$ (0.7)	$ 0.7	$ 3.4	$ 6.4	$ 8.0	$ 10.2
DCF	15%	$ (0.9)	$ (0.8)	$ (1.3)	$ (1.7)	$ (1.0)	$ (0.4)	$ 0.4	$ 1.6	$ 2.8	$ 3.2	$ 2.0
DCF	20%	$ (0.8)	$ (0.7)	$ (1.2)	$ (1.4)	$ (0.8)	$ (0.3)	$ 0.3	$ 1.2	$ 1.9	$ 2.1	$ 0.2
DCF	30%	$ (0.8)	$ (0.6)	$ (0.9)	$ (1.1)	$ (0.5)	$ (0.2)	$ 0.2	$ 0.6	$ 0.9	$ 0.9	$ (1.4)

Year	RAHR, k	11	12	13	14	15	16	17	18	19	20	Total 11-20	Total 1-20
GCF	0%	$ 14	$ 15	$ 15	$ 15	$ 14	$ 13	$ 10	$ 8	$ 3	$ -	$ 107	$ 126
		Cash inflow years...											
DCF	5%	$ 8.2	$ 8.4	$ 8.0	$ 7.6	$ 6.7	$ 6.0	$ 4.4	$ 3.3	$ 1.2	$ -	$ 53.6	$ 63.8
DCF	15%	$ 3.0	$ 2.8	$ 2.4	$ 2.1	$ 1.7	$ 1.4	$ 0.9	$ 0.6	$ 0.2	$ -	$ 15.3	$ 17.3
DCF	20%	$ 1.9	$ 1.7	$ 1.4	$ 1.2	$ 0.9	$ 0.7	$ 0.5	$ 0.3	$ 0.1	$ -	$ 8.6	$ 8.8
DCF	30%	$ 0.8	$ 0.6	$ 0.5	$ 0.4	$ 0.3	$ 0.2	$ 0.1	$ 0.1	$ 0.0	$ -	$ 3.0	$ 1.6

EXHIBIT 8.1 Example DCF Method Calculation

This outcome of a less than $2 million NPV seems too pessimistic for an opportunity that is forecast to generate more than $100 million in total GCF with a peak year value of $15 million. The obvious cause of such a low NPV is that each year is discounted by the compounding value of the factor $(1 + \text{RAHR})^n$, which for a RAHR value of 30 percent is 1.3^n, so that when, say $n \geq 10$, the factor being divided into GCF to determine the DCF is ≥ 13.8.

For projects that end, by IPO or strategic acquisition, or by a paid up license, in five years or less, this compounding effect can be serious but not catastrophic. For pharmaceutical projects, or large scale factory based technologies, where the first revenues may not occur for seven or even ten years after a technology license, using high values of RAHR make it difficult to justify an, or any, investment. This is likewise true for very long-lived technology licensing life projects for which a lump sum payment determined by an NPV is the sole or primary form of compensation. Businesses clearly find it advantageous to invest in projects that have short times to significant cash inflows. But many commercially significant opportunities just will not be realized without risk, a long term commitment, and significant near term investments.

The question logically arises, why is this aspect of the DCF Method not a "problem" when it is used in equity valuations, as we considered in the beginning of Chapter 7? There are two general answers. First, for companies with stable present earnings, there are net cash inflows beginning from the very first year post investment and likely growing gradually over time, with such growth also being evidenced in the first year or so. Discounting then occurs with all years, but there are substantial near-term cash inflows for which the effect of discounting is relatively small. Further, the projected growth component of earnings, which by definition such "growth" component increases from zero to some larger number with time, is typically comparatively small to the baseline of earning expected from the first year. For a company with a projected growth in earnings of ten percent per year (CAGR), clearly 100 percent of the initial year and 90 percent of the next year represent baseline earnings that are usually considered to be both high in dollar magnitude and low in risk. This combination of significant immediate cash inflows and low risk is not the situation for most technology investments.

The second equity situation is for companies with very low present earnings but very high growth in earnings prospects, such as the fuel cell company examples given at the beginning of Chapter 7. This combination of low, or no, present earnings and high prospects is parallel to technology licensing and, accordingly, experiences the same DCF Method challenges. For equity valuations, as with the fuel cell examples, the time periods used for anticipated realization of those expected future dramatic earnings tends to be short, such as five years, and the perceived RAHR values tend to be somewhat lower than technology licenses in part because the company and its markets exist in some already demonstrable form. If the DCF Method is used with n = 3 to 5, and RAHR less than 20 percent, the severe discounting shown in Exhibit 8.1 is greatly ameliorated. What then about all the value in the future years beyond such n = 3 to 5? Typically what is done is to assume a value of the company at the end of such period as an added value to the DCF calculation.

One can think of the utilities of Advanced Methods covered in this chapter as developing modifications to the DCF Method for circumstances where the combination of high risk and long project life provides overly pessimistic NPV projections. Before we develop the Monte Carlo and Real Options Methods, let us first consider some simpler, more direct modifications of the DCF Method.

Use of Scenarios

In Chapter 7 we considered the use of scenarios as enhancements of the DCF Method because it allowed, in principle, assessment of multiple financial models for any given opportunity that are more optimistic and less optimistic than a "base" (aka "most likely") case. Usually what is intended by consideration of an "optimistic" case is more "aggressive" business assumptions such as a higher potential market size, and/or a shorter time to market, and/or higher growth rate (CAGR), and/or lower COGS (Cost of Goods Sold), and so on. Making such assumptions should not, however, result in a lower RAHR; if anything, the RAHR value could be made larger, though usually this is not done because one is seeking to assess the sensitivity of what such more aggressive assumptions has upon the NPV value.

So, although using scenarios with the DCF Method can be used to create a range of NPV projections, by itself it does not resolve the underlying calculation that high RAHR values and distant cash flows contribute little to NPV values.

Use of Dynamic RAHR Values

Another possible modification to the DCF Method is to reduce the RAHR value with increasing time. So in the example of Exhibit 8.1, the starting RAHR value may be taken as something higher than 30 percent, say even 40 percent, for the first year or two during the period of highest risk. Then, say, starting in Year 3, the RAHR value is lowered to 30 percent, perhaps followed by 20 percent in Years 5 through 8, with all subsequent years using an RAHR value of, 10 percent. Clearly this modification "solves" the 'problem' of heavily discounting outer year GCF values, but is it a reasonable approach?

Although the logic of reducing RAHR values with time seems reasonable, the justification hinges on the controllability of the investment commitment. Implicit in Exhibit 8.1 is the assumption that all of the investment monies, namely the GCF outflows, will occur regardless of what happens during Years 1 through 6, for a total "sunk cost" of $10 million. This concept could be termed the "in for a penny, in for a pound" or "all in" model, namely: Once the project is authorized, "green lighted," then all the investment must be made before one knows anything more about the risk reward profile.

However, most investments are not made on such basis. Rather they are made on the "spend a little, learn a little model." A simple way of thinking about this is the investment of Exhibit 8.1 could be decided year by year, such that at the beginning of Year 1 the only commitment made is to expend the $1 million cash outflow during Year 1. Then at the beginning of Year 2 a separate go/no-go decision is then made regarding the $1 million investment needed for Year 2, and so forth. The advantage of such approach is that the Year 2 and subsequent year investments are, for this example, not irreversible obligations and the later year investment decisions can be made with superior information than available at the beginning of Year 1. Although such superior information could cause an investor to be more pessimistic because of less than favorable first year results.

However, if there is favorable progress during Year 1, then a DCF Method could be applied at the start of Year 2, as though this were an entirely new project, even if we then used exactly the same GCF projections as given in Exhibit 8.1 but now Year 2 is really Year 1 and so forth, making it a 19 year projection. If the results of Year 1 were favorable, the appropriate RAHR value might then be reduced to, from the 30 percent value used in this example to, say, 25 percent.

This year-by-year process would be repeated at the beginning of originally designated Years 3 through 6. If progress continued to be made, further reductions, year by year, in the RAHR value used for all future years could be justified.

This "spend a little, learn a little" financial modeling structure is compatible with "stage gate" project development, a process widely considered to be a "best practice" for new product development. Another expression commonly used is, "let's not dig big holes," meaning the development plan should not start with the premise of success justifying a huge capital investment, such as a world scale production facility. But rather, with a bench scale demonstration, followed by a "semi-works," pilot plant, and only when technology and market demonstration has occurred, by the 'big hole' factory. The development of FDA approved new pharmaceuticals has a similar staged approach, although motivated for concerns of safety, in that each "phase" of new drug development has concrete entrance criteria and commensurately, investment requirements that increase as one goes further down the path to drug approval.

However, a development plan based on the "spend a little, learn a little" model usually differs in important ways both in terms of the investment levels (cash outflows) and the time to significant returns on investment (cash inflows). This is because staging the investment in such a way to diminish risk typically requires greater total investment and longer investment periods. Risk minimization is not usually achievable without cost. In the earlier example, we assumed that after Year 1, we could simply step into Year 2 as though it were a new project Year 1 with the same investment requirements as had been originally estimated with the same commercial introduction timeline and revenue growth. However, what is likely is the need to have larger investments than originally modeled and a delay and diminishing in the cash inflows in subsequent years. Although the RAHR values year by year are decreasing, presuming success, making the denominator of the DCF calculation smaller, the GCF outflows are larger and longer in duration while the inflows are smaller and delayed than used in single-valued RAHR model of Exhibit 8.1. The net effect on NPV value may still be an improvement compared to Exhibit 8.1 but the magnitude of such improvement will be less than would be calculated by a simple year-by-year reduction in RAHR value.

Another real world effect that often arises is the added cost to a buyer (technology licensee) because, depending upon the deal structure, the seller reasonably expects to be paid additional compensation to accommodate the buyer's desire to limit its financial outlays. If the deal structure is a pure running royalty, with zero upfront payments and zero minimum royalties or other time period payments, then the buyer can delay its investment at no Dealmaking cost. Usually, as to be discussed in Chapter 10, at least some upfront payment is required, along with possibly other payments. If the buyer seeks some kind of risk-minimization structure as described in the stage gate approach, it could also require an increase in the IP payments associated with the license.

In a paper, Ashley Stevens has extensively described the use of such a stage-gating process on RAHR.[1] In this paper he contrasts such adjusted NPV, designated by raNPV (for risk adjusted NPV) with valuation models done by Hambrecht & Quist[2] Lehman Brothers[3] (the former company no longer exists as an independent company but is part of JPMorganChase, and the latter went bankrupt in 2008).

The Use of Probability Trees for Valuation

One method, with strong visual appeal, is the use of probability trees for valuation. Sometimes this modification of the DCF Method is referred to as "decision analytics."

The core idea behind the probability tree modification is to de-aggregate the RAHR into its two components: one component that represents the opportunity cost value of money, and the other component expresses all the various risk factors present.

This method is best explained from an example. Consider the example in Exhibit 8.2.

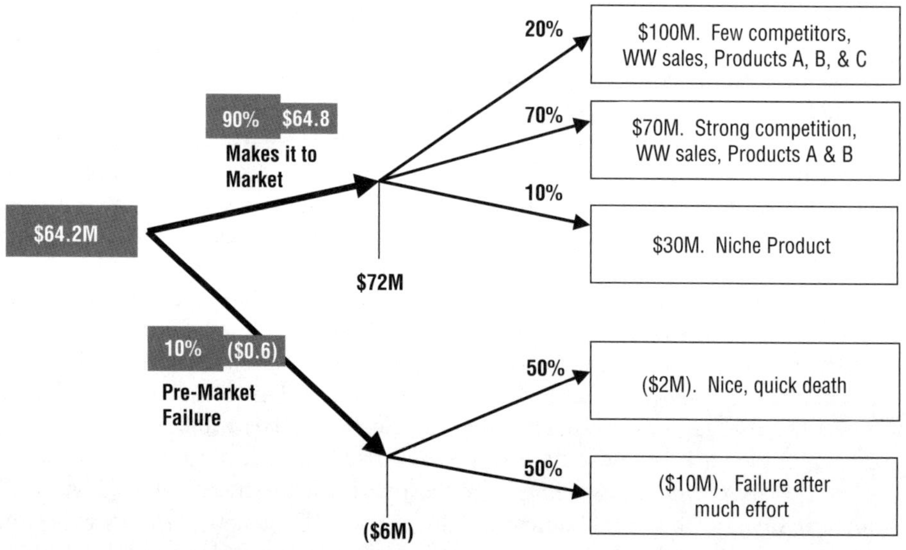

EXHIBIT 8.2 Probability Tree Valuation Example

Source: © Razgaitis, richard@razgaitis.com.

Valuation using decision trees is best viewed from right to left, from the end back to the beginning. Shown in Exhibit 8.2, in the five boxes on the right hand side, are five perceived scenarios or outcomes going from highest to lowest in value as one goes from the top to the bottom. Three of them are associated with commercial success, and two of them with failure. For purposes of this illustration, we will assume that all the monetary values associated with this figure are on an appropriated discounted basis, such as a company's WACC or at some nominal margin above such WACC as may be used by a company to apply an opportunity cost to its internal investments. As used here, "scenarios" does not mean the same thing as discussed in Chapter 7, although both usages refer to conceived future outcomes. "Scenarios" in Chapter 7 were expressed through a set of different, coherent assumptions that then were applied to the financial model to make NPV forecasts. Here, as we will see, the term "scenarios" is used in a similar but not exactly identical way.

Referring to Exhibit 8.2, for the three commercially successful outcomes shown at the top conjunction of three arrows, we can conceive of a baseline or most likely result, shown by the \$70 million outcome, but we can also readily visualize an even better possibility and one worse. Probability trees can be made to work with any number of such scenarios, but a common approach is to use two or three at a particular branch point. Failure also needs to be considered. Sometimes one uses only one failure condition, but here are shown two: a nice, quick death[4] due to obvious failure, and a slow painful one (that is often the more costly).

For each of these five scenarios, one would calculate the value of the outcome using the DCF Method of Chapter 7. It is important that in developing such scenarios that the underlying assumptions are self-consistent. In other words, if one assumes a high scenario situation, all the underlying assumptions should be logically related with this envisioned situation.

The essence of the probability tree valuation method is projecting the weighted probabilities of each of the hypothesized scenarios coming to pass. For the commercially successful three outcomes, it is common to heavily weight the mid- or baseline scenario as by definition it is perceived to be the most likely one; in this example it is assumed that there is a 70 percent likelihood of it being the outcome. Then by some similar means one assesses the probability of the high and low scenarios occurring; shown here they are 20 percent and 10 percent, respectively. The probability tree method then simply determines the value of node to the left of these three commercially successful outcomes as the weighted average of the respective probabilities multiplied by their value, namely: $0.2 \times 100 + 0.7 \times 70 \times 0.1 \times 30 =$ \$64.8 million.

A similar analysis is done for the two failure scenarios (here taken to be equally likely) yielding a weighted loss of \$0.6 million.

Finally, the method requires the specification of the relative probability of success versus failure. Here it is taken as 90:10 (90 percent probability that one of the three successful scenarios will result). The value, then, of the opportunity is simply determined by: $0.9 \times \$64.8 + 0.1 \times (-\$0.6) = \$64.2$ million.

The appeal of this method is compelling and obvious. The problem is determining the appropriate probabilities of each of the five scenarios. How would one know that the breakdown is 20 percent, 70 percent, and 10 percent for the three successes, and that 90 percent of the time one of the successes will occur? One way would be to have a very large portfolio of very similar projects for which there is an established track record. This affords the power of history with the law of large numbers. However, for technology opportunities, there is normally an inherent uniqueness about each one and it is difficult to correlate success probabilities to historic numbers, even in such circumstances where such numbers were known. Yet, people with lots of experience, the equivalent of the world-famous heart surgeon, the late Dr. DeBakey who, from a lifetime of experience, can often render just such judgment.

Applying a probability tree to Exhibit 8.1, we can take the following, illustrative approach:

- The opportunity cost of money to the buyer, namely what return it could reasonably expect to make by investing in some alternative to the technology being considered and whose return on investment is 15 percent.
- Based on prior experience, which is in effect a tool-based application of Method 1 (Industry Standards) plus Method 2 (Rating/Ranking), the probability of achieving commercial success as defined by the projected GCF values is 50 percent.
- Project failure, whose probability is then 50 percent, will have an NPV cost of a negative \$4 million.

The NPV value can then be calculated for this simple probability tree by:

$$\text{NPV} = 0.50 * \$17.3 \text{ million} - 0.5 * \$4 \text{ million} = \$6.65 \text{ million},$$

where the \$17.3 million is determined in Exhibit 8.1 by the NPV for a RAHR of 15 percent, the negative \$4 million based on experience, and the 50:50 relative probabilities by some expert judgment based in part on experience.

Such \$6.65 million NPV is a factor of more than four times higher than the Exhibit 8.1 NPV using an RAHR value of 30 percent. So even applying only a 50 percent probability of success, and including a significant cost associated with the other 50 percent probability for the corresponding outcome of failure, the NPV is estimated to be substantially higher. In this example, the difference in NPV values calculated is because of the combination of a very long project timeline, 20 years, and high RAHR value—30 percent—compared to a 15 percent value used for an opportunity cost discount rate.

The use of probability trees is a very straightforward modification of the DCF Method, and can be implemented at any level of complexity desired. In addition to having multiple parallel outcomes, such as the five we discussed in Exhibit 8.2, we could have a parallel-series structure whereby we could consider a sequence of outcomes followed by yet other outcomes dependent upon initial outcomes creating a diagram that expands rightward across the page. Instead of simply assuming "optimistic," "base," and "pessimistic," as shown, we could use multiple intermediate outcomes, such as "first customer order exceeding \$1 million," or "R&D demonstration completed by Year 3." Subsequent to such earlier outcomes, the tree would branch second and third and any number of subsequent parallel outcomes. The NPV is determined in exactly the same way as discussed with Exhibit 8.2, working from right to left, the end to the beginning, summing up the NPV value at each "node" based upon the NPV values for each resulting scenario.

The challenge of using probability trees comes not from complexity of calculation but having a reasonable basis for making the assumed probability estimates.

Suppose in our above probability tree for Exhibit 8.1, instead of a 50:50 probability split between success and failure, let us assume the outcome is failure-weighted 75:25. The probability tree calculation would then be:

$$NPV = 0.25 * \$17.3 \text{ million} - 0.75 * \$4 \text{ million} = \$1.325 \text{ million}.$$

Such a projection shows an even less favorable NPV than Exhibit 8.1 for a RAHR value of 30 percent, namely $1.6 million. This simple illustration shows that the use of probability trees does not automatically predict higher NPV values and, most importantly, the calculation is critically dependent on the relative probabilities.

For any specific situation, the ability to make supported assumptions for relative probabilities used in a tree calculation could be as defendable as that of an RAHR estimate. This is especially the situation when there exists a track record (comparables) and/or a reasonable basis for making adjusted probabilities estimates (rating/ranking) from a prior history or expert judgment. There are (at least) two "howevers": (1) Investors are calibrated to think in terms of capital put at risk for some particular promise of reward which is more compatible with RAHR-determined NPV values, and (2) it is easier and likely more tempting to use probability factors adjusted so as to predict the desired end result.

Another approach would be to combine this method with Monte Carlo. Using Monte Carlo, one can make estimates of the probability of different scenarios by doing aggregations among the (say) thousands of potential outcomes. In a sense, Monte Carlo provides a comparative probability for any particular NPV outcome based upon the uncertainty of the key assumptions used in the financial model.

Monte Carlo Method

The Monte Carlo Method, more generally known as probabilistic techniques, has a long history, primarily in engineering applications. This powerful analytical tool emerged from science and engineering analysis and was given the coined name Monte Carlo because it uses discrete probabilities to make forecasts much as a sophisticated gambler might do. Its traditional uses have been in domains for which the algebraic complexities are effectively unsolvable. In business applications, the complexity is usually not the algebra but the otherwise incomprehensible spectrum of possible future outcomes as they affect a present decision.

One key feature of Monte Carlo is that it does not produce a single-value answer. As we have seen earlier with the DCF Method, once a set of assumptions is imposed, a single-value answer results. However, what happens in practice is an extensive investigation of "what ifs" that look at the effect of certain assumptions, the creation of alternative scenarios, the sensitivity of alternative discount rates, or other changing factors. So, in practice, the DCF Method rarely is used solely to obtain a single-value answer.

In a somewhat similar, but more powerful, way, the result from a Monte Carlo analysis is a distribution of the NPV of many possible future outcomes. By analyzing such distributions one can reach judgments as to the present value of the overall opportunity even though one does not, and generally cannot, know which outcome will occur. So the uncertainty we observed in the DCF Method concerning future outcomes is not eliminated by the use of Monte Carlo. Rather, Monte Carlo provides a more powerful means of characterizing such possible future outcomes and interpreting the present value of all such possible outcomes.

Within the past 25 years, probabilistic tools have been increasingly applied to business modeling in support of decision making of many kinds, including valuation. Probabilistic calculations are very powerful ways to solve equations and situations so complex that a closed form solution is not possible.[5] With the advent of powerful and inexpensive personal computers, such sophisticated tools are now widely available although not yet widely used. However, in most MBA programs, the Monte Carlo techniques are taught, used, and required. Monte Carlo techniques will be increasingly used in license valuation contexts.

As of this writing, Monte Carlo simulation software for personal computers is not part of standard spreadsheet software packages such as Microsoft's Excel or Apple's Numbers, or other products. Some enterprising folks have created simple versions of Monte Carlo by using the "insert" "function" capability in Excel. This is relatively easy to do for simulating purely random variations in specific assumption cells. Crystal Ball and @Risk are two commercially available Monte Carlo software products that work in conjunction with Microsoft's Excel that provide a much richer capability of modeling and reporting, and are extremely user friendly.

- Crystal Ball by Decisioneering, Inc., now a division of Oracle Corporation (www.oracle.com/crystalball)
- @Risk by Palisade Corporation (www.palisade.com)

They each work in conjunction with, and require, a spreadsheet program. Different MBA programs have standardized one or the other of these Monte Carlo products; they each have a prestigious list of university adoptions. Although both products are suitable for use in technology/license valuation contexts, the examples provided in this chapter have been obtained using Crystal Ball although the methodology is common to any Monte Carlo based method.

To illustrate the Monte Carlo method we will initially use the cash flow projection example given as Exhibit 8.3. In this context, we will assume that Exhibit 8.3 is the projected situation agreed to by both seller and buyer for the purpose of valuing a technology license. It relies on the nominal value of the various income percentages shown in Column B of the exhibit based on a top-down approach using some appropriate comparables. Exhibit 8.3 shows the DCF Method calculation of NPV, based upon an assumed RAHR of 25 percent, resulting in $452,827 as shown.

In the screen shot of Exhibit 8.3 the header row just below the blue bar designation of "Microsoft Excel" is the standard Excel toolbar with menu pulldowns for Excel except for the three entries between Window and Help that have been added by Crystal Ball, namely: Define, Run, and Analyze. In the toolbar immediately below the Excel toolbar, with the symbol that looks like a small hill, are the menu pulldowns also loaded into Excel for use by Crystal Ball.

This financial model shown in Exhibit 8.3 uses the single valued assumptions shown in italics in Column B, including the RAHR of 25 percent. If the buyer and seller agreed with such assumptions and risk, they would conclude that the licensing opportunity was "worth" approximately $453K. As discussed in Chapter 7, the perspective on the RAHR selected (25 percent) determines whether the buyer would be willing to pay as much as $453K. In our consideration of the Monte Carlo

Year		1	2	3	4	5	6	Totals
Number of Units Sold (Note 1)		100	200	300	350	400	400	292 *Avg*
Average Selling Price (1)		$ 10,000	$ 10,000	$ 9,500	$ 9,000	$ 8,000	$ 8,000	*$ 9,083 Avg*
Revenues		$ 1,000,000	$ 2,000,000	$ 2,850,000	$ 3,150,000	$ 3,200,000	$ 3,200,000	$ 15,400,000
Cost of Goods Sold	*57%*	$ 570,000	$ 1,140,000	$ 1,624,500	$ 1,795,500	$ 1,824,000	$ 1,824,000	$ 8,778,000
SG&A and R&D	*35%*	$ 350,000	$ 700,000	$ 997,500	$ 1,102,500	$ 1,120,000	$ 1,120,000	$ 5,390,000
Earning Before Interest & Taxes	*22%*	$ 80,000	$ 160,000	$ 228,000	$ 252,000	$ 256,000	$ 256,000	$ 1,232,000
Provision for Taxes	*32%*	$ 25,600	$ 51,200	$ 72,960	$ 80,640	$ 81,920	$ 81,920	$ 394,240
Earnings After Tax		$ 54,400	$ 108,800	$ 155,040	$ 171,360	$ 174,080	$ 174,080	$ 837,760
Depreciation (2)	*5%*	$ 28,500	$ 57,000	$ 81,225	$ 89,775	$ 91,200	$ 91,200	$ 438,900
Increase in Investment (3)	*10%*	$ 100,000	$ 85,000	$ 30,000	$ 5,000	$ -	$ -	$ 220,000
Gross Cash Flow		$ (17,100)	$ 80,800	$ 206,265	$ 256,135	$ 265,280	$ 265,280	$ 1,056,660
Risk Adjusted Hurdle Rate, k	*25%*							
Discounted Cash Flow (4)		$ (15,295)	$ 57,816	$ 118,073	$ 117,296	$ 97,187	$ 77,750	$ 452,827
Net Present Value		$ 452,827						

Note 1 Starting with Year 2, the cell value is determined by a difference from the preceding Year
2 Taken of the Cost of Goods Sold
3 Taken of the increase in year-over-year revenues
4 Using mid-year convention

EXHIBIT 8.3 Monte Carlo Example Based on Exhibit 7.17

Method, we will make certain probabilistic assumptions of the factors in this model to obtain a richer understanding of the NPV value of this hypothetical license and in so doing will use a different, and lower RAHR value than shown.

How the Monte Carlo Method Works

The basic idea behind the Monte Carlo Method is that instead of prescribing a particular value for a cell in a spreadsheet model of a valuation, one prescribes an expression for the cell based upon some mathematical model of reality. Accordingly, a single spreadsheet model does not perform just a single complete calculation to determine the DCF values and resulting NPV, as was done in Chapter 7 leading to, for example, the above $453K NPV for Exhibit 8.3 as presently constructed. This is because in each cell where there was an assumed value in Chapter 7, there will be in this chapter, with the Monte Carlo Method, instead a probabilistic expression comprising a distribution of values for each assumption.

When we considered scenarios we were doing something similar. For example, if we developed a DCF Method for which we wanted to consider three scenarios—"optimistic," "base," and "conservative"—for which, say, we were adjusting two variables—say, the Compound Annual Growth Rate (CAGR) and Cost of Goods Sold (COGS)—then we effectively used a single spreadsheet with three values in each of two cells (CAGR and COGS cells) that would be used to calculate three different NPV values corresponding to the three scenarios. As we would do the calculation following the Chapter 7 methodology we would sequentially do three calculations of the same spreadsheet model substituting the paired values for the two assumptions corresponding to the respective scenarios. Excel software can automate this process by using its Scenario capability available under its Tools pull-down menu. Using the scenario tool, one creates a table of matched assumptions (CAGR and COGS) for each of the three scenarios being considered and the software does the respective NPV calculations using the corresponding assumptions for each respective scenario.

Monte Carlo calculations are similar to this automated scenario calculation except there is no single value in each cell that Excel can directly use. Instead there is a probability distribution function assigned to each assumption cell that is then used by Crystal Ball to provide a single numerical value that Excel can then use for each "run" (also called a "trial"). Each "run" is not, however, a "scenario," because no one NPV calculation is by itself purposeful for a valuation judgment; rather it is the distribution of NPV values that has been determined by the many "runs" that can lead to meaningful valuation insights.

What makes this approach probabilistic is that the mathematical expressions used to provide each Monte Carlo calculated "run" are structured to provide a prescribed randomness (also known as a distribution). This seems peculiar and non-productive, but it turns out to be very useful, when Excel performs calculations on thousands of runs to produce a distribution of predictions for each "forecast" cell, including of course the NPV. For the initial run (or "trial"), Monte Carlo software uses the prescribed probabilistic distributions assigned to each of the values designated as "assumptions" to calculate a single value for each respective assumption cell, which is then used to calculate the first NPV value as well as every intermediary cell dependent upon any of the assumptions. As in Chapter 7, such NPV value is simply the net sum of all the year by year DCF values. However, with Monte Carlo the discounting is not done using a RAHR value in accordance with the risk of the opportunity, because such risk has been expressed via the assumption distributions. So, instead of a RAHR value such as the table of values given in Exhibit 7.8, one gets some lesser k value that does *not* embody a risk assessment. Selecting an appropriate k value may still require judgment. As discussed in Chapter 7, a company commonly considers its WACC value as a measure of its cost of capital, taking into account both debt and equity. However, there are different assumptions that can be used to determine a company's WACC. And a company can consider that an appropriate WACC value to be the marginal WACC—that is the incremental WACC value for the next dollar of capital required—rather than its average WACC value. And a company may adopt as its practice to apply some incremental premium to its WACC value when considering any project. So, for instance, a company could calculate its average WACC value to be 10 percent, but add two points to use 12 percent for any internal investment projects without any specific additions to account for project risk.[6]

Crystal Ball then stores the calculated values of all forecast cells. The software then checks to see if the total number of calculation runs have been made, usually based on a prescribed total series of runs that have been established. Unless one is running a test to see if the financial model is doing what is expected, the answer after the first run will be "no," because there is no predictive value to the NPV from a single run. To calculate the next NPV value, Crystal Ball then again uses the probability distribution functions for each of the assumption cells to calculate a single value to be used for the second NPV calculation.

The software repeats this process until some termination condition is reached, usually specified as a total number of runs. The NPV determined from each such run can be thought of as the value of the technology in some parallel universe. By setting as a parameter a stopping point of, say, 10,000 runs, we can see a 10,000 different possible NPV values that could occur given the probability distributions we assumed for all the assumption cells we established in our financial model. When we consider the entire population of NPV values so calculated, the result is a distribution of outcomes with each of the 10,000 data points for NPV being derived from one particular DCF Method calculation.

The number of runs for the Monte Carlo calculation is arbitrary. The greater the number of runs the smoother the forecast NPV distribution simply because there are more data points available. In the early days of personal computers there was a practical tradeoff because choosing a large number of runs could require a time-consuming calculation. There were circumstances where models were set up in the evening and allowed to run overnight simply because of limited PC processor speeds. With the amazing processing speed of modern personal computers and assuming one has not created an inordinately complex financial model, the computational time difference between 1,000 and 10,000 iterations is inconsequential (perhaps a few minutes, depending upon the model) so there is no reason not to use a large number of iterations to obtain a smooth result.

The Crystal Ball software only works running on Microsoft's Windows operating system (OS). However, on the current Apple OS X on Macintosh computers it is readily possible to run a Windows OS such as XP or Vista using Macintosh emulation software such as Parallels; this requires, alas, also installing the Windows OS and a Windows version of Excel, as was done for all the examples shown here. Despite this added software burden, the calculations are astonishingly fast and the results can be readily transferred to the Macintosh operating system for use in any word processing or presentation software.

It is a good practice to perform the first several iterations one run at a time, so that you can see how the assumed values are being determined. Ensuring that such values are properly being used in all the needed intermediate calculations, and determining the NPV results. Doing single run calculations is easily done in Crystal Ball by clicking on one of its tool bar icons. Once you are assured that the model is working properly at least at the single iteration level, then the remainder of the runs can be calculated and the results viewed and interpreted.

We now need to consider in some detail how probability distributions for various important assumptions can be constructed. It turns out that the mechanics of using various distributions is very easy in products such as Crystal Ball. Such software has many preloaded distributions available with the ready means for a user to create a custom distribution. Before we consider the commonly used probability distributions, let us think further about what the randomness associated with using such distributions means.

Prescribed Randomness of Probability Distributions

Using a probability distribution for a given assumption cell is, effectively, assigning a prescribed randomness to something deemed important to an NPV calculation. Why do we think doing this is a good idea?

Although it is universally accepted that no one knows the future—"life can only be understood backwards, but must be lived forwards,"[7] and Marcel Proust wrote a world renowned 3000 page novel[8] with the underlying premise that we don't even know the past—there are many aspects of life for which we do know the future in practical everyday terms. The sun will rise tomorrow, pretty much in the east. If it is spring, summer will follow. Even in human affairs, much of life is predictable. History suggests the stock market will rise, not every day, not every stock, but overall. (Yet, a little humility is in order: The stock market in the 2007 and 2008 period is not only *not* rising every day, it's not rising every year).

There are basically three ways that one can have what philosophers sometimes term a "justified true belief" (JTB)[9] about the future: (1) a scientific law, (2) an established historical trend, or (3) a rational argument. Predicting the sun's rising and the change of seasons is an example of scientific law; there are known and knowable facts concerning the motion of the earth with respect to its own axis (rotation) and with respect to the sun (revolution), and of the tilt of the earth, and of the energy emission rate of the sun that enable predicting the "rising" of the sun, for example. In fact everyone's certainty is sufficiently high about such matters that the word "prediction" would emit a laugh: Imagine a local evening news forecast that proclaims "tonight it will be dark, but tomorrow it will be light again."

The second example of a JTB about the future implies that reliance on an established trend is similar to the use of a scientific law. Scientific laws, after all, are simply codified experience. It comes as something of a shock to some college students that there is no "proof" of Newton's Laws of Motion or of the First Law of Thermodynamics. After careful study by many people in many different contexts, no exception to these dogmas has ever been observed and so a critical mass of people have declared them "law" and everyone pretty much agrees to stop wondering about them. Reliance on an established trend to predict the future is simply an uncodified way of asserting that what happened before will happen again.

Prior to man's understanding of celestial mechanics, the existence and date of the shortest and longest days of the year (in the Northern Hemisphere, December 21 and June 21, respectively) was widely known. It appears certain that Stonehenge, for example, was constructed in such a way that at sunrise on the Summer Solstice the sun would project its light through a special keyway in the stones on that day and only that day. Other cultures many thousands of years ago similarly understood these dates and all of them did so (apparently) with either an inadequate understanding of celestial mechanics or a completely false one. What they were able to do was to capture an observation that occurs once a year, year after year, and communicate it down through a sufficient number of generations such that it was accepted as a law of life.

The rising stock market, or the existence of inflation, is this same type of prediction by extrapolation. There exist approximately 100 years of stock market history encompassing multiple wars, numerous presidential administrations and policies, countless numbers of new products being introduced and old ones being abandoned, and, yet there has been a surprisingly uniform rise in value of about 10 percent per year (not discounting for inflation) when viewed as a long term trend. Underneath such rise, there are "fundamentals" that can be used to explain why stocks as a whole are more valuable now than they were before, and why stocks on an individual basis are more, or in some cases less, valuable than in the past. So, does anyone "know" that the stock market will continue to evidence value growth by 10 percent a year? In the philosophical sense of JTB, the answer is "no." In the business sense of PDM (Prudent Decision Making), the answer is "yes," though there is clear historical evidence of year to year variability, especially in 2008, and the possibility exists for prolonged "down" periods (the so-called "bear market"). In a business context, certainty is an unaffordable luxury.[10] If there is historical data, then it is frequently prudent to predict the future and act on such predictions as though the future were known. As one of the Demotivator posters says, "Mistakes: It could be that the purpose of your life is to serve as a warning to others."[11]

When an investment decision is to be made regarding whether or not to develop a new product, business decision makers frequently have only rational argument as the basis for PDM. Although there may be both historical data for similar products or previous new product introductions and market assessments based upon surveys and trials, in almost all circumstances the commitment is made by the credibility of an argument. Thus, in the 1999 version of this book[12] it was predicted, pro forma, that the Yankees would (again) win the World Series of Baseball. This was based on a rational argument that because the Yankees won in 1998, and because off-season trades and acquisitions had made the team stronger than any other team, they should win again in 1999. Of course this was by no means certain, which is one reason why they play the game, but if the 1999 Yankees were an investment opportunity, PDM would have been to expect their winning (and they did), yet, again some humility is in order since subsequent results have not been (so far) similarly positive (for Yankee fans).

When business forecasts are made, the future values selected for cells in a spreadsheet model are some combination of extrapolations of data or experience and a rational argument as to how circumstances should turn out. With traditional, non–Monte Carlo methods, each "best guess" is but one value from a range of reasonably possible choices. Monte Carlo techniques enable the replacement of the single-valued best guess with a prescribed randomness that characterizes not only what is believed to be the most likely outcome but also includes treatment of reasonably probable but less likely outcomes. Normally the solution sought is the NPV of the project. Each time the Monte Carlo software program performs a complete NPV calculation, it will determine a somewhat different value for NPV because at least some of the cells have the prescribed randomness expression rather than a single value.

However when we examine, say, 10,000 possible NPV values from a single financial model as determined by the probability distributions used for the assumption cells we can gain a deep understanding of the effect of such prescribed randomness and make PDM of the opportunity value. As we will see, such calculation can provide reasonable estimates of the minimum and maximum NPV values, and the comparative probability for any particular NPV in between.

Let us now consider how software such as Crystal Ball can be used to prescribe randomness for any given assumption cell.

UNIFORM DISTRIBUTION A uniform distribution, or "uniform" prescribed randomness, is one that assigns equal probability to any value between prescribed upper and lower bounds. This can most easily be understood by a concrete example.

In Exhibit 8.3, we used proxy data for calculating various elements of a cash flow projection for an example technology valuation. The value used for the Cost of Goods Sold, COGS, was 57 percent. As was discussed, forecasts for COGS can be developed in many ways, including expert opinion, past history, a proxy value, a bottom-up analysis by a manufacturing engineer subject matter expert, and so forth. Regardless of the approach there is naturally some degree of COGS uncertainty. This could result because the subject technology is still under development, or a relevant manufacturing process cost is uncertain, or anticipated variability in raw materials costs, or the product yield efficiencies have a range of possible values, or changes that could occur over time in disposal or environmental costs, or the unit cost variability commonly associated with sales volume, or any other reason. So regardless of the source and "authority" of the COGS value estimated to be 57 percent, it is reasonable to consider some range in other possible values.

Suppose an examination of all the possible influences that could cause an increase or decrease in COGS from the 57 percent value we conclude that between an upper and lower bound we are equally uncertain as to any intermediate value. For this particular situation we are certain that there is no COGS value above or below certain end points, but are as uncertain as possible as to any value between such end points being more or less likely.

The probability corresponding to this kind of uncertainty is known as the Uniform Distribution. It is graphically portrayed in Exhibit 8.4.

The top figure in Exhibit 8.4 is the probability view, which shows equally probable values for COGS values between 55 and 59 percent, equally bracketing the 57 percent base COGS value of Exhibit 8.3. The bottom figure in Exhibit 8.4 is the cumulative probability view of the same uniform distribution assumption. Because the probability of any COGS value between the limits of 55 and 59 percent

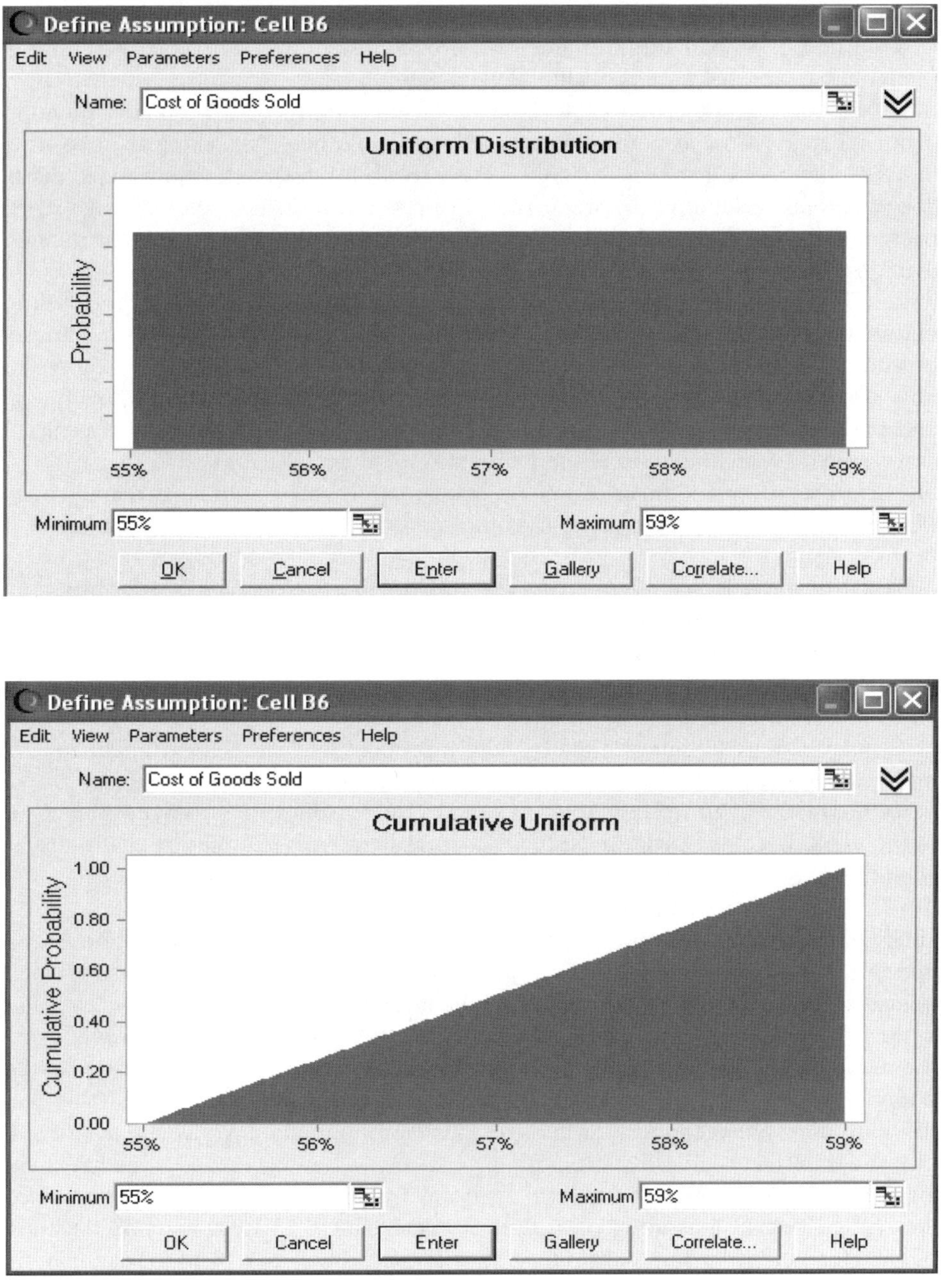

EXHIBIT 8.4 Uniform Distribution for Cost of Goods Sold for Exhibit 8.4

Source: © 1988–2002 Decisioneering, Inc. Reprinted with permission.

is equally probable, the cumulative probability begins at 0.0 (i.e., 0 percent) for a COGS value of 55 percent, and increases linearly as shown to a probability of 1.0 (i.e., 100 percent) for a COGS value of 59 percent.

Such Uniform Distribution appears to be something of a mismatch of concepts because we have both total certainty—namely there is zero probability of a COGS value to the left or the right of the probability rectangle shown in Exhibit 8.4, and total uncertainty between the left and right edges of the rectangle, because there is zero probability for any COGS value below 55 percent or greater than 59 percent with no preference for any particular COGS value between such limits. Despite this incongruity, there are circumstances where the Uniform Distribution is useful. One purpose is to see the effect on forecast NPV value caused by such total uncertainty on any particular assumption. This can be done by using only one assumption cell in a financial model, keeping all the other inputs fixed, and calculating the forecast NPV. Crystal Ball provides a capability of "freezing" any number of assumptions at their nominal, or their base value, so that even if one has constructed a financial model with many assumptions it is readily possible to study the effect of any single assumption with any desired probability distribution.

But there could also be real world situations where a Uniform Distribution could be a reasonable assumption representation. For instance, in prior experience in the manufacture of similar products based upon similar technology all the COGS experience was bounded by 55 percent on the low end and 59 percent on the high end. Or, based upon general financial operating guidelines the company will not go forward toward commercialization with a product whose COGS is 60 percent or more, and competitive pressures are unlikely to permit Gross Margins (GM) of 46 percent or more (corresponding to a COGS of 56 percent or less, since GM = 1 − COGS). Yet, between such limits, the company's experience could be that there is an almost random variation in COGS values.

TRIANGULAR DISTRIBUTION A Triangular Distribution is similar to the Uniform Distribution in that it also assumes zero probability of values below the specified lower bound and above the upper bound. It differs in that the Triangular Distribution uses a most likely value and constructs a triangle of probability that varies linearly from the maximum probability at the most likely value to zero at the upper and lower bounds. Using a concrete example, consider again Exhibit 8.3. We will use triangular distribution to predict values for the average selling price in any given year (Row 3 of this exhibit).

The financial model of Exhibit 8.3 portrays a decline in the selling price after the second year as a result of price erosion, determined by year-over-year declines of $500 for Years 2 to 3 and again for 3 to 4, and a decline of $1000 for Years 4 to 5, with no further decline after Year 5, and for the Year 2 selling price to equal the Year 1 selling price. Accordingly, by varying the Year 1 selling price we can effectively model the selling price for each of Years 1 through 5 (within the framework of the above year-over-year differences). Let us assume that as a result of market studies we are confident that the selling price can be at least $9,000 per unit, but not more than $11,000 per unit, and believe that the most likely selling price is midway between these limits, corresponding to the projection of 100 units sold in Year 1. A triangular distribution would then look like the top figure shown in Exhibit 8.5.

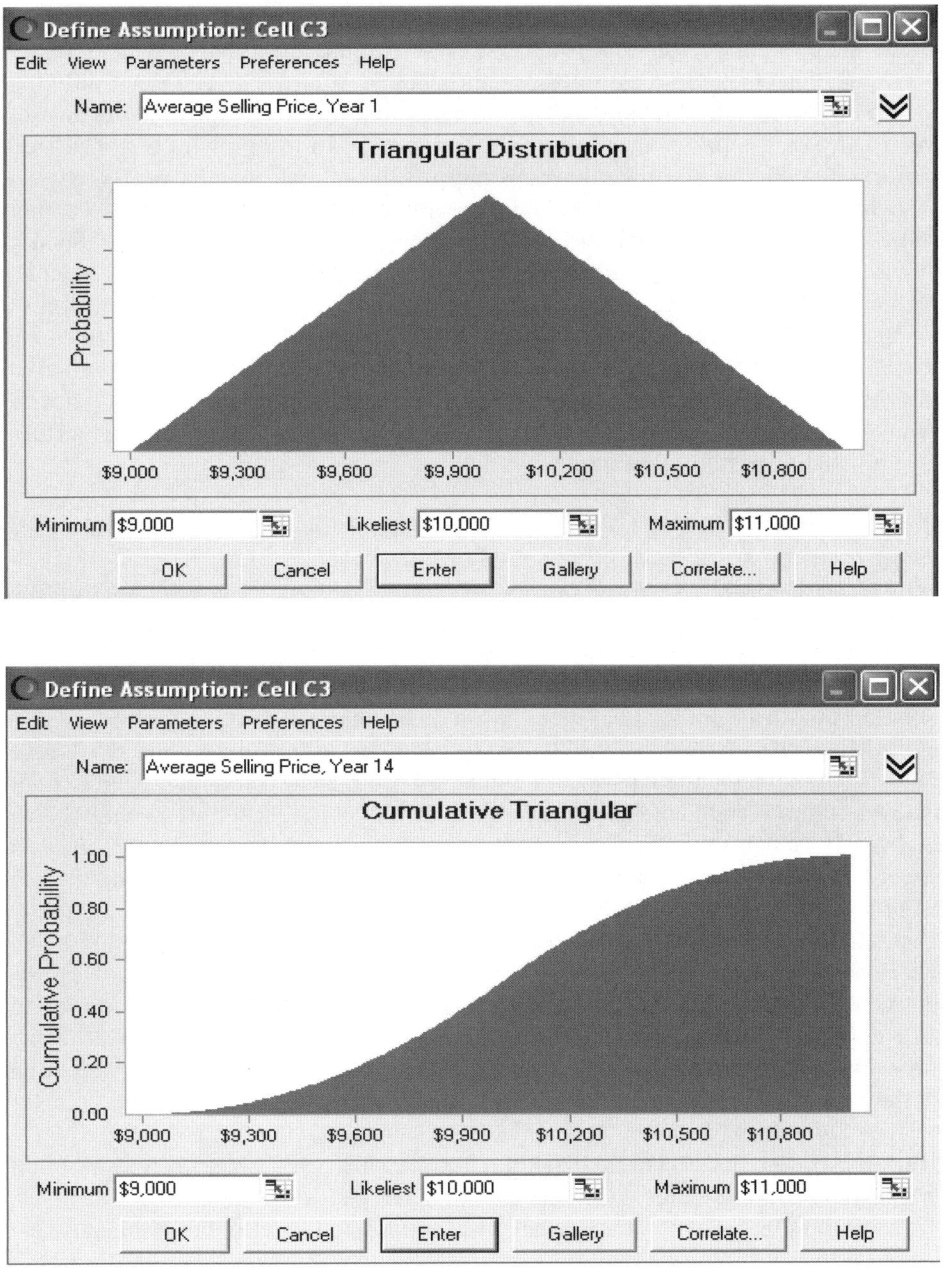

EXHIBIT 8.5 Triangular Distribution for the Selling Price in Year 1

Source: © 1988–2002 Decisioneering, Inc. Reprinted with permission.

As with Exhibit 8.4 for the Uniform Distribution, the top figure in Exhibit 8.5 shows the probability distribution, and the bottom figure the cumulative distribution.

Thus, this distribution assumes that the likelihood of the selling price differing from $10,000 declines linearly with price differential from $10,000 until, at plus or minus $1,000, the probability is zero. In comparison to the previously considered uniform distribution, the triangle distribution is appropriate when one has reason to believe that a most-likely value does exist, and that the probability of other values declines linearly for values differing from such a most-likely value. Such a distribution works well when there is a basis for confidence in the most-likely value, which corresponds to the peak of the triangle, and it is believed that outcomes become less likely in direct proportion to their divergence from the most likely value. Because it is common to hold a "most likely" outcome belief, the triangular distribution is useful for many circumstances. The triangular distribution need not be symmetric about the most likely value; it can be skewed to higher or lower values by simple choices of the end points.

HYBRID UNIFORM—TRIANGULAR DISTRIBUTION The Crystal Ball software can easily adjust even the standard distributions it makes available in its library. In Exhibit 8.6 we can see how a Uniform Distribution can be combined, in a sense, with the Triangular Distribution.

Shown in Exhibit 8.6 is how the Triangular Distribution can be "cut off" (terminated) at upper and lower bounds. This can be done in the software simply by entering the lower and upper values in the cells below the shape in the first diagram (see $9,250 on the left, and $10,750 on the right). Alternatively, one can simply "grab" the triangles shown at the base of the figure on the top and drag them to their desired position. The figure on the bottom in Exhibit 8.6 again shows the cumulative probability. When compared with its corresponding figure in Exhibit 8.5 one can see that the cumulative distribution is slightly closer to being a straight line than in Exhibit 8.5; but "cutting off" the ends of the triangle we have made the probability distribution, on average, "flatter," and thereby closer to the Uniform Distribution for which the cumulative probability is exactly a straight line.

One can think of the distribution of Exhibit 8.6 as a uniform distribution with an elevated "weighting" favoring a most-likely value, as shown by the peak of the super-posed triangle on top of the base rectangle. As discussed previously, weighting of the most-likely value need not be midway between the end points.

THE NORMAL (GAUSSIAN, OR BELL) DISTRIBUTION Another commonly used distribution is known by several names: Gaussian, normal, or bell distribution (or bell curve). This distribution, hereafter the Normal Distribution, is similar to the Triangular Distribution in that the probability peaks at the "most likely" value and declines with distance from the most likely value. However, unlike the triangle distribution, the bell distribution shows a probability that declines to zero asymptotically, not abruptly at fixed end points. Further, the probability decline is not a straight line but rather a curve that is described by a mathematical formula.

There is another important difference between the Triangular and Normal Distribution: The Normal Distribution is observed experimentally in many different physical circumstances. If one were to measure the height of a large number of people and then calculated the average height, one would find that most people's height

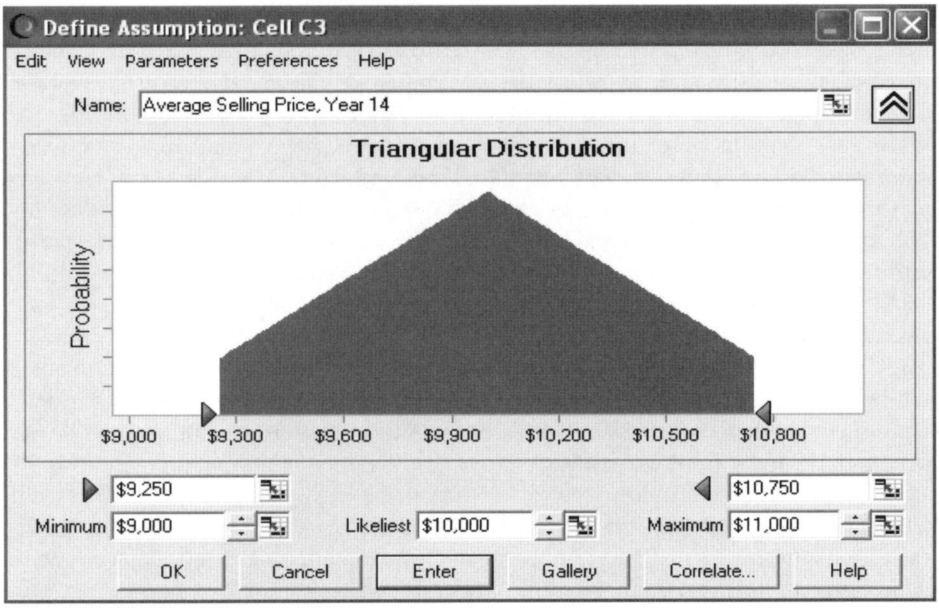

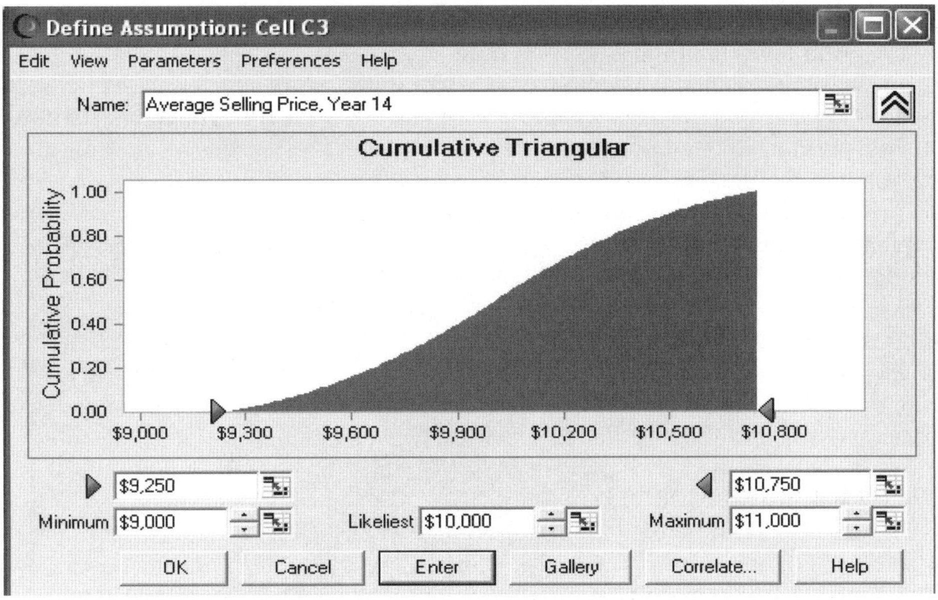

EXHIBIT 8.6 Combined Triangular and Uniform Distribution for the Selling Price in Year 1

is close to the average (median). The number of people with heights far from the mean decreases rapidly for heights increasingly divergent from the mean, more rapidly than what would be reflected by a Triangular Distribution. For example, if the mean was determined to be 5 feet 6 inches, then one would find many people who stand between 5 feet 4 inches and 5 feet 6 inches, substantially fewer between 5 feet 2 and 5 feet 4, many fewer between 5 feet and 5 feet 2, and very few between 4 feet 10 and 5 feet. The distribution of such heights, namely a declining probability with increasing difference from the mean, would closely follow a mathematical expression that prescribes the bell curve, and not the linear variation as would be evidenced for a Triangular Distribution and certainly not the even probability of a Uniform Distribution.

The use of such Normal Distribution is particularly suited when there exists a natural mean around which there is some randomness and the randomness is equally likely to be higher or lower than the mean. Although most, if not all, real world situations do not exhibit outcomes that go to plus and minus infinity—there is no probability of a human being a 100 miles tall or one inch short—the probabilities of occurrence decline so dramatically as one moves three or more standard deviations away from the mean that such impracticality is normally not a cause for concern. Even for situations where there is no "natural" mean, such a Normal Distribution can be used to express a belief that the mean or expected value is highly likely to occur with an exponentially decreasing, but non-zero, probability in the "tails." Essentially, any value is possible, but the probability of values far from the mean is much lower than values closer to the mean.

Considering again the example of Exhibit 8.3, let us assume that the number of units sold each year can be characterized by such a Normal Distribution as shown in Exhibit 8.7.

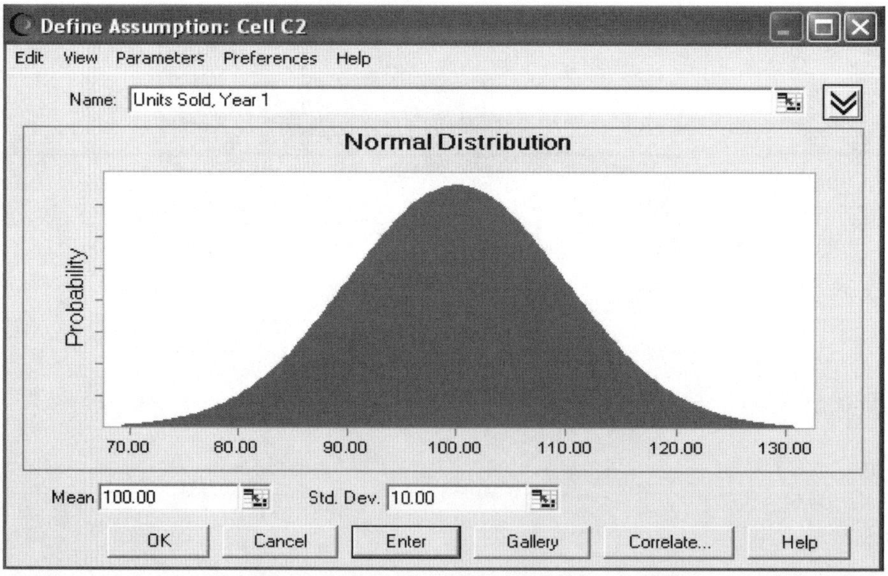

EXHIBIT 8.7 Example of Normal Distribution for Units Sold

Source: © 1988–2002 Decisioneering, Inc. Reprinted with permission.

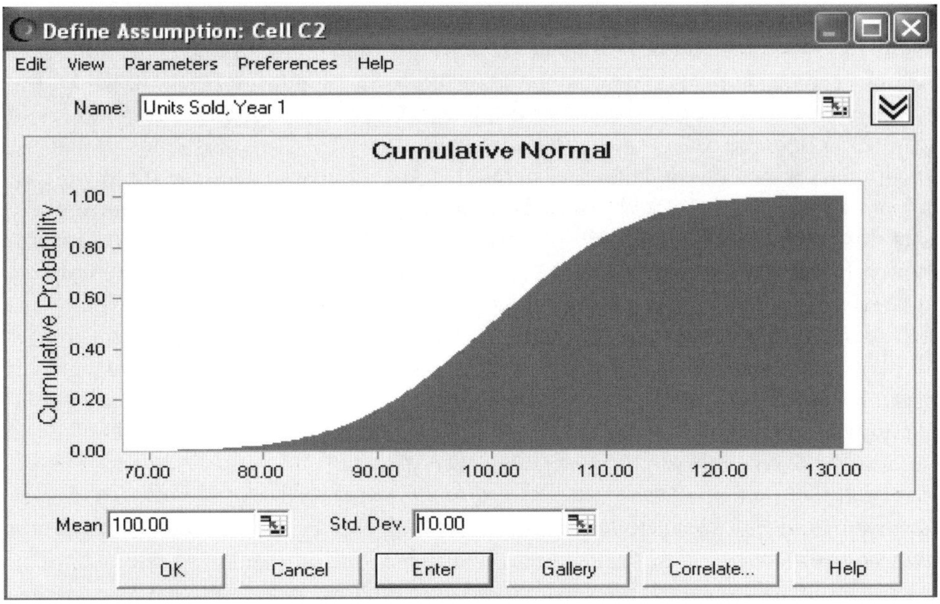

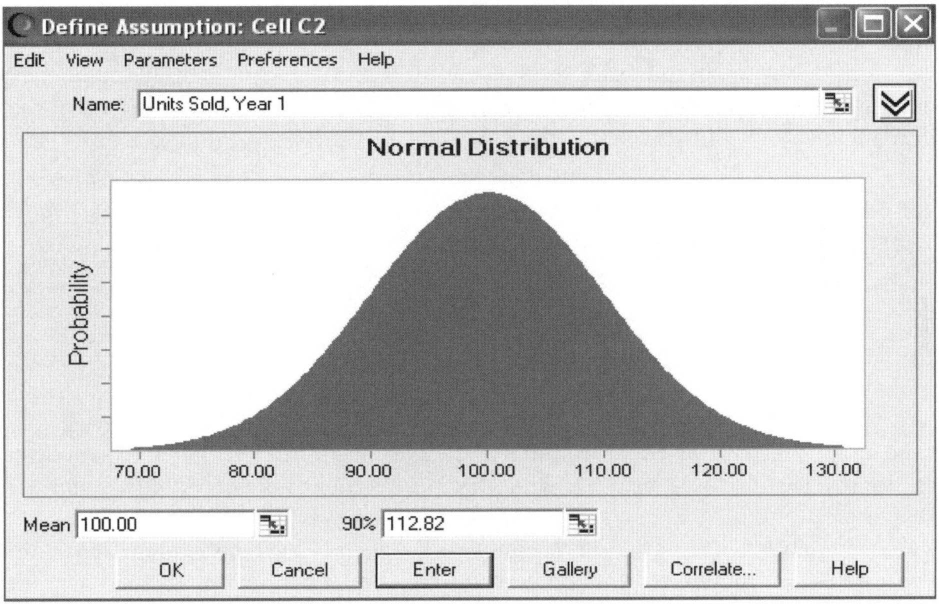

EXHIBIT 8.7 (*Continued*)

The relative slenderness of the Normal Distribution is determined by a mathematical parameter known as the standard deviation. One standard deviation, plus and minus, encompasses approximately 68 percent of the total probability of occurrence from the mean. That is, in the example shown in the first two figures in Exhibit 8.7, the selection of a standard deviation value of 10 corresponds to that the distribution which provides that 68 percent of the values selected for the units sold in Year 1 are between 90 and 110 units (plus and minus 10 bracketing the most likely value of 100). Three standard deviations, in this example plus or minus 30, encompasses 98 percent of all occurrences for a Normal Distribution. The first two figures in Exhibit 8.7 are created by specifying the mean value (here 100) and the standard deviation (here 10). The third figure in Exhibit 8.7 shows an alternative means for choosing a Normal Distribution by choosing the mean value (again 100) and an upper value (here 112.82) which is believed to encompass 90 percent of all possible values. Because the bell shape is symmetric about the mean, the value 112.82 represents 12.82 units above and below the mean of 100, and within such span 90 percent all outcomes are expected. For many purposes it is more intuitive to create a Normal Distribution assumption by taking advantage of 90 percent specification feature available.

The Toolbox

The ability to simply create graphical portrayals, in Crystal Ball, of assumption uncertainties can be pasted into presentations to illustrate a particular uncertainty unrelated to any Monte Carlo calculation. Similarly, by using the ability to insert 90 (or other) percentile values as shown in Exhibit 8.7 the particular distribution statistics are calculated and displayed by the software without having to resort to a direct calculation. Then by locating the cursor on any figure one can determine the relative probability of that particular value.

THE LOGNORMAL DISTRIBUTION The Normal Distribution exhibits some non-zero probability of values extending to both plus and minus infinity. Since many practical situations, such as prices and revenues, cannot physically evidence negative values, a commonly used distribution that is derived from taking the logarithm of Normal Distribution, results in what is appropriately known as the Lognormal Distribution.

The Lognormal Distribution is bounded by zero for the minimum value, and asymptotes to infinity for the other "bound." The distribution is, thereby, not symmetric with respect to the peak value. The peak probability does not occur at the same value as the most likely probability because of the long tail of the upper bound extending to infinity. Shown in Exhibit 8.8 is an example of the Lognormal Distribution (the second pair of figures) compared to a Normal Distribution (the first pair).

Note that both the Normal and Lognormal Distributions of Exhibit 8.8 have the same mean value, 100 units, and the same standard deviation, 50 units. However, the Normal Distribution evidences negative values of units sold (made clear in this

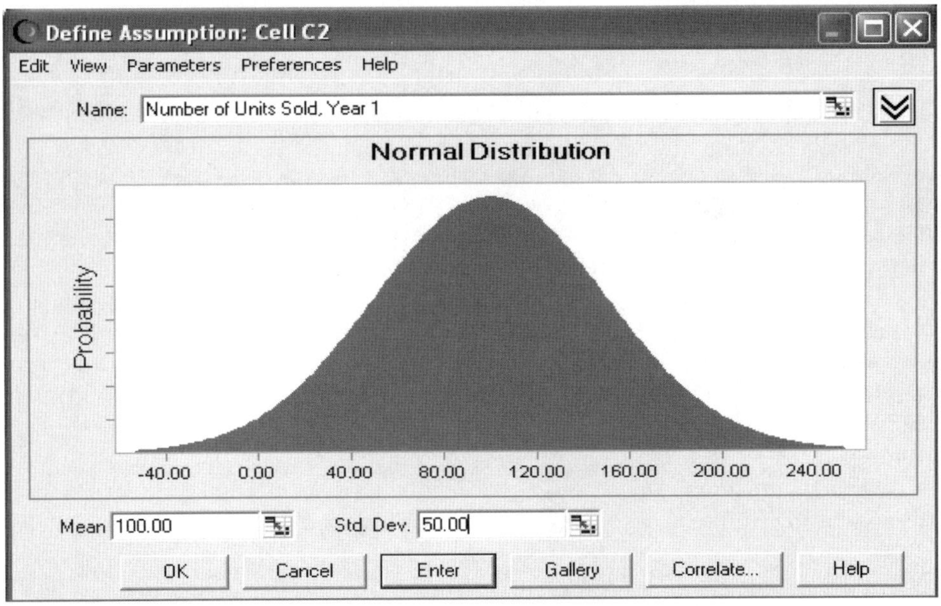

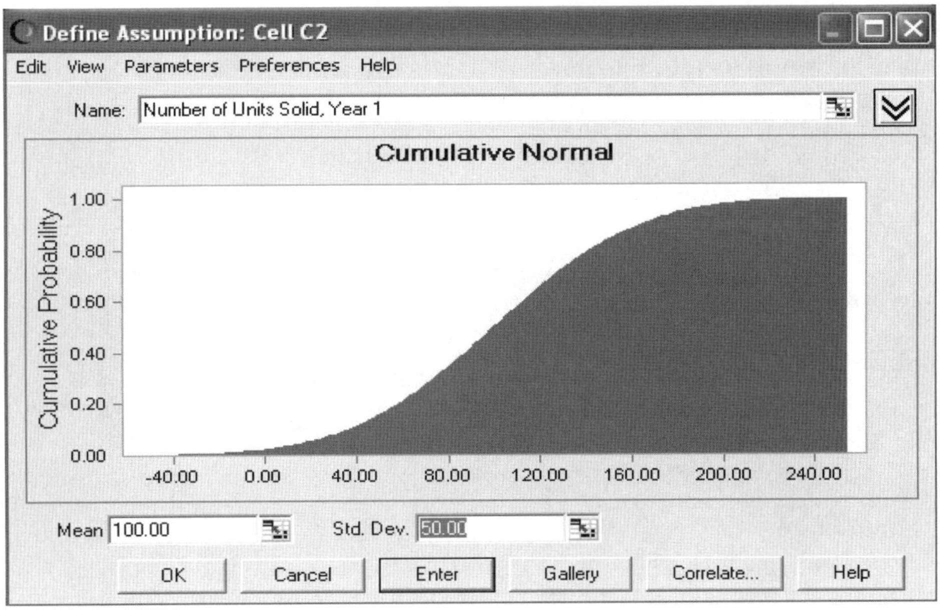

EXHIBIT 8.8 Comparison of Lognormal and Normal Distributions

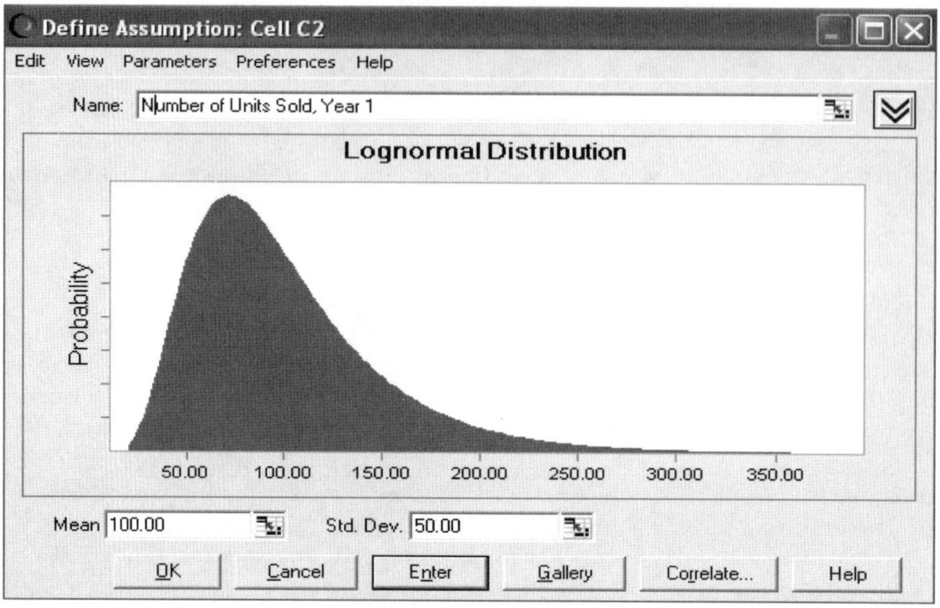

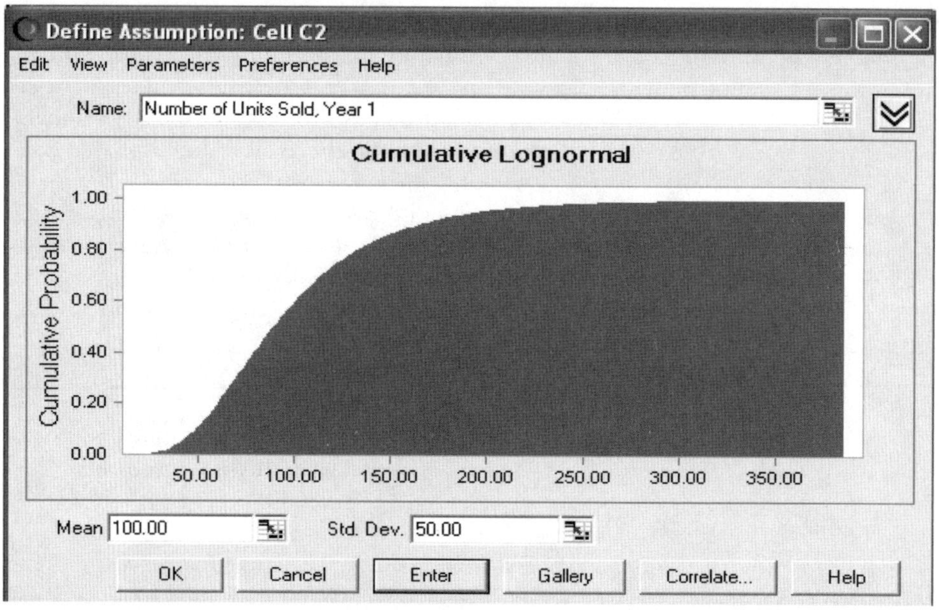

EXHIBIT 8.8 (*Continued*)

example because a very large value for the standard deviation was used). The Lognormal Distribution on the other hand by its formula cannot have values below zero units. As a result, the most likely value is not 100 as in the case for the Normal Distribution, but something substantially less (ca. 65 units). For large values of uncertainty (high standard deviations) and/or when a Normal Distribution includes a substantial probability of non-meaningful outcomes Lognormal Distribution is better suited.

THE BETA DISTRIBUTION A very useful probability distribution known as the Beta Distribution is available in Crystal Ball. Its key attributes are (effectively) a combination of the Triangle and Normal Distributions, with a smooth decrease in probability away from the peak value, similar to the Normal Distribution, but with exact upper and lower bounds like the Triangular Distribution. Further, the Beta Distribution can be make to bias (favor) either the upper or lower portions of the curve, which is approximately similar to a Lognormal Distribution, or it can be made symmetrical around the peak as in the Normal Distribution.

Shown in Exhibit 8.9 are three example configurations of the Beta Distribution that can be created by selection of the two parameters known as alpha and beta as could be used to create an assumed probability distribution for the total costs—SG&A (Sales, General and Administrative) plus R&D (Research and Development)—of Exhibit 8.3.

When alpha and beta are equal, as shown in all four figures of Exhibit 8.9, the distribution is symmetric with respect to the peak value. When these values increase the distribution is more concentrated around values close to the peak as shown by the pair where alpha = beta = 5 compared to the pair where alpha = beta = 2, and less so than the pair where alpha = beta = 20. (For alpha = beta = 1 the distribution is exactly the same as the Uniform Distribution). In all cases, the minimum and maximum values are also specified as was done for the Triangle Distribution. However, with the Beta Distribution, the relative probabilities can be adjusted so they smoothly decrease toward the zero probability end points, unlike the straight lines inherent in the Triangle Distribution.

The Beta Distribution is incredibly flexible. Shown in Exhibit 8.10 are four additional Beta Distribution examples.

The figures given in Exhibit 8.10 shows how unequal values of alpha and beta skew the probability distribution. When beta > alpha, as in the first figure on p. 366, the peak value representing the most likely total overhead costs (SG&A + R&D) is moved to lower values than the midpoint between 33 and 37 percent. In the subsequent figure, the situation is reversed with alpha > beta. As we observed in Exhibit 8.9, as alpha and beta are made larger, the probability distributions narrow around the mean. So by adjusting both the absolute magnitude and the relative values of alpha and beta affords great flexibility in creating symmetrical and asymmetrical distributions of any level of compactness or diffuseness.

The remaining two figures in Exhibit 8.10 gives examples of alternate means of shaping the Beta Distribution. Instead of specifying alpha and beta values, one can specific the value of overhead costs (in this example) for which there is only a 10 percent probability of lower values (the "minimum" cell in the pair of figures) and upper values (the "maximum" cell). As with the first pair discussed above, the

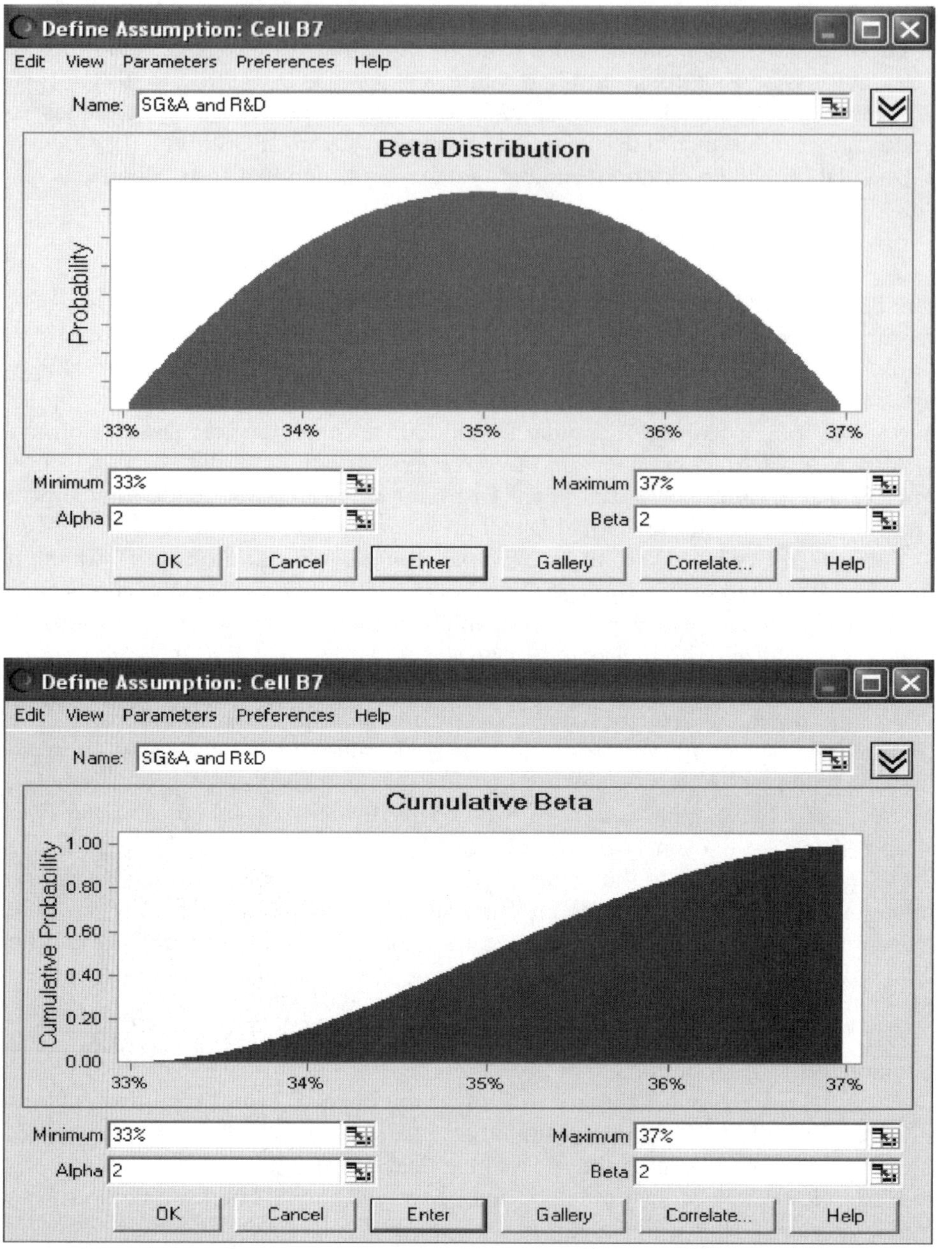

EXHIBIT 8.9 Example of Beta Distribution to Model SG&A + R&D of Exhibit 8.3 for Various Parameter Pairs (Alpha and Beta)

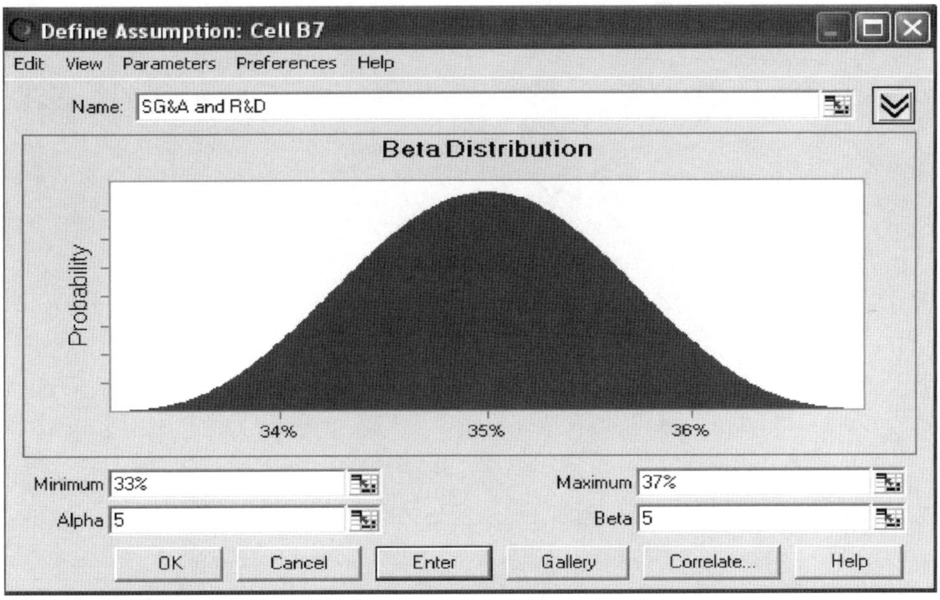

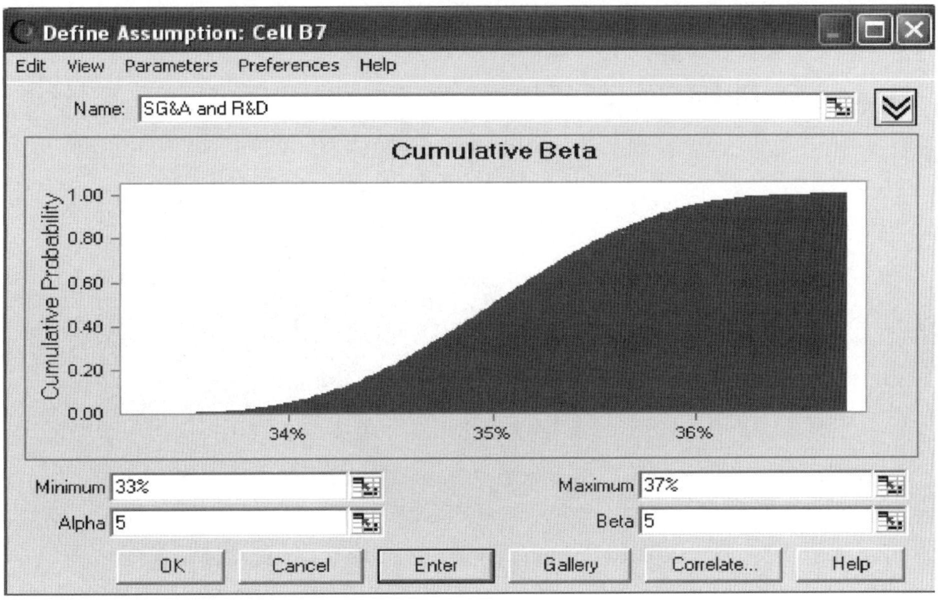

EXHIBIT 8.9 *(Continued)*

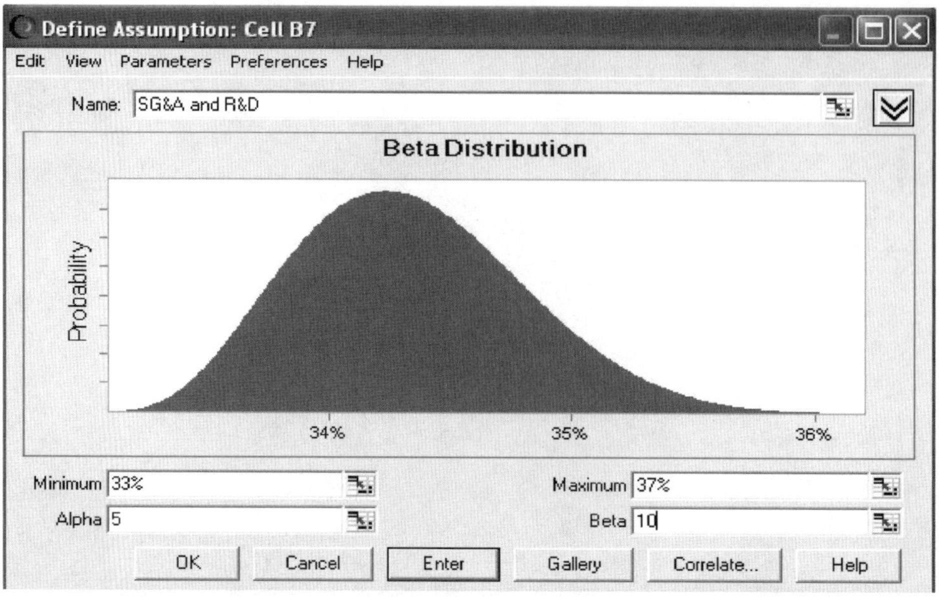

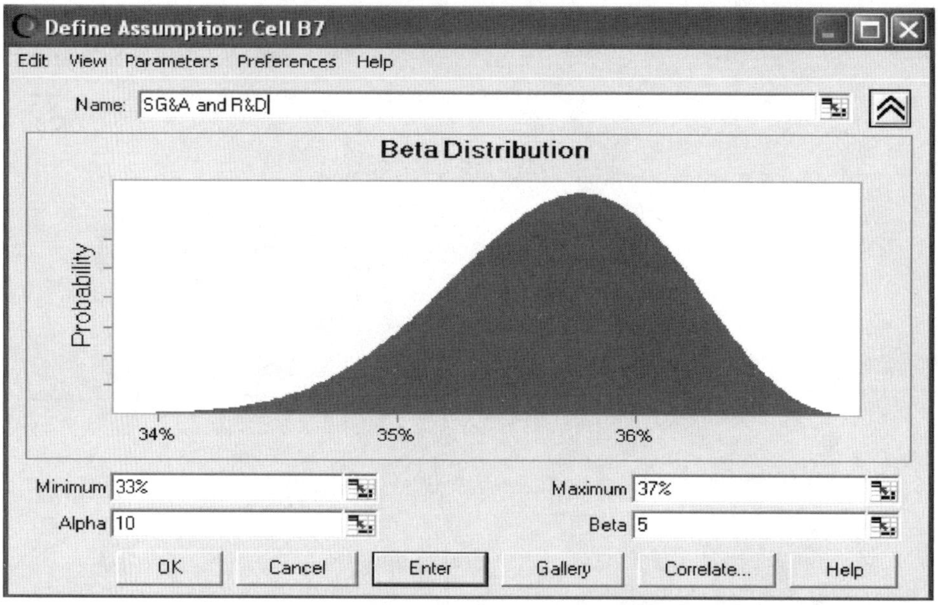

EXHIBIT 8.10 Example of Additional Beta Distribution to Model SG&A + R&D of Exhibit 8.3

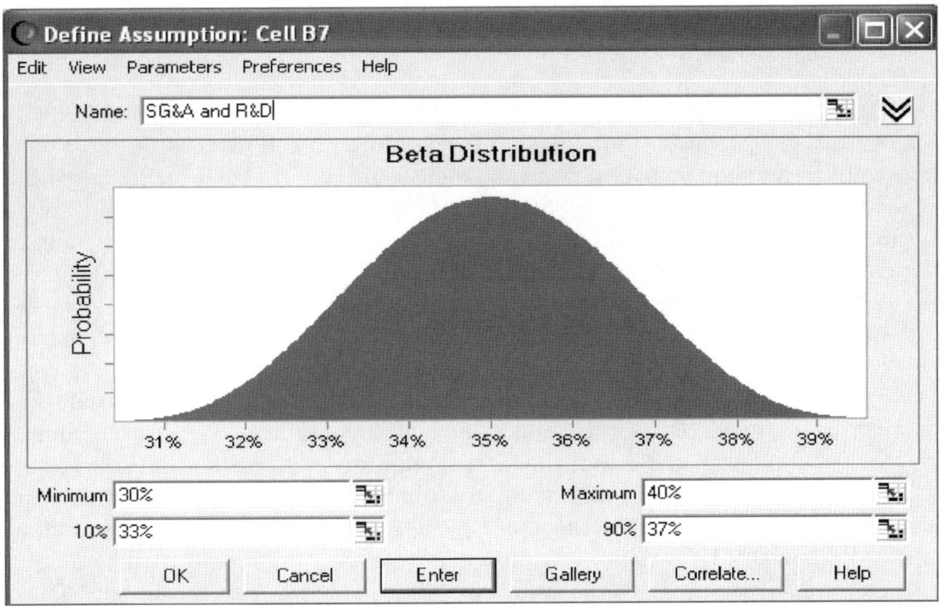

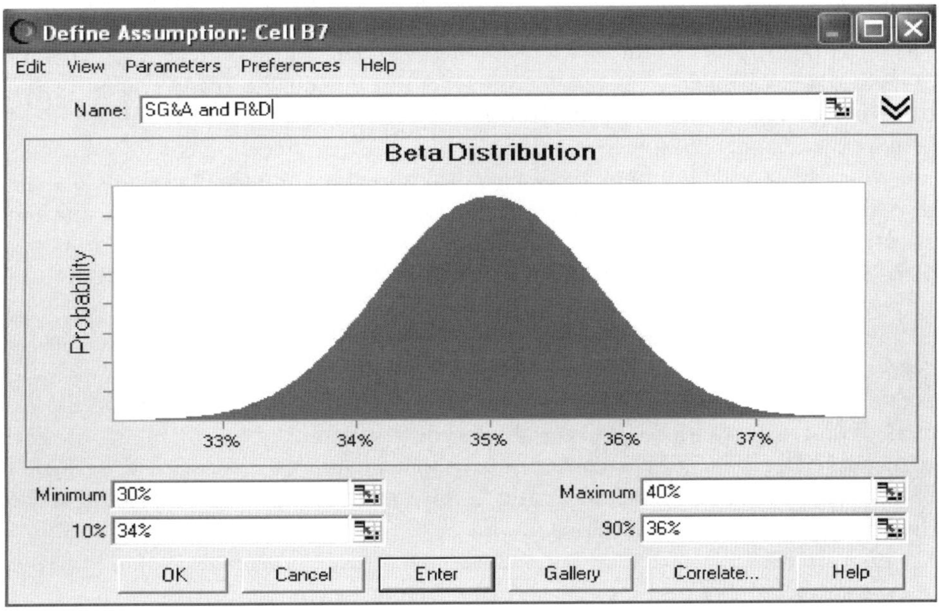

EXHIBIT 8.10 (*Continued*)

breadth of the Beta Distribution can be easily adjusted by substituting larger or smaller values in such minimum and maximum cells.

CUSTOM DISTRIBUTIONS The Crystal Ball software provides more than a dozen different types of distributions that can be readily modeled and used as we have seen above. In technology valuation contexts, there is usually no basis for identifying a particular distribution from scientific principles because the valuation is driven by business variables. Exceptions can occur. For instance, if the licensed subject matter were a pharmaceutical that was still undergoing trials, then there could be valid reason and basis on which to select a distribution that accurately represents the rate of patient cures and to use such distributions to model FDA approval, market applications, and size.

In addition to a menu of probability distributions that arise from various statistical contexts, the Crystal Ball software has the built in capability of easily creating a custom distribution that allows for the creation of any combination of probabilities at any arbitrary set of values. An example of the use of such custom distribution is shown in Exhibit 8.11 for COGS as a possible alternative to the example distribution shown in Exhibit 8.4.

This exhibit shows how the probable values of COGS can, in the alternative to the Uniform Distribution considered before, be easily modeled to accommodate almost any beliefs. The original example, shown in Exhibit 8.3, used a value of 35 percent for the single, best assumption. The figures in Exhibit 8.10 shows how one can select probabilities at three discrete values: 50 percent probability at 35 percent COGS (as before such 35 percent represents the percentage of revenues for the corresponding year that are expended as COGS), 33.33 percent probability at 34 percent costs, and 16.67 percent probability at 36 percent costs. Crystal Ball allows one to easily specify any number of pairs—as shown by the small table below the respective graphs in Exhibit 8.11, and then normalize the entire result so that the integrated probability is 100 percent. Such discrete custom distribution does not permit any values of such costs between 34 and 35 percent or between 35 and 36 percent.

The figures in Exhibit 8.11 shows an alternate means of creating a custom distribution in Crystal Ball. In that the table below the figures is filled out with the assumption values. The difference in the second figure is that one can specify the pairs of end points and, so, the straight line distribution of the probability between each pair of end points, for as many pairs of end points as desired (three such pairs are shown). The result can clearly be made to resemble certain aspects of the Uniform and Triangle Distributions.

Also shown in Exhibit 8.11 is the cumulative distributions corresponding to the respective probability distributions shown in the first two figures.

This custom distribution enables one to construct distributions based upon historical experience (data) obtained from previous licensing situations, or other new product development projects. One can create a separate Excel file of data pairs that can then be loaded directly into Crystal Ball's custom distribution. We will, later in this chapter when we use a more complex custom distribution creation that shows how to combine the use of scenarios with Monte Carlo through the application of custom distributions.

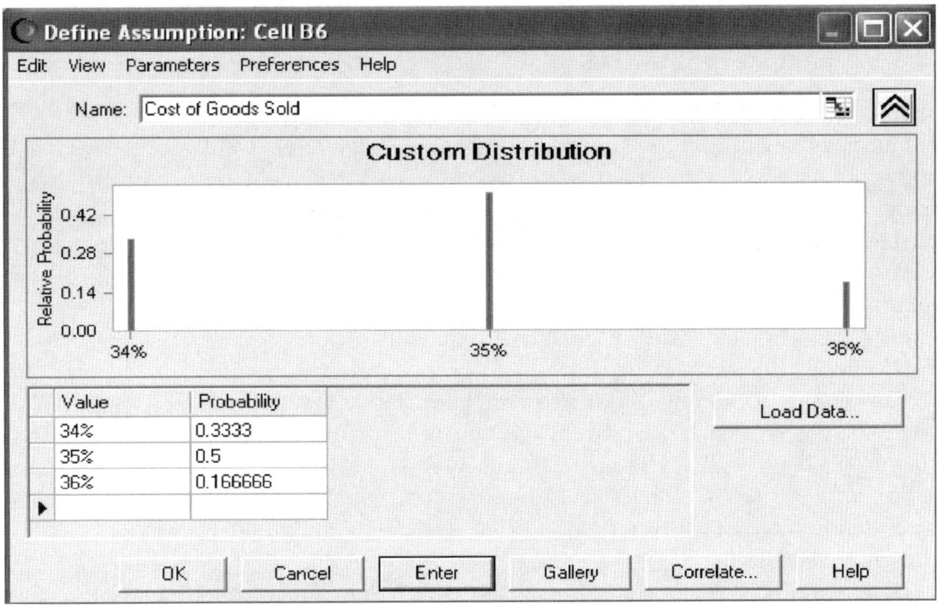

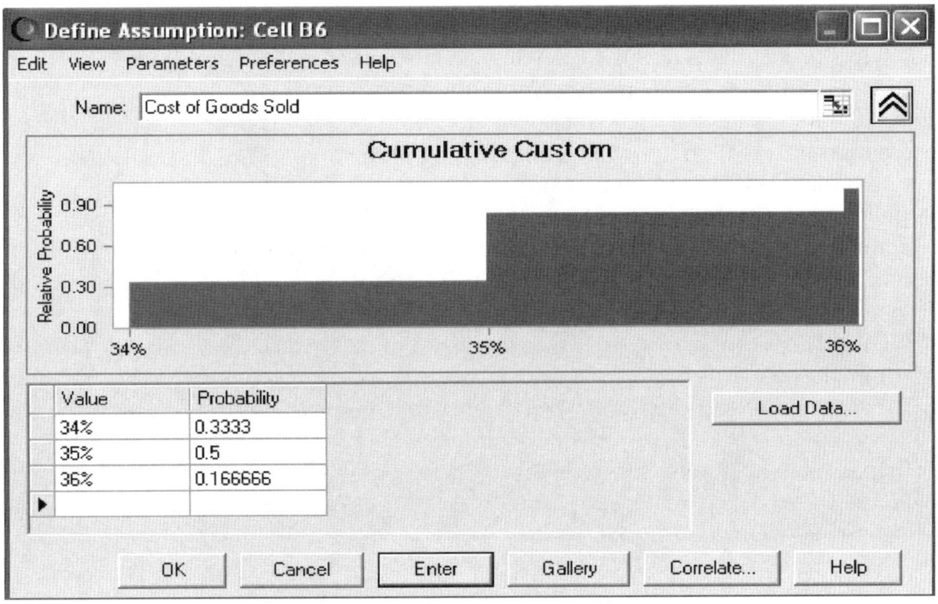

EXHIBIT 8.11 Example of Custom Distribution to Model COGS

Source: © 1988–2002 Decisioneering, Inc. Reprinted with permission.

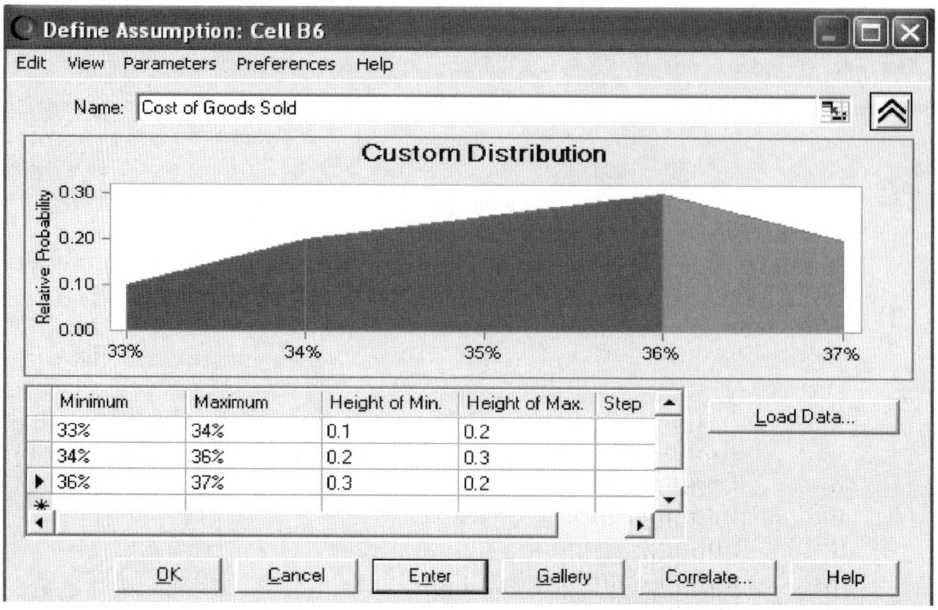

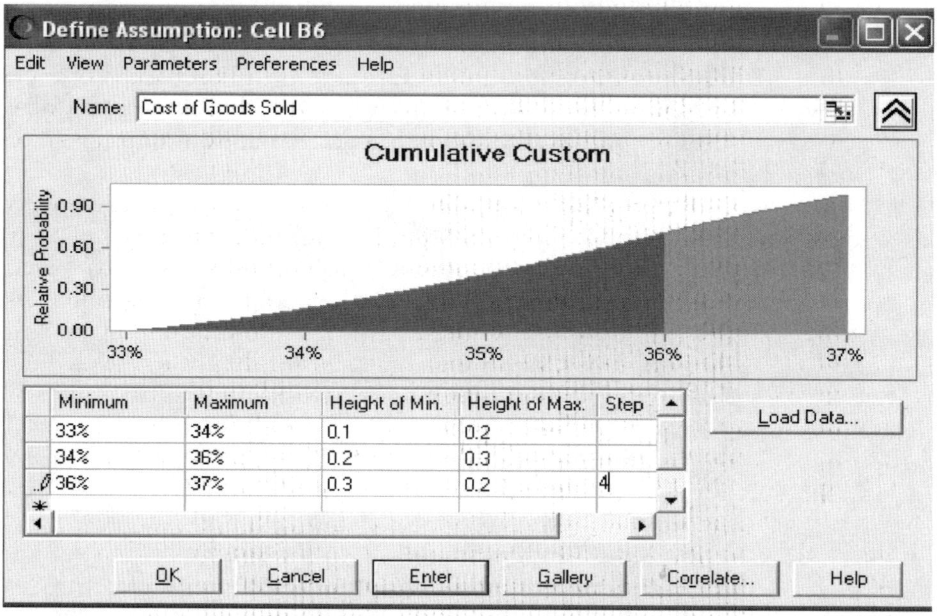

EXHIBIT 8.11 *(Continued)*

Example Monte Carlo Method Valuation Based Upon Exhibit 8.3

The ability to use prescribed randomness in the form of probability distributions for each assumption such as those given above is what makes the Monte Carlo Method powerful. Because the Monte Carlo Method builds on a financial model created in Excel, and is used to calculate NPV values, along with year-by-year projections, it is really an extension of the DCF Method of Chapter 7.

The DCF Method itself has many traditional extensions as we have seen using scenarios and probability trees. The use of spreadsheets such as Excel makes it easy, all too easy, to create dozens or hundreds of "what if" modifications of a given valuation model by changing specific assumption values, or even the entire structure of the financial model itself. When one begins thinking about the "if" in "Life," a trademark of the Met Life insurance company, there is almost no end of possibilities to consider. One of the consequences of such DCF Method extensions is trying to rationalize and grasp all the resulting calculations. Changing various assumptions can create distorted NPV predictions because various assumptions should be correlated with each other in some way. For instance it is a well known economic principle that increases in unit price are (normally) associated with decreased demand, although the exact relationship between these two variables may itself have significant uncertainty. Other assumption correlations may be less obvious.

So, creating a tall pile of spreadsheet results from DCF calculations can easily lead to the question, "Ok, I see the pile, but what does this actually mean?"[13]

The Monte Carlo method provides more powerful ways of dealing with multiple uncertainties, including correlating such uncertainties, and multiple interpretive tools that can provide both more sophisticated predictive capacity and support for exercising business, "bottom line" judgment.

IDENTIFICATION OF THE ASSUMPTION CELLS AND THEIR PROBABILITY DISTRIBUTIONS Let us now use the various probability distributions we have considered previously and apply them to the NPV model of Exhibit 8.3. In Exhibit 8.12 is a summary of the each of the assumptions we will consider as relevant to determining the NPV of the opportunity, the corresponding probability distribution that will be used to model the uncertainty and risk associated with each assumption, and the key parameters that will define the shape of the respective probability distribution.

In commercial practice additional columns would be useful, especially those that provide citation/source information that supports the probability distribution on the parameters used and some indication of the confidence level based upon such source. We will see below how another column can be added reflecting the relative importance of each assumption on the calculated NPV.

Another useful feature of Crystal Ball is that the key parameters can be loaded into each assumed distribution by making reference to the corresponding Excel cell. This is a useful feature as the key respective probability distribution parameters can be located directly into the spreadsheet financial model, often on a separate tab detailing all the assumptions and incorporating the results. An example is given as Exhibit 8.12.

Exhibit 8.12 shows in the right three columns examples of other useful information that can be included when developing an Monte Carlo model, specifically: the source (or authority) for the parameters selected and possibly the probability

EXHIBIT 8.12 Summary Table of Assumptions to be Used with the Financial Model of Exhibit 8.3

			Probability Distribution Parameters									
Cell	Assumption	Prob. Dist.	Units	Min.	Most Likely	Max.	Std. Dev.	Alpha	Beta	Source	Confidence Level	Relative Imptnce
B6	COGS	Uniform	(decimal)	0.55	-	0.59	-	-	-			
C3	ASP Y1 (Note 1)	Triangular	$	9000	10000	11000	-	-	-			
C2	Units Y1 (2)	Normal	Number	-	100	-	10	-	-			
B7	SG&A + R&D	Beta	(decimal)	0.33	0.35	0.37	-	5	5			

Note (1) Average Selling Price, Year 1 (which in turn affects the ASP for Y2 through Y5)
Note (2) Units Sold in Year 1 (which in turn affects Units for Y2 through Y6)

distribution chosen, the confidence level of the assumption parameters, and the perceived relative importance of the assumption upon the results. The confidence level can be indicated by simple H, M, or L for high, medium, or low. Likewise with the relative importance, although we will see that when using Crystal Ball the calculation quantifies the contribution of each assumption to the variance in NPV. These later columns become important when the financial model is refined, as will be discussed later.

The mechanics of loading the distributions and parameters into Crystal Ball involve selecting each assumption cell, beginning with B6 for the first row of Exhibit 8.12, and selecting the Define pulldown in the top toolbar and selecting Define Assumption. This will designate cell B6 with a distinct color used for all assumption cells. The screen then presents a gallery of all the available distribution functions. For B6 we would select Uniform. This would then lead to a screen like that shown in Exhibit 8.4. Then the parameters can be typed in by hand or by reference to the appropriate cell in the assumptions tab (as shown by example in Exhibit 8.12). This process is then repeated for every assumption cell.

IDENTIFICATION OF THE FORECAST CELLS Next, the forecast cells must be selected. In reference to Exhibit 8.3 clearly the NPV value must be selected (cell C18). When selected this cell becomes a color that is used to designate all the forecast cells. Any of the other cells can be identified as forecast values such as annual revenues and/or the gross cash flows for each year. It is useful to include a verbal description for each forecast cell (such as NPV), and the units in which the answer will be expressed (such as $, or $ Millions).

SELECTING THE RUN PARAMETERS The Monte Carlo calculation needs some kind of termination criteria. In valuation applications the most common, and simplest, criterion is the number of runs (trials). As discussed earlier, the more the merrier, as the forecast distributions become smoother with additional runs. The only downside is that the calculation takes longer. A common practice is to first do the runs one at a time, by selecting the appropriate icon in the toolbar, to be sure the cells are changing values as generally expected. Then set the number of runs to some small number like 1,000 to get a quick look at the forecast distributions. If the model appears to be working properly then the calculation can be continued to do complete, say, 10,000 runs. Unless the financial model is extraordinarily complex, such calculations can be done in a few minutes or perhaps a few tens of minutes.

EXTRACTING REPORTS Crystal Ball has useful reporting capabilities. Such reports can be customized in many ways, and saved as a separate Excel file. It is common to include in such reports all the assumptions that were used with their parameters both as a record of what caused what, but also to check to make sure that the proper values were indeed loaded into the correct assumption sell.

As we will see there are two reports that can be used to identify the relative importance that of each of the assumption cells has upon a forecast cell. One is known as a "tornado" diagram, and the other a "sensitivity" chart. We will show examples of both below.

REVISING THE MODEL One common model iteration is to consider more carefully those assumption cells that have the greatest impact upon the key forecast cells, which is typically the NPV value. This may lead to further background research to determine if a 'tighter' distribution can be supported for the most significant assumptions as this will have the most dramatic effect upon narrowing the NPV forecasts, which improves the value of any prediction.

Also different probability distributions can be tested with the more critical assumptions to gain an understanding of how important the shape of the assumed values is upon the forecast NPV distribution.

If the model is very complex the assumptions that are comparatively unimportant can be "frozen" to speed up the calculation and decrease the clutter in the reports and so improve the clarity of cause and effect.

MONTE CARLO NPV FORECAST RESULTS USING THE MODEL AND VALUES OF EXHIBIT 8.3 (RAHR = 25 PERCENT) WITH THE PROBABILITY DISTRIBUTION ASSUMPTIONS OF EXHIBIT 8.12 Exhibit 8.13 is the NPV forecast resulting from the assumption given in Exhibit 8.12 applied to the financial model of Exhibit 8.3. The graphs on the left half of Exhibit 8.13 show the relative probability (top picture) and cumulative probability (bottom picture). Relative probability figures are useful for seeing the peak(s) and tails of NPV values especially with regard to the distributions used for the various assumptions. Cumulative probability figures are useful for valuation and pricing judgments which we will discuss in later chapters on Dealmaking.

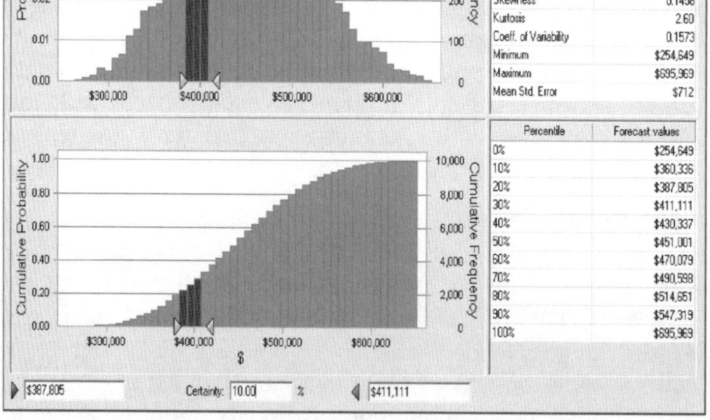

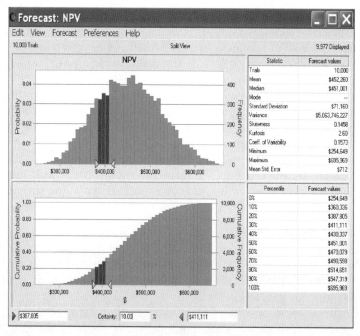

EXHIBIT 8.13 Forecast of the NPV Probability Distribution for Financial Model of Exhibit 8.3, using the Assumptions of Exhibit 8.12

The upper table on the right side of Exhibit 8.13 provides various statistics of the analysis. The number of runs, termed "trials "by the software (10,000), is shown at the top. As discussed previously, this number is generally not meaningful in terms of NPV valuation. The top graph shows a jaggedness for NPV values for relative probabilities greater than about 0.03 (on the y-axis). If we increase the number of runs (trials) to 50,000 or even higher we would expect that the NPV probability "hill" shown will become increasingly smooth.[14] The upper table gives us the mean ($452,260) and median ($451,001) NPV values, and the maximum ($695,969) and minimum ($254,649) values. Thus, the most favorable outcome of 10,000 runs, which occurs when all the assumption variables were the most favorable in terms of forecasting technology value, results in an NPV of $695,969; conversely, the very worst outcome, when every assumption within the given range and probability distribution were the least favorable, is $254,649. The other statistics provided by the software, such as standard deviation, skewness, and kurtosis, are generally not important for valuation purposes.

Depending upon whether one uses the mean or median value to measure the "average" NPV value, the result is approximately $452K, which is essentially identical to the NPV Method result shown in Exhibit 8.3. The reason for this equivalence is (1) All the assumption probability distributions were symmetric about the center, most likely value, given in Exhibit 8.3, and (2) the same RAHR value was used which, as we discussed above, should *not* be done for a Monte Carlo Method because the risk in such calculation is expressed in the assumptions. We will show the difference in the next example below.

Finally, the figures in Exhibit 8.13 show a demarcation bounded on the left by an NPV value of $387,805 and on the right by $411,111. This particular range was selected by using the cumulative 20 percentile and 30 percentile NPV values as given in the lower table on the right. The left end of the range signifies that there is a 20 percent chance that the NPV resulting from a business implementing the subject technology would experience an NPV value below $387,805, as a consequence of values of the set assumptions that were comparatively adverse. The NPV values from any cumulative percentile can be found directly from the Crystal Ball software such as from the NPV value by decades shown in the table on the lower right. By entering such 20 and 30 percentile values in the minimum and maximum cells on the figure on the lower left of Exhibit 8.13, Crystal Ball identifies the probability range between such boundaries, here ten percent—meaning that there is a ten percent probability that the NPV of a subject opportunity will occur between these two values, given the assumptions and model. We will return later to this particular range selection of 20 to 30 percentile when discussing use of the Monte Carlo projection in valuation, pricing, and Dealmaking.

"CORRECTING" THE MONTE CARLO CALCULATION FOR EXHIBIT 8.3 WITH THE ASSUMPTIONS OF EXHIBIT 8.12 USING A "K" VALUE (K = 15 PERCENT) INSTEAD OF AN RAHR VALUE (E.G., 25 PERCENT) As we saw in Chapter 7, a key aspect of the DCF Method is the specification of a risk factor by which all future cash flows are discounted. Because such factor includes risk, we generally designated such factor as RAHR (Risk Adjusted Hurdle Rate) rather than a "discount rate" (which we typically designated as "k"). So, Exhibit 8.3, which repeats Exhibit 7.17, discounts all future cash flows by the RAHR value of 25 percent. In the Monte Carlo calculation of Exhibit 8.13 we used

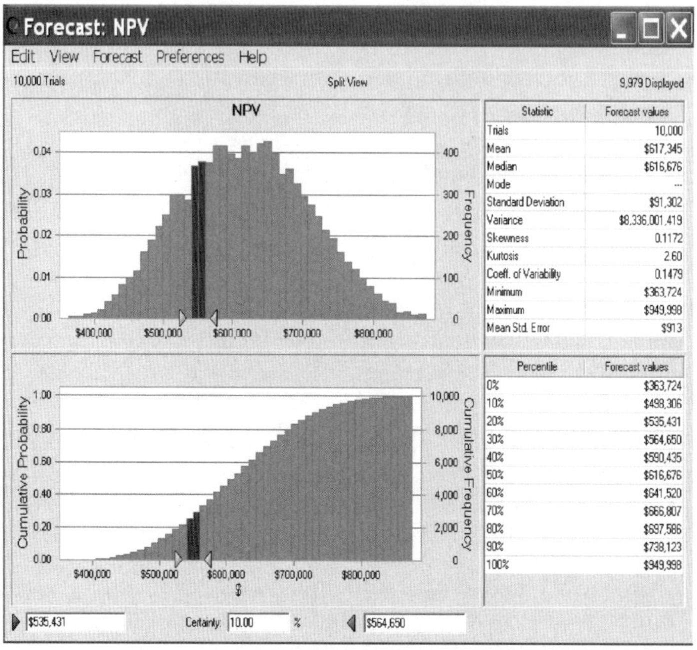

EXHIBIT 8.14 Forecast of the NPV Probability Distribution for Financial Model of Exhibit 8.3, using the Assumptions of Exhibit 8.12 but Replacing RAHR of 25 percent with a k of 15 Percent

this same 25 percent value so as to show the comparison between the Monte Carlo and DCF Methods.

Because the Monte Carlo Method expresses risk by the probability distributions in the assumptions, we can and should use a discount rate on future cash flows that does not include a risk component. As discussed above, a commonly used discount rate for a company is its WACC value or slightly above its WACC value. For illustration purposes, let us now use a k value of 15 percent instead of the RAHR value of 25 percent for the model of Exhibit 8.3 together with the same Monte Carlo assumptions we established in Exhibit 8.12. The resulting NPV distribution is given in Exhibit 8.14.

The dark shaded area shown in Exhibit 8.14 represents the NPV values bounded by the 20th and 30th percentiles, as was done in Exhibit 8.13.

Using the statistics from Exhibits 8.13 and 8.14, for RAHR = 25 percent and k = 15 percent, respectively, we can compare selected forecast NPV percentile values with the DCF Method of Exhibit 8.3. The result is shown in Exhibit 8.15.

	Monte Carlo Cumulative Percentile NPV				DCF NPV
Discount Rate	20	30	50 (Mean)	Mean	
RAHR 25%	$ 387,805	$ 411,111	$ 451,001	$ 452,260	$ 452,827
k 15%	$ 535,431	$ 564,650	$ 616,676	$ 617,345	$ 616,484

EXHIBIT 8.15 Comparison of Predicted NPV Values from the Data of Exhibits 8.13 and 8.14 and the DCF Method of Exhibit 8.3

The right-most column of Exhibit 8.15 labeled DCF NV, gives the NPV calculation using the respective discount rates (15 percent and 25 percent) directly in Exhibit 8.3. The Monte Carlo percentile values are taken directly from the statistics of the respective Exhibits 8.13 and 8.14. Because the Monte Carlo assumptions of Exhibit 8.13 were taken as symmetric around the expected value both the mean and median values shown in Exhibit 8.15 are very close to the corresponding DCF values, the difference from the mean value being only about one-tenth of a percent. So, for symmetric assumption distributions, the mean or median NPV values determined from Monte Carlo are typically very close to the DCF Method result.[15] The real power of the Monte Carlo Method even for symmetric assumptions is in gaining insight as to the NPV value for lower cumulative probabilities, as will be discussed later.

EFFECT OF UNSYMMETRICAL ASSUMPTIONS ON MONTE CARLO NPV FORECAST VALUES With unsymmetrical assumption distributions the NPV forecast is likely to be skewed rather than comparatively symmetric as shown in both Exhibits 8.13 and 8.14 in the top figures for probability distribution.

To demonstrate this, let us replace the assumption distribution for Cell B7, SG&A plus R&D expenses, in Exhibit 8.12 by changing the value of alpha. As was shown in Exhibits 8.9 and 8.10, the Beta Distribution can be readily skewed either toward higher or lower values by the relative values of the two parameters alpha and beta. For the Monte Carlo results of Exhibit 8.13 and 8.14 we used alpha = beta = 5, as given in the respective figures on Exhibit 8.10 and summarized in the bottom row

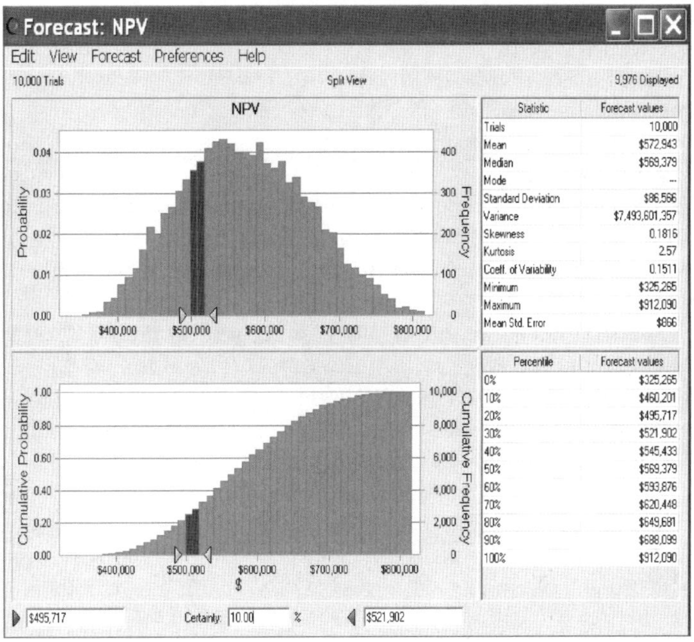

EXHIBIT 8.16 Forecast of the NPV Probability Distribution for Financial Model of Exhibit 8.3, but for k = 15 percent, and Alpha = 10 and Beta = 5 for the Beta Distribution Used in Exhibit 8.12

		SG&A+R&D Beta Dist.		Monte Carlo Cumulative Percentile NPV				DCF NPV
Discount Rate		Alpha	Beta	20	30	50 (Mean)	Mean	
RAHR	25%	5	5	$ 387,805	$ 411,111	$ 451,001	$ 452,260	$ 452,827
k	15%	5	5	$ 535,431	$ 564,650	$ 616,676	$ 617,345	$ 616,484
k	15%	10	5	$ 495,717	$ 521,892	$ 569,379	$ 569,379	$ 616,484

EXHIBIT 8.17 Comparison of Predicted NPV Values from the Data of Exhibits 8.13, 8.14, and 8.15, and the DCF Method of 8.3

of Exhibit 8.12. Let us now use the alpha and beta values shown in Exhibit 8.10 on page 366 for alpha = 10, beta = 5, which causes the SG&A plus R&D expense distribution to be skewed to right though fixed by the same upper and lower bounds (33 and 37 percent). When the Beta Distribution has unequal alpha and beta values then the most likely value is no longer the midpoint (35 percent) as given in Exhibit 8.12. Because this unsymmetrical assumption "weights" the SG&A plus R&D costs to higher values, we would expect the result to forecast an NPV distribution skewed to lower values than given in Exhibit 8.14.

The result is shown in Exhibit 8.16.

We can compare the results of Exhibit 8.16 with Exhibit 8.15 as shown in Exhibit 8.17. We see here that skewing one of the cost categories (SG&A plus R&D) to higher values results in a decrease in mean/median NPV of approximately $50K with reductions of ca. $40K at the 20th and 30th percentiles compared with the symmetric Beta Distribution.

One of the great powers of the Monte Carlo Method is the ability to express beliefs about uncertainty in very flexible terms. The Beta Function is particularly useful in this regard.

The Toolbox

Assumption uncertainty is typically expressed as some range bracketing the most likely, or expected, or "base" value. If the probability distribution used for the assumption is symmetric, with the most likely value at the midpoint of the range, then the effect is to assume values larger and smaller than the most likely value are equally likely, or symmetric. Depending then upon the relationship of such assumption in the Monte Carlo model the forecast NPV will be either symmetric or, skewed slightly because of some nonlinear effect of NPV upon the assumption. This situation is parallel to a sensitivity analysis using the DCF Method. If one wants to consider a downside weighting to any given assumption, assuming, say, a greater likelihood of assumption values below the most likely value (and "below" in the sense that such range causes lower NPV values), then only way to do this using the DCF Method is to use greater weighting of such low range calculated NPVs, using probability distribution techniques such as was shown in Exhibit 8.2.

However, using the Monte Carlo Method, skewing the distribution for an assumption with fixed assumption end points (min and max values) can be done using a custom distribution or the Beta Distribution for unequal values of alpha and beta. This capability yields a greater understanding of the sensitivity of the forecast NPV to asymmetry in an assumption. By weighting the assumption in such a manner the forecast NPV is skewed and enables one to see the effect of more frequent 'adversity' for the same most likely value and assumption uncertainty range.

USING MONTE CARLO RESULTS TO ASSESS THE COMPARATIVE SIGNIFICANCE OF ASSUMPTIONS As was introduced by Exhibit 8.12, the Monte Carlo Method is usually not a "one shot" effort. The forecast results are no better than the assumptions used, garbage in/garbage out, or great judgment in/valuable insights out. The Monte Carlo software provides a means of direct comparison of the relative importance of each of the assumptions upon any forecast value, in our case usually the NPV. There are two ways this can be done.

The Tornado Chart The first way is commonly known as a "tornado chart" because the graphical portrayal of the result resembles a side view of a tornado.

The tornado chart is developed in Crystal Ball software directly from the Monte Carlo model (such as Exhibit 8.3) and its corresponding assumptions ((such as Exhibit 8.16) and *prior to* running the actual simulation (e.g., 10,000 runs). It does this by considering each assumption one at a time, "freezing" the values of all other assumptions at their most likely/"center" value. The software then calculates the effect on the forecasts, such as NPV, by calculating the change in NPV by a change in the assumption being examined over the range specified. The software repeats this one-at-a-time calculation of the change in NPV caused by the range in the assumption. Finally, the software ranks the assumptions in their order of the greatest effect upon NPV.

Exhibit 8.18 shows the tornado diagram for the example we have been examining (Exhibits 8.3 with 8.16).

The tornado chart of Exhibit 8.18 shows that the range of the Cost of Goods Sold (COGS) assumption has the greatest effect upon the NPV range. Specifically, the "downside" input of COGS, meaning the minimum assumed valued of 55 percent, cases the NPV to be $668,206, as shown in the top row of the top table and the right edge of the top box of the tornado chart. "Downside" as used here means "minimum" value, not adversity, because, as we discussed, any reduction in the value of the COGS value will cause an increase in the NPV, which is designated by the lighter shading for the right half of the top box of the tornado chart.

The remaining three assumptions each have about the same effect upon NPV, though SG&A plus R&D is the highest and Average Selling Price in Year one the lowest. The upper table shows the quantitative effect upon NPV for the minimum and maximum values for each of these assumptions.

The lower table of Exhibit 8.18 provides NPV values for five intermediate points along the range of each of the assumptions. The midpoint of each yields the same NPV value which approximates the median value determined from the actual Monte Carlo calculation (i.e., $569,379 from Exhibit 8.16).

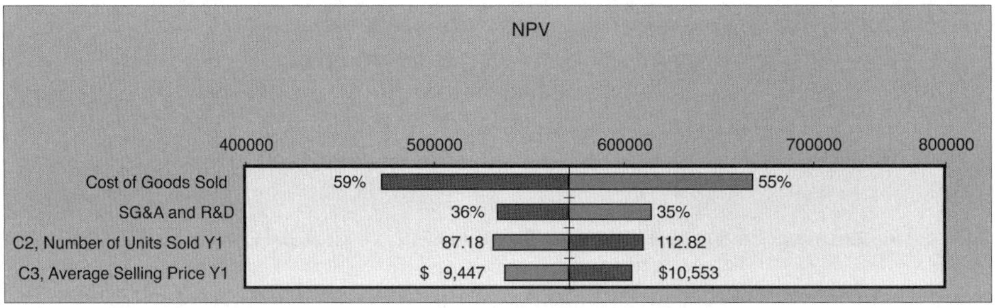

	NPV			Input		
Variable	*Downside*	*Upside*	*Range*	*Downside*	*Upside*	*Base Case*
Cost of Goods Sold	$ 668,206	$ 472,958	$ 195,247	55%	59%	57%
SG&A and R&D	$ 614,367	$ 533,539	$ 80,828	35%	36%	36%
Number of Units Sold Y1	$ 531,137	$ 610,027	$ 78,889	87.18	112.82	100
Average Selling Price Y1	$ 537,188	$ 603,975	$ 66,787	$ 9,447	$ 10,553	$ 10,000

	NPV				
Variable	*10.0%*	*30.0%*	*50.0%*	*70.0%*	*90.0%*
Cost of Goods Sold	$ 668,206	$ 619,394	$ 570,582	$ 521,770	$ 472,958
SG&A and R&D	$ 614,367	$ 588,066	$ 570,582	$ 554,261	$ 533,539
Number of Units Sold Y1	$ 531,137	$ 554,441	$ 570,582	$ 586,722	$ 610,027
Average Selling Price Y1	$ 537,188	$ 556,965	$ 570,582	$ 584,198	$ 603,975

EXHIBIT 8.18 Tornado Chart Portrayal of Assumptions Results for the Monte Carlo Calculation of Exhibit 8.16

Because the tornado chart calculation is done apart from any Monte Carlo simulation, and it is examining the separate effect of each assumption, the results do not correspond exactly to what happens as a result of a simulation. For that we need to consider the sensitivity chart.

The Sensitivity Chart Another output of the Crystal Ball software is a "sensitivity chart." This chart is produced *after* a run is complete and, thereby, shows the comparative effect of the probability distributions of the assumptions upon NPV. The results associated with the Monte Carlo calculation shown in Exhibit 8.16 is given in Exhibit 8.19.

The first key observation from Exhibit 8.19 is the ranking of the relative importance of each of the four assumptions as they have been modeled to yield the result given in Exhibit 8.18. The result shows that the COGS uncertainty has the great effect upon NPV value, followed by the remaining three assumptions of essentially equal comparative significance. The tabular data expresses these same effects in quantified form.

These results are determined by software taking into account the effect of each assumption upon NPV value as the probability distributions are being calculated. If the same simulation is run a second time, these values will change slightly because no repeated Monte Carlo simulation exactly duplicates an earlier one, whereas the tornado chart would always yield the same result.

In this example, the ranking of relative importance of the assumptions is the same from both the sensitivity and tornado charts, although this does not always occur.

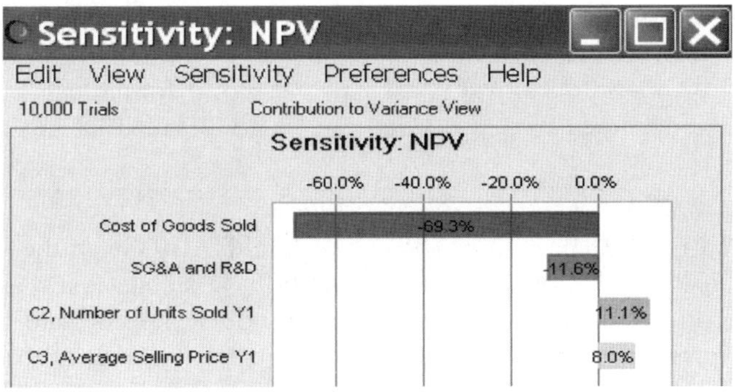

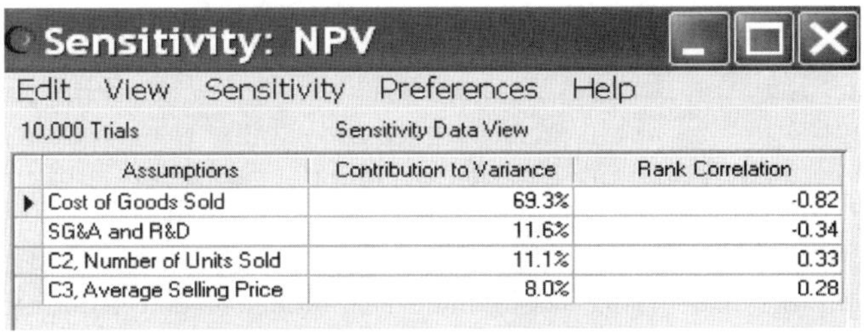

Assumptions	Contribution to Variance	Rank Correlation
Cost of Goods Sold	69.3%	-0.82
SG&A and R&D	11.6%	-0.34
C2, Number of Units Sold	11.1%	0.33
C3, Average Selling Price	8.0%	0.28

EXHIBIT 8.19 **Sensitivity Chart for the Effect of Assumptions upon NPV Values Based upon Exhibit 8.16**

The comparative importance of COGS to NPV uncertainty is driven in part by our use of a Uniform Distribution, which, as discussed, represents the greatest expression of uncertainty because all values in the range are considered to be equally probable.[16]

Clearly improvements to the Monte Carlo calculation would benefit most by any refinements achievable for the Cost of Goods Sold. This may necessitate further study into the factors that comprise COGS estimates or consideration of a more focused distribution based upon (justified) expert judgment. The use of any of the Triangular, Normal, or Beta Distributions would more heavily weight COGS values toward the center, most likely value (35 percent), and reduce the effect of COGS uncertainty upon NPV variance.

The use of sensitivity charts is very important when dealing with many assumptions because it is not always clear which ones are more significant and there are limited resources available for further research into gaining better insights into such uncertainties.

One of the limitations of sensitivity charts is that they can incorrectly prioritize the effect on NPV of the respective probability distribution if any of the assumptions are correlated; we will consider correlated assumptions below. Sensitivity charts can also be misleading for situations where assumptions are discrete such as in Exhibit 8.11 (the first figures); we will consider later examples of discrete assumptions.

FORMAL MONTE CARLO REPORTS All of the above results can be created in a single report generated by Crystal Ball. An example report for the model shown in Exhibit 8.18 is given in Appendix 8A. In Crystal Ball the report format can be customized to be over or under inclusive, as needed, and readily saved in an Excel or other software format.

FURTHER ASSUMPTIONS ANALYSIS AND THE USE OF CORRELATIONS In the examples we have been considering above, all the assumptions were modeled assuming that they were uncorrelated in a statistical sense. Of course appropriate consideration of individual probability distributions and their parameters in the context of all the other assumptions is a normal procedure. For instance, it is a well established economic principle that (for many circumstances) as the unit price of a product is made greater, the number of units sold will be reduced because customers tend to buy less of things that cost more. In the above examples, it was implicitly assumed that two of the assumptions in the financial model—average selling price and the number of units sold—were characterized by probability distributions independent of one another, as is commonly done for initial year revenue projections for a technology startup.

However, Crystal Ball has the ready capability to correlate assumptions such that the value pairs the Monte Carlo uses for such correlated assumptions satisfies both the criteria of the assumed probability distributions and the degree of correlation.

To illustrate how this works, let us again use the model of Exhibit 8.3 with the same probability distributions for each of the four assumptions except that we will change the Triangular Distribution previously used for the Average Selling Price Year 1 (ASPY1), Cell C3, to a Normal Distribution as we used for the Number of Units Sold in Year 1 (NUSY1), C2. The COGS assumption will be modeled by the Uniform Distribution of Exhibit 8.5, and the SG&A plus R&D by the Beta Distribution of Exhibit 8.10 with alpha = 10, beta = 5.

We will compare the results obtained for three cases regarding the two assumptions ASPY1 and NUSY1:

- Standard deviation of 10percent, with no correlation between them
- Standard deviation of 7.5 percent, with no correlation between them
- Standard deviation of 10 percent, with a correlation coefficient of −0.9

The standard deviation for any Normal Distribution assumption can be adjusted by substituting the appropriate value into the Crystal Ball assumption cell such as was done in Exhibit 8.7 for NUSY1: for a center (most-likely) value of 100 units, a standard deviation of 10 units corresponds to 10 percent, and 5 units to 5 percent.

The degree of correlation between any two variables can be established by clicking on the Correlate button in the same assumption window. Then, in the subsequent window a selection can be made for the other assumption(s) to which NUSY1 should be correlated, and the degree of correlation, bounded by the values of +1.0 perfect correlation, and to −1.0 perfect anti-correlation, as shown in Exhibit 8.20.

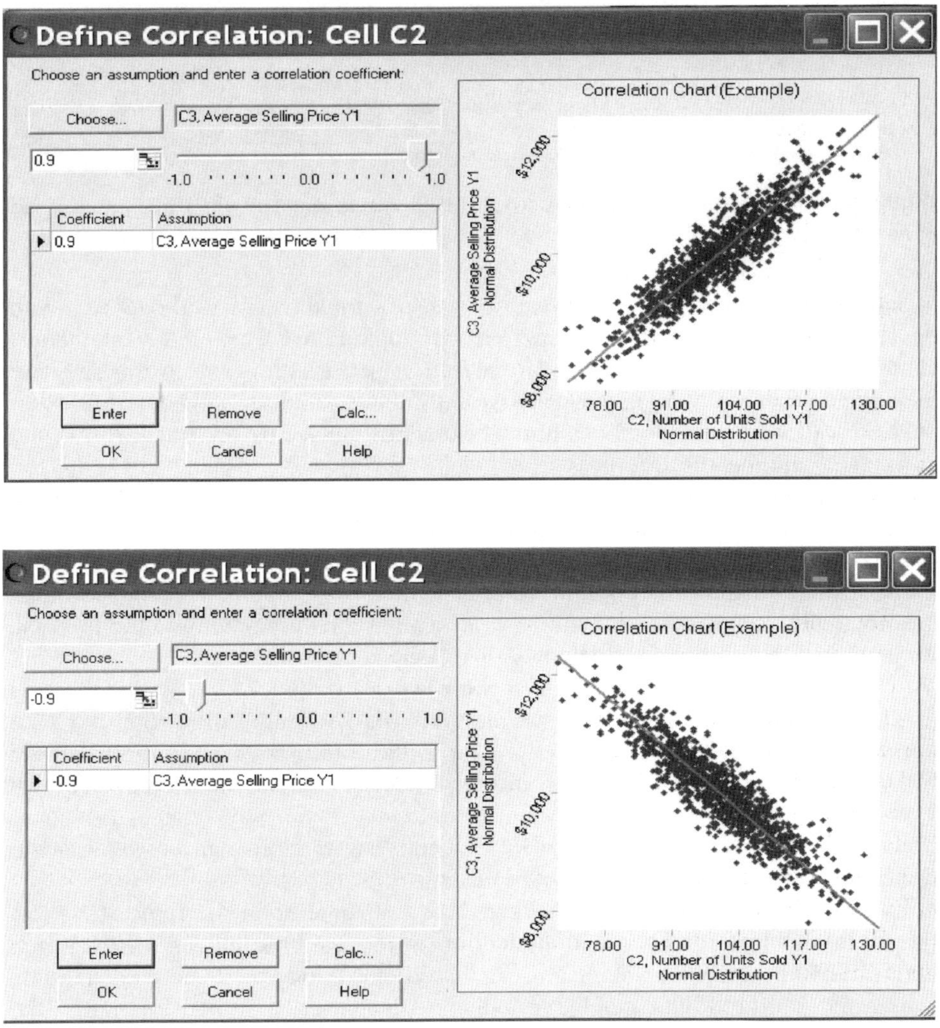

EXHIBIT 8.20 **Example Correlation of +0.9 and −0.9 of Normal Distribution Assumptions ASPY1 with NUSY1**

The top figure of Exhibit 8.20 shows the correlation between ASPY1 and NUSY1 for a correlation coefficient of +0.9 reflecting that a nearly perfect correlation between these two assumptions will be imposed by the Crystal Ball software. This means that both assumptions will be characterized by their respective Normal Distribution relationships but that when a high value occurs (statistically) for the NUSY1 there is a high probability that a high value of ASPY1 will also occur, and vice versa. The figure on the bottom in Exhibit 8.20 shows the opposite relationship characterized by the −0.90 correlation.

Exhibit 8.21 gives a tabulation of the key results from the three cases identified above.

Looking at the first two rows, we can see the effect of a reduced uncertainty in the assumptions ASPY1 and NUSY1 by comparing the forecasts of Total Revenues

Assumption*		Cell I4, Total Revenues ($Millions) Percentiles			Statistics			Cell I17, NPV ($K) Percentiles			Statistics		
Std Dev	Correlation	20	30	50	Std Dev	Kurtosis	Skew	20	30	50	Std Dev	Kurtosis	Skew
10.0%	0.00	$13.9	$14.5	$15.4	$1.8	2.96	-0.01	$481	$512	$564	$103.0	2.95	0.35
7.5%	0.00	$14.2	$14.7	$15.4	$1.4	2.97	0.04	$489	$517	$569	$ 92.0	2.62	0.22
10.0%	-0.90	$14.3	$14.7	$15.0	$1.3	3.19	-0.23	$490	$518	$567	$ 84.6	2.45	0.12

*re ASPY1 and NUSY1, both characterized by Normal Distributions around $10,000 and 100 units, respectively

EXHIBIT 8.21 Key Results for the Forecasts of Total Revenues and NPV for Three Cases of the Assumptions ASPY1 and NUSY1 Based Upon the Model in Exhibit 8.3

and NPV in addition to their respective statistics for the two values of standard deviation used for these two assumptions. By looking at the 20 and 30 percentile values for Total Revenues and NPV, we can see that a *decrease* in the standard deviation in these two assumptions causes an *increase* in Total Revenues and NPV. Such an outcome may not be intuitively obvious, so let us look at the statistics associated with these two forecasts.

The standard deviation of the forecasts is a measure of the comparative width, or uncertainty. The kurtosis is a statistical measure of the peakedness of the forecast distribution, where the value is exactly 3.0 for a perfectly normal distribution. For kurtosis values greater than 3.0 the forecast probability curve is more peaked than a Normal Distribution. The skewness is a measure of the asymmetry of the forecast; for a Normal Distribution the skewness is exactly zero.

What we see by comparing the first two rows of Exhibit 8.21 is that the reduction in standard deviation for the two assumptions ASPY1 and NUSY1 from 10 to 7.5 percent causes a reduced uncertainty in both the forecasts of Total Revenue and NPV as can be seen by a reduction in the standard deviation values, namely: $1.8 to $1.4 million for Total Revenues, and $103K to $92K for NPV. This makes sense because a reduction of uncertainty in the input assumptions can be expected to reduce the uncertainty in the output forecasts.

One of the consequences of such reduced uncertainty in the forecasts is that the "tails"—at both ends—are thinned out as more of the values are clustered about the 50th percentile value. This increased clustering about the median value causes the 20th and 30th percentile values to increase, as shown for both Total Revenues and NPV. We will return to the significance of this point.

Now let us compare rows one and three in Exhibit 8.21, namely where the same standard deviation is used for both assumptions—ASPY1 and NUSY1—but they are now anti-correlated by the coefficient of -0.9. Looking at the statistics for both Total Revenue and NPV for the third row, for the correlation coefficent, compared to the first row with no correlation, we see that the forecasts have a reduced uncertainty similar to that obtained by uncorrelated assumptions with a lower standard deviation. This result may initially appear counter intuitive. However, by establishing a correlation between assumptions that results in reduced extreme values (thinner tails) for the calculated annual revenues, which as we showed with the second row of Exhibit 8.21 causes a thinning out of the forecast tails and an increase in clustering of values near the mean. We have as a result the 20 and 30 percentile values for the third row for both Total Revenues and NPV being greater than they were for the first row (zero correlation) when using the same standard deviations for these two assumptions.

Do such correlations always decrease uncertainty? Sadly, no. The reason it does so here is that the inverse relationship between price and quantity when correlated reduces the extremes of their product, which is the year-by-year revenue. When the tails of the revenue have been thinned, then the result is tantamount to using a revenue assumption with lower statistical uncertainty. If two variables were correlated, but their correlation caused a compounding effect on uncertainty then the existence of a correlation would lead to greater NPV uncertainty.

The 20 and 30 percentile NPV values tend to be significant because these tend to be indicators of technology licensing value. As we will discuss later in this chapter, buyers are normally not very interested in paying the NPV for an opportunity corresponding to the 50 percentile value because that means that half the time they will have overpaid (if paid on a lump sum basis at the time of technology rights acquisition). A buyer will normally be highly biased to paying for opportunities for which the probability of the return exceeding the payment is far better than 50:50, which is tantamount to a coin flip. A buyer paying at the 20 percentile value has an 80 percent chance, of experiencing a return exceeding the price paid. Although we consider this in further detail later, at this point we can make several observations:

- Reducing the uncertainty of any assumption, but especially the assumptions that have the greatest influence on NPV values (as determined using Tornado or Sensitivity Charts), generally increases the licensing value to the seller as measured by, for example, the 20th and 30th percentile NPV values. Comparing rows one and two in Exhibit 8.21, the increase in NPV value is in the range of \$5 to \$8 thousand (the difference in the 30th percentile and 20th percentile values between row two and row one) as a consequence of the reduction in the shown standard deviation values for ASPY1 and NUSY1.
- Establishing a correlation between any two assumptions likewise generally increases the value to the seller as measured by NPV values at the 20th and 30th percentiles. In Exhibit 8.21 the difference between the row three and row one values in NPV is in the range of \$6 to \$9 thousand (for the 30th and 20th percentiles, respectively).
- The validity of the above generalization regarding an increase in the 20th and 30th percentile NPV values depends upon the specific assumptions and financial model, as does the magnitude of the NPV enhancement.

The Toolbox

Tornado and sensitivity charts can be used to segment assumptions into defined categories of relative significance based upon their effect on NPV. Internal R&D and business planning activities can then be re-prioritized to seek data or rational support for a less uncertain probability distribution for the high significance assumptions. Reducing the uncertainty of high significance assumptions can be accomplished by (1) narrowing the upper and/or lower bounds of the assumption range, (2) using a more narrow probability distribution within the same

(*continued*)

(*Continued*)

bounds (such as high alpha and beta values with the Beta Distribution), and/or (3) developing a correlation with other assumptions (if such correlation has the effect of being combined with a net less uncertain input to the NPV calculation).

The assumptions exhibiting a more moderate influence on NPV can be maintained "as is" while analysis proceeds on the high influence variables. It may even be possible to reduce R&D and our analytical activities for these moderate influence variables.

The probability distributions for the low importance assumptions can be replaced by single value estimates to simplify and speed up the calculation, which may be helpful for very high complexity financial models.

Valuation Judgments Based Upon Monte Carlo NPV Distributions

As we will consider in Chapter 10, there many ways to express value payments to the seller for any given opportunity. One obvious, and simple, way is a single lump sum, paid up amount at deal closing. This is most directly applicable to an NPV calculation because the payment to the seller reduces the NPV dollar-for-dollar when made as lump sum/upfront fully paid up consideration for the license.

MONTE CARLO NPV FORECAST USING THE BASELINE TEMPLATE In this section we will consider how the NPV determined by Monte Carlo can be used to value an opportunity. In Chapter 11 we will discuss this further in the context of Dealmaking. To aid our discussion let us return to the baseline template previously developed as Exhibit 7.20 and use it to perform two Monte Carlo calculations: one using only symmetric assumption distributions and one with certain of the assumption distributions being non-symmetric.

Exhibit 8.22 is a screen shot of Exhibit 7.20, but for a baseline corporate RAHR value of 15 percent, that we will use for these two Monte Carlo calculation comparisons.

Proceeding as before, the first step is to identify each assumption to be studied and ascribe a probability distribution with associated statistics that reasonably characterizes the range and nature of the uncertainties. For this analysis we will use the very flexible Beta Distribution discussed previously in this chapter. The standard parameters for the Beta Distribution are four: minimum and maximum values, in addition to alpha and beta. When the alpha and beta values are equal, the Beta Distribution is symmetric, when beta is greater than alpha the distribution is skewed toward higher values of the assumption being modeled, and when alpha and beta are made larger (equal or not) the Beta Distribution is "tighter," meaning the "tails" are thinner corresponding to greater certainty that the distribution of values will be closer to the midpoint value.

An alternative means of specifying a Beta Distribution shape is to specify minimum and maximum values, and the values for 25th and 75th percentiles. Crystal Ball software also has various other standard four-parameter specification choices and even permits a custom specification, from which the Beta Distribution, as

	A	B	C	D	E	F	G	H	I	J	K	L	M	N	O	P	Q
1	Year			1	2	3	4	5			6	7	8	9	10		
2		Assumed							Startup							Mature	10-Year
3		Ratios							Total							Total	TOTAL
4	Revenues			0.00	2.00	15.00	70.00	170.00	257.00		200.00	224.00	250.88	280.99	314.70	1270.57	1527.57
5	*CAGR Current Yr*			-	*650%*	*367%*	*143%*	*18%*			*12.0%*	*12.0%*	*12.0%*	*12.0%*	*0.0%*		
6	INCOME STATEMENT																
7	Dep-Amor(1)	*10*		0.20	1.20	4.20	8.20	10.00	23.80		11.1	12.3	13.7	15.2	16.9	69.3	93.11
8	All Other(2)			*3.00*	*8.00*	*15.40*	40.80	109.00			128.89	144.46	161.91	181.46	203.37	820.09	
9	Total Costs, $	*70.0%*		3.20	9.20	19.60	49.00	119.00	*200.00*		140.00	156.80	175.62	196.69	220.29	889.40	1089.40
10	*Total Cost, %*			-	*460%*	*131%*	*70%*	*70%*			*70%*	*70%*	*70%*	*70%*	*70%*		
11	EBIT			(3.20)	(7.20)	(4.60)	21.00	51.00	57.00		60.00	67.20	75.26	84.30	94.41	381.17	438.17
12	PFT (of EBIT)	34.0%		0.00	0.00	0.00	2.04	17.34			20.40	22.85	25.59	28.66	32.10		
13	EAT			(3.20)	(7.20)	(4.60)	18.96	33.66	37.62		39.60	44.35	49.67	55.64	62.31	251.57	289.19
14	Carry forward loss			(3.20)	(10.40)	(15.00)	3.96	37.62			77.22	121.57	171.25	226.88	289.19		
15	CASH FLOW ADJUSTMENTS																
16	Dep. Amor(1)	*10*		0.20	1.20	4.20	8.20	10.00	23.80		11.1	12.3	13.7	15.2	16.9	69.3	93.11
17	Incr WC(3)	*10%*		0.20	1.30	5.50	10.00	3.00			2.40	2.69	3.01	3.37	3.37		
18	CapEx(4)			*2.00*	*10.00*	*30.00*	*40.00*	*18.00*	*100.00*		*11.1*	*12.3*	*13.7*	*15.2*	*16.9*		169.20
19	GCF			(5.20)	(17.30)	(35.90)	(22.84)	22.66	(58.58)		37.21	41.70	46.67	52.29	58.96	236.84	178.26
20		*RAHR*															
21	DCF	*15.00%*		(4.85)	(14.03)	(25.31)	(14.00)	12.08			17.25	16.81	16.36	15.94	15.63		
22	NPV	35.88															
23																	

EXHIBIT 8.22 Baseline Template for Monte Carlo Valuation Example

shown in Exhibit 8.23, are the Beta Distribution parameters used for the Monte Carlo model of Exhibit 8.22. The two shaded rows at the bottom for the COGS distribution in Cell B9 are alternative Beta Distributions, one symmetric and one asymmetric.

The right-most pair of columns in Exhibit 8.23 shows the 25th and 75th percentile values for the Beta Distribution. So, for the first row, Revenues for Y2 (Cell E4), the Beta Distribution input parameters are the shown range ($0 and $4 million) and the alpha and beta values (4 and 4); for such parameters, the Beta Distribution provides 0 to 25th percentile between $0 and $1.52 Million, 25th to 75th percentile between

Model Input Assumptions				Beta Distribution Parameters/Values					
				Range Specification		Parameter Specification		Percentile Specification	
	Year(s)	Cell	Middle Value	Min.	Max.	Alpha	Beta	25th	75th
Revenues	2	E4	$ 2	$ -	$ 4	4	4	$1.52	$2.48
	3	F4	$ 15	$ 5	$ 25	3	3	$12.19	$17.81
	4	G4	$ 70	$ 50	$ 90	2	2	$63.05	$76.95
	5	H4	$ 170	$ 120	$ 220	2	2	$152.64	$187.36
	6	K4	$ 200	$ 150	$ 250	2	2	$182.64	$217.36
Revenue CAGR	7-10	K5-K9	12%	7%	17%	4	4	8.92%	13.08%
Costs "Other"	2	E8	$ 8	$ 5	$ 11	4	4	$7.27	$8.73
	3	F8	$ 15.4	$ 10.8	$ 20.0	4	4	$13.79	$16.21
Two COGS Distributions									
SYMMETRIC	4-10	B9	70%	60%	80%	4	4	67.58%	72.42%
ASYMMETRIC	4-10	B9	70%	60%	80%	4	3	68.94%	74.06%

EXHIBIT 8.23 Beta Distribution Parameters Used for the Assumptions in the Monte Carlo Model of Exhibit 8.22

$1.52 and $2.48 Million, and 75th to 100th percentile between $2.48 and $4 Million. For the shown minimum and maximum specification, the identical Beta Distribution would be achieved by using either the shown alpha and beta pair, or the 25th and 75th percentile pair.

Using the Beta Distribution of Exhibit 8.23 with the Monte Carlo model of Exhibit 8.22, the two NPV forecasts corresponding to the symmetric and asymmetric COGS values shown in the shaded rows of Exhibit 8.23 are shown in Exhibit 8.24.

The cumulative NPV values corresponding to the 20th and 30th percentiles of NPV are shown in Exhibit 8.24 by the shaded vertical areas. The first pair of figures on are for the symmetric COGS Beta Distribution, while the second pair are for the asymmetric Beta Distribution.

The 50th percentile value of NPV for the symmetric COGS case, namely $35.39 million, closely corresponds to the NPV determined by the DCF Method using the same 15 percent RAHR value, namely $35.88 million. The reason these values are close to one another is that all the assumptions used in Exhibit 8.23 are symmetric about their midpoint value, including the COGS distribution (only for the respective figure of Exhibit 8.24).

For the asymmetric COGS distribution, the respective figure of Exhibit 8.24, the 50th percentile value, $29.79 Million, is significantly less than the DCF Model value of $35.88 Million. The cause is simply the asymmetry of the COGS input results in more frequent high value of COGS that in turn reduces the GCF values. Put another way, using the NPV forecast values in Exhibit 8.24 for the asymmetric COGS, the DCF Method most likely result of $35.88 Million corresponds to approximately the 64th percentile, showing this value as being 14 points less likely to occur than a DCF Method or a Monte Carlo Method with symmetric assumptions would calculate.

By comparing the results for the symmetric and asymmetric NPV values at the 20th, 30th, and 50th percentiles we can see that the asymmetric NPV values are approximately $6 million less than the corresponding values for the symmetric COGS distribution: $5.99, $6.02, and $5.60 million, respectively. Whereas the minimum and maximum values differ by about half as much: $3.12 and $2.25 Million for the 0th and 100th percentiles, respectively. The NPV is reduced for the asymmetric COGS assumption distribution because (1) the skewing was to higher values of COGS, and (2) higher values of COGS result in lower GCF values because costs are subtracted from revenues. The reduction of NPV for the asymmetric COGS distribution at the extreme values of NPV (0th and 100th percentiles) is less than at the 20th, 30th, and 50th percentiles because the Beta Distribution uses specified range end points and these were unchanged.

The sensitivity charts corresponding to these two COGS distributions are shown in Exhibit 8.25.

Exhibit 8.25 illustrates two important results. First, the uncertainty (variance) in NPV is almost totally (ca. 70 percent) the result of the uncertainty caused by the COGS distribution, the Year 6 Revenue uncertainty is also an important contribution and all other assumptions are of minor consequence. Secondly, the relative contribution to NPV variance is greater for the asymmetric COGS assumption. This is caused by more COGS values for the asymmetric case being further from the mid-value.

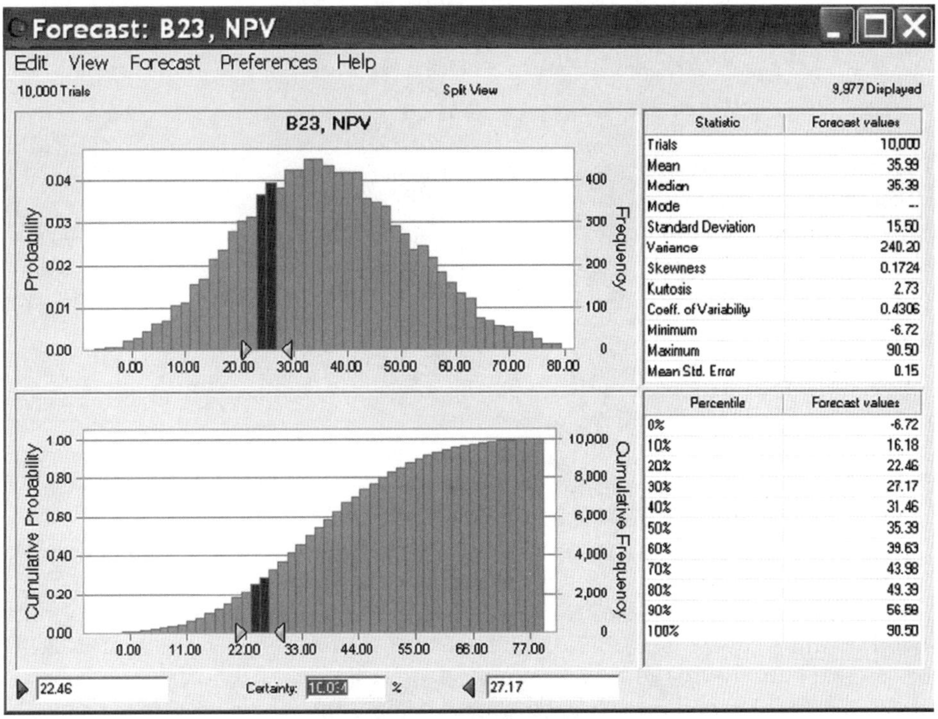

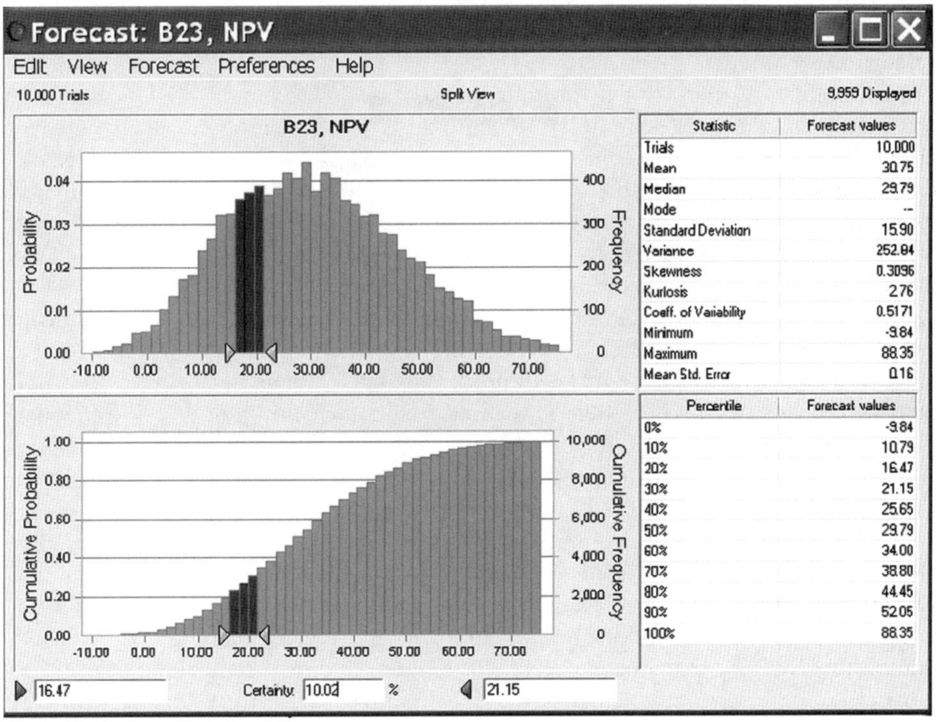

EXHIBIT 8.24 NPV Forecast for the Baseline Template of Exhibit 8.22 with the Assumptions of Exhibit 8.23

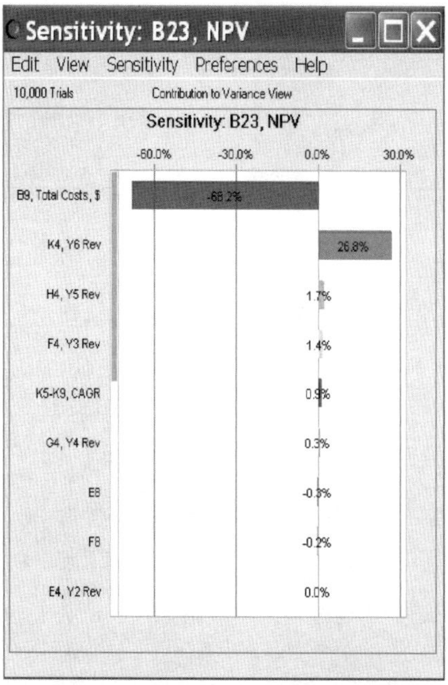

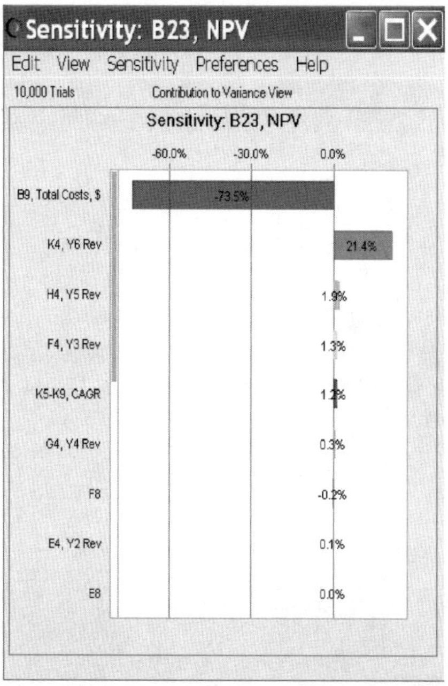

EXHIBIT 8.25 Sensitivity Charts Corresponding to the NPV Forecast of Exhibit 8.24

COGS Beta Distribution Parameters/Values | **NPV Forecast Distribution**

Range Specification		Parameter Specification		Percentile Specification		NPV Forecast Distribution			
Min.	Max.	Alpha	Beta	25th	75th	0%	20%	30%	50%
60%	80%	4	3	68.9%	74.1%	–$9.84	$16.47	$21.15	$29.79
60%	80%	8	6	69.7%	73.3%	–$6.30	$19.55	$23.48	$30.20
65%	75%	8	6	69.8%	71.6%	$1.76	$24.49	$27.58	$33.01

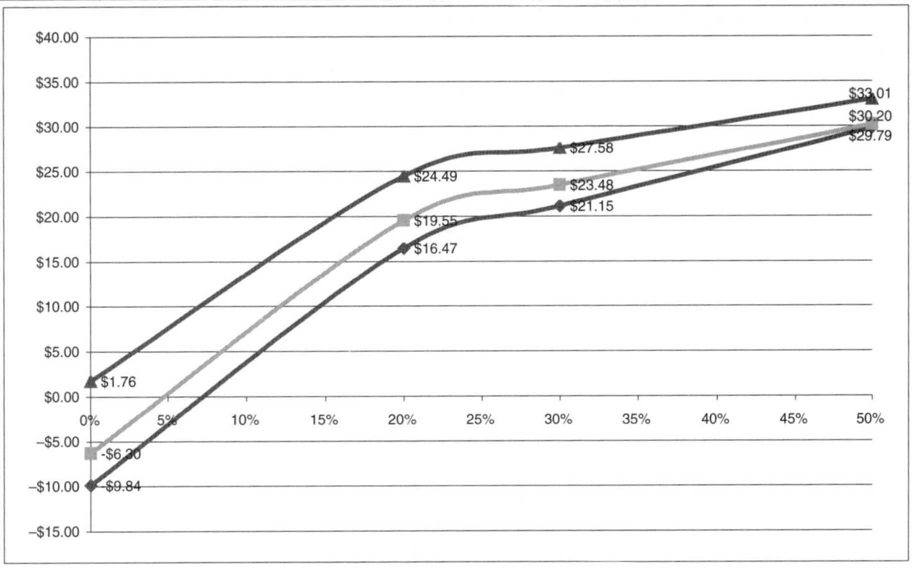

EXHIBIT 8.26 NPV Forecast for the Baseline Template of Exhibit 8.22 with the Assumptions of Exhibit 8.23 for the Three Asymmetric COGS Cases Shown

The key observations for this example are:

- The use of asymmetric distributions for assumptions can be useful in examining downside effects (adversity) upon NPV values, either in combination with changes in the assumed minimum and maximum range values or for fixed range values (as was done in Exhibits 8.23 and 8.24).
- Sensitivity charts highlight which assumptions are most significant in causing NPV uncertainty, with assumption asymmetry causing a greater contribution to NPV variance.

Finally, let us examine the effect of (1) using a "tighter" asymmetric COGS distribution, (2) and, in combination, reducing the COGS range end points. Specifically, the table shown in Exhibit 8.26 shows the three asymmetric COGS cases considered, the first of which is identical to that considered above, and the graph shows the resulting NPV forecast distribution for the shown percentile values.

Exhibit 8.26 shows how the forecast NPV values increase as (1) the COGS distribution is made tighter (by higher values of alpha and beta), and (2) the range end points on the COGS distribution is made narrower. Had this example been for symmetric COGS distributions, the effect upon the 50 percentile NPV value would have been small. However, because of the assumed asymmetric, we see an increase in the 50th percentile value, though even more dramatic increases at the 0th, 20th, and 30th percentile values, which will be important for our valuation purposes soon to be discussed.

It should be noted that because of the probabilistic nature of all Monte Carlo calculations, a replicate calculation does not yield exactly the same results. For instance, for the NPV calculation corresponding to the top row of Exhibit 8.26, replicate calculations yielded:

- 0th percentile: −$11.27, −$11.15, −$10.11
- 20th percentile: $16.54, $16.50, $16.69
- 30th percentile: $21.27, $21.35, $21.28
- 50th percentile: $29.86, $29.48, $29.68

The most significant variation is, as would be expected, at the extreme value (0th percentile above), with comparatively little variation for the other shown percentiles (ca. 1 percent, or ca. $0.5 Million).

VALUATION FROM A MONTE CARLO NPV FORECAST Let us assume that the result shown in Exhibit 8.24 represents our final best thinking about a particular technology opportunity. How can we use such a result to determine a valuation of the technology? With Monte Carlo we do not have a single NPV value, but many thousand corresponding to the number of runs used (10,000 in Exhibit 8.24). Which one(s) should be used?

We had a similar issue with the DCF Method. Although the DCF Method yields a single value of NPV, the Method commonly considers multiple scenarios, and examines the effect of varying certain of the assumptions in a sensitivity or trend line analysis. So in practice there is not normally just one NPV value even for the traditional DCF Method. Which one is "right"? As the joke goes, "When I had one watch I always knew what time it was—now with two watches I am never sure" (this joke worked better before the advent of atomic watches).

With the DCF Method the answer is often developed by selecting from a range of scenarios and trend lines a combination that represents what is believed to be reasonably conservative but not overly so and using the corresponding NPV as "the value." What "reasonably conservative but not overly so" means in practical terms is this:

- A "really conservative" value is typically the result of some combination of low and late revenue projections with little or no revenue growth, high and early costs projections with little or no cost reduction over time (so-called "learning effect"), and significant built-in contingencies for all the adverse things that could happen that one did not think of or plan for.
- The resulting NPV for a "really conservative" valuation is typically so economically insignificant or even adverse that, if such were truly reflective of what any conceivable buyer would think, it often then means that the technology has no practical value such the technology was not an "opportunity" (as we discussed in Chapter 3) in the first place.
- On the other hand, an "optimistic" value that results from comparatively high and early revenues and/or lower costs is expected to result in an NPV that reflects

significant "opportunity" value, which is why the valuation was undertaken in the first place.

- Sellers of course are inclined to sell "opportunity" by envisioning and quantifying positive economic potential to a technology. Supporting this view is that technology can become substantially more valuable than anyone had forecast, even with the most optimistic assumptions then justifiable.
- Buyers who pay sellers upfront as a lump sum irreversible payment out of the forecast NPV face the risk of realizing the forecast NPV as its return on investment above such upfront payment. (The use of running royalty structures in combination with lump sum payments is a risk-sharing alternative). Buyers are typically conservative, that is seeking to minimize their risk of overpayment for an opportunity, so they are unlikely to find persuasive an NPV value determined by an overly optimistic scenario.
- The Dealmaking value is, then, typically determined by some scenario located between the optimistic and "really conservative" outcomes, that gives the buyer reasonable confidence that it is not overpaying and the seller that it is not "giving it away" (meaning that it recognizes the buyer may realize a significant return on its investment but it will do so because it has taken significant risk and deployed precious resources).

How does this line of reasoning relate to the NPV forecast distribution of Exhibit 8.24?

- The "really conservative" value for NPV is a negative number or perhaps a very small positive number. Specifically, for the bottom 1.1 percentile of outcomes, the NPV is between −$9.84 million and zero. (This can be easily determined in Crystal Ball by entering 0 in the box by the right arrow in Exhibit 8.24 and −$9.84 in the left box, which from the table on the right is the 0th percentile NPV value, and the software shows that such range encompasses 1.1 percentile of the total outcomes, which with this combination is the worst 1.1 percentile of outcomes).
- An optimistic value for NPV would be some number greater than the 50th percentile forecast of $29.79 million. A seller would like to make note of the maximum forecast value of $88.35 million (the 100th percentile), by noting that the upper half of possibilities is a more than $60 million in excess above the $29.79 million median value.
- The buyer, if faced with the IP deal structure of a paid up/lump sum payment upon closing, would note that even for a lump sum payment of $30 million that approximately half of the time (using the many future worlds metaphor) it would have overpaid. Buyers typically want better odds than that to take on the risk.

So, although the seller can reasonably make the argument that the opportunity of Exhibit 8.24 is "worth" $30 million, the deal structure of lump sum/paid up shifts all the risk to the buyer. Although the buyer may desire to acquire the rights at no or very low risk, the seller is unlikely to find that there does not exist a reasonable buyer somewhere else willing to pay corresponding to percentile values greater than, say, the10th percentile ($10.79 Million per Exhibit 8.24). (We are assuming throughout this line of reasoning that both the seller and buyer agree that the NPV forecast shown in Exhibit 8.24 is the best present judgment of the range and probabilities of outcomes).

The Lump Sum/Paid Up Monte Carlo NPV Rule of Thumb If I the seller want a lump sum/paid up deal structure, I will have to accept an NPV at a percentile that a reasonable buyer will believe that it can pay for the technology rights and still have a strong probability of realizing a return in excess of what it paid, for the risk undertaken.[17] The most risk adverse buyer does not determine the value for the technology, just as the "low ball" bidder on a house or a business fixes the price. On the other hand, it is unreasonable to assume that there exists that buyer who has both money and loves taking great risks for low probability rewards and, thereby, would be pleased to pay the 50th percentile value or more (those folks are already fully committed to state run lotteries and Las Vegas, and likely in debt for their thrill seeking).

In the DCF Method of Chapter 7, where the NPV was determined by using an appropriate RAHR, we observed that there were two general perspectives on dividing NPV between seller and buyer: (1) The seller deserves 100 percent of the NPV because the RAHR has the justified return built in for the buyer, or (2) the NPV should be split between the seller and buyer because the RAHR produces an NPV that only minimally accounts for the risk, making the buyer "whole" so that all the excess value (NPV using such RAHR value) is the true benefit of the opportunity. The normal perspective is the first one.

Often, buyers use RAHR that provides the required internal return given the riskiness of the project. For such a situation, all excess NPV justifiably belongs to the seller. Buyers will still want to have, and seek to negotiate for, as much of the excess NPV as possible because business is all about paying $5 for $10, when and to the extent possible.

With either perspective, for the DCF Method we observed that the NPV tends to be particularly small for long-lived projects and/or high RAHR contexts. Here, with the Monte Carlo Method, we have separated the project risk from the cost of capital by the use of probability distributions for the key input variables, and used a WACC or near-WACC value to discount cash flows solely by their nominal corporate risk rate. So we now have to address the issue of how the NPV forecast distribution of percentile outcomes will be divided by a seller and buyer assuming both are in agreement with the Monte Carlo model and its underlying assumptions. There is no simple way to decide such matters. If a single one-time payment is the remuneration approach favored by the parties, then it is a matter of dividing the effects of NPV uncertainty to determine a lump sum/paid up IP fee by the seller reducing its prospective NPV realization dollar for NPV dollar. Let's consider five possible valuation norms using different domains of the NPV percentile values:

1. Seller receives the 100th percentile NPV value (rounded to $90 million for the example shown in Exhibit 8.24). This value standard would make absolutely no business sense to the buyer, as it is essentially certain (9,999 times out of 10,000) that it will realize less than it paid for the IP rights. As was discussed in Chapter 7, unless there are some extraordinary circumstances, which circumstances essentially obviate any formal valuation analysis, no rational buyer is going to provide the NPV corresponding to the absolutely best case to the seller as an

upfront payment when all projected cash inflows have been discounted by a WACC or near-WACC value.

2. Seller receives the 0th percentile NPV value (which, for the example of Exhibit 8.24 would effectively be $0, because the value is a negative $10 million).[18] Such a valuation would make no business sense to the seller because regardless of the outcome, the buyer will experience one outcome with an NPV exceeding what it "paid" all discounted by the WACC or near-WACC rate. (For the example of Exhibit 8.24, such $0 "payment" corresponds to 1.1 percentile outcome, so there would be a 99 percentile probability that the buyer will experience a return greater than $0). For our purposes, regardless of whether such 0th percentile NPV is a negative or positive number, the IP will not be valued by the *parties* at the 0th percentile or a percentile near the 0th.
3. The buyer and seller "split the difference" and use the 50th percentile value ($30 Million, from Exhibit 8.24). If the parties "split it down the middle" then the result in many Monte Carlo NPV forecasts is not much different than would have been obtained by using a straight DCF Method NPV result for the corresponding RAHR value.[19] Although splitting the difference is a certain kind of norm between competing interests, as we discussed in the Rule of Thumb Method (Chapter 6) this rarely applies in technology valuation because the parties are not in an equal standing: Once the lump sum payment is made by the buyer, all of its future return (in excess of the WACC discounting) is at risk, and the buyer faces all the work and risk of bringing the technology to market, finding and satisfying customers, collecting payment, providing needed customer service, and managing the overall business. At the 50th percentile, the buyer's perspective is that half the time it will have overpaid for the opportunity, or, there is only a 50 percent probability that it will experience an NPV that exceeds what it paid for the rights to pursue the opportunity. Again, setting aside extraordinary circumstances this split is unlikely to be acceptable to a reasonable buyer.
4. The buyer and seller agree on a lump sum/paid up payment between the 50th and 100th percentile NPV outcomes. The argument for or against the seller receiving more than half of the NPV can hinge on the cause of the uncertainty. If the surprises are more likely to be found in new markets and applications (more than considered in the model) and/or in cost efficiencies of manufacture and/or synergies with other products or processes *controlled by the buyer*, then the seller can better argue that is deserves more than the 50th percentile NPV. The rationale necessary for this argument is that the principal cause of NPV uncertainty is driven primarily by the risk associated with the buyer's performance with the technology, not the inherent risk in the technology itself or the market for products that can be made from it. Although the circumstances are not entirely parallel, it is this argument made by venture capital (VC) investors on why they should receive the significant equity apportionment that they usually do. On the other hand, the more likely circumstance is that the uncertainties, and risk, are more likely to be associated with bringing the technology to commercial fruition or as a result of new and superior products and technologies unexpectedly introduced by the competition. And, in any case, buyers, under normal business circumstances, are not inclined to undertake investments where there is a less than 50 percent probability of realizing a return in excess of what

they paid upfront to obtain. We will return to this issue when we consider the ***Approach*** of **Dealmaking** in Chapter 11.

5. The buyer and seller agree on a payment corresponding to an NPV percentile between the 0th and 50th percentile values. This is the most likely domain for agreement between the parties for the lump sum/paid up deal structure. There is no right single answer to the appropriate percentile selection. When companies consider their baseline earning projections on which public reliance will be made, the expectation standard on meeting such expectations is typically very high, perhaps in the range of 90 to 95 percent. The strong suggestion is that if "the number" forecasted is not realized, and there is not a very good "story," it could cost you your job. However, at the project or Dealmaking level, such a certainty standard would result in pursuits of only very low risk opportunities (or naïve sellers), and correspondingly modest return potential pursuits. Companies seeking high returns will correspondingly seek selected projects, in a portfolio of opportunities and recognize that high risk is often associated with such high potential returns. So, if the positive NPV zone of the Monte Carlo forecast shows large and noteworthy values, reasonable buyers could justifiably pursue the opportunity even by acquiring such rights at payments corresponding to the NPV value for probabilities for which the risk of failure exceeds to such low values of 5 or 10 percentile, but not as great as the 50th percentile value. The balance point of the seller's and buyer's reasonable application of the forecast NPV distribution is likely to be somewhere in the range of the 25th percentile value, bracketed by the 20th and 30th percentile value, which for the specific example of Exhibit 8.18 is between $16 and $21 million. At the 25th percentile, the buyer has 3:1 odds in its favor of experiencing a greater return than it paid; at the 20th percentile, the buyer's odds go up to 4:1, and down to a little better than 2:1 at the 30th percentile. Any particular buyer would of course prefer better odds, but the seller could likely perceive that this buyer is too risk averse too be the right Dealmaking partner. And the converse is likely true for a seller that aspires to percentiles greater than approximately the 30th percentile.

If we accept the principle that the bounds of 0th and 50th percentile values will likely be unacceptable to one side of a negotiation, where might a reasonable middle, and on what basis can any particular NPV percentile value be asserted as a norm or standard? We should not expect there to be a concrete answer, such as the value of pi, because the answer will be influenced by the particular negotiating context. What are the seller's alternatives? If they are poor and few, or if the seller has put this on the "just get a deal done by X" list, then the seller's willingness to accept fair value will diffuse down to lower percentiles. What are the buyer's alternatives? If this opportunity is strategic to its future, or fits with other products and present customers as well as channels, and the alternatives to the deal are speculative and distant, its reasoning will permit it to conclude fair value at higher percentiles. There is no universal percentile answer, but there is a reasonable negotiating range.

Buyers seek to buy low and sell high. (Naturalists like to characterize the survival pressure on animals as life on the "margins" of ecostructures; businesspeople think of life on and by the "spread" between the low and the high.) Additionally, buyers, like most normal people, prefer risk free opportunities. Accordingly, they will seek to negotiate NPV values that are as nearly certain to be exceeded in practice as can be negotiated. In Monte Carlo NPV cumulative probability graphs this low risk desire is by valuation points on the left side, at low values of cumulative probability. As might be expected, sellers see things in an opposite way, because they are now trying to experience the "sell high" moment, and perhaps because they see the significant upside potential as being not all that risky.

Buyers fear project failure that can occur even with a successful technology and market by the buyer having overpaid for the opportunity. Sellers who are forgoing the opportunity by selling it fear seeing a buyer gain huge financial benefits for something they acquired on the cheap. Negotiators on both sides want the deal value to be such that it is unlikely they will find themselves wearing a lifelong demerit badge as the one who did the deal that is held out as the poster child of what never should be done again.

Thus, even assuming both the seller and buyer agree on the financial model, including all the relevant assumptions, there remains the issue of where along the spectrum of probabilities should a fair trade occur? The answer lies in the alternative to the agreement, sometimes called "Plan B." If prospective Buyer #1 offers to pay no more than the 10th percentile or will walk away (really), what would a reasonable seller do? In other words, the seller is negotiating with a buyer who insists that 9 times out of 10 it must experience more in value than it paid for the opportunity, recognizing that although there is a 10 percent chance that even at such valuation the buyer will lose money, there is an equal 10 percent of possibilities at the top end. Further, Buyer #1 in this hypothetical would also have recognized that the mean value of forecasted NPV outcomes represents a substantial gain of over its proposed purchase at the 10th percentile.

From a seller's perspective, Buyer #1 looks to be (a) too greedy, (b) too risk averse, (c) operating within a different universe of assumptions, or (d) all of the above. Although Buyer #1 can point out that if the seller thinks this investment is such a great opportunity, then why doesn't the seller keep it and realize the mean value? (To which the appropriate answer should be that the seller has higher valued or better strategic fit alternative opportunities, or is simply not "in this business.") Under these circumstances, it is likely that the seller will vigorously seek out prospective Buyer #2 (and #3 and so forth) under the belief that there will be a reasonable buyer willing to value the opportunity closer to the mean than the 10th percentile offer it now has. The seller may propose to such Buyer #2 a valuation at the 40th percentile, under the reasoning that if it pursues a statistically significant number of such opportunities it can be assured an average positive return. However, for this percentile, Buyer #2 would understand that there is a 40 percent likelihood on this specific opportunity that it will realize less than it paid. Further, any buyer is likely to view as hollow the argument that if it pursues a statistically significant number of such opportunities, it will make money on the spread between the 40th percentile and the mean.[20] The reason this argument is unlikely to persuade is that the buyer is represented by a core group of humans who are not likely to live long enough to experience a mean. If a significant upfront payment for a purchased opportunity "tanks," just the first one, they could tank with it. For this reason, buyers as humans tend to be risk averse, and are unlikely to be persuaded by the seller's argument on behalf of the 40th percentile value. However, there can be exceptions, not always well advised exceptions. One exception example is the strategic-fit category.

The buyer is in some way in the business of keeping its present customers happy and finding new, more, and even better customers. Such a buyer can face a situation in which there is a product "hole" in its present family of offerings that is inhibiting satisfying fully its customers and/or gaining new customers. A buyer in such a situation may be willing to pay the 50th percentile, or even more, because of other significant benefits it will enjoy as a result of the opportunity.[21] Another example, which is a seller's dream, is Buyer A who is terrified of the implications of Buyer B acquiring the opportunity, believing that Buyer B might be willing to pay any price to do so (either out of fit or folly).

Another example, for which there are too many dead bodies to count, has been the dot.com (also known as "dot con" and "dot bomb") craze and the somewhat related telecom startup explosion. During the height of the recent startup and Dealmaking frenzy, there was a suspension of restraint by opportunity buyers perhaps in part because they performed no analysis but also because they viewed many such opportunities as "must haves." During the short term, the marketplace rewarded such buyers under the doctrine of "get big fast," "the new gold rush," "being the central switchboard of the grand thought matrix,"[22] and so forth. So, there can be both legitimate justification and crazed speculation for a buyer's willingness to value at the mean or above, but normally sellers should not count on this occurring.

If the 10th and 40th percentiles are too safe and too risky for buyers (in many circumstances), what is the right level of risk? When managers are asked to project revenues for their operating businesses, there is a common expectation that such projections will be met or exceeded essentially without fail. Sometimes such expectations are made overt ("your job depends on meeting these numbers"), sometimes it is simply reflected by the culture of the company that is intolerant of negative surprises. Though no projection is ever certain in the sense of 100 percent certainty, such risk averse contexts of projecting on existing businesses are likely using some standard such as 90 percent to 95 percent certainty, which is equivalent to saying that 18 to 19 years out of 20, I will meet or exceed my projection.[23] However, if a researcher within a company is proposing a new R&D project and is asked as to the likelihood of success, the normal expectation is that success probability is something much lower than, perhaps in some cases, at the 50 percent level, but others at the 80 percent level. For R&D projects that have very high potential payoffs, or for interesting ones that require very little investment, it is conceivable that a project advocate could accept only a 20 percent, or even a 1 percent, chance of success because of the high potential payoff and, after all, that is why they call it "research." Such 20 percent chance of success is sometimes called the "commando project," because in military settings elite commando units are sometimes committed to high stakes missions whose projected likelihood of success is only about 20 percent.

This line of reasoning suggesting low probability Dealmaking at the 10th and 40th percentiles logically leads to consideration of the 20th to 30th percentile range, bracketing the 25th percentile.[24] Why might this be reasonably acceptable to both sides? Well, one perspective would be to recognize the 25th percentile as representing a 50:50 split, in terms of probability, of the mean value. In this instance the seller would argue that if you made enough investments, you would realize the mean value but we recognize that what is on the table is one investment and, accordingly, we are agreeing to discount the probability used for computing the value to recognize the risk associated with buying just one opportunity. So, the 25th percentile is analogous to the parties meeting halfway to the mean. (Note that this "meeting halfway" is not splitting the difference between the value at the minimum and the mean, but splitting the NPV uncertainty percentile.)

The Pure Running Royalty Rule of Thumb If I the seller want to maximize the value of the technology sale, one of the ways of doing so is to participate in the risk of return as well as the delay in IP payments. The essential feature of the running royalty deal structure is that the seller gets paid as the buyer gets revenue. It is not complete risk sharing, as the seller is being paid on revenues whereas the buyer "EATs" off of the earnings on the bottom line. But running royalty payment obligations clearly do not begin until revenues begin and the magnitude of such payments scales in some way with such revenues. So this does remove some of the risk, and it certainly delays the cash outflows for the buyer. And as we saw in Chapter 7, early cash outflows have a greater influence on NPV than equivalent later cash inflows.

The incentive to the seller to participate in delayed and conditional IP payments in the form of running royalties is that its total return, the NPV of the seller, will be greater than that which may be determined by the Lump Sum/Paid Up Rule of Thumb discussed above. On this basis, the seller may reasonably argue for a running royalty corresponding to the 50th percentile equivalent return, namely $30 million.

A reasonable buyer may argue that even for a running royalty structure such 50th percentile is overpaying because the risk of achieving the net earnings (NPV) depends on all the cost elements associated with the revenues and which risk the seller is not taking because its royalty payments are conditional upon only the revenue "top line." So, the "fair value" is between the 30th and 50th percentiles, $16 and $21 million for Exhibit 8.24.

The seller can argue that the buyer will be 'steering the ship' as 'the captain' and so has control over the entire technology opportunity, whereas the seller is a passive "investor," so the 50th percentile neighborhood is indeed the fair one, though perhaps some 'haircut' to the 50th percentile value, possibly to the 40th percentile might be a reasonable compromise, bracketing $25 to $30 million for Exhibit 8.24.

The Toolbox

Monte Carlo software, such as Crystal Ball, can be used to model a range of payment outcomes for the seller. For all the examples in this chapter the valuation has been from the standpoint of the technology buyer. We will discuss later specifically how such results can be used to estimate lump sum/paid up licenses.

Licenses can also be structured as running royalties expressed as a percentage of the buyer's revenues associated with the technology either in lieu of upfront payments or, more commonly in combination with such payments.

(*continued*)

(*Continued*)

A parallel financial model can be constructed for the licensor for the situation where there will be running royalty payments. Such annual royalty payments can then be assigned as forecast cells and the total of such payments as the NPV to seller, all discounted at rate that does not include the effect of risk, such as the seller's marginal WACC.

Correspondence with Monte Carlo Forecast NPV to that Determined by the NPV Method Using the 20th to 30th percentile rule of thumb discussed above, the corresponding Monte Carlo Method NPV values can be compared to the equivalent RAHR value for the DCF Method. The underlying spreadsheet model can readily be used to calculate an NPV as a function of RAHR value by "freezing" all the assumptions in the Monte Carlo model such that the most likely (center) values for all the assumptions are used, and then using Excel's Goal Seek function to determine the implied RAHR value for any particular NPV value. Performing this calculation using the 20th percentile Monte Carlo NPV forecast of $16.47 million value results to an implied RAHR value of 20.2 percent for the DCF Method; for the 30th percentile value of $21.15 million the corresponding RAHR is 18.7 percent.

For the example we have been considering shown in Exhibit 8.21, these RAHR values in the range of 19 to 20 percent can be a reasonableness check on the Monte Carlo Method analysis given the RAHR table of Exhibit 7.7. However, this may not be the outcome for long-lived projects because of the discounting effect of large RAHR values for long periods as discussed in Chapter 7. So although it is not uncommon to make such comparison between methods, the Monte Carlo Method, properly constituted, should yield a richer and more meaningful portrayal of the value of the technology.

Such a DCF Method calculation may appear to just be a simpler way of determining a valuation, but the predictive capability of Monte Carlo generally provides a much richer understanding of the opportunity.

Is The Monte Carlo Lump Sum/Paid Up Value the Same Thing as the 25 Percent Rule? One obvious issue is the correspondence, if any, between the above described 20th to 30th percentile Monte Carlo Lump Sum Rule of Thumb, namely: is this just the 25 Percent Rule of Chapter 6 (Rule-of-Thumb Method) in a different context?

The answer is "not exactly." As was discussed in Chapter 6, there are multiple ways of looking at the authority for the 25 Percent Rule. One of them is the argument of experience, though there is no authoritative analysis that supports this value. For Monte Carlo analysis, there is zero published experience because parties do not make available their DCF or Monte Carlo Method models so there is no direct way to conclude what percentile value was used even when the lump sum/paid up value is published.

However, the undergirding idea of the 25 Percent Rule, namely that the buyer takes more of the risk and does more of the work, is similarly applied in the above Monte Carlo percentile reasoning. As we will see in Chapter 10 when we discuss venture capital deal structures, there is yet a third parallel to such 25 Percent Rule in that one norm for dividing the initial equity "pie" for a startup is 50 percent for the investors (VCs), 25 percent for management (though some of this is earned out), and 25 percent for "the technology."

One of the important distinctions between the 25 Percent Rule of Method 3 and this 20th to 30th percentile rule of thumb with the Monte Carlo Method is that within the spreadsheet model used in Monte Carlo we are directly accounting for the timing of all the cash inflows and outflows. Recall that with Method 3, the use of such 25 percent simply involves allocating 25 percent of the buyer's forecast EBIT *after* startup/rampup. One of the adjustments to such 25 Percent Rule that was discussed, was decreasing the split percentage in recognition for the magnitude of the buyer's necessary investment in the technology and the delay to its realization of mature GCFs. In fact, a direct application of the 25 Percent Rule to the baseline template we have been using (Exhibits 7.17, 8.3, and 8.22) results in multiplying the EBIT percentage for the maturity period, Years 6 through 10, by the 0.25 factor, namely:

$$\begin{aligned}\text{25 Percent Rule Implied Running Royalty} &= 0.25 * (\text{EBIT\$/Rev\$}) * 100\\ &= 0.25 * 30 \text{ percent} = 7.5 \text{ percent.}\end{aligned}$$

The above methodology would result in the same implied royalty rate even if the buyer was required to invest $1 billion and 10 years before a mature EBIT of 30 percent was forecast to be realized.

Nonetheless, the idea of "splitting the pie" in the Monte Carlo Method in a way that allocates most of the value-by-risk to the buyer who is going to do most of the work does have a similar fairness feel that is used to support the 25 Percent Rule.

Valuation vs. Price As was discussed in the opening chapters, there is a distinction between the value of sometime and the price. Value is something intrinsic, price is an offer, a concrete Dealmaking communication of value.

As can been seen in the above discussion of the Monte Carlo Rules of Thumb, there is a backward influence from "price," what a buyer may accept, to "value." This connectivity of price and value was present with all our valuation Methods. There is necessarily a consideration of a buyer's perspective in any valuation because the essential presumption is that something is worth what a willing buyer, and a willing seller, each armed with a reasonable apprehension of what is knowable and motivated in their reasonable self interest.

Seller Value Improvement Opportunities As we discussed in Chapter 3 regarding the Box and the Wheelbarrow, IP assets and payment structures are not single value, unchangeable constraints in most circumstances. Assets can be added or withdrawn, or included for a time, or for limited use. Likewise payment forms and amounts can be changed, interchanged, moved in time, made conditional (up or down), and diminished.

One of the advantages of the Monte Carlo Method is identifying areas where the IP assets as provisionally determined can be made more valuable apart from additions or other enhancements. The underlying principle of such value increase is this: Buyers will pay closer to the median value as the downside uncertainty decreases. Expressed in terms previously used, if we can shrink the uncertainty 'tail' extending from the 50th percentile to the 0th percentile on the left tails of

Exhibit 8.26, the 20th and 30th percentile values will increase even if there is no change in the median value of the forecasted NPV distribution.

There are three ways we might be able to shrink the downside uncertainty tail.

1. As a general rule, the narrower the assumption distribution the narrower the NPV forecast, which diminishes the high and low end tails of the NPV distribution (though our focus is on the low end tail as that is the area of the 20th and 30th percentile values, which is the conservative/downside value percentiles). The Uniform Distribution, as we have seen, expresses the broadest distribution of uncertainty and, for this purpose is the worst distribution. The Triangular Distribution is narrower (for the same or similar end points) leading to a "tighter" NPV distribution with thinner tails. The Beta, Normal, and Lognormal Distributions can be narrower or broader than the Triangular Distribution depending upon the value of the statistics used to define their respective shape.
2. The second way to tighten the NPV forecast distribution is by narrowing the uncertainty span of the Uncertainty, Triangular, and Beta Distributions used and the standard deviation (or equivalent statistic) for the Normal and Lognormal Distributions. These all have the effect of diminishing either the values or the frequency of such values or both in the assumption distributions that cause downside NPV values.
3. Finally, as we have discussed, a correlation that can be established between/among the assumptions may likewise have the effect of diminishing the tails. In the example we considered, it had this effect because the unit price and unit volume went in opposite directions (lower prices were correlated with higher sales) which tended to reduce the variability in the product of these two variables (representing the annual revenue). It is possible, however, for a correlation to compound adversity—in which case the effect should be included to the extent that it can be supported by data or reason, but its inclusion will not lead to an increase in 20th and 30th percentile values.

The sensitivity and tornado charts discussed already should first be used to identify which assumptions have the greatest effect upon NPV uncertainty. In Exhibit 8.12, the right-most three columns were placekeepers for exactly this purpose: (1) Source, (2) Confidence Level, and (3) Relative Importance.

- The relative importance is determined directly by the sensitivity chart, and can be expressed in quantitative terms, such as percentage contribution to NPV variance, or simply by a designation such as H, M, L for high/medium/low. The variables designated L can be either fixed or left as initially modeled. Those M variables are held at their current model distributions and values, while the focus begins on the H variables.
- The confidence level can be similarly expressed using H/M/L. Depending on the sequence of events, the initial Monte Carlo model may be developed prior to apprehension of all the relevant data from experiment, expert discussions, secondary or primary market research, in which case the confidence level may be L or M for each assumption. As further analysis proceeds, such characterizations may move up a category or two. Some care must be taken with the

context of the H/M/L scoring. What is important to a buyer is that these values are known (to the extent they can be) in terms of what must be known to proceed to commercial implementation. It may be useful to expand the categories to five (or more) where a 5 designates as high a certainty as typical of business planning for early stage products, in which case a "technology" at the state of licensing may not be justified in exceeding a 4. At the other extreme, a 1 would represent only the judgment of a generalist with reliance on any specific data or report or analysis. For those variables whose relative importance was scored L, the importance of the confidence level is low, though of course if the "right" assumption is wildly different than has been used the relative importance initially determined by the Monte Carlo model could be misleading.

- The source column is useful to identify what authority is the source of the assumption values and the confidence level for those assumptions. Again for assumptions that are low in importance, the authority/source becomes a less significant issue. When the authority is important, then due diligence on such authority and its source, or basis/rationale, of such assumption is important.[25]

Assumption triage focuses the effort and investment in model improvement on those assumptions that will make the most difference. So most Monte Carlo models undergo refinement at least in accordance with reducing the NPV uncertainty to the extent justifiable.

Another category of seller improvement acts is for the seller to take on some of the obligations of commercialization. As we discussed in Chapter 6 on the Rule of Thumb Method, there can be circumstances where the "split" is not 25 percent (or 33 percent) but more like 50 percent. One of the circumstances for such 50 percent split is software licensing where the seller may provide more than "the technology" by obligations such as ongoing second level support, training and documentation, upgrades and bug fixes, and the like. Undertaking such obligations both reduces the buyer's investment obligations and, possibly, the buyer's risk. In a similar vein, an alternate Monte Carlo model can be constructed whereby the cost burden on the buyer is reduced by such seller commitments. This step alone will shift the NPV forecast distribution to higher values. If, in addition, the overall risk of the project is reduced, as may be agreed by the parties, then an NPV percentile greater than the 30th could be agreed to by the parties.

Monte Carlo NPV Forecasts as the Basis for Revised Deal Structures The previous discussions considered only two deal structures, namely lump sum/paid up or pure running royalty. Clearly there are many other possible variations and combinations. One common structure is a combination of upfront payment and running royalty, as will be discussed in Chapter 10.

The results of a Monte Carlo analysis can provide the basis for other payment structures that can more fairly reward the parties based on the uncertainty. One example would be that the buyer pays an upfront license fee which is unconditional, an ongoing running royalty which is dependent upon and scaled on revenues, and then a conditional lump sum payment at some future date for which the overall project uncertainties have been greatly reduced for which the magnitude of such payment is scaled on some metric that relates to the NPV of the buyer realization.

The following is an illustration of how this might be done using the DCF Method in conjunction with the Monte Carlo model shown in Exhibit 8.22 with the results of Exhibit 8.24:

- Let us assume that parties agree that the NPV corresponding to the 20th percentile, $16.47 million will be used to determine the combination of up front, lump sum payment and running royalty payments.
- Further we'll assume that 10 percent of $16.47 will be paid by the buyer as the upfront, lump sum license fee, namely $1.65 million, with the balance, an NPV of $14.82, to be paid in the form of a running royalty.
- Finally, let us assume the parties agree that if the buyer experiences at least the revenues forecast in Years 6 through 10, that it will pay an added "kicker" to the seller in Year 10 equal to the 40th percentile in aggregate, namely, it will pay a total of $25.65 million, of which $16.47 million would have been paid in the combined lump sum, upfront payment and running royalties, leaving a balance to be paid in NPV terms of $9.18 million, but paid at the end of such 10th year.

Let us now see how such a calculation can be accommodated within the Monte Carlo Method. Using the baseline template.

- We use the baseline template of Exhibit 8.22, and add a buyer cost line above the EBIT line for the running royalty, where each year's payment is equal to the product of that year's revenues times the running royalty rate expressed in percentage terms, a value to be determined.
- Such added buyer royalty cost line is equal to the seller royalty revenue line, which we then discount using the DCF equation, an RAHR of 15 percent, and the midyear correction, and create a 10-year summation of these annual royalty payments.
- We next use Excel's Goal Seek function to iterate for that royalty rate percentage which will result in an NPV for the summation of the royalty payments in the exact amount of $14.82 million, the balance of the 20th percentile Monte Carlo NPV after the $1.65 million upfront payment (which amount needs no discounting because it is paid at closing). This calculation yields a running royalty rate of 2.25 percent.
- Finally, a "kicker" paid after 10 years, with an RAHR of 15 percent, and a NPV of $9.18 million corresponds to a payment, then, of $36.33 million (obtained using the basic DCF equation where $n = 10$).

So a term sheet expression of these calculations is this:

- Unconditional lump sum payment upon closing of $1.65 million.
- A 10-year running royalty rate of 2.25 percent applied to all revenues. Such payment is conditional only to the extent that no payment is due if there are not revenues, and the royalty payment in dollars is scaled on such revenue dollars using the rate of 2.25 percent.
- A final lump sum 'kicker' payment paid at the end of the 10th year in the amount of $36.33 Million 10th year dollars, if and only if, the Years 6 through 10 revenues equal or exceed that projected as the midpoint values in the baseline template.

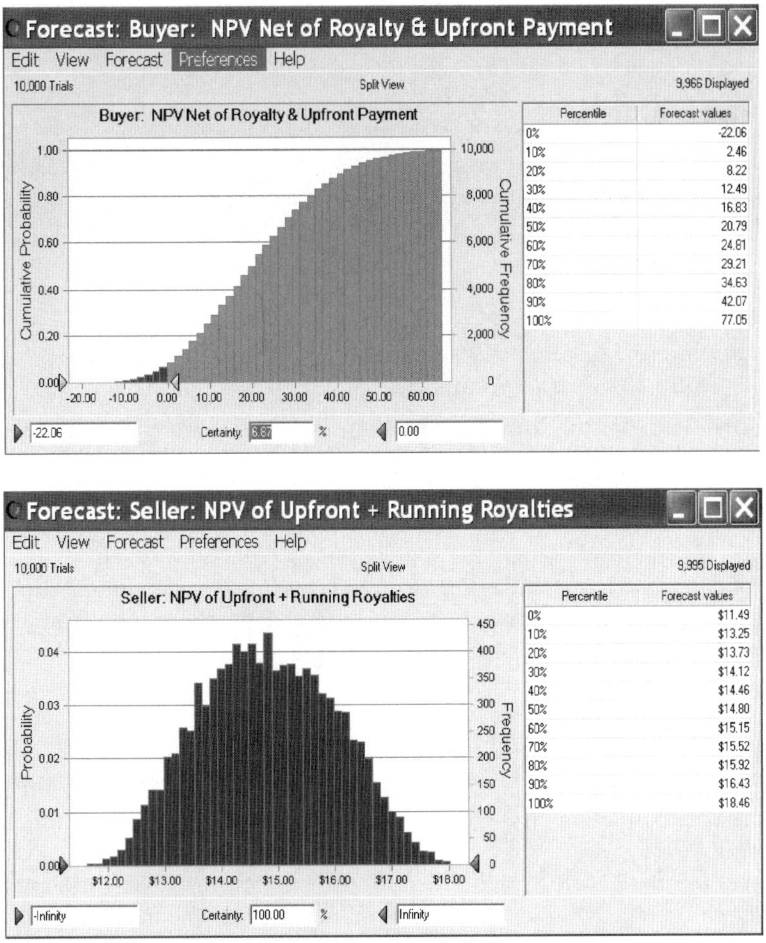

EXHIBIT 8.27 **Illustration of Running Royalty Deal Structure**

We can now use these values and rerun the Monte Carlo calculation, but now including the royalty cost deducting from the buyers revenues, and calculating the total NPV of the royalties paid to the seller. These results are given in Exhibit 8.27.

The top figure in Exhibit 8.27 shows the buyers NPV net of its running royalty payments. The shaded area represents the 6.87 percentile probability that it will experience a net loss. The bottom figure shows the frequency distribution of the NPV of the royalty payments to the seller. As per design, the 50th percentile value closely corresponds to the $14.82 million NPV royalty per the hypothetical example we are following. The percentile distribution table of the lower figure shows that the seller could experience a royalty NPV of as low as $11.49 million to a maximum of $18.46 million, in accordance with the same assumptions that underlie the baseline template we have been using. The lump sum upfront payment of $1.65 million has not been included either to the benefit of the seller or the cost of the buyer.

In Chapter 10 we will discuss deal structures in more detail. Our purposes here are meant only to show how the Monte Carlo Method can be used to provide upfront, royalty, and conditional payments based upon a negotiated percentile-based Monte Carlo value of the technology.

Scenario Models Using Monte Carlo

As we have seen already, the cost assumption typically plays a pivotal role in determining the value of a technology. Once this has been established from sensitivity or tornado charts, then further study in modeling such costs is warranted to reduce the NPV uncertainty and thereby increase the value at the 20th and 30th percentiles.

In this section, we will consider a certain kind of cost analysis that creates two Monte Carlo scenarios: One scenario is that the R&D and design for manufacturing will result in a low cost, high efficiency manufacturing process and, thereby, high GCF values and NPV. However, there is another scenario that describes a higher cost process that could be used in the event the better, lower cost process cannot be practicably developed.

MODIFICATIONS TO THE BASELINE TEMPLATE In Chapter 7 we considered how scenario analysis has several levels of appeal. One is simply the ability to see "what happens if" certain future worlds are realized. The difficulty is developing rational probabilities for each such future world envisioned. In Monte Carlo there are elegant ways of incorporating scenario modeling.

Consider again our baseline template of Exhibit 8.22. We can now consider how to incorporate scenarios in some of the assumptions. To show the effect of other assumption distributions on forecasted NPV distributions we will instead use the Triangular and Uniform Distributions and, especially, the creation of a Custom Distribution for the Total Costs that will show how a scenario perspective can be incorporated for the most-significant variable.

For this example we will examine more closely the modeling of the Total Costs assumption. If we have some basis intrinsic to our analysis of the opportunity to conclude that a 70 percent Total Costs (therefore, 30 percent EBIT) is reasonable, then it is also reasonable to use a center weighted distribution. (If our confidence level concerning the 70 percent figure was less, we might assume a Triangular Distribution with a broad range for minimum and maximum values, or a Normal Distribution with a large standard deviation.) Further, our consideration of our assumed best estimate for 70 percent Total Costs may lead us to conclude that it is more likely that deviations from 70 percent will be toward higher costs rather than lower costs. The basis of such reasoning could simply be the recognition of how difficult it is to find business opportunities that evidence 40 percent, or even 35 percent, EBITs. To provide such upward bias, we can choose a Lognormal Distribution with the mean value set at 70 percent. Although such a distribution includes some small probability that the cost ratio could exceed 100 percent, there is nothing physically impossible about such an outcome, no matter how unappealing it would be for a buyer. However, cost ratios below 50 percent are less likely and are impossible below 0 percent.

The effect of these twin uncertainty distributions clearly creates a very pronounced s-shape NPV distribution with long, thin tails. This result is reflected in the very large value of the maximum and the very negative value of the minimum. Because this simulation was done using 10,000 iterations, the extreme values occur only 0.01 percent of the time (once each out of a 10,000 parallel universes). Although the Lognormal Distribution assumed for the Total Costs is biased upward, it

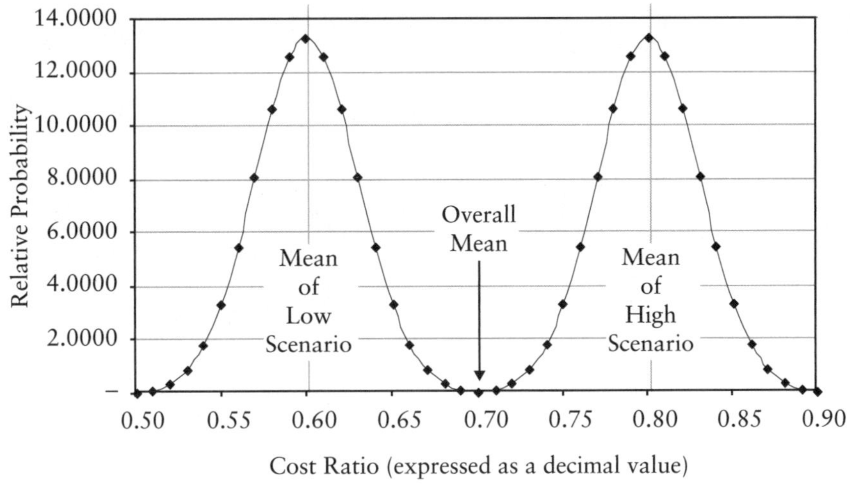

EXHIBIT 8.28 Example of a Double Hump Cost Scenario Using the Normal Distribution

has only a small effect on the mean value because the mean value of the cost ratio distribution was still assumed to be 70 percent.

One of the ways to create a scenario distribution in Crystal Ball is to use the Custom distribution function and select the option of Fit to Data. Then, by specifying the range of cells in the worksheet, the software accepts such data as the distribution. Exhibit 8.28 illustrates two adjoining normal distributions that were created in Excel using the NORMDIST function. Shown is a "camel, double-humped" double Normal Distribution for Total Costs whose overall mean value is 70 percent as before, but with the high cost ratio scenario (the adverse outcome) having its own normal distribution with a mean value of 80 percent, and the low cost ratio scenario (the favorable outcome) having its normal distribution with a mean at 60 percent. Such a situation could be conceived if there were two technologies being investigated in parallel during the first year of the project.

If the high-efficiency technology can be made to work, then we expect a very low cost ratio and highly favorable NPV returns. However, we have a backup technology we are investigating that is expected to be workable but it will cause a significant increase in costs. So, we are projecting the possibility of either technology A, or technology B becoming available, and at this point we conceive them as being equally probable (so the camel humps are the same height). We recognize that there is some range of uncertainty regarding the operating parameters of each technology, which is why there is a distribution of outcomes for each rather than just a single value at the respective means of 80 percent and 60 percent.

Exhibit 8.28 was created in Excel by creating first in Column A the x variables corresponding to the cost ratio ranging from 0.50 to 0.90 in 0.01 increments corresponding to the overall range of variability of the cost ratio. Then, in Column B, we insert the NORMDIST function with the arguments set as follows:

- The first argument is simply the corresponding cell in Column A (the particular cost ratio of interest, say, 0.55).

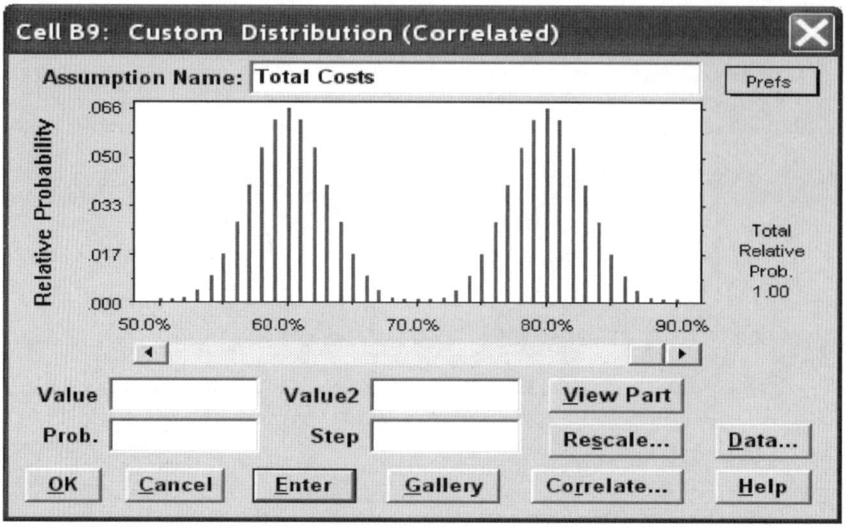

EXHIBIT 8.29 Crystal Ball Double Hump Cost Scenario Using the Normal Distribution

- Next is the mean value of the normal distribution, which for the rows in Column A corresponding to cost ratios of 0.50 to 0.70 (the first "hump"), is set to 0.60, the mean value for this first range.
- Next is the standard deviation to be used to establish the relative peakedness of the distribution. The value 0.03 (as a decimal) was chosen for both "humps" of Exhibit 8.28.
- Finally, the word "false" is entered to inform the software that we want to see the frequency distribution and not the cumulative distribution.
- Then we repeat the above steps for the second range in Column A, from cost ratio values of 0.71 to 0.90, only now the mean value is 0.80 for all these cells.
- Finally, using the graph function in Excel for Columns A and B, and selecting the scatter graph, we obtain the result shown in Exhibit 8.28.

In Crystal Ball, when the Custom Distribution is selected for the Total Costs followed by choosing the Fit option, we can then enter the entire data range developed earlier, namely, A1:B41 (A1 is the Total Costs value of 0.50, and B41 is the normal distribution value calculated by the NORMDIST function for the final cost ratio value of 0.90). This data range results in a mirror double-humped camel distribution in Crystal Ball with 41 discrete values of Total Costs (0.50, 0.51, . . . , 0.89, 0.90). Finally, the software enables by a single click to set the entire double-humped probability to 1.00 so that each corresponding cost ratio has its appropriate individual probability. The assumption screen in Crystal Ball now looks as shown in Exhibit 8.29.

Now, with all the assumptions but the Total Costs frozen, and with our two-scenario model of such Total Costs as shown earlier, we can simply allow the software to perform the simulation. The results are shown in Exhibit 8.30.

The top left graph repeats the distribution assumption for the Total Costs that was shown in Exhibit 8.29; recall that for this initial scenario example we are only

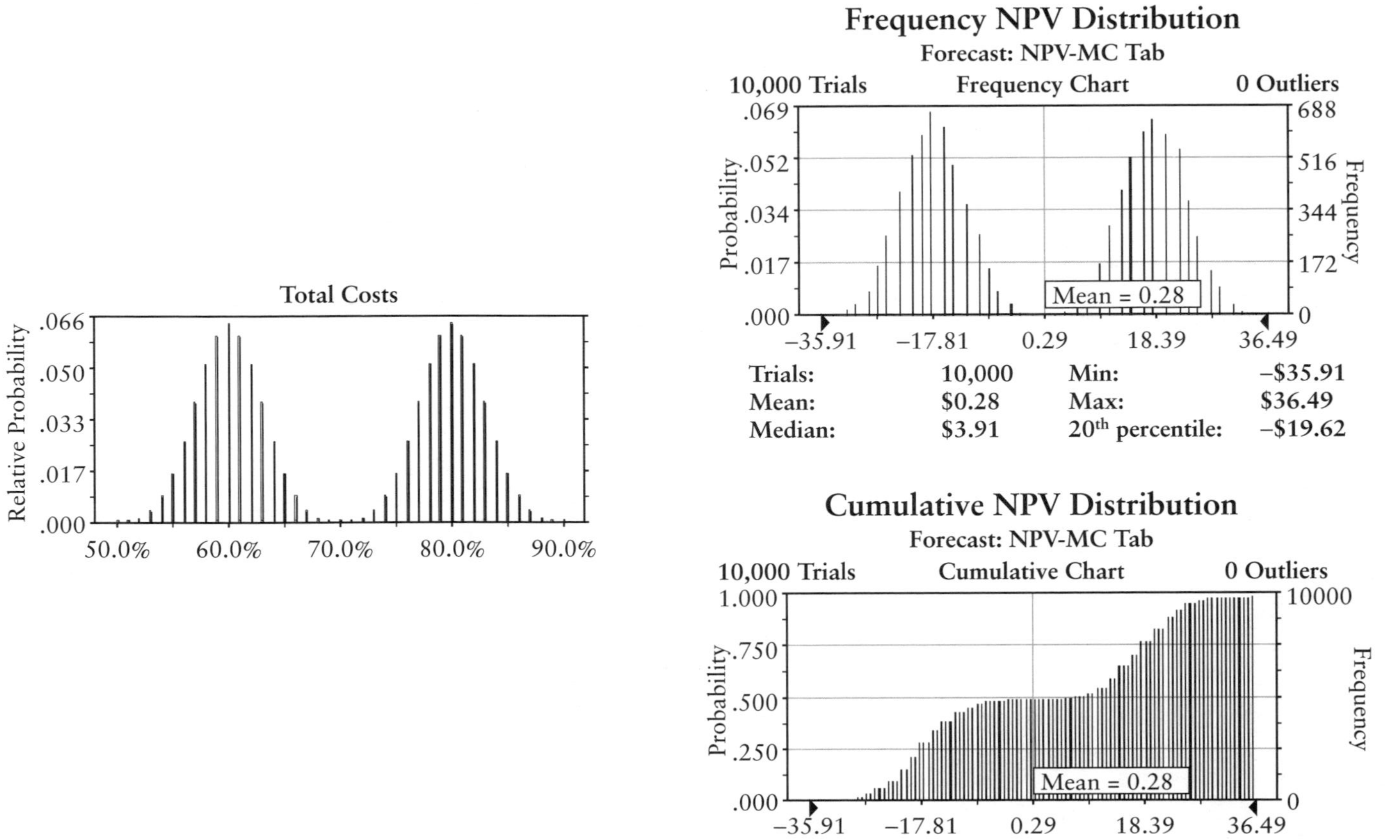

EXHIBIT 8.30 Monte Carlo NPV Model for the Double Hump Cost Scenario Using the Normal Distribution

considering the effect of such Total Costs distribution. The upper right graph shows the NPV distribution in frequency form, and the bottom graph in cumulative form. Clearly, the frequency NPV distribution mirrors the Total Costs assumption by exhibiting a double-humped shape. The corresponding cumulative distribution shows a wide, flat zone in the middle of the graph that is caused by there being essentially no NPV outcomes in the area around Total Costs of 0.70 because the twin input Total Costs distributions are centered about their respective means of 0.6 and 0.8 with a combined distribution minimum at 0.7.

The table of statistics in Exhibit 8.30 gives the corresponding effects in digital form. Note that the 20th percentile benchmark that we have been using leads to the conclusion that the opportunity would not be worth pursuing.

The result in report form is given in Appendix 8B. The NPV frequency distribution relationship clearly shows a broadening effect caused by the combination of assumption distributions. However, the overall result is still dominated by the very important Total Costs factor, especially because of the significant difference between the favorable and adverse scenarios considered. The effect on cash flow for a mean Total Costs of 0.8 is dramatic in comparison to a mean Total Costs of 0.6. Again, these results suggest the value of another method that will permit an initial payment for the right to determine which technology wins and a second payment if the favorable technology proves workable and efficient (and likely abandonment by the buyer if it does not).

If some refinement of CapEx estimates is possible, this chart suggests that the focus should be on Year 4 because it contributes about 5 percent of the NPV uncertainty. The projected revenues during Years 2 through 5 are also relatively unimportant, though somewhat more important than the effect of CapEx. Again if we were to prioritize our energies, the assumption to work on would be revenues in Year 5 followed by Year 4. However, our primary energies should be in developing the best models we possibly can for the Total Costs and then, far less importantly, the CAGR distribution. Exhibit 8.31 is an example of how such a tornado chart might be used in practice.

The left columns merely repeat the results of the tornado chart but also included is the cumulative contribution to uncertainty (variance). Then a judgment is made as to importance, as shown in the next column; this particular judgment by example shows that all assumptions that contribute less than 5 percent of the uncertainty can be ignored. (In ancient days, one would then remove such assumptions from the model because it often required a day or more to run each case; now with lighting fast PCs, there is very little to be gained by stripping out assumptions that are loaded into the model.) In the rightmost three rows are shown by the respective boxes with note references as hypothetical examples the perceptions of the level of confidence in the assumption distribution that has been used. Once such a chart is filled out, the place to begin work is where the contribution to uncertainty is high (the topmost rows) and the confidence level in the respective assumption is low (the rightmost columns). Where the confidence level is high, even for high importance assumptions, it may be that nothing more can or should be done to refine the assumption.

This result anticipates the value and power of Real Options that will be discussed in the next section of the chapter. The low projected NPV values in the previous Monte Carlo model is caused by our uncertainty as to which cost distribution

Assumption	Variance	C-Variance	Importance	High	Medium	Low	
				Confidence Level in Present Assumption Distribution			
Cost Ratio	62.60%	62.60%	Very High		Note 1		
CAGR	8.70%	71.30%	Low	Note 2			
Rev. Year 5	6.90%	78.20%	Low		Note 3		Example of 5% Significance Threshold
CapEx Year 4	4.90%	83.10%	Negligible		Note 4		
Rev. Year 4	4.80%	87.90%	Negligible			Note 5	
Rev. Year 3	3.30%	91.20%	Negligible			Note 5	
CapEx Year 5	3.20%	94.40%	Negligible				
CapEx Year 3	2.30%	96.70%	Negligible				
Rev. Year 2	2.00%	98.70%	Negligible				
CapEx Year 2	1.00%	99.70%	Negligible				
CapEx Year 1	0.30%	100.00%	Negligible				

Notes: 1. Highest priority for refinement. 2. No further refinement is warranted. 3. Some effort at refinement could be warranted. 4. Refinement is probably not warranted. 5. Together, these two account for 8.1 percent of the uncertainty and, so, some effort at refinement of revenue projects could be warranted.

EXHIBIT 8.31 Prioritizing Assumption Refining

uncertainty, or the two possible ones shown, will occur after the first year or two of further product development. Accordingly, a reasonable planning strategy could be a stage gate criterion that the opportunity will be pursued beyond the first year (or two) if and only if the more favorable Total Cost technology was successfully demonstrated. Such a buyer's strategy would lead it to seek a license structure and valuation that would give it an opportunity to invest at its own risk to establish which Total Cost outcome occurs. The seller may be inclined to provide such option approach providing it is compensated in a way and to a degree for providing the buyer a lower risk approach to the technology acquisition. This example is an ideal context for the use of Real Options.

Final Points on the Monte Carlo Model

The examples in this chapter are not intended as universal models because, as stated in the opening paragraphs, opportunities are by definition, specific. There is usually an industry norm within which the opportunity will reside that can guide some of the analysis but, in addition, it is best, and usually necessary, to perform a specific analysis on the costs and benefits and timing associated with the opportunity. It is helpful to create and use a template such as Exhibit 8.22 that can be applied to many kinds of opportunities by adjusting the assumptions and their distributions. When this template is created, then even very complex financial models can be adjusted quickly and used to prepare for negotiations or respond to the back and forth of active negotiations and to determine walk-away and Plan B triggers.

As noted previously, the model of Exhibit 8.22 did not consider the effect of terminal value. Depending on the circumstances of the transaction, this could have a very significant effect on value. When making projections beyond 10 years, if such projections are justified by perceived IP and technology life, a common technique is to treat all future value as a lump sum at the conclusion of the 10th year. Such a lump sum would be dependent on the number of years and associated cash flows for all the years beyond the 10th year that value is attributable to the opportunity seller. If the value of the opportunity is sustained only by patent protection, then the expiry of value can be tied to the associated patent life. In other cases, it may be more reasonable to assume a finite life to the opportunity for either market or competitive technology reasons. In any case, terminal value considerations are important and can be easily included in a Monte Carlo model. One way to do so was illustrated above by using the 40th percentile NPV value payment, conditional on the revenue projections being realized for the five-year "mature" period (Years 6 through 10 in that example). Although such conditionality of and form of lump sum payment at the end of the 10th year is not the same thing as a terminal value, it is another way of accounting for potential technology value for years beyond that directly forecast in the model.

The tax rate shown in all the examples was 34 percent of the EBIT. The effective tax rate of a company is a complicated and geography specific subject (not to mention the effect of political winds) and has an important effect on opportunity value because it has just the same kind of effect as an increase in cost ratio. Some parties simply standardize on 40 percent for the tax rate to remove it as a variable. Clearly a company with a lower effective tax rate, for whatever reason, can either justify paying more for a given technology opportunity or match a competing buyer's offer and enjoy a greater NPV return.

All the cash flows were discounted at a RAHR of 15 percent as shown in Exhibit 8.22. It is important that such discount value not be made large to account for risk because by the technique of Monte Carlo we are separately judging the effect of risk by valuation at selected percentile values. The use of the buyer's WACC is a logical choice for such a discount factor. However, many companies impose a discount rate somewhat higher than their WACC, with continuous changes depending on market conditions and financing operations, to standardize all their analyses on a common basis. Monte Carlo is particularly effective for this purpose as the effect of risk is accounted for independently of the discount rate used. As with the tax rate, some companies simply establish a RAHR internal standard to be used with all modeling so that it is removed as a variable from investment decision making.

One approach to the Monte Carlo method is simply to adjust, tweak, goose, and otherwise fold, spindle, and mutilate the assumption distributions, the model template, the baseline values, and anything else one can think of to get "the answer" one wants. This corruption of purpose abuses the wonderful power of Monte Carlo to give credibility to what is in effect a made-up answer. If that is your purpose, may you get only the blue screen of death on a locked-up box, probably a PC. For those seeking wisdom, the power contained in Monte Carlo modeling is incredible. It enables you to gain the best thinking of the best thinkers and develop a coherent understanding of not only what you think something should be worth but the basis of such belief and a tool that can create changes in your belief on the emergence of better data and assumptions. For you pure in heart, may your wisdom flow like the course of a crystal river through your fingers into the appropriate Monte Carlo cells and may it lead to confidence in what you can know and humility for what you cannot, and may you earn the respect of your colleagues on both sides of the negotiating table by your leadership in fact based upon reasoning and valuation.

There are many theoretical issues that can be argued about the use of Normal or Lognormal Distributions as being representative of important business variables, such as a selling price. There is no mathematical or scientific basis justifying such use. (Statistical purists have probably already discarded this book by now anyway.) However, such distributions, as well as the Beta Distribution, forecast values clustered around the expected value and, given all the other uncertainties, seems to offer reasonably useful results.

Likewise, one can argue about the interrelationship between price and volume distributions, of the year over year growth in revenues whether forecast by use of CAGR relationships or year-by-year estimates. For example, one can argue for higher unit pricing causing lower volumes and vice versa, rather than permitting both of these variables to act independently and be represented by different distributions to boot. Again the answer is that, given all the uncertainties one deals with in technology licensing, such arguments should not cause immobilization.

As we observed in the closing thoughts on the DCF Method, the power of the Monte Carlo Method should put us midway between hubris and dismissal. On the one hand, we have the wise caution—"beware of geeks bearing formulas[26]"—but on the other hand we can envision consequences from embracing ignorance and indolence because of our suspicion of math and models. The physicist Denis Diderot (1713–1784), editor of the classic French Encyclopédie, told the story of the man walking in the absolute darkness with a poor torch-lamp who encountered another man who said "It is very dark here, turn out the light!" Diderot, a champion of science and the Enlightenment, said of the second man: He must have been a theologian. (The joke, weak as it may be, applies here: A poor light in the midst of great darkness is better than no light at all.) Put in more literary terms, and to parallel the argument for a powerful, meaningful vocabulary, consider this: "The slovenliness of our language makes it easier for us to have foolish thoughts" (George Orwell). Slovenliness, like indolence, does not predictably lead to wiser judgments (or, a better life, for that matter).

Again the reader is referred to my website that has supporting information, updates, and errata relating to the Monte Carlo Method: www.razgaitis.com.

Real Option Methods

As discussed above and in Chapter 7, long-lived projects with high RAHR values result in low calculated NPVs, which can misrepresent the value of certain opportunities.

An implicit assumption with the DCF Method is that all the investment money will be spent, regardless of intermediate outcomes, namely: Once the technology-to-commercialization project is funded, either by an internal business manager or through a license or acquisition, all the costs for all years are assumed to be unchangeably committed regardless of what happens along the way. Like the pig seeing bacon advertised understands the meaning of total commitment better than the chicken seeing eggs on the menu.

In the real options book by Copeland and Antikarov,[27] they summarize a dozen companies, ranging from Enron (one wonders as to Enron's purposes) to oil companies such as Mobil, Exxon, and Texaco, (oil companies have reportedly been using real options analysis since the 1970s) to aviation industry examples such as Airbus Industrie and Pratt & Whitney, to computer companies such as Apple and Hewlett-Packard, who have all claimed to use real options methods. There are, of course, many other companies who have all used real options in one form or another but who may not have formally announced its use to the public.

Various business aphorisms have been coined to capture this idea: "don't dig big holes," "think small," "do the last experiment first," "first find a customer," "quick and dirty new product development," "stage gate product development," "phase 1 feasibility funding," "let's spend a little and learn a little (or a lot)," and so forth. All of these aphorisms have a common element of seeking to avoid making large commitments when the uncertainties are high by sequencing the opportunity in a way that makes possible relatively small investments leading to a dramatic decrease in opportunity uncertainties.

Technology Dealmaking is normally a particularly appropriate context for the use of Real Options. For internal decision making such as funding an R&D project, an NPV analysis yielding notably large positive or negative values normally makes the decision to go forward or not pretty straightforward; the tough calls are when the NPV is positive but near zero. In Dealmaking contexts, one expects that near zero NPV situations are common because sellers naturally want to maximize the payments they receive and so are motivated to price the opportunity to maximize their NPV by minimizing the NPV of the buyer; to do otherwise is called "leaving money on the table," meaning there was additional, forgone value that a willing buyer would have paid if asked and persuaded. Likewise, buyers seek to move to their account as much of the NPV of the opportunity as possible. The give and take of Dealmaking typically requires compromises on these respective self interest positions such that at the end of the process each party is motivated to consummate the deal, because it is mutually value-enhancing, but neither party feels like it has emerged with a one sided victory in the process.

Two cautionary notes are appropriate at this point of introduction. As is soon evident, this additional flexibility is not without cost. Assessing the various possible options that could be incorporated takes time and effort and may result in more complex agreements and project management. Just as was discussed when considering a la carte pricing of a Technology Box, or the possible inclusion of every possible variable in a financial, or the temptation to rerun yet another simulation, every expansion of analysis needs to be measured by the practical value of such effort and complexity. There is the need for judgment in choosing between the extremes of cursory and compulsive appropriate to the value of the opportunity and the significance of uncertainties on such opportunity value. For high potential value and significant uncertainties affecting our perception of such value, an appropriate analysis balance point moves to the more complete and complex. Yet even then, there always comes a point when one has to say "enough" and move to the next stage of Dealmaking that, as is discussed in Chapter 11, could well be a Plan B.

In *Real Options: A Practitioner's Guide*,[28] Chapter 2, written by John Stonier, Marketing Director, Airbus Industrie, recounts the change process that occurred within Airbus as it sought to improve its ability to negotiate more wisely by using real options. One of the key points of this interesting story is the effort required to communicate simply and actionably within Airbus what can be highly abstract and mathematical in real options analysis. It is the point of this chapter in this book to present real options analysis with minimal reference to equations and underlying theory in as user friendly a way as possible. The reader is encouraged to refer to the Copeland and Antikarov book, and to Johnathan Mun's book,[29] discussed in more detail later for comprehensive presentations of the theoretical foundations of real options as well as numerous examples from many different business contexts.

Stage Gate Technology Commercialization

However, what happens in many real world situations is that such commitments are made only for limited periods with any subsequent investments dependent upon intermediate outcomes. This is the essence of the stage gate project management approach, and is the norm for venture capital (VC) investors operating at the high end of the risk spectrum down to corporate investors in internal opportunities. There are exceptions, which will be addressed later, but the normal business approach is spend as little as possible while learning as much as possible so that, ideally, at each subsequent project review one understands better the future risks. If the perceived risks are still large, or worse have grown because of technology development challenges or market shifts or any other reason, the entire project may be simply terminated, saving what had been forecast as the investment required beyond what by then had been "sunk" (except for any shut-down/termination costs, which are, in effect, "sunk" as well at that point).

In all the DCF and Monte Carlo Method examples discussed to this point, we have not accounted for such stage gate investing. The Monte Carlo Method comes closer to accounting for alternative outcomes by the nature of modeling 10,000 runs (or "trials" or "future worlds"). However all such future worlds assume that the project continues to its completion, 10 years for the baseline template of Exhibit 8.22. The forecast NPV distribution determined by a Monte Carlo model shows the effect of extreme downside and upside probabilities, and everything in between, but, so far, we have not incorporated an early termination/exit in the event that the early year costs are higher and/or the early year revenues are lower with respect to the range of the respective input assumptions. (There are ways of incorporating Decision Variables and Decision Tables into Monte Carlo; the details and examples are beyond the scope of this book).

From a valuation perspective, what the stage gate process enables—where it is possible to make investments efficiently in stages—is the determining of the value of an *option* to the technology. This is the subject of this section of Advance Methods of valuation.

Introduction to Real Options

A stage gate investment is a decision to create and maintain an option on a particular technology opportunity. An option is a specific right, but not an obligation, to something—in our context, the "something" is the Technology Box (per Chapter 3) of IP rights, data, equipment, and the like, that a buyer (external or internal) is interested in. A simple example[30] is a lottery ticket. Spending $1 does not buy anything concrete in the lottery game; no bread, no milk, no 50 cents returned. The $1 buys an option on a specific sequence of numbers that may, or much more probably will not, be randomly generated on a subsequent date. If these particular numbers are not so generated, then the option has exactly zero value; this would be equivalent to a technology for which a buyer invested a total of $1 million in upfront fees, R&D, and any shutdown costs, for which there was a total failure of the opportunity such that it retained zero termination value for the buyer or any other third party.

If the later-generated random numbers match the lottery ticket numbers, then such option is "in the money," and is then worth the value of the winning payout. In the case of a lottery, there is no cost to exercise the option, one only has to go get the money, although taxing authorities will be closely behind materially reducing the winnings.[31]

The technology option can be considered in two parts, each part requiring investment by the optionee/buyer. There is first an upfront cost to obtain the option, followed by some buyer investment (in most cases) to advance the technology further toward commercialization by removing or reducing an important uncertainty, such as the one(s) causing the largest contribution to NPV variance as determined by a Monte Carlo tornado or sensitivity chart. If such results are sufficiently favorable, the optionee/buyer then must spend additional sums to exercise the option and complete commercial development of the technology.

The lottery example is one of a "financial option," whereas the technology example is known as a "real option," meaning, essentially, that it is not a financial option.

Option analysis, even with the attendant uncertainties and complexities, is a powerful method not only for determining value but also for structuring agreements. In the "double hump" Monte Carlo example earlier, we considered the value of an opportunity whose Total Costs could be very favorable (mean value of 60 percent) or unfavorable (mean value of 80 percent) based on whether or not an advanced technology succeeds. The Monte Carlo method can be used to characterize how this uncertainty of cost ratio distributions will affect NPV. However, as we saw, the result with the cost uncertainty unrealized made the value of the opportunity unattractive because if the low cost technology failed, the entire opportunity was unattractive. So, even using some standard of risk reward fairness such as the 20th percentile, or 30th percentile, or even the mean value, would lead a buyer to decline to pursue the opportunity despite the very significant economic potential. Valuation by the use of Real Options will aid us in negotiating this type of opportunity. As we see later, the use of Real Options is not just a valuation methodology but also a way of preparing for negotiations and reaching ultimate agreement.

FINANCIAL OPTIONS Financial options, or just "options," have become hugely important in the last 30 or so years. One can now readily sell or purchase an option to any particular equity as purchasing the equity (stock) itself, meaning one can buy on a stock exchange the right to buy a particular equity by or on a particular date for a particular dollar amount per share. And, not own the stock share itself, unless of course such option becomes "in the money" and one then exercises the option to buy it.

There is a vast literature on all manner of options, including, for example, relatively straightforward ones such as the European and American call (buy) and put (sell) options. Options have been a frequent and emotionally charged 'hot' topic in 2007 and 2008. The options awarded to employees, principally senior management, have been the subject of accounting-treatment debate as to whether they should be expensed as granted to reflect diminished current earnings. Certain senior management's mismanagement, or more accurately self-management, of the company assets they were entrusted with, to create stock valuation spikes that enabled them to cash in huge realizations from the value of their options even when the underlying fundamentals of the company were sick or even soon after at death's door. The significant collapse of Long Term Capital Management and more recently all manner of investment hedges/derivatives has brought adverse publicity to the use of options pricing in highly leveraged investments. The explosion of options markets and options investing even by unsophisticated investors has created concern that the increased volatility of equity investing may have led us, in effect, to Las Vegas online and, in 2008, near collapse of the world's financial markets.

Financial options and Real Options are conceptually the same thing: the present value of the future right to make a choice involving the acquisition value of an underlying asset (our focus is on the right to buy, a "call" option, as opposed the right to compel a sale, the "put" option). As discussed in Chapter 7 regarding equity (stock) value, one can think of the present value of a company as being the risk adjusted value to all future after tax earnings. So an option to each share of equity is related to the idea that such share's ultimate value derives from the stream of cash flow benefits anticipated, in proportion to the ownership interest of each share. The parallel with a Real Option is that instead of buying an option to a share of equity itself, we are considering the value of the option to own a technology or nascent product line. As seen in Chapter 7, the valuation of the latter is at its root the net present value (NPV) of the future cash flows.

TECHNOLOGY REAL OPTIONS There is one particularly important difference between financial options and Real Options: Most financial options are fungible and have an extant market that enables buyers and sellers of such options to observe a market-based determination of value and the volatility of such value for the option itself and the underlying asset. For Real Options, the underlying business opportunity is not packaged and available in a public market with published trades going back and forth on which such market value and volatility can be established. There is usually very little business history, and perhaps no present earnings or revenues and established financial statements (income, balance sheet, and cash flow) on which to perform a traditional valuation, and in many instances no history of trades (Dealmaking) of the technology at hand.

The key for a Real Options method to be effective is that there must be some future point at which the parties will know an answer that will enable them to make a more economically intelligent decision than they presently can. So in the preceding "double-hump" Monte Carlo example, if, say, after project Year 1 the answer would be known as to which of the cost ratio scenarios considered will in fact occur, we have an alternative available to the parties on how both to structure and to value a deal, namely, consider the transaction as an option to an opportunity whose value will be substantially less uncertain in one year's time. If the unfavorable cost outcome occurs, then the optionee/buyer will terminate its option. However, if the favorable cost outcome is the result, then the optionee/buyer will seek to exercise its option and acquire the IP rights.

TECHNOLOGY DEVELOPMENT STRATEGY AS REAL OPTIONS Timothy Luehrman has published a series of papers in the *Harvard Business Review* on decision-making strategy from the perspective of taking and exercising options. In his October 1998 paper, he defines an "option space" determined by two variables: one based upon NPV modified to incorporate the time value of the ability to defer investment, and the other a measurement of volatility illustrating how much circumstances can change prior to the commitment of a decision.[32]

The underlying goal is to recognize that having an option to an NPV in high volatility situations is an opportunity to spend a little and learn a little, deferring decisions of major investments until there is much higher certainty.

Professor Luehrman also describes the use of a modified NPV—APV, or adjusted present value—in modeling the present value of future returns.[33] In another article, he shows how such options relate to the Black-Scholes Model.[34]

REAL OPTION VALUATION CONTRASTED WITH A DISCOUNTED CASH FLOW METHOD VALUATION A useful, concrete example is provided in a related paper by Dixit and Pindyck.[35] The description here is adapted from their example and applied to a licensing context. For simplicity we will focus attention on the option aspects;

no time-value-of-money calculations will be made. The situation is this. A buyer is given an opportunity to acquire a license for an initial payment of $5 million after which the buyer will have to expend $10 million in additional R&D. After careful analysis, the buyer has concluded that the ultimate additional cost to commercialize the technology (after the $5 million plus $10 million) will be (C1) $40 million, (C2) $80 million, or (C3) $120 million, based upon certain assumptions. At the moment, all three outcomes are believed to be equally probable. The payoff from a successful implementation is predicted to be either (A) $50 million or (B) $130 million. Should the buyer license the technology?

Let us now consider a simple example from three different perspectives.

Perspective 1: Discounted Cash Flow View of the Six-Scenario Opportunity Let us assume that a seller and buyer are attempting to determine a fair value of an opportunity that has two present, crucial valuation uncertainties: the cost of operating the business and the size of the addressable market. With respect to the cost ratio, the parties agree that one of three outcomes will occur: (C1: $40 million) an advanced technology not yet proven will succeed and enable a low cost structure, or (C2: $80 million) a backup technology also under development will succeed although exhibiting a higher cost ratio, or (C3: $120 million) a technology will need to be acquired from a third party with the net effect of having an even higher cost ratio. At the time of the negotiation, the parties agree that the best judgment is that all three cost ratio outcomes are equally probable. This situation is parallel to the double hump Monte Carlo example considered previously, because in that case we made the Normal Distributions for the two cost ratio scenarios the same size relative to one another, and thereby equal in probability. However, here, for purposes of illustration, we have simplified the problem so that each of the three scenarios has a knowable, single value cost (instead of a distribution of possible costs).

The range of expected revenues is the second uncertainty. It is believed that there are two possibilities: (A: $50 million) a small market with correspondingly small revenues, or (B: $130 million) a large market.

These cost and revenue figures are expressed in their above-single-value NPV form by means of the DCF Method of Chapter 7, using some appropriate RAHR such as the WACC value, where the three cost outcomes represent the total cash outflows, and the two revenue outcomes the total cash inflows.

We are assuming for this example that both cash inflow outcomes and all three cash outflow outcomes are equally, and independently probably. This leads to six equally probable combined outcomes: Low Revenue (A) with each of the three Costs (C1, C2, and C3), and High Revenue (B) with each of the three Costs. Because each combined outcome is equally probably, each has a 16.67 percent of occurring (1/6th probability, each).

The parties have calculated, and agreed, that an initial investment by the buyer of $10 million in research and development (R&D) on technology and on market research necessary to determine which of the cost ratios and revenue models is the real world result.

Finally, the seller informs the buyer that it wants $5 million in a lump-sum payment to transfer all the rights to the buyer at closing.

Now, you are the buyer. How would you analyze the value of the proposed offer?

		Commercializing Cost		
		C1 $40 million	C2 $80 million	C3 $120 million
Pay off	A $50 million	$10 / -$5	-$30 / -$15	-$70 / -$15
	B $130 million	$90 / $75	$50 / $35	$10 / -$5

EXHIBIT 8.32 NPV Net Profit Table for the Real Option Example

Well, from this DCF (Perspective 1), we do straightforward math and probability ratios. In addition to the business costs of scenarios C1, C2, or C3, you the buyer will have to invest $10 million in R&D and market research and, according to the seller, pay $5 million now for ownership of the opportunity. So your costs are $15 million in addition to the C1, C2, and C3 values, namely: $55, $95, of $135 million.

These costs can then be mapped with the two possible revenues to determine the buyers NPV. Because all the revenue and costs, cash inflows and outflows, are on an NPV basis, the buyer's NPV is simply the difference of the cash inflow and cash outflow for each of the six possible outcomes. This can be summarized in what is known as a "payoff table" as shown in Exhibit 8.32.

Since, in our best judgment, each of the three cost scenarios and both of the two revenue scenarios are equally probable, each of the six paired outcomes shown in Exhibit 8.32 are also equally probable. So, the NPV of the array of six outcomes is then just the average of the six individual outcomes, or so it seems, as is shown by the simple calculation below:

$$\text{NPV of Opportunity} = (-5 - 45 - 85 + 75 + 35 - 5)/6 = -\$5 \text{ million}$$

So, as the prospective buyer, from this Perspective 1, you would conclude that the opportunity was not worth pursuing because the NPV is negative. If the seller then offered to decrease its license fee to induce you, the buyer, to "get to yes," what would it take? From the above analysis it would require the seller to reduce its price to zero! (And, even at a selling price of zero, you as the buyer should be indifferent to pursuing the opportunity because at that "price point" the NPV is exactly zero).

Perspective 2: Real Option View of the Six-Scenario Opportunity There is something wrong with Perspective 1. There are two distinct kinds of costs that were commingled in that analysis. The initial costs associated with the R&D and market development, the $10 million, are certain (within the scope of our assumptions) because without such investment the buyer will not know which combination of the six is the real world answer. The $5 million up-front license fee is also fixed, at least provisionally for purposes of the analysis. A buyer can always counterpropose an alternative fee; however, for purposes of the analysis it is legitimate to use the seller's sought for payment as a fixed, certain cost. So, as the buyer, these $15 million are the effective "table stakes" to pursue the opportunity. If agreement is reached, you the buyer will spend the $15 million no matter what the outcome.

However, the costs associated with scenarios C1, C2, and C3 are *not* committed because at the end of the initial R&D and market research, you, as the buyer, will have the *option* to proceed with the opportunity or terminate it, *and*, at that time, you will *know* (per our assumptions) which of the six now equally probably combinations is the real world result.

Consider the most obvious case of the highest cost (C3) and the lower revenues (A). The NPV of that cell is $50 million less $120 million or a net *loss* of $70 million. (Note that we have not included the $15 million as we did in the above calculation, because we are now recognizing that $15 million as a fixed, certain cost, whereas the $120 million of scenario C3 is a possibility but *not* an obligation.)

Thus we can make each cell in Exhibit 8.32 larger by $15 Million because we are going to recognize that that $15 million is an initial, fixed, certain cost of the buyer's option to pursue the opportunity. That initial $15 million is a "sunk" cost, which we will recognize to be an *option fee*. It is only after such sunk costs that you, the buyer, will have the right, but not the obligation, to pursue whichever scenario is then known.

What is the present value of these six outcomes? Before we just add them together as we did for Perspective 1, consider what choice you would make for outcomes A-C2 and A-C3? These two outcomes have the two highest cost outcomes paired with the lower revenue outcomes, a tough break. (Into every life a little rain must fall.) Both of these cells, and only these cells, reflect a negative NPV value. Accordingly, at the point of knowing that either of these outcomes has come to be, you, the buyer, would *not* further pursue the opportunity. Why would any uncompelled, rationale buyer then go forward to knowingly lose more money? The business value, then, of these two cells, is not the negative values as shown in Exhibit 8.32, because no buyer will experience them; their value, "payoff," is exactly zero, because the opportunity would be abandoned and no further costs would be incurred.

So, the key insight here is the $15 million upfront cost is sunk, and independent of the value of going forward after the option period. So we need to separately calculate the NPV value at the end of the option period, by accounting for only those outcomes that are "in the money," meaning that they have a positive NPV. Of the six possible outcomes, four have such positive NPV: all three cost outcomes for the high revenue outcome, and the one low cost outcome for the low revenue outcome. Put in words, if the high revenue outcome is found to occur, the buyer will proceed with commercialization regardless of which cost outcome because all have a positive NPV; of course the buyer aspires to the cheaper cost outcomes, but even for the high cost outcome, it is still worth going forward. However, if the low revenue outcome occurs, then the only combination for which the NPV is positive is the lowest cost outcome.

This can be summarized by two simple calculations. The first is the cost to option for the technology, namely the NPV of the option right. The second calculation is the NPV at the end of the option period based on the six possible outcomes, namely the NPV of the option exercise (what the buyer will net if it then goes forward). These calculations are as follows:

$$\text{NPV of Option Right} = -\$5 - \$10 = -\$15 \text{ million}$$
$$\text{NPV of Option Exercise} = (\$10 + 90 + 50 + 10)/6 = \$26.67 \text{ million}$$

The key is recognizing in the second calculation that one includes only the positive NPV combinations, which are the shown four, but divides by the six possible combinations.

Thus, the NPV of the opportunity is the net of the NPV of the option exercise less the cost to obtain the option right, namely:

$$\$26.67 - \$15.00 = \$11.67 \text{ million}$$

Such $11.67 million determination is dramatically different than the negative $5 million based on the analysis of Perspective 1. The difference in this Perspective 2 analysis leads to the recognition that this opportunity is an option to a future right, namely, the right without the obligation to pursue any of the resulting six combinations of cost and revenue scenarios, and that the costs associated with the license fee and R&D are sunk and therefore irrelevant to the decision to proceed with any of the subsequent six scenarios.

Therefore, by viewing this opportunity from an option pricing perspective, it is worth a positive $11.7 million to the buyer instead of the negative result found by NPV analysis. The difference is a result of the actions taken for the two darker cells in Exhibit 8.32. In the NPV case, it is assumed that the buyer would commercialize these two possibilities just as is done in the other four cells and lose even more money than the sunk $15 million in option cost. Whereas in the option perspective it is recognized that the buyer will not ever lose more than $15 million net for any outcome.

The six options are graphically shown in Exhibit 8.33.

As shown, after the "more facts period" afforded by the internal R&D investment of $10 million, there are then six options: Two of them reflect a further net loss, so are not exercised, two of them represent a recovery of some of the previous investment, and so are exercised, and two of them are dreams come true and are delightedly exercised. The weighted average of these outcomes is to bring a positive $26.7 million to the holder of the option, which must be offset by the $15 million paid to have such option, leaving a value of the option of $11.7 million as calculated above.

This result can also be shown using a probability tree structure as shown in Exhibit 8.34.

(The respective percentages have not been shown because in this example they are all equal.)

Therefore, the license fee could actually be up to $11.7 million higher and still be net positive for the buyer.

Perspective 3: A Model for a Buyer's Counteroffer If we take the $10 million for R&D and market research as immutable, that leaves $16.7 million of value (from the $26.7 million total) than can be apportioned between buyer and seller. The seller's initial proposal of a $5 million license fee payment represents in effect a 30 percent apportionment of the total opportunity value. By the previous analysis, the buyer could accept the seller's proposal concluding that under the circumstances such 30 percent apportionment was fair, or, propose a smaller apportionment of the total value as a license fee, in the traditional spirit of "more for me, less for you."

However, by recognizing the option nature of the opportunity, the buyer can, in a way, propose "more for you, and more for me." Consider the following possibility.

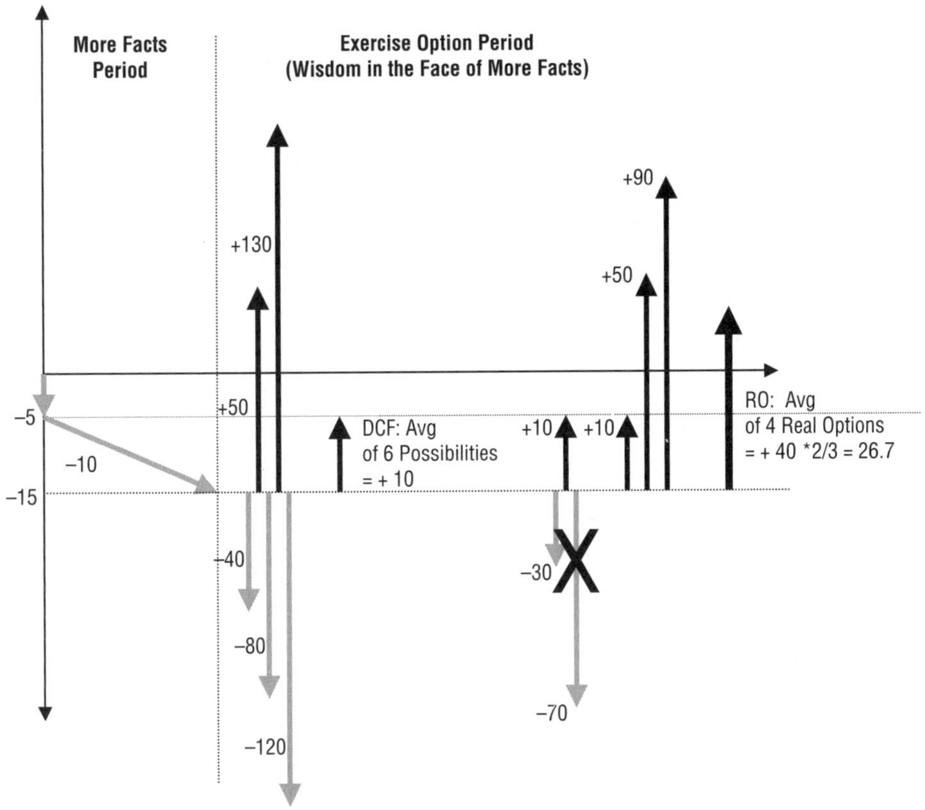

EXHIBIT 8.33 NPV DCF versus Real Option Thinking

Suppose the buyer counteroffers payment of a \$2 million up-front fee, and an additional, say, \$4 million if the buyer elects to pursue the opportunity after the initial R&D period during which it will be spending an additional \$10 million on R&D. Such a counteroffer has the following result:

NPV of the Option Right = −\$2 − \$10 = −\$12 million
NPV of the Option Exercise = (\$6 + 86 + 46 + 6)/6 = \$24 million

So, the buyer's net opportunity value by this revised counteroffer is, on a statistical basis, \$12 million, up from \$11.67 million. The seller's value is \$2 + \$4 ∗ 4/6 = \$4.67 million, down from \$5 million. The total opportunity value to be apportioned is unchanged by this rearrangement at \$16.67 million. However, in the counteroffer, the buyer proposes to pay the seller potentially a total of \$6 million, which is \$1 million more than the seller proposed; but only \$2 million is guaranteed up front. The balance of the \$4 million would be paid only if the buyer exercises the option to pursue the opportunity, which will occur the four times out of six times that the option exercise value has a positive NPV. So, six times out of six, the seller receives \$2 million up front; then four times out of six, the seller receives a second payment of \$4 million, and two times out of six he gets the opportunity returned (along with retaining the initial \$2 million). If the option is not exercised, then the buyer is out

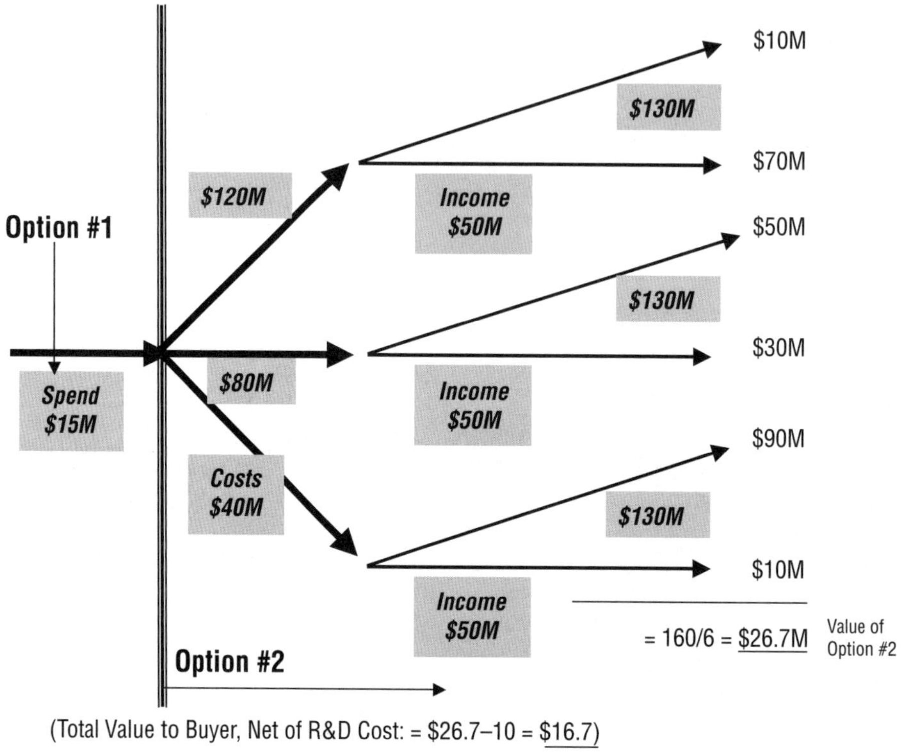

EXHIBIT 8.34 When an Option Exists, a Probability Tree Becomes a "Decision Tree"
Source: © Razgaitis, richard@razgaitis.com.

$12 million for which it gained the knowledge that the opportunity was not worth pursuing. However, four times out of six the buyer will elect to pursue his option. Notice that in two of such four times, the buyer does not earn back its option fee because the value of two of the cells is only $6 million; however, because they are positive NPV values, they are worth pursuing and have the effect of reducing the buyer's loss to $6 million (−$12 million for the cost of the option offset by a plus $6 million from the election of the option). In the remaining two times out of six, the buyer makes a substantial sum, either $86 less the $12 (i.e., $74 million net), or $46 less the $12 (i.e., $34 million net). Note there is no possible outcome (within the confines of our assumptions) by which the seller will make $4.67 million and the buyer $12 million; these are simply the mean values given the probabilities and the scenario values. The structure of such $2 million conditional payment upon the buyer's option exercise is the license fee because exercising the option means obtaining the license rights in question (or the assignment).

Such option thinking is essentially the primary motive behind the stage gate product development process. With this methodology all the activities needed to go from concept to product completion are classified into distinct stages. Of interest to us here is that each stage is defined by a "gate" that needs a priori requirements to be met before product development can continue. This gating is intended to sharply define the keys to success and apply metrics to each opportunity during each critical phase. This approach is particularly well suited to Real Options valuation and deal structures. As each gate is reached, there is an opportunity for management intervention (to continue to the next phase, terminate the product because of failure to complete the present stage, redefine the new product goals, etc.). Under an option pricing model, it is possible, in theory, to ascribe a value to passing each gate. In practice there could be a half dozen or more gates in a product development process. In technology licensing contexts it is not usual to have that many option/exercise events. However, VC funding typically comes in discrete "rounds" with each round separately valued, effectively as options to the subsequent value; there can easily be four such rounds or more between the start of VC investing and some liquidity event such as a public offering or a strategic acquisition.

This Perspective 3 discussion is an example of the interface between valuation and pricing, between analysis and Dealmaking. We will focus on this interface in the ***Approach*** chapters on Dealmaking (Chapters 10 and 11).

The simple financial example of Exhibits 8.33 and 8.34 shows how an NPV analysis sequenced around decision points is a useful means of determining a rational value based upon consideration of options. And, it shows how DCF scenario analysis can be used in a direct, 'no fancy math' way to determine Real Option value if the problem is carefully constructed. We now turn our attention to more elegant methods of calculating Real Option value.

Using the Discounted Cash Flow and Monte Carlo Methods to Determine Real Option Value

A straightforward application of the Real Option Method is to perform a pair of valuations, using the DCF or Monte Carlo Methods, as appropriate, one for the envisioned technology transaction date (the "now") and one for the value after some period of further R&D or commercial development for which there will be a much better idea of the value of the opportunity.

An example of two such period valuations would be the double hump Monte Carlo Method example considered previously. In this situation there were two possible cost structures, each with their own distribution of possible values, leading to the two separate humps. If the high cost outcome is the only practical method of manufacture then it is almost certain that the opportunity will not be worth anything. If the low cost outcome can be demonstrated then the technology will very likely have a positive NPV. In either case, we do not need to assume that all the uncertainty has been wrung out of either cost outcome, just the discernment of whether the low cost outcome is viable.

As we calculated this double hump example, the present, pre-option value is negative because of the adverse effect on NPV of the high cost outcome. Thus any option payment made by the buyer for (1) option rights to the IP, and (2) the investment required to conduct the R&D to resolve the cost outcome uncertainty, is not justified by a present option value. In a practical negotiation, this could lead a buyer to conclude that it would not be reasonable to pay any cash option fee to the seller, and to receive consideration for its investing in the necessary early R&D.

The Monte Carlo model for the double hump can be re-run using only the low cost hump to determine a reasonable value range if, and only if, such low cost outcome is demonstrated. Under these circumstances of a negative initial value, such value range could then be negotiated to be reduced by the R&D spending of the buyer.

If we consider the earlier Monte Carlo baseline template summarized in Exhibit 8.26, we saw that depending upon the COGS distribution used, and whether the 20th or 30th percentile was the valuation point, the technology value ranged from \$16 to \$28 million (rounded values). A Real Option approach could be used here, whereby the buyer initially pays only for an option right to the technology, conducts additional R&D to some point where it becomes the COGS and uncertainties are reduced whereupon it can elect to obtain its rights by exercising the option, or walk away and give up its option.

There is no simple formula for how such a two stage—option then exercise price—should be computed. One approach would be to price the option at the 10th percentile value with the exercise price being the 30th percentile value. For this example, the 10th percentile value ranges approximately from \$3 to \$13 million, depending on the specific COGS model. The R&D cost by the buyer could be credited against such option fee, assuming that all the data would be given to the seller if the buyer does not exercise the option and such R&D would be what the seller would have had to spend to obtain the necessary data.

With financial options, a remarkable development of highly accurate pricing has been developed primarily driven by a single parameter known as the volatility. We will now consider such option pricing mathematics as an example of how it might be applicable to a Real Option.

Black-Scholes Equation for Option Pricing

It can be said that rational option pricing began with a famous equation named after its discoverers, Fischer Black[36] and Myron Scholes[37] with an assist from Robert Merton[38] in a famous paper published in 1973. At the same time, just a month before the Black-Scholes paper was published, an option market was created at the Chicago Board Options Exchange (CBOE) that created a market not just for options but for the rational pricing of options. The popularity of options and the Black-Scholes equation quickly led to it being incorporated into a financial calculator offered by Texas Instruments (TI). Thus, in a matter of months, the financial world, which had been wrestling with the problem of rationally pricing options for more than 70 years, had an options market, an equation, and a calculator. This combination, something like the perfect storm, all became famous, seemingly overnight: Black, Scholes, (Merton was already famous), the equation, the TI calculator, the CBOE, and option pricing of financial securities (an important kind of financial derivative). The fame was appropriately sealed with the Nobel Prize in Economic Sciences in 1997 to Scholes and Merton (Fischer Black died in 1995). A brief biography of this award can be found at the Nobel Prize web site, www.nobel.se/economics/laureates/1997/back.html.

There are innumerable types of financial options, typically identified by colorful terms such as European, American, Asian, Bermudian—none of which has any known territorial significance. We will illustrate the European Option as it is the framework for illustrating the valuation of an option. A European Option is the right but not the obligation to buy a specified number of shares of a specific equity ("the underlying" is the jargon) on a specific date ("the expiry date") by payment of a specific share price ("the strike price"). A European Option *cannot* be exercised *prior* to the specified expiration date, and *will not* be exercised if the share price on such date is less than the specified strike price, because it would make no economic sense to do so.

THE BLACK-SCHOLES EQUATION APPLIED TO A EUROPEAN CALL OPTION TO A SHARE OF YAHOO! The simplest form of the Black-Scholes equation (hereafter, BSE1) is for a European call option. First a little background on call options. If you are interested in a particular stock, say, Yahoo! (YHOO), an interest which, in 2008, Microsoft no longer has, you can simply purchase shares on the open market. Alternatively, you could purchase not a share but an option to purchase a share ("a call") of YHOO.

Let us consider a propitious moment in time to illustrate the point. On April 3, 2000, YHOO was selling for $160.13 a share. Say that instead of buying YHOO equity on that date you instead bought only the right to buy one share of YHOO exactly a year from April 3, 2000, namely, April 3, 2001 at a strike price corresponding to its April 3, 2000 price of $160.13, such price being your cost "to call" a share of YHOO on April 3, 2001. (In technology Dealmaking the call price is the license, or assignment fee). Well, at first this seems peculiar. Why would anyone want the right to buy a share of YHOO a year hence for its present share price? Because by having the option, namely, the right to ownership but not the ownership nor the obligation to become an owner, you do not participate in any decline in the value of YHOO because if YHOO is selling for less than the $160.13 strike price you have chosen on April 3, 2001, you will let your option expire and you have lost only what you paid for the option.[39]

The important issue here is how would you, buyer of an option, and, say, me an option seller, *value* your option to my one share of YHOO? What would I the option offerer be giving up? Well, if YHOO decreases in value below the strike price (which in this example is the present price), you the owner of the call right will not exercise your right because to do so would cost you more than you could then buy somebody else's share of YHOO on the open market for, assuming you even wanted such a share. If, however, the value of a share of YHOO goes above the present April 3, 2000 price, then you as the option holder will exercise your option and pay just the strike price ($160.13 in this example), which would be less than the share is then worth. So I, as the offerer of the option, am effectively giving up the appreciation potential of the stock over the term of the option, but "own" all the downside. (So if I was confident that YHOO would decline in value, whatever I receive as payment from you for you call option would be "free" money, and provides for me some "downside" protection). What would it be worth to each of us to provide this right to you and this payment to me on April 3, 2000? This simple but elegant question is the one that Black and Scholes sought to answer by an exact equation. Because our purpose here is not to delve into the mathematical model behind their result, we merely jump ahead to their result, which is shown in Exhibit 8.35.

This form of the Black Scholes equation, which we will designate as BSE1, is only applicable to the European call option meaning, in our example, that you the holder of the YHOO call option can only exercise it on the exact expiry date, April 3, 2001; the so called American option is much more complicated mathematically because it can be exercised at any time during the year.

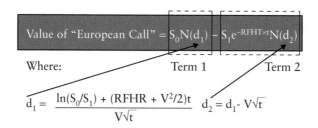

$$\text{Value of "European Call"} = \underbrace{S_0N(d_1)}_{\text{Term 1}} - \underbrace{S_1e^{-RFHT\times t}N(d_2)}_{\text{Term 2}}$$

Where:

$$d_1 = \frac{\ln(S_0/S_1) + (RFHR + V^2/2)t}{V\sqrt{t}} \qquad d_2 = d_1 - V\sqrt{t}$$

EXHIBIT 8.35 The Black-Scholes Equation for Pricing (European) Call Options

Source: © Razgaitis, richard@razgaitis.com

These BSE1 equations have the advantage of being "closed form." Closed form is a characterization of mathematical expressions in which all the unknowns can be separated onto one side of the equation with only the unknown sought for, here option (call) value, alone on the other side of the equation. Closed form equations can generally be solved exactly without the requirement of iteration or other approximation techniques

The BSE1 equation, although complex, is really amazing in its simplicity—only five input values are needed to calculate the value of the option:

1. The present price (S_0) of the underlying right (YHOO), in this example on April 3, 2000, \$160.13.
2. The strike price (S_1), namely the price chosen as the cost of exercising the option; here we have arbitrarily selected the April 3, 2000 price, \$160.13.
3. The time (t) to expiry of the option that we have selected to be 1 year hence, April 3, 2001.
4. The risk free interest rate (or risk free hurdle rate, RFHR), which is a knowable, market determined value at the time of the option (April 3, 2000).
5. The volatility (V) of the underlying right (YHOO) expressed (and here is the complicated part) as the standardized deviation of the annualized, continuously compounded rate of return of the underlying right. Volatility is a statistical measure of the price swings in the underlying equity over some recent, historic period, often 90 preceding days. Later we show how this can be calculated, but for now we simply note that such volatility is published for any publicly traded equity. For YHOO on April 3, 2000 it was 80.36 percent (which is a large number corresponding to the significant fluctuations then experienced by Yahoo's stock price).

The two calculated terms in d1 and d2 BSE1 have a physical meaning. The first term is a measure of the expected benefit from purchasing the stock itself; it is not obvious—presumably they had to do something non-obvious to deserve the Nobel Prize—but this term is a product of the stock price (S_0) and the change in the call premium with respect to changes in the stock price. The second term is the present value of the exercise price that would be paid on the expiry date. The difference between these two values is the measure of the value of the option to a share.

The calculation of the corresponding option value (the call) according to BSE1 is shown in Exhibit 8.36.

EXHIBIT 8.36 Calculation of Black-Scholes Option Value (BSE1) for the YHOO Example

Five Input Values, for YHOO at 4/3/00				
S_0	*V*	*S_1*	*t*	*RFHR*
$160.13	*0.8036*	**$ 160.13**	**1.00**	***0.0619***
Calculated Terms				
d1	**d2**			
0.4789	−0.3247			
N(d1)	**N(d2)**			
0.6840	0.3727			
Term 1	**Term 2**		**Option Value of a Call According to BSE1**	
$109.53	$56.10		$53.43	

Source: © Razgaitis, richard@razgaitis.com.

The two input values shown in italics, S_0 and V, are intrinsic to the underlying asset whose option value is being determined as of the time of sale of the option, subject to the reality that the calculation of volatility (V) requires some historic period preceding such sale date. The two bold input values, S_1 and t, are arbitrary choices of the buyer of the option. The one bold italic value, RFHR, is a universal environmental value that measures the risk free alternative available to any and all investors at the sale of the option. The N(d) values are readily calculated using the NORMDIST functions available in the Excel spreadsheet. Thus, according to BSE1, the appropriate cost for you to purchase an option right to each share of YHOO from me on April 3, 2000, based on the facts at that time, exercisable on, and only on, April 3, 2001 is $53.43. So it says. (There are now numerous places on the World Wide Web that provide a Black-Scholes calculator; see, for example: www.intrepid.com/~robertl/option-pricer3.html).

I chose this YHOO example and date because we can see in dramatic fashion what actually transpired. In Exhibit 8.37 is a graph of the actual Yahoo share price during the 12 month period of the option, starting at $160.13.

Shown at the right portion of the exhibit are four zones defined by $160 + the option value ($53) = $213, using whole dollars, and $160 less the option value = $107. Had YHOO's share price exceeded $213 a share (in your dreams), your option would have been "in the money," meaning that after buying your one share of YHOO on April 3, 2001, you would have expended a total of $53 for the option plus the $160 strike price to exercise the option or a total of $213; for any value of YHOO above $213 you would more than pay back the cost of the option. As a point of comparison to the Real Options example considered previously and illustrated in Exhibit 8.33, a YHOO share price above $213 corresponds to the two high revenue with low and moderate cost outcomes. For these two revenue and cost combinations, we found that the NPV was positive and exceeded the cost paid for the option ($15 million). Such outcome is the ideal for the optionee/buyer.

In the next zone, a YHOO share selling for between $160 and $213, you would still exercise your option on April 3, 2001, still paying $160, and to the degree YHOO is above $160 (but less than $213) you recoup some, but not all, of your cost of

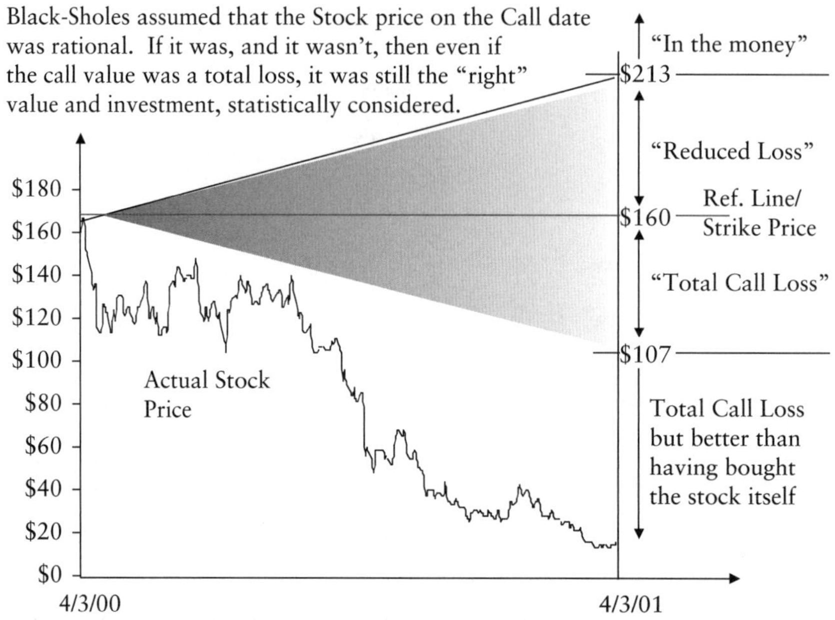
Black-Sholes assumed that the Stock price on the Call date was rational. If it was, and it wasn't, then even if the call value was a total loss, it was still the "right" value and investment, statistically considered.
"In the money"
$213
"Reduced Loss"
Ref. Line/
Strike Price
$160
"Total Call Loss"
$107
Total Call Loss but better than having bought the stock itself
Actual Stock Price
$180
$160
$140
$120
$100
$80
$60
$40
$20
$0
4/3/00
4/3/01

EXHIBIT 8.37 Value of YHOO during the Option Period Showing the Option Outcome Possible and Realized

Source: © Razgaitis, richard@razgaitis.com.

the option. This corresponds to the next two most favorable outcomes shown in Exhibit 8.33, the high revenue/highest cost and the low revenue/lowest cost, where the overall NPV of exercising the option will be negative, because the small positive NPV obtained by exercising the option will not exceed the cost paid for the option. However, nonetheless, it makes business sense to exercise the option to offset some, but not all of the option cost, because all historic costs are sunk. This seems like a very painful outcome, to undertake a project (the license) that when everything is added up years later will be viewed as a "loser." However, this is not an uncommon outcome for R&D in general. There may be many years of significant investment in a certain R&D direction for which there has been zero commercial products. At some merciful moment someone identifies a modest, but positive NPV opportunity. Should it be taken even if there is little or no chance it will "pay back" all that has been invested? The right answer is yes because the costs in the past are "sunk." If the future holds an appropriately determined positive NPV—that is an opportunity Discovery, and the past pain is just the past pain. Casey Stengel, the infamous New York Yankees manager during their glory years said: "The secret of managing is to keep the guys who hate you away from the ones who are undecided." Borrowing that idea here, the "secret" of Real Options is keeping the past away from the future.

The next two zones in Exhibit 8.37 below $160 but above $107, and below $107—you would not exercise the option because you could buy a share of YHOO on the open market for less than your option entitles you to; so you would lose the entire $53 that you paid for your option. For all three zones above $107 a share, you would have been better off having bought YHOO at $160 a share on April 3,

2000 instead of paying \$53 for the option to buy it at \$160 a share on April 3, 2001. Having paid for the option to a share of YHOO did not enable you to make a greater realization on a share of YHOO than having been a YHOO owner for each of these three zones. If so, what good is an option?

The answer lies in the bottommost zone, below \$107 a share. Here, you would have been worse off having owned YHOO than owning an option to YHOO. Since, in this specific example, YHOO (alas) "tanked," having an option instead of share ownership turned out to be a great idea because you had rights to an upside in YHOO but lost only \$53 instead of the more than \$140 that a YHOO April 3, 2000 owner lost by holding on until April 3, 2001.

WHAT DO EQUATIONS REPRESENT? "WHAT IS TRUTH?" Before turning to our primary interest of real, versus financial, options, let us first consider what equations represent. Are equations *true*? Or, as Pilate asked (demanded of?) Jesus: "What is Truth?"[40]

When we express something as an equation, what does doing so represent? Let us consider first two of the most famous equations of all time:

$$C^2 = A^2 + B^2 \text{ (Pythagorean Theorem, ca. 4th C, BC)}$$
$$F = m * A \text{ (Newton's 2nd Law of Motion, ca. 1686)}$$

The Pythagorean Theorem, which is the cornerstone equation of plane (Euclidian) geometry, says that for a right triangle (a triangle with one angle being 90 degrees), the square of the hypotenuse C (the longest side) is equal to the sum of the squares of the other two sides A and B.[41] So, for a right triangle with sides 3 and 4, the Pythagorean Theorem asserts (or, one might say: predicts) that the hypotenuse is precisely, exactly, and only 5.

Isaac Newton in the seventeenth century generally is credited with being one of the principal founders of modern science and his work was instrumental in precipitating the Enlightenment. In a series of absolutely remarkable discoveries, Newton was able to develop the underlying equations (laws) that govern the motion of bodies (in addition to numerous other discoveries such as calculus and optics). The most famous of these motion equations is that the force accelerating a mass can be determined instantaneously by taking the product of the mass times the acceleration. Or, expressing the equation differently, the acceleration experienced by a body of mass m will be simply the ratio of the force applied (F) divided by its mass (m).

Now, are these equations true? The answer is: "yes" and "no." How so?

The Pythagorean Theorem is really a corollary that derives from a hypothesized system of analysis that we now call Euclidian Geometry. If one establishes a starting set of hypotheses about a geometrical system, planar (flat) surfaces, lines of zero width and arbitrary length, and so forth, then it can be shown by proof, from such starting assumptions, that $C^2 = A^2 + B^2$. No physical triangle can be drawn exactly conforming to Euclidian assumptions so that were one to try to measure the hypotenuse of a right triangle with sides 3 and 4, it would never be quite 5.0000000..., although we would agree that such hypotenuse must be exactly 5 and it is the limitations of our physical world that makes the representation given by $C^2 = A^2 + B^2$ imperfectly expressed.[42] In addition to our inabilities to perfectly express a Euclidian right triangle in our physical world, there are many non-Euclidian applications. For instance, if we were to attempt to lay out a right triangle on, say,

North America, with short sides 3,000 and 4,000 miles long, and even looking from outer space where we might be able to neglect the effects of unevenness of the surface, we would find that the hypotenuse is not 5,000 miles. This deviation from $C^2 = A^2 + B^2$ is not due solely to our physical limitations but that the earth's surface is (roughly) a sphere and the Pythagorean Theorem is restricted to planar geometries. So, is the Pythagorean Theorem true? If I live within the geometrical world of a Euclidian geometrician, the answer is an emphatic Yes. If I carefully draw right triangles on approximately flat surfaces, say laying out a baseball infield or a tennis court, the answer is, yes for practical purposes (YFPP). If I am doing geometry on, for example, large curved surfaces, such as surveying a large tract of land, the answer is No.

Considering, now Newton's 2nd Law, $F = m * A$, we also have the two constrictions considered above with the Pythagorean Theorem, namely: (1) our most precise measurements will never quite achieve the perfect certainty and precision espoused by the equation, and (2) there is a limited domain for which the equation is applicable, known as an "inertial" (or "Newtonian") coordinate system.[43] If one were to attempt to use $F = m * A$ on, say, a merry-go-around, whose rotation makes it a strikingly non-Newtonian coordinate system, we would be confounded in our attempts. But there is a further issue with Newton's 2nd Law as modified by Einstein. Einstein showed that Newton's 2nd Law is really a special case of motion in which the speeds are small compared to the speed of light and the masses are large compared to individual atoms. At extremely high speeds approaching the speed of light, there are relativistic effects that arise that cause, among other things, for the force required to cause acceleration to approach an infinite value. At extremely small physical dimensions, there are quantum effects that permit only discrete energy levels instead of the continuity of possible speeds suggested by $F = m * A$. So, with Einstein and the twentieth century, we came to understand that Newton's 2nd Law is a regime-limited simplification of a much richer and much more complicated relationship among forces, masses, and rates of change of speed, even for a Newtonian coordinate system.

So, is $F = m * A$ true? Within a physics model known as a Newtonian universe, where our coordinate system is fixed or non-accelerating, and for "ordinary" masses and speeds, YFPP, though only because any calculation incorporating quantum or relativistic effects produces modifications too small to matter. However, when calculating the motion of a long distance projectile, or the motion of winds and weather, where the rotation of the earth gives rise to real, non Newtonian effects (so called Coriolis Forces), then the answer is "no."

Now, what about BSE1? Is the Black-Scholes Equation true? Although the details of its derivation are beyond the scope of this book, following is a summary of the assumptions that govern its applicability:

- One uncertainty (volatility)
- Volatility knowable (generally by public trade data) at time of pricing the call value
- One time period
- Constant volatility during such time period
- Volatility characterizable by a continuous-time stochastic process arising from lognormal diffusion (LND). Such LND requires no below zero values, and an

infinitely long tail representing low probability but extraordinary value potential, and causes volatility to increase with the square root of time

- The "Law of One Price" holds (two assets that have the same future value must have the same current value), or "no arbitrage" condition (known as dynamic tracking)
- European call conditions (option is exercisable only on the expiration date, not before)
- No dividends (or ongoing costs), known as "asset leakage," occur (or if they occur, BSE1 must be modified by the Merton extension)
- "Continuous time finance," meaning that prices change continuously, in infinitesimal increments, without jumps
- The present share price is rational

Let us consider first the underlying critical assumption regarding volatility. Volatility (V) in BSE1 is a required input variable for the asset in question; for Yahoo on April 3, 2000, its value was 80.36 percent. This value is calculated by a method that is shown later using historic share prices for, in this case, Yahoo. This calculation creates an inherent contradiction: How can we expect that the use of a historic input variable (volatility) will enable the prediction of a future result? The answer is: "only if the future replicates the past." So if, for example, we used a Yahoo volatility based on a then-recent history of 90 or 180 days, as is commonly done, to calculate an option value for 1 year hence, how do we know that the past is prelude to the future? We do not, but we need to assume so or we cannot go forward because we have to make a present prediction about tomorrow using only data available to us presently. And studies done of a stock's volatility show that its volatility tends to change less dramatically than its price. Any present data is either an instantaneously available number, such as share price effectively is, or it is based on some mathematical calculation on the past, however recent or distant. Underlying BSE1 is an assumption that an equity's volatility is constant over time such that a recently historic value (such as the past 90 or 180 days) is a reasonable estimate of its future volatility.

Another critical underlying BSE1 assumption is the rationality of the present share price (in the Yahoo! example this was April 3, 2000). Suppose for a moment, that the Nasdaq system processing trading during early April 2000 had some sort of "perfect storm" of Y2K and April Fools' so that there was a maelstrom of inaccurate data on the bid-and-ask price of YHOO and other financial information such as Yahoo!'s present and forecasted earnings that caused the share price to be bid as it was in our example at $160.13, whereas without such maelstrom of misinformation it would have been, and should have been, $60.13. Well, in such a case it is garbage in, garbage out. If the then-present price of YHOO was "wrong," then the calculated option value is also going to be "wrong."

Now, from the perspective of 2002, we appear to know that the historic volatility of YHOO as of April 3, 2000, as high as it was at 80.36 percent, was too low compared to the then-impending drama. Further, it appears that we know that $160.13 was not a rational price for the asset but rather some sort of reflection of a "greater fool" effect of an irrational auction fed by generally slanted information about market trends and profitability (not necessarily specific to Yahoo!).

So BSE1 is in ways similar to the Pythagorean Theorem and Newton's 2nd Law in that it is true only in a special universe that enables it to be so, for certain limited purposes.

The Black-Scholes equation has also spawned a small industry in creating modifications to BSE1, some proprietary and some published, in addition to alternative option equation theories. Much of this energy is being expended to try to create a statistical advantage on behalf of some over the many who may be buying and selling options with valuations based on the standard model.[44] So in the sense of "true" or "truth" as reflecting reality, and given the numerous assumptions required for the classic form of BSE1, such modifications are reflective of the belief that such truth-seeking is the path to financial advantage.

VOLATILITY CREATES OPTION VALUE There is an important, possibly counterintuitive relationship between volatility and option value. In our previous discussions we saw that uncertainty caused a diminution in technology value because uncertainty maps to risk, and buyers need a greater reward to take on larger risks.

But volatility has a beneficial effect upon value when determining an option value because, with an option, the buyer has a right to acquire the technology rights (paying the strike, or exercise price, in addition to the option price). If the strike price is fixed, and the volatility is high, then there exists a significant "upside" that could be shown by the end of the option period making the exercise opportunity valuable.

Although the Black Scholes equation does not directly apply to technology opportunities, it reveals the same basic trends. Substituting increasing values of volatility in a BSE1 calculator easily demonstrates the effect of increasing the option value. For the above YHOO example, we saw an option value of $53.43 for a strike price of $160.13 (which was also the current stock price) exercisable one year hence, given a risk free rate (RFHR) of 6.19 percent. Simple substitution in a BSE1 calculation shows the following, that (for example) doubling the volatility to 160.72 percent, increases the call value by 77 percent to $94.69. As the volatility increases, the call value asymptotes to the stock price at the time of the pricing of the option.

Within a Black-Scholes framework, high volatility increases option value because it increases the odds that there will be a significant future upside to the underlying equity, which an option holder can then realize by the exercise of the option. It also increases the likelihood of a significant future downside, but an option holder has the option, not the obligation, to purchase the underlying equity. So if the equity goes to zero such outcome is no different than the equity selling for a penny less than the call value since in both cases the only effect will be the expiration of the option right without its being exercised.

Likewise, the longer the option period, the greater the value of an option, all other factors being constant, for the same reason: It increases the likelihood of an upside that can be realized. The risk free hurdle rate (RFHR) has a relatively small effect on the value of an option. As RFHR rate increases, meaning there are better risk free returns available as an alternative investment, then the call value increases, and vice versa.

So if I am the owner of two equities, one with very high volatility and one with very low volatility, a call option valuation will yield a much higher value for the former than the latter. For a technology Real Option, the very high volatility parallel is an opportunity whose upside potential is very high, as determined by some scenario or sensitivity analysis using the DCF Method or by the upper percentile NPV values determined by the Monte Carlo Method.

This is intrinsically the motivation of high risk investors. DARPA (Defense Advanced Research Projects Agency) is a U.S. government agency charged with maintaining military superiority through technology. It is reported to use as one standard for investment decision making, a 10x factor improvement in performance compared to presently fielded technologies. Of course such dramatic improvements are normally associated with great technology risk, but the importance of such investments is deemed (it is reported) to justify the risk. Such 10x factor improvement potential can be viewed as very high technology volatility. Venture capitalist investors also tend to seek high technology volatility opportunities because they will yield a greater return to a VC fund to have just a relatively few wildly successful projects from a portfolio of investments than a bunch of "ok" returns.

However, even an investor seeking extraordinary potential returns by making investments in "high volatility" technologies wants to reduce the risk and committed investment dollars to the extent possible. The key to limiting the highest risk exposure is by spending as little as possible in the earliest, highest-uncertainty project development stages to gain an improved understanding of remaining risks and upside potential. Real options valuation establishes the price such investors are willing to pay at each stage of development based upon the ever more well defined opportunity volatility.

HOW TO DETERMINE VOLATILITY? Assuming for the moment that BSE1 could be a tool for valuation of technology Real Options, we need some means of estimating volatility. However, as we noted at the beginning of this chapter, Real Options differ from financial options by the absence of market based present values and a history of such values that enable calculation of innate volatility.

Volatility from Equity Comparables ("Pure Plays") What about the ability to use comparables to extract appropriate volatility values in the absence of opportunity specific data? For instance, we might find a publicly traded company that applies technology to make products for markets that are all—generally speaking—similar to the present technology and its ultimate intended use.[45] However, such volatilities will be related to the revenues, earnings, inventories, receivables, debt, and other factors comprising the company's financial statements, its management team, its intellectual property position (patents, copyrighted content and software, trademarks, etc.), its market partners and channels, trends and news from its markets and relating to its suppliers and competitors.

There is no simple way of extracting from available volatility data, for a public equity, what component of the volatility is traceable to the core question of a technology to make a product or product family to serve a market or several markets. Further, there is often an essential difference between the subject opportunity and the extant market participants. Rarely is an opportunity being analyzed and proposed that has as its value proposition that "this will be just like company X." There is normally something new and special regarding the opportunity's technology and/or manufacturing process and/or business model that allows it (or is asserted to allow it) to make something that is better, faster, cheaper, or more reliable than the incumbents, or it is making a claim to being the first to a market in which case there are no true incumbents.

Finally, the uncertainty associated with the value of a particular opportunity can be thought of as a combination of common and private risk. In the category of common risk would be those issues that any company in a similar business faces. So, all polymer companies face somewhat shared risks about general public favor or anxieties of their use of plastics and the environment, the cost and availability of crude oil (the raw material from which polymers are made), the general growth in the economy, cost of capital, and so forth. However, in the private risk category are those factors specific to the subject opportunity: Will it be protected by patents? Will it infringe someone else's patent (3,000 new U.S. patents are issued every Tuesday, any one of which could create a problem for a new entrant)? Will the technology actually work? Can a low cost manufacturing operation be created? Will there be adverse characteristics of the products made that are not presently understood (long term durability, toxicity), and so forth? It is these private risks, associated with the unique aspects of the subject technology that can play the dominant role in causing value uncertainty. In such a case, even finding an excellent pure play market comparable will not enable us to gain a picture of uncertainty about our opportunity. As I look out over my pasture, I wonder whether there is oil under the green grass, which presently consumes oil from my mowing it. If I were to form a drilling company to search for oil there, no analysis of comparables from Exxon or anyone else would provide any rational prospective investor, in such a venture, what the present value should be for a bore hole somewhere in my tall grass 60 miles west of Newark airport.

So, although the volatility data of a comparable fits the definition of this quantity in BSE1 the values for volatility so determined are unlikely to reflect the technology being valuated for a stage development.

"Volatility" Using a Probability Tree Let us consider how we might construct another form of "volatility" based upon the specific circumstances of the technology being valued.

A seller offers a technology that by, say, probability tree analysis is believed to have a present value (S_0) of $1,000. Let us further assume that such determination of S_0 was achieved by an extensive analysis of scenarios that accounted for the extent of significance of patent protection, the conclusions reached about the size of the market and value placed on the associated product compared to competitive alternatives, the technical performance that can be demonstrated at the advance prototype level, and the cost of scale up and manufacture for mass product introduction. Say, each of these four uncertainties was considered on three level outcome basis: high, medium, and low scenarios. Such four variables each with three distinct values result in 64 possible, independent combinations (assuming that the variables and their outcomes were each independent).

Let us further assume that after a one year R&D program it will be known which of these 64 possible outcomes will result. At the present time, all that is known, based on a probability tree analysis is that the expected value is simply $1,000. For convenience in illustration, we will establish each of the 64 values in the following way: We will select the worst case outcome (lowest valued outcome at the end of Year 1) at, say $10, with the next higher value higher by a factor of 1 + D, where D is a value to be determined. Then the next higher value will be $10 times the square of factor 1 + D, and so forth until we reach the 64th, and best envisioned outcome at the end of Year 1, of \$10 times the factor 1 + D raised to the 64th power. Then by adding all such end of Year 1 values and dividing by 64 we obtain the average, or expected value, of the opportunity at the beginning of Year 1, assuming, as we will here, that all 64 outcomes are independent and equally probable. (In all cases we are, for convenience, also assuming that the risk free hurdle rate, RFHR, is zero.) Using the Goal Seek function in Microsoft Excel, we can then set the average value of the 64 possible outcomes at the end of Year 1 at \$1,000 by adjusting the value of D as defined in this paragraph. So, for instance, assuming that the worst case outcome is \$10, D is determined to be 0.1075, which then determines the 64 outcomes as follows: \$10.00, \$11.08, \$12.27, \$13.58, and so forth ending with the highest value of \$6,222 (showing the powerful effect of raising a number, here 1.075, to a high exponential power). For this case, the first 46 values are less than the mean value of \$1,000, and the final, highest, 19 values exceed \$1,000.

We can now calculate a logarithmic rate of return by taking the log (LN) function in Excel of the ratio of each of these 64 values divided by the mean value (\$1,000 in all cases). Then we can take the variance of this set of 64 values (using the VAR function in Excel), and finally by taking the square root of the variance, we have the standard deviation as a proxy for the volatility (V) in BSE1. So, for this example, the resulting volatility is 1.9013 (compared to our previous example for Yahoo in which the calculated volatility 0.8036 as determined by taking the log of each day's closing price divided by the previous day's closing price).

Now, using such volatility value in BSE1, with S_0 = \$1,000 (because we predetermined this value), we can calculate the BSE1 determined call value for any chosen value of S_1; the strike price.

We can now repeat the above example by examining the effect of different volatilities. This can be easily accomplished by using the same approach of a 1 + D factor multiplied by a different value for the worst case outcome of the 64 envisioned possibilities. Using the value of \$100 for such worst case, and again normalizing the result such that the average value of the opportunity at the end of Year 1, the highest value is determined to be \$6,222. Because this range of outcomes is narrower than in the first example—namely, \$100 to \$3,645 versus \$10 to \$6,222—the volatility will be smaller, namely 1.0628 versus 1.9013.

Finally, we will consider a third set of 64 possibilities, again normalized to yield a mean value of \$1,000, obtained by starting at \$1. Solving for D results in a range of \$1 to \$8,570 and, thereby, exhibiting the highest value of volatility (2.6764).

Using these three values of volatility, and the YHOO value used above as a point of comparison, we can compute a call value corresponding to a present and strike (exercise) value of \$1,000 as shown in Exhibit 8.38.

Exhibit 8.38 shows that, for the low volatility example of the 64 outcomes, namely for a "volatility" of 1.06 (106 percent), the option value is estimated to be \$404 for a strike (exercise) price of \$1,000 (which is equal to its present estimated value).

So, we can see how a closed form equation of option pricing, in this case Black-Scholes, can compute a call price once one has established the range of possible outcomes by some other means. However, the Black-Scholes equation was derived assuming the opportunity's volatility is calculated from a time series of data, such as the closing stock price of an equity, assuming that such variation conforms to

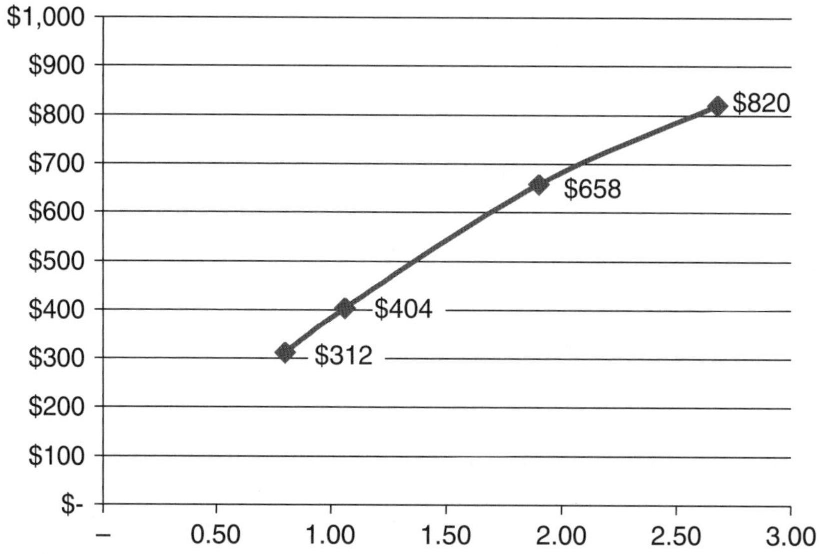

EXHIBIT 8.38 Option Value for the 64 Possibilities Example, with $S_0 = S_1 = \$1,000$, t = 1 year, RFHR = 0

a lognormal distribution. For a Real Option, a time series variation of value is not what occurs, nor do we have access to any such real time market data. Suppose that instead of the 64 outcomes we considered just above, the opportunity was a traded equity in which all buyers were evaluating the effect of the same four factors (patent rights, market, technology performance, and manufacturability) and based upon different news or perceptions were each day bidding the stock up or down. We could imagine, that in the course of a year with preliminary information about each of these factors becoming available, or simply assumed by investors, that the equity price would exhibit a fluctuation related to some degree as envisioned by 64 fixed outcomes we assumed. However, such calculation of volatility would not be equal (except by a coincidence) to the volatility as was calculated using 64 distinct outcomes compared to the mean outcome of $1,000. So, our use of the Black-Scholes equation does not have the theoretical grounding that it has (in principle, within its assumptions) for a widely traded equity. As a result, we would not expect that the calculated values for call price corresponding to the respective strike price are "right," though the trends appear generally reasonable, because we are operating outside the assumed framework for BSE1.

Other Methods for Calculation (or Estimating) Volatility Johnathan Mun devotes an appendix in his book (his Appendix 7A) to methods of making such volatility estimates.[46] In yet another book by Mun,[47] he provides additional approaches to estimating volatility (in his Chapter 4). In the Copeland and Antikarov book there is an entire chapter (their Chapter 9) on determining volatility.[48] Decisioneering, the originators of Crystal Ball and now part of Oracle, offered a software product known as Real Options Analysis Toolkit (ROATS) which contains a module for assisting in a calculation of volatility. Here, we briefly review several potentially applicable approaches.

As in many business contexts, a useful method for developing a key assumption is reasoned judgment of an individual or an expert panel. Given the mathematical sophistication of Real Options, it is a little underwhelming to rely on an opinion, however obtained, as a key input. Yet, we have to recall that the future is unknowable to us. All the inputs into all our business models involve some aspect of judgment even if it is only the selection of the market study on which we will rely, for example, to forecast future revenues. Until something is actually ready for manufacturing, we cannot be sure what its final performance will be. Until something is made and ready for shipment, we cannot know what it costs to make. Until someone buys what has been made, we cannot be sure what the market's willingness to buy and to pay will be. Filling out these cells requires judgment. Similarly, when we calculate DCF and NPV values, we have to select a discounting value (risk adjusted hurdle rate or weighted average cost of capital or some other basis). These values are also judgment calls. So, we should not object to the concept of a reasoned selection based on experience applied to a specific opportunity.

Such estimates can then be made in several ways. One traditional way is to develop a database of one's experience based on many prior opportunities, each with its unique uncertainties and knowledge of how it turned out. For companies with many opportunities of broadly comparable scope, such a database of experience can be used to make a good, or at least a reasonable, estimate for the subject opportunity. For instance, seasoned venture capitalists could easily have had the experience of participating in 20 or 50 or more investments. Based on the key variables (such as the startup's management team), venture capitalists are paid to extract such judgment to apply to new opportunities. Some have the knack for doing so.

A simple way to quantify volatility is the use of such management judgment using Crystal Ball or some other Monte Carlo software. Recall that in creating a Monte Carlo model, it is necessary to input assumed probability distributions for each of the independent variables. One can use such an assumption function for this purpose of quantifying volatility. As we discussed, lognormal distributions occur in many real life situations. By taking the logarithm of a normal distribution, the result is skewed slightly but importantly, in that no negative values are permitted but it remains unbounded at the upper limit. Exhibit 8.8 shows two distributions each for normal and lognormal assumptions.

As can be seen, for large standard deviations (volatilities), the normal distribution assumption yields negative NPV values. From a DCF perspective, this result could of course be valid because, as one knows all too well, opportunities can exhibit negative NPV values. However, from the perspective of Real Options, the future value of an opportunity cannot go below zero (not including the upfront payment made to secure the option) because a rational buyer will let its option expire at that point. However, lognormal distributions cannot have negative values even for large values of volatility.

Exhibit 8.39 shows how using Crystal Ball's lognormal distribution function a management of volatility can be easily calculated. The top panel of this exhibit shows the modeling of a lognormal distribution using the estimated NPV values for the 90th and 10th percentile outcomes.

As shown in this example, for a mean NPV value of $100 (rounded), and a 90 percent probability that the NPV value of $50 will be exceeded, the corresponding 10 percent probability is $162. So, for this example, one assumes that there is a 10 percent probability that the opportunity will be worth between zero and $50, and

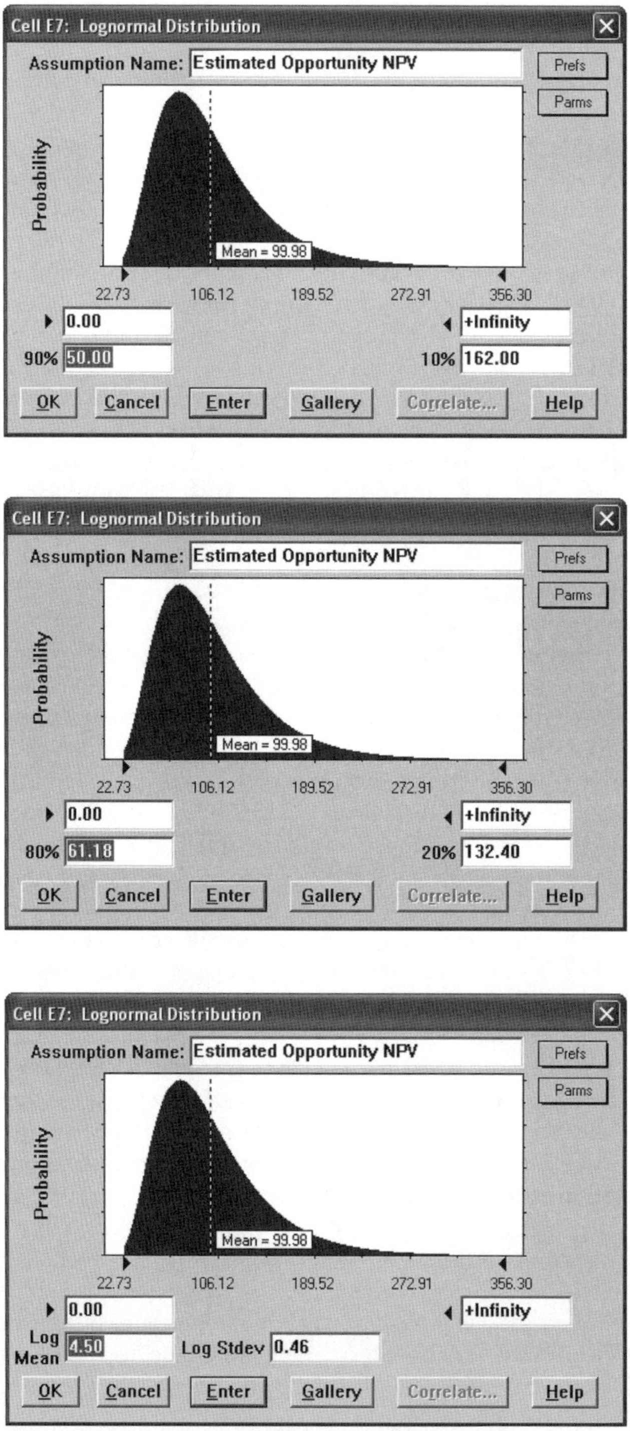

EXHIBIT 8.39 Option Value for the 64 Possibilities Example, with $S_0 = S_1 = \$1,000$, $t = 1$ year, $RFHR = 0$

also a 10 percent probability that it will be worth more than $162 with no specific upper bound. The mean (weighted average) of all such possibilities for a lognormal distribution is then simply the $100 (rounded). It should be noted that using such functionality in Crystal Ball has nothing to do with obtaining a Monte Carlo simulation; we are only using the built-in assumption capability to obtain a graphical portrayal of our assumptions and the direct calculation of lognormal volatility. The same outcome could be accomplished in Excel using its built-in functions and the Goal Seek capability. By iterating with various values of NPV for the mean, 10 percent probability, and 90 percent probability, compared to other calculations, including Monte Carlo models, that have been made, a distribution can be chosen that seems to best fit the expected range of outcomes. Then, by using the Parms input on the lognormal distribution screen, one can select other views such as the second panel in Exhibit 8.39 showing, for example, 20th and 80th percentile values, namely $61 and $132 (rounded). As discussed earlier in this chapter, buyers and sellers may gravitate to values in the range of 20th to 30th percentile outcomes. If these values do not look like best estimates, then further adjustments can be made or other percentile points selected. Once this value looks reasonable, then again using the Parms input, the calculation for lognormal standard deviation (which is simply our volatility) can be found as shown in the final panel of Exhibit 8.39, namely, 0.46 (or 46 percent).

An alternative to the above management estimation (which may or may not be based on an underlying Monte Carlo model) is to perform a calculation using Monte Carlo to convert a time series estimate of future cash flows to an estimate of outcome volatility. According to Mun, this approach was first introduced by Copeland and Antikarov. The way this approach works is as follows. For each time period, one makes an estimate for the cash flows as is normally done in any DCF analysis. Summing all such cash flows, and discounting by a rate appropriate to a Monte Carlo approach as discussed earlier in this chapter, yields an estimate of present, time zero, value. The process can be repeated to calculate such NPV value at the end of the first time step. So one now has two values of NPV: one at time zero, and one at the end of the first time step used in estimating cash flows, which is usually a year. The ratio of the NPV1 (at the end of the first time step) divided by NPV0 is less than one and is designated for convenience by X. Next, one performs a Monte Carlo simulation on NPV2, calculating the value of X for each such iteration, yielding a distribution of values for X. The Crystal Ball determined deviation of such distribution values for X is then the estimate of opportunity volatility.

An approach to using an expert panel together with benchmark equity (financial) options was described in a presentation by the author to a meeting of the Licensing Executives Society.[49]

One of the principal assumptions being made regarding volatility is the use of a single value for all possible outcomes at each time step and for all time steps. The latter assumption can be relaxed at significantly increased complexity, which is outside the scope of this book.

Beyond Black-Scholes

As we have seen, the elegance of the closed form Black Scholes equation for option value comes at the price of a set of assumptions that simply do not apply to technology valuations solutions. Other equations of other option pricing values, such as the American Option where the exercise can occur at any time during the option period, exhibit the same assumption limitations.

An alternative to an equation based calculation is to use a finite difference model known as a binomial lattice.

INTRODUCING THE BINOMIAL LATTICE FOR REAL OPTIONS A binomial lattice is a finite difference method of modeling the changing value of an opportunity as it proceeds from a starting point, say in column 1, to the next time increment in column 2 and so on to the time corresponding to the end of the option period. If such period is one year, one could use 12 columns, each representing a project month. The number of time divisions is arbitrary, but the more there are the more accurate the result, although as in all of our analyses there is a practical tradeoff of effort vs. precision.

The key idea of "binomial" is that we consider two possible values of the technology at each time for every possible value at the preceding time. So the lattice expands by a doubling of potential values with each new time increment. Each pair of two values corresponding to the next time increment exhibits one higher value as a result of future good news and, sadly, each also with one lower value as a result of bad news. Now comes a crucial simplifying assumption inherent to a commonly used form of binomial lattices: It is assumed that the good news and bad news increments are equal in magnitude, though opposite in direction, such that there always exists a future state at the same economic value (vertical position) as the starting point arrived at, either by one sequence of good news (leading upward) followed by one of bad news (leading downward), or equally by first the bad news and then the good. If these up and down increments are assumed to be equal, then every second time period has one opportunity value that is identical to (i.e., level with) the starting point. Thus, each subsequent point (or node) in the lattice becomes itself the starting point leading to two subsequent points at the end of the next time step, and so forth throughout the lattice. So the binomial lattice expands as a wedge shape getting wider with each time increment. Because such wedge is symmetric (top and bottom) usually only half the wedge is analyzed, so it looks like a right triangle with the hypotenuse angling downward as shown in Exhibit 8.40 for the Yahoo example we will now consider.

At the leftmost cell, we see the starting value of $160.13 in cell B6, which is the April 3, 2000 value of YHOO, as we considered before. In columns C through N we have monthly increments leading to the values in column O corresponding to the April 3, 2001, the expiry date of the option. The derivation of how the formulas necessary to fill out all the cell values are not important to us here. We will focus on the equations needed and the methodology. The reader is referred to the aforementioned book by Johnathan Mun for theoretical basis of the calculation.

Each cell value has a subsequent pair of values, one higher (the "up") and one lower (the "down"). The symmetric value above row 6 in Exhibit 8.40 is not shown. The value of "up" next time period cell is determined using the following equation:

$$u = \exp[V \times (\acute{y}t)^\wedge 0.5]$$

V designates volatility as we defined and used it in the preceding chapter, and ýt is the size of the time step between adjoining rows of the binomial lattice. The volatility must be based on the same time basis as used for value of ýt. Here we

	A	B	C	D	E	F	G	H	I	J	K	L	M	N	O
1	Inputs	Volatility	T, expiry	T, steps		Calculation (Eq. 7.1)		u	d					Strike Price	$ 160.13
2		80.36%	1.00	12				1.2611	0.7930						
3															
4															Net of
5	Time Step #	0	1	2	3	4	5	6	7	8	9	10	11	12	Strike Price
6		$ 160.13	**201.94**	**254.66**	**321.16**	**405.01**	**510.75**	**644.11**	**812.28**	**1024.36**	**1291.81**	**1629.09**	**2054.44**	**2590.84**	$2,430.71
7			**126.98**	**160.13**	201.94	254.66	321.16	405.01	510.75	644.11	812.28	1024.36	1291.81	1629.09	$1,468.96
8				**100.69**	126.98	**160.13**	201.94	254.66	321.16	405.01	510.75	644.11	812.28	1024.36	$864.23
9					**79.84**	100.69	126.98	**160.13**	201.94	254.66	321.16	405.01	510.75	644.11	$483.98
10						**63.31**	79.84	100.69	126.98	**160.13**	201.94	254.66	321.16	405.01	$244.88
11							**50.20**	63.31	79.84	100.69	126.98	**160.13**	201.94	254.66	$94.53
12								**39.81**	50.20	63.31	79.84	100.69	126.98	**160.13**	$0.00
13					Calculation proceeds				**31.57**	39.81	50.20	63.31	79.84	100.69	$0.00
14					to the right and down					**25.03**	31.57	39.81	50.20	63.31	$0.00
15					to expiry of option						**19.85**	25.03	31.57	39.81	$0.00
16												**15.74**	19.85	25.03	$0.00
17													**12.48**	15.74	$0.00
18														**9.90**	$0.00
19															

EXHIBIT 8.40 Binomial Lattice (Bottom Half) Corresponding to the Yahoo Example

have used 12 time steps but now we designate each one as representing 1 month, or on an annual basis, each such step is 0.08333 years.

The "down," d, is simply the inverse, namely 1/u, because of the assumed symmetry of the binomial lattice.

Further, let us use the YHOO volatility value (based on an annual period) of 0.8036. Accordingly, an equation of our previous data yields:

$$u = \exp(0.8036 \times (0.08333)\hat{}0.5) = 1.2611$$
$$d = -\exp(-0.8036 \times (0.08333)\hat{}0.5) = 0.7930$$

So the "up" value at the end of the first period shown in column C is determined by multiplying the above 1.2611 factor times the time zero value (column B) of 106.13, yielding 201.94. Likewise using the "down" multiplier of 0.7930 we find the 126.98 shown as the unfavorable outcome in column C. This process is followed to determine each remaining cell value until one reaches the final period in column N.

For the option to be meaningful, there must be a cost to exercise the right at the end of the option period. As before, we will use the exercise price as simply the starting value of the asset, namely, \$160.13. For such value, only the highest six outcomes are "in the money," that is have option value; the lowest seven have no value because their value does not exceed the cost of exercising the right to acquire the asset. Accordingly, the option value of these lowest seven is zero. The value of the highest six is simply their value, less the cost of exercising the option (\$160.13), as shown in column O.

Now the question remaining is what is the cost to acquire the option, as distinct from the earlier selected cost of exercising the option (\$160.13)? To answer that question, we need to calculate backwards to the beginning time step using the final values shown in column O and a new equation, which we will here simply take on faith. This equation calculates what is known as the risk-neutral probability:

$$\text{Risk-Neutral Probability} = [\exp(RF \times ýt) - d]/[u - d]$$

where RF is the risk free rate, and ýt is the size of the time step (0.08333 years), and u (1.2611) and d (0.7930) are the up and down factors we defined and used before. The risk free rate is a factor used in BSE1 discussed above. Let us again use 6.19 percent (i.e., 0.0619). Substituting these values in equation results in the following:

$$\text{Risk-Neutral Probability} =$$
$$[\exp(0.0619 \times 0.0833) - 0.7930]/[1.2611 - 0.7930] = 0.4533$$

Such risk-neutral probability is now used working backwards from the ending values of the lattice of Exhibit 8.40 as shown in Exhibit 8.41.

Shown in column N of Exhibit 8.41 are the final values at the end of our 12 time steps comprising our option period, as determined in Exhibit 8.40. Recall that such results were dependent only on the volatility, which is presumed to be constant and intrinsic to the opportunity under study, the size of the time step subdividing the option period whereby both the time step and option period are selected, one might say optional, values, and finally the exercise price of the option that fixes which outcomes are in the money (exercisable) and enables the calculation of their value.

Now to perform the calculations shown in Exhibit 8.41, we use additionally, the risk free probability of equations shown already as follows. The value of Cell M6 is

	A	B	C	D	E	F	G	H	I	J	K	L	M	N
1	Asset Lattice	Volatility	T, expiry	T, steps			Calculation (Eq. 7.1)	u	d			Option Lattice	Risk Free	Strike Price
2	Inputs	80.36%	1.00	12				1.2611	0.7930			Inputs	6.19%	$ 160.13
3							Calculation (Eq. 7.2)	RFP =	0.4533					
4														
5											Calculation (Eq. 7.4)			Expiry Value
6														Net of Strike Price
7	Time Step #	0	1	2	3	4	5	6	7	8	9	10	11	12
8		$ 55.08	80.58	121.14	177.93	255.11	357.14	488.86	656.22	867.50	1134.14	1470.61	1895.13	$ 2,430.71
9			29.58	47.71	75.21	115.61	172.92	251.30	354.70	487.25	654.61	865.87	1132.50	$ 1,468.96
10				14.83	25.36	42.42	69.17	109.57	167.93	248.15	353.08	485.62	652.97	$ 864.23
11					6.24	11.46	20.63	36.33	62.22	103.01	163.48	246.52	351.45	$ 483.98
12						1.98	3.96	7.81	15.20	28.99	53.83	96.18	161.85	$ 244.88
13							0.36	0.80	1.76	3.91	8.67	19.23	42.63	$ 94.53
14								0.00	0.00	0.00	0.00	0.00	0.00	0.00
15									0.00	0.00	0.00	0.00	0.00	0.00
16										0.00	0.00	0.00	0.00	0.00
17				Calculation proceeds to the left and up to starting node							0.00	0.00	0.00	0.00
18												0.00	0.00	0.00
19													0.00	0.00
20														0.00
21														

EXHIBIT 8.41 Calculating the Option Value of Yahoo from the Binomial Matrix Result of Exhibit 8.40

determined as follows:

$$
\begin{aligned}
M6 &= [N6 \times RNP + (1 - RNP)N7] \times \exp(-RF\acute{y}t) \\
&= [2430.71 \times 0.4533 + (1 - 0.4533) \times 1468.96] \\
&= \exp(-.0619 \times 0.0833) \\
&= 1895.13
\end{aligned}
$$

The result, 1895.13, is the value shown in M6 of Exhibit 8.41. To calculate the next cell, M7, one proceeds as previously only substituting N7 for N6, and N8 for N7, and so forth, for all the values in column M. Clearly, for cells below row 11, no calculation is necessary because the two corresponding cells in column N are both zero. The completion of the calculations of Exhibit 8.41 requires the previous process to be repeated for each column working from the right, the outcome of Exhibit 8.40, to the left. The result is the value shown in cell B6, \$55.08, the option value of the opportunity, the answer we have been seeking.

Using BSE1 for these same Yahoo examples, we calculated the exact answer for the option price obtaining \$53.43, slightly less than the \$55.08 shown in Exhibit 8.41 The reason these two values differ is that the Black-Scholes model embedded in BSE1 is based on a continuously changing asset value that corresponds to an infinitesimally short time step. Our model in Exhibits 8.39 and 8.41 used 12 time steps, corresponding to monthly subperiods, for the one year option period. If we shortened the size of the time steps, and thereby increased the number of such steps, our binomial matrix calculation would more closely approach the Black-Scholes exact result. This would be done, at the cost of an increasing amount of calculation effort, as will be shown through the introduction of a recently available software product discussed later. As in other situations with technology valuation, we usually face numerous other uncertainties that such calculation differences are not significant.

Real Option Conclusions and Observations

What we have sought to accomplish in this chapter are two things: developing a different framework for looking at structure and value of an opportunity and showing how to implement this framework in the practical world of dealmaking.

Every price on every thing can be thought of as an option. And many such options have options. So, an opportunity Box may have been configured and valued based on scenario analysis, probability trees, simple DCF, Monte Carlo, or some other methodology, and determined to have a best thinking, expected present value of \$100. Because such \$100 is for an opportunity that emerges in the future, as opposed to, say, a very nice dinner to be consumed in the next hour, what can be offered is an option on such \$100 Box. Depending on the configuration of the Real Option Wheelbarrow (term of the option, exercise price), the nature of the opportunity itself (volatility) and the business environment (risk free investment alternatives), an option value can be calculated. So every Box can be offered in an option structure, valued and negotiated as such.

Further, each such \$100 Box can be offered in components through options on such components, in which components could be the opportunity for the buyer to acquire additional rights such as fields and territories (or alternatively to shrink its rights). Carried to an extreme, this optioning on options approach can create an unmanageable level of complexity. But, again, there is the principle of the reasonable mean. For opportunities that are high in potential value, with high uncertainties that have a significant potential effect on value, and with practical ways of implementing subsequent management decisions to expand, contract, switch, or abandon, Real Options affords a real opportunity to do better dealmaking.

In considering real—not financial—assets, we have the following four situations and limitations with respect to applications of Black-Scholes:

1. Real assets normally do not have readily known present values because they are not subject to generally useful valuation processes such as open-market bidding. Although a DCF analysis can be used to provide an opinion of present value, based on underlying assumptions, scenarios and probabilities, as well as RAHR factors, such a result is not normally market tested as it would be (in theory) in a publicly traded equity.
2. There is limited, or no, sequence of historical data on the value of a given real asset and thereby its volatility. Further, high volatility causes the value of a financial option to increase because it increases the probability that the equity will be "in the money" for any given strike price; so volatility is a good thing. For a particular real asset, it is of course a good thing if the potential future value is greatly larger than its present value. However, volatility as calculated measures something more basic: the ups and downs of the value of the underlying asset because, presumably, of changing perceptions of the net present value of the DCF of prospective cash flows.
3. What we are normally interested in determining is at what value are we willing to sell, or buy, a real asset whose value may transform into any number of possible values, each with a relative probability. Real Options are like mathematical hydras—they spawn possibilities each one distinct from the other. Financial options also have (in theory) an infinite number of possible options but these follow sequentially and continuously from prior values.
4. Financial options cannot become negative. Real Options can. Any time a required investment can exceed the total potential return from any of the possible scenarios, then a Real Option has, for such condition, an actual negative rate of return. Unfortunately, it does occur with regularity that a technology or product asset turns out, after investment, to be deemed as having zero return potential and a sunk investment cost.

Conclusion

Do not turn to mediums or seek out spirits,
For you will be defined by them.[50]

The practice of Real Options is the subject of active research. Monte Carlo techniques are being more widely applied. The challenge is in applying such insights to the technology valuation problem at hand and dealing with the scarcity of data available to be able to exploit these tools.

However, as shown in the Monte Carlo example, it is now quite easy to develop much deeper insights into risk and reward. Some study of the software manuals is required, but experience will be gained mostly through use. The software vendors offer helpful courses and seminars. Also, insights can be gained with some simple math by viewing technology investments as options.

Our inability to define a simplified equation for valuation, as was done in Chapter 7 with the DCF Method should not be viewed as a fatal limitation of Advanced Methods. Consider the simple everyday situation of a falling leaf, a much more complex question than Newton's falling apple. What would it be like to develop the system of equations that would accurately model a particular leaf falling from any particular branch under any condition of wind, sleet, snow, or hail? All the kings horses and all the kings men, and every Intel processor made in history harnessed by the world's smartest scientists, cannot solve that simple problem at an exact level. However, a child with a $10 digital watch, a tape measure, a glass of lemonade, and several summer afternoons of observation lying on the warm grass can get an understanding of the answer that is reasonably, and surprisingly, accurate.

Valuation tools will continue to be an area for active development in order to assist businesspeople trying to make important valuation decisions in conditions of high uncertainty.

At the same time, the mathematics of Advanced Methods can lead to an implied precision and confidence that obscures the fact that these methods also rely on assumptions about the future that are plagued by uncertainty. So a little humility is again appropriate. In that spirit, below are selected reasons, in alphabetical order, for the decline and fall of the historic Roman Empire that could bear some resemblance to "Advanced Methods Hubris":[51]

- Absolutism
- Concatenation of misfortunes
- Degeneration of the intellect
- Egoism
- Hothouse culture
- Hubris
- Immoderate greatness
- Indoctrination
- Irrationality
- Loss of instincts
- Monetary greed
- Negative selection
- Over refinement
- Particularism
- Vaingloriousness

Online Resources

On my web site—www.razgaitis.com—there are several of the spreadsheets referenced in this chapter available for download. In order to run Monte Carlo simulations, you will need also a copy of the Crystal Ball simulation software that operates on top of Excel. On my web site is also a link to a free trial of the fully featured Crystal Ball software, developed by Decisioneering, which is now a part of Oracle Corporation.

Appendix 8A: Example Crystal Ball Report for Exhibit 8.18

Run preferences:
Number of trials run 10,000
Run statistics:
Total running time (sec) 57.01
Crystal Ball data:
Assumptions 4
Forecasts 4

Forecast: Average Number of Units Sold

Summary:
Entire range is from 252 to 327
Base case is 292

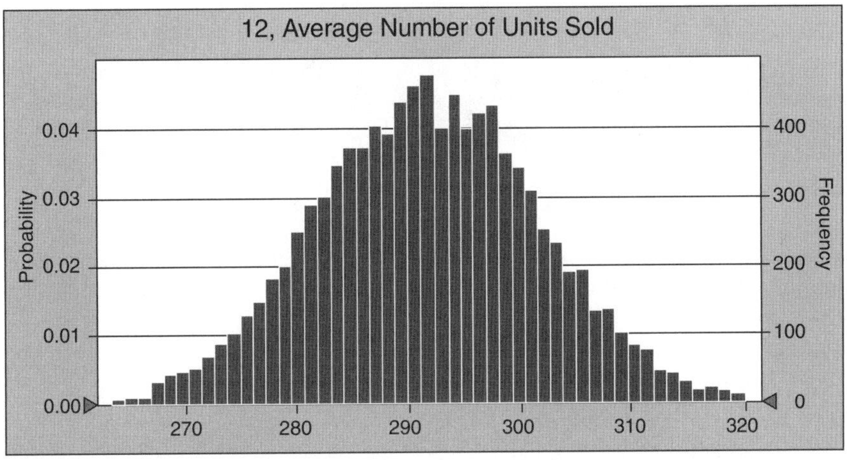

Statistics:	Forecast values
Trials	10,000
Mean	292
Median	292
Minimum	252
Maximum	327
Range Width	75

Percentiles:	Forecast values
0%	252
10%	279
20%	283
30%	286
40%	289
50%	292
60%	294
70%	297
80%	300
90%	305
100%	327

Forecast: Average Selling Price

Summary:

Entire range is from $8,093 to $10,066
Base case is $9,083

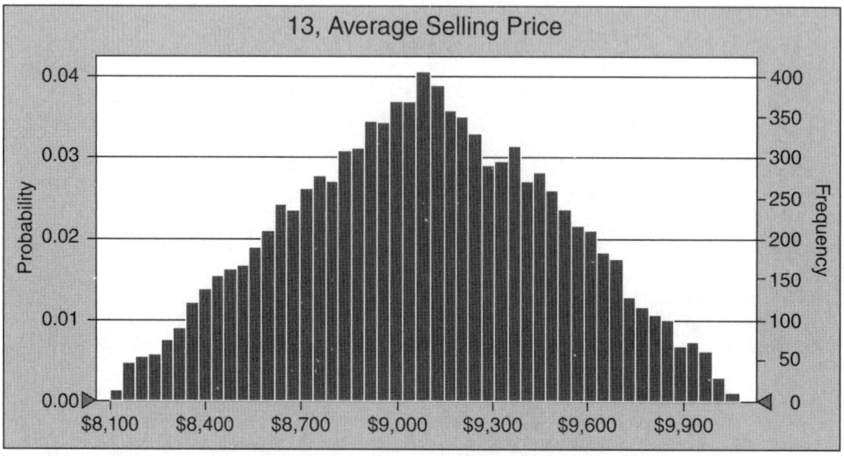

Statistics:	Forecast values
Trials	10,000
Mean	$9,080
Median	$9,081
Minimum	$8,093
Maximum	$10,066
Range Width	$1,973

Percentiles:	Forecast values
0%	$8,093
10%	$8,520
20%	$8,711
30%	$8,853
40%	$8,975
50%	$9,081
60%	$9,187
70%	$9,314
80%	$9,454
90%	$9,629
100%	$10,066

Summary:

Entire range is from $12,089,169 to $19,140,823
Base case is $15,400,000

Forecast: Total Revenues

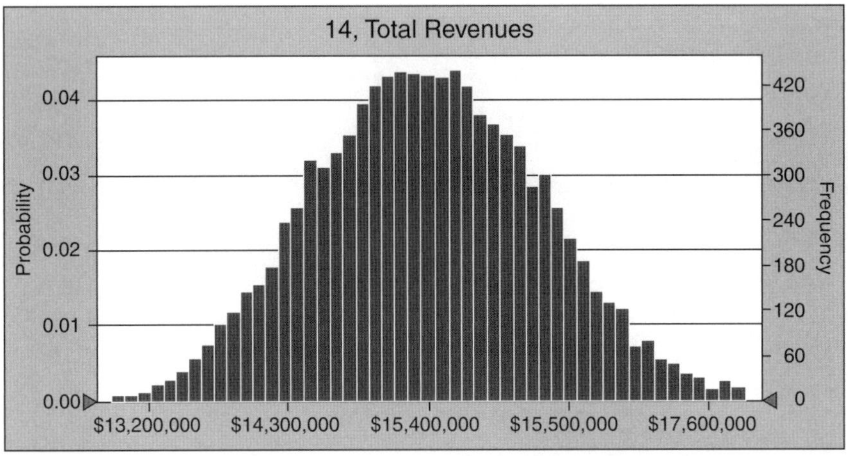

Statistics:	**Forecast values**
Trials	10,000
Mean	$15,393,895
Median	$15,380,406
Mode	—
Standard Deviation	$912,714
Variance	$833,046,104,757
Skewness	0.1054
Kurtosis	2.74
Coeff. of Variability	0.0593
Minimum	$12,089,169
Maximum	$19,140,823
Range Width	$7,051,655
Mean Std. Error	$9,127

Percentiles:	**Forecast values**
0%	$12,089,169
10%	$14,220,526
20%	$14,588,590
30%	$14,877,058
40%	$15,141,486
50%	$15,380,406
60%	$15,614,299
70%	$15,885,322
80%	$16,180,558
90%	$16,586,038
100%	$19,140,823

Forecast: NPV Cell: I17

Summary:

Certainty level is 10.00%
Certainty range is from $493,338 to $520,780
Entire range is from $328,048 to $879,382
Base case is $616,484
After 10,000 trials, the std. error of the mean is $868

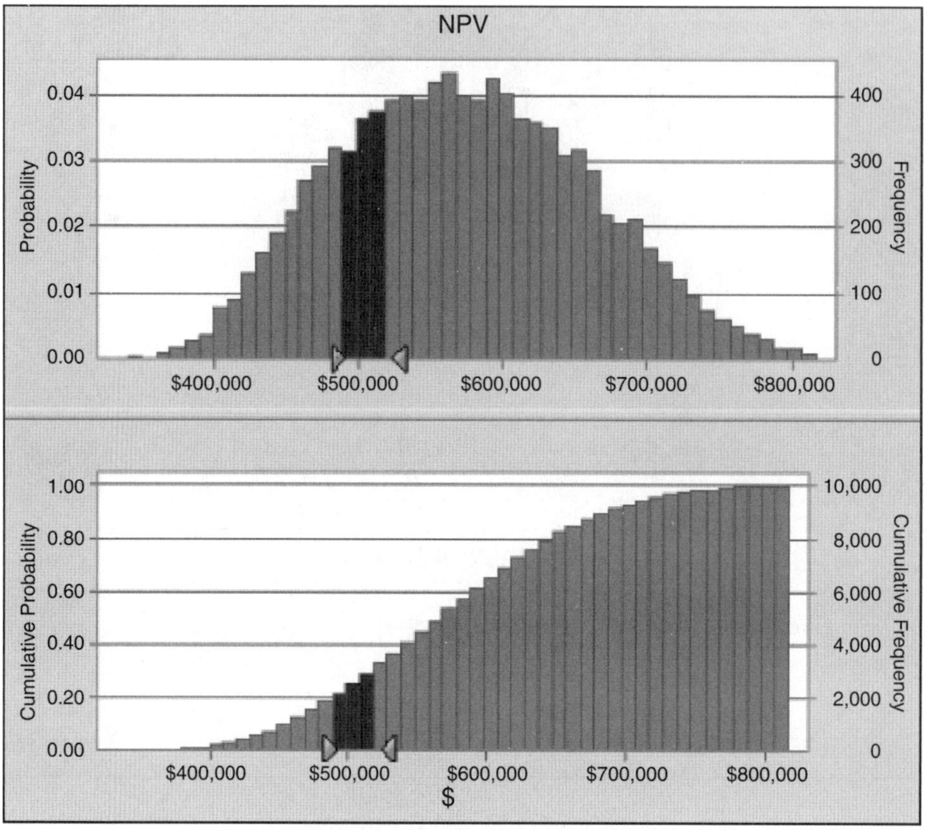

Statistics:	Forecast values
Trials	10,000
Mean	$572,784
Median	$569,974
Mode	—
Standard Deviation	$86,830
Variance	$7,539,470,458
Skewness	0.1730
Kurtosis	2.54
Coeff. of Variability	0.1516
Minimum	$328,048
Maximum	$879,382
Range Width	$551,334
Mean Std. Error	$868

Percentiles:	Forecast values
0%	\$328,048
10%	\$460,179
20%	\$493,338
30%	\$520,780
40%	\$546,370
50%	\$569,974
60%	\$594,471
70%	\$620,539
80%	\$649,737
90%	\$689,297
100%	\$879,382

End of forecasts.

Assumptions

ASSUMPTION: C2, NUMBER OF UNITS SOLD Y1 CELL: C2

Normal distribution with parameters:

Mean	100.00
Std. Dev.	10.00

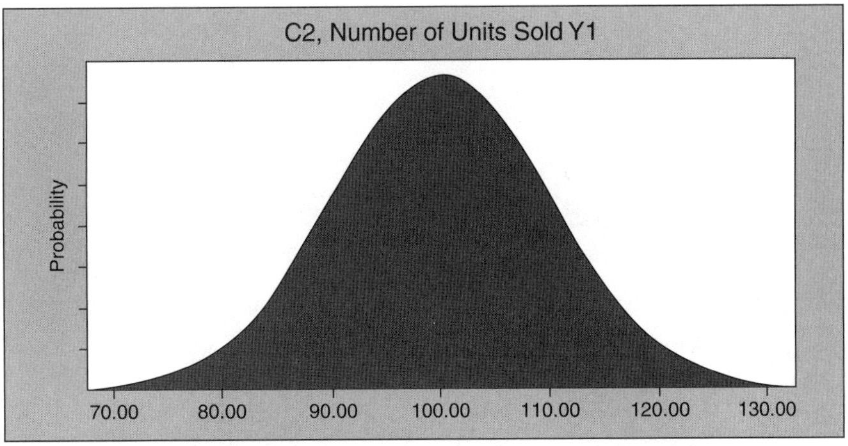

ASSUMPTION: C3, AVERAGE SELLING PRICE Y1 CELL: C3

Triangular distribution with parameters:

Minimum	$9,000
Likeliest	$10,000
Maximum	$11,000

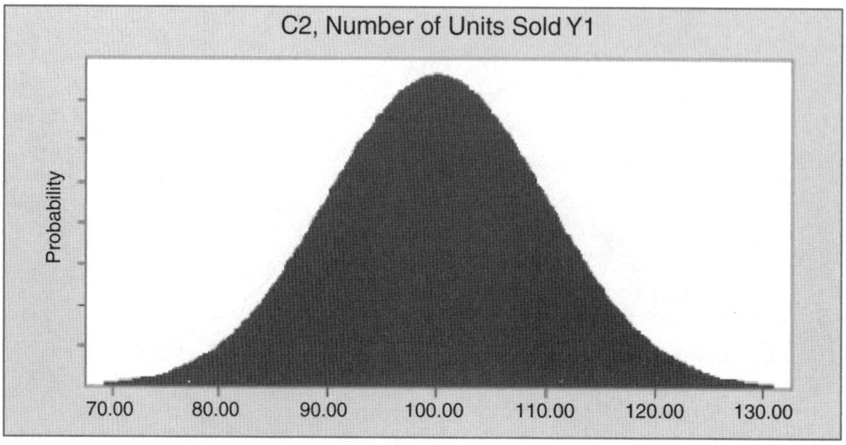

ASSUMPTION: COST OF GOODS SOLD CELL: B6

Uniform distribution with parameters:

Minimum	55%
Maximum	59%

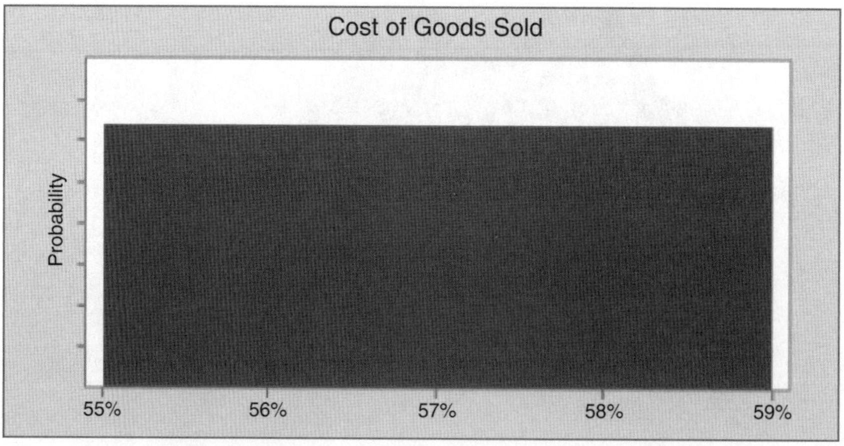

ASSUMPTION: SG&A AND R&D CELL: B7

Beta distribution with parameters:

Minimum	33%
Maximum	37%
Alpha	10
Beta	5

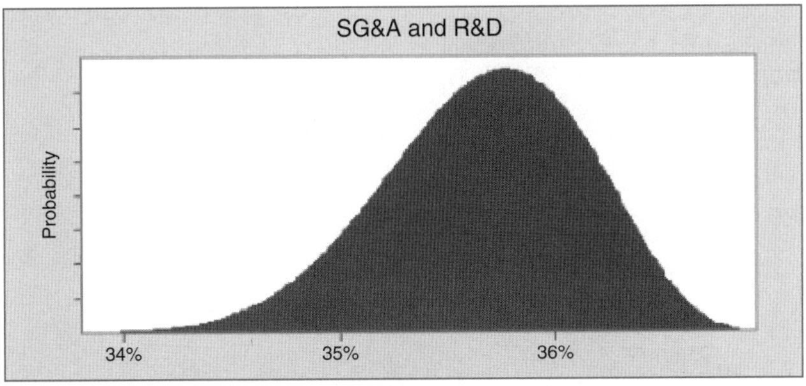

Sensitivity Charts

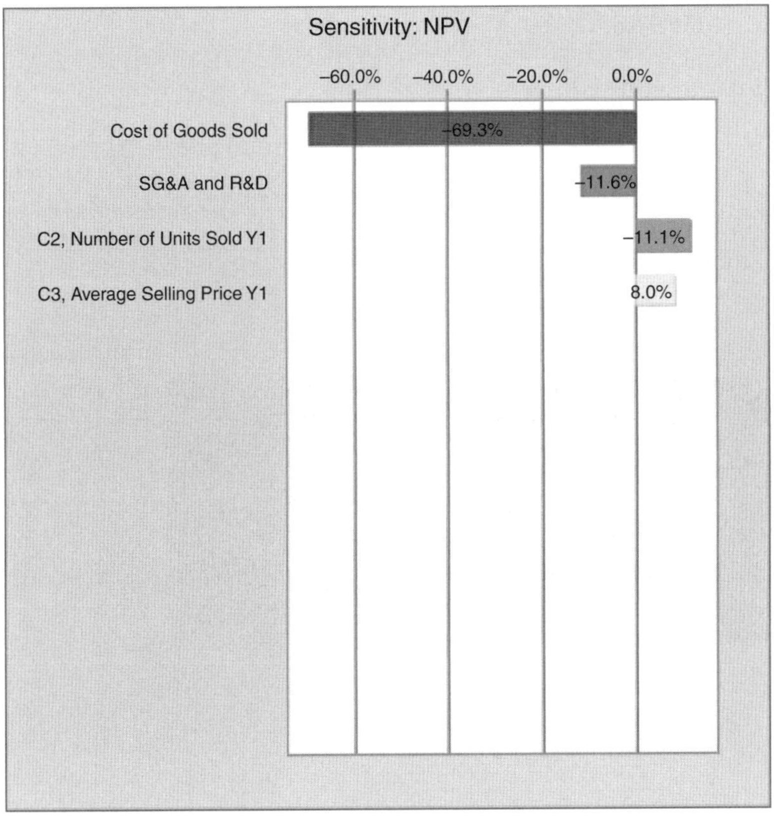

Appendix 8B: Crystal Ball Report Corresponding to the Results Presented in Exhibit 8.XX for a Double-Humped Cost Distribution Assumption

Simulation started on 10/16/02 at 22:02:16
Simulation stopped on 10/16/02 at 22:06:00

Forecast: NPV-MC Tab Cell: B22

Summary:

Display Range is from −41.34 to 56.56
Entire Range is from −41.34 to 56.56
"After 10,000 Trials, the Std. Error of the Mean is 0.20"

Statistics	Value
Trials	10000
Mean	−0.09
Median	−1.99
Mode	—
Standard Deviation	19.67
Variance	386.81
Skewness	0.18
Kurtosis	1.85
Coeff. of Variability	−221.49
Range Minimum	−41.34
Range Maximum	56.56
Range Width	97.91
Mean Std. Error	0.20

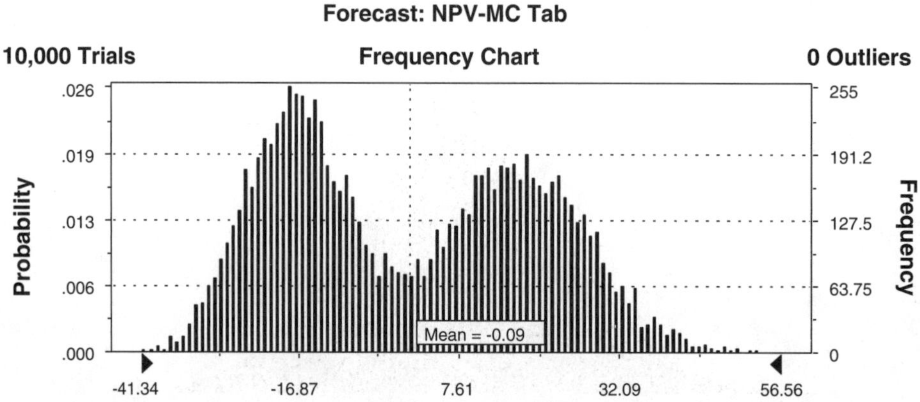

Percentiles:

Percentile	Value
100%	−41.34
95%	−27.72
90%	−24.27
85%	−21.71
80%	−19.42
75%	−17.43
70%	−15.49
65%	−13.35
60%	−10.58
55%	−7.43
50%	−1.99
45%	3.96
40%	8.16
35%	11.35
30%	14.13
25%	16.90
20%	19.66
15%	22.82
10%	26.18
5%	30.71
0%	56.56

End of forecast.

Assumptions

ASSUMPTION: CAGR CELL: K5

Normal distribution with parameters:

Mean 12.0%
Standard Dev. 4.3%
Selected range is from − Infinity to +Infinity

Correlated with:

Total Cost Ratio (B9) 0.50

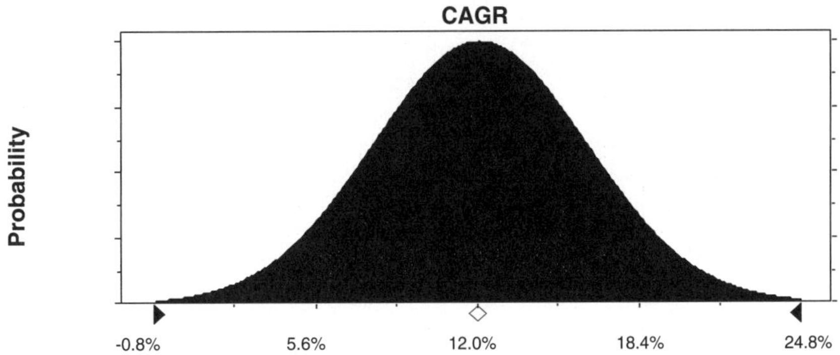

ASSUMPTION: TOTAL COST RATIO CELL: B9

Custom distribution with parameters		Relative Prob.
Single point	50.0%	0.000256
Single point	51.0%	0.000004
Single point	51.0%	0.000735
Single point	52.0%	0.000009
Single point	52.0%	0.001891
Single point	53.0%	0.000022
Single point	53.0%	0.004352
Single point	54.0%	0.000045
Single point	54.0%	0.008960
Single point	55.0%	0.000083
Single point	55.0%	0.016508
Single point	56.0%	0.000136
Single point	56.0%	0.027218
Single point	57.0%	0.000201
Single point	57.0%	0.040156
Single point	58.0%	0.000265
Single point	58.0%	0.053013
Single point	59.0%	0.000313
Single point	59.0%	0.062628
Single point	60.0%	0.000331
Single point	60.0%	0.066205
Single point	61.0%	0.000313
Single point	61.0%	0.062628
Single point	62.0%	0.000265
Single point	62.0%	0.053013
Single point	63.0%	0.000201
Single point	63.0%	0.040156
Single point	64.0%	0.000136
Single point	64.0%	0.027218
Single point	65.0%	0.000083
Single point	65.0%	0.016508
Single point	66.0%	0.000045
Single point	66.0%	0.008960
Single point	67.0%	0.000022
Single point	67.0%	0.004352
Single point	68.0%	0.000009
Single point	68.0%	0.001891
Single point	69.0%	0.000004
Single point	69.0%	0.000735
Single point	70.0%	0.000001
Single point	70.0%	0.000256
Single point	71.0%	0.000004
Single point	71.0%	0.000735
Single point	72.0%	0.000009
Single point	72.0%	0.001891
Single point	73.0%	0.000022
Single point	73.0%	0.004352
Single point	74.0%	0.000045

Custom distribution with parameters		Relative Prob.
Single point	74.0%	0.008960
Single point	75.0%	0.000083
Single point	75.0%	0.016508
Single point	76.0%	0.000136
Single point	76.0%	0.027218
Single point	77.0%	0.000201
Single point	77.0%	0.040156
Single point	78.0%	0.000265
Single point	78.0%	0.053013
Single point	79.0%	0.000313
Single point	79.0%	0.062628
Single point	80.0%	0.000331
Single point	80.0%	0.066205
Single point	81.0%	0.000313
Single point	81.0%	0.062628
Single point	82.0%	0.000265
Single point	82.0%	0.053013
Single point	83.0%	0.000201
Single point	83.0%	0.040156
Single point	84.0%	0.000136
Single point	84.0%	0.027218
Single point	85.0%	0.000083
Single point	85.0%	0.016508
Single point	86.0%	0.000045
Single point	86.0%	0.008960
Single point	87.0%	0.000022
Single point	87.0%	0.004352
Single point	88.0%	0.000009
Single point	88.0%	0.001891
Single point	89.0%	0.000004
Single point	89.0%	0.000735
Single point	90.0%	0.000001
Single point	90.0%	0.000256
Total Relative Probability		1.000000

Correlated with:

CAGR (K5) 0.50

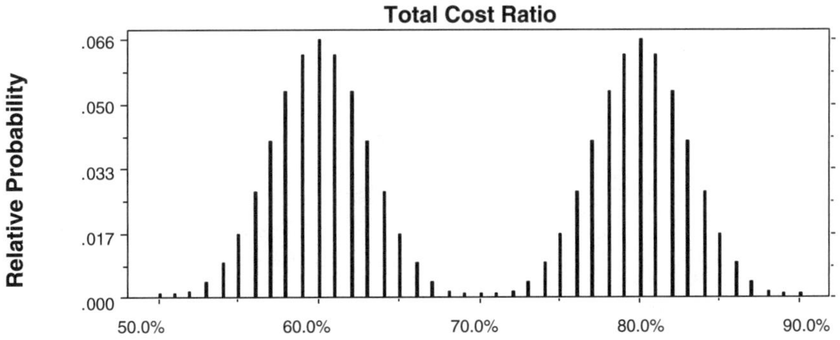

ASSUMPTION: D18: CAPEX YEAR 1 CELL: D18

Triangular distribution with parameters:

Minimum 1.80
Likeliest 2.00
Maximum 2.20
Selected range is from 1.80 to 2.20

Correlated with:

E18: CapEx Year 2 (E18) 0.50

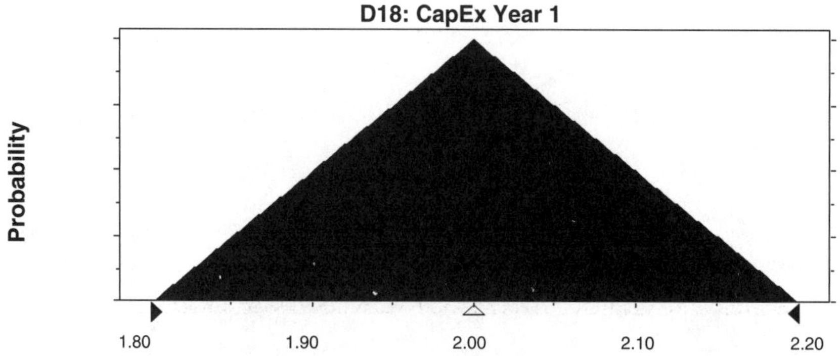

ASSUMPTION: E18: CAPEX YEAR 2 CELL: E18

Triangular distribution with parameters:

Minimum 8.00
Likeliest 10.00
Maximum 12.00
Selected range is from 8.00 to 12.00

Correlated with:

D18: CapEx Year 1 (D18) 0.50
F18: CapEx Year 3 (F18) 0.50

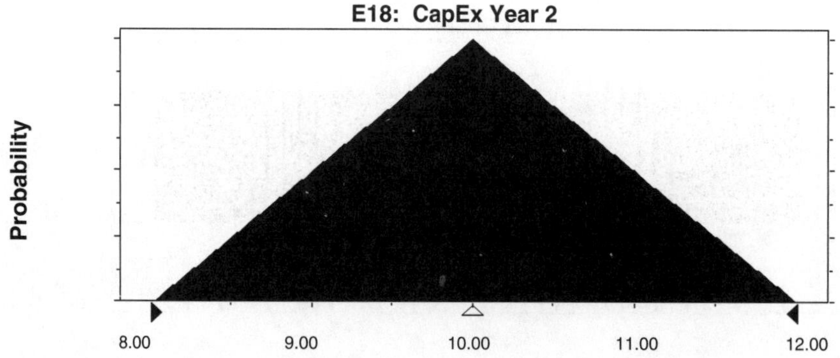

ASSUMPTION: F18: CAPEX YEAR 3 CELL: F18

Triangular distribution with parameters:

Minimum 24.00
Likeliest 30.00
Maximum 36.00
Selected range is from 24.00 to 36.00

Correlated with:

E18: CapEx Year 2 (E18) 0.50
G18: CapEx Year 4 (G18) 0.50

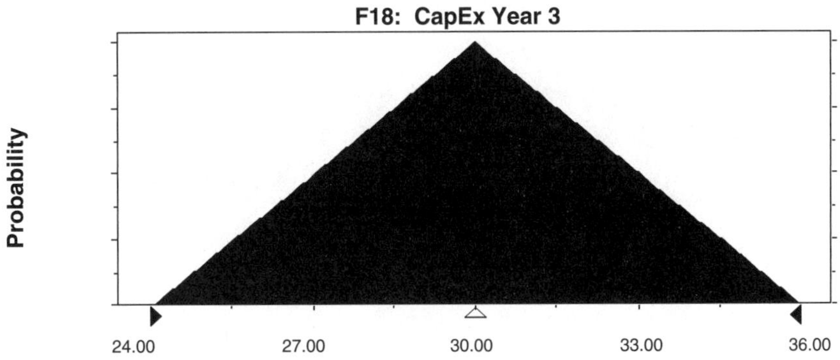

ASSUMPTION: G18: CAPEX YEAR 4 CELL: G18

Uniform distribution with parameters:

Minimum 20.00
Maximum 60.00

Correlated with:

F18: CapEx Year 3 (F18) 0.50
H18: CapEx Year 5 (H18) 0.50

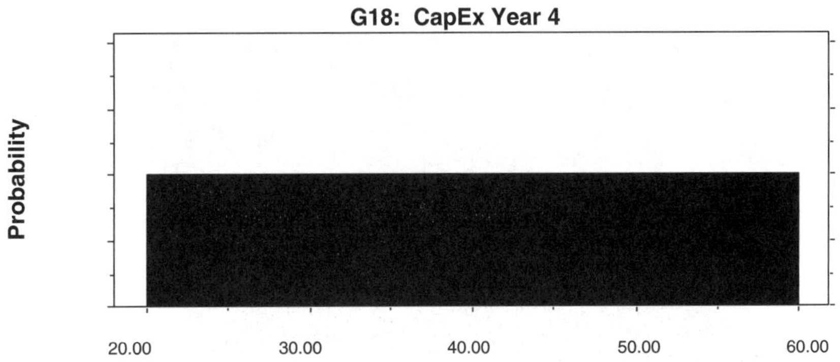

ASSUMPTION: H18: CAPEX YEAR 5 CELL: H18

Uniform distribution with parameters:

Minimum 0.00

Maximum 36.00

Correlated with:

G18: CapEx Year 4 (G18) 0.50

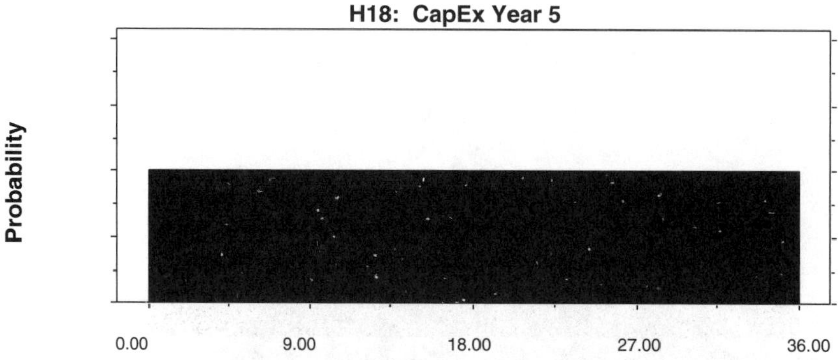

ASSUMPTION: E4: REV. YEAR 2 CELL: E4

Uniform distribution with parameters:

Minimum 0.00

Maximum 4.00

Correlated with:

F4: Rev. Year 3 (F4) 0.80

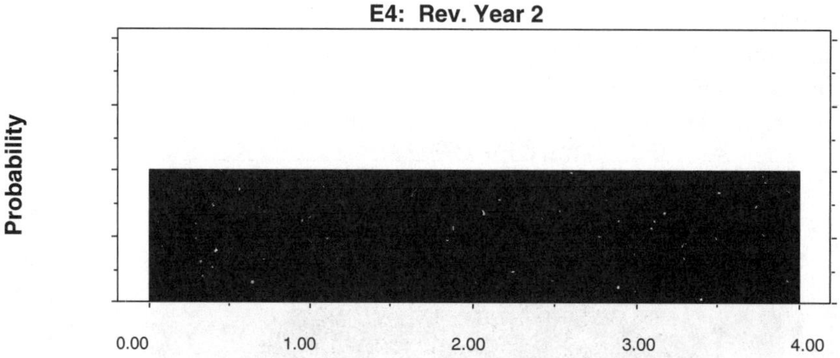

ASSUMPTION: F4: REV. YEAR 3 CELL: F4

Uniform distribution with parameters:

Minimum	10.00
Maximum	20.00

Correlated with:

E4: Rev. Year 2 (E4)	0.80
G4: Rev. Year 4 (G4)	0.80

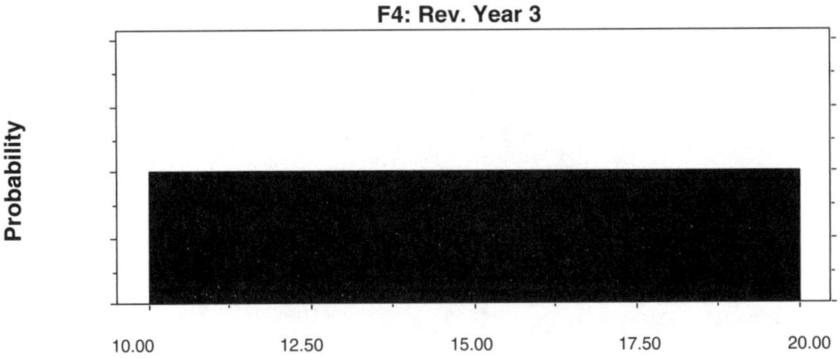

ASSUMPTION: G4: REV. YEAR 4 CELL: G4

Triangular distribution with parameters:

Minimum	50.00
Likeliest	70.00
Maximum	90.00

Selected range is from 50.00 to 90.00

Correlated with:

H4: Rev. Year 5 (H4)	0.80
F4: Rev. Year 3 (F4)	0.80

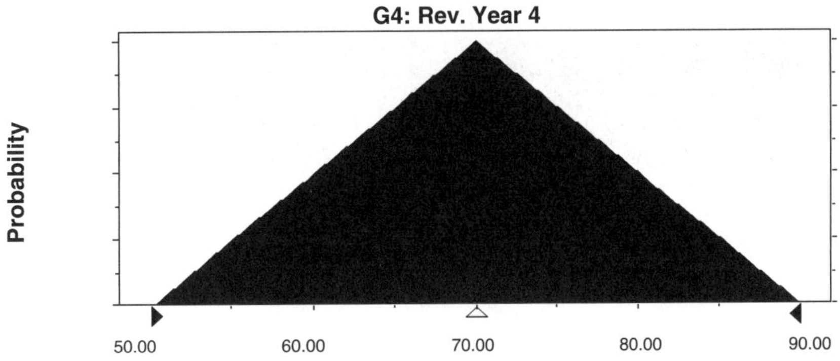

ASSUMPTION: H4: REV. YEAR 5 CELL: H4

Triangular distribution with parameters:

Minimum 120.00
Likeliest 180.00
Maximum 240.00
Selected range is from 120.00 to 240.00

Correlated with:

G4: Rev. Year 4 (G4) 0.80

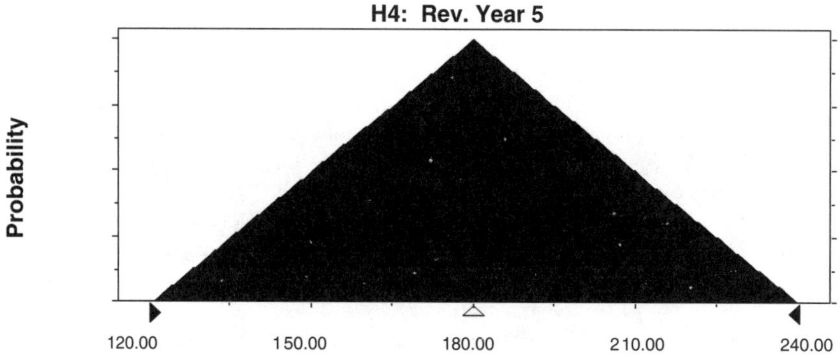

End of Assumptions

Notes

1. Ashley J. Stevens, "Risk-Adjusted Net Present Value—A New Approach to Valuing Early Stage Technologies," *Journal of Biotechnology in Healthcare*, Vol. 2, No. 4, January, 1996.
2. Larry D. Smith, "Valuation of Life Sciences Companies—An Empirical and Scientific Approach," Hambrecht & Quist Monograph, January 4, 1994.
3. Mary Tanner, "Financing Biotechnology Companies," presentation at Association of Biotechnology Companies, NYC, September 1991.
4. There is a very useful ancient Greek term: *euthanatos*. "Thanatos" means death; "eu" is a prefix that generally means "good" (as in the word "euphemism"). So, *euthanatos* means literally "good death" (and has been used as such in very controversial social policy debates—*euthanasia*). In R&D projects and technology licensing, having a financial plan that includes an *euthanatos* outcome as one scenario actually improves the NPV of the opportunity considering all the outcomes.
5. "Closed form solution" means that all the variables involved in the problem can be arranged in equations such that the value being solved for can be determined by simply substituting for all the variables. A simple form of such a solution is $z = ax + by$, where z is the thing sought, x and y are variables for which one has values (known or assumed) and a and b are known constants. For any x and y, one can always determine z in "closed form." Complex problems cannot be reduced to such simple forms.
6. A risk free cost of capital (such as 5 percent), or even an inflation rate (e.g., 3 percent), would not normally be appropriate as a k value in a Monte Carlo model. The reason such low k values are not appropriate is that the company making such investment decision, be it for an R&D project or a technology license, does not have access to investment

capital that it can acquire at such rates. As we will show in the application of Monte Carlo each assumption cell can be "frozen," meaning that only a single value is used in the NPV calculation. When all the assumption cells are frozen then the calculation reduces exactly to the DCF Method of Chapter 7, as a proxy for a "base" case (scenario). If a company used a k value such as a risk free rate of 5 percent, then the NPV calculation could only represent the NPV to an entity such as the US Government which is able to attract capital at such low rate.

7. Soren Kierkegaard (1813-1885).
8. *In Remembrance of Things Past*, or alternatively translated *In Search of Lost Time*, published in multiple volumes during the period 1913 to 1927, currently published by Modern Library, 2003.
9. Justified True Belief (JTB) deals with beliefs that are not only true (lots of people believe things that are false) but also justifiable (it is possible to hold a belief that is true but for false or unjustifiable reasons).
10. Prudent Decision Making (PDM) also requires some assessment of the consequences of being wrong. For example, the observation of long-term stock returns of, say 10 percent, is likely *not* to be prudent for purposes of projecting annual income over the forecasted lifetime of a retiree with a fixed starting investment amount, because the consequences of running out of money could be ruinous for an individual in such late-in-life circumstances.
11. Posters offered by a company known as Despair, Inc., that provides perspectives pretty much opposite to the traditional office space posters: www.demotivators.com.
12. Richard Razgaitis, *Early Stage Technologies: Valuation and Pricing*, John Wiley and Sons, 1999.
13. Here's an illustration of the challenge of representing a reality by "a pile." Suppose one is given a stack of photographs, a pile 1000 deep, of a city, say Rome, when one has never even visited Europe. Could that "pile," or any "pile" of photos, convey the reality of Rome? The answer is of course dependent on how the pile is classified and the accompanying narration. But just flaking through an unstructured sequence of photos, however lovely, would not easily lead to a coherent understanding of the city and its history.
14. A smooth NPV distribution is not always the outcome. For example, if many of the important assumptions had used "spiky" Custom Distributions, such as the examples of Exhibit 8.11, and such assumptions have an important influence on the NPV calculation, we would expect to see a certain "spikiness" in the NPV probability distributions.
15. Exceptions occur when the NPV calculation is highly non-linear with respect to even symmetrical assumption distributions.
16. However, the range is also important. If we had used a Uniform Distribution but very closely bound around the assumed center value of COGS of 35 percent, the comparative contribution to NPV value uncertainty would have been low.
17. For this discussion we are presuming the most challenging valuation (Wheelbarrow) framework of a single payment from the buyer to the seller. Alternatively, if we adopted some form of pay-as-you-go conditional payments, the valuation process can be made simpler because of a reduced reliance on a single, upfront value.
18. One can conceive of extraordinary circumstances where the seller would actually pay for the buyer to acquire the IP asset. Although this happens with some frequency when companies or divisions of companies are sold, because of excess liabilities such as personnel, environmental, and/or legal financial obligations that accompany the same, such circumstances are rare for technology licensees, and are outside the scope of this analysis.
19. In general, the assumption probability distributions are not uniformly centered about the most likely value, and even if they are, there are non-linearities typically present that result in the NPV distribution being unsymmetrical.
20. In this Monte Carlo example, the mean and median are essentially the same value, namely \$40.99 and \$40.24, respectively. In other highly skewed outcomes there could be

a significant difference between the two. For our purposes I have used mean and median interchangeably.

21. A more comprehensive analysis would include the economic effect of the opportunity being considered on all a buyer's lines of business.
22. Said by someone on behalf of a company known as Critical Path, which went public in March of 1999, reached $135/share and a market cap of $3.8 billion in October 2000, and was selling for 24 cents a share in 2008.
23. And I really, really hope that my 1 out of 20 failures does not occur my first year on the job but after I have a track record of successful projections.
24. There is a widely quoted aphorism attributed to Pareto known as the 80:20 Rule. It is widely cited in many different contexts in business books: 20 percent of one's customers are the source of 80 percent of one's profits, 20 percent of one's "to-do" list affects 80 percent of one's success, 20 percent of the employees cause 80 percent of the grief, and many other applications. The 20th percentile value has this same kind of appeal, namely, a buyer can conceive of an opportunity being fairly valued if 80 percent of the time it will receive in benefit more than it paid to acquire the rights to the opportunity.
25. During the 2008 presidential election some creative soul was widely cited as a source for an example of Gov. Palin's supposed lack of understanding of world geography. He identified himself as a Senior Fellow at the Harding Institute for Freedom and Democracy; no such organization exists. In Russia, there is a similar term of art for such "sources:" "one babushka said."
26. Although this has been attributed to Warren Buffett, it appears to have originated with Peter Klein: http://organizationsandmarkets.com/2008/11/03/beware-of-geeks-bearing-formulas/.
27. Tom Copeland and Vladimir Antikarov, *Real Options: A Practitioner's Guide* (Texere Publishing, 2001).
28. Ibid.
29. Johnathan Mun, *Real Options Analysis Course: Business Cases and Software Applications*, John Wiley & Sons, Inc., 2003.
30. A lottery ticket does not carry with it an exercise price; it does require an exercise act, namely the winning owner has to show up and claim the prize, which will be an obvious "investment" to make if the numbers are winners.
31. There is a well known email offer, generally known as the Nigerian Scan, whose operation depends upon an exercise price, namely: the email we all receive in its many variants telling us we've won the trust of some about to be exiled princess who proposes to share millions with us (a zero cost option—because "it" has been "awarded" to you by virtue of our being such trustworthy individuals), but there is a cost to exercise the option that involves you sending a cashier's check needed to overcome some obstacle. There are whole websites devoted to this scam, for example: http://potifos.com/fraud/.
32. Timothy A. Luehrman, "Strategy as a Portfolio of Real Options," *Harvard Business Review*, Sept.-Oct. 1998, p. 89 ff.
33. Timothy A. Luehrman, "Using APV: A Better Tool for Valuing Operations," *Harvard Business Review*, May-June 1997, p. 145 ff.
34. Timothy A. Luehrman, "Investment Opportunities as Real Options: Getting Started on the Numbers," *Harvard Business Review*, July-Aug. 1998, reprint 98404.
35. Avinash K. Dixit and Robert S. Pindyck, "The Options Approach to Capital Investment," *Harvard Business Review*, May-June 1995, p. 105 ff.
36. Fischer Black was at MIT in 1969 when he began to work with Scholes on mathematical models of pricing options; he was a University of Chicago business school professor at the time of publishing when the equation was named after him. Sadly, he died of cancer in 1995 prior to the award of the Nobel Prize for the discovery of the Black-Scholes

equation and method. Because the Nobel is not awarded posthumously, he was not formally joined in the award.

37. Myron Scholes was a professor at MIT during the period of developing his equation. Subsequently, he was a professor at Stanford University. He later became even more famous for his role in Long Term Capital Management, a derivative investment company for extremely high net worth individuals, whose net worth became substantially smaller through the experience.
38. Robert Merton, long associated with Harvard University, added an important contribution to the development of Black and Scholes and was recognized, along with Scholes as the recipient of the Nobel Prize for this equation. For Merton, this was his second Nobel, a remarkable achievement.
39. Another important reason for purchasing such a right—which is not our concern here—it multiplies the possible upside rate of return, so-called "increasing leverage."
40. Gospel of John, Chapter 18, verse 38.
41. It is reported that on its discovery, Pythagoras was so overtaken with emotion that he immediately went and sacrificed a bull to his god.
42. The deep significance of a simple, one might say, perfect equation able to represent imperfect, real triangles may have been one of the sources of Plato's development of the theory of "forms" and the allegory of the cave where the "truth" (the Pythagorean right triangle) resides in a different, perfect place, but we mortals are confined to the "cave" and its imperfect representation.
43. An inertial coordinate system is generally defined as one that is at rest or in uniform (nonaccelerating) motion with respect to the distant stars, and no such place on the earth meets that requirement because not only is the earth rotating about its own axis, creating a 24 hour day, it is revolving around the sun, creating a 365 day year, and the sun itself is rotating around the center of our Milky Way Galaxy, which center itself is . . . well, you get the idea. We are riding on a multilayered cosmic carousel. No person in human history has stood on Newtonian soil.
44. For those interested in the proliferation of models and equations, many can be found on the World Wide Web using a search engine with terms such as "option equation," "option theory," "Black-Scholes," or "derivatives."
45. Such match with a publicly traded company is sometimes termed a "pure play," which is a confusing term that only means it is a reasonable comparable for valuation purposes. The reference to "pure" means that the public company is narrowly focused and does also conduct significant business operations with technologies, products, and markets irrelevant to that envisioned for the technology under study.
46. Johnathan Mun, *Real Options Analysis* (New York: John Wiley & Sons, 2002).
47. Mun, *Real Options Analysis*. Johnathan Mun has also authored another recently published book: *Real Options Analysis Course: Business Cases and Software Applications,* John Wiley & Sons, 2003.
48. Copeland and Antikarov.
49. Additional information on this presentation is available at: www.razgaitis.com.
50. The entire verse is: "Do not turn to mediums or seek out spiritists, for you will be defiled by them. I am the Lord your God," from Lev. 19:31, New International Version (NIV). The two words translated by the NIV in Lev. 19:31 as "mediums" and "spiritists" are worthy of further consideration. The word translated as mediums literally means ventriloquists or, more likely, necromancers; namely, one who echoes without understanding what is heard spoken or shown in another realm. The word translated as spiritists derives from the Hebrew word for "knowing one"; this translation conveys the idea of someone who, by the use of magical arts and only by such use, can know something not humanly attainable. From time immemorial, humans have been tempted, and have succumbed, to gain advantage by seeking knowledge by supernatural, supernormal, means. This

temptation, of course, has created a not-so-small industry of charlatans of many varieties. It is well to remember that real options and the other methods and tools considered in this book are not likely to be useful to ventriloquists or their audiences, because the power of such methods is not in producing a number but a framework for understanding. Further, it is not the intention of teaching such methods to create the opportunity to disadvantage the other parties to a dealmaking opportunity. So the knowing aspect of the use of these methods is certainly appropriate, but secret knowing is neither necessary nor generally advantageous.

51. 210 Reasons for the Decline of the Roman Empire. Source: A. Demandt, Der Fall Roms (1984) 695.

CHAPTER 9

Method 6: Valuation by Auctions

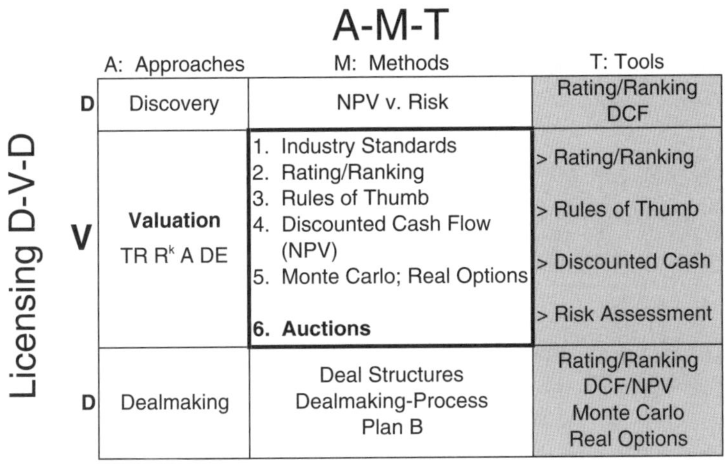
A-M-T
A: Approaches
M: Methods
T: Tools
Licensing D-V-D
D
Discovery
NPV v. Risk
Rating/Ranking DCF
V
Valuation
TR R^k A DE
1. Industry Standards
2. Rating/Ranking
3. Rules of Thumb
4. Discounted Cash Flow (NPV)
5. Monte Carlo; Real Options
6. Auctions
> Rating/Ranking
> Rules of Thumb
> Discounted Cash
> Risk Assessment
D
Dealmaking
Deal Structures
Dealmaking-Process
Plan B
Rating/Ranking
DCF/NPV
Monte Carlo
Real Options

This is our final chapter concerning the ***Approach*** of **Valuation**. Our sixth and final **Valuation Method** is the use of auctions. As we will discuss below, valuation by auctions is similar to the first **Valuation Method** considered (Chapter 4) namely, Industry Standards and its use of comparables.

The Method of Auctions also will transition us to the third ***Approach*** of this book, **Dealmaking**. The unique virtue of the use of auctions is that it provides the seller both a valuation and a buyer. So, in this sense, it combines the ***Approaches*** of Valuation and Dealmaking. If a technology owner/seller also offers an inventory of different technologies, the use of auctions can combine all three ***Approaches***—opportunity **Discovery**, **Valuation**, and **Dealmaking** (Technology/Licensing **D-V-D**)—because, in theory, bidders (prospective buyers) will (1) identify the commercial opportunities, (2) place a value on each by their bid(s), and (3) become the **Dealmaking** buyer for the seller. Even for a single technology family, bidders often will perform some aspect of opportunity **Discovery** by tailoring their bids to those aspects of the offer package that it deems valuable.

An essential distinction from the other valuation **Methods** we have considered is that the Auction Method does not provide a prospective opportunity value in advance of **Dealmaking**. There is one circumstance in which the Auction Method does provide a valuation without **Dealmaking** and that is if the winning bid does not meet the seller's reserve price. But the normal expectation for the seller is that a reserve price will protect against a market failure in the auction's bidding, so that the final, highest bid (in excess of the reserve) is both a fair market value and the **Dealmaking** price.

All these potential virtues to the Auction Method require the cooperation not only of an ultimate buyer but also of competing buyers. In our five prior **Valuation Methods**, the methods themselves can be, and normally are, conducted without the cooperation of any buyer, although such cooperation can be helpful in developing reasonable DCF and Monte Carlo based valuations. Translating a valuation to a price, as we will discuss in the closing chapters of this book, of course requires the perspective and the ultimate agreement of a buyer. But, generally speaking, valuation Methods, 1 through 5, are analyses that buyers and sellers do independently and privately until active **Dealmaking** commences. With the Auction Method, in contrast, the prospective buyers and the seller are together actively engaged in the valuation process, and the buyer provides the valuation to the seller. This differs from typical **Dealmaking** where either the buyer or the seller may begin a negotiation by positing a value or value range, although with auctions it is not uncommon for the seller to establish a price floor in its initial discussion with prospective bidding buyers.

Introduction to Auctions

While the Monte Carlo Method and the various option pricing techniques discussed in this book are fairly recent, this chapter deals with the oldest form of valuation known: obtaining bids under an auction format.

Since antiquity, auctions have been used as a simple, powerful means of determining the value of goods offered for sale. Auctioning is similar to the Industry Standards Method, Method 1, of Chapter 4 in that both methods are based on direct market determinations. However, the Industry Standards Method used market information for previous transactions as similar to the one in question as practicable. The Auction Method uses existing and pending offers for precisely the technology being valued.

In a certain sense, one can interpret typical negotiations as being "auctions." Even in mundane contexts such as bananas in a grocery store, the offering price is based upon the seller's perception of the price buyers are willing to pay, given the benefits and the alternatives. There is even a legal opinion that every purchase in a grocery store is simply you bidding the marked price on the goods at the checkout counter and the grocery store's agent, the checkout clerk, accepting your bid.[1]

There really is nothing inherent in a banana that says it should sell for 50 cents a pound (as they have, approximately, during the period 1990 through 2005). If for some reason buyers begin to want more bananas than are available, the sellers (all the sellers in the value chain) sense the demand and use it as a signal to deliver more bananas and to charge a higher price. Because bananas are perishable commodity items, the supply will eventually increase to the point where the abundance of bananas will cause sellers to reduce the price in order to clear out stock and a new market equilibrium price and demand will be established.

In offering technology for license, sellers typically call on multiple potential buyers to determine interest. The response from such inquiries can influence a seller's pricing decisions, even though no formal offer or bid has been made. Even if there are only discussions with one prospective buyer, imagine what a seller would think if that buyer said something like, "This is the best opportunity I've ever seen," "We absolutely have to have this technology," and "Hey, look, money is no object here, how much do you want?" Would not such words, or equivalent body language, be interpreted by the seller as bidding language even without formal bids? This is why, in the author's experience, the seller instead hears: "It looks very risky," "It's going to take a lot of money to get this to the market and then I'm not sure anyone is going to buy it," and "Maybe, just maybe, if we can get it for no upfront license fee and for a very reasonable royalty, I might be able to persuade my boss to take a chance on this."

The Auction Method is a way for a seller to structure a series of parallel, very short-term discussions with multiple prospective buyers and reduce all positioning statements into a simple monetary bid.

When Auctions are Feasible

Before going into the operational issues of the Auction Method, it needs to be noted that the use of the method presumes a certain bargaining power on the part of the seller. Normally, if such power does not exist, then auctioning does not work. Also, from the perspective of the buyer, it is hard to envision circumstances where the use of auctions as a valuation method should be encouraged.[2] As is often the case, court-ordered transactions, such as in bankruptcy, are exceptions to this rule. The auction takes place although the original asset owner or manager is no longer in any position of power. The court as the fiduciary for those with rightful claims determines how liquidation is to proceed and commonly uses some form of auction to dispose of assets with value.

In all five previous Methods, there is no inherent limitation on the seller in making use of the described tools and techniques. There is always the challenge of gathering data, developing models, and applying good judgment, but there is nothing about these previous methods that requires a particular circumstance for the methods to be applied by either the buyer or the seller. Also in all the previous methods, there is nothing inherently disadvantageous to either the buyer or seller in the method itself. In the case of auctions, the buyer is normally at a disadvantage; so, for auctions to work for a seller the nature of the opportunity must induce multiple, prospective buyers to take the initiative of conducting a valuation and making an offer with the knowledge that it will be competing with other potential buyers.

Buyers always hope to be in a position to buy below the market value. It is important to recognize that if a seller and buyer each independently value a particular opportunity and, near-miraculously, both conclude that it is worth $10 million on an NPV basis, that it is the nature of buyers to try to pay something less than $10 million. It has been said that business is about paying $5 for things worth $10; that is certainly the buyer's perspective. So, from a "win-win" negotiating standpoint, one might expect this situation to result in a quick settlement on the $10 million NPV. More often, what seems to happen is that the buyer will work very hard to see if the opportunity can be acquired for less than $10 million. The last thing that a buyer wants is a competitive bid situation with other buyers because such a situation would, in this hypothetical example, inevitably lead to a bid of $10 million, thus extinguishing the buyer's hope of paying $5 for a $10 item. (Lest buyers feel abandoned, a counter-measure buyers can use to avoid auctions will be briefly discussed in the last section of this chapter.) And, it should be noted, that sellers readily aspire to obtaining more than the $10 million in this hypothetical example in the event they underestimated the value of the opportunity, or there exists that mythic buyer who has a unique need of the opportunity that for this buyer, and this buyer alone, the opportunity is worth more than the $10 million.

The other special circumstance of an auction is that it presumes (1) an inherently strong bargaining position on the seller's part and (2) that the technology in question can be apprehended relatively quickly by prospective buyers. Considering first the issue of bargaining power, buyers will resist being herded into an auction. The primary reason buyers will go along with this method, when they do, is that the licensing opportunity is so compelling that passing it up is a worse option than engaging in competitive bidding.

Unless the seller can attract at least two or three bidders, the auction method is unlikely to produce a desirable result, although a sole buyer who is unaware of the nonexistence of significant (or any) competition could be induced to making a full NPV bid. Three or more bidders are optimal because it is common to have "low-ball bidders" at auctions—buyers who have not conducted a serious valuation but who bid a number so low that they are confident they can make money regardless of what it is they are buying (which by the way, is not reliably true of technology opportunities). In some cases, low-ball bidders even construct their offer in such a way as to tie up the technology for little or no money for the purpose of conducting their due diligence in a noncompetitive environment. (This approach will be included in the buyer's alternatives to auctions section.)

A variant of low-ball bids is "fire sale" bids. The term refers to the insurance industry's practice of offering for quick sale goods that have been damaged in a fire. The insured had already been paid the full value for the damaged goods; a fire sale was a way for the insurance company to recoup something on its loss. The fire sale also carried the notion that what was not sold immediately was literally trashed, so any offer above zero was considered a potential winning bid.[3] Sellers should, of course, do everything they can to avoid the fire sale perception, signaling buyers that the auction is a orderly disposal situation. Savvy buyers, as part of their due diligence, investigate the selling circumstances for exactly this reason. In the previously cited Arthur Miller play, *The Price*, the used furniture buyer does not quote a price until he is able to determine the circumstances of the sale, wherein he learns: (1) Neither heir can or will take the furniture, (2) there are no other bidders or takers, (3) the lease is about to run out on the apartment in which the furniture is being stored, and (4) the buyer's family is in a "get it over with" frame of mind. Did this affect his price? Not for nothing did an 89-year-old man spend the entire first act pumping the seller for information. (Did Arthur Miller want us to think about our self-limiting natural inclinations, causing us to sell ourselves cheaply?) (Ah, back to work....). For this reason, sellers need to provide sufficient time and auction process support that potential bidders can be identified, induced to investigate, and supported as appropriate in necessary buyer due diligence.

If an auction fails, due to a lack of bids or only low-ball bids, then the seller is at a bargaining disadvantage in seeking out subsequent buyers (assuming such buyers knew of the auction) because they would deduce that there was little or no interest by other buyers. This could lead a subsequent potential buyer to believe there was some sort of fatal flaw in the technology, or that the seller had unreasonably high expectations as to value, or simply the opportunity was so niche it was of little interest. Therefore, one of the seller's big risks in initiating an auction is that it can fail, which then can make it difficult to sell at all. At the very least, the seller might have to propose terms even less attractive than would have otherwise occurred sans auction.

The second assumption behind conducting an auction is that a buyer can reasonably apprehend the opportunity without a significant level of due diligence. To use estate auctions as a colloquial example, typical formats provide a catalog description of all the items offered for sale and an inspection period during which all bidders can examine the merchandise. When the goods being auctioned are seen and valued in a few minutes' time, then it is possible to get a large number of bidders to make the small investment in their time for the prospect of making and winning a bid. Even if a buyer's perception is that the odds of winning a bid are low, the investment required to ascertain the potential value is also low. In the case of technology, such low due diligence cost situations are rare if not nonexistent. All the risk issues discussed in Chapters 2 and 7 normally need to be evaluated through a serious investment of time and, sometimes, testing (laboratory, manufacturing, and/or market). In such circumstances, buyers tell sellers that they simply will not exert such due diligence without some reasonable chance of being able to acquire the license if the opportunity checks out and the terms are affordable. Serious buyers will often express such a position by counteroffering an option agreement (discussed in Chapter 11), together with a cash payment to maintain an exclusive right to bid for a prescribed period. To some extent, sellers can help reduce the buyer's investment requirement by creating extensive data packages and even data or disclosure "rooms" where prospective buyers can study comprehensively prepared background information. Sellers can also provide telephone or face-to-face access with potential bidders to answer questions. It is in the seller's interest to make the due diligence burdens as low as possible in order to induce as many bidders as possible. However, regardless of a seller's efforts at facilitation, technology typically requires a bidder to make an investment in the auction process with the knowledge that its competitors could be doing the same thing and it could all be for naught.

From time to time a particular auction related selling concept is tried; that of having a technology fair. At such fairs, all technology sellers are in individual booths hawking their wares to prospective invitee-buyers, a technology flea market, so to speak. There are many problems with this concept. The principal underlying hypothesis is that it is possible, while standing in front of display tables with patents and prototypes, for a buyer to conduct sufficient due diligence to make a purchase decision and engage in negotiation. Such a process works well for baseball cards, collectible dolls, and shish kabob, but not for technology.

In summary, the more complex the opportunity, the more the seller must do to make it easier for buyers to conduct due diligence, and despite such efforts, the less likely it is that enough prospective buyers will take advantage of the opportunity. Likewise, the less compelling the opportunity, the more infeasible it becomes that a group of buyers will follow a seller's schedule in reviewing the opportunity and offering bids.

Auction Examples

Let us consider several categories of valuation-by-auction examples before turning to technology auction examples.

Equity Auctions

Returning again to our use of equity examples, think of the complexity of valuing each and every company, with large ones, such as ones discussed earlier in this book (GE, 3M, TI, Eli Lilly) who make literally thousands of products. It turns out that these companies are valued minute by minute—one is tempted to say: automatically. Valuation by auction is the foundational method of valuation by the "stock market." Whether through the use of the traditional open outcry auctioning, such as the New York Stock Exchange (NYSE), or electronic trading, such as NASDAQ, these and more than a dozen other exchanges enable trading of more than 10,000 U.S. companies and dozens of other exchanges for some 17,000 companies in the rest of the world.[4]

There is a near-religious argument among economists as to whether the market is fully rational in such valuation, namely the "efficient market hypothesis." And there are recent, well known examples when dramatic re-valuations have taken place in such a short period of time, such as the dotcom bubble in 2001–2002, as well as the banking and insurance fallout in 2008 and continuing in 2009, that suggests mispricing both prior and after such drops in values. Despite such vagaries, it is generally accepted that such real time auction processes of matching willing buyers and sellers provides a reliable basis for determining value.

As discussed in Chapter 7, there are small armies of analysts that seek to develop more accurate valuations than that determined by the auction process for the benefit of their clients, who are hoping to buy low and sell high. The track record of market analysts in "beating the market" by forecasting valuations more accurately than that determined by the auction process is under whelming, for most analysts most of the time.

The overall reasonableness of such valuation-by-auction method, combined with the liquidity that stock exchanges enable, is one of the great economic strengths of our modern economy. It is not surprising, then, that the auctions are tried and used in other contexts.

Internet/Web Auctions

The development of the Internet and various manifestations of the web/dotcom economy, has created many new auction based valuation examples.

eBAY eBay began in the mid 1990s as an online kind of garage sale. One of its key features was that sellers could offer products without pricing them using online auction bidding up to standard closing hour. When all potential buyers are in the same place at the same time, each auctioned item is priced and sold within a very short time, usually measured in minutes. Such "real-time" auctions are considered to be essentially instantaneous.

eBay is not an example of a real time auction. It uses the power of the Internet to publicize instantaneously the initiation of an auction on some item, but establishes a time period, usually a few days, to permit a sufficient number of interested bidders to respond so as to create a market price.

The first item sold on eBay was a broken laser pointer for $14.83 in September 1995.[5] This remarkable transaction—to which one's initial reaction is clearly "Who knew?"—illustrates the genius of an auction valuation. As a seller establishing any price for such an item would be pure guess work. But the eBay model solves the seller's dilemma by yielding both the valuation and liquidity. However the valuation hinges upon there having been reasonable time and access for a market to be established for the item.

For our purposes what is interesting about the eBay model is how it is able to establish market prices (arguably, and for most situations) for otherwise hard to value goods.

PRICELINE Priceline (www.priceline.com) was founded in 1997 and went public in 1998 with a business model of consumers establishing the price of certain categories of services by bidding for them, reversing the traditional role requiring service providers to bid for its customers by pricing its offerings. The company offers consumers bidding opportunities on airline tickets, hotel rooms, rental cars, performance bookings, mortgages and other matters.

The Priceline model is close to a real time auction. Even if there is a delay of days or weeks from the purchase to the use of the purchase, the seller's capacity is being continually bid upon until it is fully committed.

What is particularly interesting about the Priceline business model to our context is that it illustrates auction pricing for intangibles, the right to use a seat in a jammed-full airplane leaving late with bad food and worse service.

GOOGLE IPO One of the great Internet success stories is Google. Google has exploited valuation-by-auction in two senses. Google was funded during its early period by venture capital investments, and retained earnings. As with all private companies, it was faced with three strategic choices: Stay private, be acquired by an incumbent company, or become a standalone public company through some form of initial public offering (IPO).

Google, along with many other famous technology companies (Apple, Microsoft, Cisco, Ciena, et. al) chose the IPO route. However, they did their IPO in a non-traditional way. The typical IPO follows a process whereby an investment banker works with the company desiring to go public in preparing "a book" describing the business with key financial information, and conducts "a road show" whereby visits are made to other bankers and intermediaries who represent and advise other large investors. The advising banker and company give a preliminary indication of the expected IPO price range on a per share basis and the total number shares to be offered. After such road show and follow-on discussions an IPO price is established. As we will discuss below, this process resembles a "structured private auction."

What Google did, however, was offer their stock in what is known as a reverse, or "Dutch" auction.[6] The essence of such auction is that Google invited bidders to specify what they would be willing to pay per share and how many shares they sought to buy at the specified price. The details of this do not concern us here. But what the process does illustrate is how an auction can be used to establish a price even for an entity not previously priced in the market. So unlike a traditional equity,

Google at its IPO had no market pricing history, requiring bidders to name their price purely based upon business information disclosed by Google.

GOOGLE OPERATING REVENUES What is more interesting about Google's business model is how they receive revenues. Clearly for end users all Google services and features are free. Google is paid by advertisers for providing a "clickable" ad adjoining search results responding to key words supplied by end users. The alignment of the specific advertisements with key words used in the search is a critical factor in Google's value for an advertiser. If such alignment is high, then there is a much higher probability of the end user reading the ad, and then clicking through the ad for further information, and ultimately buying the advertised product.

Clearly for Google, one crucial pricing issue is what to charge any advertiser for the right to ad placement as a function of the key word or words used in the search window. Google uses auctions whereby advertisers bid for the placement rights for various key words. A dramatic illustration of both how this is done and the real time nature of auction pricing occurred during the aftermath of the tragic killing on the Virginia Tech University campus on April 16, 2007. In the immediate aftermath, newspapers bought placements for key word searches such as "Virginia tech shooting" and "Virginia tech massacre" which, by auction rose to $5 per clickthrough. A week later, such terms were valued by auction at 6 to 8 cents a clickthrough.[7] Similar price spikes occur for "hot news" terms. It seems perverse that phrases describing a great personal tragedy become valuable to both bidders and Google because of their tragic newsworthiness, but online business models are based upon what is crudely worded as "eyeballs": what people will click to see is valuable because their attention is valuable. The business challenge that Google solved was discovering an efficient way to determine fairly a market based value using word-auctions.

Without the vehicle of auctions, especially near real time auctions, there would be no efficient way to properly determine the value of words. Even normal everyday words can have value. How much is the name "Karl Rove" worth on a search page? (This is not asking how much "Karl Rove" is worth—that's a political question, which does not concern us). The issue is how would one develop, say, a DCF Method valuation of the economic benefit gained by a clickthrough on an ad on a page using such search term? The Auction Method answers this question readily: 9 cents, in April 2007.[8] In 2009? No so much.

If Google had to compute by some traditional method the value of each possible search term it would incur significant operating costs in doing so and would no doubt face significant mispricing. By the auction method, they have shifted the burden of pricing to those who need to pay, in the same way that they have exploited the burden of producing content that it searches, to the 25 billion web pages that it indexes. It is no accident that Google's EBIT percentage exceeds 35 percent and its enterprise value is worth $100 billion (more or less).

Technology Merger & Acquisition (M&A)

Both public and private companies are known to offer themselves up for sale to other, usually larger public and private companies. This process is sometimes called "strategic acquisition" (from the buyer's perspective) or just M&A for merger and acquisition. Although such transactions can be one-to-one using any of the valuation methods discussed in this book, and in addition the "cost method" if the seller is a publicly-traded company, what commonly happens is an auction-like process where the seller seeks to engage multiple potential acquirers in near-parallel discussions wherein the seller "plays off" each buyer against all the others to try and get the highest possible bid.

Earlier in this book we reviewed some of the history of Sun Microsystems, a famous Silicon Valley company that has been through multiple boom and bust experiences. Now in 2009, according to published reports, Sun offered to sell itself to IBM and Oracle (and perhaps others). At the time of this writing, it appears that Oracle outbid IBM for Sun by agreeing to pay $7.38 billion, which amount was substantially above what Sun had been valued by the market for its equity.

The two bidders, Oracle and IBM, have been active buyers in technology M&A. Oracle has acquired more than 50 companies since it purchased PeopleSoft in June 2003. Over a comparable period, IBM has acquired 70 companies, spending a total of $27 billion in doing so. It is likely in each of these 120 some M&A events that the sellers engaged, or sought to engage, multiple bidders in a form of auction. In many cases what Oracle or IBM bought was an operating company with revenues, profits, people, and technology; so these were technology *company* M&A. In some cases the companies were so nascent that revenues were negligible, profits nonexistent, people few (but likely important), and technology was the primary asset; such cases are technology M&A.

Let us now consider some examples of pure technology auctions, which commonly have an outright acquisition, i.e. M&A, structure.

Technology Rights: Rockefeller Institute "Fat Gene"

One classic technology example of an auction that turned out very well for the seller has to do with a "fat gene" discovered by Rockefeller Institute.[9] Investigators at Rockefeller discovered a gene that appears to control obesity in mice and filed a patent application. The invention was described as "the hottest property to come out of biotech in years,"[10] a characterization not surprising given the ever popular subject of weight loss. A startup company, Millennium, sought to obtain rights to the patent. Rockefeller, reasonably concerned about obtaining fair value by an arm's length negotiation, invited the interest of more than a dozen pharmaceutical firms including Amgen, Eli Lilly, BMS, and others. The interest turned out to be very high, and Rockefeller found itself being pursued with ever increasing terms. Rockefeller conducted a series of discussions with interested parties in what emerged as a bidding process in January and February of 1995. Then on February 28, 1995, Rockefeller announced that Amgen agreed to pay a $20 million "signing fee" for a license; royalties (to be determined) were estimated at an additional $70 to $80 million. According to the Rockefeller Vice President for Academic Affairs, "Amgen purchased a scientific concept."[11]

This example has received a lot of press and may have created unrealistic expectations in some sellers. Clearly the Rockefeller auction was a case where the two necessary factors for a successful auction were present: strong bargaining power on the part of the seller, and relative ease in conducting due diligence by potential buyers; and the obvious appeal of a huge potential market is clearly an added bonus. As further evidence of seller power, in 1998 Pfizer was reported to have paid Phytopharm PLC up to $32 million for exclusive rights to an experimental drug to treat obesity based upon extracts of plants native to South America.[12] Clearly, market demand for drugs to control obesity creates intense interest in identifying promising technologies.

Other Technology Auction Examples

Although the price obtained by Rockefeller may be unusual, the use of an auction process for technology is not uncommon. The following are briefly summarized examples of auctions used to value and sell technology. They are based upon a paper by Bob Bramson which was written using publicly available information:[13]

- Exponential Technologies offered semiconductor patents alleged to cover Intel's Merced architecture. Rights were acquired by S3 for a price in the range of $10 to $12 million. Apple Computer has sued Exponential Technologies over the proceeds of the sale.
- Wang offered 200 patents organized in 34 technology groups. Certain groups sold during a so called "quiet period." Additional groups sold through the auction process.
- AR Accessories Group, Inc. sold its patents at a bankruptcy auction.
- Carl W. Cooke had a patent on a child resistant closure for pharmaceuticals. Its bankruptcy plan appraised the value of the patent at $375 million. An auction was conducted supervised by the Internal Revenue Service, but no bids were received.
- Cray Computer Corporation had patents on various technologies relating to supercomputing manufacturing packaging and processes. These patents and related intellectual property were acquired by Dasu L.L.C. for $100,000.
- IL Med had patents relating to surgical laser scanners. Under an auction format these patents were acquired by Laser Industries.
- Lamplighter Industries had patents relating to electroluminescent light technologies. The patents were offered at a bankruptcy auction and were acquired by CEL Technologies.
- Orca Technology had patents relating to disc drives which it had bought three years previously from Priam for $500,000 as part of a technology package. At a bankruptcy auction, Orca received $3.65 million by a Samsung winning bid.
- BioPolymers, Inc. had patents on medical adhesives which also were sold off also via a bankruptcy auction.
- Thinking Machines Corporation's massively parallel process patents were on track to be offered at auction. It is unclear whether such an auction took place. Likewise, VideOcart Inc.'s patent of shopping cart video display terminals was planned to be auctioned but the results are unknown.

Real time, public auctions of technology are another source of examples. Below are examples cited by Ocean Tomo[14] for its Fall 2008 auction. All cited dollar amounts include the buyer premium (10 percent), but do not include the seller's cost (15 percent plus a listing fee), and so exceed the net paid to the seller. So for a "sale" of $ one million, the buyer pays $1.1 million (and that would be the reported figure), the seller would receive \$850K (\$1 million less the selling commission of 15 percent), and the seller would have in addition paid a listing fee regardless of any transaction.[15]

- "Mikko Väänänen, a Finnish inventor, sold lots at two auctions—one related to wireless file-based multimedia messaging for \$870,320 and another related to messaging technology for \$1,681,251.
- DataNav sold a lot related to digital media for \$2,414,104,
- Carlson Wireless, sold two lots, one for \$198,000 and another for \$902,000.
- Numerous other lots go unsold because no bid exceed the seller's reserve or, in some cases there was no bid of any amount, reflecting a market failure (absence of bidders with an interest in the opportunity) or a substantial valuation misapprehension by the seller.

One final example is the recent auction of Polaroid's remaining assets in its second journey into bankruptcy proceedings. In April 2009, according to a *Wall Street Journal* story (April 17, 2009), in a court-managed auction, two fiercely competitive bidders made 28 bids and counterbids, in judge-ordained increments of a minimum of \$150,000, until, after three hours, the final number of \$88.1 million was reached. Polaroid in its prime was one of the premier technology companies, with massive IP assets around instant photography and other areas, employing more than 20,000 workers (as recently as 1978). By 2009, it was down to less than 100 employees licensing what remaining assets remained. In the subject auction, it appears that the primary asset being acquired was the brand name value of Polaroid. Dr. Edward Land, the founder of Polaroid, who died in 1991, was an inventor on more than 500 patents, second only to Thomas Edison, created an iconic technology-based product company which in its ultimate demise may have been valued only for its name.

These examples and others show not only the feasibility of using auctions but also act as another category of Industry Standard data to assist both buyers and sellers in performing technology valuations. See additional auction examples in News Sources of License Agreement Information in Chapter 4.

Auctions as Distinct from Other Types of Dealmaking

As discussed above, the Auction Method innately combines two ***Approaches*** addressed in this book—Valuation and Dealmaking—and in some circumstances also opportunity Discovery. The combination of both Valuation and Dealmaking using the Auction Method is both an advantage and a disadvantage, even in contexts where the method can be effectively used.

Although we will address Dealmaking in Chapters 10 and 11, it is useful here to consider the Dealmaking context of auctions. Exhibit 9.1, based on the work of my colleagues Dan McGavock and Bob Goldman of CRA International, and included here with their permission, distinguishes two kinds of auctions—Public and Structured Private—from other Dealmaking contexts.

The second row of Exhibit 9.1 regarding Public Auctions is the traditional model of a real time, "live" auction. The bottom row of this exhibit, Structure Private Auctions concerns an auction like process but one done for a single opportunity family, privately, and not usually in real time as will be discussed below.

Transaction Mechanism	Stage of Development (Early, Late, In-Use)	Known Interest / Demand (Low, Medium, High)	# of Qualified Buyers (Small, Medium, Large, Unknown)	Targeted Marketing Effort (Low, Medium, High)	Transaction Time (Short, Medium, Long)	Transaction Costs (Low, Medium, High)	Level of Sell-side Due Diligence (Low, Medium, High)	Expected Value (Low, Medium, High)	Advantages	Disadvantages
Online Listing	E,L	L	U	L	L	L	L	L	▪ Very low effort and cost for assets with low/unknown demand and number of qualified buyers	▪ Reliance on potential buyers to identify opportunity and express interest ▪ Limited competition resulting in lower price ▪ No deal timeline
Public Auction	E,L	L/M	U	L	S	L	L/M	L/M	▪ Low cost ▪ Short transaction time (subject to infrequent predefined auction schedule)	▪ Low targeting may result in limited competition and lower price
Mass Direct Marketing	E,L,I	L/M	U	L/M	M	L	L	L/M	▪ Low cost ▪ Allows broad targeting of large number of potential buyers at reasonable cost	▪ Limited marketing and due diligence may result in less than optimal sales price
Strategic Direct Marketing	E,L,I	M/H	S	H	L	H	H	M/H	▪ Well-suited for a small number of highly qualified potential buyers ▪ Well-suited for early stage opportunities / tech transfer ▪ Ability to convey buyer-specific value proposition maximizes sale price	▪ High cost and upfront due diligence effort ▪ Typically longer and uncertain transaction time
Structured Private Auction	L,I	M/H	M/L	M/H	S	L/M	M	M/H	▪ Targeted marketing reaches larger number of qualified buyers ▪ Defined transaction time creates sense of urgency ▪ Increased competition results in higher sales price	▪ Best for opportunities with more than a few qualified potential buyers ▪ Complicated when a post-deal relationship between a seller and one particular buyer would be advantageous.

EXHIBIT 9.1 Dealmaking Types, Including Auctions

Shown across the columns at the top of Exhibit 9.1 are various distinguishing elements for each of the five shown Dealmaking contexts:

- Stage of Development of the technology (where "in use" refers to at least initial commercial use)
- Known Interest/Demand for the opportunity
- Number of Potential Qualified Buyers
- Targeted Marketing Effort (Dealmaking resources available or budgeted for commitment)
- Transaction Time
- Transaction Costs
- Level of Sell Side (Seller) Due Diligence Support (to/for potential Buyers)
- Expected Value of the technology opportunity
- General Advantages and Disadvantages of each Dealmaking type

Briefly, each of the five Dealmaking contexts can be described as follows:

1. *Online Listing*, a passive online catalog of opportunities offered for sale, similar to Craigslist[16] but for technology IP.
2. *Public Auction*, a real time auction of technology, in person and/or by telephone bidder-buyers.
3. *Mass Direct Marketing*, similar to an Online Listing but "pushed" to prospective buyers.
4. *Strategic Direct Marketing*, the traditional form of personal marketing by the seller to multiple potential buyers, the so-called "contact sport" of technology Dealmaking.
5. *Structured Private Auction*, like Strategic Direct Marketing but deadline driven, the value is provided by offers from aspiring buyers, in response to seller-established standard contract terms with predefined offered subject matter, the Technology Box, and expected payment structure, the Wheelbarrow (terms defined in Chapter 3 and to which we will return in Chapter 10 and 11).

As might be expected with any classification schema, these five contexts are not distinguished by bright lines, nor are they mutually exclusive. A particular opportunity may be marketed by a Seller using Strategic Direct Marketing but then based on significant interest by multiple potential buyers may adapt a Structured Private Auction. Similarly, an Online Listing may be used initially and may be transitioned to one of the other Dealmaking types.

The rating/ranking used for the distinguishing elements in the various columns again are not exact, but are intended to show common experience and general rules-of-thumb. As shown, the opportunities with higher expected values are generally pursued via contexts number 4 and number 5, context number 1 is used primarily for lower valued opportunities. Clearly more Dealmaking resources and expertise in required for contexts number 4 and number 5, and the timeline is typically longer. These matters will be discussed further in Chapters 10 and 11.

At the heart of the Auction Method (context number 2 or number 5) is the establishment of an unambiguous process that prospective buyers can rely upon as being fair. Integrity in the process is essential as prospective buyers must believe that the highest qualifying bid will in fact be the successful bid. From the standpoint of a buyer, the nightmare scenario is that the seller has a hidden understanding with one of the buyers enabling the favored buyer to make a final bid after learning of all the other bids. Not only is such behavior unfair, but it also runs against the seller's own interests because it saves the favored buyer from having to make an aggressive bid by enabling that company to make only a matching or a slightly higher bid (known in the industry as a winning "McBid").

It is critical to the success of the Auction Method that potential buyers know about the opportunity, believe there is potential value in the opportunity offered and the fairness of the process being followed such that multiple buyers are willing (however reluctantly) to commit sufficient resources to perform due diligence and valuation, and to participate and so establish a market price for the opportunity.

Public Auctions (Context No. Two in Exhibit 9.1)

A simple, and traditional, form of an auction is the real time context. A time and place for binding bids is established with rules of conduct as to the admissibility of written and/or telephone bids, in addition to, or in lieu of in room bidding. An alternate form is to parallel the eBay approach by having a time-expiry auction by which bids can be made over the Internet or by express mail or hand delivery. The real time auction includes the dynamic of round robin public bidding so that each potential buyer knows the current bid price and the offer required to keep the auction going.[17]

The delivery type auction does not have this public bid feature. Such auctions can be done in a single round, meaning the winning bidder will be chosen by the seller based upon the initial and only bids. Two round delivery auctions can be used whereby only a certain number of the highest round one bidders are entitled to make a "best and final" revised bid.

Both the real time and delivery forms of auctions are here termed "public." However, any bidder can take steps to keep private its identity. In the real time form, the bidder may be identified only by some unique number, such as might be used for a "paddle" raised by the bidder indicating assent to bid the next price increment above the standing bid. The seller and/or the auction intermediary would need to know the identity of the entity bidding but such bidder may not be the ultimate assignee, and any bidder's identity could be kept secret from other bidders.

For both real time or delivery auctions, some packaging of seller IP and support for due diligence is necessary. IP rights are usually grouped into families, or in auction terminology "lots." Grouping is usually necessary as a buyer would find it untenable to bid on related patents or other IP rights one-by-each if more than one such patent or other rights are likely to be needed for a commercial product. One-by-each auctioning creates the possibility of intolerable buyer outcomes. For example if five individual patents from one seller are believed to be relevant and needed from a freedom to practice consideration and a buyer who has committed itself to the opportunity wins the bids for the first four will find itself a hostage to the bidding on the fifth patent. Some third party knowledgeable about the situation could make an all out attempt to buy the fifth patent either to block the buyer of the first four patents or to resell the fifth at some "hostage premium."

It is also important for the seller to provide some central resource of background information on the IP offered that cannot be known by a bidder. This would include retained rights by the seller, third party obligations already entered into by the seller such as potential march in rights by the Government, or some committed supply agreement. Also, because it is in the interest of the seller to attract as many bidders as possible, a seller may want to make known other background information such as prototypes, test data, market studies and surveys, potential suppliers and customers, and even legal opinions such as novelty opinions for pending patent applications and freedom to practice opinions with respect to some specific commercial embodiment.

THE MARKET REQUIREMENT Perhaps the most important requirement for either form of public auctions to be effective is sufficient publicity and marketing such that a reasonable number of potential buyers are in attendance and motivated to bid. Clearly the Auction Method does not work unless there is something approximating a "market" determination, which requires competing bids from more than one aspiring buyer with an important commercial interest in the opportunity. If all the bidders are, or the only bidder is, economically indifferent to the opportunity, the bid or bidding is likely to exhibit only nominal, even trivial offers. For the Auction Method to work for the seller, there has to be more than one buyer in attendance who has a real need for the IP/technology being offered.

THE RESERVE PROTECTION There are normally two benchmark prices pre-established by the seller: the starting bid and the reserve price. The starting bid is the published minimum initial offer that begins the auction. If something is expected to sell in the millions of dollars it usually is not a good idea to begin the bidding with a minimum bid of $10,000. The reserve price is an unpublished figure established by the seller that prevents the auctioneer from the traditional binding pronouncement—"going once, going twice . . . SOLD!"—at a price unacceptable to the seller.

Although the reserve price is not pre-published, the auctioneer must make known at some point of the bidding whether the reserve has been met and, if not, declares the opportunity withdrawn. A seller can of course elect not to have a reserve price. A no-reserve auction may attract more potential buyers because of the certainty of a sale occurring, providing the minimum starting bid is met. However, seller takes a major risk in waiving a reserve requirement because one never knows who or how many will participate in the auction with what motivations. There is a seller risk that all bidders with any significant interest in the opportunity have banded together with the strategy on not competing in the auction and instead carving up the rights bought by one designated bidder amongst themselves post auction, such as all sharing a nonexclusive license.

THE FOUR MARKET-RESERVE OUTCOMES We can combine the above two considerations—the market requirement and reserve protection—and consider the four possible outcomes in the following table:

	A market-sufficient number of qualified bidders:	An inadequate number of qualified bidders:
The reserve price was met by the highest bidder:	Desired Auction Outcome	Valuation/Selling Price is more likely to have been too low
The reserve price was NOT met by the highest bidder:	Reserve Price is likely to have been too high, with loss of a Dealmaking opportunity	Reserve Price may have protected the Seller from a below Valuation Selling Price

The key to, and design of, the Auction Method is that an opportunity price is established by a market determined price, as designated by the center column. If such occurs and the price exceeds the reserve we have the ideal Auction Method result: a Dealmaking event at the market price established by buyers.

However, these twin criteria embody dilemmas. Implicit in the Auction Method is the presumption that the market establishes the value of the technology. If so, then how does a seller establish a reserve price? Setting aside just guessing, this leads to the need for the seller to perform *some* valuation using one or multiple other methods. Assuming that such valuation considered multiple scenarios or probabilities or comparables, should the reserve be set at the optimistic, pessimistic, or most likely value, or some other benchmark such as some "walk away" threshold?

If the reserve is set high, then there is a greater possibility that it will not be met even if there is a "market" established by the bidders. Such an outcome has an opportunity cost associated with the auction process and may taint the technology in a subsequent Dealmaking campaign. If the reserve is set low, and exceeded by the bidding, then the valuation depends upon whether there was a fair market determination by the bidders at the auction. A fair market valuation benchmark requires that there be sufficient number of bidders that are representative of the opportunity value for the technology. With technology assets, there can be no assurance that such will be the case. Even for a competitive bid situation, say between two bidders each of whom has a narrow interest in the technology not because of some limitation in the technology or other markets but because that is the business focus of these two bidders. Even if they go back and forth raising the bid, the final bid could only, at best, represent a fair market value for the niche that these two were targeting.[18] How, then does a seller know whether the bidding reflected a fair market value?

PUBLIC AUCTION LIMITATIONS Public auctions can be used by both sellers and buyers for opportunities that do not matter much. In which case concerns for the seller about a proper reserve price or even whether a true market established a selling price are not that important. Likewise a buyer who is not serious about a technology may bid and buy rights for a nominal amount using some "just in case" reasoning—a Real Option value—without investing much or anything in due diligence or valuation. Such low value determination and Dealmaking is like the joke about work and wages in the old Soviet Union's economic system: "We pretend to work, and they pretend to pay us."

When opportunities are believed to be significant, then the issues suggested by the outcomes previously mentioned are real and important. The Auction Method for such circumstances does not obviate the need for valuation work by both the seller and all the prospective buyers. In addition, assuming again the value is significant, all the buyers will need to perform appropriate due diligence. And, in any case, the seller will always wonder if it could have done better for itself had it used another Dealmaking approach in Exhibit 9.1.

One of the other limitations of public auctions is the inability to tailor the offering. In a typical Dealmaking environment, such as Structure Private Auctions discussed ahead, the Technology Box and Payment Wheelbarrow discussed in Chapter 3 can undergo modification based upon the value considerations applied to each element of a transaction by both the seller and buyer. In a Public Auction the buyer is compelled to bid on the package as it is offered.

Another limitation is the difficulty of the seller's including in the package know-how/trade secrets, access to facilities, rights to solicit and hiring of key individuals associated with the technology, and so forth. This is because such assets either cannot be easily defined or made public to multiple potential bidders, or because the seller may not be willing to provide such assets to every potential bidder.

Trade secrets and know-how are not well suited to the auction format. A seller would obviously not want to make such knowledge known to all bidders, even under confidentiality agreements. And without access to what such knowledge may be a bidder is unlikely to ascribe significant value to it.

A final point of reality with public auctions of technology such as those offered by Ocean Tomo is that numerous opportunities receive no, or few, bids and are not sold; Ocean Tomo reports a selling success rate of just under 50 percent for a recent auction.[19]

For a "no sale," the seller loses its listing fee, but more importantly its time invested in supporting the auction process and an aging of the IP rights. The technology also retains a kind of taint in that any subsequent marketing to potential buyers would be with their likely knowledge that no or only low bids were offered for the opportunity at a public auction. This raises the obvious buyer question: "If this is so good, why did it go unsold?" If the answer given is "because the right people were not there," then the follow-on obvious question is "If this is so good, why weren't the right people there?"

PUBLIC AUCTION FIT Despite the limitations and concerns, there can be situations where Public Auctions make sense.

One common context is bankruptcy proceedings. Bankruptcy, a recent growth "industry," has multiple characteristics that make valuation and Dealmaking by Public Auctions a good fit: no or little available financial or other resources, a belief that the remaining technology assets have limited value, a sense of urgency, and a need for transparency. Bankruptcy courts are charged with trying to treat all claimants on a failed company's assets fairly under the law, and must do so relatively quickly at a minimum expenditure of funds and often without the availability of key principals who are most knowledgeable about the technology. Transparency is also a useful feature of Public Auctions.

Estate trustees, private inventors, and companies with "orphan" technologies can also find Public Auctions a good fit for similar reasons as bankruptcy proceedings, although transparency may not be as important a feature.

Public Auctions could also be a fit for high technology values, so called "hot" opportunities. As discussed, the Rockefeller "fat gene" attracted so much interest that the seller used a process similar to a public, real time auction. The key for this to make business sense for the seller is the founded belief that such an auction process will attract high interest by very motivated buyers.

Structured Private Auctions (Context No. Five in Exhibit 9.1)

Another kind of auction is shown by the bottom row of Exhibit 9.1, namely that of Structured Private Auction.

This form of auction can be itself subdivided into informal and formal.

INFORMAL A technology opportunity marketed to individual potential buyers without a proposed selling price is a kind of auction, here termed an informal one. What the seller is doing in such circumstances is seeking to induce any potential buyer to make the initial offer for the opportunity. The seller may be doing so because it has not performed its own valuation or as a Dealmaking strategy. Setting aside the aspect of Dealmaking strategy, does this work as a valuation method?

This approach has obvious appeal to the seller as the easiest of all valuation methods, just ask and see what happens. However, any buyer who senses that the seller does not know its value will be sorely tempted to make a very low offer such that regardless of how the present uncertainties work out, or some upward adjustments in price as a result of ad hoc bargaining, the buyer will still be very happy with the result. So ad hoc auctions are often, simply easy, low cost ways for sellers to receive very low offers. If a seller is in a "just get rid of it" mode this may be a justifiable approach. This could also make sense if the seller is in an unusual, long-term relationship with a remarkably fair minded buyer who, in such circumstances, will make a fair offer as though they were being dragged through an auction. And it is possible that the reason the seller has such a long-term relationship is that the particular buyer has been getting opportunities for 10 cents on a dollar for years.

Let us consider two situations: The seller is seeking to close the deal with the first potential buyer who is willing to name a price, and the situation where the seller will "shop around" the first price it hears. The first situation puts the seller totally under the persuasive control of the buyer. Without a valuation, the seller is literally at the mercy of the buyer's "facts" and argument as to value. This may not be important to the seller if the situation is as the described low opportunity value circumstances with a Public Auction. And there may be some special circumstances where a commercial relationship and trust exists between the seller and particular buyer that the seller has reason to trust that the buyer is offering a fair value. Such a circumstance could occur for a pure royalty based payment where an industry standard–like rate is well established. In this case the seller is basically asking the prospective buyer "Will you agree to pay the standard deal?" This could make sense if the new opportunity is believed to be either low in value or essentially identical in value to some benchmark deal.

The other situation that can take on the features of an informal private auction occurs when a seller gets an offer from a prospective buyer, and then literally takes it to other potential buyers to see if a larger offer can be induced. This is known as "shopping around an offer." Prospective buyers intensely dislike this seller tactic and work to frustrate it. A typical prospective buyer response is simply to decline to name a figure until the seller has a proposal in mind. Another is to make an offer with an immediate, or near-immediate deadline for acceptance with the assertion (threat?) that once declined there is no coming back. Buyers like having multiple opportunities for investment, and though they understand that sellers would like to have the same multiple opportunities, they do not want to facilitate it.

FORMAL The more typical Structured Private Auction is formal in nature in that all prospective buyers are informed of the seller's intention from the onset of discussions, and a procedure and schedule made known of the process the seller aspires to follow.

Any structured marketing and negotiating process has elements of an auction because there are offers, counteroffers, and adjustments in bids. However, in these circumstances both the seller and the buyer normally have some foundation for belief in the value of the opportunity and they are not relying on such foundational information to come in response to a question "What'll you give me for it?"

Sellers will need to provide a careful description of the assets offered for sale (the Box) and any limitations it seeks for the structure of payment offers (the Wheelbarrow). Such information is provided to prospective buyers in what is commonly referred to as the "Book."

Also included in such "Book" is contact information, the proposed schedule, the availability of additional information, typical legal disclaimers of warranty, and the proposed purchase agreement with all relevant attachments. Additional information could be made available by offering scheduled teleconferences or site visits, which may require a separate confidentiality agreement. As part of a site visit there can be a "data room" made available for the buyer's team to review reports and various documents that the seller wants to maintain under close control.

The seller should do everything possible to maintain the confidentiality of the number and identity of the bidders, although the bidders may surmise the identity of other interested parties. Sellers are generally best served by potential buyers not knowing who all is interested, and buyers often do not want their possible interest known to others.

Some "buyers" are really just doing competitive intelligence by participating in the process. Such buyers know or believe that someone will acquire the technology and put it into the marketplace, and they want to understand what the competitive effect is likely to be. Although such parties do not directly harm the auction process, they do take time and resources away from assisting serious prospects. Sellers have the right to exclude parties who they believe are not serious buyers. Strong nondisclosure agreements can act to dissuade some "tire kickers" because of the fear of later legal exposure if they independently develop features or products that appear to be derived from what they learned in the due diligence process. For these reasons, it is generally not a good idea for a seller to cast an overly wide net in search of buyers.

The Structure Private Auction Process normally involves written offers. The seller should create a standard form for such bids to assure that bidders respond with answers to all terms relevant to the seller. Otherwise, it can be impossible to know what exactly a buyer has bid.[20]

The seller is not precluded from proposing modifications in the winning bid although at some risk of alienation of highest bidder. Of course, the buyer is not obligated to accept such variations. However, it is possible that some changes advantageous to both parties could be found, (or at least changes that are advantageous to one and neutral to the other).

It is important upon selection of the winning bid that the consummation of the sale take place quickly as the losing bidders are likely to lose interest and go on to other projects. If for some reason the winning bidder does not complete the transaction, the seller wants to be able to conclude a deal with the next best bid. This hurdle can be cleared by having a complete agreement already drafted, one that outlines many of the key terms and requires all bidders to accept such terms for their bid to be qualified and considered for award. The U.S. Government has conducted such auctions for various contracts and in some cases even requires all bidders to sign the contract with their bid. The Government then executes only the winning contract. (It takes a lot of bargaining power to be able to do this.) In most licensing situations, the bids are sufficiently different in structure and the transaction complex enough that such pre-signed licenses are not feasible. And the various bidders could have counter-proposed asset purchase agreements that require a separate analysis by the seller's counsel. Appendix 9A, courtesy of Dale Hogue, provides a sample letter used to conduct an actual patent auction.

Sellers can further protect themselves by requiring that a nonrefundable license fee or partial licensing fee accompany a bid. If the seller accepts the bid and the buyer has a change in heart, the licensing fee is forfeited. Such a fee is sometimes known as a "breakup" fee, although that term is also used for the exit price paid by the party that terminates the deal after it has been executed. The rationale of this lost fee in an auction context is that the seller has been harmed by the buyer's refusal or inability to consummate its successful bid. When the value of the transaction is high, such breakup fee can be substantial. In the aforementioned purchase of Sun by Oracle, Oracle is reported to have agreed to a breakup fee of $260 million, or about 3.5 percent of the offer price.

One possible variation of the Structure Private Auction is the "short list" auction. The initial bidders are pared down to (usually) just two or three parties who make the "short list." Then more detailed negotiations (and possibly further due diligence) are held, and a last, "best and final" bid is made by the two or three parties. This approach is particularly useful if an ongoing relationship between the seller and buyer will be needed; the negotiating period will permit each party to discern what working with the other party will be like. Such discussions can also be helpful to a seller who is attempting to determine the likelihood of actually receiving future payments or royalties based upon a buyer's successful commercialization.

The Toolkit: The Structure Private Auction as a Valuation Tool

The Structured Private Auction Method can be used as a **Tool** in conjunction with our five other Valuation Methods, as the **Tools** that derive from those Methods can be used here.

When the seller receives multiple bids, unless they have all been structured identically, such as lump sum/up-front payments, it will need some way of making offer comparisons, using the Discounted Cash Flow equations as a **Tool**. One common need in comparing such offers with unique payment amounts at varying dates is to use the DCF calculation to "move money in time," namely all the proposed payments put in terms of their NPV (Net Present Value), so all proposals can be compared on the same basis. Of course, as part of such money movement, a risk factor must be selected which could vary from bidder to bidder depending upon the assets they can deploy in support of commercialization.

If there is a conditional element of a bidder's offer, such as a running royalty or subsequent lump payment, Rating/Ranking as a **Tool** can be useful in comparing the various bids and bidders. The Industry Standard Method can help the seller compare all the offers received with those received by others in other auctions. Finally, the seller can use the Monte Carlo Method to create multiple return scenarios with various bidders or with various options under each bid.

Auctions can also be used as a **Tool** combined with other Valuation Methods. For instance, a formal valuation could have been done using multiple Methods in preparation for a licensing campaign of Structured Direct Marketing (context number four of Exhibit 9.1), but in the course of events multiple potential buyers could begin to press the seller to conclude an immediate deal. At such point, the seller may be able to adopt the Auction Method as a **Tool** by requiring best and final bids among those expressing serious, final interest.

Auction Strategies for Buyers

As discussed above, buyers generally find auctions to be to their disadvantage and, consequently, they seek ways of avoiding such situations. There are several techniques that buyers can use to prevent auctions.

The reason sellers seek auctions is to maximize the price and to have followed a process that can be argued to have done so. Buyers, then, can meet the desires of a seller by (1) offering a "preemptive," attractive bid, and (2) providing information that will persuade the seller that their offer is in fact fair and attractive. Further, the buyer can (when legitimate) create a reasonable sense of urgency. Focusing on concluding the negotiations as soon as possible will speed the subsequent commercialization of the technology.

Every Dealmaking campaign costs the seller money reducing its net realization. A quick deal is advantageous on the cost side, and a deal done is a deal done, eliminating the always present risk of Dealmaking failure.

A buyer can also propose a Dealmaking structure and seller reward that may not be readily offered by a competitor. One example would be for the aspiring buyer to offer some unique, not solely monetary form of compensation such as a buyer's technology or other IP asset. Another example would be a form of compensation not possible by other potential bidders such as private equity from a nonpublic company. There the buyer may be able to facilitate the movement of key personnel from the seller in a way that is uniquely favorable both economically and psychologically to the seller, the buyer, and the people involved.

Auction Caution

Avoiding the cost, time, and work of performing a valuation of a technology is one obvious appeal of the Auction Method. However, as is often the case, simplifications are not also as useful as they first may appear.

Buyers are not generally fans of auctions and will work to prevent/avoid such a context. Sellers using the Auction Method of course work to overcome buyer reluctance by doing everything reasonably possible to make the auction a fait accompli. However, if there is a stumble in creating the auction, in the Public context because of poor attendance by interested parties or in the Private context by limited interest, the seller can be disadvantaged by having publicized the use of an auction. One example downside for the seller is a Structured Private Auction where a winning bidder learns that there are no other bidders or that other bidders have withdrawn. In such circumstances the lone bidder can even attempt a "down bid," namely revising unilaterally its previous winning bid. When auctions are held for the sale of operating businesses, such a down bid, or even outright withdrawal can be subject to a breakup fee paid by the buyer; but even in such circumstances a buyer may claim that there has been a "material adverse change" giving it a free exit from the prior commitment. For these and other reasons it is in the seller's interest to close on the auction as soon as possible after declaring the winner. A prompt close is often also of interest to the buyer because of the ever present fear that the seller may "shop around" the winning bid, or be induced to do so by a losing bidder.

As shown in Exhibit 9.1 and discussed, it is generally wiser to apply Dealmaking contexts number 4 and/or number 5 for more valuable technology opportunities, especially when the Technology Box has a wealth of potential assets beyond bare patent rights. And to decide if something is in the category of "more valuable technology opportunity," some form of valuation needs to be conducted.

Even if a particular opportunity is discerned to be most suitable to Public Auction (number 2), a judgment must be made as to the reserve price, the dollar figure below which the opportunity will not be sold regardless of the number of bidders.

Even with a Privately Structured Auction (number 5) where a reserve provision is not commonly used, a seller will want to have an independent assessment of expected value to guide whether any of the then received offers should be considered, or whether to restart the marketing effort. With a Privately Structured Auction it is often a good practice to provide valuation guidance to the bidders to minimize the risk of supporting due diligence efforts for a prospective buyer who is not even close to the expected value range.

Conclusion

In one sense, the Auction Method is the easiest valuation method because the seller does not *have* to calculate or develop a valuation model. However, it involves significant work of a different sort: the seller has to create and manage a valuation process that attracts a sufficient number of prospective buyers. Also, it is a good idea for the seller, and of course the buyer, to perform a valuation using the other methods described in this book. Otherwise, without such insight, it is not often obvious if the auction has produced a reasonable result, particularly with few or modest bidders. Overall, it may not be simpler, or easier, or even faster. The greatest value of auctions is that when they succeed they provide concrete evidence of market value by virtue of the fact that multiple buyers are each making offers in their own reasonable self interest. For those circumstances where it makes sense, the Auction Method can be very useful, but overall it is not the norm. Its frequent use in bankruptcy settings and other emergency liquidations is testament not to the desirability of the method but rather to the need for a rapid resolution of the sale, much like our earlier reference to fire sales.

The word "auction" derives from a Latin word meaning "to increase." According to Paul Klemperer, a professor of economics at Oxford University, "an auction is the fairest and most transparent system and will get the best price" for the seller.[21] Under ideal circumstances, this is exactly what the seller hopes to orchestrate as the result. The challenge for technology auctions is that the underlying asset is generally considered illiquid and, so, subject to mispricing as well as significant economic risk.

Appendix 9A: Bidder's Agreement

This agreement made between ________________ (hereinafter Bidder) and BID MANAGER, LLC (Hereinafter Auctioneer) is for the purpose of allowing Bidder to participate as a bidder in a live auction of U.S. Patent No. NUMBER, PATENT TITLE, now owned by OWNER NAME.

If the Bidder is the highest bidder, he agrees to pay his bid amount payable to the transfer agent, NAME AND ADDRESS, by TIME AND DATE at the above address. Payment may be by cashiers check or a wire transfer of good funds. Payment made after this time period may be accepted at the sole discretion of PATENT OWNER. If there is not timely payment or acceptance by PATENT OWNER of a late tender, PATENT OWNER may reject the bid and resell the patent at the cost of Bidder and may recover any negative difference between the ultimate sale price of said patent and the Bidder's highest offer.

Bidder agrees that he will clearly communicate his bid to the auctioneer. Once the auctioneer acknowledges the bid it is final and may not be withdrawn.

Bidder agrees to abide by the laws of the STATE pertaining to the sale of intangible property sold by auction.

The Bidder may bid anonymously. If he wishes to do so he must identify his nominee to the auctioneer in writing by DATE, no later then TIME EDT, addressed to the auctioneer at the address of the TRANSFER AGENT law firm above identified.

Bidder will be assigned a number for bidding purposes and will receive a numbered bidding card. Bidder agrees to bid by this assigned number and is responsible for retaining possession of said card and all bids made using that number. Auctioneer will not disclose the identity of any bidder.

The auctioneer will cause to be delivered an assignment of all right, title and interest in said U.S. Patent NUMBER upon payment in good funds of the successful bid price to the transfer agent. The assignment will include all rights, past and present. PATENT OWNER will warrant that there are no claims to title or licenses granted under said patent, or claims as to validity or enforceability of said patent. No other warranties or representations will be made nor indemnifications given.

Accepted by:	Accepted by:
__________________ Signature	__________________ Signature
__________________ Title	__________________ Principal Manager
__________________ Company Name and Address Tele. No.	__________________ BID MANAGER, LLC
__________________ Date	__________________ Date

Source: **Dale Hogue, Hogue Management, LLC, Hilton Head, SC, dchoguesr@aol.com.**

Notes

1. The idea being that prices cited in advertisements, flyers, circulars and the like are not sufficiently complete to be treated as contractually binding offers.
2. There is a least one case of buyer-encouraged auctions. If a prospective buyer believes that it has made a very high offer and, for reasons unique to the buyer, can afford to pay more for the technology than can other buyers, but the seller is still reluctant to sell because it believes that the technology is worth even more, then it could be in the buyer's best interest to encourage an auction, formal or informal, to dislodge the seller from its position.
3. In cases where there are significant disposal (trashing) costs, even offers below zero, (i.e., the seller pays the buyer), can actually be advantageous to the seller. This situation is what buyers dream about in alpha-state sleep.
4. www.uri.edu/library/guides/databases/mergent/mergent.html
5. http://news.ebay.com/history.cfm
6. Google was not the first to use the Dutch Auction for their IPO. Previous to Google it had been done by Overstock.com Inc and Peet's Coffee and Tea. However, at the time Google was the largest company to have used this approach.
7. The price per click statistics originated by Reprise Media, of Interpublic Group, and were cited in a *Wall Street Journal* story April 30, 2007, "Keywords: A Grow Cost for News Sites." The reason newspapers were bidding for placement near such search terms was because they sought traffic to their web pages where they could shower readers with ads from their clients.
8. Ibid.
9. The source of the information provided about the Rockefeller Institute auction is based upon *BusinessWeek* articles, March 13, 1995, p. 46; March 20, 1995, p. 100; and August 7, 1995, p. 29.
10. Ibid.
11. Ibid.

12. "Pfizer Gives Phytopharm a Boost; Pact Centers on Obesity Treatment," *Wall Street Journal*, August 25, 1998.
13. Special thanks to Bob Bramson of Bramson and Pressman for the examples cited, as given in his paper, "Patent Auctions, An Alternative Method of Generating Value from Patents," presented at the 1998 Annual Meeting of the Licensing Executives Society in Miami, October 28, 1998.
14. www.oceantomo.com/auctions.html
15. Telephone discussion with Andrew T. Ramer of Ocean Tomo, November 2008.
16. http://craigslist.org.
17. Auctions of bank-repossessed cars or homes, estate sales, or equities and commodities sold in formal exchanges is a great learning experience. One hilarious movie whose story centers on a commodity auction, orange crop futures, is *Trading Places* staring Eddie Murphy and Dan Aykroyd. The denouement by auction of brothers Randolph and Mortimer Duke, the antagonist characters and scoundrels, is a Dealmaking moment not to be missed, and is available at: www.youtube.com/watch?v=RAXdie_gifI. The YouTube clip is especially poignant as it was filmed in New York City's World Trade Center. The movie's set up lines spoken by the Dan Aykroyd character to the Eddie Murphy character is: "Think big, think positive, never show any sign of weakness, always go for the throat, buy low, sell high. 'Fear?' That's the other guy's problem; nothing you ever experienced can prepare you for the unbridled carnage you are about to witness."
18. It might be argued that included in such bids is the value of subsequent outlicensing to third parties for other markets, and, so, the winning bid does represent a reasonable approximation of fair market value. However, a buyer who is interested in rights to support a narrow product opportunity may have no awareness of how important other markets could be, or even if he does, may highly discount such value because of such limited understanding.
19. www.uprp.pl/rozne/krakow_2008/prezentacje/06.pdf
20. Some buyers create ambiguity on purpose. If a seller who does not fully understand such an ambiguous offer enters into negotiations with such a buyer, other buyers are likely to vanish and the seller could be left in a negotiating situation very different from what had been anticipated.
21. Klemperer, Paul, *Auction Theory and Practice*, Princeton University Press, 2004.

APPROACH III

Dealmaking

CHAPTER 10

Approach: Deal Structure

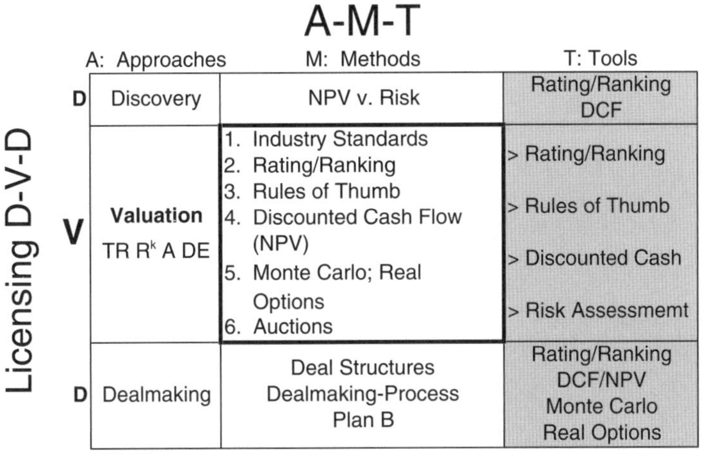
A-M-T
A: Approaches
M: Methods
T: Tools
Licensing D-V-D
D
Discovery
NPV v. Risk
Rating/Ranking
DCF
V
Valuation
TR R^k A DE
1. Industry Standards
2. Rating/Ranking
3. Rules of Thumb
4. Discounted Cash Flow (NPV)
5. Monte Carlo; Real Options
6. Auctions
> Rating/Ranking
> Rules of Thumb
> Discounted Cash
> Risk Assessmemt
D
Dealmaking
Deal Structures
Dealmaking-Process
Plan B
Rating/Ranking
DCF/NPV
Monte Carlo
Real Options

Throughout the book we have made reference to the ***A-M-T*** structure for ***Approaches***, ***Methods***, and ***Tools***. The term ***Approaches*** was used to describe the three business processes that are covered by this book, namely, opportunity **Discovery**, **Valuation**, and **Dealmaking** (hence the acronym Licensing or Technology D-V-D).

In Chapters 4 through 9, we covered each of the six Valuation ***Methods*** and how aspects of each ***Method*** can also be used as a ***Tool*** combined with other ***Methods*** as well as the ***Approaches*** of opportunity Discovery and Dealmaking.

Chapter 10 begins our closing three chapters on the third ***Approach***, namely **Dealmaking**. This chapter will focus on deal structures. It will be primarily about transforming the results of a valuation into a form that readies a seller, or buyer, for negotiation. Four principal ideas will be developed: (1) the Wheelbarrow, (2) Pricing, (3) Structures, and (4) Term Sheets.

In Chapter 11 we will address the human side of Dealmaking, and Chapter 12, integration of Licensing D-V-D: opportunity Discovery, Valuation, and Dealmaking with some concluding thoughts.

Return to the Box and Wheelbarrow

In Chapter 3, we introduced the metaphors of the Box as the seller's trade and for the Wheelbarrow as the consideration paid by the buyer. There we discussed the major categories of the Box. Definition of the Box was essential for the purpose of opportunity Discovery, our focus in chapter, 3, and for Valuation, Chapters 4 through 9. Now, in this chapter, the Box must be joined with the Wheelbarrow to establish a basis for Dealmaking.

As we will see, just as the Technology Box typically has significant complexity so also is the pricing structures expressed by the Wheelbarrow. Such complexities are neither accidental nor incidental, as complexity is normally something to be avoided. But in the face of significant risk and uncertainty, and a wide range in potential deal value, careful Dealmaking about important opportunities can justifiably include multiple compensation forms and conditions for payment.

Pricing vs. Valuation

Up to this point, we have focused on Methods and Tools of characterizing an opportunity based on its projected worth from various perspectives based on certain assumptions and financial models. This business process is often termed *valuation*. *Pricing* can be distinguished from valuation in a way similar to the distinction between a cash flow statement and an income statement (Chapters 7 and 8). A common aphorism about these two accounting statements is that "income" is an opinion, but "cash" is a fact. The parallel here is "valuation" is what I think a technology opportunity is worth, but "pricing" is the expression of value that I am asking a buyer (or a buyer asking the seller) to accept. Pricing is the process of concretizing and communicating a valuation, in the context of a deal structure, to the other side.

Why are pricing and valuation not the same thing? In simple situations, such as a one time, lump sum payment for a simple asset, they could be the same or differ only in that an appropriate gap might be used to initiate negotiations. But as a seller, I am likely to have preferences in how I am to be compensated. I may, because of my business situation, be interested only in a lump sum payment on closing, even if the NPV of such structure is substantially less than I am likely to receive by using some combination of royalty, equity, or conditional lump sum payments. Or, as a seller, for the potential of a significant upside I could be willing to receive most of my compensation in conditional forms over time. Likewise buyers can be nonnegotiable on certain payment features. Or they have a strong preference for a certain form but are open to persuasion to certain alternative forms providing the overall economics are made attractive.

Another Dealmaking driver is how the seller and buyer perceive risk and uncertainties affecting deal value and payment structure. As we discussed in Chapter 7 on the effect of RAHR (risk adjusted hurdle rate) on DCF NPV value and Chapter 8 on the effective percentile on the Monte Carlo NPV value, a party's view of risk can have a dramatic effect upon their valuation of an opportunity and, thereby, their willingness to pay both in terms of the magnitude of such payment(s) but also their timing and conditionality.

Pricing and Structure

Price is the full expression of payments made and to be made by the technology buyer to the seller. Such payments include both cash in multiple forms, such as lump sum payments on closing, royalties of sales, conditional future payments, and royalties. But payments also include noncash forms of consideration by the buyer. Usually the seller is primarily interested in the cash category—as the famous line in the movie, "Show me the money!"[1] But not always, and not entirely, for reasons somewhat similar to the buyer's interests in the Box, which is typically more than just the rights to the technology or even just "the technology" itself; returning again to the same movie for another classic line–"You complete me"—expresses the buyer's desire for obtaining all that it needs to make products successfully.

Underlying such pricing is some form of *structure* by which payment(s) will be made. The idea behind deal structure is the form and conditionality of buyer payments, which is related to but more than just payment magnitude. So behind every pricing offer is a valuation opinion, and in front of it, so to speak, is a structure.

Although there are a countless number of ways that payments can be structured, especially when considering nonmonetary forms, this chapter reviews many principal ones and attempts to provide a framework for their application.

Risk

As we have discussed, risk is a universal consideration in any valuation analysis. It is especially so with technology because by definition there is limited or no commercial evidence because it is unproven in some important ways—underlying science/R&D, manufacturability, IP rights/freedoms, and/or market demand (and other commercial issues). In addition to what is known to be uncertain, there is the uncertainty category of "unknown unknowns." In the mortgage industry there is a parallel term of art: the NINA, designating investments made to individuals with "No Income, and No Assets." Technology typically has no present income (NI); it does have "assets," but such assets may not have any commercial value without further technical and market development, and, accordingly, are clouded with uncertainty.

This combination of known and unknown unknowns is most of what is meant by *risk*, but not all of it. Even if by some means we had present certitude of both kinds of unknowns, an unattainable state, we would not, and could not, know the future. Even a proven sailing vessel casting off with a cargo known to be of commercial value in transit to an established port is not the same thing as money in the bank. (And, in 2008, we have learned money in the bank is not always what it is believed to be, and in 2009 the emergence of piracy has introduced, or more accurately re-introduced, shipping risks recently thought to be negligible).

Incomplete consideration of risk in either pricing or structure is perilous. Former U.S. Treasury Secretary and long-time Board member of Citi Group, Robert Rubin *used to say* in his speeches: "The only undervalued asset class in the world is risk."[2]

Term Sheets

The primary ***Tool*** of pricing and structure is the *term sheet*; it can be considered a pricing work product. There are two types of term sheets, internal and external.

As the name implies the internal term sheet is that used by the seller and buyer to conduct their respective internal negotiations and Dealmaking. External term sheets are ones that are shared with the other side. The purpose of both term sheets is to define explicitly in summary form the Box and Wheelbarrow and, so, establish the Dealmaking objective.

The Toolkit: Term Sheets

One of the most useful Dealmaking tools is a term sheet. It defines the Box and Wheelbarrow in terms sufficient to negotiate an agreement and construct the binding agreements. The internal term sheet is a more comprehensive tool leading to negotiation readiness, considering:

- *Range of options*, as to different configurations of the Box and Wheelbarrow, and specifically with respect to pricing and structures
- *Tradeoffs*, the willingness to accept alternatives
- *Priorities*, highlights the key 'must haves'
- *Balance*, the perceived key points of value to the other side

The external term sheet is much more succinct, usually just one or at most two pages:

- *Tailored* to the specific party with whom Dealmaking is to commence
- *Specific* as to the contents of the Box and Wheelbarrow
- *Concise* on key points, not comprehensive of all deal issues
- *Provisional*, a solid starting place but not necessarily a final or "take it or leave it" position

For these reasons the term sheet is not intended to be binding on the offerer (so it is a good practice to date it). A graphic summarization is given below:

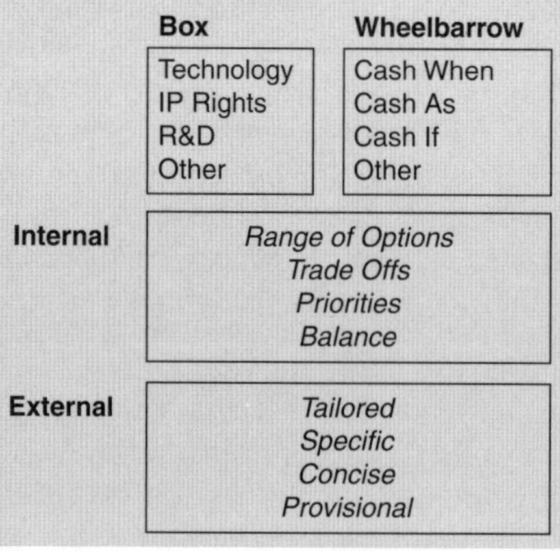

The objective of the term sheet is to provide the parties a basis for an early discussion on a deal framework. It is normally presented by the seller as its version of the deal. However, the buyer can also initiate a term sheet either because it wants to frame the discussion, or because the seller is inviting initial offers. In either case, it defines one side's perspective of what it will take to close the deal.

The provisional Box and Wheelbarrow may be inappropriate for an optimum deal between the seller and buyer. It may contain elements that represent value to the seller but do not represent value, or only little value, to the buyer. By having pricing communications in the context of a term sheet, it is more likely that these elements can be discerned and potentially removed from consideration or included but in some way that provides the buyer only what is important and allows the seller to retain some of what it values highly.

In practice, Box additions and subtractions may be both possible and value enhancing, and can take the form of "horse trading" which, in exchange for something that the buyer wants added the seller identifies something that has to be withdrawn, under a provisional presumption that the price is staying the same. Generally, such reconfiguring is not done at constant value or price. The underlying hope, often realized, is that there are potential Box contents that are more valuable to one side than to the other. It is this very hope that underlies the value of any trade, namely, each side must believe that it is better off by virtue of having done the trade or (in an arm's-length situation) no trade would occur. So the trade must be a value-increasing event. Each reconfiguration negotiation is an opportunity to create additional deal value.

There may be many possible deal configurations acceptable to the seller. Generally, there is no practicable way to express all such if/then pricing configurations. Unless there is a well recognized either/or condition known to the parties, it is usually better to keep the initial term sheet simplified to a baseline, reasonably centrist position.

The term sheet may be expressed in spreadsheet software such as Excel. This method can be particularly useful for the internal term sheet as it can contain all the other tabs comprising the negotiation readiness "Book" described in Chapter 11. The actual term sheet value can be tied directly to cells in other worksheets used for Valuation. This direct connection between valuation and proposed pricing terms can be useful when in negotiations the deal team wants to consider the impact on the term sheet by making different assumptions or restructuring the valuation model or a counterproposal from the buyer or multiple prospective buyers.

In the sections that follow we will consider four cash structures: "Cash *When*," for unconditional payments on specified dates, "Cash *As*," for expected payments conditional upon certain events, "Cash *If*," for payments which are not necessarily expected by either side, and "Cash *Maybe*" for option structures. We will also consider noncash forms of buyer consideration.

Cash *When* Pricing Structures

We will begin with the simplest form of payment Wheelbarrow: unconditional, defined cash payment or payments by the buyer. We will take as a given that both the seller and buyer has each, by one or some combination of methods, come to a determination of the NPV of the technology.

Paid up/lump Sum: Single Payment

Paid up/lump sum agreements are known by a variety of terms: cash licenses (or assignments), upfront licenses, lump sum agreements, and paid ups (as in paid up licenses). This is the simplest form of Wheelbarrow, and most closely resembles purchase "bill of sale" agreements used for real and personal property. The term "cash" does not mean currency in an envelope, but most commonly a wire transfer from the buyer's bank account to the sellers account.

For this structure to work, the buyer and seller have to "meet" at "the number" that is the one time, unconditional payment for the Box. All the uncertainty and risk is transferred to the buyer upon closing, as well as the entire upside potential; the seller's risk is reflected by what it did not receive in compensation, having accepted as full payment "the number." This can be thought of an "as is, where is" sale of rights.[3] For this reason, it can be the hardest to negotiate; but, it is the simplest to understand, and to express in agreement language. We will postpone to Chapter 11 discussion of how parties may converge on "the number." For now, we will assume they have reached agreement on it.

Why would such a structure be acceptable or even preferable to both the seller and buyer? One obvious reason, not to be discounted, is deal simplicity. The likelihood of later disputes is comparatively low because there are no subsequent payments due, and the "as is" language (more elegantly expressed) should be clear to the buyer that any disappointments will not be shared experiences.

There are other advantages to lump sum agreements. Buyers often have a preference, if affordable, to conclude the relationship with the seller and avoid the accounting issues associated with making annual, semiannual, or quarterly royalty payments. Normally, license agreements provide for auditing rights on behalf of the seller. Although there are limitations on the frequency of audits, and the seller must give fair notice before an audit, audits are still a burden on both parties. Further, the results of an audit can lead to a dispute. Furthermore, the disclosure of the buyer's sales is very sensitive business information; even though the seller, or an agreed-upon intermediary, is under confidentiality, buyers do not like having to make such detailed disclosures to anyone, particularly if the parties are competitors or have some prior conflicts.

From the seller's point of view there are also some advantages to paid up licenses. The most obvious advantage is that the seller gets its money; there is no uncertainty, or waiting, for payment. So the seller can invest such funds immediately in its other businesses, or provide returns to owners/stakeholders. The seller also avoids the cost of administering the license on its end. Although royalties should be "checks in the mail," there are administrative costs. For field of use licenses to multiple buyers, problems between different buyers can arise that will require the seller's intervention. For example, Buyer A could be exclusive in Europe, and Buyer B exclusive in the United States; however, Buyer B discovers (or thinks it discovers) that sales from Buyer A are being imported and wants the seller to put a stop to it and even negotiate reparations. If these parties have a competitive history, finding an amicable solution can be harrowing.

Other issues can relate to collecting fixed payments such as minimum royalties. Buyers are not shy about coming back to sellers and arguing for a reduction in the minimums previously negotiated. The seller can simply say "no," but if the buyer ends up terminating the license due to economic necessity, the seller may be left with a technology it cannot easily license a second time especially if key people familiar with the technology have departed.

Buyers have also been known to argue (even years later) for a reduction in royalties. New management at the buyer's company can seek to change the deal because some of the projections have not borne out or simply because they believe that previous representatives agreed to pay too much.

When licensed patents are retained in the name of the seller, there can be disputes over filing or maintaining the patent in a particular country, or dealing with oppositions (as in Europe, where such oppositions are permitted).

Infringement contentions (real or apparent) can arise. Buyers logically do not want to compete with third party infringers especially if they hold an exclusive license but even in the case of a nonexclusive license if such competitors are not likewise paying royalties. How these issues can be handled in a license agreement are outside the scope of this book, but the point here is that because of an ongoing relationship between the buyer and seller, such infringement concerns can lead to complex issues requiring further negotiation.

Issues may arise surrounding future inventions made by the seller. Even though a license agreement might clearly state that the seller is not obligated to provide such future improvements to the seller, or to offer other technologies it may invent that could be used for similar products, the buyer may believe it is entitled to such rights because it is paying royalties year by year and it views the relationship as an informal partnership. Likewise, a seller can feel restricted in its options, not because of a legal requirement, but because it does not want to alienate a company paying annual royalties into its coffers. Sellers may likewise develop expectations that it should be entitled to invention rights to developments made by the buyer in the same technology area as the license.

In general, because royalty-bearing licenses can last 10 years or more, it can be expected that the particular individuals participating in the negotiation will have gone on to other jobs during the life of the agreement. Then the interpretation of the agreement will fall to individuals who were not privy to the original negotiation and who may not feel the same commitment or enthusiasm for the deal as the originators did. For a buyer, a royalty or other obligation is another account payable, a cost of doing business. If there is a way to avoid such costs, buyers may seek to "invent around" the Box as defined in the license. Changing legal standards for patent validity– such as the KSR v. Teleflex decision[4]—could expose a seller to buyer's argument that it should no longer be paying royalties. Changing law can make it less risky for a licensee to challenge the validity of a patent it has licensed.[5]

All these issues have to be weighed against the difficulty of reaching an agreement on a lump sum payment to determine whether this form of an agreement makes the most sense. One factor not mentioned above is a subjective human one.

In some negotiations the two parties were or are adversaries and do not want to work with each other because of a lack of trust or other issues. This situation would favor a lump sum agreement so that the parties can bring the negotiating relationship to a quick close. At the other extreme are cases where the parties have a longstanding strategic relationship that is much broader than the specific license and it is in each party's interest to stay involved with the other; this view would favor some form of royalty or even equity relationship.

The primary difficulty of the lump sum form arises because all future predictions of value have to be reduced to one single number. As the future unfolds, either the buyer or the seller is likely to believe that they should have agreed to a different "number," because it is unlikely that the commercial outcome will be identical to the value ascribed in such a single payment. Another factor that could disfavor single lump sum agreements is the magnitude of the payment is painful for the buyer either because of a demand on its cash or for net income reporting. A large lump sum could also be less desirable for the seller as the entire realization from the sale occurs in one accounting period, and may later face management or shareholders asking "What have you done for me, *lately*?"

Paid Up/Lump Sum: Multiple Payments

A variation of the single payment form is to use the paid up structure but to spread the total payment into a series of *unconditional* payments. This is often still described as a lump sum agreement because all payments occur relatively near closing and do not have any dependencies.

One motivation for the buyer can be simply to divide the payment into two (or more) budget years. Accounting at the business unit level of the buyer can be one reason for this to be attractive, for both the buyer and the seller. Sometimes such distribution of payments can help reach Dealmaking closure. Although if a seller perceives a buyer readily willing to compromise on what had been a significant gap between the buyer's and seller's "number," it may be a sign to the seller that the buyer sees such later payments as being conditional. And a later dispute can be expensive to the seller even if the agreement is black-and-white clear on unconditionality; if the buyer does not pay what's owed, the seller's only recourse may be litigation.

As was discussed in Chapter 7 on the Discounted Cash Flow Method, the DCF equation is used to move monies in time. If the parties agreed on, say, a \$3 million price but to be paid in three equal payments of \$1 million each, at closing, at six months, and the one-year anniversary, then the DCF equation should be used to increase the second and third payments in this example because they have been deferred to the seller's economic disadvantage. Since such payments are unconditional, and assuming there is essentially very low buyer risk of default (such as bankruptcy), then the discount rate could simply be the seller's Weighted Average Cost of Capital (WACC discussed in detail in Chapter 7), or a small premium above the WACC (because there is always some risk).

License Maintenance Payments

A license can include an annual fee unrelated to the above progress payment category or minimum royalties discussed below. The idea is that there is a certain expense and lost opportunity to the seller by maintaining the buyer's license right. Because this is calendar driven it has an inherent simplicity compared to the above progress payment example.

One of the purposes of such maintenance payments is the recognition that regardless of the expectations at the time of original Dealmaking things can change. The champions at the buyer could move on to other opportunities, or the company itself could change strategy or have better opportunities arise. Such changes could result in a simple termination event but it also could lead to a buyer's slowing down commercial development to keep its options open. Such delay, some would say strangulation, would not be the result of unforeseen R&D, manufacturing, or market development challenges. Thus from the seller's perspective, delays imposed by the buyer for its convenience unjustly diminishes the value of the asset because technology generally is a decaying asset. An annual payment obligation puts an economic value on tying up the technology as well as keeping the buyer's "feet to the fire."

Minimum Royalties

Minimum royalties are fixed annual payments that the buyer pays the seller unless the earned royalties exceed the stated minimum. In other words, the buyer owes the seller the larger of the earned royalties or the minimum royalties.

Clearly buyers want to have low minimum royalties (or none), and they want payments to start far in the future. Sellers, on the other hand, want significant minimum royalties, approaching in magnitude to the expected earned royalties according to a pro forma income statement. They want payments to begin at a time when such earned royalties are reasonably expected.

Like everything else in a license agreement, the minimums are negotiated through back and forth bargaining. If the *pro forma* has been conservative, that is, assuming most circumstances do not turn out favorably, then the parties may agree that the royalties projected should be the minimum royalties. If the pro forma has been optimistic, then a fraction should be counted as minimum royalties. Parties seem to negotiate in the range of 25 to 75 percent of the most likely royalties, with sellers pressing for values of 50 percent or higher and buyers arguing for 25 percent.

One of the realities of licenses is that if the minimum royalties exceed the earned royalties for a number of years, the buyer can be expected to come back to the seller and ask (or demand) some relief. If the low return comes despite vigorous investment and development by the buyer, then the seller could be faced with a terminated license if it doesn't go along with a reasonable proposal. Also, a seller who gets back a technology years later as a result of a termination is often unable to license it to a third party because the market window may be gone, the key inventors may be gone, and the start up investment to a third party simply may be too large to find an interested buyer. A third party would also (quite reasonably) question what it was that made the original licensee abandon the technology and its investment.

In the case of nonexclusive licenses, buyers often argue that minimum royalties should not exist because the seller can license the technology to as many buyers as it wishes. From the seller's perspective, each license, though nonexclusive, represents a commitment made and loss of opportunity to do something else. For example, a seller could end up with just two buyers, each with nonexclusive all-fields and all-territories licenses. If one of these buyers is not practicing the technology, and without a minimum has no incentive to terminate its license, then the seller cannot take advantage of creating an exclusive license with its other buyer or induce yet another buyer to take a license to a twice-licensed Box. Such a circumstance could arise because the non practicing buyer simply wants to preserve its options to enter the market but doesn't really intend to do so, but may if some other licensee creates an attractive market. Accordingly, there is no innate reason not to have a minimum royalty even for nonexclusive licenses.

Other Payment Obligations: Bills Due

In some circumstances, the parties may agree that the seller is to perform certain tasks and be reimbursed to some extent by the buyer. One example of this would be a cost-sharing feature of subsequent patent prosecution and maintenance expenses. Another example would be a cost-sharing agreement regarding litigation expenses. Both of such examples normally derive from simple cost accounting by the seller relating with the buyer's payment being the specified apportionment.

There could be other categories of bills due that could be profit contributions to the seller. One example would be where the buyer has committed to using certain services of the seller such as R&D support, or marketing, or a seller manufacturing supply agreement. This could be done by a "take or pay" agreement (i.e., unconditional payment) using a specified hourly rate of certain categories of seller personnel multiplied by a number of hours per period, or by a price per unit of supply times the number of units to be supplied.

Another example would be the subsequent purchase of fixtures or equipment related to the licensed technology or even the factory and land on which the equipment sits. Such transaction could be part of the upfront payment at closing, but there could be reasons why the transaction needs to be deferred and become a bills due example.

Cash *When* Issues

The most obvious challenge with Dealmaking that uses only a Cash *When* is the difficulty of finding acceptable compromises between seller and buyer, especially in face of risk and uncertainty. The seller wants more cash paid, the buyer less; the contrary positions are as old as time, maybe older. The auction format, formal or informal, is one historic solution. If the seller offers the opportunity to many prospective and qualified buyers, it normally has a reasonable basis for belief that it received a fair price. When in a one-on-one negotiation, each side may attempt to assert an auction model as a fairness of standard for its respective offer: The seller contends that its proposed terms would be considered reasonable by one or more prospective buyers if the offer were to be taken to them, and the buyer contrarily asserts that although it cannot represent the nonexistence of an irrational buyer willing to pay more, it is presently offering what would be the winning bid in a context among rational buyers.

A potentially fruitful way of Dealmaking is to supplement Cash *When* structures with Cash *As*, *If*, and *Maybe* structures, as we will now consider.

Cash *As* Pricing Structures

One of the traits of technology is that there can be a significant delay between the time of Dealmaking and the time where the buyer sees any cash inflows, let alone *net* cash inflows or net *income* as we saw in Chapter 7. Such delay, and the associated risks and uncertainty, can significantly affect a buyer's willingness to pay if the payment structure is unconditional and upfront. Hence the appeal of the *as* in Cash *As* structures.

Buyers may prefer such structures because it distributes the cost of the technology to some degree over the time period of its use; however, such preference is by no means a universal rule. Sellers may find Cash *As* structures advantageous because the buyer is willing to pay more for the opportunity even on an appropriately discounted basis.

The most well known form of a Cash *As* structure is a royalty, which is a kind of rent. But there are other forms that can be thought of as different types of royalties or by other terminology such as "progress payments." We are distinguishing Cash *As* structures from the next major section on Cash *If* structures by the following guideline: The Cash *As* examples are payments expected by both the buyer and seller on the commercial realization of the technology; the Cash *If* examples are bonus-like payments triggered on some greater-than-expected commercial result.

Pure Running Royalty

The classic Cash *As* payment structure is a running royalty. The buyer's payment under this structure is determined by a simple formula that uses an agreed upon rate multiplied by the base against which such rate is to be applied. A very common form of this calculation is a running royalty rate defined as a percentage, and the base as the revenue (aka "sales") in dollars of the products made by the technology licensed. In the common language of licensing the running royalty rate percentage is often simply referred to as the "royalty." Sometimes they are called "earned royalties" or "running royalties" to distinguish them from minimum royalties or other forms of payment. However, the amount the buyer pays to the seller based on this calculation is also commonly referred to as the royalty. So if the royalty rate were 5 percent, and the revenues for the relevant period was $1 million, the royalty payment due to the seller, would be $50,000; and both 5 percent and the $50,000 payment could be referred to as the royalty, though technically the 5 percent is the royalty *rate* and the $50,000 is the royalty *payment*, and the $1 million the royalty *base*.

The adjective "pure" in reference to a royalty structure means that the buyer's only payment obligation to the seller is the royalty payment, which occurs (normally) only upon the buyer's receiving revenues from its customers. For this reason, royalties are a form of risk sharing between the buyer and seller. If the buyer never brings the technology to the market, or never receives any revenues from it, no payments are ever made to the seller.

Not all the risk is shared because, as discussed with the DCF Method, the value of an opportunity to the buyer is determined by the NPV. The buyer will normally have revenues far sooner than it begins to experience net cash inflows especially when accounting for all the pre-commercial investments required as was demonstrated in several examples in Chapter 7. So although the existence of revenues is an important benchmark, because it is evidence of a customer and willingness to pay, it does not necessarily follow that the buyer is earning even a current year operating profit.

Royalties are usually expressed as a percentage of revenues received by the buyer for the commercial use of the licensed technology, but they can also be expressed in dollars per item, per pound, per hour, or per anything. When expressed in fixed dollar amounts, it is generally a good idea to provide some form of inflation factor so that over the term of the agreement the value paid to the seller does not plummet in the event of significant inflation. In certain technology areas buyers may expect, and sellers agree, that a deflating royalty rate be used because the value and operating margins are projected to be reduced with technology maturity. It is usually a good idea to simply express the royalty as a percentage of revenues to remove inflation uncertainty and proactively include any rate adjustments based upon expected value over time as will be discussed below.

The advantages of royalties were discussed in Chapters 7 and 8. They provide an opportunity for the seller to receive more than the parties would have or could have expected because the outcome of the license has been greater than expected. Likewise, they can be an advantage to the buyer if the market turns out to be much smaller than expected. With royalty structure, it is more likely that both parties will feel that they got a fair deal years later.

ROYALTY BASE ISSUES: EMBEDDED LICENSED TECHNOLOGY Often overlooked is the importance of the royalty base. What is important to both the buyer and the seller is the magnitude of the check, not the royalty percentage itself. The magnitude of the check is determined by the royalty rate multiplied by the royalty base. Although it may appear that the royalty base is obvious, it should be recognized that the license agreement can last longer than an initial product generation, and the way products are configured by the buyer and sold to its customers can change dramatically during that term. The license agreement must carefully define both the licensed subject matter and which sales are subject to the agreed-upon royalty. If different products with different margins or with different mixes of licensed and unlicensed subject matter are envisioned, then some means of determining a fair split must be devised.

One example of such a situation is as follows. The buyer presently envisions making product A, which is covered by the definition of licensed subject matter, and then selling it to a customer who incorporates A into product B. However, in the future, the buyer decides to go into the business of making product B. Now, how shall the royalty base be calculated? If the buyer is still selling A, then that price can be used as an inferred selling price (sometimes known as a transfer price) to the part of its operations that makes product B and a royalty paid on both sales made externally and internally. If the buyer no longer sells A, then there needs to be some other means of determining a royalty base. Various methods have been used in such situations. One approach is to use a market based price for A based upon sales made by third parties. Another is to calculate a selling price by some formula such as multiplying cost of goods sold by some factor. Yet another way is to create a recipe that determines the value-percentage of B that contains A. The use of different, lower royalty rates on sales of B is yet another way. All of these approaches can be made to work, although there are complexities involved that are beyond the scope of this book.

To the extent possible, the parties should consider all the possible manifestations of the licensed technology so that an agreement can be reached on all matters at the time of the license. If not so done, or if unforeseen circumstances arise, then the parties will have to conduct a future negotiation to determine the appropriate base.

The need for future renegotiations exhibits one of the downsides of Cash *As* structures compared to Cash *When*.

ROYALTY BASE ISSUES: SOMETHING OTHER THAN REVENUES Another royalty base issue arises if a buyer proposes using something other than its revenues. One such alternative is a site license, which is in effect a lump sum/paid up license for a single location, so it is not a true running royalty structure. A variation of this is a rate paid on an hourly use basis such as a power-on meter on a production line making products from the technology. The tricky issue for the seller is knowing what revenues can result from such hourly use. The first generation plant, for example, may make 10 units an hour, each selling for $1,000, so a 5 percent royalty would yield a royalty payment of $500 an hour (10 * $1,000 * 0.05). But what if the licensee can create a second generation plant that makes 100 units an hour? Now the seller's royalty is effectively 0.5 percent.

Other royalty base issues can get even more problematic. Suppose the buyer proposes paying a royalty on its gross margin. Consider the example of forecast revenues of $1 million a year, and again for simplicity a payment agreement using a 5 percent royalty. For a traditional royalty structure based on revenues, the seller would then get $50,000 a year. Now the buyer argues that a "better" alternative, because it is "more fair," would be to use the gross margin as the base. If, in this example, the forecast gross margin (GM) is 50 percent (that is the COGS, Cost of Goods Sold, is equal to $500,000, for an annual revenue of $1 million), so it proposes to pay a 10 percent royalty on such GM. The danger to the seller in this situation is that the buyer has some control over the GM that is not completely dependent upon the technology being used which control could be used by the buyer to reduce the GM and hence the royalty payment. Proposals by the buyer to pay a royalty based upon EBIT are even more risky to the seller because there are substantial additional cost "adjustment" opportunities for the buyer. The nice thing about revenues, the so-called "top line," is it is a directly auditable figure based on third party payments. Reliance on entries "lower down" the income statement from the revenue line toward the "bottom line," royalty calculations are more difficult to audit, involving as they do a kind of buyer payment to itself, and so increase the probability of future disputes. There is an old joke that every company has three sets of books: one they use to report to their shareholders/owners, one they use to pay taxes, and one that they use to operate the business. Using a royalty base other than revenues invites the creation of yet a fourth set of books: one used to pay as low a royalty as possible.

ROYALTY BASE ISSUES: CONVOYED SALES A very contentious subject is that of licensee convoyed sales. An example of such sales is the following. Suppose the licensee is a computer printer and ink manufacturer with very limited market share in printers. Because its sales of printers are small, it is also difficult for it to have large sales of profitable inks or toner. A licensor provides them the technology and right to a new generation printer that should greatly increase their market share. The parties agree to a reasonable royalty on the sales of such printers, but then comes the matter of the inks and toner. The licensee objects to any royalty payment on such consumables under the reasonable argument that it is not licensing in such technology. However, the licensor makes the also reasonable "but for" argument, namely: Without the new printer technology you the licensee would not be selling any revenue (or as much) of such inks and toner.

In some cases the parties agree to a higher than otherwise justified royalty on the printer to account for this. In other situations, the parties might agree to a low royalty on such auxiliary (or convoyed) sales. In the latter case, the parties could compute such royalty base in a way to account for just the increase in ink and toner sales associated with the new printer technology.

ROYALTY STACKING Another important complexity to the use of the royalty structure is the "stacking" risk. Stacking occurs when a buyer needs to acquire license rights from multiple sellers for the same product. In the Rule of Thumb Method (Chapter 6) we showed how a nonsensical result occurs if multiple sellers offering rights necessary for a particular product each claim (say) 25 percent of a buyer's EBIT. Although the same concern exists for lump sum payments, the issue and risk for the buyer is clearer with pure royalty structures. One tactic used by buyers is to shift the responsibility for obtaining any subsequent needed third party licenses or, in the alternative, to reduce the agreed upon royalty because of such needed licenses. Sellers typically do not find this idea acceptable for several reasons; one is that it removes the buyer's responsibility for design around efforts to avoid third party patents when it can reasonably be done; another is that it puts the seller in the position of a guarantor of future IP rights which risk and cost have not been priced into the royalty rate negotiated with the buyer. Sellers of technology typically have not done a freedom-to-practice study (aka: a "clearance study") because at an early stage in commercialization there is not enough product specificity to do so, and there are approximately 3,000 new patents issuing every Tuesday (in the United States), so any such study would be time limited.

ROYALTY RATE ADJUSTMENTS: "WEDDING CAKES" As discussed, a royalty conveys a feeling of fairness to both the buyer and seller because it scales on revenues. In doing so there are no costs to the buyer unless it has revenues, and when it does the royalty is another fixed cost percentage just like other costs it necessarily incurs to make and sell the product.

However, buyers may argue that the *rate itself* should change because, after all, the world changes. One buyer proposal could be to adopt what is known as a "wedding cake" rate structure. These come in two "flavors," annual and lifetime.

An annual wedding cake rate works like this. If the parties agree to a 5 percent royalty, the buyer suggests that this rate should be scaled down with increasing sales as is commonly done in purchase agreements, perhaps proposing: 5 percent for the first $1 million in sales (i.e., resulting in a payment of $50,000), and 3 percent for the next $1 million in sales (an additional payment of $30,000), and 1 percent for all sales beyond $2 million ($10,000 per each additional million in sales).

There are many problems with this approach. First the underlying premise of volume discounts is sharing the economic benefit associated with large order. If the buyer places an order for paper clips, it expects to pay less per clip for a railroad boxcar full of them than it does for a single cardboard box full. Why?

Because there is a built in economy of manufacture and delivery for the paper clip vendor. Because of the buyer's large volume purchase, a volume value opportunity is credited that can be apportioned between vendor and buyer. This is a widely recognized concept—even at the grocery store: 50 pound bags of dog food are priced less on a per pound basis than 5 pound bags.

But does this make sense in licensing? No. There are no manufacturing and delivery costs or economies of scale to be shared in technology licensing. Unlike the paper clip seller our licensor-seller does not save any money or experience a greater operating margin if its "customer" (the licensee) has greater revenues during the year. The annual wedding cake is tantamount to establishing a low royalty rate for the licensee if it can generate high revenues (with respect to the wedding cake structure). The licensor can well make the argument that the technology's benefit to the licensee must be greater for greater annual sales because the licensee's fixed costs including amortization and depreciation of its investment is less on a per unit dollar of revenues so the royalty rate in a wedding cake should *increase*, not decrease.

What about declining profitability with increased sales? This can occur because, for instance, the licensee is heavily discounting the unit price of the products made by the technology. But, in the absence of data, the more likely case is increasing profitability with sales because the buyer is enjoying a volume value opportunity.

There is another wedding cake flavor that makes more sense. Sometimes buyers propose a variant of the annual wedding cake structure by scaling the royalty rate down on *cumulative* revenues over the life of the project. Using the 5/3/1 royalty rate example given earlier, this might be expressed as follows: 5 percent on the first $50 million in cumulative revenues under the license, 3 percent on the next $50 million, and 1 percent on everything over $100 million. This approach could be based on a rational examination of margins because it could happen that with time (expressible in terms of cumulative sales) that competitive pressures will erode margins and so should erode royalty rates. Traditional product lifecycle curves show the profit rate increasing rapidly with rapid growth to product maturing and then gradually declining. But there is no assurance that the licensee will in fact continue to make the product and pay royalties all the way down the increasingly low margin maturity curve, or that conventional product enhancement ("paint it blue and call it new") and/or cost savings in manufacturing or the use of alternate channels of delivery will not maintain peak or near peak profitability for a prolonged period.

The seller is cautioned to not casually adopt such structures without thinking through their potential implications, especially in the context of the total valuation determined beforehand. This is another example where the DCF Method can be very useful because all such wedding cake proposals can be evaluated and compared.

An extreme form of a wedding cake structure is a royalty cap, which works something like this. The buyer says to the seller, "After I've paid you royalties on $10 million in revenues that year (or on $100 million in cumulative sales for that form of structure), all subsequent revenues should be royalty free." This is the "enough is enough" argument and you, the seller, should not want, as the buyer's argument goes, more than the cap.

The seller's response to this should be to explore ways that both the buyer and seller can jointly contribute their profits to some charitable purpose, rather than just restricting such opportunity to the seller. The cap of the seller's profit should be similarly shared by the buyer. This usually puts an end to this line of negotiation.

ROYALTY RATE ADJUSTMENTS: "STEP DOWNS" AND "STEP UPS" The royalty rate can be scheduled to decrease on other triggers and for other reasons than sales revenue. One example of a trigger is the expiration of a certain patent or patents in the seller-licensed portfolio. This can be easy to define because patent expiration is known. However, in a portfolio of licensed patents, it may be that one or more patents expiring do not permit a competitor to make a similar product. In such case, expiration may not have a negative economic impact on the licensee justifying a decrease.

Simple calendar agreement anniversary dates can be another trigger, under similar reasoning as the wedding cake structure based on cumulative sales.

Increases in the royalty rate, "step ups," can be negotiated based upon anticipated events favorable to the buyer, such as the allowance of a key patent, or specific claims in such patent. Another example would the anticipated commercial demonstration of an improved manufacturing process based on additional R&D by the seller.

ROYALTY RATE ADJUSTMENTS: RELATED PARTY SALES A common situation is that of a licensee "selling" product to a related party, such as another division or even another company with common ownership. The reasonable concern from the licensor's perspective is that the sale price, really a transfer price, reflects fair market value as would have occurred if the parties had dealt at arm's length. There are several ways for dealing with this situation. Perhaps the simplest is to prescribe a minimum royalty amount in dollars per unit of sale, to assure that there is at least a reasonable floor on the royalty paid. Another more complex approach, but probably preferred overall, is to compute a fair market value (FMV) for the transaction based upon licensee sales to similar customers in similar circumstances where a price was established by an arms length transaction; obviously this can lead to some analytical complications and disputes.

ROYALTY RATE ADJUSTMENTS: ADD-ON FEATURES Another issue that arises is when a licensee offers the subject technology/product as an add-on to an unlicensed product or service. In such situations it may be ambiguous from a purchase order or sales agreement exactly how much was paid for the licensed subject matter. Or, in other cases, the licensor may offer the licensed product for little or no cost to its customers conditioned on some other purchase. Again some approach of a minimum unit royalty or a royalty based on FMV could be used, although there are additional complications if the licensee makes no sales solely of the licensed subject matter, as there would be no FMV data available. In such cases, the parties could develop a proxy for FMV such as some multiple like two or three of the manufactured cost (COGS), although that in turn can lead to accounting disputes as discussed earlier in this book.

ROYALTY RATE ADJUSTMENTS: ROYALTY-FREE SALES Although licensees are always seeking reduced royalty events, there are some reasonable circumstances where the parties could use such a provision. One such case is initial sales of the product, particularly if it is a very costly item for customers to purchase. It could be in both parties' interests to seed the market by having very low cost initial sales, and forgiving or deferring all or part of such early royalties is one way to do this. Licensors are advised to have some confidence that when they agree to such royalty reduction that the licensee is genuinely reducing its price on the sales, otherwise the licensor is effectively the sole subsidy of the reduction.

Another example is when sales could take place to leading opinion makers, such as to doctors in a teaching hospital. The licensee may have a well considered marketing plan of making its products available at very affordable, below market, terms because of the value of gaining opinion leaders experience with the product.

Also it is common in licensing agreements to exempt from revenues "returns and allowances." Such exemptions are used to define "net revenues" on which the royalty rate is applied.

ROYALTY RATE ADJUSTMENTS: AGREEMENTS TO NEGOTIATE ROYALTIES Because technology licenses can be entered into under significant uncertainty, parties have agreed to defer negotiations on the rates until the products and margins are better known. This can be done in a variety of ways. One is simply to agree to negotiate in good faith and, if negotiations are not successful, to submit the matter of royalty rates to some designated third party to act as an arbitrator. At this stage, both parties would submit their basis for their rates and the arbitrator would evaluate the arguments and set the rate.

Although this can appear advantageous to the seller because the buyer is advancing the technology without knowing the royalty rate that will ultimately be used, there are also advantages to the buyer. Later in the negotiations, the buyer will have a much better understanding of the value and use than the seller. Also, the buyer has the power of termination or selected use. Also, if the parties have an ongoing relationship and expect to do other deals, there should be a mutual confidence that both parties will act reasonably in the process.

Where this approach has been used the actual need for bringing in the arbitrator is rare because neither party wants to deal with the uncertainty, and cost, of a third party decision.

A variant of this approach is to provide a cap of the royalty rate with the rate to be negotiated subject to such cap. To be fair to the seller, at the same time there should be a floor, so the range is bookended.[6] When possible, the parties can also agree on principles or even a recipe for how the royalty rate will be determined within the prescribed range.

A variant of the deferred negotiation strategy is the renegotiation provision. This usually works as follows: The seller proposes that the rates agreed to will exist for a prescribed period, say five years, at which time the parties will renegotiate the license. Buyers are understandably not keen on this idea because they fear that after all the investment in manufacturing, creating the market, and developing sales relationships, excessive claims will be made by the seller. The seller can argue that the rate can also go down, benefiting the buyer, so the provision is not one sided. The key issue hinges on what happens if the parties do not agree. If the seller can effectively terminate the license by demanding an increase in royalties from 5 percent to 50 percent, then the buyer will see this as one sided because it does not have a comparable club to wield.

Two provisions can help equalize this situation. One is the use of a third party arbiter in the event negotiations break down. The other, and better, approach would be to "pre-agree" on the criteria by which any new royalty rate would be established.

For example, suppose a polymer will be introduced that initially will go into the general industrial market at low margins and at a royalty of 3 percent. However, there is a possibility that it could have medical device applications, but this will not be known for years. Although the parties could pre-agree on the royalty rate for such medical applications, there is good reason to agree to renegotiate the license in 5 years to take into account the markets being served and the margins enjoyed.

Royalty Down Payments

When creating a royalty structure, the seller typically expects a down payment on the license. This is particularly true when the license involves some form of exclusivity because the seller is then precluded from selling to others. So, "pure" royalty–only agreements are rare.

The framework for down payment thinking is similar to leasing a car or buying a house: There is a payment schedule in both cases which parallels a royalty, but there is also a required down payment for the loan originator (who has standing of a seller who has turned over something valuable to the lendee). One of the purposes of the down payment is to ensure that the buyer fulfills the commitment by risking the forfeit of the down payment. In licenses, particularly ones involving exclusivity, the seller wants to be assured that the buyer is not just "tying up" the technology without a serious intent to commercialize it. Another important reason for the down payment is that it is, or should be, a measure of what the opportunity is worth. In earlier times in the housing and auto markets, and likely in a future less-reckless lending environment, downpayments in the range of 10 to 20 percent had the effect of creating a sanity check on the lendee. If they can't afford to pay such 10 to 20 percent, how likely are they to afford, or pay, the balance, especially with accumulated interest? More recently, lenders have departed such historic standards, and we have seen the resulting peril.

How much should the down payment be? From the buyer's point of view, in many cases the opinion is that it should be as small as possible. The buyer makes the case that it will have to make significant investments in commercializing the technology, so it "cannot afford" to pay a license fee. This argument is strongly made by small start-up companies that are strapped for cash. On the other hand, the seller can say to the buyer: "Where were you when the page was blank?"[7] The seller logically believes that it has been investing in the technology for a long time and is entitled to payback in recognition for getting it to this state. Further, the seller can point out to the buyer that if the buyer's own R&D organization had created the technology, it would have already spent a significant sum before it could begin its design for manufacturing process in addition to patent prosecution and maintenance expenses.

One common basis for determining a down payment is to perform an NPV analysis and take some percentage as the down payment. A number in the range of 5 to 10 percent is common, but there is no hard and fast rule. Another approach is to take one year's royalties (at maturity) as a down payment; that is, if the royalty climbs from initial sales starting in year three to near maturity in, say, year seven and is then paying $1 million per year in royalties, parties have been known to use such a figure as the basis for the down payment.

Yet another benchmark for a down payment is to use a seller's cost-to-date for its development of the technology. The idea is that this makes the seller "whole" and the scheduled Cash *As* payments will reward both the buyer and seller. If the seller is entering the negotiations because it is closing down an R&D activity that created something of value but not something it intends to bring to the market, then cost-recovery can be perceived as reasonable. If the buyer perceives that all the R&D activities would have had similar costs in its own operation, then the buyer could likewise view such a payment standard as reasonable. However, it is possible that the seller has spent an enormous sum and created a small opportunity, or a small sum and created an enormous opportunity. In the former case the buyer would not find such costs as an appropriate down payment (or even, in an extreme case, the total NPV value of the opportunity), and in the latter case the seller may see such down payment to be too little in correspondence to the opportunity.

There are other issues with the cost down payment standard. One is that sellers typically do not know such costs, regardless of what internal accounting statements provide. The starting IP was unlikely to have been valued, nor was value ascribed to IP contributed to the project as it matured. And R&D projects often include "asides" that result from a development team exploring opportunities not directly relevant to what has been in development. Also a cost based standard does not necessarily relate to the NPV of the opportunity. If the seller has the reasonable goal of scaling a down payment to the size of the opportunity, then the project costs-to-date are irrelevant.

When determining a royalty rate using an Industry Standards Method, sometimes the parties agree to an arbitrary upfront payment that is not scaled on a DCF model because one has not been created. For instance, the seller and the buyer could agree that the subject license closely follows a certain comparable agreement that had a 5 percent royalty and, in addition, $100K as an upfront payment. Again, subject to negotiations between a willing buyer and a willing seller, the parties could agree to such terms without formally considering the $100K as a royalty prepayment.

However, buyers often argue that all down payments should be credited against royalties due. Following the example in the preceding paragraph, the buyer could insist that it pay no royalties until it receives "back" (gets full credit for) the $100K it paid as a down payment. From a seller's perspective, it is usually not a good idea not to receive any royalties once such a structure is agreed upon. Therefore, it may agree to credit some (or all) of the down payment but at a credit rate such that the buyer can credit up to half the royalties then due (as an example) year-by-year until such credit is consumed and full royalty payments are then made. This approach at least enables the seller to receive diminished royalties, beginning with the initial sales.

The discussion thus far has been about the minimum down payment under the presumption that most of the value of the technology will be paid through royalties. There are other options beyond the combinations we have considered, namely: (1) lump sum/paid up, (2) pure royalty, and (3) 5 to 10 percent down payment plus royalty. For instance, the parties could agree to a structure where a significant portion of the NPV, say 50 percent, is paid upfront with the balance as a royalty (which rate is determined by the Goal Seek process described in Chapters 7 and 8). Referring back to the Monte Carlo Method, instead of negotiating between the 20th and 30th percentiles, the parties could agree to using the 30th percentile value but half of the corresponding NPV paid upfront with the other half as a running royalty. Likewise the parties could gravitate toward the weighting of the upfront form of payment with a royalty as a kind of bonus. An example would be an upfront payment of 80 percent of the NPV, with a small royalty rate that (nominally) makes up the balance of NPV. This provides a potential upside to the seller if the revenues exceed the forecast.

Another factor in determining a down payment is the importance of immediate cash to the seller, and to the buyer. In cases where the seller is meeting or exceeding the current year's budget, there actually may be a desire to defer payments; in other cases where there is pressure to meet current year goals, a seller can be highly motivated, even too motivated, to take as large a portion of future gains in a present payment as possible. Similarly buyers who operate business units under the stricture of corporate expectations can prefer to pay more now to gain the benefit of better future operating margins, and can afford to do so because of current year earnings. Other buyers play the role of the vagrants living under a bridge and seek to defer all payments into the future when perhaps some other operating manager will have to pay them.

Progress Payments

Another kind of down payment is known as a progress payment. When the delay from the time of the license until initial sales are made is long, sellers often expect to receive some additional lump sum payments after the initial down payment but before an initial royalty on revenues would be due. One common example is in the pharmaceutical industry where new drugs go through prescribed stages (Phase 1, 2, and 3 clinical trials, and the filing of an NDA, New Drug Application). Other examples could include receipt of an initial minimum product order, completion of a factory of a prescribed capacity, approval for sale in a particular territory, or annual revenues exceeding a threshold value. As with other Wheelbarrow payments, clear definitions are needed to minimize the risk for later dispute as to whether a threshold was reached.

As the technology develops past certain thresholds, the buyer's risk decreases and reduces the RAHR discounting applied to investments needed for the next stage and tends to confirm the utility of the licensed technology. These deferred lump payments are a kind of Real Option payment structure. As each threshold is crossed there is an additional, incremental option cost to maintain the option. The final exercise price could be one final payment (in lieu of a running royalty) or the year-by-year royalty.

As with the down payment, the issue arises as to whether such progress payments are to be credited against royalties due. One simple answer is "yes" for the same reasoning already discussed. However, from an option perspective the answer is more complicated. Let us consider a simple example. The seller of a commercial real estate wants $1 million for a particular piece of urban property. A buyer agrees that this is a fair value but cannot commit to payment until and unless it can put together an investment consortium to construct commercial office space and manage it thereafter. So the buyer asks for a one year option to try to put together the financing and perhaps gain some initial approvals. The buyer proposes, and the seller agrees on a one year option price $100,000. Setting aside time value of money, risk adjusted or not, what should the buyer owe the seller one year hence if it exercises the option, $1 million or $900,000?

The "prepayment" argument, favored by any buyer, is that only $900,000 is then due to the seller. But the seller says emphatically "no" because the buyer tied up the opportunity for a year for its convenience, however reasonable, and could have walked away at no cost at the end of such year. Therefore the buyer receives more than just the property: It received *a right* to the property (for the year) and then *the property itself* (which the parties agreed was worth $1 million). So the buyer got two things, not just one. So the $100,000 option payment is in addition to the value of the property.

Clearly the practical significance of these two perspectives hinges on the magnitude of the option payment. But, assuming the option payment matters, what's the right answer? For options on equities, as we discussed with the Yahoo example in Chapter 8, and with real property, the option payment is in addition to the cost of exercising the option (the $1 million in this real estate example). With technology licensing the issue is more complicated. One reason has to do with the effect of the buyer terminating its license right. There could be a termination fee owed to the seller, and/or there could have been license maintenance fees paid. There could also have been fees to prosecute and maintain licensed patents and/or improvement patents, new R&D results, further market development and the like. All such licensee-funded achievements would typically revert to the seller upon termination. So unlike the commercial real estate example, the seller may not be left completely empty handed upon the election of a licensee/optionee declining to make a certain progress payment and thereby terminating its rights.

Cash *If* Pricing Structures

The third category of cash pricing structures is conditional payments or reduction in payments, meaning that, unlike royalties and progress payments discussed previously, there is no automatic expectation that the triggers and changes discussed here will occur.

Royalty Rate Adjustments: "Step Downs" and "Step Ups"

In the above section on Cash *As* we considered examples of anticipated royalty rate step ups and step downs. Such events can be included in agreements without an expectation that they will occur.

Although any agreement between two parties can be renegotiated, if both parties assent, it is possible for the original agreement to include a provision *compelling* a renegotiation upon some triggering event. The issue could arise when the buyer/licensee faces massive investment in commercializing the technology such that terminating the license, or threatening to do so, is not a reasonable option, yet the originally provided royalty rate could be unfair or even onerous.

The motivation behind such buyer pain is obvious. However, when the seller tries the mirror argument—namely, if this turns out to be wildly more profitable than anticipated we should renegotiate the royalty upward— it tends to fall on buyer deaf ears.

There are a variety of circumstances where it would make sense to the parties to provide in the license agreement reduced royalty rates, so-called "step downs," upon some licensee-controlled event. One example would be the conversion of an exclusive license to nonexclusive at the buyer's option. Normally, a license is negotiated to be exclusive or nonexclusive for its life. However, the parties could agree that after a fixed number of years, the license converts to nonexclusive, and at that point the royalty rate "steps down" to some lower, specified value.

Licensees are not likely to find it acceptable to have such conversion occur upon the licensor's election, but there could be instances where it would be in the parties' mutual interest, such as the instance of a large customer in the market for a second source.

One can envision a buyer/licensee seeking other step down triggers, such as market share for the licensed product, or the presence of a competing non-infinging technology. However, such conditions would be difficult to define, which invites a later dispute. Also, the predicate of the deal is that the buyer/licensee is taking the business risk of being in the marketplace. As the buyer, it will own the rights to exploit commercially the technology and, so, determine product features/functions, marketing, pricing, and so forth. Reducing the seller's royalty based on less-than-favorable outcomes could well be making the licensor suffer for less-than-stellar performance by the licensee, which performance has already harmed the licensor by the reduced magnitude of earned royalties.

Conditional royalty step ups could also be established. In the double hump Monte Carlo example at the end of the Chapter 8 we saw there was dramatic difference in buyer NPV depending on which of two manufacturing processes would be demonstrated. In that example, the opportunity only made sense if the low cost process was demonstrated which led to the idea of an option approach. But we can envision a situation where there would be a positive NPV for both manufacturing processes under development, with the more favorable one justifying a higher royalty rate. In such a situation the agreement could provide two royalty rates, the lower one for the use of a less economically attractive process and a higher one for the more efficient one.

Royalty "Kickers"

One interesting variation on royalty agreements involves a bonus factor commonly known as a "kicker." It is the seller's version of the buyer's "step down" discussed in the last section.

The situation arises as follows. The parties agree on a reasonably certain financial projection of sales, costs, royalties, and profitability, say sales of $100 million per year at maturity and a royalty of 5 percent. However, the seller believes there are other markets that could be reached by the commercialized technology that are much larger and more profitable. The buyer counters that if such additional sales occur then there will be additional royalties at the rate of 5 percent. However, the seller argues that the 5 percent figure was agreed upon by considering certain fixed investment costs and other operating costs (overhead) that do not scale up linearly with volume. Put another way, if this is a $500 million per year sales opportunity, it will be much more profitable than the $100 million scenario, and the seller would be entitled to a higher royalty rate.

One way to handle such a circumstance is by means of a kicker that adds a payment to the seller after certain sales thresholds have been reached. Continuing with this example, the parties could agree that if the sales in any given year are more than $300 million, there will be an incremental royalty of 1 percent of sales over $300 million, and a second kicker of another 1 percent for sales over $500 million. The resulting payoff table would look like this:

Sales = $100 million	Royalty = 5% = $5 million
Sales = $300 million	Royalty = $5% = $15 million
Sales = $400 million	Royalty = 5%, + 1% of $100 million = $21 million
Sales = $600 million	Royalty = 5%, + 1% of $300 million + 1% of $100 million = $34 million

In the third case above, the kicker provided an incremental $1 million over what would have otherwise been paid. In the fourth case, the kicker provided an additional $4 million.

Such kickers could be applied to a series of lump sum payments. As another example, the parties could agree that the deal will be a license fee of $6 million, paid in three equal $2 million lump sums—one at closing, one at the first anniversary, and one at the second anniversary. In addition, a kicker of an additional $2 million will be paid if sales in year five exceed $200 million. This provides some of the advantages of a royalty structure but with less complexity.

As in our discussions on royalty bases, using as the trigger or scale of a kicker, some value below the sales line on an income statement is perilous. Buyers, especially large buyers, have enormous discretion in creating bottom line numbers at the product, product line, or division level. Also, buyers are subject to reorganizations that could cause the application of bottom line provisions to be incomprehensible. Buyers should likewise be concerned about tying kickers to product profits because it opens up the possibility of a costly dispute and an interpretation beyond the limits of the original negotiation.

Royalty Buyouts

In some circumstances, the parties (especially the buyer) may seek to have a buyout provision. Such a provision is basically an option, exercisable by the buyer, to pay off the remaining financial obligations of the license by making a previously agreed upon final lump sum payment.

The way it would normally work is that there is some formula for the buyout option that varies with time. If the buyout is exercised early in the license, then the lump sum payment is large because the foregone royalties were expected to be large due to the number of years remaining. The lump sum would decline with time as the number of years bought out declines. One way this can be done is to multiply the current year royalty by some ratio of the remaining number of years. For example, the parties might agree that the buyer can buy out the license by making a lump sum payment equal to the current year's royalties in dollars multiplied by half the remaining years of the license. In other words, the buyout takes place for 50 cents on the dollar, assuming the royalties were to stay flat for the remaining life of the agreement.

The financial basis is the DCF Method. For each year of the license, the model calculates the NPV of all subsequent royalty payments using an appropriate k value. Based upon the perceived risk and estimated sales, a guideline can be developed.

Generally, such a provision is advantageous to the buyer, because the buyer has an option only it can exercise and that presumably, will only be exercised if it results in a better deal for the buyer. Sellers may find such risk acceptable if the formula used to calculate a prepayment provides a reasonable return. Care must be given to variability in royalties paid year by year. For example, it could happen that there would be a "down" year in royalties because of some problems with supplies, or a factory fire, or a one-year blip in the market; the seller would not want to enable the buyer to use a low royalty year as the basis of calculating a prepayment of the remaining royalties.

Termination Fees

License agreements are not usually entered into with the intention to terminate by either party. However, a termination provision is typical in contracts and our issue is: Should there be a cost to the terminator? The seller typically has limited termination rights, limited to some good cause, such as a material breach by the buyer/licensee. Because the licensee cannot normally be compelled to complete or continue commercialization it usually has a termination right.

A license negotiation could result in an agreement with modest upfront and limited maintenance or minimum royalty payments with the expectation that later payments would more than compensate the seller. If the licensee in such circumstance had the right to terminate its license at no cost at any time, there could create an economic disadvantage to the licensor that the parties did not envision at the time of negotiating the license. One way to protect against such result is to provide a termination fee to be paid by the licensee to the licensor in the event of its election to terminate prior to some specified date.

There are two drivers to such termination fee: the option value benefit enjoyed by the licensee, and a breakup fee of the costly negotiation. As discussed elsewhere, required payments and other investments by a licensee can be considered to be option costs, preserving its rights in the opportunity. Depending upon when and how the licensee can terminate the agreement, the payments made to that point may be sufficient to reflect the option benefit it received and the opportunity loss to the licensor. If this is not the case then it is reasonable for the seller to expect a buyer termination payment.

A somewhat parallel circumstance is termination of provisional M&A (Merger & Acquisition) agreements, *deal* breakup. Such agreements are complex and costly to negotiate. The acquiree (seller) typically discloses extensive business information including sensitive trade secrets to the acquiror (buyer). Termination fees, also known as "breakup" or "kill" fees, are invoked when a transaction agreed to is not consummated by the buyer. When a deal breakup occurs, such fees often become publicly known. They appear to be in the range of 2 to 3 percent of the transaction value though some fees have been as high as 5 percent.[8] The 2009 purchase of Sun Microsystems by Oracle was reported to include a breakup fee of $260 million (about 3.5 percent of the deal value). With M&A transactions in the multibillion dollar range, such fees are a substantial penalty for a buyer walking away from its purchase commitment.

License transactions could have a deal breakup fee for the same reason as an M&A context. But there is a separate parallel for a buyer's termination of the license, especially if it has tied up the technology during an important window of commercial opportunity for the technology and made only nominal payments prior to termination.

If a license agreement has been structured so that the buyer has made appropriate levels of payments throughout the term of the license then the seller can consider itself having been properly compensated. This can be augmented by data, improvements, and other commercial results that are conveyed by the buyer to the seller upon termination. However, if the agreement does not adequately compensate the seller for the commitment made to the buyer a termination fee can be appropriate. A universal guideline for license termination fee is difficult to establish. If the NPV of the transaction was $1 million, then a 2 or 3 percent fee is only $20,000 to $30,000, a range that might not have covered even the Dealmaking costs.

Cash *Maybe*: Options

An option is the right to make a future decision. Normally it presumes an exclusive right: If a buyer seeks an option on a license, it normally expects to receive the exclusive right to acquire such license. However, there are cases where the buyer is only seeking assurance that he can acquire a freedom to practice at some future point. In such cases an option to a nonexclusive license is sufficient.

Option agreements can be very useful in technology licensing because they allow a buyer a period of time to conduct further due diligence, including possible test marketing. During this period the buyer has the assurance that the deal will not be "sold out from under him" (the phrase refers to the retailer who repossesses a bed while the occupant is still in it). For sellers, options are both good news and bad news. The good news is that a serious buyer exists, and there has been some payment for the option. However, the bad news is that during the due diligence period the seller normally (for exclusive options) is prohibited from further marketing the opportunity (the so-called "no shop" provision) and other interested buyers must be turned away. Thus, it is possible that a more motivated buyer could offer more than the buyer holding the option but would have to be turned down. Finally, if the buyer-optionee elects not to exercise the option, other prospective buyers are likely to find out; this could cast a pall over subsequent marketing efforts. Some options require a termination fee to compensate sellers for the pall effect. Although not common, some options provide for march in provisions similar to conditional offers in real estate: If a third party shows up with a bona fide offer, then the optionee has a shortened period of time to exercise the option or lose it.

Another issue to be considered in option agreements is what happens if the buyer says yes. If the buyer wants to know all the financial and other key terms prior to exercising the option, then essentially that means the entire agreement will have to be negotiated upfront, a costly exercise in both time and money. Without such agreement, what would a "yes" entitle a buyer? Generally the answer is, only a good faith effort to negotiate within a prescribed period.

The key elements of an option agreement are (1) the scope of the option (defining the technology rights), (2) the duration of the option, (3) restrictions and obligations on the seller, (4) rights of the buyer (access to information, consultation, etc.), (5) what happens if the buyer says "yes," and (6) payment(s) by the buyer to secure the option (the Wheelbarrow).

Like upfront fees, option fees can be considered to be down payments on the opportunity. Consider a case where the parties agree that the NPV of the opportunity is $ 10 million, subject to confirmation by due diligence. They might agree to the following approach: an option fee of $250,000 upfront and nonrefundable (or creditable), an option termination fee of $250,000 in the event the option is not exercised, an upfront fee for the license of $500,000, and the balance of the value expressed in royalties. Normally the option fee does not subtract from the NPV of the deal because the buyer got more than the deal itself: It received the option to the deal, which has value of its own, and then the opportunity to acquire the deal.

Options can be very useful when two parties anticipate doing deals regularly. In that case, an almost form-like agreement can be negotiated once and used quickly many times. Such an approach also allows the option to have unspecified execution value, subject to negotiation, because parties expecting a long-term relationship have confidence that both parties have a stake in being reasonable.

Consideration Forms Beyond Simple Cash

In all the previous examples, the compensation to the seller was in some form of cash. There are in addition many possible non-cash kinds of compensation that the buyer can provide. In Chapter 3 the discussion on the Technology Box made the point that the seller should consider all the assets it can offer to a potential buyer beyond just, for instance, bare patents. The seller is likely in a unique position as the owner/developer of the technology to include assets that increase the likelihood that a potential buyer will make the investment required for due diligence (and, so, improved "deal doability"), reduce the risk perception of commercialization, and understand, more broadly, markets that the technology could be used to serve. In the same way, a buyer can make a deal more attractive to the seller by including non cash assets.

Supply Contract

One example is a supply contract. A seller could license technology to a buyer and receive as compensation the right to purchase the buyer's licensed products. This could be priced at fair market value or (as a kind of cash compensation) at a discounted price, perhaps as a partial offset to royalties due or other payment. Alternatively, the deal could be structured so that the buyer pays a royalty to the seller for sales to third parties and must supply a certain minimum quantity of the product to the seller.

Purchase Contract

Another example is a purchase contract. In this case, the buyer is obligated to buy raw materials from the seller as part of the license agreement. (Note: In both of these examples there are some potentially significant legal issues that need to be carefully reviewed by counsel.)

Other Kinds of Supply/Purchase Commitments

Both the buyer and seller have or control other assets unrelated to the subject Dealmaking. Just as with other forms of trading, the parties could incorporate such unrelated assets as a partial form of compensation. The buyer could manufacture some products that could be of value to the seller, and vice versa. Buyer IP rights, such as patents be they improvement patents or patents related to some other technology, could be another form of cash substitute. Likewise other buyer assets in the form of intangible or tangible property, or services, could be used. As discussed earlier, the ideal negotiation closure opportunities occur when one side can offer something that costs them little and the other side values it much.

Sellers prefer cash because it gives them ultimate future decision-making options. Buyers however are themselves selling products and may wish to substitute, to some extent, such products and reduce its cash outflow obligation.

R&D, Consulting Commitment

Another common form of compensation in technology licenses is the payment by the buyer for additional R&D to be performed by the seller. In many cases the reason a technology license arises is because there is an R&D capability within the seller that is not or cannot be used directly for commercial purposes. In these and other cases, the seller can be highly motivated to receive funding to support the people and labs doing such work. This can also be important to a buyer because it can speed the commercialization process and/or lead to enhanced features in a second generation embodiment.

There are numerous examples of technology sellers who perform R&D as their core "business." Included in this category would be universities, government labs, and private R&D entities such as SAIC, Inc., Battelle Memorial Institute, (formerly) AD Little, and SRI International.

One element of value to such R&D sellers is to have funding to sustain active programs within the field of the licensed subject matter or in other fields. This can lead to circumstances where the license fee(s) can be committed in a way that benefits both the seller and the buyer. For example, a portion (or all) of the upfront license fee could be committed by the seller to further a not yet investigated area related to the licensed technology and which, if successful, could become the basis for a second generation product line. By earmarking such expenditure, with terms and conditions regarding rights to new inventions, the buyer can get more for its payment than just the subject license and, thereby, justify paying more than sought by the seller just for the offered TR, the Technology Rights in TR R^k A DE. From the perspective of the R&D seller, valuation in these situations brings in other factors and rules of thumb, such as the "man year rule" or the "invention factory rule" which are outside the scope of this book.

The following question arises: Should payment by the buyer for such R&D services come out of the NPV of the deal? Using the $10 million NPV example, suppose that the seller proposes an upfront cash payment of $500,000, the balance of the $9.5 million in royalties, and that the buyer commits to funding $1 million in additional R&D at the seller's lab. From the buyer's perspective, this now looks like an $11 million deal.

What happens here depends on the nature of the R&D and the rights flowing from such work. If the $1 million in R&D was to be precisely the work that the buyer was going to have to do anyway, and the buyer obtains, for no additional consideration, all rights to the fruit of such R&D, then it should not be considered as coming out of the $10 million (assuming that is the agreed-upon figure) to which the seller is entitled. Taking the other extreme, if the R&D is not going to aid the buyer's commercialization, and the buyer receives no rights to the results, then the buyer will naturally take the position that the seller may spend its money however it likes but that it should come out of the $10 million (or elsewhere from the seller's budget), not as an additional buyer's payment.

Special Circumstances with "Cashless" Buyers

In some transaction situations the buyer is unwilling or unable to pay in cash, either on closing or in the near future. Startup companies are one notable category; even successfully backed startups are notorious for creativity in the avoidance of writing checks. Another category of cashless buyer is an economically distressed buyer who may have a very solid plan for profitability but is in a cash poor position at closing. A third example is third world and even second world companies; once one leaves North America, Western Europe, and Japan, it is common to encounter negotiating situations where the buyer is unable or unwilling to pay in hard currency, especially upfront.

In the case of startup companies, we will consider special issues of equity in exchange for TR. For distressed companies, there are usually two avenues available to make the deal economics (DE) work. One way is by delaying or reducing payments otherwise due until the commercialized technology is anticipated to yield positive net cash flow and be compensated by increased later payments because the seller in fact has become a risk capital lender as well as a technology provider. A second way is by creative investigation into non cash ways that the buyer can remunerate the seller, such as supply agreements under highly favorable terms either of the licensed technology or some other product made by the buyer.

In the case of third world companies, in addition to the two ways used with cash poor companies there has arisen a third and ancient way: barter. The way barter works in a licensing context is generally as follows. The buyer agrees to pay a third party in the buyer country using the buyer's country's currency for a determined quantity of an exportable commodity with a quantifiable value. The third party then ships prepaid the exportable commodity to a fourth party in a first world country. The fourth party then pays for the shipment by paying the technology seller in a bankable currency. There are numerous variants possible. For example, there could be multiple intermediaries buying and reselling the exportable commodity until it becomes a bankable currency to the technology seller. Another variant is that the third world company "pays" some third party not in the third world currency but with some other commodity that it makes or resells. Clearly the use of bartering is much more complex, not to mention risky, than being paid in a first world currency. However there may be licensing opportunities where a third world company is the best route to the marketplace. In such a situation entering into a barter transaction may be warranted.

Public Acknowledgment

Sellers, especially inventors at the seller, may welcome credit and publicity associated with the buyer's sales of products made by the licensed technology.

Seller Termination Rights ("March In Rights")

Sellers of an exclusive license may be able to negotiate a "march in" right to convert the license from exclusive to nonexclusive, reduce the allowed fields of use, reduce the allowed territories, and/or terminate the license entirely based on some standard of inadequacy or nonperformance by the licensee. Depending on the magnitude and timing of maintenance and minimum royalties and other periodic payments, the licensor may be harmed by a licensee's languid execution of its license rights. Some licensors, such as government agencies, require a march in provision to prevent the hypothetical situation of some oil company buying rights to the proverbial 200 mile-per-gallon carburetor solely to keep it off the market.

Such a march in right provision should reduce the seller's risk perception, which, in turn, may result in reduced buyer payment obligations, or in other situations may be the key to seller's willingness to negotiate with a "high risk" aspiring buyer in the first place.

Special Form of Cash *If*: Equity

A buyer can pay for a seller's technology using its equity. If the buyer is a public company, there is usually no point in doing so for the buyer or the seller. However for startup companies, especially those being founded or developed based upon the subject technology, equity is not available to the public, and there is the hope that a significant appreciation in value that can occur, especially by an initial public offering (IPO) of a perceived "hot" opportunity. That prospect of significant appreciation combined with agreement complexity has led some to call equity based Wheelbarrows 'the olympics' of licensing.

The 1995 to 2000 (Y2K) IPO Frenzy, and Aftermath

From the IPO of Netscape in 1995 into the year 2000 (Y2K) was a remarkable period of abundant, high risk investing by venture capitalists (VCs) and the general public through IPOs in technology equities. Through that window of opportunity came Yahoo, eBay, Amazon, and 1000 other companies most of which are no longer in existence. These internet opportunities and related businesses in optical fiber, photonics, high-speed switches and routers, as well as computers, storage, and software that made it all work, led to an explosion of investment interest by private capitalists, high risk capitalists, strategic acquirers (such as Cisco), investment bankers, and the IPO public. This led to the creation of enormous wealth in some situations, a financial black hole in others, and both (wealth, followed by a black hole) in still others.

VC STATISTICS FOR 1995 THROUGH 2000: THE FRENZY The venture capital numbers for this period are staggering. According to Vinod Khosla, a general partner with famous Silicon Valley venture capital (VC) firm of Kleiner Perkins Caufield & Beyers, in a talk given at an annual VC meeting in San Francisco in mid June 2002, here are the VC statistics for the period 1995 through 2000:[9]

- 14,463 companies received VC funding
- 978 went public (less than 7 percent)

- 1,529 were acquired (less than 11 percent; for a total with the IPOs of only 17 percent)
- 1,180 have by mid 2002 gone out of business
- 10,776 were somewhere looking for customers, money, and an exit

At its recent peak in March 2000, the "DICE" (digital information, communication, and electronics, including telecom and software/IT, but not life sciences, pharmaceuticals, health care, or biotech) public companies comprised some 44 percent of the total $17 trillion of market cap of all U.S. companies. In the three-year period 1998 through 2000, VCs invested in more than $171 billion in 17,000 deals with nearly 14,000 U.S. companies.[10]

However, as we saw with the Yahoo example in Chapter 8, by 2001 many of these companies, along with many other technology companies (such as the fuel cell examples in Chapter 7) were deeply wounded. A contemporary haiku captures the spirit of that time: *Before/One hundred million/Could not keep us in business/Jeez do we look dumb.*[11]

VC STATISTICS 2003–2007, EQUITY IN THE AFTERMATH The VC industry remained an important source of investment in high risk technology-based companies even after the boom and bust around Y2K, though it has been criticized of producing low returns for the investment risk. In the five year period 2003 through 2007, VCs have invested an average of just under $25 billion a year in over 3,000 deals a year. So lots of money is still available, though only about 25 percent of such spending is for what is considered "seed" or "startup" categories; most of the investment, both deals and dollars, are in "expansion" and "late stage" opportunities.

And the IPO exit window is not what it was. There were 87 IPOs in 2007, declining to exactly zero in the second quarter of 2008, the first such quarter since 1978.[12] In 2008, more than 80 companies *withdrew* their announced IPOs because of the unfavorable public market for startup companies. Of those that went public in 2007, less than 30 percent are, by the start of the second quarter 2008, above their IPO price.[13] A further sign of distress is the median age of VC backed companies from founding to IPO: In 2007 it reached 8.6 years, which is the highest value since 1980.[14] A similar, though not as dramatic, downturn has occurred with the other VC exit path, the "strategic acquisition."

YET, THERE WAS GOOGLE (IPO 2004) The poster child of equity based success is Google. In 2004, just a few years after the Y2K aftermath it went public[15] at $85 a share establishing a market capitalization of more than $20 billion, based upon its 2003 revenue of less than $1 billion and net income (EAT) just over $100 million. Overnight, as it were, its principal founders, former Stanford students, and Ph.D. "dropouts," Sergey Brin and Larry Page each became multi-billionaires (Google was founded by Brin and Page in 1998). Stanford University, which licensed the basic search patent (US 6,285,999B1, issued Sept. 4, 2001) to Brin and Page, received 1.76 million shares of Google, and so, realized approximately $200 million from the equity-based license depending upon when they sold their shares. In 2007 it reached its current peak stock price of more than $700 a share, more than 8x its IPO price.

The Equity of Equity

Because of the difficulty in determining one single number as an equitable valuation, and the subsequent dissatisfaction that one or the other parties can be expected to feel, it is common for the parties to instead structure the valuation so that both the buyer and the seller share some of the risk and some of the reward associated with uncertain outcomes. Royalties are a very useful and simple means of doing this, which is in fact why they exist as an option—the marketplace created the royalty concept because of the need for dealing with vast future uncertainties. This "tying together" of like interests, is one key advantage of a royalty structure. A second advantage is that it does not require the specification of one absolute dollar amount as the equitable consideration for a license; so in this sense, it is easier to reach agreements between sellers and buyers, and it is easier for both the seller and the buyer to feel that what they are to receive is fair. This latter virtue is important because, in most cases, there are multiple individuals at both companies who must approve the deal in order for it to take place. A licensing negotiator can sometimes face more difficulty trying to negotiate a consensus in his or her own organization than with the other side. Royalties and equity make this easier than lump sum payments.

COMPARISON TO CASH *AS* ROYALTIES However (and there is always a "however") royalties do not completely mirror the profitability or cash flow that will result from putting a technology into commerce. Royalties, as the term is normally used, apply to a base of sales, the so called "top line" of an income statement. Profitability, or cash flow, occurs at the "bottom line." In between are a lot of costs (and a lot of accounting). The buyer will feel success or failure, relative or absolute, by what happens principally at the bottom line.[16] Accordingly, it is possible that the seller could be quite happy with a royalty cash inflow based upon some percentage of sales, while the buyer is quite unhappy because after all the costs, including the royalty payment, the net on the bottom line is small, zero, or even negative. Because royalties are tied to sales, which occur only if there are customers, they are a step toward risk sharing between the seller and buyer, but a royalty structure does not equally balance the risks and interests between the parties. It is reasoning similar to this that leads boards and senior management to use stock options as a behavior motivating and rewarding tool, particularly for startups.

From time to time, various buyers have proposed a modified royalty structure where the royalty base is in the bottom line, EBIT, or EAT (see Chapter 7), instead of being sales based, arguing that such a net income basis is a truer reflection of the value of the license. However, because all the costs between the top line and the net income of the bottom line are largely controlled by the buyer, there are only rare and special cases where the parties agree to basing the royalty on any value below the top line and doing so is perilous to the seller as recent public accounting mischief has made all too clear.

There are certain other issues that arise with royalty agreements. Consider the following situation. The seller licenses patents and trade secrets (know-how) to the buyer and, in so doing, launches the buyer in a new business. As the technology is developed and optimized, the buyer creates and then sells products that look generally like the licensed subject matter, but such products are outside the claims of the licensed patents and the scope of the licensed trade secrets. As a result, the buyer argues that it owes the seller nothing. The seller, in looking carefully at the terms of the license agreement, concludes that although the buyer is technically correct, an unjust outcome has occurred because despite having put the buyer in business, the seller will not receive any future compensation. The buyer's response is "a deal is a deal" and I have no obligation to pay for what I am not using (i.e., I am not benefiting from the scope of the licensed patent claims or trade secret information). Equity-based agreements can help prevent this situation.

With equity agreements, the seller receives a share in the company that receives the licensed technology. If the above scenario unfolds, it would not limit the seller's future prospects because it owns stock in the company, not a royalty right in specific kinds of sales. In this sense, the consideration received by the seller is somewhat like ownership of a mutual fund comprised of anything and everything the buyer can or will create in terms of value. Even if the buyer abandons the licensed technology and instead opens a hamburger stand, as long as the corporate entity remains, the seller will retain its equity share in a burgers and fries enterprise.

Equity deals can also create a downside outcome for the seller. Consider a buyer that has two products, one based on the licensed subject matter and one developed independently. In this scenario, the licensed subject matter is wildly successful in both a top line and bottom line sense. However, the second product turns out to be a disaster and causes the loss of all the profits of the firm. Had the seller a royalty-only interest, it would have received payment possibly unaffected by the misfortune occurring elsewhere in the buyer's company, provided the buyer continued to make sales of the licensed technology. But with an equity interest, the "mutual fund" right the seller acquired could result in the destruction of all value of the company. Other concerns of sellers, which are outside the scope of this book, have to do with liability.

THE EXTREME UPSIDE OF EQUITY The extreme upside potential for equity is the common reason for potential seller interest in equity based compensation. A simple consideration can show why such extreme upside is so extreme.

Royalties are based on revenues. Using our previous 5 percent royalty rate as an ongoing example, this means that the seller receives 1/20 of the buyer's revenues in periodic payments, paid for the duration of the license. However, the present value of future distant payments trend significantly downward as we saw in the examples of Chapter 8. Using an RAHR value of 30 percent, even $100 million in buyer revenues in the eighteenth year has a present value of such royalty to the seller of less than $900,000.

The value of equity in a "hot" IPO context can also scale on revenues. In the above Google example, its IPO value was more than 20x its prior year *revenues*, an extraordinary multiple. Using a 10x multiple of IPO value to revenues, and assuming $50 million in such revenues in 5 years, resulting in $500 million in market cap, again discounted at an RAHR of 20 percent, results in an NPV of more than $200 million.

For a seller, which is preferable: negotiate for (A) a royalty based compensation, such as the 5 percent example, or (B) seek an equity share that would entitle it to some portion of the potential $500 million market cap value in five years?

Technology buyers going down the VC-funded startup path generally prefer to offer equity. This conserves scarce, costly cash, and eliminates the cost effect of royalties that decrease earning potential. Sellers, for the above reason, may find this attractive from their perspective, or they may prefer some combination of nominal cash, royalties, and a reduced equity.

Another potentially attractive feature of equity for the seller is that buyers funded by VCs are wholly focused, some might say desperately focused, on rapid commercialization and a liquidity event. The VCs and the management team are primarily compensated by equity and options to equity, aligning their interests with the seller holding equity.

Yet there are reasons why sellers can find equity structures unattractive. Startup companies, even those funded by the wisest VCs and staffed by experienced, savvy management, are fragile entities, with limited room for missteps. There are large incumbent companies also seeking great new business opportunities. Customers may not readily take the risk of committing to startups and their business models. VCs can, and do, readily "pull the plug" on funding, or find the need to raise substantial new sums that will dilute the seller's initial technology ownership share. There is a reason why companies and high net worth individuals who invest in VC funds expect average returns well in excess of 20 percent—they recognize they are taking large risks. Any seller taking equity in lieu of other more solid forms of compensation should do the same.

So, in the above calculation example, we would be advised to employ a RAHR value substantially greater than 20 percent, perhaps 50 percent or more. At 50 percent, the NPV of that IPO example is reduced from \$200 million (as calculated above) to \$65 million. And even the famous Google enumerated a long list of risks it, and any investor, faced at the time of the IPO.[17]

A Startup Capitalization Example

Equity based investment is based upon a business plan, which is the DCF (and/or Monte Carlo) Method for creating a business from scratch. Equity investors typically like to release their funding in phases, known as "rounds." A round is typically defined as a time period of 12 to 24 months, at the end of which additional funding will be needed in a subsequent round. A common business model shows the need for three or four rounds before a startup becomes publicly traded through an IPO or becomes acquired by another company.

For simplicity, let us assume the business plan shows the need for \$5 million for one year, then \$10 million for the second year, and \$20 million for the third year, at the end of which the start-up will have demonstrated sufficient sales and perhaps profits to enable it to attract an underwriter and a public market or equivalent interest from a strategic acquirer. Such a plan would ask its founding investors, those capitalizing the start-up in round 1, for \$5 million with the understanding that the plan calls for additional capital infusions totaling \$30 million before the company can stand on its own. Now the question becomes, how much of the company at founding does \$5 million buy? The easiest way to perform a valuation is to assume a number of shares outstanding. For convenience we shall use 10 million shares, a commonly used number in technology startups. So our question becomes, what is the price per share of the 10 million initial shares, and how many of such shares are awarded to the seller?

APPORTIONING THE VALUE TO STARTUP CONTRIBUTORS Generally this question is answered by looking at three primary contributions to the startup: technology, management, and money, but not necessarily in that order. For simplicity, let us consider a case where the management is not a source of any money, so their stake in the company is determined solely by their commitment to the fortunes of the company. Further, for simplicity, let us also assume that the management is not the source of the technology. In such cases, investors tend to provide 10 to 20 percent or more of the founding stock as the management share, awarded (and vested) over time, based upon meeting certain milestones. In this example, we shall assume 20 percent, or 2 million shares are so allocated. Now, of the remaining 8 million shares, how shall they be divided between the money (investors) and the technology (the seller)?

This is a negotiation between the seller (the technology owner) and the buyer (the startup investors) just like the ones considered previously in this book. What is different here is that these investors will develop a model for the future valuation of the company based on various scenarios, with a built in expectation for a rate of return (k value) from which a calculation can be made of how much of the company they should have (in their mind) given the risk they are taking. Likewise, sellers can perform the same business model assessment to determine a future cash value that can then be brought back to the present time using the DCF method (with a RAHR value appropriate to the risk). The seller then compares such DCF (or NPV) value to that obtainable from other licensing approaches, such as a royalty bearing license, to an existing company using any of the methods and tools of the preceding chapters, and decides upon the minimum number of shares that would make this equity deal attractive. If the expectations of the seller and buyer overlap, then a deal will be possible. If they do not and cannot be made to overlap by further discussion and negotiation, then no grounds for an agreement will be reached on an equity model.[18]

THE USE OF "STEP-UPS" TO CHARACTERIZE ROUND BY ROUND VALUATIONS The challenge both the seller and buyer (investors) face is that the business model is based not only on a product that does not yet exist but also on a company that does not exist with customers who also do not yet exist. Accordingly, the uncertainty in the financial model tends to be very high. One tool commonly used to develop a valuation is the use of "step-ups." Let us suppose that in this example, the seller and the buyer agree to split the remaining 8 million shares 50:50 so that the founding capital structure is as follows: 2 million shares for management (albeit earned over time), 4 million for the technology (the sellers), and 4 million for the money (the investor/buyers). Thus, $5 million invested purchases 4 million shares. This ratio fixes the initial share price at $1.25/share ($5 million divided by 4 million shares). Thus, the management allowance of 2 million shares has an initial paper value of $2.5 million, and the technology has a value of $5 million, although because there is no market for the company's stock, none of the stock is sellable (there are also legal and contractual reasons why such shares cannot be sold, but these are outside the scope of this book).

A year hence, an additional $10 million will need to be raised. To do so, the company will issue and price additional stock, which leads to the infamous "dilution" problem for the seller and for management. Here's how the dilution problem is usually stated. If the future stock is priced at $1.25/share, then to raise $10 million, it will be necessary to issue 8 million new shares, creating a total pool of 18 million shares. Now management's 2 million shares, which had been 20 percent of the company, have become 11 percent of the company, and the seller of the founding technology has seen its 40 percent initial share become "diluted" to 22 percent because its 4 million shares are that proportion of the now 18 million shares. However, the value of the company has gone up as a result of the second round of funding. There are now 18 million shares with a value of \$1.25/share or total value, known as the market capitalization (or market cap), of \$22.5 million. When the management and technology sellers multiply their respective company shares against the \$22.5 million they discover that their dollar value has not changed since the founding round, but their "say so" in company operations at the board level has been reduced by the addition of other seats for the new investors.[19]

This example of a second round of funding being priced the same as the founding round is known as "flat round" or a "step-up of 1.0." A step-up is defined as the ratio of the share price of the later round to the preceding round. Step-ups greater than 1.0 mean that the stock has become more valuable from one round to the next, and step-ups less than 1.0 mean that it has become less valuable.

Founding investors expect that the value of the shares at the time of the second round will be higher than at the founding round because the overall risk of the project should be less, and the time to liquidity should most certainly be less than faced by the founding investors. However, if there are significant problems in developing the technology or the market or building the management of the company, round 2 investors could well conclude, based upon their projections of future rewards, that the risk is as high and the time to liquidity is as long as the first round investors perceived it to be. In business terms, either nothing was accomplished during the first year, or founding investors paid too much for the technology, or the market attractiveness has deteriorated.

Founding investors normally expect a very nice step-up to occur in the course of a year because the product should be defined and perhaps even prototyped, prospective customers should have been identified, and all the key management posts filled. Continuing with this example, let us assume that the results of the first year warrant a step-up of 2.0; that is, it is possible to find round 2 investors who are willing to pay \$2.50/share, or twice what founding investors paid. In this case, the number of new shares required to raise the needed \$10 million is 4 million shares. Thus, there would now be 14 million shares, all valued at \$2.50/share. The new "market" price is based on what cash investors at the one-year juncture are willing to pay, making the total value of the company (the market cap) equal to \$35 million. The technology seller's ownership of the company has declined from 40 percent to 29 percent (4 million shares divided by the new total of 14 million shares) but its valuation has increased from \$5 million (4 million shares at \$1.25/share) to \$10 million (4 million shares at \$2.50/share). Likewise the management allowance has been "diluted" but has become more valuable.

Let us assume that during the second year significant progress is made in that a product has been completed and demonstrated and customers have placed orders necessitating another \$20 million for round 3 in order to complete manufacturing and begin running the factory. As a result, let us assume that a step-up of 4.0 is attainable, making the price \$10/share. Thus, only 2 million new shares must be printed (making a total of 16 million shares) for the round 3 investors who are putting in \$20 million, making the total value of the company \$160 million. Accordingly, the seller of the technology has been diluted to 25 percent of the company (4 million shares divided by 16 million shares, the new total) but the value of each share is now $10/share (4 times the $2.50/share at round 2) so that the total value of such shares is now $40 million.

SUMMARY OF ALL CAPITALIZATIONS AND RETURNS THROUGH IPO IN AN EXAMPLE Finally, let us assume that the company goes public at the end of the third year for $25/share, or a step-up of 2.5 over round 3, which raises $100 million. This would require issuing 4 million additional shares, bringing the total to 20 million shares. The seller would now own 20 percent of the company, which is exactly half of the starting ownership percentage, but with a publicly traded (and liquid) value of $100 million! How is it that the seller can be diluted by a factor of two and yet the value is increased by a factor of 20? The answer is that the share price has been stepped up three times by factors of 2, 4, and 2.5. Multiplying these three factors together yields exactly 20, which is why the seller's value has gone up by this factor.

Now, in order to perform the initial valuation of share price, which determines how many shares the investors providing $5 million receive and how many shares are left for the technology sellers, this model has to be analyzed to provide a basis for all the aforementioned assumptions.

The first and most important assumption is the underlying business plan. At founding, the company had to create a pro forma of its future sales and profitability. In order to obtain the IPO valuation of $500 million, for a sales multiple of 5, sales of $100 million annually would need to have been demonstrated, at the end of the third year. If the sales multiple was 10 times, then the sales needed would be $50 million.

The determination of such multiples is figured, generally speaking, using the Industry Standards Method. Fortunately, because of the public nature of IPOs, there are hundreds of IPO examples, with publicly available data. By analyzing such recently public companies (sales, growth, profitability, industry trends, etc.), investors and technology sellers can develop a range of expectations for future value based upon assumed performance. Likewise, there is a surprising amount of data available to determine step-ups. Although the companies receiving pre-IPO funding are not public, and thereby are not obligated to disclose their funding sources and valuation, normally such information is obtainable through a little digging. Sophisticated and experienced venture capitalists are much better able than technology sellers to create such models and estimates because of their experience and contacts in the industry.

Another tool for checking the overall sanity of the step-up assumptions is to use the DCF method of Chapter 7. Working backwards from the IPO, the question can be asked, what would lead the round 3 investors to pay $10/share? And, again, would a round 2 investor see $2.50/share as reasonable? Finally, would the founding round investor accept $1.25/share? Using the DCF equation of Chapter 7 we can determine that from the founding of the company until the IPO event, the founding investor receives an ROI of 171 percent, which corresponds to a 20 "bagger" (multiple) in just three years. Would a 171 percent ROI make a founding investor happy? Yes and no. If it was guaranteed, and the value of other comparable guaranteed returns was 5 percent, then of course the answer is "yes." But because it is not guaranteed, such an investor would review all the assumptions in the business plan and determine how speculative or realistic they are. If they were reasonable, then the answer should still be "yes," but investors would not be shy about trying to get an even better deal, especially if there are even better opportunities available to them elsewhere. In the late 1990s, the overall range of ROI for the more successful venture capital investors was over 40 percent, a number obtained by a mixture of outcomes, some at 171 percent and some total losses.[20]

Using the same equation for the round 2 investors, their ROI is 216 percent overall return is even higher than the founding investors', because their capital was tied up for only two years. Finally, the round 3 investor experiences a 150 percent return.

In order to refine the assumptions, one would need to look carefully into the business plan and ascertain what risks will occur at what point in time and with how much money invested. The plan should be that the ROI of the founding investors should be higher than any of the later investors because joining the party at start-up entailed the highest risk. Statistically speaking, some start-ups will never have a Round 2 and will fail out of the starting gate, losing all the founding capital, which is why investors who join only in the later rounds should normally receive a lower rate of return.

By adjusting the ROI projected for each round's investors in the context of the expected risk at that point, this model can be refined to provide a more rational prediction. Then, by comparing the return to the founding investor, compared to their alternatives, and to the technology seller, compared to their alternatives, the relative balance between their initial contributions can be analyzed. If the technology is genuinely the substance of the start-up company, then it is not unusual for the technology seller to receive founding shares equal to the investment, or even higher. On the other hand, if the investment yet required to commercialize is large and progress is likely to be slow, then founding investors will not fund a deal that allocates so much of the stock to the technology. To do so would not leave room for later investors to infuse additional needed money at attractive rates of return.

DILUTION ISSUES Earlier we considered the effect of dilution, and we now need to return to the subject to consider what happens when things go more poorly than expected. If the step-ups are greater than 1.0, then the value of founding shares increases with each round. As the discussed example shows, even as the percentage of the company owned goes down, the value of shares held goes up. That is the magic of step-ups.

For flat rounds, where the step-ups are exactly 1.0, the technology seller's ownership is diluted as a percentage, but the value of the shares held is unchanged. This is because there are more shares issued but the value of the shares remains what it was in the preceding round, and the startup company has more money infused to support its operations and further development.

If a technology seller wanted a deal where its ownership percentage is unchanged even with the infusion of later investors, the founding investor would receive very poor returns on its investment because the dilution that occurs would come out of the founding investors' shares. Unless the percentage awarded to the technology seller was extremely low, then no investor is likely to want to fund the start-up company.

There is one other means that a technology seller, or founding investor, can use to avoid dilution: Continue to invest in the company in all later rounds to maintain a larger share of ownership. Such a provision is common in start-up deals. The difficulty that arises is that technology sellers are not always in a position to make such investments, whereas founding investors exist for the purpose of making such investments. Ordinarily, founding investors are also second and third round investors. Perhaps they maintain their share, perhaps they are diluted a little as other investors are admitted to the club, but technology sellers, who have the right to match investments, often may not have the means or will to do so. Another valid reason why technology sellers choose not to invest in subsequent rounds is to maintain a balanced portfolio. Because of risk, VCs are diligent about holding stakes in many different companies for each fund that they raise. A particular technology seller does not normally operate in this way and so may have only one or a few equity stakes by virtue of its R&D. To additionally invest scarce discretionary cash in later rounds of one of the opportunities puts them increasingly in an "eggs all in one basket" situation.

Assuming that such funding is secured through legitimate means using fair market value negotiations at each of the subsequent rounds, technology sellers are not innately harmed by their inability to maintain their share. However, if the start-up is a success they will regret not having found the funds somehow and somewhere.

There is another phenomenon, however, that should be of great concern to a technology seller. In all the previous examples, the step-ups have been 1.0 or greater. What happens if progress during the year has been poor, or the market looks more distant, or competitors have emerged that were unexpected or stronger than expected? It is entirely possible for legitimate business reasons that the value in a later round is less than at the founding round. If this happens, then a true dilution will occur to a holder of previous round stock who does not invest to maintain his or her share: not only will the share of the company as a percentage decline but the aggregate value of their share holdings will also decline.

In such a situation, frustration arises when the adverse round is a result of management blunders over which the seller had no control. It should be recognized that technology sellers are not normally going to have a controlling interest or right to manage the company. In many cases, the reason for a start-up in the first place was that the technology seller wanted to put the technology in someone else's hands to develop and commercialize it. Otherwise, there would be no licensing situation. In essence, even though the technology seller may have one or more board seats and may express its opinion on various strategic matters, it is an opinion only. Decisions at the board level are made by the board majority. As a result of some bad decisions, the technology seller may, in retrospect, perceive that its dilution in value is unfair. However, the other owners also have incentive to increase the value of the shares (because they own shares too), so usually the board's decisions can be expected to have been made in good faith. An effective defense in such circumstances is for the technology seller to invest in subsequent "down rounds."[21]

There is, unfortunately, another kind of down round known in the industry as a "cram down" round. One technique that founding investors can use to unjustly dilute technology sellers (and management) is to lead a second round of funding at a valuation substantially below the founding round valuation. In the previous discussion, if instead of the second round being priced at $2.50/share, a step-up of 2.0, it was priced at 25 cents a share, a step-"up" of 0.20. After the infusion of second round capital, primarily from the founding investors perpetrating this plan, the original allocation of stock among the founders has been significantly altered to the detriment of those founders who are not able to make the second round cash investment.

There are numerous such issues present in equity deals, more so than in the other pricing structures we have discussed. Although there are various protective techniques that can be negotiated by technology sellers, they are outside the scope of this book. The general lesson here is to know with whom you are dealing. The same holds true for the management. This segment will receive a significant share of the founding stock, and the success or failure of the company will depend in large part on their skill, their industry, and their ethics. So, "Who am I dealing with?"—ever present in any licensing negotiation—is an even more significant question in an equity transaction.

Industry Standards and Rating/Ranking Valuation Methods

For equity investments there is a unique window into valuation available. When a company intends to go public, it must file a document with the SEC known officially as an S-1 but commonly known as a "Red Herring." This document is typically over 100 pages in length and loaded with information on the company, its market, its current and historic financial performance, as the previously cited Google S-1 contains. Further, once the company becomes publicly traded there is a simple means of establishing its valuation.

When performing valuations of startups, parties commonly look to such public documents as S-1s for comparables. Also, in the VC industry, there are many term sheets that are preferred and floated about that become part of individual consciousnesses. Further, there are so many VC investments, even at their diminished scale today, that the law of large numbers makes it possible to find comparable agreements. The challenge is making the appropriate comparison given the different investment situations.

One of the most famous companies to go public, and in many ways the precursor and enabler of the Internet revolution, was Netscape. The company was formed on April 4, 1994. It went public via an IPO just 16 months later on August 8, 1995 priced at $28 a share creating a market capitalization of just over $1 billion, having cumulative *losses* of nearly $13 million and never having shown one quarter of profitability. By November 1995, Netscape was selling for over $100 a share and worth more than $4 billion, though still not profitable. Its share price at that time was 325 times (!) its projected 1996 earnings. The financial statements filed by Netscape in its S-1 together with several other relevant pages are provided at: www.razgaitis.com.

In a widely reported story, in 1997 Microsoft introduced their bundled competing product, Explorer, and succeeded in crushing Netscape. In November 1998, Netscape announced that it was being acquired by AOL and the acquisition was consummated on March 26, 1999, for a value of $10 billion at closing. So in just under five years as an independent company Netscape went from a raw idea to product to a public company to the highest of high flyers in the internet market place to being in the center of the Microsoft bullseye to disappearance as a stand-alone company but at a very substantial valuation and ultimately to being grounds of a legal finding against Microsoft for antitrust misbehavior. There are not many companies who have that kind of excitement in 100 years, let alone five. But the creators of Netscape (James Clark, Mark Andreessen, James Barksdale, the VC firm of Kleiner Perkins, and others), suggested dramatically new possibilities:

- It was possible, and even desirable, to go public in less than a year and a half
- It was possible to be highly valued without having shown a profit, but by having a great story and widespread name and product use and recognition

- The new recipe for success was "get big fast"
- It need not require very much investment (about $30 million) to make a valuable company (about $1 billion), but timing is everything
- VC investors can facilitate "gold rush" like value-creation and copycats
- The Internet was the hottest hot thing in memory and money

Equity with an Existing Company

The governing assumption in the previous discussion is that the startup company is being created at the time of the license for the purpose of commercializing the licensed technology. Earlier, licensing to a public company was briefly discussed. What remains to be considered is the intermediate situation: licensing to an already existing, pre-public company in exchange for stock.

In this circumstance, the startup company is effectively restarting its operations (perhaps abandoning its previous technology for the subject license). The founding valuation needs to be considered by all the parties as though it was a fresh start. The fact that significant sums were expended in a fruitless endeavor should not penalize the technology seller. Sunk costs are irrelevant. The restarted up company can argue that it has now established a management team and some market awareness that deserves recognition. That may be so. On the other hand, it is possible that the management team assembled is not particularly suited to the new direction of the company, or that the management has demonstrated only a lack of business acumen in its previous efforts. In any case, the seller should consider all these arguments just as though it was a true startup, and value each party's contributions independently.

Another possibility is that a pre-public company seeks the seller's license to create a second product or to enhance its first product. Instead of paying a cash license fee or royalties, the buyer instead may propose issuance of stock. In this circumstance, the seller should consider that it is, in effect, a second or third round "funder" by infusing the company with technology and rights. The seller should assess all the valuations that have gone into the company to date, the business plan and its financial performance as of the negotiation date, and determine what is the highest stock price, or fewest number of shares, it needs in order to get a fair return at the time of an IPO or strategic acquisition.

Such analysis is difficult for the seller because it necessarily involves performing due diligence on a company, its management and technology, and its business plan, without the advantage of having been part of the company's formation. Further, the seller may not have sufficient knowledge about the existing technology in the pre-public company to enable a fair assessment of its worth. The seller in these circumstances is really playing the role of a later-round venture capitalist without the experience and tools that come with doing this for a living. For these reasons, this form of valuation is more difficult than either getting stock in a true startup or stock in a public company. In the former case, the founding technology is the seller's, and should be known; in the latter case, the value of the shares is determined by a public market and so it is known. This intermediate situation may have both little-known technology and hard-to-know share price.

The uncertainties might possibly be narrowed by performing due diligence, perhaps with support from an outside consultant. If the uncertainty remains large, then this can be reflected by a high RAHR value in a DCF calculation. If the buyer's offer can meet the seller's requirements through an appropriately high discount rate, the seller then needs to decide whether it wants to take a high risk opportunity. Such decisions are always best made when alternatives exist.

It should be noted that all six valuation methods discussed in this book can be applied to determine equity valuations, just as they can be used to determine a royalty or any other form of compensation. However, the non-liquidity of stock and the complexity of ownership bring with them a whole array of other business issues; those most directly related to valuation were considered in this chapter.

Balancing Simplicity with Comprehensiveness

Clearly, if any one license agreement attempted to incorporate all the various structural tools described in this chapter, in addition to others that can be conceived, the agreement would likely be so complicated as to defy comprehension, agreement, and management.

Simpler agreements are easier to negotiate in the sense that there are fewer issues to work on, they can be understood and communicated to all stakeholders more easily, and then, importantly, years later third parties responsible for their implementation can comprehend them. So, in general, simple agreements are good things.

However—and there is almost always a however—simple agreements normally do not take into account all the vagaries of the future which one or both parties may be concerned about because without such taking into account the agreement could become unfair. Many of the structural issues discussed in this chapter have arisen from this motive, to ensure the agreement remains fair under some if/then situation. Also each party in a negotiation has things that are uniquely important to them, either in the Box or in the Wheelbarrow, for either or both the buyer and seller. Incorporating such priorities into the agreement, even at the addition of complexity, can make the negotiation easier because a need has been accommodated. Also, a concern about future fairness alleviated, or even a compensation for making some other concession as a means of reaching agreement closure has occurred (which is sometimes difficult to do without the use of such structure provisions).

So each negotiation and agreement represents some balance between KISS (keep it simple stupid) and providing for every possible issue and eventuality. Perhaps Albert Einstein said it best when he commented on ideal physics models: They should be made as simple as possible, but not simpler.

Conclusion

In this chapter we considered many of the ways that the economic value of a technology can be structured. The wonderful flexibility of technology licenses enables parties to customize the terms of payment to meet their respective goals. In many instances, the issues addressed in this chapter are a delight to work out because it becomes a mutual discovery process for how to meet the needs of all stakeholders.

The term sheet is a power tool for developing pricing and structures:

- Defines the Box and the Wheelbarrow
- Connects valuation and pricing

- Distinguishes proposed transaction from historic practices
- Creates internal clarity, congruence, and commitment
- Frames negotiation planning
- Qualifies prospective buyers
- Provides checkpoints to the negotiation process
- Focuses "the eye on the prize"

Likely the all-time record for a structured financial transaction initiated by a term sheet was the $25 billion invested by the U.S. Government in each of multiple banks in a new class of preferred stock paying annual dividends of 5 percent. The term sheet, prepared by the Government, was presented to each of the bank CEOs, and ultimately signed by each CEO, all in just one hour, 3 to 4 p.m. on October 13, 2008, and formalized in separate agreements just days later.[22] Such term sheet negotiation may be unprecedented; but a term sheet is a tool that can crystallize a Dealmaking event, and get to closure on essential terms.

In the next chapter we will cover the negotiation process of transforming internal and external term sheets into living agreements.

Notes

1. From the movie *Jerry Maguire*.
2. Quoted in the *Wall Street Journal*, November 29, 2008, "Rubin Under Fire, Defends His Role at Citi: 'Nobody was Prepared' for Crisis of '08," p. A1.
3. Here is one memorable definition of "as is where is," as I heard it proclaimed in warning to me at an automobile auction: "If after you buy it, it breaks in two, we give you both halves." (I bought it anyway).
4. The U.S. Supreme Court addressed the patent obviousness standard in KSR International Co. v. Teleflex Inc., 127 S. Ct. 1727 (2007).
5. The U.S. Supreme Court in Medimmune, Inc. v. Genentech, Inc.; 549 U.S., 117 S. Ct. 764 (decided Jan. 9, 2007); and, subsequently, the U.S. Federal Circuit in Sandisk Corp. v. STMicroelectronics, Inc., 480 F.3d 1372 (Fed. Cir. 2007).
6. An example "bookend" structure would be as follows. At the time of the licenses the parties reach agreement on the most (reasonably) pessimistic and optimistic projections for the use of the technology, and these correspond to a royalty rate of 1 percent and 5 percent respectively. The agreement could then provide for a royalty rate to be negotiated at the time of commercial introduction that would be bound by these values. The parties could further provide a formula, or basis, by which future events or findings could be used to determine the neighborhood or even exact value in this range.
7. Reportedly said by Truman Capote to a film director who was changing the storyline of the screenplay of a Capote book.
8. The *Wall Street Journal* in July 2008 reported on the 15 highest breakup fees since 1995, based upon data supplied by *Dealogic*, for M&A transactions exceeding $40 billion. Such fees ranged from a low of 2.5 to a high of 4.6 percent. http://blogs.wsj.com/deals/2008/07/17/how-the-anheuser-busch-breakup-fee-measures-up/.
9. "Talk about Scary," in the *Digits* column of Ann Grimes, *Wall Street Journal*, June 20, 2002, p. B5.
10. Source: MoneyTree Venture Capital Profile for United States, PricewaterhouseCoopers/Venture Economics/National Venture Capital Association, published June 30, 2008.

11. An anonymous haiku submitted to a web site dedicated to failed dot com companies.
12. Source: National Venture Capital Association, and Thomson Reuters.
13. "A Silicon Valley Slowdown," *New York Times,* April 9, 2008.
14. "A Cringing Quarter for Venture Capitalists," *New York Times,* July 1, 2008.
15. www.sec.gov/Archives/edgar/data/1288776/000119312504073639/ds1.htm
16. There are some exceptions to this broad statement that are outside the scope of this book.
17. www.sec.gov/Archives/edgar/data/1288776/000119312504073639/ds1.htm
18. Investors in startup companies are often not interested in a royalty relationship. They realize that the company will be a cash burner for many years and want to structure the company to limit such cash outflows. Royalty is simply another cash outflow. Accordingly, investors will attempt to defer royalties until the company is profitable, or encourage reducing or eliminating the royalty in lieu of stock.
19. In many cases the "new" investors are the old investors putting in additional money.
20. Article in the *New York Times* dated 10/21/01 citing Venture One, Thompson, National Venture Capital Association.
21. There are, in addition, various down round protections known as "ratchet" provisions. Such provisions act to revalue, in whole or in part, previous round investments. Ordinarily only the founding investor expects to be the beneficiary of such provisions. A thorough discussion of such matters is outside the scope of this book.
22. "The Moment of Truth, U.S. Forced Big Banks to Blink," *Wall Street Journal*, October 15, 2008.

CHAPTER 11

People, Process, and Lessons Learned

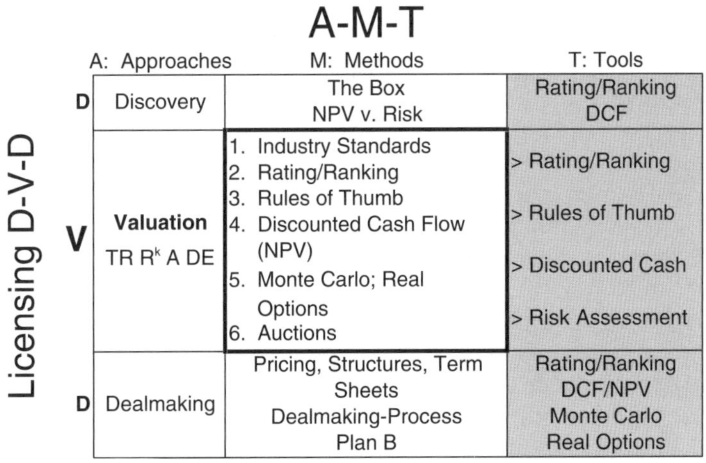
A-M-T
A: Approaches
M: Methods
T: Tools
Licensing D-V-D
D
Discovery
The Box
NPV v. Risk
Rating/Ranking
DCF
V
Valuation
TR R^k A DE
1. Industry Standards
2. Rating/Ranking
3. Rules of Thumb
4. Discounted Cash Flow (NPV)
5. Monte Carlo; Real Options
6. Auctions
> Rating/Ranking
> Rules of Thumb
> Discounted Cash
> Risk Assessment
D
Dealmaking
Pricing, Structures, Term Sheets
Dealmaking-Process
Plan B
Rating/Ranking
DCF/NPV
Monte Carlo
Real Options

In Chapter 10 we reviewed four key ideas relating to the ***Approach*** of Dealmaking: (1) the Wheelbarrow (and Box), (2) pricing (vs. valuation), (3) structures (for pricing), and (4) term sheets (internal and external).

In this chapter we will start from the existence of term sheets from Chapter 10, and continue with Dealmaking focusing on the process for negotiation, negotiation itself, as well as the post-Dealmaking relationship, and specifically four additional key ideas: (1) deal team, (2) deal targets, (3) deal plan, and (4) Plan B.

The objective of this chapter, and any negotiation, is to configure the Box and Wheelbarrow to maximize value for both the seller and buyer, and reach an agreement that both parties can live with and see as fair. With the acronym ***TR R^kA DE***, we previously designated the DE as Deal Economics; we can also view it as Deal Equity in our present context, meaning fairness to both sides of Dealmaking.

Introduction

Negotiation is a very popular subject for books and articles. These range from pop psychology to theatrical imagery to game and bargaining theory branches of economics research. The first category focuses on the human-to-human interaction, including simple acts of greeting and courtesy. Here's one: the eyebrow wink, the act of lifting one's eyebrow on approaching another person to establish contact and rapport. It has been studied in many cultures, including that of apes, and is generally taken as a friendly precursor to verbal and physical contact. Political consultants, in particular, counsel their clients to do "eyebrow pushups" to "open up the face." Tips on human behavior are probably helpful in general terms, but as the Chinese saying goes: "Talk doesn't cook rice."

The second category uses the imagery of theatre with actors playing roles, reading scripts, and communicating a story persuasively. We will say something about this when we cover "deal team" below.

The third category includes studies on the Prisoner Dilemma, Bayesian Equilibrium, and now made famous by a biography and movie, as well as a Nobel Prize, Nash Bargaining. There has been great interest in economic theory, but it is impractical in contexts of a complex range of interests and issues such as our Box and Wheelbarrow and where the time and resources that can be justifiably committed to negotiation are limited.

Our focus here is on practical business negotiations, hence the preferred term of Dealmaking. Such negotiation is a business process, like sales and marketing, in addition to R&D. In fact the very word, negotiate, originates from the Latin word to transact business in contrast to acts of leisure: neg- (Latin for "not") and otium (for "leisure"). Like any business process there are best, or at least better, practices and lessons that can be learned.

We can think of the process as achieving in price our preparatory conclusions of value. But Dealmaking is more than this. It includes price discovery, much as we discussed in Chapter 9 on auctions.

There is a citation from Shakespeare on almost every imaginable topic, including pricing and valuation. In his play set in the Trojan War, *Troilus and Cressida*, the character Troilus asks: "What's aught but as 'tis valued?" King Hector replies: "But value dwells not in particular will, it holds his estimate and dignity as well wherein 'til precious of itself as in the prizer."[1] Troilus's perspective seems to be that there is no value except by expression of a buyer. Troilus is a pricing guy (who was betrayed by his beloved and ultimately killed, demonstrating certain perils of the market method). Hector, more an internal valuation guy, expresses the contrary belief that value resides intrinsically, which bears as much consideration as the value perceived by any external entity. So we might anticipate that at the end of a Dealmaking campaign some wonder at the difference found between price and value. Care in valuation, and a process for Dealmaking, lessens that probability and the gap when it occurs.

Dealmaking Challenges: Survey Data

The Licensing Foundation of the Licensing Executives Society of the United States and Canada has undertaken annual surveys of its 6,000 members on various issues relating to licensing. Among such issues investigated, was Dealmaking adversity, specifically: (1) impediments to the initiation of Dealmaking, (2) breakdowns in negotiation, and (3) post-Dealmaking disappointment (deal remorse, similar to the well known phenomenon of buyer's remorse, though in Dealmaking remorse is an equal opportunity emotion).

All cited percentages and statistics below are approximate. The reader is referred to the published papers for exact values and detailed discussion.[2,3,4,5]

IMPEDIMENTS Getting to the point of substantive negotiation is not easy. Survey respondents gave the following responses for 2003. During that year, only 25 percent of identified technology licensing opportunities had identified potential buyer-licensees. And of those opportunities with identified potential buyers, only 25 percent of the opportunities had begun the negotiation process; the most common reason cited, in more than 25 percent of the cases, was insufficient Dealmaking resources. So, based on these data, we have an indication of another kind of 25 Percent Rule pointing to the challenge of getting any deal done for technology opportunities. Even with opportunities for which substantive negotiations had occurred, more than 40 percent did not result in a successful deal.[6]

BREAKDOWN Breakdown refers to situations where substantive negotiations were begun but for whatever reason never successfully consummated. Many factors can cause deal breakdown. Money is only one of them—cited approximately 25 to 33 percent of the time, only slightly higher than the inability to agree on nonfinancial terms, cited about 20 percent of the time. Delays in Dealmaking and inconsistent positions, likely caused by inadequate preparation, were cited with a frequency of about 15 to 20 percent.[7]

REMORSE Remorse refers to the perspective of either the buyer or seller looking back on Dealmaking consummated just in the preceding year. When asked "With the benefit of hindsight, which of the following contract characteristics would you now, on average, structure differently?" The most frequently cited for the year 2003 by sellers was payment *structure* (more than 50 percent), followed by business milestones (45 percent), and payment *amounts* (33 percent), with numerous other issues cited more than 15 percent of the time (restrictions on field of use, geography, or duration, and other terms of use; technical milestones; grant backs). For buyers the responses were led by payment *amounts* (50 percent) and then *structure* (45 percent), followed by field of use restrictions and both technical and business milestones (25 to 30 percent).[8]

Data for the year 2005 showed higher frequency of response. For sellers, there were three deal terms that were cited at more than 40 percent frequency: business milestones, technical milestones, and field of use restrictions. Cited at more than 30 percent frequency were payment amount and structure, as well as degree of exclusivity.[9] Recall that these are hindsight regrets within one year of the respective deal. When asked for the three most common reasons why the remorse answers were given, the most common response was that the other side is not putting their promised effort into the technology (cited by over 50 percent). This was followed by revised business strategy and new market information (both at 40 percent). At about 30 percent frequency were new information on the technology performance and mistakes made in licensing; at 20 percent was a revised view of the most profitable licensing strategy.[10]

DEAL DEMISE In the 2006 Survey, the respondents were asked about deals that went "bad," and why. By "bad," we mean deals requiring substantial renegotiation,

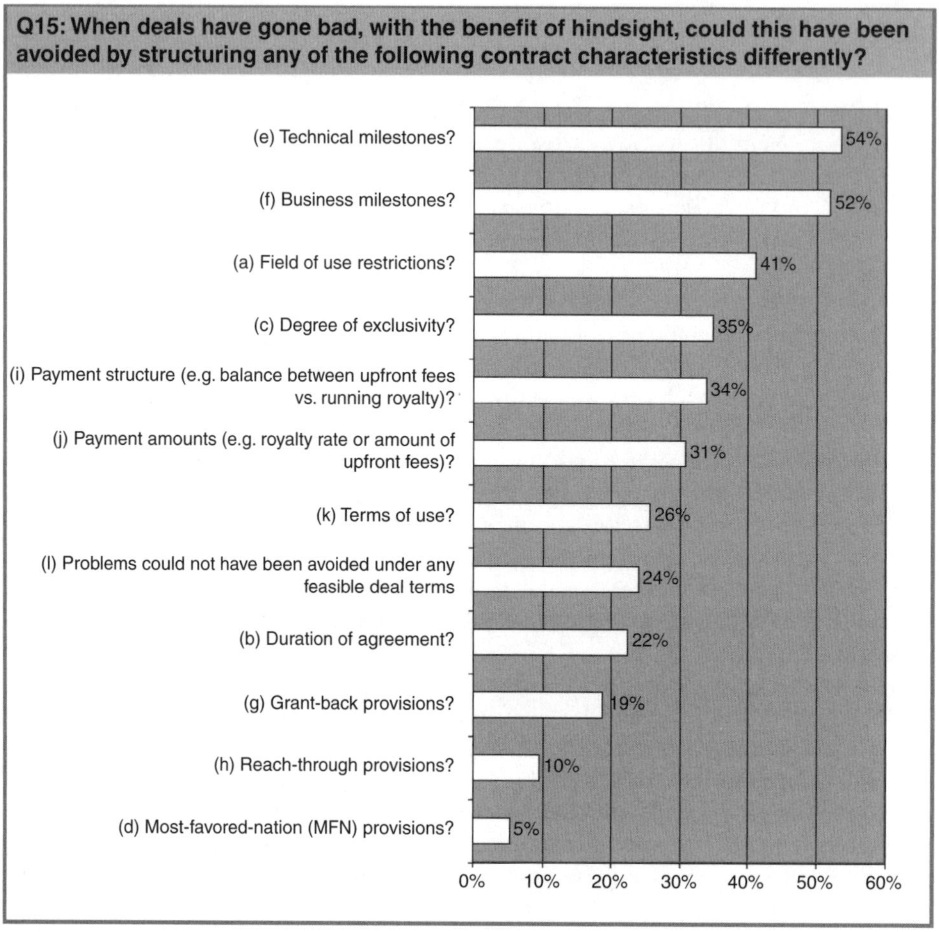

EXHIBIT 11.1 2006 Survey Results of Sources of Deal Remorse

or those ending up in arbitration, or even the deal being effectively abandoned by one or more of the involved parties.

The response to the key sources of deal demise is shown in Exhibit 11.1.[11] Similar to the findings cited under deal remorse above, both technical and business milestones were very important factors, here cited more than 50 percent of the time. Payment amounts and structures were cited about 33 percent of the time. And unavoidable demise was cited with a frequency of 25 percent.

In Exhibit 11.2 are the reasons the survey respondents gave as to why any one or more of the deal features cited in Exhibit 11.1 occurred. The leading reason is a revision in deal strategy (more than 60 percent). Because respondents could only cite three reasons, the dispersion of responses shows the diversity of causes in deal remorse. One significant reason, similar to the results cited above, is serious mistakes made in negotiation (nearly 30 percent).

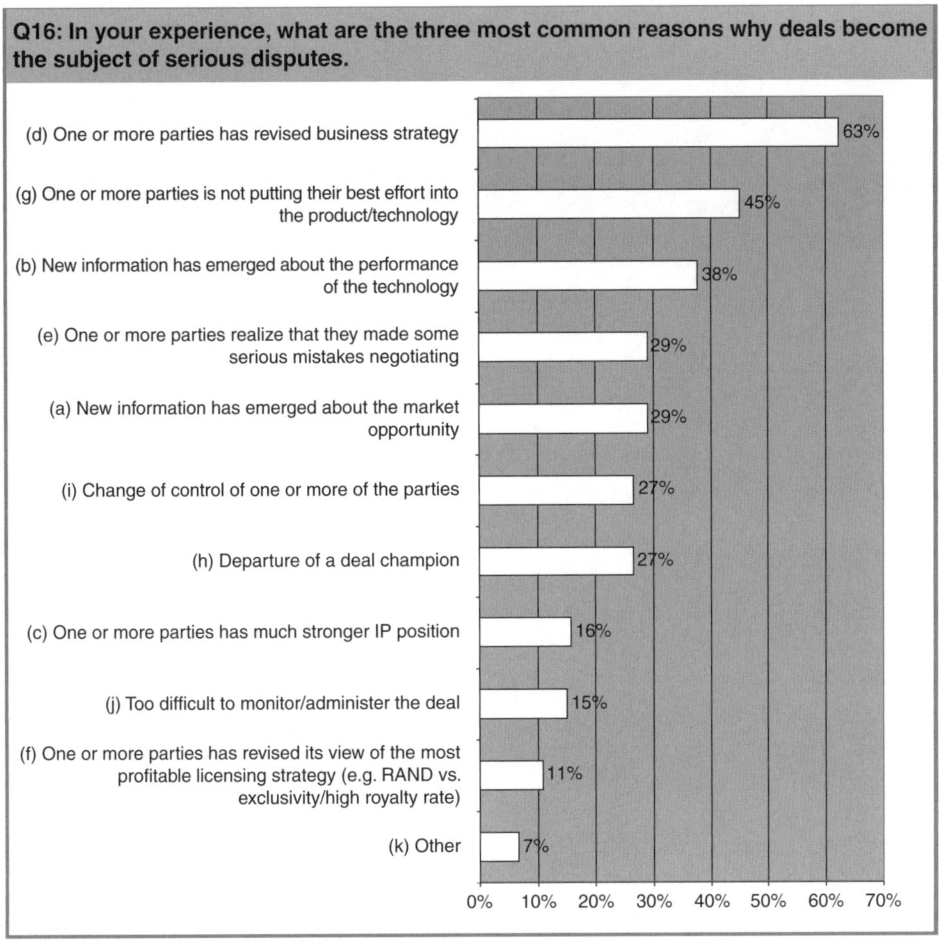

EXHIBIT 11.2 2006 The Most Common Reasons for Deal Demise

Importance of Dealmaking as a Business Process

The above data, which is generally consistent with the experience of technology Dealmaking professionals, illustrates the challenges in creating deals that work out well. It is commonly appreciated that R&D is not easy, and "failure" is just part of the process. IP risks occur both in terms of loss of one's own IP protection as well as the emergence of third party IP claims. Likewise products that are made and "work" are known to fail in the marketplace for any number of reasons.

Risk is inherent in operating a business. A reading of the Google-identified risk factors in its IPO S-1 document, cited in Chapter 2, is characteristic of challenges technology startup companies face. We should add to all such risks the Dealmaking risk of a technology moving from its seller-owner to a buyer-licensee.

In Chapter 10, the four keys discussed—Wheelbarrow, Price, Structure, and Term Sheets—are important parts of Dealmaking preparedness, and risk reduction. In the following sections of this chapter, we will address four other keys: Deal

Team, Deal Targets, Deal Plan, and a Plan B. We will close the chapter returning to the cited Licensing Foundation survey results for 2006 by summarizing Dealmaking advice and counsel.

Deal Team

Technology Dealmaking involves an unusual confluence of disciplines and practices. Underlying the technology are some scientific principles, made manifest in some practicable form, with a certain exactness and ability to be replicated. Protecting the technology involves IP law, patents, trade secrets, copyrights (such as for software or procedure documents) and may include trademarks and other forms. The Dealmaking agreements need to be done in accordance with contract law. Clearly the valuation and pricing aspects involve finance and even accounting. Recognizing and prioritizing opportunities, and developing business and financial models for them, needs business development and marketing skills. And, the Dealmaking process itself requires people skills of communication, especially listening, applied with wisdom and judgment.

Seven Dealmaking People

One of the most ancient, and foundational, questions is: Who is there "out there?" The study of this famous question is known as ontology. In pop psychology books on selling or negotiating, this question is addressed by contrasting various personality types such as "analytical" versus "entrepreneurial," or role types such as "gate keeper" versus "decision maker." Here, we look at this important matter from the perspective of direct deal responsibilities.

In most negotiation contexts there are often seven different people "out there":

1. Lawyers
2. Profit and loss managers
3. Business developer ("bus dev"), deal initiator
4. Deal manager
5. Financial analysts
6. Inventors, content creators
7. Those impossible to classify

First, we have lawyers. Agreements in our culture and time have sufficient complexity, and normally importance, that require that they be reduced to writing in formally structured documents. Further, such writing must be done in a way that independent third parties, subsequent deal managers, and potentially judges and juries and other dispute resolvers, can, at any later time, divine the intentions and duties of the parties. Ultimately, the words and sentences of most agreements will receive the thought and reflect the fears of lawyers. Their skills are exceedingly useful in creating language that is understandable, which is surprisingly difficult to do (as someone once said: "English resists meaning"). They also often bring a "what if" questioning as to a seemingly endless stream of possible adverse turns of events. (In human psychology this focus on the possibility of adverse events is known as "awfulization"; if someone personally close to you has this trait, and you remain cheerful and unswayed in your optimism, you may be a candidate for sainthood.) The underlying aspiration for such awfulization is to avoid adverse surprises (risks) and as much as possible avoid all duties and obligations by shifting them to the other side. This situation is the legal equivalent of the analyst we discuss later who similarly, in the extreme, aspires to deals that give nothing but get everything, or the CFO whose strategy for business success is cash all checks, pay no bills.

Next we have managers. Although everyone is a manager, what is meant here are those persons who have profit and loss (P&L) responsibilities. Frequently, they are either the owners of the selling company's books of what is being dealt, or will be the owners on the buy side. After the deal is done, they are the ones who will enjoy, or suffer, a substantial portion of the economic gain, or loss, flowing from the deal, and the attendant glory or shame.

The business developer in this context is understood to be the deal creator (or generator). He or she is the point person for wanting this deal done, and could be the P&L manager, or (as discussed later) the deal manager or even the inventor; in different circumstances any of these seven people could be the deal creator.

In the middle of our list is the deal manager. He or she is the person who is responsible for Dealmaking. In this sense he or she is a project manager, which is a useful concept for reasons to be discussed later. I have used the singular on purpose as there normally is, and in any case should be, just one person who is the deal manager. That person may have a support team whose members are sometimes termed "second chair" negotiators, but for a concerted negotiation to lead to a deal, there should always be one person who is the recognized project leader.

Next are the financial analysts. They have a very specific interest in the numbers of the deal. Financial analysts span a wide range of perspectives and roles. Some reflect the treasury and accounting functions in the buying and selling companies. Some "work the numbers" for the respective business units affected in a P&L sense by the deal being envisioned. Still others are focused on the numbers directly related to the deal itself (deal numbers). In Dealmaking, there are often three sets of numbers: those from the chief financial officer's (CFO's) perspective of the company's books, those from the P&L manager's scorecard, and those of the deal manager. As is discussed later, these first two sets of numbers—the CFO's and the P&L manager's—frequently influence the deal pricing, but it is the deal value, not some internal set of books, that is negotiated and forms the terms on which agreement is reached; how those terms affect P&L and company financial statements are consequences of a deal, but should not be the cause of the deal terms.

Next we have the people whose content, key contributions, or even inventions are the very subject of the deal. In many instances, their participation in the negotiation is important to their respective sides of the negotiation because they assist in developing financial and business models of the future, as is discussed later. They are also important in the communication of the opportunity to the other side and in the due diligence process that has as its primary objective an accurate understanding of the present stage of development, the important future uncertainties, and a characterization of the future risks. As discussed in Chapter 3, they also play an important role, often with the P&L managers, in developing the content of what will be sold or bought. Such content can be configured to include multiple technologies and associated forms of intellectual property (patents, trade secrets and know-how, copyrighted content and software), physical assets (plant, property, and equipment), and key people who may serve as deal resources and even as post deal transition resources or who may become permanently associated with the implementation of the opportunity.

Finally, others are often involved in the deal who are impossible to classify. They can be inside or outside consultants, a trusted pair of eyes and ears sent by the chief executive officer (CEO); or some not otherwise gainfully employed person who in some unknown way has an ability to get him or herself included in various deliberations and work steps, and others. Every deal manager has experiences of this seventh category of people; there should be a web site—www.7thcategorypeople.com?—to collect these experiences, and rants.

Although we are all to some degree captive to our education and training, in general the roles played are not perfectly correlated to our formal degrees. A lawyer may be the deal manager or the P&L manager. The financial analyst could have been, in an earlier life, an inventor. Deal managers arise from many different career paths. We each bring both our histories and our duties to the job at hand. It is generally helpful to know who shows up and who they are in the matter. Well managed deal teams normally require these multiple perspectives and insights.

Four Dealmaking Voices

Deals are balances. One kind of balance is between risk, generally taken as a possibility or probability of an adverse outcome, versus the possibility of highly successful realizations. Generally, the two people focused on the risk side of the balance are the lawyers and the financial analysts. Typically by training, disposition, and responsibility, these two team members are prone to identifying risk, "awfulizing" it, and developing propositions to transfer it to someone else, trying to avoid it by some other means, or otherwise minimizing it. They are usually the voice of caution in Dealmaking. In many circumstances, they may prefer or appear to prefer "no deal" as the preferable option. Characterizing them as pessimists is probably too sweeping because it may not be reflective of their personalities as much as their responsibilities. A more accurate concept, using a presently invented word, is that they are "pessi-missive," meaning that it is their mission in the subject negotiation to cause the team to consider the probabilities and consequences of undesired and even worst case outcomes. (Pessimism derives from the Latin word *pessimus*, which means "worst"). Opportunities are fragile things. Overbearing pessimism can extinguish good opportunities, especially during the early stages before they have established some momentum.[12]

On the other side of the risk–opportunity balance normally are the business developers and inventors (though inventors on the buy side can be negatively biased against not-invented-here opportunities). Their natural inclinations are to discount risk often expressed by the confidence that solutions exist to any potential exigencies and a "nothing ventured, nothing gained" can-do optimism. Using a coined word, we can characterize their role on the team to be "opto-missive," meaning it is their mission to reason toward the opportunity that can reasonably be realized while recognizing that nothing is certain, as they say, but death and taxes. (Optimism derives from New Latin *optimum*, meaning "greatest good.") There has to be a present visceral belief in a future good to sustain the momentum toward deal realization.

Well managed negotiating teams have effective considerations of voices on both sides of the risk–opportunity axis. As discussed in Chapters 7 and 8, the use of scenarios and developing ranges for keep assumptions, requires considering and characterizing both downside and upside possibilities. Between the worst and highest such possibilities there are many rational intermediate possibilities whose value and likelihood are important deal considerations. A team overweighted with risk considerations by "pessi-missives" will undervalue their selling opportunities and underbid, and thereby likely lose, excellent buying opportunities. Overweighting with "opto-missives" can result, when present in sellers, in unreasonable deal expectations, in buyers overpaying and even pursuing opportunities that should not be embraced. Great Dealmaking teams are just that, teams comprised of voices that play an important role but do not dominate the balance.

Another balancing axis is past versus future perspective. Profit and loss managers are commonly the owners of historical positions or results and, accordingly, bring a historical perspective to an opportunity analysis and a concern for how a deal may affect existing financial books. One common historical perspective is the cost associated with the subject opportunity as contained, for example, on the seller's books, or how the prospective transaction will immediately impact the buyer's books or the buyer's previous representations. On the buy side, the P&L manager often is concerned with the implications of investments previously made whose value could become infertile as a consequence of the proposed deal. Although the axiom "all sunk costs are irrelevant" is widely accepted, the business developers on a negotiating team tend to be fervent in its acceptance because of their innate future orientation. Generally these people are hired—and make their reputations—on making something new happen. What is in the past is, for them, not their primary concern. Everyone brings his or her history to the present considerations, but on a deal team, there are often those primarily concerned about "retro-spective" impacts and those focused on "pro-spective" opportunity. (*Specio* is Latin for "to see" or "to know," and is the root of the word "science.") The "retro-spective" view is important for harmonizing the present deal in the context of previous decisions and present situation.

The absence of such harmonization can make Dealmaking difficult. Historic valuations, regardless of how well founded, can be a significant internal barrier when they exceed what a rational buyer will pay. A simple example for a technology suffices. Lucent, the hardware and software company derived from the original AT&T company, sold its Marlboro, Massachusetts, facility in 2002 for $28 million, which was about half of its replacement cost and only about one-third of what it would have sold for at the most recent peak just three years earlier during the dot com and telecom boom.[13] According to the cited *Wall Street Journal* article, Lucent was reportedly pleased with the outcome because the sale "reduced our overall cost structure and [made] the most efficient use of our capital." Although no doubt disappointed that their realization was below what recently could have been, and could well have been a charge against its earnings, selling it in the past when it was worth more is not an available present option. And the future for AT&T is about (then) developing a business model in the face of a dramatically changing market, not worrying the adverse outcome from an investment made and now unneeded.

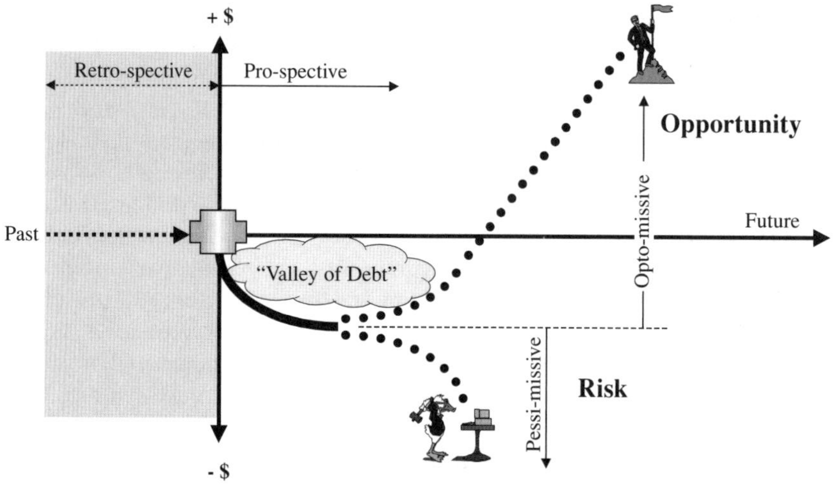

EXHIBIT 11.3 Two Axes of Dealmaking

Harmonizing the present perception of future opportunity with the past is always an available option. Such harmonization is sometimes a key internal negotiation pre-Dealmaking.

A graphic illustrating these two axes is shown in Exhibit 11.3.

Although the past, and the "retro-spective" view, is unchangeable, it can affect the present perception of a proposed deal. From the seller's perspective Dealmaking may require several aspects of "retro-spective" reconciliation. One area of concern is how the selling price compares with existing numbers on the company's books. In many situations, the public books of a public company will be unaffected either because the subject deal value does not meet a test of materiality or because the selling asset had not been shown at any value. However, the books that are used to run the business and measure internal performance could reflect values that will need to be aligned in some way with the deal value. For instance, if the deal calls for a modest upfront payment and then progress milestone, annual, or royalty payments in the future, the immediate financial realization on such operating books could be significantly less than, say, R&D or business development costs that have been collected in a project account or charged against the operating expenses of a business unit or division. Such an immediate shortfall could affect year end bonuses and other judgments management may reach about stewardship of company investment resources. If someone in the seller's organization fears "taking a hit" financially, or otherwise, because of the immediate impact of a transaction, that historical perspective will influence negotiation planning and perhaps ultimate deal terms or even deal prospects. Another kind of "retro-spective" issue is the meaning ascribed to the sale itself. Does this event mean that some "we" failed in our commercialization efforts? Was our plan more ambitious than our delivery? Does this say anything about the fidelity, or reliability, of our previous promises and forecasts? Might this transaction now call into question future revenue or earning projections of the selling company because they included significant contributions from the now about-to-be-sold asset? Does this say anything to our inventors and business developers about our company's growth prospects, or confidence in its marketing skills or in its complementary technology, or in its liquidity? Does this sale mean certain careers are ending or being sidelined? So, despite the mantra of "sunk costs are irrelevant," if these costs, and plans, are associated with people, then these issues, and others, are likely matters that a deal manager must manage as part of the overall process, primarily by resorting to future total benefit being greater than doing no deal or a different deal.

Likewise the buyer may have important "retro-spective" issues. Does this purchase reflect a failure on the buyer's R&D team? If so, why is it spending so much on its R&D? Did the buyer miss the market opportunity and is it now paying a premium to cover its mistake? Given the checkered history of mergers, is the buyer paying for something that has a high probability of disappointment? Given the M&A and IPO business history of the period 2000 through 2002 when drastic overvaluations occurred, does the buyer know what it is doing and is it paying a fair price? Is this transaction inconsistent with a strategic vision or business plan previously put forth to investors or employees or customers or suppliers? Will this be taken as a competitive threat to a key ally?

Looking toward the "pro-spective" future, there is often a negative return position for the buyer before there is the anticipated positive return; such negative return is shown by the area in Exhibit 11.3 annotated as "the valley of debt," as in "Though I walk in the valley of death . . ." humorously adapted from the 23rd Psalm. The "pessi-missive" view tends to focus on those outcomes that never survive such "debt valley." The "opto-missive" view sees that wonderful, high earning outcome when every variable breaks just in its favor and, as for the valley of debt, it is just "a bump in the night."

> *The primary point here is that all four kinds of these voices are normally present and their presence properly balanced makes for an effective Dealmaking team. For deal managers balancing these voices, responding to reasonable and obsessive concerns of one's* internal *team can be more exhausting than the external negotiation. As one of the Demotivators charts perversely captures it: "Madness does not always howl; sometimes it is the quiet voice at the end of the day saying, 'Hey, is there room in your head for one more?'"*[14]

When any one perspective overwhelms an appropriate, balanced consideration for its opposite, then it is likely that the Dealmaking team will have a distorted perspective on the opportunity, to its detriment. And, finally, at the end of the day, a decision has to be made to get anything done, and such decision is unlikely to be perceived by everyone as being the absolute wisest course of action.

The Nut, the Number, the Bogie, the Toe Tag

There is an interesting term that is used in fields as diverse as theatrical productions and rental property management and it is "the Nut." The Nut, and one wonders of its origin, is the cash inflow number that must occur to cover just the ongoing expenses of operation. A more elegant accounting term would be "break-even cash inflow," but the somberness of the Nut is useful to our discussion. Looming over the seller in many Dealmaking experiences is this very Nut, namely, that monetary figure that must be recovered on the particular deal to clear the books, or to rescue some P&L situation within the seller's organization.

Sometimes this break-even cash inflow is known as the Bogey.[15] Sometimes it is known as the "toe tag," meaning that you as the Dealmaker will get that number or it will become your corpse's identification.

Regardless of the term of art that is used, the dilemma of the must-have number is that it casts a shadow over value and deal options because of requirements, needs, or expectations external to the deal event or even to its intrinsic value. In a sense it is the global politic that, in certain circumstances, can override all other considerations.

Who owns the Nut? Sometimes it is the P&L manager who will be credited with the proceeds from the transaction. Sometimes it is the CFO, or even the CEO, who will absorb such proceeds and report an overall profit number to shareholders and investors. Sometimes it is the deal manager who, for some reason, needs, or feels the need, to create a career number. Sometimes it is just a number that has emerged out of an inventor's head as an appropriately spectacular signifier of his or her contributions. On the buy side, the number, as might be anticipated, is some extraordinarily low figure that reflects the great bargain expectations placed on the deal manager. It can also reflect the buyer's cash outflow projections, including Wheelbarrow costs, pending new product revenues and profits. In either situation, the power of the Dealmaking methods and tools to be discussed is the ability to create a rational framework against which such external, and often unfounded, asserted values can be tested, contrasted, and corrected. There is an old joke about propaganda published by the former Soviet Union in its official newspaper Pravda: "Comrade, this latest material is so good we're believing it ourselves." The goal of the deal manager is to overcome these backdrop expectations that often are the metaphorical equivalent of propaganda by creating a business model that becomes defendable and ultimately believable by both sides of the negotiation.

Deal Targets

As a seller of anything, one's concern is always the question "Who is my customer?" For a Box of exclusive rights, one needs only one customer-buyer; for nonexclusive licensing Boxes, the answer can be a few to many. We will consider here the exclusive case.

For ease in collecting statistics, let us consider for the moment only buyers in the United States. If I presume that my buyer is a business, U.S. census statistics suggest that there are some six million potential buyers if we consider all firms with employees regardless of their legal form, which of course does not include not-yet-into-existence startups that could be formed. With the frightful possibilities made available by commercial email lists, I could presumably acquire the means to send a deal proposal with one mouse click to six million inboxes. Assuming for a moment that such a proposal would be at least viewed, what would be the reaction of this universe of prospective buyers? Well, of course, the almost universal value ascribed would be even less than zero, meaning that, were it possible, this vast group of non-buyers would consider or acquire the opportunity only if they were paid to do so simply because they have no business interest in the area.

Next we would find a category of nominal buyers who would have sufficient interest to invest in reviewing the opportunity but their interest and the opportunity fit is such that their perceived value, at the last, would be nominal or zero. If the opportunity was offered for free, or near free, they could be interested, a kind of "just in case" very low-cost option. They might respond with a nominal offer to buy patents for some figure approximating what they would have spent to get a patent had they made the original invention(s).

A more suitable category would be our "target buyers" who, because of the specific envisioned business benefits associated with the opportunity, would immediately perceive this offer as something worth pursuing.

Finally, one might imagine a single, unique ideal buyer for whom this opportunity fits like a key into an extraordinarily valuable door lock available only to that company. This scenario is the business-to-business equivalent of the metaphorical "soul mate" concept used in human affairs.

As will be discussed later regarding a Plan B, it is a wise Dealmaking practice for a seller to have multiple potential buyers under consideration. Using the described categorization, this means that of the population of "target buyers" and the one, or very few, "ideal buyer(s)," a selection must be made as to the number and identity that will be targeted for contact and at least initial discussions.

There are two temptations that generally should be resisted: Seize on one and only one target buyer, or, at the other extreme, make a very long list and pursue them all. The ideal, as in much of our discussion in this book, is the golden mean between extremes. Here such a mean could be 5 to 10 potential buyers. The list is short enough that an appropriate level of analysis on each prospect is manageable that will enable an intelligent contact and follow-on discussion to occur. Yet, providing the opportunity is itself attractive and the selection of the target list has been done well, there should be enough prospective parties interested that an appropriate use of Plan B can be accomplished, as will be discussed.

In Chapter 5 on the Rating/Ranking Method we saw how a spreadsheet could be used to develop an expert judgment on the value and relative importance of various factors. Rating/Ranking is a useful Tool for identifying potential target buyers. An example of how this could be done is shown in Exhibit 11.4. The motivation for a systematic process of identifying buyers is (1) the Dealmaking challenges discussed above (from the Survey data), (2) the significant investment cost in conducting a Dealmaking campaign, and (3) the obvious seller desire to realize the maximum potential value from the opportunity.

Each considered potential buyer is in a separate row. The rightmost, shaded columns are then used to summarize key facts about each potential buyer. The first set of such shown in the graphic include annual revenues in relevant markets, compound growth rate, gross margin, profitability measure (EBIT), and R&D spending. The next set of criteria assesses the company's Dealmaking history with examples, and personal contacts known to the seller. Other important criteria (not shown) could include general information about the company's strategy or key business needs, and complementary patents it owns or controls relevant to the subject opportunity.

Shown in the two three-headed columns to the left in Exhibit 11.4 are Rating/Ranking criteria and for calculated values: Each column headed C (C1, C2, etc.), captures the value scored for each company of the respective criterion. W, the weighting on each criterion, and WC the result obtained by multiplying the first two columns. An example of C1 could be the ability to dominate the market(s) that are relevant to the subject opportunity and C2 could be the ability to master the underlying technology (-ies) that will successfully convert the subject opportunity

Rating/Ranking Score							Considered Alternatives					Metrics of Alternatives						
C1	W1	WC1	C2	W2	WC2	Score	Rank	Cat.	Grp	ID	Company	Rev. $	CAGR %	GM %	EBIT %	R&D $	Deals	Contacts
							1	A										
							2	A										
							3	B										
							4	B										
							5	B										
							6	B										
							7	B										
							8	B										
							9	B										
							10	C										
							11	C										
							12	C										
							13	C										
							14	C										
							15	C										
							16	C										
							17	C										
							18	C										
							19	C										
							20	C										

EXHIBIT 11.4 Illustrative Spreadsheet for Applying Rating/Ranking to Identify Target Buyers

into a finished manufacturing operation. If the criteria are deemed approximately equal in importance, then the weighting column can be eliminated, thereby simplifying the analysis. Alternatively, if the relative importance of the various criteria is simple, then the weighting can be done at the time of calculating the final score.

For important candidates, a separate, spreadsheet tab can be dedicated entirely to facts about the company such as its publicly filed financial statements, or even the results of market surveys. Opportunity marketing information, such as key deal team contacts and background information, can also be conveniently placed within dedicated worksheet tabs.

The middle columns of Exhibit 11.4 show the group to which the company belongs, its ranked order (when the Rating/Ranking process is completed), and its Dealmaking priority: A companies are the ones perceived to be ideal fits, B companies solid target fits, and C companies deemed less likely or at least lower in priority. Often when a long list of candidate companies are considered, they can be usefully distinguished as belonging to different types or subgroups. Grouping the companies according to some taxonomy can be useful for multiple purposes. The Rating/Ranking criteria and weighting might change because the appropriate business model for a deal could be different for one group of companies. When observing a highly ranked candidate it is useful to think of other possible companies that might belong to the same group and that had been overlooked in an initial assessment of deal alternatives.

It is generally a good practice to include in the list of alternatives some that do not include a deal with any third party. For instance, one alternative is simply to wait for some prescribed period, say a year. Another alternative is to retain the opportunity and develop it further or completely. Other alternatives could include aggregating the opportunity with something larger, such as a technology being aggregated with a product line or a division, and offered only as a whole; another alternative could be to deaggregate the opportunity and offer for sale or license, say, just the rights to certain patents or other intellectual property. These nondealmaking alternatives may simply have been a priori ruled out. Still it is useful to include them here as a benchmark by which to gauge the relative attractiveness of various alternatives. Including these alternatives is especially valuable when Plan A has not worked out and one is forced to consider various Dealmaking Plan Bs, as we will discuss later in this chapter. The question often arises: Is such pursuit really worth doing? Keeping track of buyer alternatives is useful during opportunity marketing especially if/as the recognition occurs of new potential buyers.

It helps to remind ourselves of the Aristotelian mean:

> *We must also remember... [to] not look for precision in all things alike, but in each class of things such precision as accords with the subject matter, and so much as is appropriate to the inquiry. For a carpenter and a geometer investigate the right angle in different ways; the former does so in so far as the right angle is useful for his work, while the latter inquires what it is or what sort of thing it is; for he is a spectator of the truth.*
>
> Book 1, Chapter 7, *Nicomachean Ethics*

Negotiating Plan

A Dealmaking readiness "Book" addresses the eight keys of Chapter 10 and 11: Box/Wheelbarrow, Price, Structure, Term Sheets, Deal Team, Deal Targets, Negotiating/Deal Plan, and Plan B. In this section we want to consider some aspects of the Negotiating/Deal Plan.

Negotiating Sequencing

In Chapter 9 we identified five broad contexts for Dealmaking, and focused on the two auction contexts, Real Time Public, and Structured Private. The focus here is on the traditional, Strategic Direct Marketing.

The ten steps of such marketing are generally as follows:

1. *Starting from the described target list and initial contacts, screening for potential interest*. Such screening occurs without formal written documents (although table napkins have an illustrious history). It can occur in an informal encounter or, more typically, by telephone. Email can be useful to set up a time for a telephone call, but email alone does not provide for the kind of communication exchange needed.
2. *Nonconfidential, brief, writing that characterizes the "scene" of the opportunity*. Writing creates something concrete that can be pondered on in private and shared with others whose opinion will matter. Such writing, which I refer to as an Opportunity Memorandum (distinguished from the formal Offering Memorandum), gives the readers a perspective that fits with their business operations and their customers. It provides some weight behind the initial discussion to answer the always present "so what?" question.
3. *Confidentiality agreement specific to the opportunity*. It is customary in business communications to keep confidential the communications with other parties about prospective opportunities as a matter of professional courtesy and ethics. However, there are some good reasons for formal confidentiality agreements, such as protecting the seller's ability to pursue future patenting, maintaining a valuable trade secret, preventing premature disclosure of an interest in selling, not providing competitors with advantageous information, and so forth.
4. *Confidential writing that discloses key elements of what is contended to be proprietary to the seller*. This disclosure could be done at a face-to-face meeting or by letter. Such a disclosure should have the purpose of creating awareness in the seller as to why a negotiation is necessary to secure the business benefits characterized in the Opportunity Memorandum. Normally the seller does not disclose everything confidential or all the facts behind the opportunity because it is still not clear how serious the interest is.
5. *Term sheet and detail disclosure*. Prospective buyers often seek to understand the seller's proposed terms prior to "deep dives" into the opportunity. Sellers may share a similar interest for a similar reason—to avoid wasting time. However, sometimes sellers want to wait until there is a deeper context developed from which such terms can be better understood. It is generally a good idea not to provide copies of the term sheet or to delve too deeply into the expected value range until the prospective buyer has done some initial work to confirm its potential interest. Buyers often want to have an early idea of seller expectations.

So there may need to be some range of value discussion. However, sellers are cautious about just citing some number. As we have discussed, typical deal structures are more complex than just one number.

6. *Initial negotiation and due diligence.* At this point, the prospective buyer should have concluded that (1) this opportunity fits their business, (2) the opportunity makes sense, and (3) there appears to be something proprietary to the seller that would be worth acquiring. Both the buyer and seller should have reached a common understanding on at least this level prior to beginning initial negotiations or due diligence. As in the previous stage (5), these two activities are paired because they can occur in either order (diligence first or last) or semi-simultaneously. If there are some key business terms that either party is seeking that, based on the term sheet in stage 5, appear to be key deal issues, then it is often a good practice to work on them first to gain confidence that, if the due diligence is satisfactory, an agreement is likely to be possible. However, until due diligence is completed, there is often substantial uncertainty as to the total value, and even all the prospective deal issues. Although due diligence is a common term of art for a buyer's activities, in many business deals there can be important due diligence activities by the seller.
7. *Detailed negotiations and formal agreement drafting.* As previously discussed, these two activities are paired because they can occur sequentially or semi-simultaneously. Lead negotiators who are also attorneys appear to prefer detailed negotiations by means of formal agreement drafting. Lead negotiators who have sales and marketing in their backgrounds and orientations generally prefer detail negotiations instead of (at least for their part of the Dealmaking) formal agreement drafting.
8. *Final negotiations and agreement.* In the previously described (7) activities, which can last over many weeks, there is commonly a list of items that requires either side to consider with other parties within their respective organization or there has been incomplete assent by both parties on (or even outright disagreement). In stage 8, all these areas are to be communicated and resolved or the Dealmaking process will be stalled or even terminated.
9. *Execution and asset transfers.* This stage should normally be a straightforward process of dotting i's and crossing t's, but there are often last-minute issues that arise either because some matter had been forgotten, or some issue already resolved has returned, or legal wrangling occurs regarding making the English and legal language work in conformity with the agreed provisions.[16] There is a phenomenon of "buyer's remorse" known to all automobile salesmen. Shortly after a purchase commitment has been made, it is human nature to wonder if one did the right thing. Before the purchase, the buyer had the universe of possibilities in front of him or her, and now, by making a commitment, that universe has shrunk. Sellers can experience the same thing, though it appears to occur less often, perhaps because sellers are typically the initiators of the entire Dealmaking process. Both parties can have the internal churning of "Did I get the best deal I could have?"[17]
10. *Agreement maintenance.* Complicated deals commonly have after-deals, just as earthquakes have aftershocks. They can range from informal clarifications to the need for a formal amendment or even (according to at least one side) to a complete renegotiation.

All ten steps or stages are important to a negotiation. Our focus here in a discussion of sequencing, is the heart of the negotiation process that takes place in stages 6, 7, and 8. Of all the deal issues that require mutual assent, how should they best be sequenced in a negotiation? There are four possible strategies:

1. Start somewhere, anywhere.
2. Start from page 1.
3. Work from the easiest to the most difficult issues.
4. Work from the most difficult to the easiest issues.

The start-somewhere strategy reflects the belief that it is not particularly important to choose or sequence but to get started.[18] Start from page 1 is the strategy favored by the checklist oriented, especially when working on standard deals such as template license agreements. The more interesting sequencing strategies are the final two. Is it better to work the most difficult issues first or last?

The argument made in support of saving the most difficult issues until last is to create momentum by agreeing on some simpler matters. The idea is to first lift the 5-pound weights, get comfortable doing so, let the blood flow to warm those muscles, and then move to the 10 pounders. By the end of the process, you will be prepared to chalk up, notch up, and try to heave up some Olympic weights. The compelling counterargument is that little significance is established by lifting 5-pound weights if one's goals are Olympic; we would be better off getting to the really important issues first, reaching agreement on these matters or, if no agreement is possible, seeking another way to reconfigure the entire approach to make agreement become possible, or moving on to Plan B (soon to be discussed). For the seller, if there are multiple potential buyers, as well as excellent Plan B's, then it makes sense to tackle the hardest issues first to get to an early realization of whether a deal is likely to be possible. Another benefit of early work on the hard issues is that they may take time to work through which time may be invested in parallel with other Dealmaking activities. A potential downside of starting on hard issues is the risk of one side or another souring on the entire effort because it is not yet clear that many other deal issues will be resolved easily. A term sheet is useful in highlighting the important deal issues, leading to an early understanding, in most cases, of which issues may be both complex and more difficult for one or both sides to accept.

Issue Explosion

Some negotiations experience an emergence of many issues separating agreement between the parties. In some instances, the mere large number of such issues can be a signal to the parties that agreement is not likely within the presently envisioned framework of the agreement. In other cases, such issue explosion could arise because of motives, perhaps not altogether pure, by one side of the negotiation. Such a strategy is generally a bad faith effort by the issue-proliferating side to create a blizzard of objections, or concerns, for the purpose at some later stage of conceding on many or even all of them as bargaining ploys to gain certain concessions from the other side on a very major issue. The underlying idea is that one side concedes many issues and creates a concession bank account that it can then draw on, perhaps in one massive withdrawal, to achieve the concession it really seeks from the other side. This strategy is sometimes called the "bones" strategy, as in throw the dog a bone to keep it happy, and is equivalent in moral standing to the now widely discredited "cookie jar" strategy of some companies in managing their reported earnings by recognizing a revenue (a cookie) at convenient moments each reporting quarter to manage investor illusions.

However, a particular agreement framework for a particular opportunity for particular parties can genuinely lead to a vast number of legitimate negotiating issues that could be disproportionate to one side. In such cases, the sheer number of issues should cause the parties to reconsider the big picture before attempting to go through any resolution sequence. Generally speaking, there are three possible sources for legitimate issue explosion:

1. Wrong parties for the given opportunity
2. Wrong opportunity for the right parties
3. Wrong framework for the right opportunity for the right parties

These scenarios are akin to the situation of a poorly performing employee. One possibility is that the employee simply is the wrong person for the job. However, the problem could be a good employee in a wrong job. Finally, the employee and employer and the job could all be made to work well if the job is restructured in some way. In a similar way, issue explosion is a sign to deal managers that something is wrong either with respect to the pairing of these two particular parties, or the deal framework, or both.

Negotiating Values

The three A's of professional services sales are: Ability, Availability, and Affability. We tend to overlook the third one: People buy from people they like, whenever they are able to do so. Jerry Mulen, producer of *Jurassic Park* and *Schindler's List* and many other movies, talks of negotiating with prospective directors and storytellers as "sitting down and listening to their [the collaborator's] heart" and "assembling a team to tell a story you have a passion about" and "friendships that survive the project." This point drives the seeking of win–win deals.

Communication fidelity is always an issue when dealing with individuals and groups who negotiate on behalf of their self interest. The challenge is not the silence, namely, what you are not told about the other side's position; although silence can inhibit opportunity Discovery, it is the truthfulness of the communications received that is important. Over the years, there have been many attempts to find simple attributes that can, without raising suspicions, detect an untruthful statement. Eye movements and blinking, for example, have had popular adherents. An interesting study was performed with subjects to see if one ear or the other could detect truthfulness; amazingly, one study reported that there was a left ear advantage to recognizing the truthfulness of a statement.[19] Until some technology is developed that is accepted for Dealmaking, we will have to rely on more traditional measures. Although I am not aware of studies that have been done in the context of business negotiations, I believe that deal teams interacting with each other in multiple encounters do, in fact, become attuned to communication fidelity. Loss of trust, deserved or not, is normally very damaging for deal closure prospects.

Deal/Agreement Complexity

Deals that involve conditional future consideration, such as milestone payments, or royalties, or royalties that are subject to future adjustments, or any of the other ways of configuring the Wheelbarrow, or even the Box, create additional agreement complexity. Such additional complexity may be sufficiently important to one or both parties because of future uncertainties that it is a good idea to include the feature. However, if each deal compromise, or each idea by a deal team member, results in a new feature for the Wheelbarrow, the agreement can get unmanageably complex.

Albert Einstein claimed one of the keys to discovery in physics was *making it [model] as simple as possible, but not simpler*. Aristotle emphasized the importance of "the mean," meaning that ideal point of balance between extremes, for example: Courage being "the mean" between cowardliness and foolhardiness. In like manner, a good Dealmaking agreement is as simple as possible, but not simpler, reflecting a "mean" between the complexity of every possible contingency and interest, and no consideration of "what if."

Agreements tend to be long lived and administered by people who were not directly involved in the negotiations. They have to be comprehensible. And the clearer they are the less likely there will be future disputes.

Active Learning

A final point of advice is on the aspect of listening, learning, and flexibility. The point of Dealmaking is developing and using **Approaches, Methods**, and **Tools (A-M-T)** to enable deals done, not a priori positions to be defended at all costs, especially in the face of contrary evidence.

In the ancient play *Antigone*, Sophocles has the character Haimon appeal to his father, the authoritarian King Creon:

> *"I beg you, do not be unchangeable: do not believe that you alone can be right. The man who thinks that, the man who maintains that only he has the power to reason correctly, the gift to speak, the soul—a man like that, when you know him, turns out to be empty. It is not reason never to yield to reason!"* (Haimon to his father Creon who has sentenced Antigone, his betrothed, to death.)
>
> *Antigone*, Scene III

Plan B

Everybody needs a Plan B. And, the best time for one is before you need one.

Auctions and Betrothals

Before developing a plan for Plan B, let us first consider two polar negotiating situations: auctions and betrothals. Auctions are as old as commerce and as new as www.ebay.com. As discussed in Chapter 9, for sellers, there is aspiration for many simultaneous aspiring buyers making offers creating a kind of free-for-all environment, with an immediate and final resolution.

Now, let us consider the polar opposite of auctions: "betrothal" Dealmaking. The term betrothal negotiations in Dealmaking means that, for reasons and forces (apparently) beyond the control of the deal manager, there is a pre-established expectation that Seller X and Buyer Y will price, negotiate, and consummate this deal. This XY betrothal may be at the behest of the infamous lunch or golf outing or Outward Bound bonding of CEO-X and CEO-Y who agree to agree and assign down the responsibility to get the Dealmaking done, or equally as likely, a principal inventor at X is good buddies with an R&D manager/inventor at Y and decides this is certain to be an ideal fit.

The temptation for the deal team in this situation is to resignedly accept the mission and get the best deal possible. However, in general, even with such expectation constraints, it is still a good idea to develop a Plan B analysis. For instance, one of the most constraining of deal constraints is litigation between X and Y that CEOs have directed their teams to settle. Is a Plan B possible in such a case? Yes, and the side that does it better has an advantage. In this case the Plan B is simply to point out the costs, rewards, and risks of not settling and either continuing to pursue the litigation or creating some alternative form of dispute resolution to a negotiation. Without a Plan B what can one side do to a fabulously unreasonable and fixed position taken by the other side, which then just waits for acquiescence?

Two other common sources of betrothal negotiation are the favorite Company Y for Seller X and the so called match made in heaven (which may also be called the "soul mate deal"). In the favored company example, there is some favorable working history or perhaps ongoing collaborations that create a context that is attractive to one or both sides. Such trust and experience is helpful in overcoming many communication hurdles and may also be useful in valuation or agreement construction by referring to and using previous transactions. However, opportunities tend to be opportunity specific. It may well be, and probably is, that in this specific instance companies X and Y will determine, if they each perform a Plan B analysis, that one or both will conclude that this opportunity has greater value with some third party. Without such Plan B analysis, it is almost certain that a suboptimal though easy deal will result. And if it does subsequently become disadvantageous to either side, then the deal will in fact have harmed the relationship.

The other example, the soul mate deal, occurs when what looks to be the ideal buyer Y, from the perspective of seller X, has independently concluded that its ideal opportunity is the subject opportunity being offered by X. This situation is that of the seller of a Buckminster Fuller hard-to-sell geodesic house in rural nowheresville finding a prospective buyer who has been searching all his or her life for a Buckminster Fuller geodesic house in nowheresville. Should such parties still do a Plan B? Yes, although in this example the seller would probably be advised to do his or hers quite quickly. The experience in Dealmaking, like marriage, is that initial appearances may not correlate well with ultimate experience. Further, a soul mate buyer characteristically comes to that realization and discerning the absence of a seller, Plan B will be inclined to exploit the advantage (CFOs on deal teams are typically quite skillful at providing such buyer voicing).

Plan B Analysis and Tools

It is said that every investor in a startup asks of itself "first the exit," meaning consideration of how a liquidity event will occur. A Plan B analysis is a similar question. There is a reason why the discussion of identifying the target (and ideal) buyers are Plan A. However, what happens if none or one of those Plan A buyers are, in the end, seriously ready to negotiate? A Plan B is about answering that question. It is a good idea to do such a plan at the outset, but it is increasingly important if/as the Plan A list of potential buyers shrinks to two or less. The famous football coach Vince Lombardi stressed conditioning because, he said, "Fatigue makes cowards of us all." In Dealmaking, having no Plan B, has that same effect. It is hard to say "no" even to unreasonable requests of the other side when one's alternatives are a blank page.

The starting point for a Plan B is the creation of a broader range of possibilities than the focused list of Plan A. It is surprising how rarely (and poorly) this is sometimes done. One possible reason is the thought-constraining experience of education in which we tend to learn that there is always a best answer, and that the teacher is the one who knows it. There are creativity experiments done with early elementary school students, such as third graders, in which they will be asked to suggest how a particular problem can be solved. What follows is something like an explosion of ideas, often with humor, and normally with enthusiasm. (If you are a parent with children in this age range who, say, want a horse; just ask them, seriously, "How could we keep one here?" and you will be amazed at the range of answers.) However, in these same experiments done with late elementary school students, say, seventh graders, the creativity is (commonly) curtailed and classes tend to think of no or only marginally variant alternatives. This change has been attributed to a general transformation from joy and wonder to fear and judgment (which may be the ultimate point of Cervantes' *Don Quixote*).

In business contexts, especially when a lot is at stake, and especially when a senior company official is present, this combination of fear and judgment can constrict the creation of a list of options to the few obvious and timid suggestions. The initial list of companies that did not make the Plan A cut is a starting point for Plan B candidates. Also, starting from the scoring criteria that led to the high scores for the Plan A candidates leads to the question: what other companies, or kinds of companies, that we have not considered would score well on this criteria? This could be asked of colleagues by identifying the key traits believed to be the most important.

Another useful source of Plan B candidates are Plan A companies who decline interest in the opportunity for any reason. A good question that can be asked over the phone, as people don't tend to answer such questions in writing, is "If you were me, who would you call on to determine their interest in this opportunity?" Even the more traditional question of "Help me understand why you are not interested in this opportunity so I can better prioritize my focus?" can lead to thinking about better or at least alternative prospective buyers.

Plan B Implementation

PLAN B CAUTION As with any good practice, there can be a dark side to having a Plan B. One obvious one for Plan B analysis is that one can become stuck in analysis, as in paralysis by analysis. There can be too many alternatives under serious consideration. Or there can be too many factors being scored and weighted. Or there can be too long a debate as to the significance of the differences in scoring.

When the opportunities are potentially significant and the future opportunity can be difficult to characterize or widely varying in value depending on the perspective used, then a serious effort in such analysis is appropriate and warranted. But time is often a critical factor. So having established procedures and trained deal teams and even access to outside consultants, together with a reasonable standard of certainty, is important to keep the opportunities from being sidetracked by study.

Another less obvious caution is the loss of deal focus. Most high value, high complexity deals experience times of discouragement bordering on despair. Issues thought to be resolved seem to reappear. Hard issues for which there appeared agreement on a resolution principle or process cannot seem to be resolved. Harsh words or other foul behavior can sour relationships. Feelings known as post-deal remorse (as in buyer's remorse) can appear even before deal closing is in sight, perhaps expressed late at night as "Why are we even thinking of doing this deal?" Having a ready Plan B, which is a good thing, can in such cases cause a deal manager or deal team to give up at the point of adversity on what would otherwise, with determination, have been a very good deal. At this stage, the Plan B alternative(s) can appear better than they are simply because you have not begun the hard work of negotiating with such fresh faces.

Having quantified at least the top candidates on the Plan B list can be useful at such junctures to reinforce the reason why this particular opportunity was your Plan A in the first place. Difficulty in negotiation may be just that—difficulty.

PLAN B FROM THE BUYER'S PERSPECTIVE Although much of the previous discussion has been in the context of the seller's perspective, a Plan B is important for prospective buyers as well. Without such alternatives, the buyer deal team can assume that their very careers are on the line such that no deal means no career because there is no alternative in view. Although such a scenario can be usefully motivating, it is also a dangerous practice that will cause deal teams perhaps to ignore red flags, and/or overpay. We witnessed in high visibility technology companies numerous acquisitions that in retrospect were simply not well considered.

When the buy-side deal team has been charged with acquiring the best available X, in which X is a technology or product, creating alternatives and a Plan B Rating/Ranking is very similar to the process described for the sell-side deal team. When the alternatives are very disparate investments with perhaps loss of deal team cohesion, it becomes more difficult.

PLAN B AND LIFE Exhibit 11.5 is a reproduction of a black and white painting by Raphael Soyer,[20] perhaps incongruous here in the context of technology Dealmaking, but worth your careful reflection.

Depicted are two women shown on a common black floor but silhouetted against two very different vertical panels, one black (the unopened shade) and one an unshaded, light-transmitting window. The ballerina on the right is dressed for ballet practice, with her hair up; the one on the left is dressed in street clothes with her hair down. One has her head down, looking into the practice room, the other's is up and looking outside. One is holding with both hands what appears to be a garment associated with her work, the other is holding the shade with one hand, almost like a wave (or a salute?) and reaching outward with the other. On the third vertical panel, the rightmost one, is a second white panel balancing the panel

EXHIBIT 11.5 *Ballerinas* by Raphael Soyer

Painting by Raphael Soyer, courtesy of the Seattle Art Museum. © The Seattle Art Museum, gift of Mrs. Helen Eisenberg. Reprinted with permission.

with the "outward" woman on the left; on this third panel is some sort of message, which echoes in the outward woman's also light panel and contrasts in the "inward" ballerina's dark panel. The inward ballerina appears almost weighted down by the dark panel, as if it were pressing her into the dark floor; even her shoes, shown as dark, appear almost like weights that have locked her into the practice room. The outward ballerina, in contrast, has white shoes that not only contrast with the floor but she is shown barely within the confines of the floor and the shoe color suggests that a freeing break has been made.

And, so? We are processing in this picture a deep idea of response to imposed, dramatic change. Why two ballerinas, as opposed to two, say, writers or welders? Because, I think, there comes a time, usually surprisingly soon, when the ballerina's profession shuts off the professional opportunity for employment, for compensation, for expression; the calendar is simply less kind to ballerinas than to writers or welders. What happens at the moment of the "writing on the wall" when the realization occurs that Plan A can no longer work?[21] This painting conveys the two basic responses available to us: the inward resignation versus the outward, new opportunity perspective. In this book centered on options, albeit investment options, it is appropriate to close with a deeper look at what options should mean.

For high value, high complexity Dealmaking, this business process can become an all consuming pursuit. It is not uncommon that as a result of forces beyond one's control or anticipation, the process can lead to frustrating apparent or real dead ends. That perception is the inward ballerina, stuck in the room, hands almost bound to what no longer can work, dressed for no other purpose, eyes on no other prize.

There is another perspective possible. Somewhere there is a shade that can be undrawn, and a window that opens to something else. There exists a Plan B. A cornerstone idea of Plan B is that there are other opportunities, always, hidden behind drawn shades that can, and should, be considered. Look one last time at the outward, now former, ballerina at the window. Between her and that window, a small barrier in front of her feet, is pictured a radiator, shown by the alliteration of light and dark vertical lines. Those lines convey an image of miniature jail bars. With the shade drawn, those lines could have looked like tall bars hidden by the shade; with the opened shade, they are seen for what they really are—a small barrier.[22]

So, in the spirit of this book, I envision a new symbol posted on that bulletin board in the rightmost panel: $\exists$B. The symbol $\exists$, is used in mathematics to designate existence, literally, "there exists" as in: $\exists$ an even number greater than two. A Dealmaking best practice is posting $\exists$B in front of every analysis: Beyond this opportunity, which we are hotly pursuing, there does exist a Plan B. Its existence, though solely perceptual, has a reality because of the conviction that it can be made to exist experientially. The inward ballerina, perhaps as her first step toward acceptance, may be less imprisoned by the garment in her hands and more conducting a funeral and placing the remnants of Plan A in what looks very much like a miniature sarcophagus. Perhaps that is always the necessary first step.

And there are some, few situations where $\exists!$A (namely, the symbol $\exists!$ is used to designate unique existence, so here there exists uniquely/only Plan A). So the heart and soul must be in pursuit of Plan A. That is what makes it A. And without such pursuit, one becomes a dilettante, always dabbling, never realizing the difficult opportunities. But the commitment to A should be sheltered by the B, whenever possible. Such realization leads to better execution of the A, and the courage to know when to "fold 'em" and pursue the B.

Concluding Advice from Technology Dealmakers

The previously discussed Licensing Foundation Survey for 2006 asked fill-in-the-blank questions for the top three best and worst Dealmaking practices for three periods: before, during, and after the deal. Highlights of these responses follows:[23]

1. *Before the Deal*. The predominant best practice observation can be summarized by "do your homework." This was expressed by more than 100 phrases containing words like know, understand, research, due diligence, study, analyze, prepare, plan, identify, evaluate, develop, estimate, assess, define. For example,

18 responses began with the word identify(ing), 26 with know(ing)/knowledge, 8 with prepare/preparation, 13 with research(ing), 34 with understand(ing). As might be expected, there was a variety of things that were identified as the object of to know/understand/etc. Although the market was the most frequent word mentioned in this context probably followed by valuation, the span of things "do homework" on, was deep and wide: key decision makers, goals, walkaways, other party's needs, patent position, competitors, IP strengths, BATNA.[24] It should also be noted that there was frequent response of people issues: build a project team, "courtesy wins in the long, run, no matter how painful the interaction," face to face meetings, being flexible/creative, and the like. Worst practices were in many ways the best practices turned upside down: no preparation and poor people skills. Common words that captured such lack of preparedness were assume(ing), cursory, ignorant (ance), unaware, sloppy, unclear. One response captured such unpreparedness as follows: "'make me an offer (no preparation)." On people matters, words used were arrogance, bad faith, close-minded, bluff, shoot from the hip.

2. *During Negotiation.* Many of the responses captured the best practice idea of being wholly sentient, most often expressed by listening, but also including other forms of observation (body language). People issues were even more important here: Be courteous, ethical, flexible, polite, respectful, patient, positive, discuss/don't argue, honesty, humor, open (ness). These practices relate to another common observation regarding the practice of flexibility, which may again point to the greater complexity of IP dealmaking than other kinds of business negotiations. The worst practices included many references to assume (reflecting here perhaps more a lack of listening rather than as above a lack of preparation). Other worst practices included dirty little tricks, bait and switch, arguing, bullying, changing people on the negotiating teams, changing terms, delay, ego, getting insulted ("it isn't personal, stay positive"), nickel and diming.
3. *After the Deal.* The most common best practice centered on communicating (ion). Among the terms and phrases used in this regard were various forms of follow up, maintain(ing), monitor(ing), manage(ing), staying connected. For the worst practices, characteristic words used were complacency, assume(ing), failure to (follow up, communicate, etc). On the people side, there were two particularly poignant pieces of advice of behaviors to avoid: continued antagonism, and its opposite, crying over spilled milk—human feelings all too easily experienced from dealmaking that had limited degrees of freedom for one of the parties.

Notes

1. *Troilus and Cressida*, II ii., based on a medieval legend that retells the fall of Troy to the Greeks, originally told in Homer's *Iliad* and *Odyssey*. Troilus was the son of the king of Troy and Cressida was the betrayer of his love, whereupon Troilus was killed in the Trojan War. Alas.
2. "U.S./Canadian Licensing in 2003: Survey Results," by Richard Razgaitis, *les Nouvelles*, December 2004, p. 139ff., and www.licensingfoundation.org.

3. "U.S./Canadian Licensing in 2004: Survey Results," by Richard Razgaitis, *les Nouvelles*, December 2005, p. 145ff., and www.licensingfoundation.org.
4. "U.S./Canadian Licensing in 2005: Survey Results," by Richard Razgaitis, *les Nouvelles*, December 2006, p. 233ff., and www.licensingfoundation.org.
5. "U.S./Canadian Licensing in 2006: Survey Results," by Richard Razgaitis, *les Nouvelles*, December 2007, p. 641ff., and www.licensingfoundation.org.
6. "U.S./Canadian Licensing in 2003: Survey Results."
7. Ibid.
8. Ibid.
9. "U.S./Canadian Licensing in 2005: Survey Results."
10. Ibid.
11. "U.S./Canadian Licensing in 2006: Survey Results."
12. It is appropriate to repeat a well-worn pith attributed to James Branch Cabell (1879–1958): "An optimist proclaims that we live in the best of all possible worlds; and a pessimist fears that this is true."
13. "Office Buildings Sell at Bargain Prices," *Wall Street Journal*, October 29, 2002, p. A2.
14. www.demotivators.com, by Despair, Inc.
15. "Bogie" as used, likely derives from a military context in which it is used for the enemy targeted.
16. A great quote, for which I do not recall the citation, complicates much of Stages 8 and 9: "English resists meaning."
17. There is even a pathology that poisons Dealmaking whereby one side concludes that if the other side has agreed, they must have been willing to make it more favorable, which leads to the contradiction that the only time I know that I have gotten the best possible deal is if the other side walks away!
18. This strategy could also be called the Mt. Vernon strategy. George Washington's home, available for touring, is maintained by an approach called "Mt. Vernon method." It consists of starting wherever one starts, and keeping going through the room you are now in, cleaning and fixing as necessary, and then progressing from room to room. Wherever you stop at the end of that day, you just pick up the next day, and so on in perpetuity.
19. F. Fabbro, et al., "Hemispheric Asymmetry for the Auditory Recognition of True and False Statements. Neuropsychologia 31" (1993): 865–870. The experiments were done with 48 right-handed adjust subjects, 24 males and 24 females.
20. 1945, the original is in the Seattle Art Museum, Seattle, Washington.
21. I see the note on the right panel, as the writing on the wall, as being the list of the ballerinas selected for the performance season and neither ballerina in our picture made the "cut."
22. The vertical lines also convey to me the marking of time, somewhat as a prisoner might do by ticking off the days and years of confinement.
23. "U.S./Canadian Licensing in 2006: Survey Results."
24. BATNA: Best Alternative to a Negotiated Agreement, which is another way of saying a "Plan B."

CHAPTER 12

In Conclusion

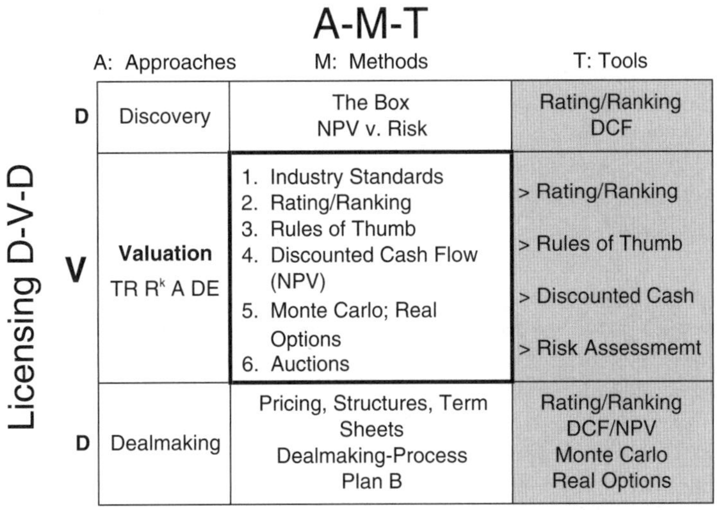
A-M-T
A: Approaches
M: Methods
T: Tools
Licensing D-V-D
D
Discovery
The Box
NPV v. Risk
Rating/Ranking
DCF
V
Valuation
TR R^k A DE
1. Industry Standards
2. Rating/Ranking
3. Rules of Thumb
4. Discounted Cash Flow (NPV)
5. Monte Carlo; Real Options
6. Auctions
> Rating/Ranking
> Rules of Thumb
> Discounted Cash
> Risk Assessmemt
D
Dealmaking
Pricing, Structures, Term Sheets
Dealmaking-Process
Plan B
Rating/Ranking
DCF/NPV
Monte Carlo
Real Options

This final chapter briefly reviews the key points of Technology Licensing D-V-D, namely the ***Approaches*** of opportunity Discovery, Valuation, and Dealmaking, and the valuation **Methods** and **Tools** that have been described and applied.

The usual goal of all the covered A-M-T, ***Approaches-Methods-Tools***, is a deal structured and priced fairly capturing the exchange of value, and structured in a form that makes sense for one's business context and objectives. In this final chapter we will try succinctly to fit these A-M-T elements together.

We will begin by considering the idea of a quest, a searching for opportunities and the appropriate values and structures to make them tradable.

Approach of Opportunity Discovery as a Quest

The D's of Technology Licensing D-V-D—opportunity Discovery and Dealmaking—are not so much a linear business process that hits a target. They are more like *quests*.

The concept behind and embodied within the word *quest* has a long and rich history in literature. Its root connects with many familiar words like *question*, *quarry* (as in hunted animals or ore in mines), *conquest, inquiry, and inquest*. It is central to one of the greatest book titles of all time, if not one of the greatest books of all time: *Fides Quaerens Intellectum* (Faith Quarries [for] Understanding, as indeed it does).[1] In the medieval period, the idea of a *quest* was central to many books and was made especially famous in the novel *Don Quixote* by Cervantes.[2] More on Cervantes' character Don Quixote and his sidekick Sancho Panza later.

The *quest* idea has similarities to the word *adventure*, from which we get *venture* as in venture capital (VC) a term less than 100 years old. And to the word *discover*, our word here for the business process/**Approach** of apprehending an important business opportunity. *Discover* comes from Latin, the conjunction of *dis* + *cooperire* (to cover), so it means literally to *un-cover.*

And *quest* is conceptually also related to *entrepreneur.* Entrepreneur comes from French as the composite of *entre* (between) + *prendre* (to take), so its root is a journey-idea.

Most business activities are about getting done something that was a predetermined "to do." So we mostly work at the "how" of some preexisting "what." The application of **Methods** and **Tools** is exactly about such "how," which in this book has been the V for valuation. The ***Approaches*** of opportunity Discovery and Dealmaking also have important elements of a quest, venture, discovery process than just a "how to do" something.

Here are some distinctions of a discovery/quest driven process:

- An act of creation/invention is necessary for success.
- High uncertainty environment; it is unclear what will be found, if anything.
- A general goal is in place as a motivation/purpose, but a specified result/configuration is missing.
- A kind of faith that that which is being sought will be found and recognized ("I'll know it when I see it").
- A journey-like experience (the object of the quest is a pursuit, rather than just answering a static waiting).
- The enemy of success tends to be things like distractions and discouragement, especially in the face of uncertainty.
- The keys to success include courage and wisdom.

There is a famous, largely legendary, story distinguishing two of our key concepts in the context of a quest. It is the story of Roland and Oliver, who were charged with the defense of Charlemagne's southern flank. Because the story dates to circa 800 A.D., and despite recent copyright extensions by the U.S. Congress to accommodate various powerful suppliants, the copyright has expired and is, so far, freely available on the Internet. In this story we see the mythos of two contrasting responses to the struggles and dangers of a quest. Roland in his brashness evidences (from the Latin) *fortitudo* (courage and determination in the face of adversaries, from which we get the English word *fortitude*), but not *sapienza* (wisdom). Oliver, Roland's right-hand man, and lifelong friend, in contrast, displays both *fortitudo* and *sapienza.* The story of two men, like the *Ballerinas* of Raphael Soyer in Chapter 11, enables the author to highlight the consequences of the missing trait of *sapienza* in Roland, which leads to his utter defeat and death, and the death of his friend, Oliver, despite Roland's *fortitudo*, even, it can be argued, because of his *fortitudo.*

We are raised in a culture of thinking of the "right answer" and the "right way" to get there. College classes, after all, are filled with homework problems and examinations. They are graded in some form of right and wrong. Those who get a lot of "wrongs," do not generally make it through the education process. So we are engrained to pursue the "right" method to obtain the right answer. A quest has a different architecture. The problem is often quite ambiguous. Instead of it being neatly defined at the start, it is more of an "I'll know it when I see it" situation. Instead of the right method, there is the greater significance of the right character qualities in our pursuit and motives. The right answer becomes the outcome of discovering that problem, conquest, or challenge that the person charged with the quest was uniquely called to do, and accomplish by the best of his or her character and abilities.

In many business activities, especially of large bureaucratic companies, such sense of adventure and wonder has been extinguished in our longing for certainty or at least predictability. In contrast, people who are drawn to opportunity Discovery—a kind of entrepreneurship—find its appeal because, in contrast to common business environments, every day can be quest-like. It's no accident that entrepreneurs and management, especially in large, old companies, are often at odds and in states of mutual incomprehension. The conflict is an old one, between the hunter-gatherer and the land farmer. The latter survives by methodically following procedure, while the former needs some method, but the hunt leads where it will. The conflict is a recurring story theme. In the James Bond stories the lab guy Q (apparently for Quartermaster—the archetypical "home office" procedures guy) is frequently distressed by the various equipment catastrophes occurring in Bond's adventures. Q: "Now pay attention 007..." "please read the instruction manual..." "be careful..." (re the new Lotus-submarine); to which Bond reminds Q to the effect that "the field" wherein he does His Majesty's work is not a benign environment.

Don Quixote was asked why he endured the struggles of travel seeking to help and save. He replied: "The exercise of my profession does not allow or permit me to go about in any other manner. Tranquility, luxury, and repose were invented for pampered courtiers, but travail, tribulation, and arms were invented and created only for those whom the world calls knights errant." (Such sentiment likely will resonate with deal managers). And later, when asked "Couldn't your grace be one of those who stay put to serve their king and lord in court?" he replies:

> *Look my friend, not all knights can be courtiers and not all courtiers can or should be knights errant; there has to be some of each in the world... courtiers without leaving their chambers or passing beyond the threshold of the court, travel the entire world by looking at a map, nor spending a* blanca *or suffering heat or cold, hunger or thirst; but we the true knights errant, measure the earth with our own feet, exposed to the sun, the cold, the wind, and the inclemencies of heaven, both night and day, on foot and on horseback, and we know our enemies not only in portraits but in their actual persons, and no matter the danger and regardless of the occasion we do battle with them, not worrying about trifles or the laws governing duels.*

Miguel de Cervantes, *Don Quixote*[3]

A final thought on the idea of a quest. There are two conflicting joys in life: successfully predicting how things will turn out and discovery of not previously known successes. Financial analysts, especially those with a strong accounting affection, and such feelings of attraction are possible, generally find more joy in the first situation, namely, accurately predicting how things will turn out. There is the delight of analysis, complete and accurate. For such folks, one of the most pleasant sentences is "Everything is on plan," much like the unsmiling customs agent affirming "Your papers are in order." Order, control is the mantra. For those with this bent, it is the methodological preparation for Dealmaking that is the satisfying part, especially by valuation exactitude. The messiness of human encounter and compromise, and surprise and change is both tortuous and torturing. However, for those whose joy lies in discovery, the delight is the pursuit, and the more and sooner the better; for those with this bent, preparation is painful, but horse trading, gamesmanship, and inventing new opportunities or new twists on existing opportunities is where the fun lies.

Opportunity Discovery and Dealmaking include both these perspectives. **Methods** and **Tools** enable a preparatory framework, but it is a framework that enables in-progress discovery and adaptation. So, for those more comfortable with pre-deterministic analysis, we seek to expand that perspective to include ways of enhancing or discovering opportunity stemming from the analysis, and for those more from the "I'll know it when I see it" school, we seek to empower you with **Tools** and **Methods** that will enable you to pursue in a more directed way and to be able to make wiser choices in the heat of pursuit. And, on this point, our objective is, after all, a deal done as Aristotle noted:

> *For dogs do not delight in the scent of hares, but in the eating of them, nor does the lion delight in the lowing of the ox, but in eating it.*
>
> Book 3, Chapter 10, *Nicomanichean Ethics.*

If there is one additional key to a successful quest it is this: a learner's heart. Knowledge, especially the possession of what is held to be certain knowledge, is a door closed to learning. So there is a certain conflict here. If the "slate" of the mind is truly blank, *tabula rasa,* then learning is almost impossible because there is no framework for processing knowledge or ability to exercise discernment between what is true and false, important and not, even relevant and not.

One of the important roles for **Methods** and **Tools** is that they provide a framework for knowledge, but with such framework is the recognition that these are representations of the world, not the world itself, let alone the future codified. Not everything important can be quantified and multiplied, but in business that is where we start.

Approach of Valuation: A Review of the Six Valuation Methods

Briefly, let us review the six valuation Methods we have considered.

Method 1: Industry Standards (Chapter 4)

The Industry Standards Method requires the identification of an appropriate comparable agreement, or industry norm. This Method has strong and obvious appeal, partly because of its simplicity but also because we are inbred with the idea that there exists a true, market price if we can but discover it.

However, we recognize that with technology valuation and pricing:

- Most technology agreements are not published and, so, are not available for study. And when they are published, they may not comprehensively describe the deal Box and Wheelbarrow. So, available agreements are likely to be incomplete and biased.
- Patents and other IP rights are, by nature, unique. No two patents can be identical, nor is it likely that two trade secrets or copyrighted software are either exactly or substantially the same. Opportunity Boxes created by sellers, or sought by buyers, are highly specific so much so that the same underlying opportunity may not be offered in the same way to two different buyers. And different buyers, and sellers, can value and price unique to their own interests and perceptions, especially with regard to risk and uncertainty. So even a given opportunity may not be comparable to itself!
- Published averages, whether obtained by survey or some calculation of a selected published population of agreements, can be meaningless.

In many cases, no single agreement exists that closely matches the subject valuation. Therefore, a common practice is to create a comparable family of agreements from available individual ones upon which *judgment*—that key idea—can be exercised. Such judgment is the interpretation that interpolates and extrapolates from any relevant existing data to predict how the market would have valued the subject opportunity had it been given a chance to do so, incorporating all the *mutatis mutandis* (changes as need be changed) for a meaningful comparable valuation.

Method 2: Rating/Ranking (Chapter 5)

Rating/Ranking is about systematizing comparisons. So it is useful in the judgment required with Method 1, and as a **Tool** in many other contexts.

There is a useful metaphor for this process. Airplanes reference their positions from fixed ground stations that emit a special signal. These signals, known as VORs, are coded in such a way that an onboard instrument can determine the heading, or direction, of the airplane moment by moment relative to the ground station. Originally, such VOR stations were used as byways whereby pilots would "hop" their way across the country flying from one VOR to the next until they got close enough to their destination that they could use visual observation or other forms of navigation. Then a very bright guy came up with a simple but powerful idea: Instead of flying from VOR station to VOR station, why not use the VOR signals and create virtual stations anywhere, ideally in direct lines toward the destination? This was the birth of what is now known as R-NAV.

However, we recognize certain limitations:

- The Rating/Ranking Method relies upon well founded distinguishing criteria/factors, and method for scoring and decision making.
- Scoring (rating) and judgment (ranking) is prone to bias, especially for the subjective version of the Method.
- A Rating/Ranking result does not directly compute a value.

Yet, Rating/Ranking is a lot like a value navigation R-NAV. If one can find a comparable agreement, or better yet, a family of them that happen to be located closely in scope and time to the Box under analysis, it has the potential of finding a valuation VOR located at one's objective. It is more common to find useful points of reference from previous agreements (similar to the scattered VOR stations). Analyzing the agreements through analysis such as Rating/Ranking—perhaps coupled with other Methods and Tools–one can create a metaphorical R-NAV site directly where one needs to go.

Method 3: Rules of Thumb (Chapter 6)

The Rule of Thumb Method is commonly employed for three valuation purposes. First, it can be used as a starting point for deriving a royalty rate, based upon an analysis of the benefit to the buyer. Second, it is a sanity check on a number created in some other way. For instance, the seller's use of the Industry Standard Method coupled with Discounted Cash Flow can create a valuation that does not take into consideration what proportion of the expected financial benefit to the buyer is being allocated in royalties and equity. The Rule of Thumb Method can check the reasonableness of other methods. Finally, Rules of Thumb can be used as an early basis of agreement between a seller and buyer to frame subsequent detailed financial analysis. For instance, if the parties can agree at the earliest stage of due diligence and negotiation that they will apply the 25 Percent Rule with the value 25, then this process agreement can create confidence that a deal can ultimately be struck and a fair final number calculated. Conversely, if a prospective buyer discerns early in the process that the seller aspires to 50 percent or 75 percent of the profits, and such a high range is clearly incompatible with the nature of the opportunity, the buyer can focus on realigning the seller's perspective or else cut off further investment in due diligence.

However, we recognize certain important limitations:

- The Rule of Thumb Method does not expressly account for required buyer investment and risk. As we see with the DCF Method, the forecast net cash inflows and associated risk have an enormous effect on value.
- There needs to be an accounting for the relative contribution of the Technology Box to the buyer's value. There can be significant additional technology and IP rights needed for value realization that cannot be simply ignored.

Yet the idea of some "rule" seems natural to us. In 2008, piracy has emerged as an expanded "industry." One notable example was the capture and offer-for-ransom of a super tanker laden with $100 million of oil.[4] Although we do not have access to the pirates' valuation methodology (it seems doubtful that they used Monte Carlo), their offer for safe return was—what would you have guessed?—$25 million. Had they heard of the 25 Percent Rule, or did we all learn it from the same ancient practice?

Method 4: Discounted Cash Flow, DCF (Chapter 7)

The DCF Method is based on creating pro forma models of estimated net cash inflows. Such models are the basis of establishing business plans required for seeking investment and subsequent management and reporting of results. The flexibility and power of spreadsheets can readily accommodate any appropriate level of complexity and completeness. The DCF Method and NPV calculation is considered the "gold standard" of business valuation.

However, there are certain limitations:

- Many key value drivers such as buyer investment, operating cost, and revenues and growth in such revenues, are difficult to estimate, and have limited comparables.
- Certain assumptions can have an enormous influence on value, and the uncertainty associated with such assumptions cannot be confidently made narrow.
- Every reasonably possible scenario may not have been conceived or considered, or if considered weighed properly in terms of its relative probability.
- Risk assessment (RAHR) is critical to determining value, but is difficult to assess. The future has a way of surprising us all.

The DCF Method (and its related equations) is highly useful as a **Tool** to support pricing structures involving multiple payment forms such as upfront and progress payments, royalties, as well as other forms of consideration.

Method 5: Advanced Methods: Monte Carlo, Real Options (Chapter 8)

The Monte Carlo Method builds off of a DCF model but with a much richer portrayal of assumption uncertainties through probability distributions. This leads to a different perspective of the effect of risk, separating the cost of capital from the explicit uncertainty risk associated with the technology. Monte Carlo Tools such as tornado diagrams and sensitivity charts help prioritize further analysis of the most important assumptions. Monte Carlo provides a powerful visual tool of opportunity and risk, and makes more readily understandable related implications on value.

The use of Real Options has great appeal because of its ability to take measured risks with less risk capital while preserving the right to realize high value opportunities. But, unlike financial options that can be valued by well recognized financial methodologies such as Black Scholes and its modification, no simple correlate exists for Real Options.

Method 6: Auctions (Chapter 9)

Finally, the Auction Method is a way of creating an incontrovertible comparable, or as in the metaphor used earlier, creating a VOR site at the perfect location, by having the market bid for the specific opportunity. With perfect information, and multiple bidders, this process should yield a fair value to both the buyer and the seller. And when/as the Method works well, it establishes a value and price and buyer, all at the same time, for it can be viewed as combining the ***Approaches*** of Valuation and Dealmaking. Unlike the other valuation **Methods**, real time public auctions *cannot* practically be used without a Dealmaking event because the value, and price, is determined by a bidder's final price, when it exceeds a seller's reserve.

Real Time Public Auctions are well known for many kinds of assets, from equities to broken laser pointers to rare works of art, and have been applied to technology as well.

However, such auctions have limitations:

- The technology must be structured simply, and the opportunity sufficiently attractive to cause multiple buyers to make the investment and take a risk of participation.
- The method does not obviate the need for a seller valuation unless it takes the significant risk of not using a reserve price.
- There is no certainty that a market price has been established, or that the seller would have done much better had it followed a more conventional Dealmaking ***Approach***.

Structured Private Auctions are similar to traditional technology Dealmaking, even indistinguishable from such when the seller has the fortune of multiple, aggressive aspiring buyers. But following such a Dealmaking strategy can combine elements of the use of auctions with one or more other valuation Methods.

What About Cost (as a Method)?

Reinforcing a key point made in Chapter 3 about cost, it must be remembered that costs are, with special exceptions, irrelevant. A famous line in the Disney movie *The Lion King* occurs after a monkey (Rafiki) hits the lion (Simba) on the head with a stick. Simba screams, "Owwww!!!! What did you do that for?" Rafiki replies, "Who cares! It's in the past." Rafiki's personal skills may be lacking, but he knows something important about perspective as to value.

It is easily conceivable that a seller has already made enormous investments in getting the technology to its present state, and these costs would not have to be laid out by the buyer. One reason this must arise is simply poor project and investment management on the part of the seller. Another reason is that the seller's timing was poor; the cost of creating a new technology is heavily dependent on when one starts. In starting too late, one misses the window. If one starts too early and is the so-called pioneer, one has to invent everything and endure a long gestation period before the market is ready. Numerous other reasons can exist. The seller may have locked into a needlessly complex and expensive way of creating the technology because of the mindset of the inventors or corporate policy.

On the other hand, a low cost project might "get lucky" in that it creates something of significant value quickly and for a very modest investment. This is normally not a fortuitous accident: Key capabilities that already exist were previously paid for at the seller's labs.

In both of these extremes, the cost basis of the project will have no bearing on a valuation. In the former case, no rational buyer will pay more than an opportunity is worth, looking only forward in time; the buyer perceives itself as striking a deal to benefit itself, not to undo the misfortunes of the seller. In the latter case of the "fortuitous" project, no rational seller will sell it for less than it is presently worth just because its costs were low. Sellers recognize that, just as in each life a little rain must fall, so does a little extra sunshine from time to time. Realizing fair value for sunny days helps compensate for the rainy times.

Yet there are certain circumstances where a cost analysis is worth performing. Often within the seller's organization there are stakeholders who approve or influence the approval of a deal. These stakeholders may be cognizant of the project's official costs and they will want to know why the seller is receiving less than it spent or why it is getting a smaller ROI than expected. There can be circumstances where in-process R&D has been booked as a balance sheet asset; upon disposition, there could be an adverse balance sheet effect. Such circumstances would indicate the need for a cost analysis.

Performing the cost analysis will help stakeholders in the selling company to come to one mind on the valuation. Such a process may require reconciliation with earlier (and not-to-be-realized) ROI expectations. Even if R&D expenses do not show up on the seller's official balance sheet, they can show up in key people's bonuses and so affect behavior. As discussed in Chapter 11, license negotiations include negotiations within one's own organization. For the seller, such negotiations involve reconciliation of already sunk project costs with proposed selling prices or terms offered by the buyer.

Another reason to analyze cost is to determine how a buyer might value an opportunity. What are the buyer's alternatives to a negotiated agreement with the seller? One simple alternative for the buyer is to do nothing, which is equivalent to investing its funds in buying down its debt or buying back its stock. Another option is to invest in a completely different project unrelated to the one offered by the seller. A third option, and a crucial issue with regard to perceiving the value of the seller's technology, is to create the same or similar business opportunity as might result from a deal with the seller but to do so independently of the seller. This can be done by following a different technology path, or by following the same path but working around the seller's patents and/or independently recreating the seller's trade secrets.

The seller's project costs might be a useful starting point for estimating what it might cost a buyer to recreate the technology. If it will cost the buyer X to recreate the seller's technology, then the buyer will not pay much more than X unless there is a significant time-to-market advantage in doing so or some other barrier to buyer's use of the technology. Other reasons to consider technology licensing would be if there is significant risk that the buyer's recreation might not work, or there is significant risk that the scope of the seller's patent claims might not be avoided, or the buyer wants to maintain good will between the parties because of broader business objectives, or for some other reason.

Accordingly, one could seek to answer two cost questions: (1) What did it cost the seller to this point? (2) What would it cost the buyer to recreate the seller's technology, if it could use it without a deal with the seller? However, it is rare that either of such figures will be the basis of a final agreement. The seller and buyer will be inclined to reference the answer to the first question only when it would advantage its negotiation position, but the other side will likely find the argument unpersuasive for the reasons given above. On the other hand, the answer to the second question could be a basis for buyer-seller agreement.

But "cost" is not a "method." It may not even be a meaningful number, given business practices associated with its computation.

The "Best" Valuation Method(s)?

An old observation, and one that worked better before the advent of digital technologies, goes like this: When I had one watch I always knew what time it was, but now that I have two, I never know. A more elegant version, and one that has some factual foundation based on the legendary regular walking habits of Immanuel Kant,[5] is a daily walker into town resets his watch based on a store's grandfather clock. After decades of doing this he happens upon the shopkeeper and asks how he sets the clock. His reply is that he uses the factory noon whistle. To which the walker replies, "I use your clock to blow that whistle."

With multiple valuation Methods, and multiple "answers" possible even for one given Method, how do we determine (or divine?) and defend a specific value as expressed in an external term sheet?

Some Valuation Method Issues and Dangers

HOW DO WE KNOW *ANYTHING*? One of the foundational questions of philosophy is what is truth or its close corollary: What do I know and how do I know that I know it? This latter question falls within the discipline of epistemology, meaning a theory of knowledge.

Earlier, we considered the matter of uncertainty as an inherent element in future planning. Here we want to briefly consider another aspect of uncertainty dealing with the valuation and pricing methods as well as outcomes.

Epistemology is one of the core philosophical subjects that in the Western tradition dates back to at least the 400 B.C. Greek classics. Epistemology deals with the question of what can be known and how one can know it, but not with the specifics of what it is that one is trying to know. For us here, the epistemological question is this: What is knowable from the use of these valuation Methods, and how do we know that we know?

In our scope of technology valuation, there are two, polar opposite erroneous answers to the first of these questions: (1) nothing is knowable, or (2) epistemic certitude is possible. The first response has the effect of declaring valuation of technology as an utterly futile effort. This is the equivalent of you thinking of a number between one and a million and inviting me to predict the number. In this situation, nothing is knowable; regardless of my tools and endurance, I am not going to generate a better guess than the first number that enters my head. But is technology valuation really this epistemologically bleak? In general, the answer is no; the future may be dark, but it is not black.

What about the other extreme of contending that epistemic certitude is achievable? There is an old cartoon (*Miss Peach*) in which an elementary school mathematics teacher asks a student: "Quickly, Johnny, how much is 9 times 7?" To which the mathematically unaccomplished, but perhaps future senior management material, student replies, "High 50s, low 60s, somewhere in there." For many purposes, is this not an OK answer?

The answer depends on what are the implications of being wrong. If the difference between the low 60s and 63 is life and death, then the lack of certitude is pretty important. This is usually the case about the basic science and its technological expression of what is being offered in the Box. Technology is usually not very valuable if it works rarely, or only some of the time.

What about technology valuation? Valuation is in a real sense the end of a long chain of uncertainties. There is likely to be some uncertainty in the performance of the technology, the cost of manufacture, the magnitude, growth rate, and margin of associated revenues, scope of IP rights, competitive response, the emergence of alternative technologies, and so forth. Each of such uncertainties is a kind of compound interest, as we saw with Monte Carlo models. So by the time we get to the point of specifying some exact value for worth, we have the effect of accumulated uncertainty.

An example of the difference in the value of exactitude between what science can produce, or may even need, and that which everyday practical application uses can be seen by returning to the example of the value of pi. We all learned it to be 3.14 plus a boundless number of subsequent digits, which could be ignored for purposes of carpentry and paper drawings. Undaunted, mathematical sciences have pursued exactitude with the value of pi to literally now more than one *billion* significant figures. However, just knowing pi to 39 decimal places (40 significant figures) is sufficient to calculate the circumference of *the universe* to the diameter of a single atom. (That would seem to be sufficient exactitude for most of us, but mathematicians, undaunted by practical reason, are seekers of ultimate Truth).

One of the virtues of having six valuation Methods, and each Method enabling multiple results, is the opportunity for comparing results. Each of the Methods reviewed has its strengths and weaknesses, and can be more or less useful to any particular valuation context. By using more than one Method, one frequently gains insight into a valuation that does not occur by the use of only one Method. Even though these multiple methods will almost surely lead to multiple values, they are also likely to lead to a deeper understanding of the key factors driving the value and how the process can be refined to develop a wiser answer.

So, in technology valuation, the epistemological aspiration is neither futility nor certitude, but rational coherence—where multiple Methods produce a value or value range that makes sense from such multiple perspectives.

As discussed in Chapter 4, just taking the average of multiple views can be misleading, or even nonsensical. So does one choose one method as "supreme" or just average all the numbers? The answer lies in a search for coherence. For any given valuation situation, there are varying categories of information available each with potentially different confidence levels. Although it is generally a good idea to look at a valuation from the perspective of multiple Methods, one generally gains an understanding when performing such valuation that the available data, or Dealmaking environment, just creates greater confidence in the values obtained by such preferred Method. So, for instance, we might value an opportunity by a combination of Industry Standards, Rules of Thumb, and Discounted Cash Flow, perhaps with each one using some aspect of Rating/Ranking, and result in three different value models. But in performing this calculation, we come to believe that the availability of very relevant comparable agreements causes us to have a higher confidence in the Industry Standards Method. In such case, we could be well served to consider what was it that caused our valuation by Rules of Thumb and Discounted Cash Flow to deviate from what we believe is a most reasonable estimate.

This kind of thinking and subsequent method analysis of methods used is what is meant by a search for coherence. There is no one method that is the gold standard of technology valuation for any and all circumstances, although for reasons discussed earlier the DCF Method and related Monte Carlo Method are highly regarded when reasonable models and assumptions can be established.

Coherence is a process of seeking to apply practical wisdom to the array of results produced by each individual method used.

In Chapter 5 on Rating/Ranking we considered three "worlds": Certainty, Complete Uncertainty, and Probability. The **Method** of Valuation is the expression of a deep conviction that certainty is unavailable to us, but we are not in complete uncertainty; we can construct a term sheet based upon reasonable probabilities, which is all that is generally available to us in the business world.

PATTERN FIXEDNESS We are by nature pattern makers. With few exceptions there are no stellar groupings in the night sky,[6] no dippers, no bears, no archers, no teapots. Yet in the most ancient of documents we know that three millennia ago cultures identified these by terms just like ours. Pattern making is how we grasp things, and create mental order. It is the essential task of the financial modeling necessary for the DCF and Monte Carlo Methods.

The danger is pattern fixedness. Once those models are made real to us, they are difficult to be unmade, or even recognized by the maker as only models. And chances are the dealmaker on the other side of the table has a very different model fixed in their thinking. Unless by some coincidence these competing models yield respective term sheets with congruent price and structure someone is going to have to see the other's point of view for progress to be made.

Another unhelpful feature with patterns is there tends to be a strong historical element in them. We naturally tend in creation to recreate what we know/think based on our prior experience. Think about the following poetic insight, where the underlined terms (my emphasis) relate to the idea of our self-made patterns and models:

> If I see before me
> The <u>nervature</u> of past life
> In one <u>image</u>, I always think
> That this has something to do
> With truth. Our brains, after all,
> Are always at work on some quivers
> Of <u>self-organization</u>, however faint,
> And it is from this that an <u>order</u>
> Arises, in places beautiful
> And comforting, though more cruel too,
> Than the previous state of ignorance.[7]

The "comforting though more cruel" in valuation and subsequent Dealmaking is in its fixedness.

There may be no cure, but there are at least two helps: the deal team, and the great Dealmaking question: "Please show me where I'm wrong." (An invitation that is irresistible to the other side of any dispute.) The deal team in internal negotiations can perform wonderful service in challenging perspectives as well as assumptions. There is a good reason why kids are blessed by having two parents, who see almost every issue differently. And our famous literary adventurer, Don Quixote, had his squire Sancho Panza; it was and is the first great "buddy story." Here's some Sancho advice:

- "... the person who cut us down still has the scissors in his hand."[8]
- "That's exactly what I hate most ... charging at hundred armed men like a greedy boy attacking half a dozen melons. Good Lord ... There are times to attack and times to retreat, and not everything's 'Charge for Santiago and Spain!'"[9]
- "... when they give you the calf, run over with the rope."[10]

QUANTIFICATION, RATIONALITY, AND HYPERRATIONALITY What are we to conclude from this discussion of the quest? Can we, should we, just wander our landscapes and if it feels good do it? No, there is math and method. Implicit in the idea of math and method is rationality, namely, that the quantification that emerges from the mathematical and structural approaches described in this book guides one to the best choice in any given set of circumstances. Hyperrationality is sometimes used to characterize an analytical approach in which only factors that can be expressed numerically and processed mathematically are considered because nonmathematical matters are deemed unimportant or irrelevant. As was discussed in Chapter 5 on Rating/Ranking we neither live in Certainty World nor Complete Uncertainty World, but a place better characterized as Probability World.

Returning for Aristotelian Wisdom we have this counsel (emphasis mine):

> *It is the mark of an educated man to look for precision in each class of things just so far as the nature of the subject admits; it is evidently foolish to accept probability reasoning from a mathematician and to demand from a rhetorician scientific proofs.*
>
> Book 1, Chapter 3, *Nicomachaen Ethics*

Deciding on an Appropriate Level of Analysis

Using any of the described methods, it is possible to engage in an endless analytical exercise, leading to paralysis by analysis. This quote from Ross Perot captures well the analysis frustration he experienced as a Board Member of GM, a 20 year old prescient anticipation of that company's current predicaments:

> *I come from an environment where, if you see a snake, you kill it. At GM, if you see a snake, the first thing you do is go hire a consultant on snakes. Then you get a committee on snakes, and then you discuss it for a couple of years. The most likely course of action is—nothing. You figure the snake hasn't bitten anybody yet, so you just let him crawl around on the factory floor.*[11]

An appropriate question to ask is: How much of my resources are justifiably spent on analysis? Or, put another way, what is an appropriate cap on transaction costs, of which valuation analysis and other preparedness activities are the initial component?

Let us consider a simple example. Suppose there is a technology that a seller expects could result in a royalty of probably more than $100,000 per year, but probably less than \$1 million per year; this is colloquially termed a six-figure deal. Further, it is believed that such royalties might be paid over a period of five to ten years starting three to five years hence. Using such approximate numbers, a seller might estimate that it should be able to receive an upfront licensing fee of at least \$100,000, so in current year terms the deal should be worth at least that much money. Over the life of such a license, the NPV could be roughly estimated as, say, seven times the DCF of a \$300,000 royalty payment (on the conservative side of midway between \$100,000 and \$999,999), occurring seven years hence (about midterm of the royalty payment after four years of further development). Using 7 as the multiple on the DCF is a somewhat conservative estimate of the number of years that a royalty would be paid. Overall, the risk level of the royalty stream (as an example) may be estimated to be 30 percent. Thus, the NPV may be calculated as follows:

$$\text{NPV} = 7 \times \$300{,}000/(1 + 0.3)^7 = \$330{,}000.$$

Such an estimate of potential impact can be done quickly, especially with experience, and used to gauge priority and significance. It can be argued that the range in the assumed values is so vast that the calculated result is meaningless. It can also be argued that the entire process has become circular because the calculation assumes the value which is to be determined to decide whether or not it is worth the effort to determine the value. However, making judgments about the importance of things without genuinely knowing the importance of things is something we all do every day and is the essence of the ***Approach*** of opportunity Discovery covered in Chapter 3. When you get a telephone call soliciting the "opportunity of a lifetime" do you invest time in figuring it out or not?[12] Sometimes it is impossible to invest all the due diligence time needed. Early, best guess judgments and selections must be made.

Following up on this example, if it is reasonable to assume, as a ballpark estimate, a current year value of \$100,000 (assumed to be conservative) and a lifetime NPV value of \$330,000 (modestly conservative), what is the appropriate level of investment to make a deal? Like many things, there is no hard and fast rule. One way to look at this from the seller's perspective is, what is the opportunity worth without a license agreement? If it is zero, then if there is even a 50 percent chance of reaching an agreement with a buyer under the previous terms, it is worth spending up to 50 percent of those figures. For sellers that think appropriately in NPV terms, that would put a cap of \$165,000 on the transaction costs; for sellers who think in terms of current year expenses and revenues, the cap would be \$50,000. More accurately, the seller should view investment in creating a deal like any other investment made and, so, should be reasonably justified on an ROI basis. This might place the operational caps at 80 percent of these figures (\$40,000 and \$134,000).

Of course the goal of any seller is to determine rational behavior to maximize benefit, not to compute the worst tolerable performance. A way of valuing the benefit of perfect information is needed. Let us consider what might be meant by perfect seller information in a licensing valuation context. A good working definition of that number would be the most that any one buyer would be willing to pay after completing due diligence and hearing the seller's persuasive argument and that would allow the transaction to take place in a reasonable amount of time with reasonable selling costs. In many cases, such perfect valuation information would cause three to five buyers to take a serious look at the opportunity. Three might make serious counteroffers, all within a three-month period, and all with terms and conditions generally acceptable to the seller.

How would such perfect information differ from, say, the example proposed earlier? Because in that example the probable annual royalties varied by a factor of 10 ($100,000 to just under $1 million); this would correspond to a royalty rate variation of 0.2 to 2 percent or 0.5 to 5 percent, a huge range. For the seller to be reasonably safe in quoting a figure, it would have to select a number at or close to the top end of the range. Such a figure may be so high as to dissuade any bidder. Alternatively, considering the range of 0.5 to 5 percent, what should the seller do if an early prospective buyer offers 1.5 percent "firm and final"? Most sellers, under these circumstances, would view the investment of several tens of thousands of dollars as a prudent investment.

Sellers often find themselves at an information disadvantage with respect to the buyer. By definition, the buyer is planning to put the technology into commerce, so it should know many of the key issues of manufacturing and sales as well as marketing. If the opportunity is really significant, the buyer is not likely to tell the seller that it is valuing the opportunity too modestly.

Therefore, it is good practice for the seller to perform some preliminary analysis of potential significance to make a general determination of the value at stake. This can be done semi-quantitatively as shown in the previous example, or even more qualitatively by creating and using "high," "medium," and "low" categories. Then a seller can adopt deal investment levels and methodologies appropriate to the categories. For example, for a high opportunity (say, a potential of seven figures or more, i.e., $10 million or more), an extensive valuation will be performed using multiple cross-checking methods and using outside experts to provide additional resources and confirmation. For a medium category (a six-figure deal), the seller could use one method, perhaps with external support and validation.

For low categories (a five-figure deal), judgment could be based upon an afternoon of thinking and consulting the records of previous deals (including networking with colleagues and friends). Also, for each of these categories a budget for selling and transaction costs should be established. Clearly for a five-figure deal one could spend more than the value of the deal in internal staff costs, especially for legal costs. If a seller has numerous opportunities in the low category, then it would be wise to create a very standard valuation approach with form licenses that are not subject to negotiation or customization to avoid consuming value in transaction costs. Also, there are some situations in which the opportunity is literally not worth the cost of creating the agreement to transfer the rights.

And, maybe, your initial judgment was flat wrong. (Welcome to the adult world of business).

Approach of Dealmaking

Valuation versus Pricing

As discussed, we have used the term "valuation" to mean the worth of an opportunity and "pricing" as a communicated offer. When buying from street merchants in some countries, especially areas frequented by tourists, a seller's initial price can easily be ten times the product's value. In such circumstances, the number of potential buyers is practically endless. Sellers in such circumstances have little to lose by quoting enormous prices because there is literally always another buyer around the corner (or perhaps on the next cruise ship). Further, if the buyer is not responding favorably, the price can be dropped quickly, often, without losing the transaction. Such backpedaling by a seller normally causes a buyer to distrust the seller's representations. In the case of street goods, this is generally not a significant loss because the trust was probably not high in the first place, but, more importantly, the buyer can conduct rapid due diligence without the "assistance" of an untrusted seller. Consequently, it should be no surprise that street sellers the world over have learned to deploy strategies of high price multiples.

How would such a strategy work in licensing a technology? Not well. First, the number of potential buyers is normally not large and certainly not endless. Therefore, it is generally not a good idea to risk losing any buyer's interest by quoting unreasonably high numbers.

In addition, technology licensing requires significant levels of due diligence by buyers. Buyers are not inclined to make such investments if they have reason to believe that the seller is just looking for naïve or desperate buyers. Further, trust is an important element in most licensing transactions. A buyer will tend to devalue an opportunity if it concludes that the seller is hiding or misrepresenting information. There are serious adverse results to being too aggressive in pricing.

So, although a seller can count on not being offered more than it asks, it does not serve its own interests to ask for much more than it is perceived to be worth. A very reasonable approach to finding the middle ground is for the seller to value an opportunity several times under varying levels of optimism, the so-called scenario analysis. A common approach is a low scenario, a high scenario, and a most likely scenario. The low and high scenarios are usually labeled according to the assumptions made about them. For example, the low scenario could be "niche market, United States" and the high scenario "mass market, worldwide." For a seller to select a price valuation at the high end is reasonable, providing that there is some basis for making such an assumption. During the course of discussions with prospective buyers, the feasibility (or not) of the optimistic assumptions can be tested.

Obviously, buyers may disagree with the seller's assumptions, particularly for the more optimistic scenarios. However, buyers generally will respect a reasoned approach. Further, if the seller's assumptions are communicated to a buyer, then the buyer can move forward by developing its own most likely scenario and present those findings to the seller. If the seller says, "I want 100" and the buyer says, "I'll give you 10," convergence will be difficult if not impossible. If instead the seller says, "You will be able to sell licensed products for three major applications in all the industrialized countries of Europe, Asia, and America, and so it is worth 100," then the buyer can reply, "If I believed I could, I would agree with your number, but here is where I can see applying it. . . ." And so on.

Although the pricing discussion has been primarily focused on a seller's position, pricing is also an activity performed by the buyer. "Low ball" offers by a buyer often poison the relationship with the seller and can, in particular, offend inventors whose technology is being sold. Even if the buyer later makes a more reasonable offer, offended inventors (and others) can sometimes sabotage negotiations. Although some buyers might relish the prospect of getting something for almost nothing, most sellers are not naïve and, furthermore, they have long memories.

Marketing and Selling Strategies: Seller's View

Although "marketing" as a term seems to carry a more professional image, what a seller really is doing is "selling." Marketing has more to do with creating future products and services that the target segments will want. Selling is getting a buyer to take what exists on the shipping dock. Theodore Leavitt has put this succinctly: "Selling is getting rid of what you have; marketing is making sure you have what you can get rid of."

Selling as an activity focuses on the specific "product" in the sales bag and how it will benefit specific customers. This process leads a seller to consider how the intrinsic features of the technology translate to the benefit of the buyer and the buyer's customer. It is helpful to consider the buyer as a value-added reseller (VAR) as the term is used in the information technology industry. The key attribute of VAR-thinking is that the buyer is an intermediary to the ultimate customer and, as an intermediary, has to contribute to and benefit from the value delivered to such customer. It is generally a very good idea for the seller to be able to express in income statement terms (such as used in the DCF Method) how the buyer will make money with the technology. This is the basic concept behind the phrase, "Sell the benefits, not the features."

Another key aspect of selling is market segmentation. Not all categories of buyers will view the same opportunity as equally valuable. An astute seller will focus on the category of buyers that is most likely to be interested in becoming a licensee and that will put the highest value on the opportunity because they can extract the greatest benefit. Next we will consider four distinct buyer segments.

One poor buyer category that is frequently but unwisely considered is the ultimate customer. To make this concrete, let us consider a technology for making a special-purpose laser. Sellers can often more easily identify potential customers of such lasers than potential licensees who would want to build and sell such lasers. The identity and enthusiasm of potential customers can be helpful in attracting licensees, but rarely will such customers find the opportunity so compelling that they will seek to become laser manufacturers.

A better buyer for this category is a company that presently uses similar technologies but for other markets and applications. Again using the laser example, let us suppose that the laser is particularly suited to medical applications, both diagnostic and treatment. If a prospective buyer exists that already makes lasers, but only for the industrial laser market, then it can be a significant stretch for that buyer to enter the medical market. This is because there are many aspects of the medical market that would be unknown to the company, such as FDA approval processes, the buying needs and patterns of hospitals and doctor's offices, the economics of the industry, especially the important involvement of third party payers, and so forth. Also, having trade name value and company recognition definitely plays a role. Finally, one needs an experienced sales force to call on the ultimate customer. Thus, although it is a positive that the prospective buyer understands lasers, its lack of experience in the niche market is usually a significant barrier.

An even better buyer segment would be a company making high tech devices for the medical industry. Even if it does not presently make lasers, it inherently possesses an in-depth understanding of the market environment and customer requirements, and it is the perspective that is generally more important and difficult to obtain. If needed, the buyer could have some or all of the laser manufacturing contracted out to one of its vendors. Obviously, the best buyer segment would be a company already making lasers for the medical industry because it would have both the technology and the market understanding, but finding such a buyer is not always possible.

Using such perspectives, a seller needs to develop a sales strategy. Because it will be necessary to induce a buyer to make a significant due diligence investment, it is helpful to be able to show the prospective buyer how and why the opportunity is beneficial. To do this intelligently requires some effort on the seller's part and limits the number of prospective buyers that could be cost-effectively analyzed. Usually a seller should consider more than just three or four buyers; depending upon the potential significance of the deal, a reasonable upper limit might be in the range of six to ten. If a seller were to choose six in the laser example, the distribution should favor the last two buyer segments. A reasonable distribution would be as follows: two or three companies that make lasers for the medical market, one or two companies that make other high tech equipment for the medical industry, and possibly one company that is experienced in making and selling lasers for many markets, but not the medical market. This approach benefits the seller by providing different perspectives from different segments; however, most of the selling energy goes into the most-likely-to-succeed category.

Another selling question that arises is determining what size companies are most likely to be serious buyers. In other words, should a seller approach the existing market leader, a strong number 2, or a market laggard? There are two generalizations that can be useful to answering this question. First, the size of the opportunity should be scaled to the prospective buyer. For instance, if the seller's expected price is going to be seven figures, it is generally not fruitful to consider buyers whose annual revenues are just seven figures. Big opportunities, particularly ones that will require large R&D and developmental investments, will need the resources and grand visions of big companies. Likewise, profitable but small opportunities seem to be more attractive to smaller prospective buyers; bigger companies are generally not interested in licensing opportunities that, even if successful, will be almost undetectable on their income statements.

The second generalization deals with the attitude of market leaders. It appears to be both a human and corporate trait that large size and success lead to hubris and the belief that one knows more than anyone else. Compounding this, market leaders normally have a vested interest in maintaining the status quo. Although there can certainly be exceptions, it is not surprising when market leaders turn down an opportunity, and later that decision proves to be a short-sighted judgment. At the other end of the market share spectrum, the smallest companies are often so limited in their resources that they are unable to effectively implement opportunities. Generally, the companies ranging number 2 through number 4 in terms of market size frequently are better targets than the market leader or the smallest players.

Opportunity Discovery: The Buyer's View

The high cost of conducting due diligence, coupled with the high mortality of even the most promising projects, makes a strong argument for a strategic approach for a buyer. If every prospective opportunity has to be analyzed from first principles, then the cost of analysis will be high and the likelihood of failure will be equally high. However, if licensing opportunities can be investigated from a pre-established framework of company priorities and strongest assets, success becomes more likely.

By being proactive, a buyer can increase its odds for being the first in line to negotiate. By having a checklist of key functions, features, and benefits sought, together with an understanding of the customer needs it seeks to meet, the buyer is also better able to quickly recognize significant opportunities.

An ability to understand the value of a license early in the process enables the buyer to do a reality assessment. In some cases such an assessment may actually precede the seller's own valuation activities (which from a seller's perspective, is not a preferred method). By being early, the buyer can create momentum for a quick and early deal that can induce the seller to accept a lower price than it might have otherwise. This is particularly so in a royalty-based agreement where the buyer can make the case that in its hands the technology will be exploited more fully and immediately because of the strategic fit and the proactivity of the buyer.

Dealmaking Readiness

Prior to a negotiation, there are certain basic preparations that are part of "Dealmaking readiness." The first two are obvious but often are not carefully thought through: (1) What do I have to offer? (the Box) and (2) What do I want in return? (the Wheelbarrow). As discussed in Chapters 3 and 10, there are many things that can be offered and sought. Even if one considers only money, it comes in many forms. As discussed in Chapter 11, it can be tied to company value (equity), to sales (royalty), to profitability (a kicker), to fields of use and territories granted. Money can be fixed payments or conditional, and weighted to occur early (or not).

The nature of the buyer's commitment is another important element of a deal. Often this shows up as the diligence requirement of the license. This means that if the buyer/licensee does not fulfill the specified requirement, the license can be terminated, or made nonexclusive, or some penalty payment is made, depending upon what is negotiated. This is an example of an important "want" of the seller and "offer" of the buyer.

Another kind of commitment is future assistance by the seller, either in the form of tech transfer, troubleshooting, and/or improvement inventions. The ability of the seller to provide such assistance may be critical to the buyer's decision to enter the license agreement at all, no matter what the price.

Although it's not possible to think of everything in advance of a negotiation, preparation can often make the difference between deal closure and failure. Don Quixote has spoken well: "Tis a common proverb . . . that diligence is the mother of good fortune."[13]

Plan B

The alternative analysis, sometimes called a "Plan B Analysis," should always be: What happens if there is no deal? What are our alternatives, and the likely value of such alternatives, if we cannot reach an agreement with this party? For sellers who negotiate with only one prospective buyer and who believe that there are no other alternatives possible, this process reveals the vulnerability of not having a tenable Plan B. Accordingly, sellers should always sell and negotiate with a legitimate Plan

B, even if it is significantly less desirable than Plan A. Without a Plan B, the seller can be convinced to accept a very low valuation because "something is better than nothing," (if their Plan B is truly nothing). In many situations, buyers inherently have a Plan B. That Plan B can be to invest its money in some completely unrelated but profitable project.

A Plan B can be embodied in the internal term sheet, as a completely alternative deal structure, less desirable than the one proposed but an acceptable alternative. In some cases this may require consideration of a range of possible "adders" that could be included in the deal, such as additional fields of use, or additional patents or software. In some cases it could be a completely alternative Wheelbarrow, such as an all-equity transaction as a Plan B to a convention license fee and royalty approach.

All of these Box and Wheelbarrow elements are interrelated. One cannot value and price each possible variation, because there are likely to be too many possibilities. But, likewise, it is generally a good idea to have more than just one way of looking at the transaction, particularly with multiple prospective third parties. Don Quixote, again: "It seems to me, Sancho, that there is no proverb that is not true, because all of them are judgments based on experience, the mother of all knowledge, in particular the one that says: 'One door closes and another opens.'"[14]

Buyer-Seller Value Creation and Convergence

If we were in the earth's orbit looking outward into the furthest reaches of the universe, with views now afforded by the amazing Hubble Space Telescope (HST), we would be, or should be, struck by several amazing questions. Perhaps the most famous question is why is there something instead of nothing? This question is beyond the scope of this book, but there is a second foundational question that we do want to consider: Why is the something pulled together in bodies, groups, and clusters?

Specifically, let us consider the HST picture shown in Exhibit 12.1.

This absolutely spectacular picture was taken by the HST on April 1 and 9, 2002, as part of a NASA servicing mission. The elongated shape that dominates the picture is a galaxy of stars popularly known as the Tadpole[15] Galaxy (UGC10214). That galaxy is located 420 million light years from us in the direction of the constellation Draco. The elongated tail of the Tadpole is 280,000 light years long, which is more than a million trillion miles, just that line right there in this book. There are two particularly remarkable features of this particularly remarkable photograph that we want to point out. First, that long tail was caused by something else in this picture. In the upper left portion of the main body of the Tadpole Galaxy can be seen a small, compact interloper galaxy shown by the arrow. These two galaxies have had a close encounter. Despite their vast dimensions and open spaces, the forces exercised by the stars and other matter in each galaxy are believed to have unwound, partially, the spiral arm structure of the Tadpole into that amazing tail.

The other particularly noteworthy feature in this picture is the background elements. If you look closely at those small dots and smears, there are approximately 6,000 galaxies extending outward perhaps 13 billion light years, presenting us with an image that existed just a short time, relatively speaking, after the Big Bang. Recall that we are seeing this large number of galaxies by viewing only a tiny cone of

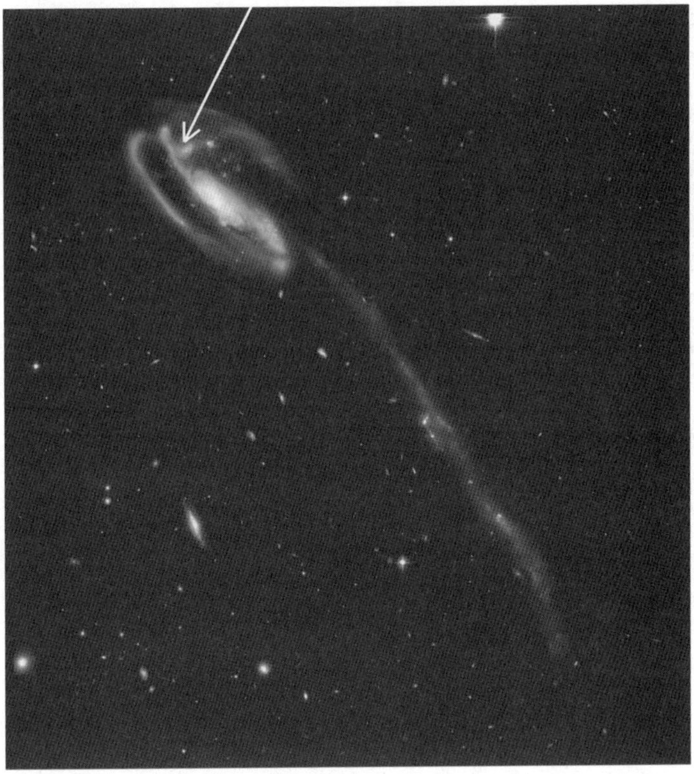

EXHIBIT 12.1 Hubble Space Telescope Photograph
Source: http://antwrp.gsfc.nasa.gov/apod/ap020502.html

the sky. By contrast, our little group of galaxies, known as the Local Group, that includes our Milky Way Galaxy, of which our solar system is just a tiny part, is one star in 100 million stars, and includes the dramatic neighboring Andromeda Galaxy, and only about 18 other galaxies.

So, why after the Big Bang doesn't the universe look like the playroom of a group of preschoolers after a busy day? The question is not "Are the stars out tonight?" but "Why are the stars grouped?" The answer lies in a force we call gravity. For these stellar bodies this gravitational force is really very weak because it decreases with the square of the distance and as we have seen the distances are vast beyond imagination. So the forces on each star imposed by all the other stars in the universe are very, very small. But, these forces exist and over time they result in the accretions we see as galaxies and other structures.

Now, returning to our imaginary earth orbiting platform, let us train our camera downward on the object shown in Exhibit 12.2.

The two pictures are of the same place, New York City taken in 2002.[16] The one on the left was taken at night. Even in these relatively low resolution pictures, one can see the three primary New York airports (JFK, LGA, and EWR) and the large outer belt highway into New Jersey (I-287). Now, why are these pictures in this book?

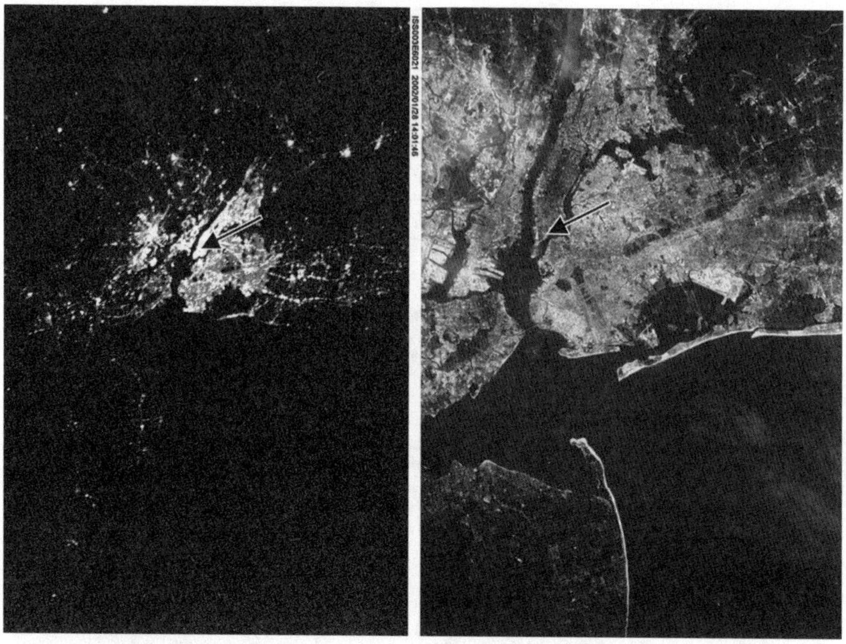

Earth Sciences and Image Analysis, NASA-Johnson Space Center. 11 Oct. 2002. "Astronaut Photography of Earth - Display Record." <http://eol.jsc.nasa.gov/scripts/sseop/photo.pl?mission=STS036&roll=39&frame=14> (13 Oct. 2002).

Earth Sciences and Image Analysis, NASA-Johnson Space Center. 11 Oct. 2002. "Astronaut Photography of Earth - Display Record." <http://eol.jsc.nasa.gov/scripts/sseop/photo.pl?mission=ISS003&roll=E&frame=6021> (13 Oct. 2002).

EXHIBIT 12.2 Astronaut Space-Based Photograph of New York City
Source: http://eol.jsc.nasa.gov/sseop/use.htm

Just as the deep space pictures evidenced an attractive force that creates clusters instead of chaos, so the earthward pictures show the same general effect. But instead of gravity from principles of physics, there is an attraction from the principles of economics. There is no reason for New York City to exist as we see it. People have not crammed themselves into this high-rent district to be within fortified walls as with medieval cities; it is quite the opposite as the events of September 11, 2001 have shown us. Why are they there?

The answer for this city, and the countless others, is to pursue opportunity. New York City began as a place for traders, originally Dutch traders. It expanded and grew because that city, like the United States itself, welcomed many others who sought the opportunity to trade. Commonly the trade was their labor for the liquidity to buy from those markets whatever they desired. In these New York City pictures but not clearly visible, or well remembered, is little Ellis Island, where millions of immigrants, my parents among them, came to America with the dream of pursuing opportunities, their opportunities. The terrorist attacks on September 11, 2001 were horrific in their human toll. And the primary targets were the World Trade Centers, places created and energized by creating such Dealmaking opportunities that benefit both sides of the deal.

There is a gravity for Dealmaking that draws us to one another under the belief that what I can give you, you will so value, that you can see the equity in giving to me what I will value. There are some solitary souls out in the woods converting string-bean hulks into shoe laces by some laborious process. We wish them well. But, for most of us, we would rather do what we do best so that with a tiny portion of our earnings we can buy a lifetime's supply of shoe laces, among other things of value, and go forward with more interesting pursuits.

There is, then, something special in Dealmaking. As a seller you are of high value to a buyer and vice versa, because what you can offer can create greater value in the hands of the ideal partner, given an ideal deal. It does not always work out that way, between all combinations of sellers and buyers and all opportunities, but it does it often enough that it attracts us to one another seeking additional (and better) opportunities. In the global, mobile, 24/7 village we now share, this Dealmaking gravity additionally exists in the form of voices over wire and fiber, printed sheets of paper that stream out of little, cheap boxes located on 100 million tables, of bits parsed into an Internet protocol that echo thousands of miles in only seconds and essentially for free to any of nearly a billion unique web addresses. Nothing replaces face-to-face dealings, at least not yet. But the communications revolution enables us now to do better, faster, and cheaper what we have gravitated to do all along.

Sellers and prospective buyer positions commonly do not overlap when negotiations begin. If both parties have performed valuations based upon some rational methodology, and both have identified underlying assumptions, then there is reasoned basis for the hope that with an open exchange of information convergence can take place. It can be the buyer's valuation increasing to meet the seller's, or it can be the reverse. In other cases it might be movement by both parties, not just in the spirit of compromise, but due to a better understanding of the opportunities and risks.

Convergence is illustrated in Exhibit 12.3, which is based upon a similar figure in a book by Smith and Parr.[17]

Early in this book, we introduced the acronym TR R^k A DE, where TR stood for Technology Rights, DE for Deal Economics (or Equity), and R for the risk characterized by the risk adjusted hurdle rate (k). The final element in the acronym is the A: A stands for the Art of the deal. Once the buyer's and seller's valuations overlap, a deal should be possible. The art of the process is discovering ways that make the deal as valuable as possible to both parties and to do so quickly.

Respect the Deal Team, on Both Sides

Very little needs to be said on this point, except as to its importance. The pile of historical stupidity resulting from disrespect would be high indeed. One of the great themes of *Don Quixote* is how each, Don Quixote and his squire Sancho Panza, transform their beginning mutual bewilderment to, at the end, deep understanding of the wisdom of the other's perspective. Before this end state, here is the clear exasperation of Don Quixote, as a type of dealmaker instructing his analyst:

> *Sancho, perform the investigation I have told you to, and do not concern yourself with any other, for you know nothing about the course, lines, parallels, zodiacs, ellipticals, poles, solstices, equinoxes, planets, signs, points, and measurements that compose the celestial and terrestrial spheres; if you knew all these things or even some of them you would see clearly which parallels we have cut, how may zodiac signs we have seen, and how we have already left behind and are leaving*

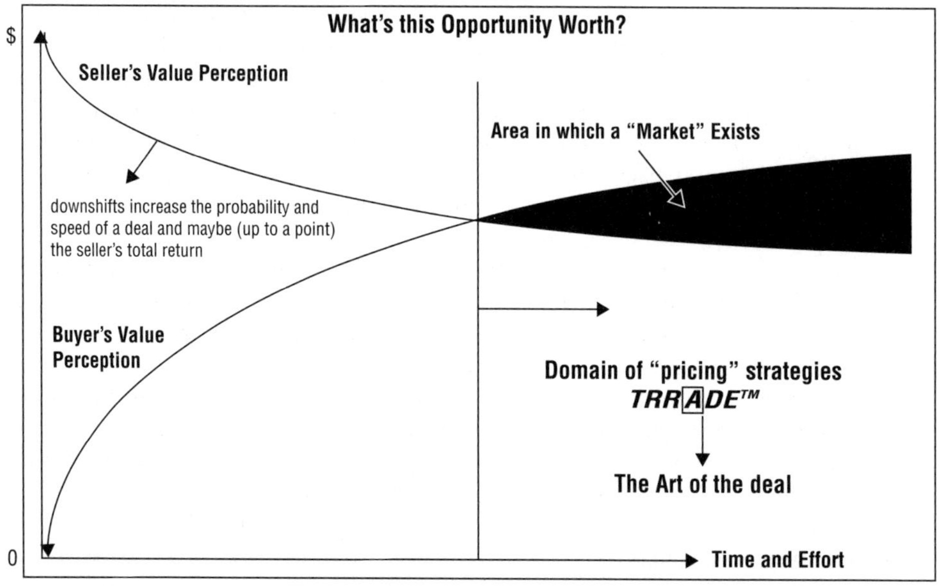

EXHIBIT 12.3 Illustration of the conditions for which a negotiation opportunity exists
Source: Based on Figure 5.1 in Smith and Parr, *Valuation of Intellectual Property and Intangible Assets*, John Wiley & Sons, Inc., 1999.

behind now. And I tell you again to probe and go hunting, for in my opinion you are cleaner than a sheet of smooth white paper.[18]

The book *Don Quixote* cannot be recommended too highly, especially the recent translation by Edith Grossman with an introduction by Harold Bloom, from which the quotes in this chapter have been taken. Try reading it with the following provisional frame:

- Don Quixote, as the inveterate deal chaser, looking for that career capstone deal
- Sancho Panza, as the junior financial analyst, or the just out of school lawyer, trying to make sense of the world he has entered
- Lady Dulcinea (literally: *sweetness, dulce = sweet*) who is Don's lady in waiting, and perfect in his eyes in all respects (and illusorily so), as the technology
- Rocinante (literally: *the former nag; rocin = nag, ante = former)*, Don's long suffering horse, as his term sheet "vehicle"

Also recommended is the well known song—"The Impossible Dream"—from the movie (with Peter O'Toole as Don) and oft performed play, "Man of La Mancha" (Don's hometown).

Closing Thoughts

In theory, there is no difference between theory and practice. But, in practice, there is.[19]

In case Technology Licensing D-V-D seems complicated, the reason is 10,000 hours. As popularized in a current book,[20] but a well known principle based on published academic research, it takes a significant investment in any discipline to develop mastery. There is no formal academic department of program for this discipline though aspects of it are part of law school programs with IP emphasis, and many of the financial aspects are derived from standard business finance and accounting fundaments. But technology Dealmaking and all its preparatory aspects are highly interdisciplinary, with levels of complexity such that no one person is expert in all aspects of even any one given opportunity. It is a high interpersonal process involving all the key players comprising the interdisciplinary aspects and of course the negotiation aspects of communicating and ultimately persuading both the other side and one's own side on any final agreement.

Mentoring is an important source of learning. Active learning from one's colleagues and negotiation adversaries can be a particularly enhanced form of real time mentoring. Experience does come and with it can be some particularly sweet and satisfying moments, as captured by two final quotes from Cervantes's *Don Quixote*:

> A perro vijo no hay tus, tus *(You don't need "here boy, here boy," with an old dog).*[21]
>
> *I'm bringing money, because if I've had a good lashing, at least I left riding the horse.*[22]

A complete catalog of possible mistakes would consume a lot of trees. But six compiled about 2,000 years ago by the Roman philosopher Cicero (Markus Tullius Cicero, 106–43 B.C.) contain some useful counsel for us. Cicero's world was very different from our and yet the human failure modes are surprisingly similar. Below are his six mistakes, with my comments in brackets connecting them to our context here:

1. *The delusion that personal gain is made by crushing others* [lost opportunities to convert dissent into learning].
2. *The tendency to worry about things that cannot be changed or corrected* [lack of balance in the pursuit for certainty and/or completeness].
3. *Insisting that a thing is impossible because you cannot accomplish it* [one-person "teams" of just me].
4. *Refusing to set aside trivial differences* [yes, even then].
5. *Neglecting development and refinement of the mind, and not acquiring the habit of reading and studying* [learning new tools/methods, willingness to listen to the power of a better argument].
6. *Attempting to compel others to believe and live as we do* [negotiating as bludgeoning into submission the other side, and dissent]."

Finally, you bought this big (not so) expensive book and were looking for a number? Douglas Adams in his book *The Hitchhiker's Guide to the Galaxy* embodied a quest to find the secret of the universe, which turned out to be a number (spoiler[23]). For technology valuation, I have been asked for "the number" many times. My standard answer is: 3.14. It's the best I can do without additional information, and three significant figures are all one needs for most practical circumstances.

Website Resources

The reader is invited to visit my website: www.razgaitis.com.

On the site are the inevitable errata, bibliographic resources, certain Excel templates that were used in Chapters 7 and 8, and a link that can be used to obtain a free trial license to Crystal Ball from Oracle (no charge to you, no benefit to me). Also, from time to time, I have added news from current events concerning valuation and Dealmaking.

Notes

1. St. Anselm of Bec, later Archbishop of Canterbury (1033–1119).
2. Miguel de Cervantes (1547–1616), a contemporary of Shakespeare—they died almost simultaneously in one of history's quirks. His book *Don Quixote* is considered by many scholars to be not just the first novel but the best work of fiction in the world (so voted in 2002 by 100 major writers from 54 countries).
3. Miguel de Cervantes, *Don Quixote*, A New Translation by Edith Grossman, HarperCollins Publishers, 2003, p. 87.
4. The Sirius Star, owned by a Saudi Arabian shipping company, and carrying more than two million barrels of crude oil, was seized by Somali pirates on November 15, 2008. The pirates demand was, apparently, value-based: "What we want for this ship is only $25 million because we always charge according to the quality of the ship and the value of the product," said pirate spokesman Abdi Salan, in a telephone interview.
5. "According to an anecdote, Kant's life habits were so regular, that people used to set their clocks by him as the philosopher passed their houses on his daily walk [in the city of his birth, life, and death: Königsberg]—the only time when the schedule changed was when Kant read Jean-Jacques Rousseau's *Emile*, and forgot the walk." Source: www.kirjasto.sci.fi/ikant.htm.
6. The lovely Pleiades is one, a stellar nursery. The Andromeda Galaxy is another; with good eyes and a clear night, you can see 2 million light years. A light year is a really long way. The moon is just over a light second, that is, it takes light about 1.3 seconds to reach the earth from the moon. Our sun is 8.3 light minutes away, meaning if the sun turned off at just this moment we would not see it go off for 8.3 minutes because there is a 93 million mile spherical shell of photons always present and streaming outward. So a light year is about six trillion (i.e., million million) miles, an incomprehensible distance.
7. The opening lines of a poem by W.G. Sebald (1944–2001) entitled "Dark Night Sallies Forth," published in the *New Yorker* magazine, 6/17 & 24/2002, p. 126.
8. *Don Quixote*, p. 703.
9. Miguel de Cervantes, *Don Quixote*, A New Translation by Edith Grossman, HarperCollins Publishers, 2003, p. 483.
10. Ibid., p. 788.
11. Ross Perot, "The GM System Is Like a Blanket of Fog," *Fortune*, 15, February 1988, pp. 48–49.
12. The author once received a collect long distance call from a man living in a homeless shelter in Florida who convincingly described the general outline of the "invention of the century." The deal was that he would offer negotiating rights in exchange for a Western Union transfer of $500, but that the deal had to be done now because the shelter lunch line was closing in two minutes. How does one decide such things?
13. *Don Quixote*, p. 399.
14. Miguel de Cervantes, *Don Quixote*, A New Translation by Edith Grossman, HarperCollins Publishers, 2003, p. 153.

15. Again calling on Dr. Einstein, he discovered in his work on relativity that what we call the force of gravity is the effect of space curvature caused by local masses. So stellar and other masses curve the space around them off to infinity and such curvatures in space cause the masses to move not in straight lines, which we interpret as the result of gravitation.
16. The slight blurring just below the southern tip of Manhattan is a consequence of a small cloud in the picture that coincidentally and approximately spans the distance between Manhattan and the Statue of Liberty.
17. Based on Fig. 5.1 in Smith & Parr, *Valuation of IP & Intangible Assets*, John Wiley & Sons 1989 (p. 129).
18. *Don Quixote*, p. _____.
19. Jan L.A. van de Snepscheut. I am indebted for this quote to a Web site of interesting quotes collected by Dr. Gabriel Robins at: www.cs.virginia.edu/~robins/quotes.html.
20. Malcolm Gladwell, *Outliers*, Little Brown and Company, 2008.
21. *Don Quixote*, p. 680.
22. Ibid., p. 928.
23. Here is reported to be his explanation: "The answer to this is very simple. It was a joke. It had to be a number, an ordinary, smallish number, and I chose that one. Binary representations, base thirteen, Tibetan monks are all complete nonsense. I sat at my desk, stared into the garden and thought '42 will do'. I typed it out. End of story."

APPENDIX

List of Abbreviations and Trademarks

A-T-M	Approaches-Tools-Methods
BP	Basis Points
BRIC	Brazil, Russia, India, China
CAGR	Compound Annual Growth Rate
CapEx	Capital Expenditures
CAPM	Capital Asset Pricing Model
CMT	Constant Maturity Treasury
COGS	Cost of Goods Sold
DCF	Discounted Cash Flow
Dealmaking	The Approach of pricing, marketing, negotiating, and reaching agreement
EBIT	Earnings Before Interest and Tax
EAT	Earnings After Tax
GCF	Gross Cash Flow
GM	Gross Margin
IEEE	Institute of Electrical and Electronic Engineers
IP	Intellectual Property
IPO	Initial Public Offer
ITU	International Telecommunications Union
JTB	Justified True Belief
k	Discount Rate
Licensing D-V-D	Opportunity Discovery-Valuation-Dealmaking
LTM	Last Twelve Months
M&A	Merger and Acquisition
Methods	Systematic procedures for performing a valuation
MWACC	Marginal Weight Average Cost of Capital
NEWCO	New Company formed
NPV	Net Present Value
NRSRO	National Recognized Statistical Rating Organization
PDA	Personal Digital Assistant
PDM	Prudent Decision Making
PFT	Provision For Tax
PPE	Plant Property and Equipment
RAHR	Risk Adjusted Hurdle Rate
Revenues	Sales

R&D	Research and Development
Tools	Methods useful for application in other contexts
SG&A	Sales General and Administrative overhead
T-Bill	U.S. Treasury Bill (debt instrument)
TR R^k A DE	Technology Rights, Risk, Art, Deal Economics/Equity
VC	Venture Capital
VCs	Venture Capitalists
WACC	Weighted Average Cost of Capital
YFPP	Yes For Practical Purposes

Trademarks

@Risk
Apple, Inc.
Crystal Ball
iDealmaking
Licensing D-V-D
Macintosh
Microsoft
Excel
Word
Windows XP
Windows Vista
NASDAQ™
Oracle
Parallels
TR R^k A DE
Technology D-V-D

Bibliography

Additional resources are provided and updated at www.razgaitis.com.

Licensing

AUTM Technology Transfer Practice Manual, 2nd Ed., Association of University Technology Managers, 2003.

The LESI Guide to Licensing Best Practices: Strategic Issues and Contemporary Realities. Goldscheider, Robert, Ed. John Wiley and Sons, 2002.

A Primer of Basic Valuation Tools and Considerations, Sec. 9,3, pp 861ff, "Intellectual Property Management in Health and Agricultural Innovation," published by MIHR and PIPRA (Centre for the Management of Intellectual Property in Health Research and Development, and Public Intellectual Property Resource for Agriculture), sponsored by The Rockefeller Foundation and the Ewing Marion Kauffman Foundation, 2007.

Parr, Russell L. and Gordon V., Smith. *Intellectual Property: Valuation, Exploitation, and Infringement Damages*, John Wiley and Sons, 2005.

General Books on Strategy, Uncertainty, and Negotiation

Dixit, Avinash K., and Barry J. Nalebuff. *Thinking Strategically.* New York: W.W. Norton and Company, 1991.

Dixit, Avinash K., and Robert S. Pindyck. *Investment Under Uncertainty.* Princeton, NJ: Princeton University Press, 1994.

Raiffa, Howard. *The Art and Science of Negotiation.* Cambridge, MA: Harvard University Press, 1982.

Ury, William, and Roger Fisher. *Getting to Yes; Getting Past No.* Cambridge, MA: Harvard University Press. [Drs. Ury and Fisher are also the developers of and have been frequent presenters at the Harvard executive education short courses on negotiation.]

Real Options

Amram, Martha, and Nalin Kulatilaka. *Real Options: Managing Strategic Investment in an Uncertain World.* Boston, MA: Harvard Business School Press, 1999.

Copeland, Tom, and Vladimair Antikarov. *Real Options, A Practitioner's Guide.* Texere Publishing, 2001.

Moore, William T. *Real Options & Option-Embedded Securities.* John Wiley & Sons, 2001.

Mun, Johnathan. *Real Options Analysis, Tools and Techniques for Valuing Strategic Investments and Decisions.* John Wiley & Sons, 2002. [This book is effectively a companion text to Decisioneering's Real Options Analysis Toolkit software; Dr. Mun is an employee of Decisioneering.]

Financial Options

Chriss, Neil A. *The Black-Scholes and Beyond Option Pricing Models.* McGraw-Hill, 1997.

Chriss, Neil A. *The Black-Scholes and Beyond Interactive Toolkit.* McGraw-Hill, 1997.

Lowenstein, Roger. *When Genius Failed: The Rise and Fall of Long-Term Capital Management.* Random House, 2000. [Not a book on Real Options methods, but a compelling history of a company, Long Term Capital Management, founded to create market-beating returns using derivatives based on options value by Black-Scholes type of analysis.]

General Finance Texts

Brealey, Richard A., and Stewart C. Myers. *Principles of Corporate Finance.* McGraw-Hill, 1988.

Luenberger, David G. *Investment Science.* Oxford University Press, 1998.

Friedlob, George T. and Lydia L.F. Schleifer. *Essentials of Financial Analysis.* John Wiley and Sons, 2003.

Pratt, Shannon P. *Cost of Capital: Estimation and Applications*, 2nd Ed. John Wiley and Sons, 2002.

Venture Capital

Metrick, Andrew. *Venture Capital and the Finance of Innovation*, John Wiley and Sons, 2007.

Timmons, Jeffrey and Stephen Spinelli. *New Venture Creation: Entrpreneurship for the 21st Century.* McGraw-Hill 2006.

Recommended Classic Literature

Miguel de Cervantes. *Don Quixote.* Edith Grossman translation. Harper Perennial, 2005.

Sophicles. *The Oedipus Cycle: Oedipus Rex, Oedipus at Colonus, Antigone.* Harvest Books, 2002. Available at many sites online.

Aristotle. *The Nicomachean Ethics.* Penquin Classics, 2003. Available at many sites online.
Plato. *Theaetetus.* Focus Publishing, 2004. Available at many sites online.
Plato. *The Republic.* Hackett Publishing Company, 2004. Available at many sites online.
The Bible. http://bible.org/category.php?scid=5&category_id=71&parent_id=0 contains the Net Bible, a modern internet-based translation from more than 30,000 extant ancient Aramaic, Hebrew, and Greek texts, freely downloadable including 60,000 translator notes, and available from Amazon on its Kindle reader, and available in hardcopy from its publisher www.bible.org, 2006.

Valuation Methods

Arnold, T. "Basic Considerations in Licensing," in *The Law and Business of Licensing: Licensing in the 1980s* 2A-73 (1984).
Bayes, "Pricing the Technology," 1977 *Current Trends in Domestic and International Licensing* 369.
Bowler, J. "Payments for Technology," 1980 *Les Nouvelles* 241.
Cruver, D. "The International Marketplace." (September 16, 1983).
(Handout at The Society for Marketing Professional Services, Tenth Anniversary Convention, Dallas, Texas).
Evans, "Packaging and Pricing Technology," 1984 *Domestic and Foreign Technology Licensing* p. 77.
Evans, "Pricing the Technology," 1977 *Current Trends in Domestic and International Licensing* p. 361.
Evans, L. "Turning Patents and Technology Into Money," (Handout at The First Annual Licensing Law and Business Institute. February 26–March 2, 1979).
Farley, "Price Fixing and Royalty Provisions in Patent Licenses," 34 *J. Pat. Off. Soc'y* 46 (1952).
Finnegan and Mintz, "Determination of a Reasonable Royalty in Negotiating a License Agreement: Practical Pricing for Successful Technology Transfer," Vol. 1, No. 2 *Licensing Law and Business Report* 13 (1978).
Goldscheider, R. "The Art of 'Licensing Out," 1984 *les Nouvelles* p. 84.
Goldscheider, R. *Technology Management Handbook* (1984) (In particular, see Chapter 9, "Royalties and Other Sources of Income from Licensing").
Hadji, S.B. "Licensing as a Profit Center," 1985 *les Nouvelles* p. 193. Interview with Donald R. Cruver, Partner, Blask, Cruver & Evans, Houston, Texas (July 17, 1986).
Janiszewski, H. "Licensee Evaluation of Payments," 1978 *les Nouvelles* p. 248.
Leprince, P. "How Evaluation of Process Technology Affects Licensing," 1974 *les Nouvelles* p. 182.
Marlow, R. "Matrix Approach to Pricing," 1978 *les Nouvelles* p. 11.
Matsunaga, Y. "Determining Reasonable Royalty Rates," 1983 *les Nouvelles* p. 216.
McKie, "Pricing and Packaging the Technology," 1984 *Domestic and Foreign Technology Licensing* 93.
Orleans, G.P. "Pricing Licensing of Technology," 1981 *les Nouvelles* p. 320.

Rahn, R.W. "Determining the Royalty—What is Done and What in Fact Should Be Done," in 2 *The Law and Business of Licensing* 657 (1980). (Excellent! He lists 46 factors ranked by usage by licensing executives.)

Root & Contractor, "Negotiating Compensation in International Licensing Agreements," Vol. 22 No. 2 *Sloan Management Review* 23 (1981).

Scaglione, P. "Licensor View of Royalty Rates," 1981 *les Nouvelles* 231.

Index